HANDBOOK
ON THE
HISTORICAL BOOKS

HANDBOOK ON THE HISTORICAL BOOKS

Joshua

Judges

Ruth

Samuel

Kings

Chronicles

Ezra–Nehemiah

Esther

Victor P. Hamilton

Baker Academic
a division of Baker Publishing Group
Grand Rapids, Michigan

© 2001 by Victor P. Hamilton

Published by Baker Academic
a division of Baker Publishing Group
P.O. Box 6287, Grand Rapids, MI 49516-6287
www.bakeracademic.com

Paperback edition published in 2008
ISBN 978-0-8010-3614-9

Printed in the United States of America

The Library of Congress has cataloged the hardcover edition as follows:
    Hamilton, Victor P.
        Handbook on the historical books : Joshua, Judges, Ruth, Samuel, Kings, Chronicles, Ezra-Nehemiah, Esther / Victor P. Hamilton.
           p.   cm.
        Includes bibliographical references and index.
        ISBN 10: 0-8010-2257-6
        ISBN 978-0-8010-2257-9
        1. Bible. O.T. Deuteronomy—Criticism, interpretation, etc. I. Title.
    BS1275.2 .H45 2001
    222′.06—dc21   2001035582

Dedicated to
all the students I have had the privilege of
teaching in biblical studies at Asbury College
over the last thirty years

Contents

Abbreviations

ABD	*Anchor Bible Dictionary*. Ed. D. N. Freedman. 6 vols. New York: 1992
ANET	*Ancient Near Eastern Texts Relating to the Old Testament*
BA	*Biblical Archaeologist*
BAR	*Biblical Archaeology Review*
BASOR	*Bulletin of the American Schools of Oriental Research*
BEATAJ	Beiträge zur Erforschung des Alten Testaments und des antiken Judentum
BETL	Bibliotheca ephemeridum theologicarum lovaniensium
Bib	*Biblica*
BI	*Bible Illustrator*
BibInt	*Biblical Interpretation*
BJRL	*Bulletin of the John Rylands University Library of Manchester*
BRev	*Bible Review*
BSac	*Bibliotheca Sacra*
BTB	*Biblical Theology Bulletin*
BT	*The Bible Translator*
BZ	*Biblische Zeitschrift*
BZAW	Beihefte zur Zeitschrift für die alttestamentliche Wissenschaft
CAD	*The Assyrian Dictionary of the Oriental Institute of the University of Chicago*
CBQ	*Catholic Biblical Quarterly*
CBQMS	Catholic Biblical Quarterly Monograph Series
CT	*Christianity Today*
CTM	*Concordia Theological Monthly*
EncJud	*Encyclopaedia Judaica*. 16 vols. Jerusalem: 1972
EvQ	*Evangelical Quarterly*
ExpT	*Expository Times*

9

Fs.	Festschrift
GTJ	*Grace Theological Journal*
HAR	*Hebrew Annual Review*
HBT	*Horizons in Biblical Theology*
HeyJ	*Heythrop Journal*
HSM	Harvard Semitic Monographs
HTR	*Harvard Theological Review*
HUCA	*Hebrew Union College Annual*
IDB	*The Interpreter's Dictionary of the Bible*. Ed. G. A. Buttrick. 4 vols. Nashville: 1962
IDBSup	*The Interpreter's Dictionary of the Bible: Supplementary Volume*. Ed. K. Crim. Nashville: 1976
IEJ	*Israel Exploration Journal*
Int	*Interpretation*
JAAR	*Journal of the American Academy of Religion*
JANES	*Journal of the Ancient Near Eastern Society*
JAOS	*Journal of the American Oriental Society*
JBL	*Journal of Biblical Literature*
JETS	*Journal of the Evangelical Theological Society*
JFSR	*Journal of Feminist Studies in Religion*
JJS	*Journal of Jewish Studies*
JNES	*Journal of Near Eastern Studies*
JNSL	*Journal of Northwest Semitic Languages*
JPS	Jewish Publication Society
JR	*Journal of Religion*
JSNT	*Journal for the Study of the New Testament*
JSOT	*Journal for the Study of the Old Testament*
JSS	*Journal of Semitic Studies*
JTS	*Journal of Theological Studies*
LTQ	*Lexington Theological Quarterly*
NICOT	New International Commentary on the Old Testament
OSt	*Oudtestamentische Studiën*
PEQ	*Palestine Exploration Quarterly*
PSB	*Princeton Seminary Bulletin*
RB	*Revue biblique*
RefR	*Reformed Review*
RelSRev	*Religious Studies Review*
ResQ	*Restoration Quarterly*
RevExp	*Review and Expositor*

RTR	*Reformed Theological Review*
SBLDS	Society of Biblical Literature Dissertation Series
SBLMS	Society of Biblical Literature Monograph Series
SBLSP	*Society of Biblical Literature Seminar Papers*
SBLSS	Society of Biblical Literature Semeia Studies
SJOT	*Scandinavian Journal of the Old Testament*
SJT	*Scottish Journal of Theology*
TBT	*The Bible Today*
TDOT	*Theological Dictionary of the Old Testament.* Ed. G. J. Botterweck and H. Ringgren. Trans. J. T. Willis, G. W. Bromiley, and D. E. Green. 8 vols. Grand Rapids: 1974–
ThTo	*Theology Today*
TJ	*Trinity Journal*
TynB	*Tyndale Bulletin*
TZ	*Theologische Zeitschrift*
UF	*Ugarit-Forschungen*
USQR	*Union Seminary Quarterly Review*
VT	*Vetus Testamentum*
VTSup	Supplements to Vetus Testamentum
WTJ	*Westminster Theological Journal*
ZAW	*Zeitschrift für die alttestamentliche Wissenschaft*

Preface

It is common in Christian circles to refer to the corpus of biblical books from Joshua through Esther as the Historical Books. This large unit begins with Israel's entry into Canaan under the leadership of Joshua, and concludes centuries later with exiled Israel putting down roots in Persia.

There is no shortage of books dealing with this period of biblical Israel. For example, the standard bearer in this field has for some time been John Bright's immensely popular *History of Israel*. It appeared first in 1959, then in a second edition in 1972, in a third edition in 1981, and most recently in a fourth edition in 2000.

Suffice it to say, numerous histories of Israel have been written before, concurrent with, and since Bright's that take a much more skeptical approach to the historical claims of this unit of Scripture. Some of the more recent and radical histories fail to discern any real, verifiable history here at all! Such interpretations distinguish between biblical Israel and historical Israel.

At the other end of the spectrum are those biblical scholars for whom Bright's conservative *History of Israel* is not conservative enough. For them, even the historically conservative John Bright makes too many concessions. Hence, they have produced their own histories, which reflect belief in an inspired and inerrant Bible.

So we can say that of the writing of histories of Israel there is no end. Surely, there is something here to satisfy everybody's taste, from that of the minimalist to that of the maximalist.

I have absolutely no interest in adding another history of Israel to the already flooded market. What I have tried to produce is something that will serve as a supplement and companion volume to Bright's, or some other, history of Israel. Those whose exclusive interest is in the area of historical issues and arguments will find some of those matters addressed in this volume, but that is not my primary focus.

Instead, using the principles of disciplines such as rhetorical criticism and inductive Bible study, I have tried to get at and uncover the thrust and message of these books of Scripture. For example, I do not think one will find in Bright's, or in any other, history of Israel, an examination of the structure of Judges, and how the fleshing out of that structure illuminates the movement within and the theological message of Judges.

My primary target audience is the undergraduate college student who is beginning advanced biblical studies. The seminary student and pastor will also find, I trust, ideas and insights that will assist them in their encounter with and exposition of this portion of Scripture.

For those wishing to engage in further research in the scholarly literature, I have appended a bibliography to each chapter. Here the reader will find a listing of commentaries and major studies as well as shorter studies (most often those found in the academic journals of the discipline of biblical studies). Of necessity, I have limited most of my entries to those written in the last several decades, and by choice, I have limited my entries to those written in English.

I must express my appreciation to many people for their assistance in writing this book. First, I thank the Faculty Development Committee of Asbury College for recommending me for a sabbatical so that I might complete several segments of my manuscript. Thanks go also to Mr. Jim Kinney, director of Baker Academic, and to the competent and professional editorial team at Baker Book House for their much appreciated help in seeing this project to completion.

I have had the gift of immeasurable stimulation from many fellow biblical scholars who have produced commentary on these books of the Bible. My indebtedness to them is reflected in bibliographical notations throughout my own commentary.

Finally, I am honored to thank Shirley, my wife of many years, for all of her help. Not only did she provide constant encouragement, but she also typed the entire manuscript. Thus, very literally, the production of *Handbook on the Historical Books* has been a joint project.

Joshua

The name "Joshua" (Hebrew, *yehoshua*ʿ) means "Yahweh [*yeho*] is salvation." His original name, the one given to him after he was born in Egypt, was "Hosea" (Hebrew, *hoshea*ʿ [see Num. 13:8, 16; Deut. 32:44]), meaning "salvation, deliverance." Thus, sometime after the exodus from Egypt, Moses expanded the name Hosea by prefixing to it a form of the Tetragrammaton, YHWH, and so gave him a distinctly theophoric name. His new name, then, becomes a constant reminder of who Israel's real deliverer is.

Moses, mighty, indispensable leader that he is, nevertheless is mortal, will one day die, and therefore must have an appropriate successor. We know that Moses had two sons, Gershom and Eliezer (Exod. 2:22; 18:3, 4), but they are mentioned infrequently in the Bible, and neither one seems suited to succeed their father (possibly because their mother was the Midianite Zipporah). Instead, it appears that Joshua is the one who will one day complete the work that his predecessor started but was not permitted by God to finish. Accordingly, for many years Joshua will serve as an underling to Moses, being prepared for that moment when he will inherit his predecessor's mantle. It may be significant, in partially explaining some of the early turbulence of the post-Joshua Judges period, that Joshua, for one reason or another, never developed a mentoring relationship with a subordinate, as Moses had done with him.

Several key events narrate the ways and means through which Joshua would be prepared for his own ministry later on.

(1) *Exod. 17:8–16*. As they continue toward Canaan, the Israelites are suddenly attacked by the Amalekites, an Edomite-related nomadic peo-

ple who view the encroaching Israelites as a threat to their own security. Moses' directive to Joshua is to select an ad hoc group of men (they have no professional soldiers) who will engage the Amalekites in battle at the base of the hill, while Moses moves to the top of the hill, divine rod in hand. This is, in fact, the only incident in which Joshua engages in a military enterprise prior to entering the Promised Land. But this is his first exposure to a crisis that involves engagement with others who, on paper, would appear to have the upper hand.

That Joshua is not identified by parentage would seem to indicate that he is, as early as this incident, already a prominent person. Nun, his father, has little claim to fame, but Elishama, his grandfather, filled a major role in the days of the wilderness wandering (Num. 1:10; 2:18; 1 Chron. 7:26–27).

(2) *Exod. 24:13*. It is Joshua's privilege to join Moses, partway at least, as Moses reascends Mount Sinai to receive the tables of stone from God. Surely, Joshua does not continue on to the summit with Moses, but he ascends higher than do the elders and Aaron, perhaps bringing him as close as possible to an experience of the divine glory that rests there.

This verse identifies Joshua as Moses' servant or attendant (*mesharet*), a term used again for Joshua's relationship vis-à-vis Moses in Exod. 33:11; Num. 11:28; Josh. 1:1. Perhaps the closest parallel to this is the notice in 1 Kings 19:21 that Elisha followed Elijah and "ministered" to him (*wayesharetehu*, from the verb *sharat*, as is *mesharet*), only later to succeed Elijah (2 Kings 2:15–16), as Joshua does Moses. The reference in Exod. 17:9 shows that this could be impromptu military service, whereas here it implies more of a demonstrably religious service. Moses taking Joshua with him to a higher point on the holy mountain may parallel Jesus taking three of his disciples with him into a deeper recess of the garden where he too would meet God (Matt. 26:37). That a *mesharet* could have a cultic role is proved by passages such as Ezra 8:17 (a temple servant), Ezek. 44:11 (sanctuary ministers), and Joel 1:9, 13 (a priest who ministers at the altar of the sanctuary).

We shall observe that in all these references to Joshua in Exodus, Numbers, and Deuteronomy, Joshua is never seen apart from Moses, and never dialogues with anybody but Moses. Even in the beginning of the book that bears his name he is still identified as Moses' attendant, even though the latter is deceased (Josh. 1:1). By contrast, Moses is introduced there as "the servant of Yahweh." Not until the ending of the book of Joshua (24:29) does Joshua's identification label shift from "servant of Moses" to "servant of Yahweh."

(3) *Exod. 32:17*. In the golden calf debacle Joshua plays one minor, inconspicuous role. From somewhere on Sinai's slopes he hears sounds rising from the people in the camp below and believes they are the noise of war. Maybe he had heard similar noises when they were attacked by the Amalekites (Exod. 17:8–13). But Moses, with a greater sense of perception, identifies the sounds as singing. It was not a crisis but a celebration, and the senior of the two turns out to be correct. From this point on in the incident Joshua becomes a silent observer of how forcefully Moses confronts the sin of idolatry among God's people.

(4) *Exod. 33:11*. Exodus 33:7 speaks of a tent that Moses would pitch outside the camp. It was the place where God could be sought, and was intended primarily for Moses. The glory of God was revealed at the entrance to this tent (vv. 9–10) rather than in the interior. When Moses returned again to the camp, Joshua would stay behind and not leave the tent. The text does not state why he was stationed there or what his function there was. He receives no revelation, unlike Moses. He is simply there with Moses, as he was in Exod. 24:13 and 32:17. Possibly, there is an analogy with young Samuel, whose bed was in the inner sanctuary where the ark of God was positioned (1 Sam. 3:3). It appears that this incident in Exodus 33 is a miniature of that in Exodus 19. Both take place "outside the camp" (Exod. 19:17; 33:7). The people "present" themselves (*natsav*) before God (Exod. 19:17; 33:8). God descends in a cloud and speaks from that cloud (Exod. 19:9; 33:9). And both times, Joshua is there, silently, with Moses (Exod. 24:13; 32:17; 33:11). (See Haran 1960: 57.)

(5) *Num. 11:24–29*. For a second time (cf. Exod. 32:17), Joshua makes an honest mistake. Observing the spirit resting upon Eldad and Medad, who were prophesying even though they had not gone out to the tent, Joshua urges Moses to forbid them to continue. This brings to mind the disciples who forbade a certain individual to practice exorcisms because of his departure from acceptable ways of doing this kind of thing (Mark 9:38; Luke 9:49). But in neither case, as both Joshua and the disciples were to discover, can God be bound to conform to our expectations or placed in a box of our making.

Joshua is identified in v. 28 as both the attendant of Moses and as "one of his chosen men." This latter expression can just as well be read "an attendant of Moses, from his youth," depending on how one reads the letters *b-kh-r*. Such a reading is made possible by the fact that in Exod. 33:11 Joshua is not only servant to Moses, but also is called "a young man" (*na'ar*). This term might also point to Joshua's youthfulness, unless *na'ar* is used here in the sense of one who attended upon his lord in war (MacDonald 1976: 153–54).

(6) *Num. 13:8, 16; 14:6–9.* Joshua is picked by Moses as one of the spies sent to reconnoiter Canaan-land. So, he is released from duties at the tent of meeting. And, along with Caleb, he presents the minority report to Moses: "If God is in this, let's go for it, the staggering opposition notwithstanding." What motivates Joshua and Caleb on this occasion is not only their faith and their larger view of God, but also their observing of the humiliation of Moses and Aaron, who, when rebuked by their people, fall on their faces before the assembly (14:5). Once again, Moses' reaction, or lack thereof, casts a shadow on Joshua.

Some commentators have suggested that there are two accounts of the spying of Canaan conflated in Numbers, a JE one and a P one. So, in 13:30 it is only Caleb who speaks up, while in 14:6–9 it is Joshua and Caleb who speak up. Again, in 14:24, Yahweh mentions only Caleb (not Joshua), who will be allowed to enter the Promised Land, whereas 14:30 extends this privilege to both Caleb and Joshua. In the retelling of this incident (Deut. 1:19–46), Caleb alone will see the Promised Land, in opposition to his contemporaries (1:35–36), while Joshua will see the Promised Land because he served Moses (1:38).

It is possible to argue for the unity of the passage by suggesting that Joshua did not originally speak up because his close connections with Moses would have discredited his position as biased. That the issue raised by the naysayers in 14:2–4 ("Why is God doing this to us?") is even more serious than that raised in ch. 13 ("Is the land conquerable?") may explain why on this occasion Joshua chose to join the fray with Caleb.

It is interesting that when Caleb and Joshua are mentioned together, Caleb's name normally comes first (Num. 14:30; 26:65; 32:12; Deut. 1:36–38). "Joshua and Caleb" is found in Num. 14:6, 38. It appears that Joshua stands not only in the shadow of Moses, but also in the shadow of Caleb.

(7) *Num. 27:18–23.* Informed that he will not see the Promised Land because of his own rebellion (vv. 12–14), Moses asks God to appoint a successor (vv. 15–17)—and this is a rare time when Moses prays referring to God in the third person rather than the second person, no doubt because of the reminder of his sin and its consequences in vv. 12–14. God instructs Moses to take Joshua, lay his hands upon him, and commission him to be, eventually, Moses' surrogate. Joshua is not to be a second Moses or an alter ego for Moses, for only some of Moses' authority/power/charisma (v. 20) is to be transmitted to Joshua. And unlike Moses, who received divine guidance directly, Joshua is to stand before Eleazar the priest as the latter consults the Urim (v. 21).

In the beginning of this incident Joshua is described as one "in whom is the spirit," or more literally, "in whom there is a spirit" (v. 18). This is what equips Joshua for his future position of leadership. (After Moses places his hands on Joshua, Joshua is "full of the spirit of wisdom" [Deut. 34:9], but this is after his commissioning. This spirit is present before his commissioning.) One might suggest that the spirit Joshua possesses, even before his investiture, is either some divinely endowed talent/ability (cf. this use of "spirit" for Joseph in Gen. 41:38, and Bezaleel in Exod. 35:31), or else "spirit" is a synonym for "courage" (cf. Josh. 2:11; 5:1). Joshua is the person to succeed Moses, because of a God-given ability, or a God-given courage, or both.

In Numbers, Moses is to do the commissioning (27:18–19), but in Deuteronomy, Yahweh does the commissioning (31:14, 23). This is not a case of either/or, but rather, both/and. Joshua must experience both the impression of the hands of Moses and the inundation of the Spirit of Yahweh.

The main divisions of Joshua are clear:

1. Preparation for entry into Canaan-land (1:1–5:15)
2. Entry into Canaan-land (6:1–12:24)
3. Allocating Canaan-land (13:1–21:45)
4. Holding on to Canaan-land (22:1–24:33)

1. Preparation for Entry into Canaan-land (1:1–5:15)

A. 1:1–18. The first chapter is comprised of a series of speeches.

1. God speaks to Joshua (introduction [1:1]; speech [1:2–9]).
2. Joshua speaks to his officers (introduction [1:10]; speech [1:11]).
3. Joshua speaks to the Transjordanian tribes (introduction [1:12]; speech [1:13–15]).
4. These tribes respond to Joshua (introduction [1:16a]; speech [1:16b–18]).

The first three of these speeches highlight the fact that the land is something Yahweh is "giving" or "has given" to Israel (vv. 2, 3, 11, 13, 15), or that Moses already gave them (vv. 14, 15). While not an emphasis confined to this chapter (e.g., 2:9, 24), the prolific attention paid in the introductory chapter to the land as divine gift is not without significance. It suggests that the successful penetration and occupation of Canaan is the result of a donation rather than of a conquest. In fact, even to speak of the events in the first half of Joshua as a "conquest" may be a misnomer. Gift gives the credit to God; conquest gives the credit to humans.

The longest of the four speeches is that of Yahweh to Joshua (1:2–9). It is composed of two different, but complementary, emphases: first, God's guaranteed promises to Joshua (vv. 2–5), and second, Yahweh's encouraging word and torah word to Joshua (vv. 6–9). In the first part God speaks to Joshua about God (the verbs are mostly in the indicative mood, future tense), while in the second part God speaks to Joshua about Joshua (the verbs are mostly in the imperative mood). This shift from indicative (what God promises to do) to imperative (what Joshua must do) parallels the same structural movement in the last chapter of Joshua: 24:1–13, what God has done (verbs in the indicative mood, past tense); 24:14–15, what the people must do (verbs in the imperative mood).

Thus, the three elements here are (1) description of the task (v. 2), (2) an assistance formula (vv. 3–5, 9), and (3) an encouragement formula (vv. 6–8). Taken together, these three elements constitute a genre of literature throughout Joshua through Chronicles known as an "installation genre" (Porter 1970: 102–32; McCarthy 1990: 31–41).

In a book whose first half is devoted to a narration of matters heavily militaristic, it is interesting that Yahweh's commissioning of Joshua is so decidedly unmilitaristic—not a word about military strategy. The bulk of the second half of Yahweh's message to Joshua is always to keep before him the torah of Moses, and walk in its teachings. Nothing here indicates that Yahweh has an additional word for Joshua that he had not revealed to Moses. On the contrary, for Joshua, the torah of Moses assumes "the normative role of a closed corpus of divine law" (Childs 1979: 245).

The two speeches of Joshua that follow (vv. 11, 13–15), by virtue of their content, are the functional equivalent of what Genesis said of Abram after he received promises from God: "And he [Abram] believed Yahweh" (Gen. 15:6a). It could be said of the Joshua who speaks in ch. 1 that "Joshua believed Yahweh."

Just as Josh. 1:3–5a (God speaking to Joshua) = Deut. 11:24–25 (Moses speaking to Israel), so the third speech here (1:12–15) has many affinities with Deut. 3:18–20. Both are speeches to the two and one-half Transjordanian tribes, and both distinguish between the land east of the Jordan as gift and the land west of the Jordan as gift. Sometimes God is the donor, and sometimes Moses is the donor. But in both speeches the emphasis is first on Yahweh's gift, then Moses' gift (Polzin 1980: 78–79).

Deut. 3:18–20	Josh. 1:13–15
1. v. 18: God gives Transjordan	v. 13: God gives Transjordan
2. v. 19: Moses (?) gives Transjordan	v. 14: Moses gives Transjordan
3. v. 20a: God gives Cisjordan	v. 15a: God gives Cisjordan
4. v. 20b: Moses (?) gives Transjordan	v. 15b: Moses gives Transjordan

In the final speech (vv. 16–18), representatives of these tribes pledge faithfulness to Joshua, and that they will be as supportive of him as they were of Moses. With the transition, Joshua need not fear any diminution of commitment. That would help maintain the confidence of a new leader of a congregation that has recently lost its shepherd of four decades.

B. 2:1–24. Apparently acting on his own, Joshua, himself a former scout (Numbers 13–14), sends out two spies clandestinely to gather tactical information about Jericho. These two spies, who are never identified by name, are called "men" by both the narrator (2:1; 6:22) and the king of Jericho (2:3). They are also labeled "young men" (ne'arim) in 6:23. This latter term more than likely does not emphasize the age of the spies (Joshua sent out two lads/youths), but rather their military function as part of Joshua's entourage.

Two points of interest emerge from the first half of v. 1. The first is the information that Joshua dispatched the two scouts from Shittim, Israel's last stop in the wilderness wanderings. The ancient site has not yet been identified by archaeologists, but according to the first-century A.D. Jewish historian Josephus (*Antiquities* 5.1) it is located sixty stadia (approximately seven miles) from the Jordan. Numbers 25:1–3 informs us that it was at Shittim that the Israelites "played the harlot" (*zanah*) with the women of Moab. And, of course, from Shittim ("Harlotville") the two Hebrew spies will spend their time in Jericho in the house of a harlot (*zonah*).

A second item of interest is how one evaluates Joshua's decision to scout out Jericho, presumably to bring back vital information about the walled city's vulnerability, or lack thereof, to siege. His action may be judged negatively as a lack of trust in the word of God. That is, why does a targeted city need to be scouted when (in the preceding chapter) Yahweh has given almost unconditional guarantees of success (e.g., "no man shall be able to stand before you")? Or, his action may be judged positively. That is, the promises of God do not negate human responsibility; rather, they advance it along the lines of "faith without works is dead."

The two spies lodge in the house of Rahab. Some evidence suggests that *zonah* describes Rahab as an innkeeper/hostess rather than as a prostitute (Wiseman 1964). The source of this idea is in (1) the Jewish Targum's rendering of *zonah* in Joshua 2 as *pundeqita*, derived from the Greek verb *pandokeuein*, "to keep an inn" (an interpretation endorsed by Josephus [*Antiquities* 5.7–8]), and (2) the (implausible) connection of *zonah* with *mazon*, "food." It is preferable, however, to retain the traditional understanding of *zonah* as "prostitute," and think that Aramaic "innkeeper" for Hebrew "prostitute" is either a euphemism or a double entendre that connects bars or inns with places where harlots could be found (Cohen 1971: 114).

Whether intentionally or unintentionally, the spies' decision to stay at the house of a prostitute works to their advantage. It provides them with cover. It provides them with access to intelligence information (harlots will be more sympathetic to outsiders and guard the privacy of their "guests").

Throughout the narrative Rahab shines as an exemplary individual, especially when she is contrasted with the two male spies, who may be characterized as "two incompetent buffoons" (Zakovitch 1990: 96), or "a singularly incompetent set of spies" (McCarthy 1971: 173).

As a woman who outwits a man or a group of men (the king of Jericho and his posse), she parallels the likes of the midwives who duped the pharaoh about the alacrity of the birth of Hebrew boy babies (Exod. 1:15–19), or Rachel, who tricked her father, Laban, into believing that it was the flow of her menstrual period that prevented her from rising and thus exposing the concealed household gods (Gen. 31:35). As a woman who saves a man (or men) from other men, she parallels the likes of Michal, who saved David from Saul by means of her own ruse (1 Sam. 19:11–17), or the unnamed woman who hides the pro-David Jonathan and Ahimaaz, who are being hunted by some pro-Absalom agents (2 Sam. 17:15–20).

Possibly the best parallel to this event is that recorded in Genesis 19, the Sodom story. Both stories focus on the night (Gen. 19:1, "in the evening"; 19:2, "spend the night" [2x]; 19:4, "before they lay down"; 19:5, "tonight"; 19:33, "that night"; Josh. 2:1, "and lodged there"; 2:2, "tonight"; 2:5, "when the gate was to be closed at dark"; 2:7, "the gate was shut"; 2:8, "before they lay down"). In both stories two *mal'akim* (messengers/angels) approach a city that is destined to be destroyed, with only one individual and his or her family to be spared (Gen. 19:1; Josh. 6:17, 25). At first the messengers who come to Lot offer to spend the night outside "in the street" (Gen. 19:2), the Hebrew word for which is *rekhov*, very close in spelling to Rahab's name, *rakhav*. But the contrast between Lot and Rahab cannot be missed. Throughout the narrative Lot is hesitant, bungling, unsure of himself, and not taken seriously by some family members. Rahab, on the other hand, is aggressive, a take-charge person, an individual of faith. Her faith is her salvation. God's remembrance of Abraham is Lot's salvation (Gen. 19:29) (Fields 1992: 21–26; Hawk 1991: 64–65).

Rahab does not do what she does because she is impressed with the spies. Rather, her awe is with the Lord of the spies. Her stunning and testimonial words in v. 9 recall, in chiastic fashion, a portion of Moses' and Israel's doxological song to Yahweh after deliverance at the sea:

Exod. 15:15–16	Josh. 2:9
all the inhabitants of Canaan have melted away.	The fear of you has fallen upon us.
Terror and dread fall on them.	All the inhabitants of the land melt away before you.

Although the word "covenant" does not appear in ch. 2, the arrangement she exacts from the spies is essentially that (Campbell 1972: 243–44). The exchange includes (1) a preamble, "for the Lord your God is . . ." (v. 11); (2) a prologue, "we have heard . . ." (vv. 9–11); (3) stipulations, "swear to me . . ." (by Rahab, vv. 12–13), "you shall . . ." (by the spies, vv. 18–20); (4) sanctions, salvation for Rahab's family if they keep the oath (vv. 18–20); (5) an oath (vv. 14–17); (6) and a sign (vv. 18, 21), the scarlet cord hung in her window.

The spies seem to have forgotten Moses' earlier warnings about not making covenants with or showing any mercy to indigenous peoples when Israel enters the land (Deut. 7:1–5; 20:16–18). No exceptions! But may justice ever be tempered by mercy? It would appear in numerous places of the Old Testament, especially Deuteronomy, that if pure justice alone rules the day, then Israel, because of their sins, should never have inherited the land. Nevertheless, God gives Israel the land because of (1) his promissory, conditional convenant; (2) the wickedness of the nations; and (3) his promise to that effect to Israel's founding fathers and mothers. The exact same three factors are here: (1) the spies make such a promise to Rahab; (2) in transgressing God's law, Israel demonstrates wickedness; (3) Rahab's family is saved only because of a promise made to Rahab. Thus, in many ways Rahab is a microcosm of the macrocosm Israel (Polzin 1980: 86–90).

Subsequent religious traditions never speak of Rahab pejoratively, and condemn her neither for her *métier* nor for her act of deception perpetrated on her king. On the contrary, in Christian biblical tradition she is an ancestress of Messiah (Matt. 1:5), is one of only two women to be included in Hebrews' who's who of the old covenant faithful (Heb. 11:31), and has the privilege of being the only one whom James couples with Abraham to show faith and works operating in tandem (James 2:21–25). Similarly in Jewish tradition, specifically in *Megillah* 14b (*Megillah* is the tenth treatise/tractate in the section of the Mishnah known as "Moed/Festivals"), we read that Rahab married Joshua after she became a proselyte, and became the ancestress of eight prophets who were priests, two of whom were the prophet Jeremiah and his contemporary, the prophetess Huldah. And in 15a of the same tractate Rahab is listed with Sarah, Abigail, and Esther as one of "four women of surpassing beauty in the world." Like Robin Hood among outlaws, Rahab is "an antitype of the dominant image: a whore with a heart of gold" (Bird 1989: 131).

C. 3:1–4:24. For a second time the Israelites encounter a "water hazard" on their trek from Egypt to Canaan. The difference between the Re(e)d Sea and the Jordan River is that the former represents an exit, and the latter an entrance. The sea points to that territory to which they must never return. The river points to that territory which lies before them and toward which they must press. At the sea the enemy is behind them; at the river the enemy is before them.

Israel's responsibilities in this river crossing are amazingly minimal—basically putting one foot in front of the other. There is, however, one mandate they must follow right at the outset. In 3:5, Joshua tells the people, "Sanctify yourselves, for tomorrow the Lord will do wonders among you." The sequence is clear. Before God works marvelously in the sight of Israel the people of God must sanctify themselves on the preceding day. That exact sequence appears after Israel's setback at Ai: "Sanctify yourselves for tomorrow. . . . In the morning you shall come forward tribe by tribe, and the tribe Yahweh takes. . . ." (Josh. 7:13, 14).

The same emphasis is present in the manna/quail story of Numbers. God instructs Moses to say to his people, "Sanctify yourselves for tomorrow, when you will eat meat" (Num. 11:18). Similarly, Job 1:5 relates that it was the practice of Job to send a message to his children to sanctify themselves. Then, rising early in the morning (of the next day), Job would offer whole burnt offerings on their behalf. In a similar fashion, Jacob tells his household to get rid of their alien gods to "purify" themselves (using *tahar* rather than *qadash*, as do the references above), before going on to Bethel (presumably the next day) to build an altar (Gen. 35:2–3).

In preparation for the theophany at Sinai, Yahweh instructs Moses, "Go to the people and sanctify them today and tomorrow . . . for on the third day Yahweh will come down on Mount Sinai in the sight of all the people" (Exod. 19:10, 11). This passage focuses on laundering one's clothes and abstaining from normal sexual congress as evidences of consecration. But all of these passages contain the same emphasis: the precondition for the descent of God and the moving of God in power and miracle is that his people are fully consecrated to him and sufficiently holy.

There are differing ways of dividing the material in these two chapters. One writer (Polzin 1980: 95) suggests the following:

Episode	Event	Reference
1.	Israel journeys to/through/over the riverbed	3:1–17
2.	Joshua sets up twelve stones beyond the river	4:1–8
3.	Joshua sets up twelve more stones in the riverbed	4:9–14
4.	Priests exit the river and the waters of the Jordan return	4:15–18
5.	Twelve stones set up at Gilgal	4:19–5:1

An alternative is the following (Winther-Nielsen 1995: 175, 190):

Episode	Event/Theme	Reference
Stage	March to the Jordan	3:1
1.	Preparatory orders	3:2–5
2.	Crossing orders	3:6–13
3.	Descent (into the river)	3:14–17
4.	Stone orders	4:1–10
5.	Priests and ark cross while people look on	4:11–14
6.	Ascent (from the river)	4:15–18
Closure	Arrival of Gilgal	4:19–24

A glance at most of the modern commentaries on Joshua (especially that of Soggin) reveals that their writers fail to discern any internal unity in these two chapters. What they do discern is disarray, inconsistencies, and the like. For example, is there one crossing or multiple crossings of the Jordan? The language of 3:17 and 4:1 describes the crossing as a fait accompli ("had finished crossing"). Yet, we find a subsequent reference to the people and the priests crossing the river in 4:10–13, 18.

Or what about the memorial stones? First, standing by itself in 3:12, is an instruction to Joshua to select twelve men from the twelve tribes, with no purpose given for their selection. Then, after the crossing (4:1), Joshua is instructed a second time to choose twelve men (4:2), this time with the stated purpose that the twelve are to take up twelve stones from the river's dry bed and carry them to the spot where they will encamp for the night (4:3). Joshua does what he is supposed to do (4:4–7), and the twelve do what they are supposed to do (4:8). Then, surprisingly, we read in 4:9 that Joshua, without directives from Yahweh, sets up twelve stones in the middle of the Jordan. Finally, we read in 4:20 that Joshua set up the twelve stones from the Jordan at Gilgal.

Such analyses have led many scholars to the conclusion that the account of the crossing of the Jordan is a conflation of stories written by different people at different periods, possibly by someone living around the time of King Josiah of Judah (late 600s B.C.), and frequently dubbed the Deuteronomist[1], and by someone else living after Josiah, possibly during the days of the exile in Babylon, a writer called the Deuteronomist[2].

A closer reading of the text, however, reveals the unity of the narrative. Thus, a literary analysis of the event suggests that in 3:1–4:14 the emphasis is exclusively on the entourage "crossing over" the river. By contrast, in 4:15–24 the emphasis is exclusively on the entourage "coming up out of" the river. To match this emphasis on descent and ascent, Joshua twice explains the significance of the stones. First (4:6–7) they are a powerful stimulant, jogging Israel's memory about their Lord and his faithfulness and commitment to his people. Second (4:20–24), they are a powerful object lesson to "all the peoples of the earth" (v. 24), that they too might know the power of Yahweh's hand.

What about the stones Joshua is said to have set up in the middle of the Jordan (4:9)? There is no evidence to suggest that v. 9 is intrusive in the text (Saydon 1950: 203). Perhaps Joshua is here acting autonomously, and without rebuke from Yahweh, as did the spies in the previous chapter when, on their own, they made a covenant with Rahab. But this objection is raised: of what practical value would be an underwater memorial? This suggestion, by the way, is as old as the Septuagint, with its rendering of 4:9 as "Joshua set up twelve *other* stones" (*allous dōdeka lithous*).

Then again, the twelve stones of 4:9 may be the same as the twelve stones of 4:8. This is brought out in the NIV rendering, which offers a harmonized reading in the text proper ("Joshua set up the twelve stones that had been in the middle of the Jordan") and consigns the literal reading to a footnote ("Joshua also set up twelve stones").

Prominent in these two chapters is the emphasis on the ark. It is mentioned sixteen times: nine times in ch. 3 (vv. 3, 4, 6, 8, 11, 13, 14, 15, 17), and seven times in ch. 4 (vv. 5, 7, 9, 10, 11, 16, 18). At the head of this liturgical procession into the river is the ark, carried by the Kohathite Levites (Num. 4:15). Like the pillar in wilderness days under Moses, the ark functions as a symbol of God's presence in the river crossing and subsequent invasion under Joshua. That an item symbolizing the presence of God leads this procession means, in effect, that God gets to Israel's problem before Israel gets to the problem.

A further connection between the deliverance under Moses and Joshua's leadership here is the reference to "dry land" that is experienced both times. Interestingly, the Hebrew uses two different words for the dry land through which Israel under Moses traversed—*kharavah* (Exod. 14:21) and *yabbashah* (Exod. 14:22). Those same two words, in the same order, are used for "dry land" in Josh. 4:18 and 4:22 (Coats 1985: 143).

We learn in 3:15 and 4:18 that the time God led Israel across the Jordan was at "flood stage during the harvest" (i.e., sometime in the spring; cf. 4:19). This piece of information says something about God, and it says something about appropriate strategy. God stems the river's flow not in the middle of a summer drought, but just when spring snow melts off in the highlands to the north, swells the breadth and depth of the Jordan, and increases its currents. And strategically, crossing the river at floodstage would catch the peoples living on the river's other side more off guard and unprepared than they would be in the hot, dry season, when the Jordan would be shallow enough to cross, at least in places, by fording. (For rivers that could be waded through, see Gen. 32:22 and Josh. 2:7.)

D. 5:1–15. In 5:1 is a description of the responses of the kings of the Amorites and of the Canaanites of the Cisjordan upon hearing the news that Yahweh had dried up the Jordan, thus enabling the Hebrews to cross over. In language remarkably similar to that of Rahab earlier (2:10–11), we read that "their hearts melted and there was no longer any spirit in them." On both occasions it is the hearing of what God has done for and among his people that motivates the response. Other occasions in the book of Joshua show where "hearing" leads, rather, to belligerence against Israel (9:1–2; 10:1–5; 11:1–5) or tricking Israel (9:3–27). Thus, the nations have the choice between two responses to the presence of Israel in their midst: submission or resistance. Those are precisely the same two choices that Yahweh and his word place before Israel.

Three items of interest follow. First, Joshua circumcises the people of Israel, that is, those who had been born after the exodus from Egypt (vv. 2–9). Second, Passover is observed (vv. 10–11). Third, the manna ceases (v. 12). These are interesting preparations for battle and engaging the enemy! First, at a time when they will need all of their maximum physical strength, the fighting men are subjected to the pain that comes with circumcision later in life (see v. 8)—any fighting will be postoperative. Second, at a time when the focus is on the future, the Passover celebration places the focus on the past. Third, at a time when rations may be all that is available, God cuts off the food supply!

It was, of course, imperative that circumcision (vv. 2–9) precede Passover observance (vv. 10–11). The regulation is that the uncircumcised may not participate in the Passover (Exod. 12:43–49). But circumcision functions here more than merely as a prelude or a prerequisite. It is vital at this point to demonstrate that Israel belongs to Yahweh and not to Egypt. They are not pharaoh's property. All of this takes place after the Jordan is crossed, at a site on the west bank of the river, and after God has displayed his power. In fact, the name Gilgal is connected with the fact that here God "rolled away [*galloti*] the reproach of Egypt" from the Israelites (v. 9). The Hebrew word for "reproach" (*kherpah*) refers frequently to verbal abuse, and hence covers words like "taunt, slander, insult, shame" (e.g., 1 Sam. 17:26; 25:39; Ps. 15:3; 69:20). The word *kherpah* refers to the devastating destruction of someone by speech, and here must refer to the degrading insults heaped on the first generation Israelites by the Egyptians. Now, God has liberated his people from the tragic and lingering effects of such abuse. He has not only taken Israel out of Egypt, but now takes Egypt out of Israel.

It is not a mystery why, on the day after Passover and eating for the first time, the produce of the land (the manna) should cease (v. 12). It is now time for Israel to take responsibility for their own life. Freedom means responsibility and a cutting away of some props heretofore vital—much as a parent who, teaching a child to ride a two-wheel bicycle, knows a day must come when the training wheels have to come off; or a flight instructor says to a student pilot, "Take it up yourself."

The chapter concludes with the sudden appearance of a "man" to Joshua who shortly identifies himself as commander of Yahweh's forces (vv. 13–15). God's presence is revealed in Scripture sometimes through theophany and epiphany. These two words, though related, are distinct. The first, "theophany" (from Greek, *theophaneia*, "manifestation of God/deity"), refers to a revelation of God that includes a spectacular display of awesome power, usually in a natural cataclysm, such as God's destruction of Sodom (Genesis 19), or God's revelation in the burning bush (Exodus 3), or his descent in fire and smoke on Sinai (Exodus 19). By contrast, "epiphany" (from Greek, *epiphaneia*, "manifestation, revelation") need not be spectacular or include natural phenomena. Thus, God's appearance to Joshua in 1:1–9 falls into the category of epiphany, while the commander's appearance to Joshua in 5:13–15 falls into the category of theophany.

The man is as mysterious to Joshua as was the man whom Jacob encountered, also by a river. Jacob's question to the man, "What is your name?" (Gen. 32:29), matches Joshua's question, "Are you for us or for our adversaries?" (v. 13). The man's "Why is it that you ask my name?" (Gen. 32:29) to Jacob matches the "No" (v. 14) to Joshua (i.e., the man has not come to take sides, but to take over).

An even closer parallel to an earlier event is God's word to Moses and Joshua to remove their shoes because the ground on which they stand is holy (Exod. 3:5; Josh. 5:15). The command to remove one's shoes may reflect either that sandals, because of the impurity deriving from the hide of a carcass, were taken off before entering the sacred sanctuary, hence contributing to the idea that the priests ministered barefooted before Yahweh, or that shoes are symbols of power, dignity, and ownership (Brichto 1969: 225–26), symbols that must now be removed and placed at the feet of one greater than Joshua. Apart from the shoe removal, another parallel is the timing of the two incidents. Both occur at the threshold of a crucial mission: for Moses, leading his people from Egypt; for Joshua, leading his people into Canaan.

Interestingly, the Hebrew word for "remove" (*nashal*) in Exod. 3:5 and Josh. 5:15 is used again transitively in Deut. 7:1 to describe Yahweh's removal of the nations (i.e., clear away, dislodge) when Israel enters the land. The one whom God will use to remove the nations first must remove his own sandals.

This introductory section of Joshua, chs. 1–5, is bracketed by direct revelations to Joshua, which are designed not only to encourage Joshua, but also to remind Joshua that the battle really is Yahweh's (1:1–9; 5:13–15).

One might appropriate these final three verses of ch. 5 by reflecting on these three ideas:

1. Look at Jericho, and see your problem.
2. Look at Jesus, and see God's provision.
3. Look at Joshua, and see your position ("fell, worshiped").

2. Entry into Canaan-land (6:1–12:24)

A. 6:1–27. From their camp at Gilgal just to the west of the Jordan, the Israelites are instructed by Joshua, who is instructed by Yahweh, to march against Jericho. As in Moses' era, Yahweh does not speak directly to his people, but only through his chosen mediator. The strategy is clear enough. For six consecutive days one circuit is to be made around Jericho's perimeter per diem. Those who are to make the march fall into three different groups: (1) an advanced military unit (*khaluts*), (2) seven priests with seven trumpets in front of the ark, and (3) a military rearguard (*me'assef*). (This form of military deployment [vanguard-middle-rearguard] is reflected in Isa. 52:12, which speaks of Yahweh's position to Israel thus: "for Yahweh will go before you, and the God of Israel will be your rearguard [*me'assifkem*].")

The armed groups are to do nothing but promenade. The seven priests, however, are to blow their trumpets. Everybody else is to be silent. On the seventh day the entourage is to make seven circuits around the city. Following a signal from Joshua on this seventh day, the people are to raise a shout, a war cry. Thereafter, the walls of Jericho will collapse, permitting the Israelites to enter the city and gain victory over the Jerichoites, exempting only Rahab and her family from devastating punishment.

If, as we saw in Joshua 5, it was odd that, on the eve of battle, would-be soldiers are subjected to painful circumcision and God puts a halt to the food supply, is not the strategy given to Israel for laying siege to Jericho equally strange? Simply circumambulating the targeted city for a week! In fact, one might argue that Joshua 6 does not describe military strategy at all—unless it be psychological warfare—but rather a cultic event. The walls of Jericho will fall when the revealed ritual is properly enacted and executed (Coats 1985: 148).

Accordingly, ch. 6 in no way accentuates the bravado or militarism of Israel. What it does accentuate is the certainty of victory, and that victory is only because of Yahweh's promise to Joshua (v. 2), a promise repeated by Joshua to his people (v. 16). On both occasions, God's promise to do something in the imminent future is put in a Hebrew verbal form that suggests it has already happened: "I *have given* Jericho into your hand"; "Yahweh *has given* you the city." Exactly the same phenomenon is present in 1:3 ("I have given to you") and 2:24. Hebrew grammarians have various names for this use of the perfect tense: a perfect of certitude, a perfective of confidence, a perfective future—a means of expressing a vivid future when the action is considered "as good as done." God's promissory word is "as good as done."

The divisions are clear enough:

Introduction, 5:13–15: Joshua falls before Yahweh's commander
Episode One, 6:1–5: Yahweh's word about how Jericho will fall before Joshua
Episode Two, 6:6–11: seven circuits around Jericho on day one
Episode Three, 6:12–14: circuits around Jericho for days two through six
Episode Four, 6:15–20a: seven circuits around Jericho on day seven
Episode Five, 6:20b–21: walls collapse, Jerichoites destroyed
Episode Six, 6:22–25: Rahab and her family spared
Conclusion, 6:26–27: Joshua's imprecation and reputation

As in Joshua 4, a command-fulfillment emphasis extends throughout the chapter (Culley 1984: 36; Niehaus 1988: 39–42):

Yahweh gives directives to Joshua (vv. 3–5).
Joshua transmits Yahweh's directives to Israel (v. 7).
Israel implements those directives (vv. 8–9).

Joshua gives directives to Israel—no shouting (v. 10).
Joshua instructs Israel when to shout (v. 16).
Israel shouts (v. 20).

Joshua instructs Israel to destroy Jericho (v. 17a).
Joshua instructs Israel to destroy also Jericho's commodities (vv. 18–19).
Israel destroys Jericho and its commodities (v. 21).

Joshua instructs the people to spare Rahab (v. 17b).
Joshua instructs the two spies to spare Rahab (v. 22).
Rahab (and her house) is spared (vv. 24–25).

This pattern suggests that throughout this event neither Joshua nor any member of the procession walking around Jericho acts autonomously, especially the walkers. Only three individuals speak: God, Joshua, and the narrator. Israel, or a portion thereof, marches, blows trumpets, and shouts, but never does Israel talk. The emphasis, then, is upon faithful implementation of orders received from a superior. Other matters of interest are discussed minimally. For example, "The great and colossal event that is the climax of the story, the fall of the walls of Jericho, is reported in one very brief and unadorned statement (v. 20b)" (Wilcoxen 1968: 49)—about a half dozen words in English, and just two words in the Hebrew (*wattippol hakhomah*).

There is one word (appearing in both verbal and nominal form here) that calls for extended comment: *kharam* (verb) and *kherem* (noun). In v. 17 Joshua tells his people that Jericho and anything within it is to be *kherem* (noun). In v. 18 Israel is told to keep herself away from those things that are *kherem* (noun) lest Israel be "kharamed" (verb). Verse 21 then states that Israel "kharamed" Jericho. There is no consensus on how to render *kharam/kherem* into the best English equivalent, or whether or not it should always be translated the same way. A look at some modern versions illustrates the diversity of choices.

kherem (6:17)	*kherem* (6:18)	*kharam* (6:21)
KJV: be accursed	the accursed thing	utterly destroyed
NKJV: doomed to destruction	the accursed things	utterly destroyed
RSV: be devoted for destruction	the things devoted to destruction	devoted to destruction
NRSV: be devoted for destruction	the things devoted to destruction	devoted to destruction
NAB: under the Lord's ban	anything that is under the ban	observed the ban
NEB: under solemn ban	anything that is forbidden under the ban	destroyed everything
REB: under solemn ban	anything that is forbidden under the ban	destroyed everything under the ban
JB: set apart under a ban	the ban	enforced the ban

NJB: devoted under the curse of destruction	the curse of destruction	enforced the curse of destruction
NAS: under the ban	the things under the ban	utterly destroyed
NIV: be devoted	the devoted things	devoted
TEV: be totally destroyed	anything that is to be destroyed	killed
Berkeley: a devoted portion	the devoted portion	destroyed everything as a devoted portion
Boling: under the ban	something banned	put everything under the ban
Butler: under the ban	the banned goods	set everything under the ban

The most common translations for the noun are "things devoted for destruction" and "the things under the ban," while for the verb the most common choices are "utterly destroy" and "put under the ban." Although we do not use the expression "under the ban" in current vernacular, it is a meaningful term. One dictionary lists these definitions for the noun "ban": (1) ecclesiastical interdict, anathema, or excommunication; (2) a curse, bringing evil, as from a supernatural power, specif., a curse upon something devoted to destruction; (3) an imprecation; profane exclamation; malediction; (4) a prohibition made by authority; an official interdict, sometimes involving a sentence of outlawry; (5) condemnation or prohibition, as by public opinion. Perhaps the most curious of all the above is the NIV's choice of "[be] devoted." It is difficult for us to think of "devote" as meaning "to give something over to God by totally destroying it," especially when we recall New Testament uses of "devote" such as "they devoted themselves to the apostles' teaching" (Acts 2:42).

The root *kh-r-m* appears about 80x in the OT, 29x as the noun *kherem* and 51x as the verb *kharam*. The book of Joshua has more uses of both the noun (13) and the verb (14) than any other Old Testament book. And all but two of the twenty-seven Joshua references (2:10; 22:20, which refers back to ch. 7) fall within chs. 6–11. The book with the second most occurrences after Joshua's twenty-seven is Deuteronomy's ten (8x for the verb: 2:34; 3:6 [2x]; 7:2 [2x]; 13:16; 20:17 [2x]; 2x for the noun: 7:26; 13:18). I mention the book with the third highest number of occurrences, First Samuel, only because all eight occur in its fifteenth chapter, which relates Saul and Samuel's slaying of the

Amalekites and their king, Agag (7x for the verb: vv. 3, 8, 9 [2x], 15, 18, 20; 1x for the noun: v. 21). (Additional statistical information may be found in Lohfink 1986: 180–99; Fretz 1986: 7–44; Mitchell 1993: 52–66.)

The root has turned up only occasionally in other Semitic languages. The name in Akkadian of a certain type of sequestered priestess called a *ḥarimtu* and the attendant status of *ḥarimutu* (see *CAD* H 101–2) suggest the idea of "separate, set aside" for the root.

The extrabiblical use of *kh-r-m* closest to its use in Deuteronomy and Joshua is in the Moabite/Mesha inscription (i.e., a war context). King Mesha of Moab (ninth century B.C.) is describing his victory over Israel, and in one place boasts of the slaying of "7,000 men, boys, women, girls, and maid-servants for I *had devoted them to destruction* for (the god) Ashtar-Chemosh [*ky lˁshtr kmsh hḥrmth*]" (*ANET*, 321).

The concept of *kherem* may be defined as "the status of that which is separated from common use or contact either because it is prescribed as an abomination to God or because it is consecrated to Him" (Greenberg 1971: 344). Because "to dedicate" something or someone to God has inherent in it the idea of irrevocability or irreversibility, *kherem* is the "ultimate in dedication" (Milgrom 1990: 428). It is handing something over to God, with no "ifs, ands, or buts" and renouncing of any further claim on the item.

The land that God promised to Abraham's descendants is a land that is already populated by a group of people, collectively subsumed under the label "Canaanites." Had Canaan been deserted or unoccupied in Joshua's day, there would have been no need for such encounters as appear in Joshua. But what is to be done if group A wishes to lay claim to property currently possessed by group B, assuming that peaceful coexistence and fraternization are not options? And what is to be done if the inside group does not roll out the welcome wagon for the outside group?

Israel's God had already addressed that point, but interestingly, the verbs used to describe policy vis-à-vis the insider group shift. Thus, in Exod. 23:28, 29, 30, 31 and 34:11, God promises to "drive out" the indigenous peoples, the word for which is *garash*. Note that in Judg. 2:3 God promises that he will *not* "drive out" the nations, reneging on his earlier promise, but only because of Israel's sinful disobedience. Neither Exod. 23:23–33 nor 34:11–16, passages dealing with Canaan's indigenous peoples, uses *kharam*, only *garash*. The verb points clearly to expulsion versus extermination. Although *kharam* is used once in Exodus (22:20), this verse is addressed to Israelite idolaters, and not to the occupants in Canaan.

One passage in particular in Numbers (33:50–56) speaks about Israel ridding the land of its current peoples, collectively called "all the inhabitants of the land." The verb used here is *yarash* (vv. 52, 53, 55), which, when followed by the phrase "all the inhabitants of the land," means "dispossess" (vv. 52, 55), but when followed by the phrase "the land" means "take possession of" (v. 53). Like Exodus, Numbers never uses *kharam* of the Canaanites, although it uses *kharam* to describe Israel's gifts to God to his sanctuary (18:14; 21:2, 3, these latter two verses referring to Israel's vow to *kharam* to God the towns under the sway of the king of Arad in the Negeb if Israel can regroup and defeat them). This verb *yarash* is used frequently in Judges 1 to describe Israel and their inability to drive out various groups of people throughout Canaan (vv. 19, 27, 28, 29, 30, 31, 32, 33). Judges 1 never says, "Israel could not *kharam* them."

When we turn to Deuteronomy, the verb of choice is *kharam* (3:6; 7:2 [2x], 26 [2x]; 13:15, 17 [against Israel!]; 20:17 [2x]). Deuteronomy 7:2 and 20:17 are the only two places in the Old Testament where the infinitive absolute form of the verb precedes, for emphasis, the finite form of the verb—"'kharaming,' you shall 'kharam.'" Deuteronomy eschews both *garash* and *yarash* when it focuses on how to deal with the people already living there. So there are three different ways in which the Israelites take the land from the Canaanites: (1) expulsion (*garash*), (2) eviction (*yarash*), and (3) annihilation (*kharam*).

While *kharam/kherem* carries several different nuances through the Old Testament, easily the dominating one is that of an act of warfare and destruction, with all of its instances in Deuteronomy—Second Kings falling into this category, and overall about 85 percent of its eighty uses throughout the Old Testament (Mitchell 1993: 55). It is a "means of gaining God's favor through expurgation of the abomination, through justly deserved punishment of the subversive enemy, external to the people of Israel or internal" (Niditch 1993: 57).

The reason for such a dramatic command in the above passages is reasonably consistent: "they will make you sin against me" (Exod. 23:33); "they will make your sons also prostitute themselves to their gods" (Exod. 34:16); "they will trouble you" (Num. 33:55); "that would turn away your children from following me" (Deut. 7:4); "so that they may not teach you to do all the abhorrent things that they do for their gods" (Deut. 20:18). It appears, then, in Exodus, Numbers, and Deuteronomy that for Israel, the command of *kharam* (or whatever verb is used) against the Canaanites functions primarily as a prophylactic. It is the one sure way of preventing moral and spiritual contamination. There is little emphasis on Israel's potential to influence the nations for good, but much emphasis on the nations' potential to influence Israel for evil. The concern is not that Canaan will act like Israel, but that Israel will act like Canaan and be conformed to its image.

For those interpreters who are inclined to doubt the historicity of the events described in Joshua 6 (i.e., the chapter does not record actual history), any moral issue raised by *kharam* in Deuteronomy and Joshua becomes a non-issue in our response to the Old Testament's picturing of God. The *kharam* becomes a "utopian program that reflects the ongoing bitter struggle with the Canaanite religion and culture from the time of Elijah until the time of Josiah" (Weinfeld 1991: 52), or a "theological-historical statement about God's gift of the land to Israel, by means of a theological-novelistic narrative" (Goldingay 1994: 42).

For those interpreters who attribute a high degree of historicity to Joshua 6, even if the event has been shaped by later editors before it reached its final form, *kharam* raises serious moral and apologetic questions. Did Yahweh, the one whom Jesus called "Abba," command the genocide of pagans, or did the Deuteronomists believe that their God commanded such mass extermination of polytheists? Is Yahweh a deity of both *milkhamah* (battle) and *shalom* (peace)?

There are few portions in the narrative sections of the Old Testament (from Exodus through 2 Chronicles) in which Israel is not found engaged in warring battle. They are ubiquitous. Most are defensive; a few are offensive. It is interesting that so few battles Israel engages in, outside of Joshua, are the *kharam* type. For example, none of the many judge-led battles in Judges is a *kharam* war (although the verb is present in the opening chapter [1:17] and in the last chapter [21:11]), except for the war effort led by Deborah and Barak (Judges 4–5), and this is fought on the disputed boundary of where Israelite and Canaanite interests touched. In Joshua, *kharam* wars are common because they are with Canaanite groups, while *kharam* wars in Judges are nonexistent because wars are with non-Canaanite groups (Kaufmann 1960: 251). This may explain why Deuteronomy records no command to utterly destroy the Philistines, and why in Judges–Kings no Israelite king "devoted to destruction" the Philistines. Thus, it is important that such wars of extermination not be carried out on a wide scale or become national policy.

In fact, the book of Joshua itself points out that among all its battles, only Jericho and Ai are attacked directly and "kharamed." All of the remaining battles (chs. 9–11) are actually defensive operations precipitated by the Canaanites responding belligerently to Israel's presence (9:1–2; 10:1–5; 11:1–5). The Canaanites must choose between two responses to the presence of Israel: (1) submission and acceptance (e.g.,

Rahab, the Gibeonites [ch. 9]); (2) resistance and aggression (e.g., Adoni-zedek [ch. 10], Jabin [ch. 11]). When they choose the latter, Israel launches a counteroffensive, and then "kharams" the aggressor. These kinds of dynamics raise the question of whether or not the book of Joshua unequivocally endorses wars of extermination. Unlike Deuteronomy, the book of Joshua never condemns the Canaanites as decadent. What it condemns is their failure to respond affirmatively to Israel's presence. And, of course, the Israel of Joshua must choose between the exact same two alternatives regarding God's torah: either gracious acceptance (with the attendant blessings) or recalcitrant resistance (with the attendant terrible consequences) (Stone 1991: 25–36).

Because the New Covenant community is made up of a body drawn from earth's tribes and nations rather than from a particular sovereign state where church and state merge, the war of Joshua 6 and 8 must be viewed as a part of the Judeo-Christian unusable past. At the same time, "The very power of these examples to shock and appall us as history is perhaps their most important characteristic as theology, since here we find the ferocity of spiritual war made unbearably real to us. No eloquence could drive home more powerfully the fact that God's war now, and His judgment to come, are alike total: that for us the world, the flesh and the devil are enemies to fight to the death, and that the last judgment will make this *herem* absolute" (Kidner 1985: 107–8).

The above quotation, with which I am in agreement, reinforces that it is both wrong and useless to use an incident like that in Joshua 6 to pit in some gnostic fashion the God of the Old Testament against the revelation of God in Jesus Christ in the New Testament. The horrors of Gehenna will be no less than those of Jericho.

What does a story like Joshua 6 tell us about God and about ourselves (see especially Fretheim 1983: 71–74, from whom I draw heavily)?

First, God has sovereignly determined to be dependent upon imperfect sinful human beings in bringing to pass his plans for his creation and for history.

Second, God works in his world with what is available to him, and that includes both flawed human beings and flawed structures by which any society operates; God perfects neither before working through them and using them.

Third, we will probably never have a perfect understanding of what it means to be an instrument of God in the achieving of his purposes.

Fourth, for God to be absent from such tragedies as war would be more a cause for despair than anything, because for God to withdraw from such realities means that human beings and human beings alone are now solely responsible for achieving their own brand and reading of justice and the pursuit of their own agendas.

Fifth, God must accept part of the responsibility for the violence perpetrated against Jericho, much as he must for the violence heaped on his own Son, for behind both was a divine promise and a divine determination. Jericho is not destroyed primarily because of its sinfulness, but because of a promise of the land by God to the patriarchs. Jesus was not crucified primarily because of any Jewish high priest or a raging mob, but because of the eternal will of his Father.

B. 7:1–8:29. After the successful taking of Jericho, the next city to be taken is nearby Ai. But, shockingly, Israel's troops are routed. Only after discerning the cause of the humiliating defeat and dealing with that cause can Israel regroup, make a second approach, and this time be victorious. So this unit is about the movement from defeat (7:1–5) to victory (8:1–29), and exposing the necessary steps to be pursued so that defeat gives way to victory. Chapters 7–8 present a stunning contrast with ch. 6, especially when victory is played off against defeat. The causes of victory are faith, obedience, and courage (ch. 6); the causes of defeat are self-confidence and covetousness (ch. 7).

The opening verse of ch. 7 explains the specific sin that aroused God's wrath, and is the necessary background for what follows in 7:2–8:9. It begins with a general statement that indicts Israel (v. 1a), then moves to a specific statement that identifies Achan as the guilty perpetrator and the nature of his sin (v. 1b). For some reason, this introductory verse identifies three ancestors of Achan's genealogical tree: Carmi > Zabdi > Zerah. The last individual, Zerah, was one of the twins born to Judah by Tamar (Gen. 38:30). One possible connection of Zerah with events in Joshua is that he emerged from Tamar's womb with a crimson thread (*shani*) on his hand, the same colored material used to describe the cord that Rahab was to hang in her window (Josh. 2:18, 21).

It is important to notice that while later in the narrative Yahweh says, "Israel has sinned" (v. 11), and Achan confesses that he has sinned (v. 20) (both use the verb *khata³*, v. 1 does not indict for sin. Rather, it says that Israel "broke faith" and "acted unfaithfully." The verb is *ma'al* and its cognate noun is *ma'al*. The sin or crime of *ma'al* is that which is covered by the guilt offering (Lev. 5:14–6:7). A *ma'al* is the misappropriation of sacred property. Yahweh is deeply offended when something rightfully belonging to him is misappropriated. Thus, *ma'al* is always a sin against God. It would be preferable to translate Achan's act of "taking" (7:1, 11) as one of (mis)appropriating what had been "kharamed" to Yahweh. Levitical law provides for the forgiveness of acts of *ma'al*, provided there is sacrifice and full restitution plus 20 percent. But there is no forgiveness for Achan, his confession of sin notwithstanding. Perhaps the reason for the difference is that Achan's sin was intentional *ma'al* that violated the *kherem* against personal enrichment from Jericho's spoils, whereas the acts of *ma'al* addressed by Lev. 5:14–6:7 are inadvertent ones.

For a second time Joshua sends spies to scout a targeted city. Their report, upon returning, is that Ai is a "pushover," an almost guaranteed victory that will require only a modicum of Israelite troops (7:3), a far removal from the Yahweh-glorifying report that the two spies brought back from Jericho (2:24). To what degree should Joshua himself be faulted for failing to discern the cockiness and inaccuracy of the spies, although in the narrative that follows he never comes under indictment? Also, to what degree must Joshua accept partial blame for the thirty-six or so Israelite war casualties at Ai (7:5)? Proverbs asserts repeatedly that one mark of a good leader is relying on advice, getting all the available counsel (Prov. 11:14; 15:22), especially before waging war (Prov. 20:18; 24:6). If victory is achieved through good advice, defeat is encountered through bad advice.

The decisiveness of the setback moves Joshua and the elders to pray prostrated before Yahweh (7:6–9). Interestingly, he never rebukes the spies. Is this Joshua's way of saying to himself, "I made a mistake, I should have known better"? Joshua 7:7–9 is an example of a type of prose prayer in the Old Testament whose concern is that God has done something, or is on the verge of doing something, to somebody that in the judgment of the one praying is questionable; hence, a battery of questions are fired at God: "Why? . . . What if? . . . Then what?" (Ballentine 1993: 118–39). Joshua's prayer has analogues with those of Abraham (Gen. 18:22–33) and of Moses (Exod. 32:11–14; Num. 11:10–23, esp. vv. 10–15; 14:13–19). All of these prayers share three features: (1) a crisis provoked by a breach in one's relationship with God that, if not rectified, will have dire results (Josh. 7:1–5); (2) a response to God in prayer by an intercessor that includes questions addressed to God that take issue with God (Josh. 7:7–9), and to which God responds (Josh. 7:10–15); (3) an explanation or resolution of the crisis (Josh. 7:1, "Yahweh's anger burned against the Israelites," now resolved by Josh. 7:26, "Yahweh turned from his burning anger").

Apart from these structural parallels, however, Joshua's prayer fails to rise to the level of that of his predecessor Moses. In fact, one commentator has suggested that it is more of a harangue than a prayer (Boling 1982: 224). For example, Joshua's "Why have you brought this people across the Jordan at all?" (v. 7) finds echoes in "Why is Yahweh bringing us into this land to fall by the sword?" (Num. 14:3), spoken not by Moses, but by Moses' congregation. In his praying, is Joshua modeling Moses or Israel?

Yahweh's response to Joshua (vv. 10–15) contains some information, but not exhaustive information. Yahweh incriminates all of Israel because they have violated the ban and so have come under the ban themselves (vv. 10–12). Not until the evil is eliminated can Israel expect a reversal of fortunes (endings of vv. 12, 13). Suddenly, the enemy has shifted from without to within. The means by which the villain or villains will be determined is apparently by the drawing of lots, although lots per se are never referred to here. Yahweh never says, "You suffered a setback at Ai because of Achan of Judah."

The Old Testament talks of several methods of determining guilt, which, by contemporary procedures of jurisprudence, seem strange (de Ward 1977: 1–19). For example, one way to determine the guilt of a woman suspected of adultery was to subject her to an ordeal that involved drinking muddied water (Num. 5:11–31). Ascertaining guilt by lot casting falls into that category. Apart from this incident, there are only two other instances in the Old Testament where guilt is determined via lots. During a lull in battle against the Philistines, Saul inquires of God whether or not he should again engage the Philistines (1 Sam. 14:37), and God does not respond. From such divine silence Saul concludes that somebody has sinned, and lots are cast to find the perpetrator (1 Sam. 14:41), who turns out to be Saul's own son Jonathan (1 Sam. 14:42). Jonathan's response is that he had eaten some honey (1 Sam. 14:43), a violation of the oath Saul had earlier placed on his troops (1 Sam. 14:24), but an oath to which Jonathan was not privy (1 Sam. 14:27). Only the people's decision to ransom Jonathan, presumably by the form of a substituted animal, spares Jonathan from death. The other instance of lot casting to determine culpability is that done by the sailors on board the ship from Joppa to Tarshish. The sailors have enough religious orientation to know that the horrendous storm on the Mediterranean they are fighting has been divinely sent, and that because of somebody on board. The casting of lots reveals that the culprit is Jonah, or that he is able to identify the culprit (Jon. 1:7).

Thus, all three incidents follow the same basic pattern:

Crisis	Questions asked	Lot casting	Culprit revealed	Problem resolved
Joshua 7: setback at Ai	"why . . . what" (vv. 7, 9)	vv. 14–18	v. 18b	Achan, his household, and possessions totally destroyed

1 Samuel 14: divine silence	"why" (v. 41)	vv. 41–42	v. 42b	Jonathan ransomed
Jonah 1: storm at sea	"why . . . what . . . where" (v. 8)	v. 7a	v. 7b	Jonah thrown overboard

The progression mentioned in Joshua 7:14 for apprehending the offender follows this order: (1) tribe (*shevet*); (2) clan (*mishpakhah*); (3) houses/households (*batim*). The *shevet* is Judah. The *mishpakhah* is the Zerahites. The *batim* are Achan and his immediate family. The lot flushes Achan and his secret sin out of hiding.

On the surface, Achan's first words are commendable. First, he makes public confession that he is the one who sinned against Yahweh (v. 20). Then, he follows immediately with an explanation of how he sinned (v. 21). His language is remarkably like that of Eve when the Genesis narrator describes her trespass: "So when the woman *saw* . . . she *took* . . ." (Gen. 3:6). Achan says, "When I *saw* . . . I *took*. . . ." What Achan adds, but which the Genesis narrator does not, is that in between the visual act and the appropriating act he "coveted" (*khamad*) what Yahweh had forbidden. The emotion of *khamad* precipitates the action of *laqakh;* the movement is from coveting to taking. The first is the cause; the second is the effect (cf. James 4:2). We need to be clear that the Scripture never teaches that a deep desire for something, otherwise normal and acceptable, is itself illegitimate. A profound desire for more of God is certainly never to be proscribed. It is proper for a believer to say he or she "covets" an interest in the prayers of another believer. What the Scripture does teach is that a deep desire for something that belongs to somebody else (cf. the tenth commandment) is that which makes it illegitimate. This is the essence of Achan's sin—desiring (and then appropriating) something that belongs to somebody else (i.e., God).

Under normal circumstances confession and repentance avert, or at least mitigate, punishment. But not here. This is not a normal circumstance. The nature of the items he took are not the problem. The first item was a beautiful mantle from Shinar, a place name connected with Babylonia in Gen. 10:10; 11:2; Dan. 1:2 (curiously, the Septuagint renders Shinar not as a place name, but with the Greek *poikilēn*, "multicolored," the same used in the Septuagint of Gen. 37:3 for the coat Jacob made for Joseph). Additionally, Achan seized silver and gold. Possibly, Achan is guilty of a double sin. Joshua's earlier directive was twofold: Israel was to utterly destroy virtually everything and everybody in Jericho (6:17), but the silver and gold were to go into Yahweh's treasury

(6:19). In keeping the mantle, Achan violated the first part of Joshua's order, and in helping himself to some silver and gold, he defied the second part. What makes his act of seizure unredeemable surely has something to do with the fact that what he took was to be devoted completely to, or reserved for, God and God alone. This is a more likely suggestion than, say, his act of public confession came too tardily and only after he was put on the spot.

What makes this incident mysterious is that his sons and daughters (for some unexplained reason, his wife is not mentioned), the absconded articles, his animals, and his tent all suffer judgment. Achan himself is stoned (and subsequently incinerated?); everybody and everything else associated with him is burned (7:25), a penalty that is imposed elsewhere only in the case of serious sexual offenses (Gen. 38:24; Lev. 20:14; 21:9).

Various explanations have been offered as to why the perpetrator's children, domestic animals, and tent either perish or are destroyed. The narrative nowhere claims that the children collaborated with their father. And certainly, the oxen, sheep, and donkeys were not in on the usurpation!

The standard, time-honored explanation, rooted in the writings of H. Wheeler Robinson, is that this part of the narrative is an illustration of "corporate personality"; that is, because ancient Israel did not tend to distinguish between the individual and the group, their thinking subordinated the individual to the group and subsumed the former in the latter. Accordingly, a group is seen to function as a single individual. This idea is generally discredited today, at least as conceptualized by Robinson, and its possible application to Joshua 7 has been vitiated.

Close to the preceding suggestion is the idea that this part of Joshua 7 illustrates that relatives or employees, and not just living quarters and animals, could be considered personal property. This would be true of slaves, daughters, and even wives. So understood, Joshua 7 tells of the destruction of Achan and all his "property."

A third possibility is that the crime of Achan falls into a category not covered by Israel's normal legal system. Hence, what we have here are drastic, highly abnormal measures for an unusual case.

A fourth possibility focuses on the importance of the violation of the *kherem* regulation and the attending consequences in Joshua 7. It suggests that "the tabooed status from the misappropriated objects spread to Achan's family and his possessions" (Kaminsky 1995: 86). "He, his family, his domestic animals and his tent, had to be destroyed, since all incurred the *herem* status. This is not a case, then, of vicarious or collective punishment pure and simple, but a case of collective contagion of a taboo status . . . though, to be sure, the actual guilt of the misappropriation was Achan's alone" (Greenberg 1960: 24; see also Krasovec 1984: 67–68). Here, then, is a fundamental difference between the concepts of collective responsibility and contagion liability. In the first, those who bear the guilt of the offense of another do not constitute, just by their presence, a threat to the community's well-being. On the other hand, those who bear contagion liability are, by their very presence, a threat to the community, and therefore face elimination (Jackson 1972: 164).

Chapter 7 ends with the name of the place where all of this took place. The place of execution and cremation is the Valley of Achor (vv. 24, 26). In v. 25 Joshua asks Achan, "Why did you [sg.] bring trouble [ʿakar] on us? May Yahweh today trouble [ʿakar] you [sg.]." Therefore, "the place is called Valley of Trouble [ʿakor] until this day." (v. 26). Sadly, the very first name given by an Israelite to a site after entering the land is "Valley of Trouble," or "Devastation Valley." Hardly an auspicious beginning! In fact, so connected is Achan (ʿakan) with Achor (ʿakor), that the Septuagint consistently in Joshua 7 calls him "Achar," the same label that identifies him in 1 Chron. 2:7.

Past failures, however, need not be set in concrete. The prophet Hosea envisions a day when Yahweh will bring Israel to spiritual renewal (2:14–23). One portion of that divine promise (v. 15) says, "I will give her back her vineyards and make the Valley of Achor a door of hope." Apart from the reference to Achor, one notes another allusion in Hosea's prophecy to Joshua 7 in that the Hebrew for "her vineyards" (kerameyah) recalls the name of Achan's father, Carmi (karmi), "my vineyard." Achor had, for a long time, one claim to fame. It was the place where Israel first sinned upon entering Canaan. But in Hosea's forecast that memory and reputation are laid to rest. The spatial topography of Joshua 7 in Hosea serves "as both prism and outline for a more interior journey that would restore Israel, and guide her towards a renewed covenantal fidelity with YHWH" (Fishbane 1985: 361). This is who the God of Scripture is—the one who can turn a valley of trouble into a door of hope.

With the rectification of *kherem* violation behind, Joshua can now turn his attention to a second assault on Ai (8:1–29). The narrative includes . . .

1. Yahweh's command to lay siege against Ai (8:1–2).
2. The troops who will set the ambush are sent ahead (8:3–9).
3. The next morning the main army moves on Ai (8:10–13).
4. Joshua and the main troops feign defeat and retreat (8:14–17).

5. Ai is captured and burned; the king is spared, but his troops, caught in an ambush, are slaughtered (8:18–23).
6. The noncombatant occupants of Ai are put to the sword (8:24–28).
7. Ai's king is executed (8:29).

Some significant differences exist between the accounts of the battle first against Jericho, then against Ai. In the Jericho account the miraculous is heavily stressed. Otherwise impenetrable walls need only be circuited by trumpet-blowing, ark-toting priests and screaming warriors for them to collapse. No siege weaponry needed here! In the Ai account the miraculous is not ignored, but it is downplayed. Here, the emphasis is on military strategy, logistics, setting up an ambush and catching the enemy in between, what in military terms is called a pincer movement. God works through miracle; God works through human planning and strategizing.

Another difference is that at Jericho, even before the invasion starts, the people are instructed to "kharam" Jericho and everything in it to Yahweh (6:17). No such command precedes the order to attack Ai, unless it be Yahweh's oblique "You shall do to Ai and its king as you did to Jericho" (8:12). It is true that *kharam* is used in the Ai narrative, but only after the confrontation is finished (8:26).

This second difference points to a third that is quite unexpected. In the Jericho narrative the Israelites were strictly forbidden to accumulate for themselves any booty from the spoils of war. Achan, of course, violated that ban. In the Ai narrative the case regarding booty is just the opposite. Here, the Israelites are allowed to keep for themselves the spoil and livestock of Ai (8:2, 27). In other words, "Achan is executed for doing at Jericho what every Israelite is given permission to do at Ai" (Polzin 1980: 114). Achan's actions perpetrated at Jericho are sinful. Achan's actions, had they been perpetrated at Ai, would have been perfectly normal and acceptable. The Ai incident, with its green light for retaining spoil for one's personal benefit, has its closest parallels with Deut. 2:34–35 and 3:6–7, both of which speak of the legitimacy of plundering the livestock and booty of a city or town that has been "kharemed" (see also Josh. 11:11–14). Such permission is limited to booty as the consequence of victory, never the goal of victory (Mitchell 1993: 78).

A fourth difference is the contrast between two characters who emerge respectively from within the larger narratives, Rahab and Achan.

	Status	Sex	Relationship to Yahweh	New status
Rahab	outsider	female	fearful and faithful	insider
Achan	insider	male	fearless and faithless	outsider

The story of the capturing and razing of Ai, spread over Joshua 7–8, has in its various components parallels with antecedent and subsequent events (Begg 1986: 320–33, from whom I draw the parallels below). The two events narrated by Moses in Deuteronomy 1–11 in which Yahweh threatens to annihilate his people for sinning is the retelling of the spy story from Numbers 13–14 in Deuteronomy 1 and the retelling of the golden calf story from Exodus 32 in Deuteronomy 9. All three events follow this pattern:

Defection-disaster	Interlude-return	Restoration-triumph
sending the spies (Deut. 1:19–46)	elimination of the exodus generation (2:1–16)	Israel defeats Sihon and Og (2:17–3:11)
the golden calf (Deut. 9:8–14, 22–24)	elimination of the calf, and Moses' intercession (9:15–21, 25–29)	God rewrites the tablets (10:1–11)
Ai (Josh. 7:1–5)	elimination of Achan (7:6–26)	victory at Ai (8:1–29)

The similarities between Joshua 7–8 and Deut. 1:9–3:11 are especially clear (Begg 1986: 324–25):

1. There is the sending of spies and their report (Deut. 1:22–25; Josh. 7:2–3).
2. Israel advances only to be routed, and the chasers become the chased (Deut. 1:43–44; Josh. 7:4–5).
3. Defeated Israel weeps (Deut. 1:45); Joshua laments (Josh. 7:6–9).
4. Israel's behavior arouses Yahweh's fury (Deut. 1:34; Josh. 7:1).
5. Yahweh withdraws his presence (Deut. 1:42; Josh. 7:12).
6. There is confession of sin by the guilty party (Deut. 1:41; Josh. 7:20–21).

7. The elimination of the guilty is required if Israel's fortunes are to be reversed (Deut. 1:46–2:16; Josh. 7:24–26).
8. Yahweh, once the problem is rectified, tells Israel to move again against the enemy, and promises his assistance (Deut. 2:18–25; Josh. 8:1–2).
9. Israel is attacked by the enemy (Deut. 2:32; 3:1; Josh. 8:14–16).
10. Israel defeats the attackers (Deut. 2:33; 3:3; Josh. 8:21–23).
11. There is application of *kherem* to a hostile population (Deut. 2:34; 3:6; Josh. 8:26).
12. Enemy cattle are taken as spoil (Deut. 2:35; 3:7; Josh. 8:27).

The two stories, taken together, make some powerful points: (1) human advice has the potential to lead to disaster; (2) defeats can be turned into triumphs, but only when sin is dealt with appropriately and God's ways are honored; (3) sins of attitude (Deuteronomy, negativism; Joshua, cockiness) can be as destructive as sins of action; (4) in engaging the enemy, the bottom line is the presence or absence of a blessing God.

C. 8:30–35. With two victories in hand, it is time for Israel to abandon militarism, at least temporarily, and engage in public acts of worship (vv. 30–31) and in a fresh hearing of the word of God first given to Moses (vv. 32–35).

Joshua's first act after the conquest of Ai is altar building on Mount Ebal. After inscribing a copy of the law of Moses on stones, Joshua reads it to the entire assembly, half of whom are stationed in front of Mount Gerizim and half in front of Mount Ebal (v. 33). Gerzim, approximately 2,600 feet high, rises above the city of Shechem on the south. Ebal, approximately 2,800 feet high, rises above the city of Shechem on the north. The blessing is to be pronounced on Gerizim, possibly because Gerizim is on Shechem's south side (see Deut. 11:29; 27:12–13), that is, the right-hand side for one facing eastward; conversely, the curse is to be pronounced on Ebal, on Shechem's north side, that is, the left-hand ("sinister") side. Also, Gerizim is more lush and fertile than Ebal. Since both hills are composed of monolithic limestone, there would be plenteous stone available for Joshua on which to inscribe the Torah. The distance from Ai to Shechem/Ebal/Gerizim is about twenty miles due north. Joshua does what he does in fulfillment of the command that Yahweh had given to his predecessor Moses (Deut. 27:1–13).

This brief episode points to the importance of balance and inclusivity in a community's worshiping experience. There is a balance here between times of festive celebration in worship, the offering of sacrifices to God (vv. 30–31), and times for the solemn hearing of the word of God (vv. 32–35). There is also balance, rather than selectivity, in the hearing of that word. For it is a word that speaks not only about the possibility for blessing, but also the possibility for curse (v. 34).

Inclusivity is evidenced here by the words "all Israel" (v. 33). It is an occasion that cuts across lines of ethnicity ("alien as well as citizen," vv. 33, 35), gender ("the women," v. 35), and age ("the little ones," v. 35).

The emphasis on Joshua's obedience, doing just as Moses earlier commanded (vv. 31, 33, 34, 35), is a refreshing contrast with the immediately preceding event, where Israel, or Achan, did not do as Yahweh commanded. At the same time, the occasion of worshiping God and reflecting on his word does not prevent the Israelites from promptly being hoodwinked in their own encampment at Gilgal by the Gibeonites (ch. 9), because they failed to seek Yahweh's will and direction in the matter at hand (9:14). In 8:30–35 (Shechem) God's word is honored; in 9:1–15 (Gilgal) seeking God is ignored. In juxtaposing these two episodes, the text suggests this warning: "Beware of Gilgal after Shechem."

D. 9:1–27. From Shechem, the action shifts to the city of Gibeon, which is approximately seven miles southwest of Ai. The chapter opens with a stunning contrast of two diametrically different responses by various peoples in Canaan toward the presence of the Israelites. First, one group chose the path of resistance and formed a military coalition to launch an offensive attack against Israel (vv. 1–2). The other group, the Gibeonites, chose the path of nonresistance and acceptance of Israel, and eventually exacted a covenant from them (vv. 3–15). Unlike their counterparts, the Gibeonites, like Rahab, have not only heard of Joshua (v. 3), but also, more importantly, have heard of Joshua's Lord (vv. 9–10, 24). If the other kings had heard of that same divine power and reality, they chose to ignore it—to their detriment.

It is the Gibeonites who take the initiative, rather than waiting to be attacked by Israel. Verse 4 states that the Gibeonites acted with guile, cunningly, with a ruse. The word for this is ʿormah, which is quite close to the word used in Gen. 3:1 for the "cunning" serpent (ʿarum). While the root ʿ-r-m carries condemnatory force in places (e.g., Exod. 21:14, the murderer who kills "with guile," the exact same expression as in Josh. 9:4), in other places it carries the idea of a virtue, such as prudence, shrewdness, cleverness (Prov. 1:4; 8:5; 22:3). So, are the Gibeonites treacherous or clever?

Their plan was a great one. They donned costumes that gave the Israelites the impression that they were defenseless travelers from a far country who wandered into Israel's camp at Gilgal. Their props included worn-out sacks, carried by their donkeys, worn-out wineskins, worn-out sandals and clothes, and some dry and moldy food. Furthermore, they ask Israel to "make a covenant" with them (v. 6), something Joshua later does (v. 15).

The expression "make a covenant" is literally "cut a covenant." Since the phrase is followed by the preposition *l* (*karat berit l*), it means literally, "make a covenant *to*." This is the expression used when a covenant is made between non-equals, a superior and a subordinate party. When the parties to a covenant are equals, the expression used is either "make a covenant *with*" (*ʾim*) or "make a covenant *between*" (*ben*). Here, it is the Israelites who will impose the terms of the covenant, should it be granted, on the Gibeonites. A good parallel to this is found in 1 Sam. 11:1, where the besieged Jabesh-gileadites say to Nahash and the Ammonites, "Make a covenant with us [literally, 'cut a covenant to us'], and we will serve you." The Gibeonites reinforce their inferior status by frequently mentioning to Joshua that they are his "servants" (vv. 8, 9, 11).

Joshua's decision to "make a covenant to" the Gibeonites is a clear and serious violation of Yahweh's earlier dicta to Israel to *not* "make a covenant to" any nations once they are settled in Canaan (Exod. 23:32; 34:12; Deut. 7:2).

The ruse perpetrated by the Gibeonites has a number of parallels with the account of Israel's covenant renewal in the plains of Moab, narrated in Deuteronomy 29.

Deuteronomy 29	Joshua 9
the clothes on your back have not worn out (v. 5)	worn-out clothes (v. 5)
the sandals on your feet have not worn out (v. 5)	worn-out, patched sandals on their feet (v. 5)
you have not eaten bread (v. 6)	dry and moldy provisions (v. 5)
you have not drunk wine (v. 6)	torn and mended wineskins (v. 4)

One point that emerges from these parallels is that Joshua 9 pictures the Gibeonites as looking "like Israel would have looked had it not been for Yahweh" (Hawk 1991: 89). Furthermore, the Gibeonites are aware of what Yahweh did to the kings Sihon and Og in the Transjordan (v. 10), which is precisely the two battles Moses recalls in his address in Deuteronomy 29 (v. 7). Again, those present at the covenant renewal ceremony in Deuteronomy 29 include not only elders and (male) officials, but also children, women, and the aliens who "cut your wood and draw your water" (v. 11). This latter phrase is the one used in Joshua 9 to describe the status imposed on the Gibeonites by Joshua (vv. 21, 27).

Finally, we note that the Gibeonites know, somehow, about that part of Moses' writings in which God instructed Israel to employ *kherem* against the inhabitants of Canaan (v. 24). This may explain why the Gibeonites repeat that they have come from a "distant land" (just a few miles away!) in vv. 6, 9. According to Deut. 20:10–18, only cities within the boundaries of the Promised Land are to be "kharamed" unconditionally (vv. 16–18). By contrast, towns situated outside these boundaries, that is, towns that are "far" (*rekhoqot*) from Israel, may escape *kherem* if they surrender, and instead be put into forced labor (vv. 10–15). In Josh. 9:6, 9, the Gibeonites claim they are from a land that is *rekhoqah*. It is as if they are "using the biblical law so as to circumvent it" (Fishbane 1985: 207). (Unfortunately, the Gibeonites are not alone in so abusing Scripture and misapplying it to fit one's own agenda.)

Both chapters talk about covenants: God's covenant with Israel (Deuteronomy 29); Israel's covenant with the Gibeonites (Joshua 9). What guarantees the perpetuation of Israel's covenant with the Gibeonites is not the worthiness of the Gibeonites, but rather, the irrevocable nature of Joshua's promise and commitment, the swearing of an oath (vv. 15, 18, 19). It should not take too much imagination to see that this is precisely the basis of Yahweh's covenant with Israel—not the worthiness of the latter, but the gracious, promissory, oath-taking actions of the former. "Israel *is* Gibeon writ large" (Polzin 1980: 120).

Undoubtedly, the chapter highlights the trickery and the adroitness of the Gibeonites. It all begins with a (mis)quotation by some Gibeonites who recite the words of their elders back home to Joshua. This is one pattern of discourse using quotations in which X quotes Y to Z, using what is not only an unverifiable quotation, but also what is an outright lie (Savran 1988: 24).

The quoted speaker (X)	The original speaker (Y)	The hearer (Z)	The deception
Josh. 9:11: Gibeonites	Gibeon's elders	Joshua	"Take provisions in your hand . . ."
1 Sam. 19:17: Michal	David	Saul	"Let me go. Why should I kill you?"

The quoted speaker (X)	The original speaker (Y)	The hearer (Z)	The deception
1 Sam. 21:2: David	Saul	Ahimelech	"No one must know anything . . ."
2 Sam. 1:7–9: an Amalekite	Saul	David	"Come, stand over me . . ."
2 Sam. 16:3: Ziba	Mephibosheth	David	"Today the house of Israel . . ."
1 Kings 13:18: a prophet	an angel	a man of God	"Bring him back with you . . ."
2 Kings 5:22: Gehazi	Elisha	Naaman	"Two members of a company . . ."

But surely the narrative is about more than a Gibeonite ruse and Israelite carelessness, as important as this emphasis is. In contrasting Gibeon's submission to Israel with the belligerence of others against Israel, the passage becomes "an object lesson in responsiveness to Yahweh's actions and warnings against resistance" (Stone 1991: 34). Those who submit survive; those who resist perish. That is a foundational teaching of all of Scripture.

E. 10:1–43. The next portion of Joshua details aspects of Israelite campaigns and conquests in the southern portions of Canaan. But unlike the campaigns described in chs. 6–9 (in central Canaan), in which Israel initiated the conquest, here, the campaigns are defensive rather than aggressive in nature. (The same holds true, by the way, for the northern campaigns to be described in ch. 11.) There is in ch. 10 no word from Yahweh to Joshua instructing him to employ *kherem* against Jerusalem or any other southern Canaanite city.

On the contrary, the Israelites find themselves once again at war, but only to come to the assistance of a covenant subordinate, Gibeon, who is the object of an aggressive attack launched by a military coalition of five kings. This coalition targets Gibeon rather than Israel. The confrontation is with the former rather than the latter. This is understandable, because from the perspective of these five Amorite/Canaanite kings, the Gibeonites are the defector while the Israelites represent the main power. Their goal is not to annihilate Israel, but to punish and restore the delinquent Gibeonites.

The chapter includes the following episodes:

1. Adoni-zedek, king of Jerusalem, panics after hearing what Joshua did to Ai and of his pact with the Gibeonites (10:1–2).
2. Adoni-zedek's panic moves him to spearhead the formation of a military coalition in order to attack Gibeon (10:3–6).
3. Joshua, when solicited for his intervention, comes to the defense of the Gibeonites, and defeats the aggressors and slaughters them (but not their kings), primarily because of Yahweh's sending of a shower of tremendous hailstones (10:7–11).
4. Joshua's miraculous ability to stop the sun and the moon, thus prolonging the hours of daylight, enables him to rout the aggressors (10:12–15).
5. The five kings flee the scene of battle and seek refuge in a cave, only to be discovered by Israelite soldiers, who incarcerate them in the cave. Shortly thereafter, the kings are released from the cave, only to be executed, with their corpses first suspended from trees and then thrown back into the cave, which is then permanently sealed (10:16–27).
6. A listing of seven southern Canaanite cities that fell to Joshua and the Israelites: Makkedah (10:28); Libnah (10:29–30); Lachish (10:31–32); Gezer (10:33); Eglon (10:34–35); Hebron (10:36–37); Debir (10:38–39).
7. A summarizing statement of Joshua's southern battles (10:40–43): by region (v. 40), by territories (v. 41), by chronological framework (v. 42).

Hearing about something God has done provokes one of two diametrically different responses. Such hearing provokes either awe, acceptance, and submission (as in Josh. 2:10; 5:1; 9:3–4, 9–10), or hostility and resistance (as in 9:1–2; 10:1–3; 11:1–5). It never provokes indifference or cynicism. Stung by the defection of their ally the Gibeonites, five Amorite city-states marshal their forces to discipline their breakaway neighbors. The Old Testament records two other instances where five kings joined together in a coalition: Gen. 14:2 and Josh. 13:3. But unlike the coalition formed in Joshua 10, these two pentad-coalitions existed primarily for defensive purposes, for repelling the enemy and stalling outsider penetration into their territory.

Joshua's response to the Gibeonites' SOS is immediate and generous. To fend off "all" the kings of the Amorites (v. 6), he moves "all" his mighty warriors from Gilgal to Gibeon by night (vv. 7, 9). Several things of interest are present here. First, Joshua places a higher premium on the reliability of his word than he does on "letting the chips fall where they may." That is to say, by refusing to respond to the

Gibeonites' pleas for assistance, he would have permitted their fellow Amorites to do to the Gibeonites what Joshua and the Israelites would probably have done to them, had they not been tricked by the Gibeonites' ruse.

A second thing of interest here is that Yahweh's "Do not fear them. . . . Not one of them shall stand before you" (v. 8) comes after, not before, Joshua's departure from Gilgal with his troops (v. 7). Thus, the promise of God does not authorize Joshua's movements; rather, it affirms them. This is to be expected. When people give their word, they do not need to ask God's guidance and will on whether or not they should honor that word.

Joshua and Israel do not fight alone. Surprisingly, no mention is made of the Gibeonites joining the fray, notwithstanding that it was their "sell-out" to Israel despite their numerous warriors that worried Adoni-zedek (v. 2). But who does fight with Joshua and Israel is none other than Yahweh. The Amorites suffer two kinds of casualties: those who die by the sword, and those who die by an "act of God," in this case, a devastating rain of great (hail)stones "thrown" from heaven (v. 11), with the casualties in group two outnumbering those in group one. Yahweh's action of "throwing down huge stones" (*shalak ʾavanim gedolot*) contains exactly the same phrase that is used later in the chapter (v. 27) when Joshua has the corpses of the five kings "thrown" (*shalak*) into the cave whose aperture is then sealed with "large stones" (*ʾavanim gedolot*).

The text does not make clear how the hailstones fell on the fleeing Canaanites but totally missed the pursuing Israelites. This element is part of the miraculous here too. It echoes the plagues in Exodus. There seems almost to be an invisible shield that prohibits the pestilence (Exod. 9:4, 6), hail (Exod. 9:26), and darkness (Exod. 10:23) from affecting the Israelites and their livestock. The bottom line is that the Old Testament affirms strongly its belief in the concept of divine intervention in warfare, an idea by no means unique to biblical faith (Weinfeld 1983: 121–47; Younger 1990: 208–11).

The best-known section of this chapter is Joshua asking the sun and moon to stand still until such time as Joshua might vanquish the enemy, and the heavenly bodies complying (vv. 12–14). The most likely interpretation of this is that Joshua believes he needs an extension of daylight to finish the battle. The stoppage of the sun would vouchsafe him victory.

While there are numerous places in the Old Testament where the utilization of darkness is a stratagem in battle (e.g., Gen. 14:15, Abram against the kings; Josh. 8:3, Joshua against Ai; Judg. 7:9, Gideon against the Midianites; 1 Sam. 11:5–10, Saul against the Ammonites; 1 Sam. 14:36, Saul against the Philistines; 1 Sam. 26:7, David against Saul; 2 Kings 6:14, the king of Aram against Elisha; 2 Kings 8:21, Jehoram against the Edomites; 2 Kings 19:35, the angel of Yahweh against the Philistines), there seems also to be the tradition of calling off the battle after sunset (2 Sam. 2:24–28).

Verses 12–14 begin with a prose introduction (12a), followed by a poem (vv. 12b–13a), followed by a comment in prose on the event (vv. 13b–14). Some portion of these three verses, ranging from a maximum of all three verses to a minimum of some portion of one of these verses, is said to be excerpted from the "Book of Jashar." There is only one other reference in the Old Testament to this book, and that is 2 Sam. 1:18, where David's lament over Saul and Jonathan is introduced with "He [David] ordered that The Song of the Bow be taught to the people of Judah; it is written in the Book of Jashar."

The Book of Jashar, that is, "The Book of the Righteous," is one of several books referred to by Old Testament writers that fall into the category of lost literature. Other examples are the "Book of the Wars of the Lord" (Num. 21:14), the "Book of the Annals of the Kings of Israel" (1 Kings 14:19, and cited 18x in the Old Testament), the "Book of the Annals of the Kings of Judah" (1 Kings 14:29, and cited 15x in the Old Testament), the "Book of the Acts of Solomon" (1 Kings 11:41), and the "Book of the Prophet Nathan" (1 Chron. 29:29). Because the references to the Book of Jashar and the Book of the Wars of the Lord always occur in conjunction with poetry, it is possible that these two books in particular were anthologies of early songs that rehearsed the story of Israel's battles in the earlier portions of national existence, conceivably a poetic epic beginning with the Hebrew conquest under Joshua and culminating in David's monarchy. The authors/compilers of Joshua and Second Samuel knew the Book of Jashar and quoted from it.

Debate continues over several portions of this episode. For example, in the phrase "he said in the sight of Israel" (v. 12), who is "he"? Who speaks to the sun and moon? Joshua (the probable answer)? God (a possible answer)? A similar problem surfaces in the phrase *'ad yiqqom goy 'oyevaw* (v. 13), which is traditionally translated "until the nation [*goy*] took vengeance on their enemies [*'oyevaw*]." One might also take Yahweh as the subject of the verb, and read, "until he had avenged himself upon the people of his enemies," or even take Joshua himself as the subject of the verb: "until he [Joshua] had taken vengeance upon the host of his enemies" (Peels 1995: 86–92).

But the most crucial issue is the identification of what actually happened. The possibilities are two. One is the interpretation provided by the prose comment of v. 13b: "the sun stopped [moving] in mid-heaven, and did not hurry to set for about a whole day." The other interpretation suggests that what happened at Gibeon was a celestial blackout in daytime, a solar eclipse, that threw the invading army into panic (Margalit 1992: 466–87). This explanation, while it has many commendable features, has the drawback of reading the prose comment of v. 13b as a complete misunderstanding of what actually happened.

We can propose that the attempt to discover what "actually happened" is a futile one, and one that the text does not demand. Assuming for the moment that the text speaks of the earth halting its rotation, may we not understand this as one of Scripture's uses of pictorial language that conveys the idea of a mighty God who can marshal the celestial bodies to assist his people? God uses hailstorms (times of darkness) and sunlight hours (times of light) to bring to naught the enemy (Howard 1993: 89; Barr 1977: 243–45, who chides some "fundamentalist" writers for adopting what is essentially a liberal-rationalist form of argumentation).

Favoring the interpretation of Josh. 10:12–13 as a reference to sun stoppage rather than solar eclipse is that this motif occurs elsewhere in Mediterranean literature. For example, one might refer to Agamemnon's prayer to Zeus (*The Iliad*, 2.412–15): "Most glorious and mighty Zeus, god of the Black Cloud, Lord of High Heaven, grant that the sun may not set and darkness fall before I bring down Priam's palace, blackened with smoke, send up his gates in flames, and rip the tunic on the breast of Hector with my bronze." Later in *The Iliad*, during a brief respite in the battle between the Trojans and the Achaens, we read, "Here the ox-eyed Queen of Heaven, now told the tireless Sun to sink into the Stream of Ocean. The sun had been disposed to linger, but at last he set, and the brave Achaeans enjoyed a respite from the grim struggle and the give-and-take of war" (18.239–42).

There may be a similar reference in the Canaanite Baal-Anath texts from ancient Ugarit (ʿnt:V:25–26). It occurs in a passage where Baal, the only important Canaanite god without a palace, persuades Anath to appeal to Asherah to ask El (the head of the pantheon) to authorize the god of craftsmanship, Kothar-wa-Hasis, to build Baal a palace. Anath agrees and is successful. As she approaches El, these two lines appear:

nrt. ʾilm.shpsh [ṣhrr]t
laʾ.. shmm[.] by [d. bn. ʾilm. m]t

Here are three representative translations of the two lines, which in the mythology of Canaan refer to Mot, the god of death, and his dominance over Shapash, the sun-goddess.

- H. L. Ginsberg, *ANET*, 137:
  Even the God's Torch Shapsh
  [Who wings] the expanse of heav[en],
  Is in El's Beloved Mot's hand.
- J. C. L. Gibson, *Canaanite Myths and Legends* (Edinburgh: 1977), 53:
  Shapash, the luminary of the gods [did grow hot]
  The heavens were wearied by the hand [of divine Mot].
- C. H. Gordon, *Ugarit and Minoan Crete* (New York: 1966), 56:
  The Luminary of the Gods, Sun, [burn]s.
  The heavens stop on [account of the god mo]t

(Gordon, in his *Ugaritic Textbook*, [Rome: 1965], 426, connects Ugaritic *la* with Hebrew *la'ah*, and renders the phrase "the heavens were weakened/stopt," as in Josh. 10:12–13.)

The last part of ch. 10 (vv. 28–43) narrates briefly other phases of Israel's conquest of cities throughout southern Canaan (Younger 1990: 226–28; 1995: 255–64). Throughout this section one repeatedly encounters phrases like "he [Joshua] utterly destroyed every person in it" (v. 28); "he left no one remaining" (v. 28); "he struck it with the edge of the sword, and every person in it" (v. 30); "leaving him no survivors" (v. 33). Given the pervasiveness of similar "exhaustive" language in other Near Eastern battle accounts, it is fair to say that one should interpret such phrases as hyperbole.

This is borne out by the fact that the two cities listed last, Hebron and Debir, which Joshua was supposed to have destroyed completely, turn up again in the first chapter of Judges (Hebron, 1:9–10; Debir, 1:11–15), and are subdued after Joshua's death by Caleb and Othniel. Rather than argue for a blatant inconsistency between Joshua and Judges (de Vaux 1978: 627), one could say that Joshua 10 highlights the first stages of military victory, while Judges 1 focuses on the much more difficult and lengthy task of gaining full political control over these same cities. Note that the final verse of Joshua 10 states that after these various and sundry conquests, "Joshua returned, and all Israel with him, to the camp at Gilgal." That is, Israel did not yet take up residence in any of these cities, even though they conquered them.

Further, note the information given in 10:42 that "Joshua took all these kings and their land *pa'am 'ekhat*." If one translates this Hebrew phrase as "in a single campaign" or "at one time," then it is certainly to be distinguished from the northern campaign in which Joshua "made war a long time with all these kings" (11:18). However, the exact same expression occurs in Josh. 6:3, 11, 14 to refer to the "once" or "one time" that the Israelites marched around Jericho. Assuming that the phrase means the same in ch. 10 as in ch. 6, then 10:42 is saying that Joshua took these cities "one time" or "once," implying that subsequent battles may be necessary in order to gain full control. The expression "*at* one time" would require the preposition *b*, as in 2 Sam. 23:8 ("whom he [David] killed at one time").

F. 11:1–23. In several ways, the account of Israel's victories in northern Canaan (11:1–20) parallels that just described in ch. 10.

Ch. 10	Ch. 11
1. A coalition of five kings headed by one king, Adoni-zedek of Jerusalem, is formed to attack Israel's ally, Gibeon (10:1–5).	A coalition of five kings headed by one king, Jabin of Hazor, is formed to attack Israel (11:1–5).
2. Both kings are moved to action because of what they have heard (10:1).	(11:1)
3. Yahweh tells Joshua, "Do not fear them" (10:8).	(11:6)
4. Yahweh uses the verb *natan* ("give") in the perfect ("for I have handed them over to you") (10:8).	Yahweh uses the verb *natan* in participial form ("I will hand over all of them") (11:6).
5. Joshua launches a defensive war and comes upon the enemy suddenly (10:9).	(11:7)
6. Joshua defeats the coalition (10:10–27), plus he conquers other cities in the area (10:28–39).	Joshua defeats Hazor (11:8–11), plus nearby cities (11:12–15).
7. Summarizing statement (10:40–43).	(11:16–20)

There are two novel elements in this chapter. One is the notice that the Jabin-led coalition came against Israel with horses and chariots (vv. 4, 6, 9) at the "waters of Merom" (thought by some archaeologists to be about ten miles west of Hazor). This is the only mention of horses and chariots in all the battle scenes depicted throughout Joshua. And while there is no hailstorm or stoppage of the sun and moon here, one wonders how a horseless, chariotless army could gain a stunning victory over the enemy who possessed both of these in abundance. That is the miracle here. We should more than likely interpret the reference to the Israelites cutting the hamstrings of the horses and burning their chariots (v. 9) as the means by which Israel managed to defeat these northern Canaanites, rather than interpreting that activity as the result of their victory over the invaders.

The other new element here is the reference to Joshua's elimination of the Anakim from the hill country of both Judah and Israel (vv. 21–22). Part of the population of Canaan before Israel's conquest, the Anakim were known and feared for their size (Num. 13:32–33; Deut. 1:28; 2:10).

Thus, in this chapter Israel faces an enemy who has two different kinds of superiority: weaponry (vv. 1–20) and size (vv. 21–22).

But lest the Israelites be tempted to boast that they deserve a pat on the back for the victories accomplished, the narrative gives the credit to Israel's Lord. In language reminiscent of Yahweh's treatment of pharaoh in the days of Moses and the exodus, v. 20 states that it was Yahweh who "hardened their hearts" so that these Canaanite cities would engage Israel in battle, and so be destroyed.

G. 12:1–24. This chapter summarizes Israel's victories under Joshua's leadership, first in the Transjordan area (vv. 1–6), then in the Cisjordan area (vv. 7–24). The first reviews the events of Deut. 2:24–3:17, especially the defeat of Sihon of Heshbon (Deut. 2:24–37), and of Og of Bashan (Deut. 3:1–7). The second encapsulates the events of Joshua 6–11, and lists thirty-one kings of captured territories.

This chapter seems to be on par with other ancient Near Eastern literature, where it would not be uncommon to find an onomastic list of cities and defeated lands that a given king conquered. In fact, we have instances where two different inscriptions describe the same king's list of conquered areas. When the two lists are compared, one notices that one city may be listed in one list but not the other, suggesting that the listings are selective and partial (rather than inaccurate). This may explain why in ch. 12 we find, for example, a listing of Joshua's defeat of the king of Megiddo (v. 21), not a word of which was mentioned in ch. 11. That simply points to the selective, as opposed to exhaustive, narration of the northern campaigns in Joshua 11 (Younger 1990: 230–32).

This section of Joshua, chs. 6–12, has highlighted Israel's engagement of Canaan's cities and their inhabitants. Against insuperable odds, ranging all the way from impenetrable walled cities to armies with horses and chariots, Israel has plugged away until the task was finished. Had Yahweh not been at the center of the engagement, Israel would not have even made it across the Jordan, never mind confront and vanquish cities and peoples with resources far greater than Israel's. Israel has neither horses nor chariots. But what Israel does have, which Canaan does not, is Yahweh.

We may summarize these seven chapters of Joshua by focusing on the faith theme, and following the phrasing of Baxter (1960: 264):

ch. 6: the fall of Jericho—faith triumphant
ch. 7: the sin of Achan—faith disabled
ch. 8: the fall of Ai—faith reempowered
ch. 9: Gibeon's guile—faith endangered
chs. 10–12: the fall of southern and northern Canaan, and summary—faith all-victorious

The Conquest as Historical Event

If a lay biblical reader were asked to summarize the thrust of Joshua 1–12 she or he might describe the contents this way: Joshua 1–12 tells of the conquest of Canaan and the Canaanites by the Joshua-led Israelites, who came across the Jordan from the east, took control of the central portions of the land, and then extended that control over southern and northern portions of Canaan. This conquest was swift, total, and brief, with everything being accomplished in the adult lifetime of one man.

However, many biblical scholars and archaeologists interpret these chapters differently, in fact, quite differently. At one end of the spectrum are those moderately critical historians who believe there is a good nucleus of historical truth in Joshua 1–12. That is, we can be certain that a Joshua-led group of Israelite tribes (not necessarily all twelve of them) succeeded in breaking down the resistance of the Canaanites in three campaigns: one in the center of the land (Jericho, Ai, Gibeon), a second in the territory of Judah (Makkedah, Libnah, Lachish Gezer, Eglon, Hebron, and Debir), and a third in Galilee, especially at Hazor. While not overthrowing the Canaanites, these battles exhausted them to the degree that the invading Israelite tribes (however many there were) were able to establish sovereignty in the hilly regions of Samaria, Judah, Galilee, and eventually extend that control beyond these limited toeholds. This position, then, would affirm the essential historicity of chs. 1–12, while freely admitting the presence of nonhistorical fictive elements such as (1) etymological explanations of place names paraded as historical information, or (2) battles that were actually later (say, in the days of the judges and that were retrospectively attributed to Joshua), or (3) even all "supernatural" events.

At the other end of the spectrum are those scholars who take an almost nihilistic view of this portion of the Old Testament. For them,

Joshua 1–12 is not partially inaccurate; it is totally inaccurate in terms of giving information about what "actually happened." In fact, historically speaking, the material is so fallacious that we must abandon altogether even the basic idea of a conquest. Israel never conquered the Canaanites. No walls tumbled down. No cities were circuited. No communities were put under *kherem*. No stones were raised up.

Accordingly, in place of the *conquest* model (hideous, anyway, because of its militancy), alternate models are proposed as a more objective interpretation of what actually took place.

One of these alternates is what we shall call the *immigration* model. The fundamental thesis of this model is the contention for a long (two centuries at least), relatively peaceful infiltration and immigration of different groups at different times (either Israelites or potential Israelites), some eventual amalgamation with indigenous peoples, and, only much later, in the time of David, the consolidation of Israel as the victor via military triumph. The line of distinction, if there was one, between the indigenous Canaanites and the immigrants had nothing to do with religion or theology or ethics or worldview. Rather, it had to do with residents versus (semi)nomads and farmers versus herders. What diminished the mutual suspicion of both groups of each other and contributed to more ecumenism and intermixing was that the intrusive group took on the modus vivendi of the residential group, that is, pastoral nomads became anchored farmers.

Another model that has been proposed to explain what "really happened" we shall call the *revolt* model, or the *social revolution* model. In this model, the Israelites turn out to be, at least for the most part, native Canaanites of a more servile type who, when they could stand the oppression of their "Solomons" no more, revolted against their rich taskmasters and their city-states, joined forces with some groups of invaders or immigrants, and carved out their own niche in Canaan. It is proposed that here we have the classic case of the Marxist teaching of the revolt of the peasants against the rich, land-monopolizing bourgeoisie. What the fugitives from Egypt contributed to this revolt was their worship of a god they called YHWH, a god who was shortly embraced (via conversion?) by the members of this oppressed, marginalized coalition as their consensual deity and who would unite them in a common cause. In such a model, "Canaanite" becomes a metaphor for "the haves," the hierarchy, the oppressor. Their religion is Baalism. "Israelite" becomes a metaphor for "the have-nots," the egalitarian, the beleaguered. Their religion is Yahwism.

So, we have three different approaches to the interpretation and evaluation of Joshua 1–12: (1) the conquest model, which we may iden-

tify as the archaeological approach; (2) the immigration model, which
we may identify as the history of traditions approach; and (3) the social
revolution model, which we may identify as the sociological approach.

Each one has its proponents. The conquest model (a complete and
unified achievement) is the traditional interpretation, and clearly enjoys wide acceptance among more conservative scholars. Its major and
more notable supporters have included the likes of W. F. Albright,
G. E. Wright, John Bright (especially his magisterial *History of Israel*
[3rd ed., Philadelphia: 1981] and his *Early Israel in Recent History Writing* [London: 1956]), and two late Israeli biblical scholars, Y. Kaufmann (*The Biblical Account of the Conquest of Palestine* [Jerusalem:
1953]), and Y. Yadin (*Military and Archaeological Aspects of the Conquest of Canaan in the Book of Joshua* [Jerusalem: 1965]). In more recent times, one might point to a scholar like J. Bimson, and to his book
Redating the Exodus and the Conquest (Sheffield: 1981).

The immigration (history of traditions) model first gained notoriety
through various writings of the German Old Testament scholar Al-
brecht Alt in the 1920s and 1930s, and was given a wider hearing in M.
Noth's well-received *History of Israel* (Eng. trans., Edinburgh: 1958),
and more recently in J. A. Soggin's *History of Ancient Israel* (Eng.
trans., Philadelphia: 1984), 152–53, and in M. Weippert's monograph
on the settlement of the Israelite tribes in Palestine (Naperville, Ill.:
1971).

The social revolution (sociological) model was given ventilation by
G. E. Mendenhall, especially ch. 7 of his *Tenth Generation* (Baltimore:
1973), and subsequently by his student N. K. Gottwald in *Tribes of Yahweh* (New York: 1975) and *The Hebrew Bible: A Socio-Literary Introduction* (Philadelphia: 1985), 272–76.

Now, the proponents of models two and three readily agree that
their reconstruction of the appearance and settlement of Israel in
Canaan differs radically from that of the canonical account found in
Joshua 1–12. They take their positions not because they bring an
inbred skepticism to the text's historicity or because they bring a
bias against "supernatural" explanations of otherwise "natural" events.
They may well entertain such a presupposition, but that is not the controlling factor.

There are at least four reasons why alternative models to the canonical model have been suggested:

First, there seems to be some contradiction/tension between the account of the "conquest" as narrated in Joshua 1–12 and as told in Judg.
1:1–2:5. In the former, the conquest is a unified assault against all the
land of Canaan, which is eminently successful. In the latter, by con-

trast, various tribes appear to act independently, some concurrent with Joshua, some after his death. And for the most part these campaigns, at best, meet with minimal success. Note how frequently in Judges 1 the reader encounters the phrase "X did *not* drive out the inhabitants of Y."

Second, some of the narratives in Joshua 6–11 lack, for some commentators, historical credibility when attention is paid to the full text. Take, for example, the account of the southern campaign in Josh. 10:1–43. In response to a request from the besieged Gibeonites, Joshua and his soldiers advance under the cover of darkness from Gilgal to Gibeon, a distance of about twenty miles and uphill all the way (v. 9). Even though his soldiers were sleepless the night before, they chase the enemy down the road of Beth-horon and from there to Azekah and Makkedah, a pursuit covering a distance of approximately thirty-five miles (v. 10). Then, surprisingly, we read in v. 15 (a verse *not* found in the Septuagint) that Joshua and all Israel returned to their base camp in Gilgal, only to resume operations in the Makkedah area in vv. 16–27.

Third, adherents of models two and three believe they can discern traces of their reconstruction in the biblical account itself. Those who appeal to the immigration model find support for that concept in verses like Judg. 1:19: "Judah took possession of the hill country, but could not drive out the inhabitants of the plain, because they had chariots of iron." This reflects the idea that the original immigrants at first settled in the sparsely populated mountain regions. One might also appeal to the fact that the patriarchs, unlike their successors, lived in harmony with the resident population, and even intermarried with Canaanites (Genesis 38).

Those who opt for the social revolution model would appeal to Canaanite "converts" to Yahwism such as Rahab and her family (Joshua 6), Canaanite "allies" who, while not becoming Yahwists, supported Israel (Joshua 9, Gibeonites), and Canaanite "neutrals" who never engaged in hostile action against Israel (there is no reference anywhere in Joshua to the Israelites invading Shechem [in the hill country of Ephraim], the site at which Joshua oversaw the great covenant renewal service [ch. 24]).

Fourth, the trump card used most frequently to write the obituary of the conquest model is archaeology. Long thought to be the greatest evidence to support a conquest, archaeological excavations now, for many scholars, deliver the coup de grâce to the idea of a conquest. In particular, scholars cite the evidence, or more precisely, the lack of evidence, at (1) Jericho (Joshua 6), (2) Ai (Joshua 8), and (3) Hazor (Joshua 11) to buttress their case against the military conquest model.

Before we progress further, let us recall the dates assigned to the various archaeological periods in Palestine that relate to Joshua. Despite some minor disagreement in dating, especially when dealing with subdivisions, the following represents a consensus:

Early Bronze Age (EBA)	3000–2100/2000 B.C.
Middle Bronze Age (MBA)	2100/2000–1550 B.C.
MB I	2100/2000–1900 B.C.
MB IIa	1900–1700 B.C.
MB IIb	1700–1600 B.C.
MB IIc	1600–1550 B.C.
Late Bronze Age (LBA)	1550–1200 B.C.
LB I	1550–1400 B.C.
LB IIa	1400–1300 B.C.
LB IIb	1300–1200 B.C.
Iron Age (IA)	1200–300 B.C.

For those who read the exodus from Egypt and the invasion of Canaan as historical events, two possible dates (again, with minor modifications) are suggested for these events: (1) the earlier date, that is, the exodus from Egypt took place in the fifteenth century B.C., probably during the tenure of the Eighteenth-Dynasty Pharaoh Thutmose/Thutmosis III (1490–1436 B.C.), with the conquest under Joshua following forty years later; (2) the later date, that is, the exodus from Egypt took place in the early thirteenth century B.C., probably during the tenure of the Nineteenth-Dynasty Pharaohs Seti I (1302–1290 B.C.) or Ramses II (1290–1224 B.C.).

We are not interested here in arguing the merits of the early date versus the late date, or vice versa. Both seem to have a measure of support from biblical and extrabiblical evidence. It is one of the few issues in Old Testament studies on which even very conservative scholars disagree with each other. What we will observe is that to accept the early date is to say that the conquest under Joshua took place sometime during LB I (1550–1400 B.C.). To subscribe to the late date is to say that the conquest under Joshua took place sometime during LB IIb (1300–1200 B.C.).

Of the three "problem" cities cited above, Ai (said in Joshua 8 to be conquered by Joshua) is the most conspicuous. Joshua 7:2 describes Ai as "near Beth-aven, east of Bethel." Between Bethel (the modern village of Beitin?) and the desert to its east there is a site, one large mound, now called et-Tell (which is an Arabic translation of the Hebrew "Ai," "ruin(s)"), which most think is ancient Ai. If that equation is correct, then those archaeologists who have excavated et-Tell have discovered a huge gap in occupation here between the EBA, when Ai was quite a large city, and the IA, when a tiny Israelite settlement was established. In other words, throughout the entire LBA, Ai was unoccupied! In our judgment, the results of excavation at et-Tell present the stiffest argument against the historicity of a biblical event. Of course, the final word is seldom in on an archaeological excavation, and even the equation of Ai with et-Tell may one day have to be abandoned. But for the moment, the evidence is negative.

What about Jericho? Three different extended periods of excavation have taken place at Jericho in the twentieth century. The first was conducted by a group of German and Austrian archaeologists over the years 1907–1911. Their conclusion matched that of more recent archaeologists at Ai: Jericho was unoccupied throughout the LBA. A British archaeologist, John Garstang, represents the second phase of excavation at Jericho, and his work spans the years 1930–1936. He corrected his predecessors by excavating the remains of a LBA settlement (most of which had eroded). Furthermore, he identified a collapsed wall of Jericho as a LBA wall, and labeled it as the fallen wall of Joshua 6. The third phase—for many, the most definitive—of excavation at Jericho was done by Garstang's prize pupil, Kathleen Kenyon, from 1952–1958. She disagreed with her mentor's conclusions at two vital points: (1) Jericho was unoccupied, or minimally occupied but not fortified, from the middle of the LBA to the end of IA I, and (2) what Garstang thought were LBA fortifications were, in fact, from MB IIb IIc, a millennium earlier at least.

Her conclusions notwithstanding, Kenyon writes about her discovery of a house and some tombs at the latest LBA occupation of Jericho: perhaps she had chanced upon "part of the kitchen of a Canaanite woman, who may have dropped the juglet beside the oven and fled at the sound of the trumpets of Joshua's men" (1957: 265).

Kenyon's conclusions vis-à-vis Jericho's occupation and especially its final destruction date are in process of reevaluation, particularly in the work of Bryant Wood (1990a: 44–58; 1990b: 45, 47–49, 68). Wood agreed with Kenyon that City IV at Jericho met a violent end, but unlike Kenyon, who dated this destruction to about 1550 B.C. (the end of the MBA period), Wood dated it to around 1400 B.C. (thus arguing indirectly for the early date of the exodus/conquest briefly alluded to above). He based his conclusions on four lines of evidence: (1) ceramic data that included a significant number of examples from LB I (1550–1400 B.C.); (2) the stratigraphy of City IV—there are too many occupational phases (twenty of them) for MBA Jericho to be squeezed into the one hundred years of MB III (or the latter part of MBIIb and the first part of MBIIc; 1650–1550 B.C.); (3) scarab evidence (scarabs are tiny Egyptian amulets shaped like a dung beetle with an inscription on them) from a cemetery northwest of Jericho extending from the eighteenth century B.C. (the Thirteenth Dynasty) to the early fourteenth century B.C. (the Eighteenth Dynasty), suggesting that the cemetery was in use to the end of LB I; (4) a single carbon-14 sample from the destruction debris that was dated to 1410 B.C., plus or minus forty years. Also, Wood comments on the abundance of grain found in the destruction, evidence, he believed, that correlated closely with the Joshua story of Israel invading shortly after the spring harvest.

In sum, one may say that the archaeological data from Jericho cannot serve as a decisive argument against the conquest of Jericho by the Israelites. On the contrary, archaeological data from Jericho, unlike from Ai, serves to buttress the biblical account.

The third city that calls for comment is Hazor, located nine miles north of the Sea of Galilee. According to Josh. 11:10, Hazor's greatness is indicated by the phrase "was the head of all those kingdoms." Along with Jericho (Josh. 6:24) and Ai (Josh. 8:19), Hazor (Josh. 11:11, 13) is one of only three cities that Joshua conquered and then burned—which indicates, by the way, that Israel came not to destroy the land, but to occupy it and preserve it in as best condition as possible. In the various levels of occupation at Hazor, then, archaeologists look for both destruction evidence and burning evidence.

All excavators at Hazor agree that the city (Stratum XIII of the "Upper City" and IA of the "Lower City") was violently destroyed in the mid-thirteenth century B.C. (LB IIb), and subsequently gave way to evolving as a small, unfortified village.

Now, what is to be done with this evidence? One school of thought suggests that because Judg. 4:2 identifies another Jabin (Jabin II?) as "king of Canaan who reigned in Hazor" (at least a couple of generations after Joshua), and whom Barak and Deborah attacked and prevailed against, one of two things must be true: either (1) archaeology provides support for Joshua 11, that Israel may have attacked and razed Hazor in the 1200s B.C., but archaeology provides no evidence to support the story of Judges 4; or (2) what the destruction level of Stratum XIII reflects is Barak's attack on Hazor, and in fact, the story as described in Joshua 11 never took place. It is a literary story (inspired by Judges 4–5), not a historical one.

Another school of thought takes a different approach, believing you can have your archaeological cake and eat it too. It is possible to look for an earlier destruction level at Hazor than that of Stratum XIII/IA, and in fact, Stratum II (possibly around the time of Thutmosis III, fifteenth century B.C. [LB I]) shows such evidence. Thus: Stratum II, Joshua; Stratum XIII, Barak. What is absent from this particular stratum, however, is any evidence of burning.

Perhaps one might identify Stratum XIII as reflecting Joshua's campaign of Hazor without having to sacrifice the historicity of the Jabin/Hazor account in Judges 4–5. Note that unlike the Jabin of Joshua 11, the Jabin of Judges 4 is called "king of Hazor" (4:17), but more frequently "king of Canaan" (4:2, 23, 24 [2x]). Furthermore, Barak's battle in Judges 4 involves not Jabin in Hazor, but Sisera in Harosheth-ha-goiim and near Wadi Kishon. There is little, or nothing, on Hazor! This might indicate that Jabin II's Hazor was much smaller than Jabin I's, or that Jabin II ruled the *region* of Hazor, but from a different, nearby town in the area (Waltke 1990: 192–93).

The differences (mounting to contradiction) that have been maintained between the conquest account in Joshua 1–12 (unified, quick, all-victorious) and that in Judg. 1:1–36 (local, protracted, mixed results) are, in our judgment, exaggerated. For one thing, "mixed results" are present in Joshua 1–12 (cf. 7:2–5). For another, abundant evidence elsewhere in Joshua indicates that much land remains to be conquered after Joshua has disappeared from the scene, both extra-Palestinian territories (13:1–6, 13), and territories in Canaan proper (15:63, the Jebusites of Jerusalem; 16:10, Canaanites in Gezer; 17:12–13, Canaanites in the territory of Manasseh; 19:47, the Danites succumb and have to relocate).

Joshua upbraids no less than seven tribes who had not yet taken possession of their inheritance (18:2–3). And in his farewell address (ch. 23), Joshua speaks of those nations that yet remain (v. 4), which one day Yaweh will push back and drive out (v. 5). And for any disobedience from Israel, God will cease dispersing such nations; rather, they will become a snare and trap (vv. 12–13). Such sentiments recall earlier words that Yahweh will drive out the nations not by blitzing, but "little by little" (Exod. 23:30; Deut. 7:22). Even the thirty-one defeated kings in Joshua 12 represent "not a conquest in depth, merely a cropping of the leadership" (Kitchen 1978: 90). And note also that in the introduction in ch. 12 to Israel's victories in Transjordan (under Moses), one reads, "These are the kings whom the Israelites defeated, *whose land they occupied*" (v. 1). By contrast, in the introduction to Israel's victories in Cisjordan (under Joshua), one reads, "The following are the kings of the land whom Joshua and the Israelites defeated" (v. 7). Conspicuously absent is "whose land they occupied," except in the proleptic announcement of v. 7b. Thus, it seems plausible that we need to distinguish between a swift military sweep throughout the land (Joshua 6–12) with the subsequent permanent occupation of the land and a much slower and more difficult process at that (some latter portions of Joshua and Judg. 1:1–36).

3. Allocating Canaan-land (13:1–21:45)

In this large section dealing with the division of the land among the tribes of Israel, God speaks only twice (13:1–7; 20:1–6). Joshua, too, speaks rarely (17:15, 17–18; 18:3–7, 8b). It is the narrator we hear mostly in these nine chapters.

A. 13:1–33. Verses 1–7, which deal with the nine and one-half tribes' need to press ahead and possess all the land as their inheritance, contrasts with vv. 8–33, which deal with the full conquest of Transjordanian lands (vv. 8–14), and the allocation of the inheritance to the two and one-half tribes occupying these territories (vv. 15–33). Both sections end (vv. 14, 33) by noting the anomalous situation of the tribe of Levi: a tribe without territory of its own, but whose members live in other towns and cities of the land (see Deut. 14:29). The Levites can attribute their landlessness to divine decree. The tribes west of the Jordan have no such excuse.

It is striking how the Transjordanian tribes, much smaller in number and sometimes relegated to a subordinate position to their Cisjordanian brothers and sisters, serve both as a model and a rebuke to their more celebrated west-bank peers. The west-bankers need to move on and "get their act together," as their counterpart east-bankers have already done.

Relationships between the Transjordanian and Cisjordanian tribes were not always cordial, both within and without the book of Joshua. In Numbers 32, Moses is grieved by the proposal of the tribes of Gad and Reuben that they be allowed to settle in Transjordan because of its excellent pasture land (vv. 1–5). He is indignant, and compares the Gadites and Reubenites with the spies of Numbers 13–14, whose demoralizing report threatened the unity of Israel (vv. 6–15). Only after they agree to participate in the conquest (vv. 16–19), does he agree to their proposal (vv. 20–24). The same friction appears in Joshua 22, where again the southern Transjordanian tribes appear to their orthodox kin to be guilty of apostasy by building an altar on their side of the Jordan (22:10, 16). Joshua even goes so far as to suggest that their (Transjordanian) land might be "unclean," and if they cross over the Jordan they would be on clean land (22:19).

B. 14:1–15:63. After a general introduction to the distribution of the land west of the Jordan (vv. 1–5) comes a description of the land assigned to Judah (14:6–15:63), with Caleb figuring prominently throughout (14:6–15; 15:13–19). Judah's allotment is presented in two formats: (1) a boundary inventory in which boundaries are determined by natural features such as mountains or rivers (15:1–12); (2) a combination of city inventories (naming individual settlements) and regional inventories (identifying regions by name) (15:20–63).

The point is made clearly that Judah and the other Cisjordanian tribes receive their tribal areas by lot (14:2). Throughout chs. 14–21 the Hebrew word for "lot" (*goral*) occurs twenty-six times, which represents the largest cluster of the seventy-seven uses of the word in the Old Testament.

This practice is in conformity with the method of apportioning land spelled out in Num. 26:52–56. There the rule is given that the location of each individual tribal area is determined by lot (vv. 55–56), but the size of each tribal area is determined by population (vv. 53–54). Thus, each tribe receives its location from God. The reason for this approach is clear enough. Because each tribe's location has been designated by God, nobody can claim prejudiced or unfair treatment, that they have been victimized by having a less fertile area of ground to farm.

It is interesting that Caleb is highlighted twice in this section. Numbers 13:6 and 34:19 clearly identify Caleb as Judahite. Other references identify him, or his father, as a "Kenizzite" (Num. 32:12; Josh. 14:6, 14; and implied in Josh. 15:17 [= Judg. 1:13], "Othniel, son of Kenaz, the brother of Caleb"). Genesis 36:11, 15, 42 identify the Kenizzites as originally an Edomite clan. Is Caleb Judahite or Kenizzite? Either Caleb comes from a clan of foreigners (Edomite stock) who lived in the area of Hebron and who gradually were absorbed into the tribe of Judah, or else the Kenizzites were part and parcel of the Judahite stock as far back as the patriarchal period. If it is the former, then Caleb functions in Numbers and in this portion of Joshua much like Rahab does in an earlier portion of Joshua—a courageous, faithful outsider (non-Israelite) who at some point in her or his life became an insider (a worshiper of Yahweh).

Caleb's victorious conquests of the Hebron region, as described in Josh. 14:6–15 and 15:13–19, suggest the following overview:

- Caleb's life was the victory of a *preserved* life: "the Lord has kept me alive these forty-five years. . . . And here I am today, eighty-five years old" (14:10):

—Caleb is alive physically, in mind, in spirit, in vision
—God preserved Caleb in a situation of unbelief (14:8)
—God preserved Caleb in a situation of unpopularity (14:7)
- Caleb's life was the victory of a *powerful* life: "I am still as strong today as I was on the day that Moses sent me" (14:11)
- Caleb's life was the victory of a *prosperous* life: "Then Joshua blessed him and gave Hebron to Caleb . . . for an inheritance" (14:13).

Caleb gains not only an inheritance but also a son-in-law, Othniel, to whom he gave his daughter Achsah in return for Othniel's attacking and conquering Debir/Kiriath-sepher (Josh. 15:15–19 // Judg. 1:11–15). Achsah, like Jacob (Gen. 27:19), convinces her father to give her a blessing/present (15:19) on this occasion. That gift is upper and lower springs of water. This may be an illustration of a custom in which a bride receives a gift from her family, such as Laban "giving" to Leah and Rachel a servant/maid (Gen. 29:24, 29), or pharaoh "giving" Gezer as a dowry to his daughter (1 Kings 9:16). But the Hebrew verb that the NRSV translates as "she urged him" (*sut*) most often carries pejorative tones with meanings like "allure, incite, beguile, instigate against," as in Satan "inciting" David to number the people (1 Chron. 21:1). This indicates that Caleb's actions were far from spontaneous and cultural. Achsah's timing is perfect. She asks her father for a gift "at what is psychologically the optimum moment, immediately after the victory has been achieved, when Caleb is most inclined to grant her request" (Mosca 1984: 22).

C. 16:1–17:18. This portion of Joshua deals with the territory apportioned to the Joseph tribes, or the Josephites. Actually, the tribe of Joseph was split into two tribes, Manasseh and Ephraim, named after Joseph's two sons (Gen. 41:50–52). Together they are assigned the area in the central hill country north of Jerusalem, with the Ephraimites occupying the more southerly sections of the region and the Manassehites the more northerly.

Some similarities exist between this section and the preceding one dealing with the apportionment of Judah. For one thing, the recall in Josh. 17:3–6 of Moses' earlier seeking guidance from God (see Num. 27:1–11) on the question of inheritance of property by women has a double connection with the preceding unit. First, we have back-to-back cases of women inheriting property: Achsah as a blessing/gift from her father (Josh. 15:19), and the daughters of Zelophehad from Moses by virtue of a divine oracle (Josh. 17:3–6). But in another way, the daughters of Zelophehad parallel Achsah's father, Caleb. Both are outsiders who nevertheless receive a divine inheritance—Caleb by virtue of his ancestry as a Kenizzite and the daughters of Zelophehad by virtue of their sex. Another similarity is the notice that like the Judahites (Josh. 15:63), neither the Ephraimites (Josh. 16:10) nor the Manassehites (Josh. 17:12) could dislodge local Canaanite groups.

However, major differences also appear between the two sections. For one thing, although Josh. 15:63 states that the Judahites did not drive out the Jebusites from Jerusalem, that is not a negative commentary, because according to the outline of the tribal frontiers, Jerusalem lay outside the territory of Judah (see Josh. 15:8; 18:16). By contrast, Josh. 16:10 and 17:12 note that Ephraim/Manasseh did not drive out peoples living within their borders, peoples whom they should have been able to expel.

For another thing, a world of contrast stands between the spirit of Caleb requesting the hill country (Josh. 14:12) and the Josephites demanding from Joshua a double portion of land (Josh. 17:14–18). For Caleb, his request is born out of his faith in and commitment to the Yahweh of Israel (Josh. 14:7–11). By contrast, the Josephites are ingrates, whiners, and complainers. They think they are entitled to a bigger piece of the pie (Josh. 17:14). Joshua responds with both graciousness and bluntness. In essence, he says, "Your territory is large enough; go clear it if necessary. Stop complaining, since the apportionment of the land is already equitable, based as it is on population" (Josh. 17:15, 18).

D. 18:1–19:51. These two chapters describe the inheritance of land for the remaining seven tribes:

1. an introductory section in which Joshua dispatches three individuals from each of these tribes to survey the remaining land and report back to him, whereupon a lot will be cast to determine their inheritance (18:1–10)
2. the territory of Benjamin (18:11–28)
3. the territory of Simeon (19:1–9)
4. the territory of Zebulon (19:10–16)
5. the territory of Issachar (19:17–23)
6. the territory of Asher (19:24–31)
7. the territory of Naphtali (19:32–39)
8. the territory of Dan (19:40–48)
9. an allotment for Joshua himself (19:49–50)
10. a summarizing statement (19:51)

For the first time in the Old Testament, the city of Shiloh, located in Ephraim and about twenty miles north of Jerusalem, appears (vv. 18:1, 8, 9, 10; 19:51). Unlike some other cities mentioned in Joshua—say,

Shechem (ch. 24)—Shiloh has had no connections whatsoever with earlier patriarchal traditions, nothing to give it a sense of sanctified tradition. Shiloh represents new beginnings, new opportunities. Here, Joshua sets up the "tent of meeting," (which, interestingly, in 1 Sam. 1:9 and 3:3 is called a "temple," suggesting maybe that the tent of meeting existed alongside the temple, or was a part of the temple complex). Archaeological finds suggest that in the premonarchic period of Israel, especially at the beginning of Iron Age I, a dramatic proliferation of permanent settlements occurred in the central hill country occupied by Ephraim/Manasseh. Within a three- or four-mile radius of Shiloh stood no fewer than twenty-two new settlements. Shiloh most likely became the regional center for the area and possibly served as the first and only interregional, transtribal religious center before the Jerusalem temple.

Even as the land's distribution is described, "glitches" remain. Joshua upbraids these seven tribes for their slowness and slackness in possessing what God has given them (18:3; cf. 16:10; 17:12). The end of this unit states that the Danites "lost" their territory (19:47), and at least some of them emigrated northward (see Judges 18). That not all Danites left is reflected in the story of the Danite hero Samson (Judges 13–16); nevertheless, the announcement of Dan's setback in Josh. 19:47 is far from celebratory. Thus, in this larger section of Joshua (chs. 14–19) we have seen a unit of Scripture that "begins with the success of Judah and concludes with the failure of Dan" (Hawk 1991: 112).

E. 20:1–9. With the land now apportioned to the tribes, attention is turned to a matter of civil law: the provision of six cities of refuge for one guilty of involuntary homicide. For the first time since 13:1–7, God speaks (20:1–6), indicating that civil law, as much as moral/religious law, is a result of divine revelation.

Three earlier passages have already addressed this issue:

Num. 35:9–28. Three unnamed cities of refuge are in Transjordan and three unnamed cities are west in Cisjordan. Asylum is given only to the involuntary murderer. The individual who kills with premeditation is put to death by the "avenger/redeemer" (go'el), that is, a next of kin of the deceased, who acts as an agent of the state. This is all to be implemented after the Jordan is crossed (v. 10).

Deut. 4:41–43. Moses chooses three cities of refuge in Transjordan: Bezer (in Reubenite territory), Ramoth in Gilead (in Gadite territory), and Golan in Bashan (in Manassehite territory).

Deut. 19:1–13. The Israelites are commanded to set apart three unnamed cities of refuge after the conquest and occupations of the land, but nothing is said about cities of refuge in Transjordan, possibly because they were already mentioned in 4:41–43.

Joshua 20:1–9 follows suit and builds on these three passages. It is especially close in structure to the first two passages, in which the city-of-refuge law follows the completion of land allotment:

- Numbers 34 (borders of the Promised Land and its tribal divisions) > Num. 35:9–28 (cities of refuge)
- Deut. 3:12–22 (allotment of tribal areas in Transjordan) > Deut. 4:41–43 (cities of refuge)
- Joshua 13–19 (the division of the land) > Josh. 20:1–9 (cities of refuge)

It departs, however, from the earlier passages in three ways. First, it is the only passage to name all six cities, three in Cisjordan in a north-south direction (Kedesh, Shechem, Kiriath-arba/Hebron), three in Transjordan in a south-north direction (Bezer, Ramoth, Golan). Second, the separation of the cities of refuge is attributed to the Israelites: "*they* set apart . . . *they* appointed." Third, a distinction is made between the three Transjordan cities of refuge and the three west of the Jordan, and this is indicated by the verbs that are used. While the three Transjordan cities are "appointed" or designated" (literally, "given" [*natan*, 20:8]), the three Cisjordan cities are "set apart" (literally, "sanctified" [*qadash*, 20:7]).

What all these passages affirm is that the right of asylum is limited to those who commit unpremeditated manslaughter. They are not put to death; rather, they take refuge in one of the cities until the death of the high priest (v. 6). (Interestingly, the biblical Hebrew word for "refuge," *miqlat*, means in modern Hebrew an "(air-raid) shelter".) By contrast, if a tribunal (v. 6) determines that the taking of a life was premeditated, the murderer is turned over to the avenger/redeemer for execution. This is a clear case of the punishment fitting the crime. The deliberate homicide is deliberately put to death. The involuntary homicide, who took somebody's life by chance (and not by choice), must wait the chance of the high priest's death before obtaining release from the city of refuge (J. Milgrom, *Numbers* [Philadelphia: 1990], 510).

There is some possibility that God's mark on Cain (Gen. 4:15b) anticipates these later references to the cities of refuge. Cain is afraid that someone will seek to take his life in retaliation for what he did to Abel ("anyone who meets me may kill me"). In both Genesis 4 and in the cities of refuge passages God supplies protection for somebody else's life against the

avenger of blood. In Numbers 34, Deuteronomy 3, and Joshua 20 God
supplies cities to protect the accused against the threat of a blood avenger.
Clearly, God's mark on Cain is meant to provide him protection. Is it a
mark somewhere on his body? Or could the mark refer to the city Cain
built (Gen. 4:17)? Because in Genesis 4 a sign narrative is followed by a
city narrative, possibly, "Cain's city may have been intended as the 'sign'
that gave divine protection to Cain" (J. Sailhamer, "Genesis," in *The Expositor's Bible Commentary*, vol. 2 [Grand Rapids: 1990], 67).

A brief allusion to the cities of refuge is in Heb. 6:13–18, where the
writer is discussing the absolute certainty and truthfulness of God's
promise and oath. It is in such a God that believers may "take refuge"
(v. 18) or "have fled for refuge" (KJV). The Numbers, Deuteronomy,
Joshua passages suggest some comparisons between the cities of refuge and Christ our refuge (Schaeffer 1975: 195–200).

- A place of refuge must be available and accessible for those who
  need it.
- A place of refuge must exist for all people, not just for one group
  (see Num. 35:15 and Josh. 20:9, which state that the alien is entitled to the same protection of basic rights as the Israelite).
- No protection exists for one who has taken the life of another and
  broken the law outside the safety net of the place of refuge.
- Central to the significance of a place of refuge is the presence of a
  living high priest.

The first stanza of the hymn "How Firm a Foundation" captures
these nuances:

> How firm a foundation, ye saints of the Lord,
> Is laid for your faith in his excellent Word!
> What more can He say than to you He hath said,
> To you who for *refuge to Jesus have fled*?

F. 21:1–45. The final administrative matter to be dealt with is the assignment of forty-eight cities to three subgroups of Levites. Leaving
matters related to the Levites for last, and only after details related to
the lay tribes have been dealt with, is a common pattern:

Lay tribes	Levites
Census (Num. 1:1–46)	Levites not numbered (Num. 1:47–54)

Arrangements and order of march (Numbers 2)	Levitical arrangement and order of march (Numbers 3–4)
Second-generation census (Num. 26:1–56)	Census of second-generation Levites (Num. 26:57–62)
Conquest and apportionment of land (Num. 33:50–56)	Levitical cities (Num. 35:1–8)
With precise boundaries (Num. 34:1–15)	
Under supervision of chieftains (Num. 34:16–29)	
Distribution of land (Joshua 13–20)	Levitical cities (Joshua 21)

Although the Levites were an ecclesiastical tribe, they were not a monastic order. They were a tribe with families, and hence they needed enough real estate on which to build houses and land on which to graze their animals in lieu of a specific territorial allocation.

Like minority groups today who have owned land in rich, urban areas, only to see that land appropriated by wealthier majority groups, it would have been easy for the lay tribes to exploit their clerical brothers. To prevent the dispossession of the Levites, the law stated that the Levites could redeem at any time any urban dwelling they had been forced by need to sell (Lev. 25:32). This is in contrast to an urban dwelling sold by anybody else, which could be redeemed only until a year had elapsed since its sale (Lev. 25:29–30). Furthermore, if a sold or mortgaged dwelling was not redeemed by a Levite, the property reverted to the original Levite owner at the Jubilee (Lev. 25:33).

Numbers 35:1–8 is the primary unit on these Levitical cities, and of which Josh. 21:1–42 is the implementation (and see also 1 Chron. 6:54–81). Actually, the sequence in Numbers and Joshua is reversed. Numbers 35 moves from Levitical cities (vv. 1–8) to cities of refuge (vv. 9–15); Joshua moves from cities of refuge (20:1–9) to Levitical cities (21:1–42).

One fundamental difference stands between the legislation of Num. 35:1–8 and Josh. 21:1–42. According to Num. 35:8, the larger the tribe (in population? in territory?), the more Levitical towns it has; the smaller the tribe, the fewer Levitical towns it has. This is patently not the case in Joshua 21, where the distribution is equitable rather than proportional: forty-eight towns are distributed almost equally among the tribes, four cities per tribe regardless of size. (I say "almost equally" because Judah and Simeon receive nine cities [v. 16], and Naphtali three [v. 32].) More than likely, Joshua 21 has adapted the Numbers 35 legislation to the historical realities and circumstances of its day.

Numbers 35, but not Joshua 21, specifies that the area allotted to the Levites includes not only the cities/towns themselves (vv. 2–3), but also pasture land that extends one thousand cubits in each direction from the exterior edge of the town's wall (vv. 4–5), giving a two-thousand-cubit (approx. one thousand yards) perimeter for the pastureland (see J. Milgrom, *Numbers* [Philadelphia: 1990], 502–4):

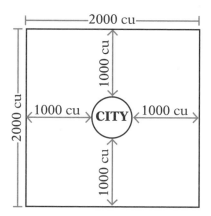

It is unlikely that only Levites lived in these forty-eight Levitical cities. Gezer, for example, one of the forty-eight cities (Josh. 21:21), contained Canaanite population until Solomon's time (1 Kings 9:16). Rather, we should understand that there were Levites living in each of these cities who performed some particular function in that city. As those devoted to the service of the nation in spiritual matters, it would be imperative that the Levites live among, rather than isolated from, the people.

Neither Numbers 35 nor Joshua 21 makes any comment on what function the Levites fulfilled in any of these cities, nor contains any reference to their sacred vocation. Basing his view on 1 Chron. 26:29–32, which speaks of the employment of Levites in David's day "for everything pertaining to God and for the affairs of the king," Mazar (1960: 202) suggests that "Levitic cities are a kind of provincial administrative cities, in which the Levites were appointed 'for all the work of the Lord and for the service of the king'; they were largely responsible for the supervision of the royal estates and the collection of taxes." Aharoni (1962: 273) similarly understands Joshua 21 to be a reference to the Levites as an arm of the civil service of the united monarchy: "The Levitical cities were established probably principally as royal Israelite centers near the borders intended for strengthening the kingdom's authority by promulgating Yahwistic worship, national solidarity and loyalty to the Davidic dynasty at Jerusalem." While this explanation may well be true of what the Levitical cities evolved into by the time of David and Solomon, it does not clarify their raison d'être prior to the beginnings of the monarchy. All that we can say for certain is that these towns served (1) as a domicile for the Levites, and (2) as a place for pasturing their animals. This is the crystal point of Josh. 21:2—"towns to live in, along with their pasture lands for our livestock." It would be quite conceivable that a Levite would reside in one city and officiate in another (Haran 1961: 52).

The last three verses of the chapter, vv. 43–45, not only conclude ch. 21, but also chs. 13–21, or chs. 1–21, or even further back than that, the promise(s) God made first to Abraham (Brueggemann 1977: 71):

Promise	Fulfillment
"Go from your country and your kindred and your father's house to the land I will show you" (Gen. 12:1).	Thus the Lord gave to Israel all the land he swore to their ancestors that he would give them. . . . Not one of all the good promises that the Lord had made to the house of Israel had failed; all came to pass" (Josh. 21:43, 45).
↓	↓
Starts with trustful departure	Ends with glorious possession
↓	↓
Sojourners	Heirs

These last few verses are affirmations about Israel's Lord, Yahweh. He is the subject of almost every verb in it. He is land giver and rest giver, swearer, promise maker and promise keeper. It is not that these three verses are blissfully ignorant of or evasive about earlier statements about Israel's failure to drive out this or that people. Those hard facts of faithlessness and slackness remain. But while a flawed performance must haunt Israel, nobody can suggest to Yahweh how he might improve his track record.

4. Holding On to Canaan-land (22:1–24:33)

A. 22:1–34. Thus far in the book of Joshua, excepting the incident involving Achan, Israel's crises have involved confrontation with external foes. In the majority of these Israel emerges as the victor. In this particular chapter the crisis is internal, a dispute between the Transjordanian tribes (already alluded to in 1:12–15, 4:12–13, and 13:8–32) and the majority Cisjordanian tribes.

The issue is twofold. First, are the Transjordanians guilty of apostasy in building an altar in their territory in defiance of the law of Deuteronomy that prohibits worship at any altar outside of that in the central sanctuary (in Cisjordan), as stated in Deuteronomy 12? See Josh. 22:10–11.

Second, are the Transjordanians, just by the fact of their living on the east side of the Jordan, located beyond the borders of the chosen land? Note this challenge of Phinehas and the ten chiefs to the Transjordanians: "If your land is unclean, cross over into the Lord's land, where the Lord's tabernacle now stands" (v. 19). That sounds as if Transjordan is *not* part of "the Lord's land." Furthermore, the narrator clearly distinguishes between "the land of Canaan" and "the land of Gilead," the home of the Reubenites and Gadites, east of the Jordan (vv. 9, 32), implying that the latter is not a part of the former. Again, expressions like "the whole assembly of the Israelites" (v. 12), or "the whole congregation of the Lord" (v. 16), or "the whole congregation of Israel" (v. 18) clearly exclude these Transjordanians. "Whole" equals "west of the Jordan."

So the crisis is totally internal. No worry here from Canaanites. It is about a potential schism spawned by a religious act and geography. If history is any teacher, the book of Numbers makes it transparent that internal crises (Numbers 11, 12, 13–14, 16, 20) carry a far greater potential to sidetrack the advancement of God's people than does an external crisis (Numbers 22–24). A Korah is more dangerous than a Balaam. God turns curse into blessing, but does not turn rebellion into blessing.

The chapter begins innocently enough (vv. 1–9). Joshua, now that the conquest is completed and the two and one-half Transjordanian tribes have fulfilled their commitment to their west-bank kin, sends these easterners back to their home. He sends them on their way with an exhortation (v. 5), a blessing (v. 6), and copious possessions (v. 8).

The crisis starts to emerge in v. 10, and is narrated in the form of a chiasmus (Jobling 1986: 98):

    (a) v. 10: Transjordanians build an altar
      (b) vv. 11–12: Cisjordanians threaten war
        (c) vv. 13–15a: Cisjordanians send a delegation to investigate
          (d) vv. 15b–20: Accusatory speech by the delegation
            (e) vv. 21–29: Transjordanians respond and
              clarify their action
          (d^1) vv. 30–31: Accepting speech by the delegation

(c^1) v. 32: Return of the delegation to the Cisjordanians

(b^1) v. 33: Withdrawal of the Cisjordanian threat of war

(a^1) v. 34: Transjordanians name the altar

The charges brought against the Transjordanian altar builders are severe. Phinehas, son of Eleazar and grandson of Aaron (Exod. 6:25; Josh. 24:33), heads the delegation. He is an appropriate choice. He has already acted once as the protector of Israel's cult when it faced possible contamination via unacceptable behavior (Numbers 25; 31). Later Jewish literature commends Phinehas for his zeal: (1) Sir. 45:23–24, "Phinehas son of Eleazar is third in glory because of his zeal in the fear of the Lord, because he stood firm when the people revolted, with a staunch and courageous heart; and in this way atoned for Israel . . . and secured to him and his descendants the high priestly dignity forever"; (2) 1 Macc. 2:26, "In his [Mattathias'] zeal for the law he acted as Phinehas did against Zimri son of Salu"; (3) 4 Macc. 18:12, "And he spoke to us of Phinehas, the zealous priest." Both Phinehas and, later, Elijah were "zealous" for their Lord (Num. 25:11, 13; 1 Kings 19:10) in rooting out the evil that was threatening to invade and engulf the community. One wonders if Saul of Tarsus was expressing himself as Phinehas-like or Elijah-like when, in the context of describing his attempts to destroy the church of God, which he viewed as threat, he says, "I was far more zealous for the traditions of my ancestors" (Gal. 1:14).

The charges are threefold. (1) The Transjordanians are guilty of apostasy. They have "turned away (shuv) from following the Lord" (vv. 16, 18, 23, 29). The exact Hebrew expression used here (shuv me'akhare) is not a common one. Apart from Joshua 22 it occurs in Num. 14:43; 32:15; 1 Sam. 15:11; 1 Kings 9:6; Jer. 3:19, and it always appears in speeches, never in narrative. (2) The two and one-half tribes are guilty of "rebellion" (vv. 16, 18, 19 [2x], 29). The Hebrew verb marad is used but 25x in the Old Testament, and more often in Joshua than in any other book, and only in this twenty-second chapter (5x). (3) The third charge is that of "breach of faith" (vv. 16, 22, 31). The word ma'al refers to the misappropriation or misuse of sacred property, and it was used earlier of Achan's ma'al against the kherem of Jericho (7:1).

In fact, using what we may call analogical exegesis or argument, the delegation recalls, using the a fortiori logical argument, two broad historical analogies to buttress their accusation: the sin at Peor (v. 17 and Numbers 25) and the sin of Achan (v. 20 and Joshua 7). What is at stake here is the possibility of divine wrath against all Israel. Just as Achan acted alone, but many others perished as a result, so the activities of the Transjordanians is not a private matter, but one for which Yahweh will judge all Israel. Or to put the issue a bit differently, if one individual (Achan) could, via his unfaithful actions, threaten the existence of all Israel, how much more could two and one-half tribes do so! Hence, this act of religious malfeasance must be aborted promptly.

The delegation, however zealously motivated, is misinformed. It turns out that the Transjordanians did not build an altar for sacrifices (vv. 26, 29). Rather, they built the altar purely as a witness to their west-bank kin, both to their contemporaries and especially to future generations of west-bankers, that the Transjordanians too are loyal Yahwists and that their living east of the Jordan is not illicit, and does not place them outside of the Lord's land (vv. 24–25).

This explanation is wholly acceptable to Phinehas and his group (vv. 30–31). It is to the credit of this Phinehas-led delegation that at least it investigated and talked and clarified before it declared war. Indeed, "in order to be Israel, it is better to talk than to fight" (Boling 1993: 250). Church history offers many unfortunate illustrations of clashes between believers that were precipitated by nothing more than a misunderstanding.

B. 23:1–16. What Yahweh said to Joshua and what the narrator said about him in 13:1, Joshua says about himself ("I am now old and well advanced in years," v. 2), as does the narrator again (v. 1). Joshua will shortly deliver a farewell address, a valedictory, to "all Israel" (v. 2), who are represented by various leader groups ("elders, heads, judges, officers," the same groups mentioned in 24:1). The reason why representatives are styled "all Israel" is to show that what follows is for the benefit of all Israel's citizens, not just their leaders. Yet, it is still not clear that "all Israel" includes Transjordanian Israel (remember the near civil war of the preceding chapter), for according to v. 4 the nations still to be dispossessed by Israel are located "from the Jordan to the Great Sea in the west."

Three admonitions stand out in this farewell address. The first is Joshua's exhortation to the leaders to be unflinching in their commitment to observing everything in "the book of the law of Moses" (v. 6). Yahweh had given Joshua himself exactly the same counsel in 1:8. The terms used for God's word vary from "the book of the law" (1:8), to "the book of the law of Moses" (23:6), to "the book of the law of God" (24:26). Thus, Moses' words and God's words are indistinguishable or interchangeable. And the references to "the book of the law" in the first chapter of Joshua and in the last two frame all other events narrated throughout the book.

Joshua's second exhortation is that the people of God vigilantly maintain separation from Canaanite peoples (vv. 7, 12). Specifically, it appears that what he has in mind is intermarriage—for Joshua, the place where inevitably compromise and religious defection start.

Third, Joshua exhorts his people to love their God fervently (v. 11), following a parallel injunction to the Transjordanian tribes in 22:5. To love God is a common phrase, especially in Deuteronomy (5:10; 6:5; 7:9; 10:12; 11:1, 13, 22; 13:3; 19:9; 30:6, 16, 20). While certainly including affection and emotion, at the heart of loving God is the sole recognition of God as God to the exclusion of any rival. Thus, love connotes loyalty.

C. 24:1–33. Joshua's last act, after his farewell address of ch. 23, is to gather representative leaders of the tribes to Shechem, a city located in the heart of the territory of the Joseph tribes. It is about forty miles north of Jerusalem at the pass between Mount Gerizim and Mount Ebal. There are only three other references to Shechem in Joshua: (1) 17:7, Shechem is connected with the boundary of Manasseh; (2) 20:7, Shechem is one of the cities of refuge; (3) 21:21, Shechem is one of the Levitical cities. There are no references to Shechem in that portion of Joshua which narrates the conquest of the land of Canaan (chs. 6–12), suggesting either that the Israelites, rather then conquering Shechem, entered into a peaceful entente with them as with Gibeon (ch. 9), or that in the selective accounts narrated in chs. 6–12, the one at Shechem is not included. While not mentioned per se in the text, the reference in Josh. 8:30 to Joshua building an altar on Mount Ebal puts that action adjacent to Shechem. Earlier in the book of Joshua two other cities took on a degree of special sanctity: (1) Gilgal (4:20; 5:9–10; 9:6; 10:7, 9); (2) Shiloh (18:1, 8, 9, 10; 19:51; 21:2; 22:9). But here the focus is on Shechem.

Why the attraction to Shechem? The key may be found in references to Shechem in the patriarchal traditions. The first identified place Abram reaches in the Promised Land is Shechem, at which he builds an altar (Gen. 12:6–7), in essence sanctifying Shechem. Later, Jacob, after his odyssey in Mesopotamia, returns to Canaan, and that inevitable meeting with Esau. One of his first activities is to go to Shechem, where he purchases some property, and builds an altar (Gen. 33:18–20). Before he leaves Shechem for Bethel, he instructs his household to "put away the foreign gods that are among you" (Gen. 35:2), gods that he subsequently buries "under the oak that was near Shechem" (Gen. 35:4). These last two pieces of information are quite close to Joshua 24, where Joshua first exhorts his people "to put away the gods your fathers served" (v. 14), and then places a large stone as a witness under the oak near the sanctuary at Shechem (v. 26). Thus, the experiences of later generations (under Joshua) parallel those of the founding fathers—altar building, putting away false gods, purchasing and possessing land. And the God who appeared to Abram at Shechem is the same faithful God whom Joshua at Shechem will urge his people to serve.

The first twenty-eight verses of the chapter are mostly dialogue between Joshua and the people, in the form of challenge and response:

>   vv. 1–15: Joshua's challenge to tribal leaders
>   vv. 16–18: leaders' response to Joshua
>   vv. 19–20: Joshua's challenge to tribal leaders
>   v. 21: leaders' response to Joshua
>   v. 22a: Joshua's challenge to tribal leaders
>   v. 22b: leaders' response to Joshua
>   v. 23: Joshua's challenge to tribal leaders
>   v. 24: leader's response to Joshua
>   [vv. 25–26: covenant made; covenant stipulations put in a book;
>   large stone set up under the sanctuary oak]
>   v. 27: Joshua's challenge to tribal leaders
>   [v. 28: dismissal of the tribal leaders]

But it is Joshua who gets the first word (vv. 1–15) and the last word (v. 27). And in the twenty-five of the twenty-eight verses that are dialogue, Joshua speaks in twenty of them, while the tribal leaders speak in only six of them. Joshua initiates; they respond. In the one verse in this incident that uses the word "covenant" ("So Joshua made a covenant with the people that day" [v. 25]), the Hebrew for "made a covenant with" is *karat berit le*, literally "cut a covenant to." Whenever this expression is used to describe a covenant formulated between human beings, the one who "cuts" the covenant is the superior party, who confers the treaty as a favor or imposes it (as with the covenant Joshua "cut" with the Gibeonites at their request [Josh. 9:6–7, 11, 15–16], or the covenant/treaty Nahash the powerful Ammonite agreed to "cut" with Jabesh-gilead [1 Sam. 11:1–2]). Similarly, Israel is instructed not to "cut" a covenant with the Canaanites after they have conquered them (Exod. 23:32; 34:12, 15; Deut. 7:2). By using this phrase, v. 25 makes it clear that Joshua is totally in control of this situation, and he alone can dictate the terms Israel must meet in order to serve Yahweh supremely.

The first twenty verses present a particularly fascinating dynamic on commitment. Joshua takes the longest unit in this dialogue, vv. 1–15, first to summarize God's great acts, the *magnalia dei* on behalf of Israel (vv. 1–13), then to exhort (vv. 14–15). Grammatically, the emphasis in vv. 1–13 is on the declarative and the indicative. In vv. 14–15 the emphasis is on the imperative that flows out of the declarative and the indicative as result flows out of cause. Exactly the same progression occurs in Josh. 1:1–9, with its shift from declarative/indicative (vv. 1–5) to imperative (vv. 6–9). The progression in 24:1–15 is from the past/then (vv. 1–13) to the present/now (vv. 14–15).

Joshua's reporting and recalling of the past—actually, quoting God—covers events from Abraham's time until his own:

vv. 2–4: Abraham, Isaac, Jacob
vv. 5–10: exodus from Egypt, passage through the sea, drowning of the Egyptians, wilderness wanderings, Transjordanian victories, Balaam's "blessing"
vv. 11–13: crossing the Jordan, taking Jericho, victories over Cisjordanian peoples, the gift of land

It is interesting that Joshua, or Yahweh via Joshua, omits any reference to the Sinai event in Exodus 19–24, while including events that lead up to it (vv. 6–7) and follow it (vv. 8–10). The reason for this deletion may be that a heavy element of the Sinai covenant was the law and the severe retribution that would follow for violating that law. In vv. 2–13 Joshua's concern is not with threatened repercussions for treaty violation, but with a rehearsal of God's good and gracious acts. It is also interesting that Joshua adds a few novel facts. For example, he states in v. 11 that the Jerichoites "fought" against Israel, something that Joshua 6 never claims.

From this survey of the past, Joshua moves to his "Now therefore revere the Lord and serve him" in 24:14. And between v. 14 and v. 24 the word "serve" will appear fourteen times. Joshua challenges the people to serve Yahweh, in light of what Yahweh has done for them and their ancestors.

Neutrality is not an option. The people must either choose to serve Yahweh or choose to serve other gods. Hence comes Joshua's famous exhortation: "Choose this day whom you will serve" (v. 15), using a word used earlier to refer to Joshua's choosing thirty thousand warriors to attack Ai (8:3). It is striking how rarely the Old Testament speaks of human beings choosing a deity (apart from Josh. 24:15, 22, see Judg. 5:8; 10:14), while references to God's choosing of individuals and groups are legion.

But at least in Joshua 24, Joshua is "pro-choice." But what kind of choice is it?

- It is an *independent* choice: "Choose this day whom you will serve" (v. 15).
- It is an *intelligent* choice: "Think of all that God has done for us in our history [vv. 2–13] and remember that he is a holy, jealous God [v. 19]."
- It is an *implemented* choice: "Put away the gods your ancestors served" (v. 14).
- It is an *influential* choice: "As for me and my household, we will serve the Lord" (v. 15).
- It is an *immediate* choice: "Choose this day whom you will serve" (v. 15).

The leaders respond enthusiastically (vv. 16–18). They have no intention of forsaking Yahweh. And just as Joshua/God earlier included them in past events in which they did not literally participate, for they were not yet born (e.g., "and afterwards I brought *you* out," v. 5b), here they include themselves in these events (e.g., "who brought *us* and our ancestors up from the land of Egypt," v. 17a). This actualization of past events so that later generations experience the results of those events is no different from when one sings the spiritual "Were You There When They Crucified my Lord?" and the answer is yes.

Ostensibly, the dialogue could stop here at v. 18. Joshua has spoken (vv. 1–15) and the people have responded affirmatively (vv. 16–18). But now, to everybody's surprise, Joshua's response is not, "Amen," but rather, "You cannot serve the Lord" (v. 19)! Talk about throwing cold water on enthusiasm!

Why can they not serve the Lord? Is there some shortcoming in their commitment to service? Apparently not. The problem with serving God is not ourselves, but God. That is, God insists on being God. Joshua does not say, "You cannot serve the Lord because *you are*. . . ." He says, "You cannot serve God because *he is*. . . ." He is what? Three things:

1. He is a God who is *holy*, which means he will not tolerate those who choose to serve him and yet continue to traffic with and tolerate the unholy in their lives.
2. He is a God who is *jealous*, impassioned, a word used earlier in the second commandment of the Decalogue ("a jealous God" [Exod. 20:5; Deut. 5:9]), which means that for those who choose to serve him he will be a God who is intolerant of rivalry or unfaithfulness.
3. He is a God who will *not forgive your transgressions* (which is just the opposite of what Moses says about the attributes of the

merciful God in Exod. 34:7 and Num. 14:18: "forgiving sin and transgression"), which means that for those who choose to serve him he will not be a God who routinely forgives sin so that grace may abound (see Rom. 6:1).

Thus, far from discouraging the people's desires to serve God, Joshua is simply reminding his people forcefully that all service of God must be rendered on God's terms, not on terms of one's own choosing. After another round of dialogue in which the leaders reaffirm their desire to serve Yahweh (vv. 21–24), Joshua makes a covenant with them, writes the stipulations in "the book of the law of God," and sets up a large stone near an oak by the sanctuary, which serves as a witness to this covenant (vv. 25–27).

This stone stands as a witness against the people lest in the future they deny they ever made such a commitment ("if you deal falsely with your God, " v. 27b). The Hebrew verb for "deal falsely with" (*kakhash*) was used earlier in 7:11 to refer to whoever "acted deceitfully" by taking some of Jericho's devoted things. Its basic meaning is "to act with deceit," and it connotes denial of the truth (Gen. 18:15, "But Sarah denied, saying, 'I did not laugh'"), or the fabrication of an untruth (1 Kings 13:18, "Then the other said to him, 'I also am a prophet as you are. . . .' But he was deceiving him"). Especially relevant for the verb's use in Josh. 24:27 are uses elsewhere where it means "to deny falsely," in the context of oath taking (Ps. 59:12; Hos. 4:2).

The book ends, as it began, by calling attention to somebody's death (Moses, 1:1; Joshua, 24:29–31; Eleazar, 24:33), and to Joseph's burial (24:32). It is to Joshua's credit that Israel carried through on their commitment to serve Yahweh well beyond Joshua's time, knowing, as they did, "all the work that the Lord did for Israel" (v. 31b).

Eleazar ("God has helped") has appeared frequently in the book of Joshua (14:1; 17:4; 19:51; 21:1), all in connection with the distribution by lot of the land among the tribes. He is always mentioned in conjunction with Joshua, and his name always precedes that of Joshua in the cited passages (and so too in Num. 32:28; 34:17). As Joshua has been successor to Moses, so Eleazar has been successor to Aaron. Joshua holds his position by divine selection, while Eleazar holds his position by birth. To that end, transfer of authority from Moses to Joshua involved Moses laying his hands on Joshua (Num. 27:18), while transfer of authority from Aaron to Eleazar involved Moses stripping Aaron of his high priestly vestments and putting them on Eleazar (Num. 20:26). Eleazar, we know, will be succeeded by his son Phinehas (v. 33). But who will suceed Joshua?

Bibliography (Joshua)

Commentaries and Major Studies

Auld, A. G. 1998. *Joshua Retold: Synoptic Studies.* Old Testament Studies. Edinburgh: Clark.

Boling, Robert G. 1982. *Joshua.* Anchor Bible 6. New York: Doubleday.

Bright, John. 1953. "Joshua." In *The Interpreter's Bible.* Vol. 2. Nashville: Abingdon. Pp. 539–673.

Butler, Trent C. 1983. *Joshua.* Word Biblical Commentary 7. Waco, Tex.: Word.

Gray, John. 1967. *Joshua, Judges and Ruth.* New Century Bible. London: Nelson. Pp. 15–200.

Hamlin, John. 1983. *Inheriting the Land.* International Theological Commentary. Grand Rapids: Eerdmans.

Hawk, L. Daniel. 1991. *Every Promise Fulfilled: Contesting Plots in Joshua.* Literary Currents in Biblical Interpretation. Louisville: Westminster/John Knox.

———. 2000. *Joshua.* Berit Olam. Collegeville, Minn.: Liturgical Press.

Hess, Richard. 1996. *Joshua.* Tyndale Old Testament Commentaries. Downers Grove, Ill.: InterVarsity.

Huffman, John. 1986. *Joshua.* Mastering the Old Testament. Ed. L. J. Ogilvie. Dallas: Word.

Ironside, Harry. 1950. *Addresses on the Book of Joshua.* New York: Loizeaux.

Miller, J. Maxwell, and Gene M. Tucker. 1974. *The Book of Joshua*. Cambridge Bible Commentary. Cambridge: Cambridge University Press.

Mitchell, Gordon. 1993. *Together in the Land: A Reading of the Book of Joshua*. JSOT Supplement 134. Sheffield: JSOT Press.

Nelson, R. D. 1997. *Joshua: A Commentary*. Old Testament Library. Louisville: Westminister/John Knox.

Noth, Martin. 1953. *Das Buch Josua*. Handbuch zum Alten Testament 1/7. Tübingen: J. C. B. Mohr.

Polzin, Robert. 1980. *Moses and the Deuteronomist: A Literary Study of the Deuteronomistic History*. New York: Seabury. Pp. 73–145.

Redpath, Alan. 1955. *Victorious Christian Living: Studies in the Book of Joshua*. Westwood, N.J.: Revell.

Schaeffer, Francis. 1975. *Joshua and the Flow of Biblical History*. Downers Grove, Ill.: InterVarsity.

Soggin, J. Alberto. 1972. *Joshua*. Old Testament Library. Trans. R. A. Wilson. Philadelphia: Westminster.

Wiersbe, Warren. 1993. *Be Strong*. Wheaton, Ill.: Victor.

Winther-Nielsen, Nicolai. 1995. *A Functional Discourse Grammar of Joshua: A Computer-Assisted Rhetorical Structure Analysis*. Coniectanea Biblica Old Testament Series 40. Stockholm: Almqvist and Wiksell.

Woudstra, Marten H. 1981. *The Book of Joshua*. NICOT. Grand Rapids: Eerdmans.

Shorter Studies

Auld, A. G. 1978. "Textual and Literary Studies in the Book of Joshua." *ZAW* 90:412–17.

Baxter, J. Sidlow. 1960. *Explore the Book*. Vol. 1. Grand Rapids: Zondervan. Pp. 235–72.

Beek, M. A. 1994. "Joshua the Savior." In *Voices from Amsterdam: A Modern Tradition of Reading Biblical Narrative*. SBLSS. Ed. M. Kessler. Atlanta: Scholars Press. Pp. 145–53.

Boling, R. G. 1993. "Levitical History and the Role of Joshua." In *The Word of the Lord Shall Go Forth: Essays in Honor of David Noel Freedman in Celebration of His Sixtieth Birthday*. Ed. C. L. Myers and M. O'Connor. Winona Lake, Ind.: Eisenbrauns. Pp. 241–61.

———. "Joshua, Book of." *ABD* 3:1002–15.

Bright, John. 1981. *A History of Israel*. 3rd ed. Philadelphia: Westminster. Pp. 105–82.

Childs, Brevard. 1979. *Introduction to the Old Testament as Scripture.* Philadelphia: Fortress. Pp. 239–53.

Coats, G. 1987. "The Book of Joshua: Heroic Saga or Conquest Theme?" *JSOT* 38:15–32.

Coogan, Michael. 1990. "Archaeology and Biblical Studies: The Book of Joshua." In *The Hebrew Bible and Its Interpreters.* Vol. 1. Ed. W. H. Propp, B. Halpern, and D. N. Freedman. Biblical and Judaic Studies. Winona Lake, Ind.: Eisenbrauns. Pp. 19–32.

Good, E. M. 1962. "Joshua, Book of." *IDB* 2:988–95.

Gottwald, N. K. 1995. "Theological Education as a Theory-Praxis Loop: Situating the Book of Joshua in a Cultural, Social, Ethical, and Theological Matrix." In *The Bible in Ethics: The Second Sheffield Colloquium.* JSOT Supplement 207. Ed. J. W. Rogerson, M. Davis, R. and M. D. Carroll. Sheffield: Sheffield Academic Press. Pp. 107–18.

Greenspoon, L. J. 1983. *Textual Studies in the Book of Joshua.* Harvard Semitic Monographs 28. Chico, Calif.: Scholars Press.

Gunn, David M. 1987. "Joshua and Judges." In *The Literary Guide to the Bible.* Ed. R. Alter and F. Kermode. Cambridge, Mass: Belknap/Harvard. Pp. 102–21.

Hess, Richard S. 1995. "Studies in the Book of Joshua." *Themelios* 20, no. 3:12–15.

Howard, D. M., Jr. 1993. *An Introduction to the Historical Books.* Chicago: Moody, Pp. 59–98.

Kissling, P. J. 1996. *Reliable Characters in the Primary History.* JSOT Supplement 224. Sheffield: Sheffield Academic Press. Pp. 69–95.

Mullen, E. T., Jr. 1993. *Narrative History and Ethnic Boundaries: The Deuteronomistic Historian and the Creation of Israelite National Identity.* Atlanta: Scholars Press. Pp. 87–119.

Ngan, L. L. E., et al. 1998. "Joshua." *RevExp* 95:161–284.

Rowlett, L. 1992. "Inclusion, Exclusion and Marginality in the Book of Joshua." *JSOT* 55:15–23.

Scroggie, Graham. 1950. "The Land and Life of Rest." In *Keswick Week 1950.* London: Marshall, Morgan and Scott. Pp. 45–56, 87–98, 139–51, 183–92.

Strange, J. 1993. "The Book of Joshua: A Hasmonean Manifesto." In *History and Traditions of Early Israel: Studies Presented to Eduard Nielsen.* Ed. A. Lemaire and B. Otzen. Leiden: E. J. Brill. Pp. 136–41.

Vaux, Roland de. 1978. *The Early History of Israel.* Trans. David Smith. Philadelphia: Westminster. Pp. 473–680.

Wenham, G. J. 1971. "The Deuteronomic Theology of the Book of Joshua." *JBL* 90:140–48.

Joshua 1–2

Barnes, P., 1995. "Was Rahab's Lie a Sin?" *RTR* 54:1–9.

Bird, P. 1989. "The Harlot as Heroine: Narrative Art and Social Presupposition in Three Old Testament Texts." *Semeia* 46:119–39, esp. 126–32.

Campbell, K. M. 1972. "Rahab's Covenant." *VT* 22:243–44.

Chirichigno, G. D. 1987. "The Use of the Epithet in the Characterization of Joshua." *TJ* 8:69–79.

Coats, G. W. 1985. "An Exposition for the Conquest Theme." *CBQ* 47:47–54.

Cohn, H. 1971. "Rahab." *EncJud* 13:1513–14.

Culley, R. C. 1992. *Themes and Variations: A Study of Action in Biblical Narrative.* SBLSS. Atlanta: Scholars Press. Pp. 110–14.

Fields, W. W. 1992. "The Motif 'Night as Danger' Associated with Three Biblical Destruction Narratives." In *Sha'arei Talmon: Studies in the Bible, Qumran and the Ancient Near East Presented to Shemaryahu Talmon.* Ed. M. Fishbane and E. Tov. Winona Lake, Ind.: Eisenbrauns. Pp. 17–32.

Hawk, L. Daniel. 1992. "Strange Houseguests: Rahab, Lot and the Dynamics of Deliverance." In *Reading between Texts: Inter-texuality and the Hebrew Bible.* Ed. D. N. Fewell. Louisville: Westminster/John Knox. Pp. 89–97.

McCarthey, D. J. 1971. "The Theology of Leadership in Joshua 1–9." *Bib* 52:165–75. (Repr. in *Institution and Narrative: Collected Essays.* Analecta biblica 108. Rome: Pontifical Biblical Institute Press. 1985. Pp. 193–203.)

———. 1971. "Some Holy War Vocabulary in Joshua 2." *CBQ* 33:228–30. (Repr. in *Institution and Narrative: Collected Essays.* Analecta biblica 108. Rome: Pontifical Biblical Institute Press. 1985. Pp. 204–6.)

McKinley, J. E. 1999. "Rahab: A Hero/ine?" *BibInt* 7:44–57.

Moran, W. L. 1967. "The Repose of Rahab's Israelite Guests." In *Studi sull'Oriente e la bibbia offerti a G. Rinaldi.* Ed. G. Buccellati. Genoa: Editrice Studio e Vita. Pp. 273–84.

Nelson, R. D. 1981. "Josiah in the Book of Joshua." *JBL* 100:531–40.

Newman, M. L. 1985. "Rahab and the Conquest." In *Understanding the Word: Essays in Honor of Bernhard W. Anderson.* Ed. J. T. Butler, E. W. Conrad, and B. C. Ollenburger. JSOT Supplement 37. Sheffield: JSOT Press. Pp. 167–81.

Tucker, G. M. 1972. "The Rahab Saga (Joshua 2): Some Form-Critical and Traditional-Historical Observations." In *The Use of the Old Tes-*

tament in the New and Other Essays. Durham, N.C: Duke University Press. Pp. 66–86.

Wilcoxen, J. 1968. "Narrative Structure and Cult Legend: A Study of Joshua 1–6." In *Transitions in Biblical Scholarship*. Ed. J. C. Rylaarsdam. Chicago: University of Chicago Press. Pp. 43–70.

Wiseman, D. J. 1964. "Rahab of Jericho." *TynB* 14:8–11.

Zakovitch, Y. 1990. "Humor and Theology or the Successful Failure of Israelite Intelligence: A Literary-Folkloric Approach to Joshua 2." In *Text and Tradition: The Hebrew Bible and Folklore*. SBLSS. Ed. S. Niditch. Atlanta: Scholars Press. Pp. 75–98 (and a response to this article by F. M. Cross, "A Response to Zakovitch's 'Successful Failure of Israelite Intelligence,'" pp. 99–104).

Joshua 3–5

Brekelmans, C. 1989. "Joshua v 10–12: Another Approach." *OSt* 25:89–95.

Brichto, H. C. 1969. "Taking-off the Shoe(s) in the Bible." In *Proceedings of the Fifth World Congress of Jewish Studies*. Vol. 1. Ed. P. Peli. Jerusalem: World Union of Jewish Studies. Pp. 225–26.

Coats, G. W. 1985. "The Ark of the Covenant in Joshua: A Probe into the History of a Tradition." *HAR* 9:137–57.

Peckham, B. 1984. "The Composition of Joshua 3–4." *CBQ* 46:413–31.

Saydon, P. 1950. "The Crossing of the Jordan." *CBQ* 12:194–207.

Winther-Nielsen, N. 1964. "The Miraculous Grammar of Joshua 3–4." In *Biblical Hebrew and Discourse Linguistics*. Ed. R. D. Berger. Winona Lake, Ind.: Eisenbrauns. Pp. 300–319.

Joshua 6 (especially *Kherem*/War)

Bienkowski, P. 1990. "Jericho Was Destroyed in the Middle Bronze Age, Not the Late Bronze Age." *BAR* 16, no. 5:45–46, 69.

Boyd, Gregory A. 1987. *God at War: The Bible and Spiritual Conflict*. Downers Grove, Ill.: InterVarsity.

Coats, G. W. 1985. "The Ark of the Covenant in Joshua: A Probe into the History of a Tradition." *HAR* 9:137–57.

Cowles, C. S. 1995–1996. "Canaanite Genocide and the God of Love." *The Preacher's Magazine* 71:44–49.

Craigie, Peter. 1978. *The Problem of War in the Old Testament*. Grand Rapids: Eerdmans.

Culley, R. C. 1984. "Stories of the Conquest: Joshua 2, 6, 7 and 8." *HAR* 8:25–44.

———. 1992. *Themes and Variations: A Study of Action in Biblical Narrative*. SBLSS. Atlanta: Scholars Press. Pp. 114–17.

Fretheim, T. E. 1983. *Deuteronomic History*. Interpreting Biblical Texts. Ed. L. R. Bailey and V. P. Furnish. Nashville: Abingdon. Pp. 61–75.

Fretz, M. 1986. "*Herem* in the Old Testament: A Critical Reading." In *Essays on War and Peace: Bible and Early Church*. Ed. W. Swartley. Elkhart: Institute of Mennonite Studies. Pp. 7–44.

Goetz, R. 1975. "Joshua, Calvin and Genocide." *ThTo* 32:263–74.

Goldingay, J. 1994. *Models for Scripture*. Grand Rapids: Eerdmans.

Hanson, P. 1984. "War and Peace in the Hebrew Bible." *Int* 38:241–61.

Holladay, William L. 1995. *Long Ago God Spoke: How Christians May Hear the Old Testament Today*. Minneapolis: Fortress. Pp. 117–135.

Kang, Sa-Moon. 1989. *Divine War in the Old Testament and in the Ancient Near East*. BZAW 177. Berlin: Walter de Gruyter.

Kaufmann, Y. 1960. *The Religion of Israel*. Trans. M. Greenberg. Chicago: University of Chicago Press. Pp. 169–77.

Kidner, F. D. 1972. "Ancient Israel at War (and Occasionally Peace)." *His* 33:14–16.

———. 1985. "Old Testament Perspectives on War." *EvQ* 57:99–113.

Lilley, J. P. U. 1993. "Understanding the *Herem*." *TynB* 44:169–77.

Lohfink, N. "Harem." In *TDOT* 5:180–99.

Malamat, Abraham. 1979. "Israel's Conduct of War in the Conquest of Canaan According to the Biblical Tradition." In *Symposia Celebrating the Seventy-Fifth Anniversary of the Founding of the American School of Oriental Research*. Ed. F. M. Cross. Cambridge, Mass.: American Schools of Oriental Research. Pp. 49–52.

Martin, G. H. 1989. "Dedicated to Destruction," *BI* 16, no. 2:24–25.

Mazor, L. 1988. "The Origin and Evolution of the Curse upon the Rebuilder of Jericho." *Textus* 14:1–26.

Milgrom, J. 1990. *Numbers*. JPS Torah Commentary. Philadelphia: The Jewish Publication Society. Excursus 44, "The Status of 'Herem.'" Pp. 428–30.

Niditch, S. 1993. *War in the Hebrew Bible: A Study in the Ethics of Violence*. New York: Oxford University Press.

Niehaus, J. J. 1988. "Joshua and Ancient Near Eastern Warfare." *JETS* 31:37–50.

Reid, Daniel G., and Tremper Longmann III. 1996. "When God Declares War." *CT* (October 28) 14–21.

Stern, P. D. 1991. *The Biblical Herem: A Window on Israel's Religious Experience*. Brown Judaic Studies 211. Atlanta: Scholars Press.

Weinfeld, M. 1993. "The Ban on the Canaanites in the Biblical Codes and its Historical Development." In *History and Traditions of Early Israel: Studies Presented to Eduard Nielsen*. Ed. A. Lemaire and B. Otzen. Leiden: E. J. Brill. Pp. 142–60.

Wilcoxen, J. 1968. "Narrative Structure and Cult Legend: A Study of Joshua 1–6." In *Transitions in Biblical Scholarship*. Ed. J. C. Rylaarsdam. Chicago: University of Chicago Press. Pp. 43–70.

Wood, B. 1990a. "Did the Israelites Conquer Jericho? A New Look at the Archaeological Evidence." *BAR* 16, no. 2:44–59.

————. 1990b. "Dating Jericho's Destruction: Bienkowski Is Wrong on All Counts." *BAR* 16, no. 5:47–49, 69.

Joshua 7–12

Auld, G. 1995. "Reading Joshua after Kings." In *Words Remembered, Texts Received: Essays in Honour of John F. A. Sawyer*. JSOT Supplement 195. Ed. J. Davies and W. G. E. Watson. Sheffield: Sheffield Academic Press. Pp. 167–81.

Ballentine, S. E. 1993. *Prayer in the Hebrew Bible*. Overtures to Biblical Theology. Minneapolis: Fortress.

Barr, James. 1977. *Fundamentalism*. Philadelphia: Westminster.

————. 1990. "Mythical Monarch Unmasked? Mysterious Doings of Debir King of Eglon." *JSOT* 48:55–68.

Begg, C. T. 1986. "The Function of Josh 7, 1–8, 29 in the Deuteronomistic History." *Bib* 67:320–33.

Bimson, John J. 1991. *Redating the Exodus and Conquest*. 2nd ed. JSOT Supplement 5. Sheffield: Almond.

Coote, Robert B., and Keith W. Whitelman. 1987. *The Emergence of Early Israel in Historical Perspective*. Sheffield: Almond.

Culley, R. C. 1992. *Themes and Variations: A Study of Action in Biblical Narrative*. SBLSS. Atlanta: Scholars Press. Pp. 117–20.

Dever, W. "Archaeology and the Israelite 'Conquest.'" *ABD* 3:545–58.

Fensham, F. C. 1964. "The Treaty between Israel and the Gibeonites." *BA* 27:96–100.

Finkelstein, Isaac. 1988. *The Archaeology of the Israelite Settlement*. Trans. D. Saltz. Jerusalem: Israel Exploration Society.

Fishbane, Michael. 1985. *Biblical Interpretation in Ancient Israel*. Oxford: Clarendon.

Fritz, V. 1987. "Conquest or Settlement?" *BA* 50:84–100.

Gottwald, Norman. 1985. *The Hebrew Bible: A Socio-Literary Introduction*. Philadelphia: Westminster. Pp. 261–76.

Greenberg, Moshe. 1960. "Some Postulates of Biblical Criminal Law." In *Yehezkel Kaufmann Jubilee Volume*. Ed. M. Haran. Jerusalem: Magnes. Pp. 5–28. (Repr. in *The Jewish Expression*. Ed. J. Goldin. New Haven: Yale University Press, 1976. Pp. 18–37.)

Grintz, J. M. 1961. "Ai Which Is beside Beth-Aven." *Bib* 42:201–16.

———. 1966. "The Treaty of Joshua with the Gibeonites." *JAOS* 86:113–26.

Hess, R. S. 1993. "Early Israel in Canaan: A Survey of Recent Evidence and Interpretations." *PEQ* 126:125–42.

———. 1994. "Achan and Achor: Names and Wordplay in Joshua 7." *HAR* 14:89–98.

Holladay, J. S., Jr. 1968. "The Day(s) the Moon Stood Still." *JBL* 87:166–78.

Jackson, B. 1972. *Theft in Early Jewish Law*. Oxford: Clarendon.

Kaminsky, J. S. 1995a. *Corporate Responsibility in the Hebrew Bible*. JSOT Supplement 196. Sheffield: Sheffield Academic Press.

———. 1995b. "Joshua 7: A Reassessment of Israelite Conceptions of Corporate Punishment." In *The Pitcher Is Broken: Memorial Essays for Gösta W. Ahlström*. JSOT Supplement 190. Ed. S. W. Holloway and L. K. Handy. Sheffield: Sheffield Academic Press. Pp. 314–46.

Kaufmann, Y. 1953. *Biblical Account of the Conquest of Palestine*. Trans. M. Dagut. Jerusalem: Magnes.

Kitchen, K. A. 1966. *Ancient Orient and Old Testament*. Chicago: Inter-Varsity.

———. 1977. *The Bible in Its World*. Downers Grove, Ill.: InterVarsity.

Krasovec, J. 1994. "Is There a Doctrine of Collective Retribution in the Bible?" *HUCA* 65:35–89.

Lapp, Paul W. 1967. "The Conquest of Palestine in the Light of Archaeology." *CTM* 38:283–300.

Lemeche, Niels Peter. 1985. *Early Israel: Anthropological and Historical Studies on the Israelite Society before the Monarchy*. VTSup 37. Trans. F. H. Cryer. Leiden: E. J. Brill.

Liver, J. 1963. "The Literary History of Joshua ix," *JSS* 8:227–28.

Livingstone, D. 1970. "Location of Biblical Bethel and Ai Reconsidered." *WTJ* 33:20–44.

Margalit, B. 1992. "The Day the Sun Did Not Stand Still: A New Look at Joshua x 8–15." *VT* 42:466–91.

Mendenhall, G. E. 1970. "The Hebrew Conquest of Palestine." In *Biblical Archaeology Reader*. Vol. 3. Ed. E. F. Campbell Jr. and D. N. Freedman. Garden City, N.Y.: Doubleday. Pp. 100–120.

Merrill, E. 1982. "Palestinian Archaeology and the Date of the Conquest: Do Tells Tell Tales?" *GTJ* 3:107–21.

Peels, H. G. L. 1994. *The Vengeance of God: The Meaning of the Root NQM and the Function of the NQM-Texts in the Context of Divine Revelation in the Old Testament*. Leiden: E. J. Brill.

Savran, G. W. 1988. *Telling and Retelling: Quotation in Biblical Narrative*. Bloomington: Indiana University Press.

Stec, D. M. 1991. "The Mantle Hidden by Achan." *VT* 41:356–59.

Stone, L. 1991. "Ethical and Apologetic Tendencies in the Redaction of the Book of Joshua." *CBQ* 53:25–36.

Sutherland, R. K. 1992. "Israelite Political Theories in Joshua 9." *JSOT* 53:65–74.

Van Seters, J. 1990. "Joshua's Campaign of Canaan and Near Eastern Historiography." *SJOT* 4:1–12.

Thompson, T. L. 1992. *The Early History of the Israelite People*. Leiden: E. J. Brill.

Waltke, B. K. 1990. "The Date of the Conquest." *WTJ* 52:181–200.

Ward, E. F. de. 1977. "Superstition and Judgment: Archaic Methods of Finding a Verdict." *ZAW* 89:1–19.

Weinfeld, M. 1967. "The Period of the Conquest and the Judges As Seen in the Earlier and Later Sources." *VT* 17:97–113.

Weippert, M. 1971. *The Settlement of the Israelite Tribes in Palestine*. Studies in Biblical Theology 21. London: SCM.

Wright, G. E. 1946. "The Literary and Historical Problem of Joshua 10 and Judges 1." *JNES* 5:105–14.

Yadin, Yigael. 1963. *The Art Of Warfare in Biblical Land in the Light of Archaeological Study*. 2 vols. Trans. M. Pearlman. New York: McGraw and Hill.

———. 1965. *Military and Archaeological Aspects of the Conquest of Canaan in the Book of Joshua*. 3rd ed. Jerusalem: World Jewish Society and the Israel Society for Biblical Research.

Yeivin, S. 1971. *The Israelite Conquest of Canaan*. Istanbul: Nederslands Historisch-Archaeologisch Instituut in Het Nabije Oosten.

Younger, K. Lawson, Jr. 1990. *Ancient Conquest Accounts: A Study in Ancient Near Eastern and Biblical History Writing*. JSOT Supplement 98. Sheffield: JSOT Press.

———. 1995. "The 'Conquest' of the South (Jos 10, 28–39)." *BZ* 39:255–64.

Zevit, Z. 1983. "Archaeological and Literary Stratigraphy in Joshua 7–8." *BASOR* 251:23–35.

Joshua 13–19

Auld, A. G. 1978. "Textual and Literary Studies in the Book of Joshua." *ZAW* 90:412–17.

Hess, R. S. 1994a. "Asking Historical Questions of Joshua 13–19: Recent Discussion Concerning the Date of the Boundary Lists." In *Faith, Tradition, History: Old Testament Historiography in Its Near Eastern Context*. Ed. A. R. Millard, J. K. Hoffmeier, and D. W. Baker. Winona Lake, Ind.: Eisenbrauns. Pp. 191–205.

———. 1994b. "Late Bronze Age and Biblical Boundary Descriptions of the West Semitic World." In *Ugarit and the Bible: Proceedings of the International Symposium on Ugarit and the Bible, Manchester, September 22*. Ugaritisch-Biblische Literatur Band 11. Ed. G. Brooke, A. Curtis, and J. Healey. Münster: Ugarit-Verlag.

Mosca, P. G. 1984. "Who Seduced Whom? A Note on Jos 15,18/Jd 1,14." *CBQ* 46:18–22.

Na'aman, Nadav. 1986. *Borders and Districts in Biblical Historiography*. Jerusalem: Simor.

Joshua 20

Cohn, H. 1971. "City of Refuge." *EncJud* 5:591–94.

Greenberg, M. 1959. "The Biblical Conception of Asylum." *JBL* 78:25–32.

Spencer, John R. 1992. "Refuge, Cities of." *ABD* 5:657–58.

Joshua 21

Aharoni, Y. 1962. *The Land of the Bible: A Historical Geography*. Trans. A. F. Rainey. London: Burns and Oates.

Albright, W. F. A. 1945. "The List of the Levitical Cities." In *Louis Ginzberg Jubilee Volume*. New York: American Academy for Jewish Research. Pp. 49–73.

Auld, A. G. 1979. "The Levitical Cities: Texts and History." *ZAW* 91:194–206.

———. 1990. "The Cities in Joshua 21: The Contribution of Textual Criticism." *Textus* 15:141–52.

Ben Zvi, E. 1992. "The List of the Levitical Cities." *JSOT* 54:77–106.

Boling, R. 1985. "Levitical Cities: Archaeology and Texts." In *Biblical and Related Studies Presented to Samuel Iwry*. Ed. A. Kort and S. Morschauser. Winona Lake, Ind.: Eisenbrauns. Pp. 23–32.

———. 1993. "Levitical History and the Role of Joshua." In *The Word of the Lord Shall Go Forth: Essays in Honor of David Noel Freedman in Celebration of His Sixtieth Birthday*. Ed. C. L. Meyers and M. O'Connor. Winona Lake, Ind.: Eisenbrauns. Pp. 241–61.

Haran, M. 1961. "Studies in the Account of the Levitical Cities I. Preliminary Considerations." *JBL* 80:45–54.

Greenberg, M. 1968. "Idealism and Practicality in Numbers 35:4–5 and Ezekiel 48." *JAOS* 88:59–63.

———. 1971. "Levitical Cities." *EncJud* 11:136–38.

Mazar, B. 1960. "The Cities of the Priests and Levites." *Congress Volume: Oxford 1959*. VTSup 7. Leiden: Brill. Pp. 193–205.

Milgrom, J. 1982. "The Levitical Town: An Exercise in Realistic Planning." *JJS* 32:185–88.

———. 1990. *Numbers*. JPS Torah Commentary. Philadelphia: The Jewish Publication Society. Pp. 502–4.

Miller, J. M. 1987. "Rehoboam's Cities of Defense and the Levitical Cities." In *Archaeology and Biblical Interpretation: Essays in Memory of D. G. Rose*. Ed. L. G. Perdue, L. E. Toombs, and G. L. Johnson. Atlanta: John Knox. Pp. 273–86.

Spencer, John R. 1992. "Levitical Cities." *ABD* 4:310–11.

Joshua 22

Jobling, D. 1980. "The Jordan a Boundary: A Reading of Numbers 32 and Joshua 22." In *SBLSP 1980*. Chico, Calif.: Scholars Press. Pp. 183–207.

———. 1986. "'The Jordan a Boundary': Transjordan in Israel's Ideological Geography." In *The Sense of Biblical Structural Analysis in the Hebrew Bible*. JSOT Supplement 39. Sheffield: JSOT Press. Pp. 88–134.

Kloppenbury, J. S. 1981. "Joshua 22: The Priestly Editing of an Ancient Tradition." *Bib* 62:347–71.

Snaith, N. H. 1978. "The Altar at Gilgal: Joshua xxii, 23–29." *VT* 28:330–35.

Joshua 23

Koopmans, W. T. 1988. "The Poetic Prose of Joshua 23." In *The Structural Analysis of Biblical and Canaanite Poetry*. JSOT Supplement 74. Ed. W. van der Meer and J. C. de Moor. Sheffield: JSOT Press. Pp. 83–118.

Joshua 24

Brekelmans, C. 1991. "Joshua xxiv: Its Place and Function." In *Congress Volume: Leuven, 1989*. VTSup 63. Ed. J. A. Emerton. Leiden: E. J. Brill. Pp. 1–9.

Brueggemann, W. 1993. *Biblical Perspectives on Evangelism*. Nashville: Abingdon. Pp. 48–70.

Edelman, D. 1991. "Are the Kings of the Amorites 'Swept Away' in Joshua xxiv 12?" *VT* 41:279–86.

Fretheim, T. E. 1983. *Deuteronomic History*. Interpreting Biblical Texts. Ed. L. R. Bailey and V. P. Furnish. Nashville: Abingdon. Pp. 75–86.

Giblin, C. H. 1964. "Structural Patterns in Jos 24,1–25." *CBQ* 26:50–69.

Koopmans, W. T. 1990. *Joshua 24 as Poetic Narrative*. JSOT Supplement 93. Sheffield: JSOT Press.

Kraus, Hans-Joachim. 1966. *Worship in Israel*. Trans. G. Buswell. Richmond: John Knox. Pp. 136–41.

McCarthy, Dennis J. 1978. *Treaty and Covenant*. Analecta Biblica 21. Rome: Pontifical Biblical Institute. Pp. 221–42, 279–84.

Mendenhall, George. 1955. *Law and Covenant in Israel and the Ancient Near East*. Pittsburgh: Biblical Colloquium. Pp. 41–44.

Muilenburg, J. 1959. "The Form and Structure of the Covenantal Formulations." *VT* 9:347–65, esp. 357–60.

Nielsen, E. 1959. *Shechem: A Traditio-Historical Investigation*. Copenhagen: G. E. C. Gad. Pp. 86–134.

Sperling, S. David. 1987. "Joshua 24 Re-examined." *HUCA* 58:119–36.

Van Seters, John. 1984. "Joshua 24 and the Problem of Tradition in the Old Testament." In *In the Shelter of Elyon: Essays on Ancient Palestinian Life and Literature in Honor of G. W. Ahlström*. JSOT Supplement 31. Ed. W. B. Barrick and J. R. Spencer. Sheffield: JSOT Press. Pp. 139–58.

Vaux, Roland de. 1978. *The Early History of Israel*. Trans. David Smith. Philadelphia: Westminster. Pp. 667–72.

Judges

This book of the Bible stands out from its predecessor in the canon by virtue of its title. Unlike "Joshua," whose title is simply the name of a prominent individual, "Judges" is named after an office, "judge," which is put in the plural. While the Hebrew Bible has no book called "Prophets," unlike the New Testament, which has a book called "Acts of the Apostles," there is a good parallel for a title like "Judges," and that is, of course, "Kings"—one word, in plural form, and indicating influential leaders.

The fact that Judges, unlike Joshua, does not bear a personal name in its title may be quite significant (note also the presence of Ruth after Judges, at least in the order of the books of the Old Testament in Christian tradition). Unlike the era of Joshua, no one individual is dominant enough to cast a shadow over the entire book. In fact, what does cast a shadow over Judges is the absence of such a leader. The episodic and ephemeral appearance of charismatic judges notwithstanding, just about everything "after the death of Joshua" is downhill. If Judges ends by saying, "In those days there was no king in Israel" (21:25), in effect it begins by saying, "In those days there was no Joshua in Israel." "No Joshua" is retrospective. "No king" is prospective, suggesting that maybe filling the vacuum of "no king" (toward which the last chapter points) will be the solution to the vacuum of "no Joshua" (with which the first chapter begins).

Another difference between Joshua and Judges is that the former begins with a clearly designated event that marks its beginning ("After the death of Moses" [1:1]), and ends with an equally clearly designated event that marks its terminus ("Joshua . . . died" [24:29]; "Eleazar . . .

died" [24:33]). Judges, too, opens with a recapitulatory death notice ("After the death of Joshua" [1:1]). However, no death announcements appear in the last chapter of Judges. This means that the last five chapters of Judges (17–21), usually dubbed "appendices," do not function to chronologically terminate Judges, as does ch. 24 of Joshua for that book. In that sense, closure is not brought to Judges.

The earliest event in Judges, and really a prelude to the book, is the death of Joshua. The last event, and one of the few in this book that can be dated with any degree of specificity, is the one referred to in 18:30, the context for which is a stinging indictment of the idolatrous shrine at Dan. Verse 30 ends by saying, "Jonathan . . . and his sons were priests to the tribe of the Danites *until the time the land went into captivity.*" This last phrase probably refers to the displacement of the northern kingdom of Israel at the hands of the Assyrians toward the end of the 720s B.C. And it also suggests that whoever put this material together in Judges, at least in its final form, was somebody who lived after 722–721 B.C.

There are twelve "judges" in the book of Judges, whom we shall call, primarily on the basis of how much space is devoted to each, "major" and "minor" judges.

Major Judges	Minor Judges
1. Othniel (3:7–11)	1. Shamgar (3:31)
2. Ehud (3:12–30)	2. Tola (10:1–2)
3. Deborah (4:1–5:31)	3. Jair (10:3–5)
4. Gideon (6:1–8:35)	4. Ibzan (12:8–10)
5. Jephthah (10:6–12:7)	5. Elon (12:11–12)
6. Samson (13:1–16:31)	6. Abdon (12:13–15)

Almost all uses of the noun "judge(s)" (*shophet/shophetim*) are confined to the introductory 2:16–19 (plural: vv. 16, 17, 18; singular: vv. 18, 19). The only other place in Judges where "judge" occurs as a noun is in 11:27, and there it applies to Yahweh ("Let the Lord, who is *judge,* decide today").

The verb "judge" (*shaphat*) is confined to the stories of the judges themselves in 3:7–16:31, but even there it is used minimally and spasmodically. Of the six major judges, the verb is used only with Othniel (3:10) and Deborah (4:4) without any chronological notice. With two of these judges it is used with a chronological note twice ("Jephthah judged Israel six years" [12:7]; "He [Samson] judged Israel . . . twenty years" [15:20; 16:31]).

In the two lists of six "minor" judges (10:1–5; 12:8–15) the verb is used without chronological notice with Ibzan (12:8), Elon (12:11a), Abdon (12:13), and with a chronological note with Tola (10:2); Jair (10:3); Ibzan (12:9); Elon (12:11b); Abdon (12:14). Putting all uses of the verb "judge" together, we see thirteen uses of it, five with the major judges, eight with the minor judges. Statistically at least, more attention is given to the judging done by the minor judges than to that done by the major judges.

Another word used besides "judge" is "deliver, save," and it occurs as noun and verb both in the introductory 2:16–19 and in the stories of the judges. Thus, 2:16 speaks of Yahweh raising up judges who "delivered them," and 2:18 of judges who "delivered them from the hand of their enemies." The judges who are styled as "deliverers" of their people are Othniel (3:9), Ehud (3:15), Gideon (8:22), and Samson (13:5, but only in a promissory, predictive sense). None of the minor judges are called "deliverers" except for Shamgar (3:31). Thus, the judges, some of them at least, are deliverers, saviors, suggesting that their role may be more a military one than a juridical one.

The book of Judges falls into three distinct units of uneven length, which we may outline as follows:

1. In Those Days There Was No Joshua in Israel (1:1–3:6)
   A. The results of this territorially (1:1–2:5)
   B. The results of this spiritually (2:6–3:6)
2. In Those Days There Were Judges in Israel (3:7–16:31)
   A. Othniel (3:7–12)
   B. Ehud (3:12–30)
   C. Shamgar (3:31)
   D. Deborah and Barak (4:1–5:31)
   E. Gideon (6:1–8:35)
   F. Abimelech (9:1–57)
   G. Two lists of minor judges (10:1–5; 12:8–15)
   H. Jephthah (10:6–12:7)
   I. Samson (13:1–16:31)
3. In Those Days There Was No King in Israel (17:1–21:25)
   A. The results of this: spiritual and tribal migration (17:1–18:31)
   B. More results of this: an all-Israelite civil war (19:1–21:25)

1. In Those Days There Was No Joshua in Israel (1:1–3:6)

A. 1:1–36. One of the first things the reader of Judges observes is that the book appears to have two introductions, the first addressing events that happened "after the death of Joshua" (1:1a, introducing 1b–2:5), and the second addressing events that start during the lifetime of Joshua and continue beyond his death and into future generations (2:6a, with its "when Joshua dismissed the people," introducing 2:6b–3:6). In other words, in 1:1 Joshua is dead, but in 2:6 he is alive (and then dies again [2:8]), as the narrative suddenly backtracks, rewinds the tape, providing a kind of a momentary flashback.

For an analogy of a double introduction to one book, one may point to Genesis, which interpreters often claim has two introductions, 1:1–2:4a and 2:4b–25. It is fashionable among commentators to do two things with Judges' double introduction. The first is to suggest that the two units have little, if anything, in common with each other, and that 1:1–2:5 is an alternate account of Israel's conquest clashing with that presented previously in Joshua (speedy, complete conquest [Joshua 6–11] versus slow, partial conquest [Judg. 1:1–2:5]).

The second suggestion many commentators make is that the real introduction to Judg. 3:7–16:31 is 2:6–3:6; that is, it is the Deuteronomist(s) who composed 2:6–3:6. By contrast, 1:1–2:5 is an earlier document, a sort of a tendentious Judahite document vis-à-vis the conquest of Canaan, and it was added arbitrarily to 2:6–3:6 in later times merely as an appendix. Thus, according to this reconstruction, Judges begins (1:1–2:5) and ends (17:1–21:25) with appendices. Now by definition, an appendix is a nonvital, expendable organ. Thus, Judges' first and last five chapters may be expunged without serious damage to the original heart of the book.

Our point of disagreement with these suggestions is not with the view that 1:1–2:5 and 2:6–3:6 may come from different hands. Rather, it is with the idea that the "bookends" of Judges have not been intentionally integrated with what follows or precedes. In what follows, we shall attempt to make the case for integration versus appendixing (and see the perspectives of Eslinger, Stone, and Webb, who so read the final form of the book).

To begin with, we note that the introductory words to ch. 1 are "After the death of Joshua," which is very similar to the beginning of Joshua ("After the death of Moses") and Second Samuel ("After the death of Saul"). Three key periods are identified in Old Testament history via the use of this formula: (1) the post-Moses era (for the most part, a glorious one); (2) the post-Joshua era (for the most part, an embarassing one); (3) the post-Saul era (which combines the features of (1) "glorious" and (2) "embarrassing").

In the absence of a heroic Joshua the people do the natural and good thing—they "inquired of the Lord, 'Who shall go up first for us against the Canaanites?'" (Judg. 1:1b). To "inquire [*sha'al b*] of the Lord" more than likely refers to seeking the will of God by the use of the Urim and Thummim, those two small objects that could be thrown like dice to solicit a response from God. The Urim and Thummim could be consulted for a simple yes-or-no reply (see Josh. 18:6), but on other occasions they were consulted for additional and quite explicit information (in addition to Judg. 1:1, see 1 Sam. 10:22 [they reveal Saul's hiding place]; 2 Sam. 2:1 [they reveal the city to which David is to go]; 2 Sam. 5:23–24 [they reveal the complex military strategy David is to use against the Philistines]).

This specificity of response occurs here in Judg. 1:1. Inquiring of Yahweh, via the Urim and Thummim, results in the designation of the tribe of Judah as the first tribe to go up and engage the Canaanites. What is of great interest here is that exactly the same "inquiring of God" (via the Urim and Thummim) takes place toward the end of the book (20:18). Exactly the same question is asked ("Who of us shall go up first to battle against the . . . ?"). And exactly the same divine response is given: a specific tribe is designated, and it is Judah again.

But there is a profound difference between 1:1 and 20:18, and that difference will tell us, in a nutshell, where the people of God are going in the post-Joshua days of the judges:

> 1:1: "Who shall go up first for us *against the Canaanites*, to fight against them?"
>
> 20:18: "Who of us shall go up first to battle *against the Benjaminites?*"

A book that starts with a reference to an offensive war by a united nation against a common enemy ends with a reference to that same nation at war with itself. Benjaminites, part of the family of God, have become Canaanites.

Several things about the structure of Judges 1 require attention. For one thing, the victorious tribe of Judah (vv. 2–20) is contrasted with the less successful and less achieving northern tribes of Israel (vv. 21–36). Victories for Judah after Joshua's death take place in Bezek and over its leader/king, Adoni-bezek (vv. 4–7); in Jerusalem (v. 8); in Kiriath-arba/Hebron (v. 10); in Kiriath-sepher/Debir (vv. 11–13); in Zephath/ Hormah (v. 17); in Gaza, Ashkelon, and Ekron (v. 18).

The only nonvictorious note sounded in the Judah portion of the chapter is v. 19b: "[Judah] took possession of the hill country; but could not drive out the inhabitants of the plain because they had chariots of iron." But even this single admission needs qualification. First, that v. 19 begins by stating that "the Lord was with Judah" would seem to indicate that the lack of success is not due to divine disfavor with Judah and hence the withdrawal of his presence, leaving Judah to fend for herself. Second, the text is ambiguous about the real reason for Judah's inability to drive out the inhabitants of the plain. Was it because of the latter's superior armaments in a place suitable to their employment (a flat plain), or was it because of Judah's failure of vision?

Two other items reinforce this ambiguity. First, the phrases "*could not* drive out" of 1:19b and "*did not* drive out" (used of the northern tribes in the second half of the chapter—vv. 27, 28, 29, etc.), though using the same Hebrew verb (*yarash* in the Hiphil/causative stem) are different in the original. For those in the second half of the chapter, the Hebrew uses the straightforward perfect form of the verb, *lo' horish*, "did not drive out." By contrast, 1:19b uses an infinitive rather than a finite form of the verb (*lo' lehorish*). So, 1:19b "uses an infinitive without specifying the verbal agent of the verb because it was impossible to relate failure explicitly to Judah" (Weinfeld 1993: 396).

The second item qualifying 1:19b is brought out by comparing it with Josh. 17:18: "The hill country shall be yours . . . for you shall drive out the Canaanites, though they have chariots of iron, and though they are strong." Note here that Joshua is speaking not to Judah, but "to the house of Joseph, to Ephraim and Manasseh," that is, those tribal areas north of Judah and near the southern Galilee area (note the references in Josh. 17:16b to Bethshean and the Valley of Jezreel). If Judg. 1:19b is alluding to Josh. 17:16–18, then it is simply saying that the Judahites failed to take an area that was far beyond their own borders, hardly a damning indictment. Furthermore, "The presence of iron chariots is the closest approach to a legitimate excuse for failure in gaining possession of territory that can be found in Joshua or Judges" (Stone 1988: 217).

In the description of the military forays of the northern tribes in vv. 21–36, matters are quite different. Seven times the narrator says that a certain tribe did not drive out the inhabitants of a certain place or places (vv. 21, 27, 28, 29, 30, 31, 33). It is failure after failure. In fact, there are twenty-one towns/cities reported not to have been conquered in vv. 21–36. Specifically, the tribes of Asher (seven cities) and Manasseh (five cities and their surrounding settlements) are cited for the highest number of failures. Additionally, because we read that some northern tribes, rather than driving out the inhabitants of the land, instead put them to "forced labor" (vv. 28, 30, 33, 35), we can conclude that the northern tribes chose this alternative. Presumbably, if they were strong enough to impose upon them forced labor, then they could have expelled them if they wanted to. Thus, the explanation of failure is not inability, but unwillingness.

Even the one account of a conquest by the "house of Joseph" (1:22–26), the taking of Bethel, is a "mixed bag." The sending out of spies first, encountering a local resident with whom and with whose family a "deal" is worked out in return for vital information, and the subsequent destruction of the city beg comparison with the story of Jericho and Rahab (Joshua 2 and 6). But note also the differences between the two accounts (Gunn and Fewell 1993: 160). First, Rahab makes a confession of faith in Yahweh, the God of Israel, and it is this persuasion that empowers her to entertain the Hebrew spies. The anonymous "man of Bethel" makes no confession. He is an opportunist, not a convert. Second, Rahab gives no vital data about the city of Jericho. She merely talks about God and her family. The man of Bethel, on the other hand, "showed them the way into the city." Third, Jericho is placed under the ban and left in ruins. Not so Bethel. The informant leaves the targeted city and builds another one with the same name elsewhere, a second Luz.

One also observes a process of degeneration in vv. 22–36 in terms of Israel's relationship with the indigenous Canaanites.

1. Victory, however mitigated, for the house of Joseph (vv. 22–26)
2. Dominance, but not expulsion, by Manasseh and Ephraim: Canaanites continue to live in land (vv. 27–28)
3. Dominance, but not expulsion, by Ephraim: Canaanites live among them (v. 29)
4. same with Zebulon (v. 30)
5. Asher and Naphtali live among the Canaanites (vv. 31–33)
6. Dan repulsed by the Canaanites/Amorites, and confined to the hill country (v. 34)

Thus, the move is from victory (1) to partial victory (2, 3, 4), to substantial losses (5), to defeat (6). What begins in triumph (1) ends in confinement (6).

A second thing to notice about Judges 1 is that the mentioning of the various tribes moves in a south-to-north direction:

Dan (v. 34)
↑
Naphtali (v. 33)
↑
Asher (vv. 31–32)
↑
Zebulon (v. 30)
↑
Ephraim (v. 29) (actually, Manasseh is on top of Ephraim)
↑
Manasseh (vv. 27–28)
↑
house of Joseph (= all the northern tribes) (v. 22–26)
↑
Benjamin (v. 21)
↑
Judah (vv. 2–20)

We find exactly the same south-to-north sequence in the story of the major judges in 3:7–16:31:

Samson, from Dan (13:1–16:31)
↑
Jephthah, from Manasseh (10:6–12:7)
↑
Gideon, from Manasseh (6:1–8:35)
↑
Deborah, from Ephraim (4:1–5:31)
↑
Ehud, from Benjamin (3:12–30)
↑
Othniel, from Judah (3:7–11)

Not only are both ch. 1 and 3:7–16:11 arranged in a south-to-north direction, but each unit begins with a Judah that is both an exemplary tribe (1:2–20) and has an exemplary judge (Othniel, 3:7–11), and ends with a Dan that is both a lackluster tribe (1:34) and has a wild, unrestrained judge (Samson, 13:1–16:31). Here is a picture of a nation deeply fractured. To use New Testament language (Romans 8), part is living life in the Spirit, and part is living life in the flesh. One expels the enemy; the other cohabits with the enemy. One is incisive; the other is tolerant.

The third, and final, thing to note about Judges 1 is that much of its material is extracted from Joshua in the form of either quotations or allusions. Most often there is some modification in Judges 1 of the Joshua reference, and this modification is usually strategic. The direct quotations are:

1. Judg. 1:10, 20 = Josh. 15:13–14 (and 14:6–15): the taking and giving of Hebron

2. Judg. 1:11–15 = Josh. 15:15–19: Debir, Caleb, Achsah, and Othniel
3. Judg. 1:21 = Josh. 15:63: inability to drive out the Jebusites
4. Judg. 1:27–28 = Josh. 17:11–13: Manasseh's failure to conquer
5. Judg. 1:29 = Josh. 16:10: Ephraim's failure to conquer

Let us note, briefly, some of the comparisons that emerge:

1. Josh. 14:6–15 and 15:13–14 emphasize Joshua's giving Hebron to Caleb, while Judg. 1:20 says Judah (the "was given" is a third-plural verb) did this, obviously because Joshua is dead (1:1). Joshua 15:13 states that it was Caleb who drove out the three sons of Anak: Sheshai, Ahiman and Talmai. Judges attributes this feat to both Judah (1:10) and to Caleb (1:20), but names the three only in the Judah reference.
2. Caleb "went up" against the inhabitants of Debir in Josh. 15:15, but in Judg. 1:11 "they [Judah] went up against the inhabitants of Debir." Joshua 15:17 identifies Othniel as "son of Kenaz, the brother of Caleb." Judges 1:13 expands that to "son of Kenaz, Caleb's younger brother" (as again in 3:9). This addition in Judges is necessary for the chronology of Othniel, whose judgeship begins after eight years of oppression (3:8), and whose death follows forty years of rest (3:11). Interestingly, this event, which is dated to during Joshua's lifetime in Josh. 15:15–19, is placed in Judges "after the death of Joshua," unless v. 1a be read as an editorial title to the book rather than merely to ch. 1.
3. Josh. 15:63 states that "the people of Judah could not drive out the Jebusites, the inhabitants of Jerusalem," while Judg. 1:21 says that "the Benjamites did not drive out the Jebusites who lived in Jerusalem," after having noted earlier that Judah had taken Jerusalem (1:18). Note also the Joshua reference "Judah could not drive out" (i.e., inability) versus the Judges reference "Benjamin did not drive out" (i.e., unwillingness, or at least an act of omission). According to Judges, Judah took Jerusalem (1:18). Benjamin failed to hold on to it (1:21). Not until David's time is Jerusalem totally reclaimed (2 Sam. 5:6–9).
4. Judges turns Josh. 17:12, "Manesseh could not take possession of those towns," into "Manasseh did not drive the inhabitants of . . ." (1:27), again shifting the explanation from inability to unwillingness, as in (3). Also, Judges deletes the information of

Josh. 17:11, that the towns from which the Manassites could not expel the Canaanites were "within Issachar and Asher."

5. Judg. 1:29 deletes the last line of Josh. 16:10, ". . . to this day, but have been made to do forced labor."

Thus, the three features of Judges 1 (the contrast between Judah and the northern tribes, the south-to-north description, and the quotes from Joshua) all in their own way emphasize the radically different situation in Israel following the death of Joshua. The tribe of Judah, from which David will eventually emerge, models effective and authentic discipleship. Judah's northern counterparts, by comparison, model ineffectiveness, compromise, and accommodation. But the narrator of ch. 1 reports all of the incidents matter-of-factly, without comment or evaluation of any kind. He neither commends nor chastises. He is descriptive, not prescriptive. That latter task will belong to the angel of the Lord.

B. 2:1–5. At the beginning of Judges, Yahweh speaks because the people inquired of him (1:1, which we shall call oracular divine speech). But now Yahweh speaks, via his intermediary, on his own initiative (which we shall call non-oracular divine speech, and which occurs again in Judges only in 2:20–21; 6:7–10; 10:11–14).

As with other passages of Scripture, Yahweh and his angel/messenger are interchangeable: "Now the angel of the Lord . . . said, 'I brought you up from Egypt.'" Compare, for example, the story of the angel/messenger finding Hagar in the wilderness (Gen. 16:7), the conversation that follows between the two (Gen. 16:8–12), and Hagar's words, "So she named the Lord who spoke to her" (Gen. 16:13). Here is a case where God himself appeared in the form of a human being, one who could be seen by a mortal.

One instance of oscillation between Yahweh and his angel/intermediary that includes an actual observable appearance in Judges is found in ch. 6. The angel "came and sat" near Gideon (6:11). The two then converse (6:12–13). Then the text says, "Then the Lord turned to him and said . . ." (6:14). Another Judges text with the same crossover is Judges 13, where the incident moves back and forth among "man," "angel of the Lord," "man of God," and "God."

There are, however, other texts in which the angel and God are interchangeable, but with no mention of an actual appearance (e.g., Gen. 22:11–12, 15–18). Whether or not one perceives a (human) appearance in 2:1 is dependent on what one makes of the statement "Now the angel of the Lord went up from Gilgal to Bochim" (2:1). One other thing about the angel's presence in 2:1–5 is that it is one of the very few places where the angel appears to the community. Usually, the angel appears to individuals (e.g., Abraham, Hagar, Jacob, Moses, Gideon, the wife of Manoah).

The purpose of the angel's mission is underscored by v. 1 saying that the angel *went up* (*'alah*) from Gilgal to Bochim. It is a verb used frequently in ch. 1 (vv. 1, 2, 3, 4, 16, 22), and, most importantly, every time it is used there it is referring to military assault, to "go up" in the sense of "move out against, invade." Presumably, the verb carries that same martial sense in 2:1. But in a shocking reversal, Israel, in ch. 1 the subject of going up, becomes in 2:1 the object of a going up. Those who earlier laid siege are now under siege, but from no normal, mortal opponent.

The distribution of this verb in Judges 1–2 is nicely laid out by Webb (1987: 103):

A$_1$ 1:1–2: the assembled Israelites ask Yahweh, "Who will *go up?*"

B$_1$ 1:3–21: Judah *goes up*.

B$_2$ 1:22–36: Joseph *goes up*.

A$_2$ 2:1–5: the messenger of Yahweh *goes up* to indict the assembled Israelites.

There is one basic difference between the two times that Yahweh or his representative speaks to Israel. The first (2:1–3) is a proclamation: the angel speaks *to* Israel. The second (2:21–22) is a monologue: Yahweh speaks *about* Israel. The difference between a divine proclamation and a divine monologue explains why there is some kind of a response by Israel after 2:1–3 and none after 2:21–22.

The angel, speaking on Yahweh's behalf, begins by talking about himself and Yahweh's previous acts of benefaction—the exodus from Egypt in fulfillment of his promise to Abraham, Isaac, and Jacob, and his commitment never to be a covenant-terminating, covenant-violating God. He continues by talking about Israel's acts of malfeasance, which contrast blatantly with his acts of benefaction. Israel, against his orders, has made a covenant with the inhabitants of the land and has not torn down their altars (2:2). All of the "not" phrases in Judg. 1:19–33 ("could/did not drive out") connect with the one "not" sentence of the angel's indictment, "You have not obeyed [listened to] my command." Israel's sin, whatever its final manifestation, is a sin of not listening. Whenever God's voice and word are muted or ignored, the repercussions become almost unfathomable.

One of those repercussions is that Yahweh will not drive out the nations (v. 3). If Israel does not "drive out" the nations, neither will Yahweh. If Israel does not *yarash* the inhabitants (the verb used throughout ch. 1), Yahweh will not *garash* them (the verb used in 2:3). No *yarash?* Then no *garash*. Thus, the leaving of the nations as "adversaries" and "a snare" is a penalty, a consequence, for Israel's faithlessness. Israel's "lifting up their voices and weeping" (v. 4) appears a little vacuous, occasioned more by what the angel said in v. 3 rather than by what the angel said in vv. 1–2. It is the leaving of the nations in adversarial roles and not their own sin that they find disquieting. There are a lot of tears, but no repentance.

In essence, the angel tells Israel that if they had done what they did not do (1:19–33), then they would not have done what they did do (2:2). Israel may be sheep without a shepherd—there is no Joshua around—but that does not let Israel off the hook.

C. 2:6–3:6. Three items immediately separate 2:6–3:6 from 1:1–2:5. For one thing, the writer in 2:6–3:6 frequently presents his own analysis and evaluation of Israel's behavior (among the many examples: "The Israelites did what was evil in the sight of the Lord and worshiped the Baals" [2:11]). By contrast, the writer in 1:1–2:5 avoids analysis and evaluation, which he leaves to the angel of Yahweh, and whom he quotes on that in 2:1–3. So, 1:1–2:5 (or 1:1–36, anyway) reads more like a compendium of historico-geographical facts, while 2:6–3:6 reads more like a discourse. This distinction should not be pushed too far, however, for we have observed in our earlier analysis that the writer of 1:1–2:5 is more than an assembler of objective facts. Without ever using "preaching" language per se, his structuring of his data is done in such a way that his evaluation of Judah in contrast to the northern tribes is quite transparent. The reader is not unprepared for or caught off-guard by what the divine representative says in 2:1–3.

The second item separating 2:6–3:6 from 1:1–2:5 is that while the latter is replete with quotations and allusions from Joshua, the former has only one quotation from Joshua (Judg. 2:6–9 = Josh. 24:28–31). Also, 2:6–3:6, but not 1:1–2:5, is filled with phrases and vocabulary found in Deuteronomy. Some examples of this are:

> 2:7 and 2:10: "who had seen/did not know all the (great) work that the Lord had done for Israel"; Deut. 11:7: "your own eyes that have seen every great deed that the Lord did"
>
> 2:11: "the Israelites did what was evil in the sight of the Lord" (also 3:7, 12; 4:1; 6:1; 10:6; 13:1); Deut. 4:25: "thus doing what is evil in the sight of the Lord your God" (also 9:18; 17:2; 31:29)
>
> 2:12 and 2:19: "follow other gods"; Deut. 8:19: "and follow other gods" (also 11:28; 28:14)

2:12: "the gods of the peoples who were all around them"; Deut. 6:14: "do not follow . . . any of the gods of the peoples who are all around you" (also 9:18; 31:29)

2:12: "and they provoked the Lord to anger"; Deut. 4:25: "and provoking him to anger" (also 9:18; 31:29)

2:17 and 3:4: "obeyed the commandments"; Deut. 11:13: "if you will only heed/obey his every commandment" (also 11:27, 28; 28:13)

2:19: "and behave worse than" (or, "act more destructively than"); Deut. 4:16: "so that you do not act corruptly" (or, "so that you do not act destructively") (also 4:25; 31:29)

2:20: "have transgressed my covenant"; Deut. 17:2: "and trangresses his covenant"

2:21 and 2:23: "drive out the/these nations," with Yahweh as subject (Deut. 4:38; 9:4, 5; 11:23; 18:12) and with Israel as subject (Deut. 7:17; 9:1; 11:23)

2:22: "to walk in the way of the Lord"; Deut. 8:6: "by walking in his ways" (also 19:9; 26:17; 28:9; 30:16)

2:23: "not driving them out at once/quickly"; Deut. 9:3: "so that you may drive them out quickly"

The third element that distinguishes 2:6–3:6 from 1:1–2:5 is that 1:1–2:5 is replete with names of individuals and places: Adoni-bezek, Caleb, Achsah, Othniel, the man from Bethel, and about thirty place names. By contrast, the account in 2:6–3:6 is more general, less tribally oriented and more nation oriented. If 1:1–2:5 is a close-up of post-Joshua Israel, 2:6–3:6 is a wide-angle panorama of post-Joshua Israel.

This unit, 2:6–3:6, begins with a flashback to the final portion of Joshua's career (vv. 6–9), which is a quote from Josh. 24:28–31. But several things stand out when the two passages are placed side-by-side. For one thing, Judg. 2:6–9 varies the sequence of the parallel verses in Josh. 24:28–31 thusly:

Judg. 2:6–9		Josh. 24:28–31
v. 6	=	v. 28
v. 7	=	v. 31
v. 8	=	v. 29
v. 9	=	v. 30

Judges 2 makes v. 31 of Joshua 24 a prescript to Joshua's death, rather than a postscript to Joshua's death, as it is in Josh. 24:31. This shift places into even bolder relief the contrast between the faithfulness of the generation of Joshua and his contemporaries vis-à-vis the following generation. Unlike the next faithless generation, Joshua and his generation "knew" (Josh. 24:31) and "saw" (Judg. 2:7) Yahweh's (great) work he had done. That is, they had both existential and observational experience of Yahweh's mighty acts. They have believed because they have seen first-hand, are eyewitnesses of, something God has done dramatically. In one sense, seeing is believing, but Jesus' words to Thomas may be recalled. In response to Thomas's statement that seeing is the sine qua non for believing, Jesus asks rhetorically, "Have you believed because you have seen me?" (John 20:29a). And then he adds this beatitude: "Blessed are those who have not seen and yet have come to believe" (John 20:29b). The post-Joshua generation is a Thomas-like generation.

The information in v. 10 about "another generation" after them that knew neither Yahweh nor his work recalls a parallel in the opening chapter of Exodus—a double death notice of a significant person followed by somebody who does not know Yahweh:

Gen. 50:26: "And Joseph died."	Josh. 24:29: "Joshua died."
Exod. 1:6: "Then Joseph died."	Judg. 2:8: "Joshua died."
Exod. 1:8: "Now a new king arose over Egypt who did not know Joseph." And this king, or a successor, later states, "I do not know the Lord" (5:2).	Judg. 2:10: "Another generation grew up after them who did not know the Lord or the work he had done for Israel."

If Judges 2 intends the reader to picture the succeeding generation as corresponding to the new pharaoh, then it clarifies what is meant by "know" in v. 10. Does it mean "not know" in the sense of "be ignorant about" or "never eyewitnessed it," or does it mean "ignore, refuse to accept the reality of"? One cannot be faulted fully for ignorance, but one can be faulted fully for willful rejection.

The rest of this unit (2:11–3:6) spells out how a generation that does not "know" Yahweh behaves and how Yahweh responds to that (mis)behavior:

Israel's behavior (cause)	Yahweh's response (effect)
2:11–13 (forsook Yahweh, followed gods)	2:14–15 ("his anger kindled" [v. 14])

2:16–19 (after death of each judge, returned to following gods)	2:20–3:6 ("his anger kindled" [v. 20])

Everything written here about the post-Joshua generation(s) is censure. We encounter here for the first time the phrase "the Israelites did what was evil in the sight of the Lord." Never do we see "the Israelites did what was good in the sight of the Lord." The evil that they did is apostasy (vv. 11–13) and not listening to the judges, thus opening Pandora's box (vv. 16–19).

God graciously and continually raised up judges to rectify the situation, not because of any repentance from the people, but because of the kind of God he is: "for the Lord would be moved to pity by their groaning because of those who persecuted and oppressed them" (2:18b). "Groaning" (i.e., an appeal for help and respite) does not mean penitence and godly sorrow. If post-Joshua Israel is to survive from generation to generation, it will not be because of any up-and-down cycles of rebellion and repentance, but because of Yahweh's merciful actions, which guarantee perpetuity—actions from a God whose judgment is always accompanied by his grief and pity (Fretheim 1983: 90, 94–95).

The judges are successful (vv. 16, 18–19), but only to a limited degree (v. 17). The judges successfully deliver Israel from plunderers (v. 16) and from oppressive enemies (v. 18), but not even the judges can deliver Israel from the greatest enemy of all—Israel itself (v. 17)! Philistines, Moabites, Midianites, Canaanites, and Ammonites are not nearly as formidable foes.

Three reasons are listed for the leaving of the nations (Stone 1988: 254):

1. a punitive one: "because this people have transgressed my covenant" (2:20–21)
2. a probative one: "in order to test Israel, whether or not they would take care to walk in the way of the Lord" (2:22–23; 3:4)
3. a pedagogical one: "to test all . . . who had no experience of any war in Canaan . . . to teach those who had no experience of it before" (3:1–2)

For this state of affairs Israel was responsible (vv. 20–21), but so is Yahweh, who, to begin with, did not hand these nations over even to Joshua (2:23b); in fact, he has "left" them (2:23a; 3:1a). The Hebrew actually says that Yahweh has "given them rest"—rest for the nations, turbulence for Israel.

The last two verses of the unit (3:5–6) summarize 1:1–3:4:

(1) 3:5–6a ("the Israelites lived among the Canaanites . . . and their daughters they gave to their sons") = 1:1–2:5

(2) 3:6b ("and they worshiped their gods") = 2:6–3:4

2. In Those Days There Were Judges in Israel (3:7–16:31)

A. Othniel (3:7–11)

Several items set Othniel apart from the other major judges. First, he is the only judge from Judah, and so once again, as in ch. 1, Judges precedes in a south-to-north direction. Second, the Othniel episode is the one judge segment of the six in which the behavior of the judge is totally exemplary. Othniel plunges a dagger into nobody, nails nobody's head to the ground, puts no demand or test on God, makes no foolish vow, and does not consort with harlots. As in 1:1–3:6, where Judah is the model tribe, so in 3:7–16:31 the Judean judge is the model. Both one tribe and that tribe's judge become the standard against which to measure all the other tribes and all the other judges.

Enforcing Othniel's uniqueness vis-à-vis his counterparts is the note about his family in 3:9 (cf. 1:13):

Othniel: son of Kenaz, Caleb's younger brother (3:9)
Ehud: son of Gera (3:15)
Deborah: wife of Lappidoth (4:4); Barak son of Abinoam (4:6)
Gideon: son of Joash the Abiezrite (6:11)
Jephthah: son of a prostitute (11:1)
Samson: son of Manoah (13:2)

The clue here is Othniel's connections with Caleb (he is Caleb's nephew) and Caleb's connections with Joshua. From the days of Moses to the opening chapters of Judges there have been three generations: (1) that of Moses, (2) that of Joshua and Caleb (2:7, 10a), and (3) another generation (10b):

Generation one, that of Moses and those exiting Egypt, is a faithless generation. All perish for sin except for Joshua and Caleb.
↓
Generation two, that of Joshua and Caleb (holdovers from generation one), those conquering Canaan, is a faithful generation.
↓
Generation three, the post-Joshua one, "those who did not know the Lord or the work that he had done for Israel," is a faithless generation.

Joshua and Caleb are survivors of a faithless generation, but they immensely impact their own generation and those who outlive them (2:7). They model obedience and righteousness. Similarly, Othniel, who lives in Israel after the death of Joshua and the elders who outlived Joshua, models true judgeship for all who follow him in that position. There never is another Joshua, a survivor of a faithless generation, and there never is another Othniel, a survivor of a faithful generation.

The Othniel unit in Judges, more so than any other unit in 3:7–16:31, uses all the key phrases for the cycle of the judges.

Othniel's career establishes the pattern. All other judges vary from this fundamental pattern to a greater or lesser degree. Note, for example, that of the twelve subsections in the Othniel story, nine of them are duplicated in the Jephthah story, seven in the Ehud story, but only five in the Samson story. Thus, 3:7–16:31 is not one record played over six times with merely cosmetic changes. "If there were no variations, characters in the narrative would be determined by the cyclical plot pattern. They would be absorbed by the repetition rather than stand out from it and would, consequently, all look alike. In other words, character depiction and variance from pattern are closely interrelated" (Kort 1988: 30).

The Othniel unit begins in vv. 7–8 with a general to specific statement. Verse 7a is general ("did evil"). Verse 7b is the specific—what kind of evil. Verse 8a is general (Yahweh's anger kindled). Verse 8b is the specific—the manifestation of that anger. Cushan-rishathaim, Israel's subjecting foreign king and then defeated king, functions much like Nebuchadnezzar (and Babylon) in Jeremiah. He moves from being an instrument of judgment to an object of judgment. Cushan-rishathaim is a mystery king. His name means "Cushan of double wickedness," or "Cushan of double dastardliness," or "Cushan of compound criminality" (Stone 1988: 282). His name rhymes with his country—Cushan-rishathaim of Aram Naharaim (Cushan of double wickedness from Aram of double rivers).

In response to the "cry" of his people, which we should interpret not as pentience, but nevertheless as a real outcry to God for help against an oppressor, Yahweh "raises up" a deliverer (v. 9), whom he then gifts with "the spirit of the Lord" (v. 10).

The Old Testament knows of two types of leaders, those who inherit their office (i.e., kings and priests), and those who enter their office via some kind of direct experience with God (i.e., judges and prophets, who receive God's spirit or his word, or occasionally both). The expression "raised up for" in v. 9 is the same (Hiphil stem of *qum*, plus preposition *le*) elsewhere for the appointment of a prophet: "The Lord your

	Othniel	Introduction	Ehud	Deborah	Gideon	Jephthah	Samson	Shamgar	Tola	Jair	Ibzan	Elon	Abdon
the Israelites did evil in the eyes of the LORD	3:7a	2:11a	3:12a	4:1b	6:1	10:6a	13:1a						
they forgot the LORD their God and served the Baals and the Asherahs	3:7b	2:11b, 12b; 3:6b				10:6b, 13a, 14a							
the anger of the LORD burned against Israel	3:8a	2:14a, 20a				10:7a							
so that he sold them into the hands of Cushan-Rishathaim king of Aram Naharaim	3:8b	2:14b (gave over), 14c (sold)		4:2a (sold)		10:7b (sold)	13:1b (gave over)						
to whom the Israelites were subject for eight years	3:8c		3:14										
but when they cried out to the LORD	3:9a		3:15a	4:3b	6:6b, 7	10:10a							
he raised up for them a deliverer; Othniel son of Kenaz, Caleb's younger brother, who saved them	3:9b	2:16, 18a	3:15b					3:31	10:1 (Qal *qum*)	10:3a (Qal *qum*)			
the Spirit of the LORD came upon him	3:10a				6:34 (took possession of)	11:29	13:25 (began to stir); 14:6, 19; 15:14 (rushed)						
so that he became Israel's judge and went to war	3:10b			4:4		12:7 (six years)	15:20; 16:31 (twenty years)		10:2a (twenty-three years)	10:3b (twenty-two years)	12:8, 9b (seven years)	12:11 (ten years)	12:13, 14b (eight years)
the LORD gave Cushan-Rishathaim king of Aram into the hands of Othniel, who overpowered him	3:10c		3:28b	4:7	7:7b, 9b, 15b	11:30b, 32b							
so the land had peace for forty years	3:11a		3:30b	5:31c	8:28b								
until Othniel son of Kenaz died	3:11b	2:19a	4:1a		8:32	12:7b	16:30		10:2b	10:5	12:10	12:12	12:15

God will raise up for you a prophet" (Deut. 18:15); "I will also raise up for them a prophet" (Deut. 18:18); and see Jer. 29:15 and Amos 2:11.

The note in v. 11 that the land had rest for forty years, followed by Othniel's death notice, points to the enduring effectiveness of Othniel's judgeship. The same complement is given to Ehud (3:30b), Deborah (5:31c), and Gideon (8:28c), but is glaringly absent from the end of both the Jephthah and Samson stories (see chart above). By contrast, Judges refers only to the length of their respective judgeships (Jephthah, six years [12:7]; Samson, twenty years [15:20; 16:31]). This, along with other data in Judges, strongly suggests that the movement in 3:7–16:31 is not cyclical but linear, and that in a precipitously downward direction.

B. Ehud (3:12–30)

Seven basic units form the Ehud story:

1. Israel serves the Moabites and Eglon for eighteen years due to their acts of evil (vv. 12–14)
2. God raises up Ehud as deliverer who is a tribute-bearing, dagger-toting envoy to Eglon (vv. 15–16)
3. Ehud presents the tribute (the dagger will follow!) to the obese king (vv. 17–18)
4. Ehud murders Eglon (vv. 19–23)
5. Eglon's lifeless corpse discovered by his courtiers (vv. 24–25)
6. Ehud-led Israel engages Moabites in victorious battle (vv. 26–29)
7. Summarizing statement (v. 30)

The Ehud story shares several items with the preceding Othniel story. Like Othniel, Yahweh "raises" Ehud up to his position of deliverer (the only two judges with whom this phrase is used). Again, like the Othniel section, the Ehud story ends by stating (before it records his death [4:1]) that the land had rest for eighty years, thus again emphasizing the success of Ehud's judgeship rather than merely the duration of his judgeship, as with some of the later judges.

But there are differences as well between the two. For one thing, while 3:7b in the Othniel unit specified the "evil" as forgetting Yahweh and worshiping Baals, no such specificity is present in 2:12. What the nature of the evil was we are not told.

A second difference is that there is no reference to the "spirit of the Lord" coming on Ehud, as there was with Othniel (3:10a), an omission in Judges that Ehud shares only with Deborah. It cannot be without some significance that the two judges who, apart from Othniel, are most successful, most untainted by flaw or defect, most luminous, operate without explicit reference to Yahweh's spirit.

A third difference, albeit a necessary one, is the insertion of "again" in the opening, common formula, "The Israelites *again* did what was evil in the sight of the Lord." Two things may be said about the "again." First, does it mean resumption of a previous behavioral pattern (the cycle of evil and apostasy starts all over again after an interlude), or does it mean continuation of a current behavioral pattern (Israel continued to do evil)? The data of 2:18–19 seems to argue for the former ("But whenever the judge died, they would relapse" [v. 19a]), but the data in 2:17 seems to argue for the latter ("Yet they did not listen even to their judges, for they lusted after other gods" [v. 17a]).

The second item to be noticed about this adverb is that the one place where "again" does not occur in this formula in Judges, apart, of course, from 3:7, is 6:1 (Stone 1988: 302), that is, after the career and judgeship of Deborah and before the introduction of Gideon. Its absence there may well be a way of highlighting the ministry of Deborah. So effective was her leadership that the cycle of sin was broken, at least for a good, long while.

Ehud is a Benjaminite by tribal association, and a left-hander by bodily orientation. Since "Benjamin" means "son of the right hand," Ehud is really a left-handed right-hander. Actually, the Hebrew text does not say he was "left-handed," but rather, "hindered, impeded, handicapped [ʾitter] in his right hand." Like some of the judges who follow him, Ehud represents an anomalous, subordinate segment of his society (Jobling 1989: 128). Ehud is a left-hander in a world of right-handers. Deborah is a woman, and a leader at that, in a world of men (leaders). Gideon is the youngest son in a world of older brothers. Jephthah is the son of a harlot in a world of "legitimate" children. Samson is a nonshaving, non-intoxicant-imbibing ascetic Nazirite in a world of "normal" people.

The people who are first the oppressors of Israel, and then their victims, are the Moabites and their bulky king, Eglon. Relationships between Israel and Moab were hardly ever cordial (Brettler 1992: 296–97). With the exceptions of Deut. 2:9, where Israel was told not to harass Moab or engage them in battle on their way to Canaan, and 1 Sam. 22:3–4, where David leaves his parents with the king of Moab as he seeks refuge from Saul, and Ruth the Moabite, all other Old Testament references picture Moab(ites) negatively. According to Gen. 19:37, Moab has its origin in an incestuous sexual act in a cave involving a drunken father and his older daughter. Balak, king of Moab, did his best, albeit unsuccessfully, to render Israel impotent (Numbers 22–24). One of Israel's greatest acts of apostasy involved the Moabite women of Shittim (Numbers 25). Deuteronomy 23:3 prohibits admission to Yahweh's assembly of any Ammonite or Moabite, even to the tenth generation. David subjugated the Moabites (2 Sam. 8:2), but sporadic fighting would later break out between Israel and Moab (2 Kings 1:1; 3:1–27; 13:20–21; 24:2). Frequently, the prophets castigated Moab in their oracles (Isa. 15:1–16:14; Jer. 48:21–47; Ezek. 25:8–11; Amos 2:1–3).

Judges 3 contributes to this depiction of Moab by describing Eglon as a "very fat man" (v. 17) who is duped by Ehud. "Eglon" reflects the word *'egel*, "calf"; so Eglon is quite literally "the fatted calf" (such as the father in Jesus' parable had prepared for the homecoming of his lost son [Luke 15:23]). Furthermore, the Moabite soldiers share their king's corpulence. The word that the NRSV uses to describe them in v. 29 as "strong" (*shamen*) is actually another word for "fat" or "stout."

Also, both Eglon and his troops are made to look like fools. Rising from his chair to meet the tribute-bearing Ehud, and believing Ehud to have an oracular message from God, Eglon and his large body become an easy target for Ehud's dagger. Similarly, his servants wait in silence outside his room, believing that his protracted silence is because he is using the toilet, a belief advanced, no doubt, by the release of the anal feces in Eglon's death spasm ("and the dirt came out" [v. 22d]). Again, the kingless Moabites, ten thousand of them, are lured to their grave by Ehud and his small army when they find themselves trapped in a setting from which there is no escape (v. 28). Interestingly, the verb used to describe Ehud's "thrusting" his dagger into Eglon (v. 21) and for Ehud's later "sounding" the trumpet to rally his troops (v. 27) is the same (*taqa'*).

But Judges is careful to make the point that Israel defeated Eglon and the Moabites not because the latter were a bunch of stupid, blundering, overweight idiots. Rather, Ehud and his kin are victorious because of a divinely raised-up deliverer (v. 15), and because Yahweh is the victory granter (v. 28). The outcome would have been the same even if Eglon and the Moabites were slender and suave paragons of astuteness.

Ehud's weapon is a "sword with two edges" (v. 16), literally, "two mouths" (possibly another oblique reference to Eglon—anybody that big needs two mouths!). It is short enough ("a cubit in length") to be hidden by being strapped against the left-hander's right thigh. This is different from the normal sword of that period, which was curved and would be used for slashing one's enemies (Yadin 1963: 254–55). The word from God that Ehud claims to have is actually the concealed sword. The connection of "word from God" with a two-edged dagger invites comparison with the New Testament claim that "the word of God is living and active, sharper than any two-edged sword, piercing until it divides soul from spirit, joints from marrow" (Heb. 4:12).

Ehud has been variously described by interpreters: "duplicitous" (Klein 1988: 40); "cleverly ruthless" (Stone 1992: 335); "boldly resourceful" (Alter 1981: 38); "not particularly likeable" (Polzin 1980: 160); "deadly cunning" and "a devious assassin" (Webb 1987: 130, 132); "a great warrior with special skills" (Amit 1989: 106).

C. Shamgar (3:31)

Sandwiched between the Ehud and Deborah stories is the one-verse reference to Shamgar son of Anath. His only other mention in Scripture is in Deborah's song in 5:6 ("In the days of Shamgar son of Anath . . . caravans ceased and travelers kept to the byways").

Two items are credited to him. He killed six hundred Philistines with an oxgoad and he delivered Israel. This second accolade he shares with Othniel (3:9c). The first remark appears to be present in the pre-Samson reference in 10:11, "And the Lord said to the Israelites, 'Did I not deliver you from . . . the Philistines?'"

Yet, he remains an elusive individual. Is "Shamgar" even an Israelite name? Many scholars think it is not. And does the reference to his parent, "son of Anath," have any connection with the famous Canaanite goddess of the same name?

Two observations may be advanced on Shamgar's judgeship. First, his weapon is a primitive one. He uses an ox-goad, for which the Hebrew uses the phrase *malmad habaqar*. The first of these two words, *malmad*, is from the verb *lamad*, "teach, learn," but whose original meaning is "to train." Hence, *malmad habaqar* is "that which is used for the training of the oxen." The text suggests that Yahweh honors those who use what they have and what is available to them rather than excusing themselves from commitment with "If I only had . . ." or some other evasive statement.

The second thing to be said is that Shamgar shares with Samson a battle against the Philistines. But there is one major difference. Samson will only *"begin* to deliver" Israel from the Philistines (13:5), whereas Shamgar "delivered Israel." Thus, Shamgar is eminently more successful against a common foe than is Samson. Yet, while the judge with mitigated success against the Philistines rates four full chapters in Judges (13–16), the judge with delivering success against the Philistines rates one verse. Shamgar is a minor judge with a magisterial ministry. That he is placed between the judgeships of Ehud and Deborah may reinforce the perception of Judges' editor/compiler that the era of Ehud-Shamgar-Deborah is head and shoulders above that of the remaining judges (Stone 1988: 365).

D. Deborah and Barak (4:1–5:31)

The story of Deborah and Barak appears twice in Judges, first in a prose account (4:1–24) and then in a poetic version (5:1–31). Chapter 4 tells the story and ch. 5 sings the story. Narration gives way to celebration. The only parallel to this in the Old Testament is the account of the exodus from Egypt, told first in prose (Exod. 12:37–42; 13:17–14:31), then in poetry (Exod. 15:1–21). Our comments will focus first on the prose, then on the poem.

1. 4:1–24. Several things separate the Deborah story from the others in Judges. For one thing, the death notice about the previous judge, Ehud, does not so much end the Ehud story as it does introduce the Deborah story: "after Ehud died" (4:1b). Putting Ehud's death notice in the Deborah story links these two judges, and is a further evidence of their qualitative superiority over the following judges. Judges emphasizes more the success of Ehud's judgeship than his death by (1) stating the land had rest for eighty years (3:30b), that is, well beyond his lifetime, and (2) reducing Ehud's death notice to an almost parenthetical remark in the Deborah story: "The Israelites again did what was evil in the sight of the Lord—by the way, Ehud had died" (Stone 1988: 345).

For another thing, as with Ehud, never does the text say that the spirit of Yahweh came upon Deborah—the only two judges for whom this formula is absent. And yet, these "spiritless" judges are the exemplary judges! Deborah is a "prophetess" (4:5). This does not of itself suggest her possession of Yahweh's spirit. Rather, it suggests that her supernatural possession is the word of God rather than the spirit of God. In this respect, she is like Samuel, who has the divine word, but who is never associated with the divine spirit. Note that the spiritless Ehud, too, claimed to have a word from God (3:20b). In 4:6b the narrator quotes Deborah quoting God. While other judges talk to God or about God, Deborah is the one judge who speaks for God. She is his mouthpiece.

A third thing is that the formula "the Lord raised up a judge/deliverer," present in the introduction (2:16a, 18a), with Othniel (3:9b), and with Ehud (3:15b), is missing here (and throughout the rest of Judges). The absence of the phrase in the prose account may be tempered somewhat by a line in the following poem that the NRSV renders as "because you *arose*, Deborah, *arose* as a mother in Israel" (5:7b). The Hebrew construction is a difficult one, and may also be translated "because I,

Deborah arose, arose as a mother in Israel," or even "until you raised me, Deborah, up, raised me up as a mother in Israel."

The fourth thing to notice is that Deborah is the only major judge whose death is never mentioned (see 3:11b; 4:1b; 8:32a; 12:7b; 16:30 for the others). Given the information of 2:19a ("but whenever the judge died, they would relapse"), the absence of a death announcement for Deborah may be Judges' way of underscoring the effectiveness of her tenure.

A fifth thing setting the Deborah story apart is that the oppressing nation is actually in Israel's own borders. The enemy is the Canaanites, led by their Hazor-based king, Jabin, and his commander, Sisera. Compare this situation with the other judges:

Judge	Oppressing Nation
Othniel	Mesopotamia
Ehud	Moabites
Gideon	Midianites
Jephthah	Ammonites
Samson	Philistines

Finally, this portion of Judges begins with the spotlight on a woman, Deborah, and ends with a woman, Jael (vv. 17–22). Both of their spouses are named. Deborah is "wife of Lappidoth" (v. 4). Jael is "wife of Heber" (v. 17). But neither husband says or does anything. Each stands in his wife's shadow. "Lappidoth" may not even be the name of Deborah's husband. The word *lappid*, meaning "torch, fire," is a non-Semitic loanword in early Hebrew (compare Greek *lampades*), brought by the technically superior Philistines, who introduced new kinds of torches and lamps to Palestine. We could render *ʾeshet lappidot* as "woman of torches" (van Wolde 1995: 240) or "woman of fire," that is, "a spirited woman" (Fewell and Gunn 1990: 391) or "fiery woman" (Rasmussen 1989: 93). If Lappidoth be retained as the name of Deborah's spouse, then his presence in no way "illuminates" the narrative.

Jael's husband, Heber, is equally quiet. All that gives him notoriety is his wife. "Heber" is very close to the Hebrew word for "associate, friend." While there is peace between the clan of Heber and King Jabin of Hazor (v. 17b), Jael turns out to be a "Heber" more to Israel than to the Canaanites by smiting Sisera in her tent.

The reader will observe here (v. 11) that Heber is called a "Kenite," and the Kenites ("the Cainites") are the descendants of Hobab, Moses' father-in-law. In Judg. 1:16 and 4:11 and in Num. 10:29 Moses' father-in-law is Hobab ("loved one, friend, client"). Elsewhere, this same person is identified as Reuel, a priest of Midian (Exod. 2:18), and as Jethro (Exod. 4:18; 18:1–12). Numbers 10:29 further identifies Reuel as the father of Hobab. Thus, who is Moses' father-in-law: Hobab, Reuel, or Jethro? And is he a Midianite or a Kenite? One solution to this enigma is to attribute the differences in names to different literary sources behind our Pentateuch (e.g., Hobab in Numbers 10 from the J source and Jethro in Exodus 4 and 18 from the E source). Another approach, however, suggests that the father-in-law has two names, Hobab and Jethro, and that Reuel is either the clan name or the father of Hobab/Jethro (Num. 10:29), thus necessitating reading "daughters" and "father" in Exod. 2:16–18 as "granddaughters" and "grandfather." What then of Midianite versus Kenite? Midianite appears to be the name not of one people but of a confederation of peoples, one of which is the Kenites. For some evidence to support this, note that Enoch (Hanoch) is the son of Cain (Kenite) in Gen. 4:17, and a Hanoch is the son of Midian in Gen. 25:4. Kenite means "smith," individuals who worked the mines in the areas of Sinai and Midian. That they were also a guild of itinerant craftsmen and metalworkers is evidenced by their presence as far south as Arad in the Negeb (Judg. 1:16), and as far north as Kedesh near Elon-bezaanannim in Naphtali (Judg. 4:11).

After the introduction (vv. 1–3) Deborah first appears. As prophetess, it is not surprising that she speaks for God. Rather than lead the troops herself, she assigns that responsibility to Barak ("flash of lightning") from Naphtali (vv. 4–7). There is one possible ambiguity in Deborah's charge to Barak. Who is the "I" in "I will draw out Sisera . . . I will give him into your hand" (v. 7)? Yahweh? Deborah?

Barak's response is interesting: "If you will go with me, I will go; but if you will not go with me, I will not go" (v. 8). It is common to interpret Barak's words as cowardice. This may be the case, but not necessarily so. His words sound much like Moses' words to God: "If your presence will not go, do not carry us up from here. For how shall it be known that I have found favor in your sight, I and your people, unless you go with us?" (Exod. 33:15–16). As a prophetess with unmediated access to God, Deborah's presence is both welcomed and salutary. Again, since Barak has not heard Yahweh speak this word, he is "being asked to risk his life as well as the lives of ten thousand men on the strength of this woman's unconfirmable word. Barak's conditional proposal, then, is a test: if Deborah is willing to stake her own life on this word, then he will believe and obey" (Fewell and Gunn 1990: 398).

To Barak's response comes Deborah's counterresponse: "The road on which you are going will not lead to your glory, for the Lord will sell Sisera into the hand of a woman" (v. 9b). Here is another ambiguity in Deborah's talk. What woman? Presumably Deborah, we think, and so does Barak. We are surprised, and Barak is surprised, and maybe even Deborah herself is surprised, to find out later who this woman is.

The battle scene is described in vv. 10–16. Ten thousand Israelite infantry descend from the safety of Mount Tabor against Sisera's nine hundred chariots of iron mobilized by the river Kishon. Once again, Deborah is a stimulus to Barak (v. 14), this time, however, intentionally deleting any reminder about Yahweh selling Sisera into a woman's hand. Israel is victorious, with credit going to Yahweh (v. 14c; 15a). Deborah has "initiated and forced the battle; God has won it; and Barak remains with a mopping-up operation to his credit" (Sternberg 1987: 277).

Sisera manages to escape the slaughter and flee to Elon-bezaanannim, where he seeks refuge and cover, not in the tent of Heber his ally, but in the tent of Heber's wife, Jael (v. 17). Jael is like Ehud. She pretends to be the sympathetic hostess, just like Ehud pretended to have a word from God; and like Ehud with Eglon, she singlehandedly murders the gullible and unsuspecting Sisera.

Jael invites the fleeing and distraught Sisera into her tent ("Turn aside, my lord, turn aside," in which there is a similarity of sound between "turn aside" [*surah*] and "Sisera" [*sisera*ʾ] [v. 18a]), reassures him of her care ("have no fear" [v. 18b]), and covers him with a rug, both for warmth and for concealment (v. 18c). She gives him milk instead of the water for which he had asked (v. 19b). Once asleep, she hammers a tent peg into his temple. The same verb (*taqaʿ*) is used in v. 21 for Jael's driving the tent peg into the side of his head as was used in 3:21 for Ehud thrusting the sword into Eglon's stomach. And the Hebrew word for "into his temple" (*beraqqato*) contains the name of Barak (*baraq*). Jael is "a heroine who offers milk instead of water, death in place of sleep, a corpse instead of a captive" (Polzin 1980: 166). Interestingly, when Barak does show up (v. 22), he has no reaction and says nothing. He only observes, reinforcing the idea that at best, Barak's contribution is "a junior partnership in a female enterprise" (Sternberg 1987: 283).

The text never comments on any motivation of Jael in her elimination of Sisera (Amit 1987: 97; Culley 1992: 102). Her words to Barak in v. 22 ("Come, and I will show you the man whom you are seeking") indicate that she has some knowledge of what has been going on. Did she do it to protect her honor and that of her husband (Matthews 1991: 17)? After all, Sisera is alone with Jael in her tent, and he ordered her to be dishonest, as Abram had done with Sarai (Gen.12:10–20). He is an obvious refugee, hiding from somebody. Or did she do what she did out of commitment to the God of Deborah and Barak, thus allowing the story to extol "the heroics of an ordinary person choosing the Lord's side" (Stone 1992: 335; compare these remarks on Jael: Heber "had a loyal Yahwist wife" and "Jael was a covenant loyalist" [Boling 1975: 97, 100])? Or, is Jael caught between a rock and a hard place? What would Sisera do to her if she rebuffs him? On the other hand, what happens to Jael when the Israelite pursuers come to her tent and find she has given aid and comfort to the enemy? "Her best bet for survival . . . is to turn Sisera's presence in her tent into proof of her own personal allegiance to the victors. The body of Sisera will be her trump card" (Fewell and Gunn 1990: 396).

2. 5:1–31. While in English translation "Deborah and Barak . . . sang on that day" sounds like two singers, the verb "sang" here is not plural. It is feminine-singular, "And she sang, Deborah, and Barak." It is like Num. 12:1, where the English translation says, "Miriam and Aaron spoke against Moses," implying a plural verb for "spokc." Actually, the verb is feminine-singular, "And she spoke, Miriam, and Aaron, against Moses."

It is amazing how much God does for his people again and again throughout the books of Joshua and Judges (and First Samuel). Act of deliverance follows act of deliverance. Equally amazing is how few are the expressions of praise and gratitude for those divine interventions. They are limited to this song of Deborah (the only act of praise in Judges) and the song of Hannah (1 Samuel 2:1–11), thus leading Ballentine (1993: 222) to say, "Only with Hannah and Deborah is there any praise in the canonical presentation of Israel's history between settlement and kingship."

As is to be expected, some differences exist between the prose account in ch. 4 and the poetic account in ch. 5. Some of the more significant are the following.

(1) Tribal participation: Chapter 4 mentions the mustering of ten thousand troops from Naphtali and Zebulon (v. 6), while ch. 5 boosts the level of the militia to forty thousand (v. 8) and includes the tribes of Ephraim, Benjamin, Machir (= Manasseh) (v. 14), and Issachar (v. 15). The poetic account also castigates four tribes for not joining in the battle (Reuben [vv. 15b–16], and Gilead [= Gad], Dan, and Asher

[v. 17]). Judah, Simeon, and Levi are never mentioned in either account.

(2) How the battle was fought and won: Chapter 4 reports the battle in most general terms: "The Lord threw Sisera and all his chariots and all his army into a panic" (v. 15), using a verb (*hamam*) that connotes panic and confusion, and that frequently occurs in the descriptions of divine war (Exod. 14:24; Deut. 7:23; Josh. 10:10; 1 Sam. 7:10). Chapter 5 says that "the stars from heaven fought against Sisera" (v. 20) and "the torrent Kishon swept them away" (v. 21). God's powerful actions through these heavenly and terrestrial bodies "evoke an aura of miracle, of cosmic involvement in the process of history" (Brenner 1990: 134).

(3) Geography: Chapter 4 states that Barak led his ten thousand warriors from Mount Tabor (v. 14), which is just southwest of the Sea of Galilee and on the northern rim of the Jezreel Valley. Chapter 5 locates the action at "Taanach, by the waters of Megiddo" (v. 19), which is on the southern rim of the Jezreel Valley.

(4) Sisera: Chapter 5 deletes the fact recorded in ch. 4 that Jael slew Sisera only after he "was lying fast asleep from weariness" (v. 21). Also, the milk that Jael brought to Sisera she brought in either "a skin" (4:19) or a "lordly bowl" (5:25).

(5) The prose account never refers to Sisera's mother waiting for her son to return from battle with the spoils of war (5:28–30).

It is difficult to divide the poem into clear, distinct units or stanzas. Two of the more penetrating attempts are those of Globe (1974: 495–96) and Coogan (1978: 143–66, and followed closely by Webb 1987: 140–41).

Globe:

> I.   vv. 2–11d: an introductory thanksgiving hymn
>   A. vv. 2–3: calling on the people to hear the poet's praise
>   B. vv. 4–5: Yahweh, the source of Israel's help
>   C. vv. 6–8: the oppression of Israel
>   D. vv. 9–11d: a call to Israel to celebrate their God
> II. vv. 11e–18: the muster of the Israelite tribes
>   A. vv. 11e–15c, the assembly of the tribes and the participants
>   B. vv. 15d–18, censure for four tribes, honor for two tribes
> III. vv. 19–31: the battle and its aftermath
>   A. vv. 19–23: the battle and the rout
>   B. vv. 24–27: Jael kills Sisera

    C. vv. 28–30: a taunt of Sisera's anxious mother

    D. v. 31: a conclusion

Coogan/Webb:

I. vv. 2–8

    A. vv. 2–5: hear the song; Yahweh is the coming divine warrior

    B. vv. 6–8: prebattle conditions in Israel

II. vv. 9–13: a summons to join in the battle

III. vv. 14–18: the response of the tribes, positive and negative

IV. vv. 19–23: the battle

V. vv. 24–31

    A. vv. 24–27: the death of Sisera

    B. vv. 28–30: Sisera's mother waits in vain

    C. v. 31: concluding invocation of Yahweh

The poem begins by extolling those who volunteered and dedicated themselves to the cause of the moment, moving the poet twice to exclaim "Bless the Lord!" (vv. 2, 9). This is the thrust of the first line of v. 2, "When locks are long in Israel" (mysteriously rendered in the NIV as "When the princes of Israel take the lead," but probably taken from the first line of v. 9). It is probably an early reference to Naziritism. The militia (probably we should render "people" as "fighting force/men" in vv. 2, 9, 11, 13) fighting in these wars would dedicate themselves, and this dedication would include not shaving the hair on their head.

If the poem begins by talking about the dedication of the fighting force, it continues by talking directly to God (vv. 4–5). He is the God who comes from the arid regions of Seir and Edom of the south. God has moved with his people. As they have marched from the southern wilderness to Canaan, so has he. That divine presence makes all the difference.

The next few verses (6–11) are difficult both to translate and to interpret. It appears that having spoken about the infantry (v. 2) and Yahweh (vv. 3–5), Deborah now talks about herself. We are inclined to think that in vv. 6–7a she is describing the cessation of open settlements (*perazon* [v. 7a]) in her land because of fear of attack (and here following the NIV in v. 7a, "village life in Israel ceased," rather than the NRSV, "the peasantry prospered in Israel"), an attack due to the apostasy of her people alluded to in v. 8 ("when new gods were chosen").

But that all changed when Deborah came on the scene. She is the divinely raised-up deliverer ("because you arose, Deborah" [NRSV]; "until I, Deborah, arose" [NIV]). Both the well-to-do (v. 10 ab) and the poor (v. 10c) are summoned to sing of God's great victory (v. 11ab) and the return to normal, tranquil life in the open villages (v. 11c). Even the absence of defensive ("shield") or offensive weapons ("spear") is not critical in winning this battle, for the battle is the Lord's (v. 8c).

The victory already celebrated (vv. 10–11) is now recounted in some detail, beginning with the mustering of the tribal troops (vv. 11–15b), moving to a statement or inquiry about tribes who did not get involved (vv. 15c–17), another commendation of the two principal tribal participants (v. 18), the account of the battle (vv. 19–22), and finally, a curse on the city of Meroz (v. 23), a city presumably in the vicinity of the battle. Why one city should be cursed for noninvolvement while whole tribes are merely asked about noninvolvement is not clear.

The rest of the poem, except the last verse, focuses on two women, Jael (vv. 24–27) and Sisera's mother (vv. 28–30). Notice the play-off in v. 26 and v. 27 between the subjects of the staccato verbs: "*she* put . . . struck . . . crushed . . . shattered . . . pierced; *he* fell . . . lay still . . . sank . . . fell . . . sank . . . fell dead." This is a graphic illustration of parataxis in poetry (see Hauser 1980), in which phrases and/or clauses are placed side by side without any connectives such as "and." The presence in v. 27 not only of parataxis, but also of repetition (sank . . . fell, . . . sank . . . fell, . . . sank . . . fell), "produces an effect of slow motion that mimics Sisera's death agony" (Alter 1985: 45). The language is graphic and brutal. As Halpern (1988: 81) has stated, "A more epicurean relish over Sisera's collapse could not be expressed." This section is a mother in Israel (v. 7d) praising the deed ("most blessed of women be Jael") of a mother of the Kenites.

Contrasting with Jael is the mother of Sisera (vv. 28–30) looking out the window of her palace. Her ignorance of why her son has not yet returned from battle matches the ignorance of Eglon's servants as to why he stayed so long in the bathroom (3:24–25) (Polzin 1980: 167). Her hunch is that her son is delayed because he is gathering up some spoils from war, specifically, "a girl or two" for the men and embroidered dye stuffs for the ladies. The Hebrew for "a girl or two" is actually "a womb, two wombs," thus in Sisera's mother's estimation, reducing the captured Israelite women to "body parts, receptacles for male invasion" (Fewell and Gunn 1990: 407).

The poem concludes, as it began (v. 4), by addressing God directly. If vv. 24–30 contrast Jael with Sisera's mother, v. 31 contrasts Yahweh's enemies with his friends/lovers. This final verse is hardly a suspicious tack-on to the poem. Rather, "It is a liturgical statement climaxing and ending the poem and a paranetic extension and universalizing of the specific victory celebrated in the song" (Miller 1973: 101).

The Deborah/Barak story concludes, "And the land had rest for forty years" (v. 31c). Note briefly three things here. First, Deborah is the only judge whose death is not recorded. Second, the word "again" is *not* used in the formula "the Israelites did what was evil" that introduces the Gideon story (6:1). Third, as with the judges ahead of Deborah, the years of rest in the land are greater than the years of subjugation to an oppressor, but this pattern breaks down later in Judges. There is no rest for the land after Jephthah and Samson.

Years of subjugation	Years of rest for the land
Othniel: 8 years (3:8)	40 years (3:11)
Ehud: 18 years (3:14)	80 years (3:30)
Deborah: 20 years (4:3)	40 years (5:31)
Gideon: 7 years (6:1)	40 years (8:28)
Jephthah: 18 years (10:8)	none
Samson: 40 years (13:1)	none

E. Gideon (6:1–8:35)

The next character in Judges is Gideon, from the tribe of Manasseh. His name is from the verb *gadaʿ*, "cut down, cut off, break," and has the *-on* suffix that Hebrew grammarians refer to as "the characterizing suffix/affix" (as in Eglon, Samson). So his name means "destroyer, shatterer" or even "hacker, hewer, chopper." In the one place where Gideon literally lives up to his name, the cutting down of the Asherah pole adjacent to his father's altar to Baal (6:25–32), the text uses the verb *karat* (vv. 25, 28, 30) rather than *gadaʿ*. By contrast, Deut. 7:5 ("hew down their sacred poles") and 12:3 ("and hew down the idols of their gods") both used the verb *gadaʿ*. The pagan icons are to be "gideoned."

Outside of Judges 6–8, Gideon never again appears in the Old Testament as "Gideon." He does, however, have another name, Jerubbaal ("let Baal contend/sue/make a complaint"), conferred on him by his father (6:32). If Cushan-rishathaim (3:8) is Cush of "double wickedness," then Gideon is the judge of "double name." Twice, both names occur together (7:1; 8:35): "Jerubbaal (that is, Gideon)." But in ch. 9 only

Jerubbaal appears. Later on yet, there is remembrance in 2 Sam. 11:21 of Jerubbaal. Actually, the Septuagint Greek reads "Jerubbaal," but the Hebrew has "Jerubbesheth," replacing "-baal" with "-besheth." Thus, Jerubbesheth means "let shame contend," with the removal of the -baal element, as in Ishbaal/Ishbosheth (1 Chron. 8:33 and 2 Sam. 3:7). Thus, Gideon's name with patently pagan vestiges ("let Baal contend") endures in the scriptural narrative, while "Gideon" slips into oblivion.

The following episodes fill up the Gideon narrative:

1. Midian humbles the evildoing Israel, causing Israel once again to cry to Yahweh (6:1–6).
2. Yahweh sends not a judge but a prophet, who speaks of God's gracious acts and Israel's refusal to listen (6:7–10).
3. The angel of the Lord reveals himself to Gideon and commissions him, to which Gideon responds with an objection and a sign request (6:11–18).
4. The sign given is divine fire, which completely consumes Gideon's present/*minkha*, alleviating Gideon's uncertainty but filling him with fear (6:19–24).
5. Gideon/Jerubbaal tears down at night his father's altar to Baal and the nearby Asherah pole, and so provokes the ire of the residents of Ophrah (6:25–32).
6. Clothed with the spirit, Gideon assembles a fighting force mainly from the northern tribes of Manasseh, Asher, Zebulon, and Naphtali to engage the Midianites and others by the Valley of Jezreel (as with Barak in ch. 4) (6:33–35).
7. Gideon seeks further confirmation from God by the fleece of wool and the threshing floor (6:36–40).
8. Yahweh reduces Gideon's fighting force of twenty-two thousand by some 98 percent, leaving him with just three hundred of the original troops (7:1–8).
9. Accompanied by his servant Purah, Gideon goes at night to the Midianite camp, where he overhears a Midianite tell a fellow Midianite a dream whose interpretation predicts victory for Gideon (7:9–14).
10. Gideon and his troops, armed with trumpets, empty jars, and torches, attack the Midianite camp at night, throwing the latter into panic and rout (7:15–23).
11. Ephraim joins their northern neighbors and adds the finishing touches, killing two Midianite captains, Oreb ("raven") and Zeeb ("wolf"), and presenting their heads to Gideon as war trophies (7:24–25).

12. The Ephraimites scold Gideon for their last-minute summons to battle by Gideon, but are satisfied by his proverblike response to their censure (8:1–3).
13. After his defeat of Midian, Gideon and his three hundred warriors cross the Jordan in pursuit of two fleeing kings of Midian, Zebah and Zalmunna (8:4–12).
14. Returning with his two captives, Gideon rebukes and punishes severely the Cisjordanian/Manassite cities of Succoth and Penuel for their earlier refusal to offer assistance in the form of food when he went after the two Midianite kings (8:13–17).
15. After Gideon's oldest son, Jether, refuses to kill the two captured Midianite kings, Gideon does so himself to avenge their earlier murdering of his brothers (8:18–21).
16. Gideon rejects the offer of hereditary rule, but makes an ephod from the people's contribution of jewelry and cloth items to which the Israelites prostitute themselves (8:22–28).
17. Gideon fathers a large family (seventy-one sons in all, including Abimelech, mothered by his Shechemite concubine); he dies (8:29–32).
18. Israel relapses immediately into idolatry after his death. Gideon has no postmortem influence. Nobody shows loyalty either to Yahweh or to Gideon's household, his good work for Israel notwithstanding (8:33–35).

Unparalleled in any other judge story is the length of the description of the severe oppression that the camel-riding Midianites brought on Israel for seven years (episode 1, 6:1–6). That oppression took the form of depredations of livestock and on pasture land, depriving Israel of crops ("no sustenance"), sheep (for food and clothes), oxen (for farming and plowing), and donkeys (for transport), and forcing them to hide out in places like mountains and caves (6:2–4). The result for Israel is impoverishment and destitution.

God's displeasure with his people is indicated by the fact that he first sends not a deliverer to save, but a prophet to indict. And while the unexpected emergence of a prophet here may be compared with the opening reference to "Deborah the prophetess" in the preceding unit (4:4), Deborah does not fulminate against Israel as does this anonymous prophet. The words of this prophet are much closer to those of the angel of the Lord in 2:1–3 than they are to Deborah's. Both speak in the first person for God. Both begin by stressing God's gracious deliverance acts for his people (2:1, 6:8–9). Both sound the warning against false covenants/gods (2:2ab; 6:10a), a warning that went unheeded (2:2c; 6:10b).

Gideon's call by God, via the angel of the Lord (episode 3, 6:11–18), is not without Old Testament parallel. Possibly the closest parallel is the call of Moses, which shares at least six elements with that of Gideon (Habel 1965: 297–305).

	Moses	Gideon
1. divine confrontation	Exod. 3:1–4a	Judg. 6:11–12a
2. an introductory word	Exod. 3:4b–9	Judg. 6:12b–13
3. commission	Exod. 3:10	Judg. 6:14
4. objection	Exod. 3:11	Judg. 6:15
5. reassurance	Exod. 3:12a	Judg. 6:16
6. a sign	Exod. 3:12b	Judg. 6:17

The most patent difference between the two is (6), where in Exod. 3:12 God volunteers to give Moses a sign, while in Judg. 6:17 Gideon requests a sign. Throughout this call narrative cracks appear in Gideon's character. His response to the messenger's claims and commands are "why" (v. 13), "where" (v. 13), "how" (v. 15), and "show me" (v. 17). First, Gideon throws questions at the messenger: "If the Lord is with us, why has all this happened to us? And where are all his wonderful deeds?" (see Macartney 1948: 68–77.) These are not exploratory questions. They are angry, defiant, confrontational questions. Then, Gideon looks for an escape route by appealing to his insignificant roots ("My clan is the weakest in Manasseh, and I am the least in my family"). And finally, he tests the messenger (v. 17), even after hearing words that any Israelite would have recognized as divine speech (vv. 14, 16).

Interestingly, Gideon is not censured for his questions or his sign demand. Rather, the angel's response is (1) a challenge (v. 14), (2) a guarantee of the Lord's presence and victory over the Midianites (v. 16), and (3) consumption by fire of Gideon's sign/present (episode 4, 6:19–24). That Gideon, even before raising a hand, is assured of victory by the divine messenger indicates that "the tension in the story does not reside in whether or not Gideon will succeed, but rather in *how* he will succeed" (Culley 1992: 105).

It is odd that Gideon's father would have his own altar to the Canaanite Baal, plus an Asherah pole near it. (An "Asherah pole" refers to Asherah, the female element of divinity in Canaanite religion, who was the wife of El, the head of the pantheon at Ugarit. The term refers to either a tree [Deut. 16:21] or a wooden pole [Exod. 34:13], which was removed either by cutting it down [*karat*, Judg. 6:25; *gada͑*, Deut. 7:5] or by burning it [Deut. 12:3].)

If his father's possessions are suspect, so is the new name he gives his son: Jerubbaal (6:32). Here we have the oddity of a Hebrew, who himself has a Yahwistic name, "Joash" ("Yahweh has given"), giving his son a Baal name! And Gideon hardly commends himself to the reader by destroying the pole and altar at night for fear of both his family and the townspeople of Ophrah (6:27).

That the spirit of the Lord takes possession of Gideon (episode 6, 6:33–35) should harbinger better things ahead. Actually, Judg. 6:34 says, "And the spirit of the Lord clothed [*lavash*] Gideon." This verb is used again with the spirit of God coming on somebody only in two later sources in the Old Testament: 1 Chron. 12:18, "then the spirit clothed Amasai," and 2 Chron. 24:20, "then the spirit of God clothed Zechariah son of the priest Jehoiada." To clothe, or to invest, means to authorize, to empower.

But in spite of his charismatic endowment, Gideon remains skeptical. Hence, his two famous tests involving the fleece of wool and the threshing floor (episode 7, 6:36–40). The first test is the more predictable one: wet fleece, dry ground. The fleece would normally retain the night dew and moisture, while the ground would absorb it. The second test (dry fleece, wet ground) is, then, the more abnormal.

Believers, trying to ascertain God's will, often do so, they say, by "putting out a fleece" (à la Gideon). "If you want me to do this, then let such-and-such happen." Whether Gideon's fleece serves as a model of one way of finding God's will has advocates and opponents. Perhaps something in the text will tilt the matter toward the latter. First, note the decided preference for "the Lord" or "the Lord your God" so far versus "God" in the Gideon story: 6:1, 6, 7, 8, 10, 11, 12, 13, 14, 16, 21, 22, 23, 24, 25, 26, 27, 34 ("angel of God" does occur in v. 20.) Suddenly in this incident "Lord" is replaced exclusively by the more generic "God" (vv. 36, 39, 40). Second, although Gideon is the only judge to whom God speaks directly in Judges, this is one of only two incidents (the other is 7:13–14) in which "the deity is described as sending a communication without any divine words being reported" (Polzin 1980: 171–72).

While Gideon, having assembled a large number of troops, prepares to engage the enemy in battle, Yahweh pulls a surprise on him (episode

8, 7:1–8). Yahweh first reduces Gideon's army from twenty-two thousand to ten thousand (7:3). Those who return home do so because they are the "fearful and trembling" ones. This dismissal reflects the teachings on waging holy war as spelled out in Deut. 20:8: "Is anyone afraid or disheartened? He should go back to his house, or he might cause the heart of his comrades to melt like his own." But Gideon himself is still fearful (7:10)! The final chopping, as God "cuts down" the size of Gideon's army, reduces the troop number from ten thousand to three hundred (7:6). Those who lap water from their hands, go; those who kneel to drink, stay. To be sure, God is trying to teach Gideon that he is a God who can save by little or by much, and that counting on God is more important than counting noses. But there is more. As Tanner (1992: 157) has observed, "The reduction of the army does more than emphasize God's ability. . . . It is dealing with a struggle within Gideon." If he found it hard to believe God with a force of twenty-two thousand, what will he do with a meager force of three hundred?

What finally brings Gideon to full belief is a dream he overhears one Midianite telling another Midianite (episode 9, 7:9–14). But that is certainly both ironic and pathetic. "Hearing the promise from a Midianite soldier convinced him, but not hearing it directly from God" (Tanner 1992: 159). But then again, this may be but another way in the Gideon story by which Yahweh speaks to his servant: (1) a prophet; (2) an angelophany; (3) fire; (4) direct speech; (5) the dew; (6) an overheard dream and its interpretation (Standaert 1996: 200).

The actual account of Gideon's attack (episodes 10, 11; 7:15–25) describes a nocturnal campaign. This tactic reflects the nomad's dislike of nighttime fighting. His three hundred troops are armed only with musical instruments ("trumpets"), household commodities ("jars"), and incendiary devices ("torches"). Unexpected noise (during the tranquil night) and unexpected light (during the dark night) are Gideon's weapons.

A victorious war behind him, Gideon finds himself faced with an internal threat to Israel's intertribal unity (episode 12, 8:1–3). Ephraim protests being excluded from the first military rally of tribes. Actually, the verb "upbraided" in 8:1 is *rib*, the verb in the first part of Gideon's other name, *yerubba'al*. The Ephraimites contend with Gideon. It is not just that the Ephraimites feel slighted; their absence may mean a loss of their share of the war spoils.

The accusation of the Ephraimites against Gideon may be compared with their accusation later against Jephthah (12:1). Gideon's way to solve the crisis is more salutary than that of Jephthah. The latter, concerned only to exonerate himself, slaughters forty-two thousand of the malcontents (12:6)! Gideon, by contrast, assuages deep emotional feelings by placing a premium on the Ephraimites' role thus far—they killed two of the Midianite captains, Oreb and Zeeb. They are mollified by Gideon's proverblike expression "Is not the gleaning of grapes of Ephraim better than the vintage of Abiezer?" Interpreted, that seems to say, "The limited effort of the strong is better than the major effort of the weak" (Fontaine 1982: 82). Indeed, "A soft answer turns away wrath, but a harsh word stirs up anger" (Prov. 15:1). Further, "To make an apt answer is a joy to anyone, and a word in season, how good it is!" (Prov. 15:23).

The next few episodes (13–15, 8:4–21) describe Gideon's crossing the Jordan in pursuit of the Midianite kings Zebah and Zalmunna. We the readers assume that Gideon, lacking any specific divine directive, does this only to complete his victory over the Midianites, the safe escape of two major figures being a flaw in an otherwise successful campaign. But that is not the reason at all. We discover, to our surprise, that Gideon pursues these two fugitives for personal motivation, to avenge the death of his own (half-)brothers at the hands of Zebah and Zalmunna (8:18–19). The narrative has nowhere referred to Gideon's brothers, dead or alive. And in the process, he reaks havoc against the contract-breaching, nonsupporting Manassite towns of Succoth and Penuel (familiar from the Jacob story in Genesis: 32:22–32 [Penuel/Peniel]; 33:17 [Succoth]), leading Klein (1988: 62) to say, "This judge seems to have no compunctions about torturing or killing those Israelites who have doubts in him."

On the surface at least, Gideon, on the heels of his victory, rejects an offer from his people to establish hereditary, dynastic leadership (episode 16, 8:22–28). But that being the case, is it not ironic that Gideon names his son by the Shechemite concubine "Abimelech," that is, "my father [is] king" (8:31)? The desire of the Israelites to put into the head office of the land an individual who has been eminently successful in war finds a parallel in America and the movement of General Eisenhower to President Eisenhower.

But what Gideon does do is offer "an alternative to his own rule: his own religion!" (Stone 1992: 337). Like Aaron, who collected jewelry to make the golden calf (Exod. 32:1–4), Gideon collects earrings from the people, and together with materials taken from the Midianite camels and kings, makes an ephod (8:24–27). Ordinarily, the ephod is an apronlike garment worn by the high priest that covers the loins and is suspended from two shoulder pieces. It is made of gold, of blue, red, and purple woolen threads, and of fine linen (Exod. 28:6–14). There is also a linen ephod worn by an ordinary priest (1 Sam.

2:18; 22:18; cf. 2 Sam. 6:14 [David]), and an oracular ephod (1 Sam. 23:6–14), although the same basic garment may be intended in all these texts. Judges 8:27 makes Gideon's ephod seem to be a statue; yet it is possible that merely the ornamental garments gave the object a statuelike appearance.

In any case, the ephod turns out to be an idolatrous cult implement. Interestingly and sadly, the only other place in Judges where the root *zanah* ("go a whoring after," KJV) is used to describe promiscuous idolatry, apart from the introductory 2:17, is in the Gideon story. The verb is present in 8:27, "And all Israel prostituted themselves to it there," and in 8:33, "As soon as Gideon died, the Israelites relapsed and prostituted themselves with the Baals" (Stone 1988: 303).

Gideon exits the scene, and the forty years of peace for the land (8:28c), while welcomed, is confined clearly to Gideon's lifetime—"rest for forty years in the days of Gideon." Those who outlive and live after Gideon (8:33–35) look much like the generation that comes after Joshua.

The climactic charge brought against the Israelites in these post-Gideon days is that they did not "exhibit loyalty" to the house of Jerub-baal/Gideon (v. 35). The Hebrew word for "loyalty" is *khesed*. This charge of no *khesed* means one of two things: either Israel as a whole did not come to the rescue of Gideon's seventy sons from Abimelech and Shechem (ch. 9) (Sakenfeld 1978: 57), or once they found out about the massacre, they did nothing to bring the murderers to justice (Clark 1993: 222).

F. Abimelech (9:1–57)

The death of Gideon and his refusal of royal dignity (8:23) open the door for his concubine's son, Abimelech from Shechem (8:31), to seize that power in Shechem and do so by an act of massive fatricide—killing his seventy half-brothers. That all this violence and illegal usurpation should take place in the city of Shechem, where Joshua earlier had led his people in the renewal of their covenant vows to Yahweh (Joshua 24), makes Abimelech's actions even more heinous. It is certainly no accident that Yahweh never appears or speaks, or is mentioned in this chapter. Jotham uses "God" (v. 7), as does the narrator (vv. 23, 56, 57), but neither employ "Yahweh."

Following Boogart (1985: 52–53) with a few minor changes, we may outline the Abimelech story as follows:

I. Opening Narrative (vv. 1–22): the evil of Abimelech and of Shechem's lords

A. vv. 1–6: the elimination of potential rivals via fratricide

B. vv. 7–21: Jotham's poetic fable and its prosaic application

C. v. 22: Abimelech is allowed to rule for three years

II. Transition (vv. 23–25): God sends an evil spirit, which will result in future retribution on Abimelech and on Shechem's lords

III. Closing Narrative (vv. 26–41): retribution visited on Abimelech and on Shechem's lords, and vv. 23–25 actualized

A. vv. 26–41: Gaal ben-Ebed challenges Abimelech, only to be routed by Abimelech

B. vv. 42–45: Abimelech murders the ordinary people of Shechem

C. vv. 46–49: Abimelech kills the lords at Migdal-Shechem as they seek refuge

D. vv. 50–54: Abimelech himself is killed

E. v. 55: everybody "goes home" after Abimelech's death

IV. Conclusion (vv. 56–57): God has repaid Abimelech and the guilty Shechemites for their dastardly deeds, thus fulfilling Jotham's curse on them

Abimelech uses his Shechemite connections to the fullest to persuade the "lords" of Shechem (the leading citizens or some kind of small presbyterian council) that it is in their best interest to have one ruler rather than seventy, monarchy rather than polyarchy. They agree not only with his argument, but also with the means of eliminating the opposition, which they bankroll by taking funds from their temple treasury (v. 4). The fraternal rivals gone, Abimelech is made king (v. 6).

One brother, Jotham, escapes the bloodbath and goes to nearby Mount Gerizim, where he utters his famous fable (Vater Solomon 1985: 114–25). While the majority of fables involve talking animals, this one involves talking plants/trees. The olive tree, the fig tree, and the (grape) vine all reject the invitation to reign over their fellow trees. Finally, the bramble bush readily accepts and invites all the other trees to seek protection under the shade of his kingship. The bramble bush being the fourth after a preceding three (olive, fig, grape, bramble) seems to be another illustration in the Old Testament of a threefold reference that climaxes with the fourth. Recall Delilah's four attempts to wrest from Samson the secret of his strength, with only her final one being successful (Judg. 16:6–9, 10–12, 13–14, 15–21); or Yahweh's call of young Samuel, the divine source of which is perceived only on the fourth time (1 Sam.

3:4–5, 6–7, 8–9, 10–14); or Noah's sending out from the ark a raven and then a dove three times, and on this last time the dove does not return (Gen. 8:6–7, 8–9, 10–11, 12); or Job's four tragedies, of which the last one is the climatic one (Job 1:13–15, 16, 17, 18–19).

But do thorns offer protection? Why allow "Rex Thorn" to reign? The issue here is the stupidity of the coronators. The fable is "directed primarily against those who were foolish enough to anoint a worthless man as king, and, secondarily, against the worthless king himself" (Maly 1960: 304). A thorn promising protection will become a thorn in the side, but the convincing rhetoric of the candidate blinds them to reality.

For three years, while Abimelech rules, God does nothing to change the situation (v. 22). (Compare Absalom's avenging the rape of his sister Tamar, but not until two years later [2 Sam. 13:23].) It is of interest that while the previous verses have used the verb *malak* (and noun *melek*, "king") frequently (v. 6, "they made Abimelech king"; vv. 8, 10, 12, 14, "reign over us"; v. 15 "if . . . you are anointing me king over you"), v. 22 does not use the verb *malak* for "reign, rule." Rather, it uses the verb *sarar*, which "denotes the exercise of power at a level lower than that wielded by kings" (Stone 1988: 382). Abimelech is no king, but a tyrant.

This time God sends not his benevolent spirit to empower and equip, but an "evil spirit" between, not *on*, Abimelech and his Shechemite supporters (v. 23). The concept of an evil spirit sent from God finds a parallel with Saul. After the departure of the spirit of the Lord from Saul, there came "an evil spirit from the Lord" to torment him (1 Sam. 16:14; cf. similar phraseology in 1 Sam. 16:15; 18:10; 19:9). In fact, at many points the kingship style and career of Abimelech matches that of Saul (O'Connell 1996: 291–92). What the seventy brothers are to Abimelech, David is to Saul (or so thinks Saul): rivals. In both cases, Yahweh sends an evil spirit on a king lacking integrity and righteousness. Both kings slaughter large groups of people. Jotham's fable matches Samuel's rebuke of Saul. Both kings, while seriously wounded, request an armor bearer to end their life (Judg. 9:54; 1 Sam. 31:4).

We should not understand "evil spirit" as referring to some supernatural force or demon sent by God as a wedge. Nor is the evil spirit sent by Satan or some other cosmic archdemon. The sender is God. What "evil spirit" means here is a disruptive, alienating, and gradually burgeoning divisiveness between a king and his crowners. Amicability gives way in stages to hostility.

The first to attempt to put a chink in Abimelech's armor comes in the form of Gaal son of Ebed (v. 26–41). He is, however, hardly a foe to challenge Abimelech. He is a laughable, pathetic figure, possibly intoxicated at the time (v. 27), and it appears that the "antidote is worse than the poison" (Klein 1988: 74). Abimelech quickly and effortlessly dispatches him.

But such challenges to his position only enrage a pathological Abimelech and send him on further rampages, first against the citizenry of Shechem (vv. 42–45), and then against approximately one thousand men and women hiding out in a temple at the Tower of Shechem (most likely a tiny city located in the area of Shechem's jurisdiction) (vv. 46–49).

It is difficult to sheathe anger and retaliation once they have been unsheathed. Thus, Abimelech attacks Thebez (v. 50–55), a town located about twelve miles northeast of Shechem. Abimelech almost succeeds again in a mass killing. This time, however, he is thwarted by a woman up in the tower who "throws" (interestingly, the text does not say "drops") a millstone on his head, crushing his skull (v. 53). His death hardly encourages mourning. The text simply states, "When the Israelites saw that Abimelech was dead, they all went home" (v. 55)—no weeping, no burial, no lamentation, no repentance (Polzin 1980: 174).

Janzen (1987) has caught the irony of this incident by noticing the various uses of the adjective "one" throughout the chapter, the preposition "on" (ʿal), and the noun "head":

v. 2: "Which is better . . . or that one [ʾekhad] rule over you?"

v. 5: "Jerubbaal killed his brothers on [ʿal] one [ʾekhat] stone."

v. 18: "You have killed his sons on [ʿal] one [ʾekhat] stone."

v. 37: "Gaal spoke, 'one [ʾekhad] company [roʾsh] is coming'"

v. 53: "But a certain [ʾakhat] woman threw an upper millstone on [ʿal] Abimelech's head [roʾsh]."

v. 57: "God made all the wickedness . . . fall back on their heads [roʾsham]."

The retribution visited on Abimelech moves beyond simply the one who kills with a stone himself being killed by a stone. Here, as Janzen (1987: 35) states, "One who would rule Shechem *single-handedly* as its *head* (v. 37), and who to that end killed seventy brothers upon (ʿal) a *single stone*, in the end is killed by a *single* woman who drops a *millstone*, upon (ʿal) his *head*."

The last two verses of the chapter (vv. 56–57) give a theological verdict. All that happened to Abimelech (v. 56) and to the lords of Shechem (v. 57) is the result of God punishing them for their ruthlessness and wave of carnage, beginning with that perpetrated on Gideon's surviving family. The punishment fits the crime.

The italicized words in "God *repaid* Abimelech for the *crime* he committed" (v. 56) and "God *made* all the *wickedness* of the people of Shechem *fall back* on their heads" (v. 57) are the same in Hebrew. Both use the Hiphil of *shuv* + *ra'ah*. Thus, literally, "God returned the evil of Abimelech" and "All the evil of the men of Shechem God returned upon their heads." The construction appears again, in Gen. 50:15, on the lips of Joseph's brothers: "What if . . . he pays us back in full for all the wrong we did to him?" and in 1 Sam. 25:39: "The Lord has returned the evildoing of Nabal upon his own head."

G. Two Lists of Minor Judges (10:1–5; 12:8–15)

Including Shamgar (3:31), whom we have already discussed, five other judges receive brief mention in chs. 3–16: Tola (10:1–2); Jair (10:3–5); Ibzan (12:8–10); Elon (12:11–12); Abdon (12:13–15). It is common to refer to these six individuals as the *minor* judges to distinguish them from their six counterparts, the *major* judges. This distinction, however, is arbitrary, as much as the distinction between major prophets (e.g., Isaiah, Jeremiah) and minor prophets (e.g., Hosea, Amos). The biblical text itself never makes such a dichotomy.

There have been several attempts to distinguish between these two groups of judges vis-à-vis their office and responsibility. For example, one suggestion, advanced by the brilliant scholar Martin Noth, is that we have in these two sets of judges two distinct groups. Noting that the major judges engage consistently in battle and are spirit-inspired in contradistinction to the minor ones, he suggests that they were charismatic leaders who appear sporadically on the scene in premonarchic Israel when crises emerged, and who were not judges at all. These gifted leaders represent the anthithesis of institutionalized, routinized governmental administration. By contrast, the minor judges were real judges, the proclaimers of the law to the nascent Israelite community. Only when the traditions about the charismatics and the judges were conjoined by the Deuteronomistic historian was the title of the latter extended to the former.

Noth's reconstruction, while appealing and containing more than a germ of plausibility, is increasingly suspect, if only because the attempt to assign military responsibilities to one group and juridical/civil responsibilities to the other lacks the necessary confirming evidence, and appears not to be supported by the text itself. Hauser (1975: 190) seems more on target when he suggests, "The only legitimate distinction between these categories is one which refers to the *length* and *style* of the literary material preserved in the case of each figure."

The form in which the minor judge figures appear, exluding Shamgar, is as follows, with "PN" indicating a personal name and "*n*" indicating a number (and see Halpern 1983: 190):

I. Introduction

    A. After PN_1 arose PN_2 (+ tribal/geographical detail) (10:1, 3), or,

    B. After him PN (+ tribal/geographical detail) judged Israel (12:8, 11, 13)

II. A notice about children (10:4 [after III]; 12:9, 14)

III. The length of the judging
He judged Israel *n* years (10:2a, 3b; 12:9d, 11b, 14c)

IV. Death and burial
PN died and was buried in (place name) (10:2b, 5; 12:7b, 10, 12, 15)

Some of these four elements are also present in a few of the major-judge units. For example, the Jephthah story contains elements III (12:7a) and IV (12:7b). The same goes for the Gideon unit, which contains elements II (8:30) and IV (8:32). Element III is present in the Samson story in 15:20 and 16:31c.

The presence of parallels between major- and minor-judge units suggests that the distinction between these two should not be forced. Also, note that the parallels are with the Gideon-Jephthah-Samson portion rather than with the Othniel-Ehud-Deborah portion, suggesting some kind of connection between these lesser-known judges and the three last, more prominent ones.

In fact, the three placements of the minor judges come at interesting points:

I. Ehud (3:12–30)—Shamgar (3:31)—Deborah (4:1–5:31)

II. Gideon and Abimelech (6:1–9:57)—Tola, Jair (10:1–5)—Jephthah (10:6–12:7)

III. Jephthah (10:6–12:7)—Ibzan, Elon, Abdon (12:8–15)—Samson (13:1–16:31)

Or, we may observe how the minor judges are bookends to the Jephthah story:

Tola, Jair (10:1–5)—Jephthah (10:6–12:7)—Ibzan, Elon, Abdon (12:8–15)

Thus, the first minor judge comes between Ehud and Deborah, two eminently successful judges. Tola and Jair come between two judges with major flaws in their character and performance. The last three minor judges come between Jephthah, a seriously flawed judge, and Samson, a parade example of charisma gone sour.

It is only with the first and second set of minor judges that the verb "deliver, save" (yashaʿ) occurs—with Shamgar in 3:31 and with Tola in 10:1. In fact, Tola appears specifically to save Israel from the bloody, macabre effects of Abimelech's rule ("After Abimelech, Tola . . . rose to deliver Israel"). That there is no reference to the land enjoying rest after Abimelech's reign would indicate that the "after" points not merely to "some time later" but to a more "intimate temporal sequence" (Mullen 1982: 194). No minor judge in the third set is said to deliver Israel.

Nor is it said of any judge in the last set that "he arose," as in 10:1, 3. The use of the verb qum ("rise") in the Qal stem there finds its best parallel with 2:16, 18 (the introduction), 3:9 (Othniel), and 3:15 (Ehud), all of which use the Hiphil stem of qum for the divine upraising of the judges.

Also, the total years of the first two minor judges' judging (Tola, 23 + Jair, 22 = 55) is over twice that of the last three minor judges (Ibzan, 7 + Elon, 10 + Abdon, 8 = 25). All this provides further evidence of the fact that, if Gideon-Jephthah-Samson do not "stack up" against Othniel-Ehud-Deborah, neither do Ibzan-Elon-Abdon against Tola-Jair-Shamgar.

With the exception of Shamgar, none of these minor judges engages in military action. At least, the text records none. They simply "judged Israel" or "judged Israel n years." Military action is probably implied for Tola in 10:1, simply because everywhere else "deliver" is used in Judges it refers to military action (2:16, 18; 3:9, 15, 31; 6:14, 15, 36; 8:22; 13:5; see also, in a bit different light, "deliver" in 10:11, 12; 12:2–3 [Hauser 1975: 199]).

And yet, the war machine is quiet with these minor judges. None of them, so the text, ever were the recipient of a divine afflatus and empowerment. They simply did their job without fanfare, did their job well, and did it sucessfully. Their only claim to fame in Scripture's annals is a verse or two with a modicum of details. Perhaps their presence in Judges indicates that one of the fundamental needs of the people of God is "order, not heroics; character, not charisma" (Stone 1992: 339).

H. Jephthah (10:6–12:7)

The Jephthah story has five major units:

1. 10:6–16: Israelite evil (v. 6) provokes Yahweh's response of judgment via the Ammonites (vv. 7–9), which in turn evokes Israel's repentance (vv. 10, 15–16a) and a second response from Yahweh (vv. 11–14, 16b).
2. 10:17–11:11: Under siege by the Ammonites, the residents of Gilead by consensus select Jephthah to be their military leader, only after Jephthah elicits a guarantee of permanent civil leadership if victorious in battle.
3. 11:12–28: Jephthah attempts, unsuccessfully, to resolve the dispute with the Ammonites through diplomacy.
4. 11:29–40: Upon receiving the divine spirit, Jephthah makes his infamous vow that if he returns victorious from battle, he will offer whoever comes out of his house to meet him upon his return as an offering to Yahweh, and so he sacrifices his daughter.
5. 12:1–7: Jephthah responds to the complaints of the Ephraimites by a massive slaughtering of the malcontents; he dies and is buried somewhere in Gilead.

(1) In some ways, the first of these five sections, 10:6–16, parallels other introductory portions of the judge stories. Israel is "sold" into the hands of an oppressor because of infidelity, because of "again doing evil" before Yahweh. Israel "cries" to Yahweh and he responds.

However, several items set this introduction apart from others. First, this is the only place where Yahweh sells/gives over his people for oppressive judgment to two nations: "and he sold them into the hand of the Philistines and into the hand of the Ammonites" (v. 7b). Since only the latter appear in the Jephthah story, and the former appear in the ensuing Samson story, then possibly we should read these few verses as prelude to both the Jephthah and Samson stories.

Second, this is the only time where we are not only told that Israel cried to Yahweh, but also are informed of the content of that cry. Not once, but twice (vv. 10, 15), Israel acknowledges "we have sinned," and once tells Yahweh specifically the nature of that sin ("We have abandoned our God and worshiped the Baals"). While communal confession ("we have sinned") is common enough in the Old Testament (Num. 12:11; 14:40; 21:7; Deut. 1:41; 1 Sam. 7:6; 12:10; 1 Kings 8:47; Neh. 1:6; Jer. 14:20; Dan. 9:5, 8), this is the only place where such confession is recorded in the book of Judges.

One may debate whether confession of sin or the acknowledgment of the presence of sin is the same as the repudiation and repentance of sin (and this Judges passage does use confession language rather than repentance language); nevertheless, the confessional cry appears genuine if their appeal "deliver us this day" (v. 15b) includes a desire for deliverance not only from the Ammonites, but also from the evil that brought on the Ammonites.

The third unique item here is God's response. He is far from pleased. On the contrary, he appears to reject their confession, and instead counsels them to call on these surrogate gods they have pursued to see if they are saving and delivering gods (v. 14).

Verse 16 is a difficult verse to interpret, especially because of its second half. The first part is clear enough and self-explanatory, and the actions described therein commendable: "they put away the foreign gods among them and worshiped the Lord." There is no problem if one reads the last part of the verse as "and he could no longer bear to see Israel suffer" (NRSV) or "and he could bear Israel's misery no longer" (NIV). That is, God responds to their confession and putting away of foreign gods with "enough is enough." Compassionate Yahweh finds Israel's continued misery unendurable (Webb 1987: 48).

Others, however, read the phrase differently: "he grew annoyed [or impatient] with the troubled efforts of Israel" (Polzin 1980: 177); or "his soul became short [or aggravated] at Israel's toil" (Stone 1988: 320–23; 1992: 340). According to this reading, Yahweh's response to Israel's sin, oppression, and confession is not compassion, but extreme aggravation.

The problem lies in how best to translate the verb qatsar ("to be short") (15x in the Old Testament) and the noun ʿamal ("labor, toil") (55x in the Old Testament) in this verse. The closest verbal parallels to Judg. 10:16b are Num. 21:4 and Zech. 11:8, because all three have the verb qatsar with the subject nephesh ("soul"), followed by a word to which the preposition be is prefixed and which expresses the cause of the shortness/impatience: "the people became impatient on [because of] the way" (Num. 21:4); "for I had become impatient with them" (Zech. 11:8). Judges 16:16 uses the verb qatsar and the subject nephesh, but not the preposition be attached to a following word: "After she had nagged him . . . he was tired to death."

Perhaps the passage is intentionally ambiguous, for it may designate either Yahweh's growing impatience with those troubling Israel, or Yahweh's growing impatience with Israel's self-imposed troubles. Those who favor the first interpretation distinguish sharply between Yahweh's first response (vv. 11–14) and second response (v. 16b), a move from rejection to compassion. Those who favor the second interpretation will read Yahweh's second response as reinforcing his first.

(2) In 10:17–11:11 we meet Jephthah. From the start he is a paradox. Negatively, he is "the son of a prostitute" and his father is "Gilead" (which is another way of saying, "who his father was, nobody knows; it could be just about any Gileadite man who had visited this unnamed prostitute"). Positively, he is "a mighty warrior." Thus, he combines "the desirable with the unacceptable" (Exum 1989: 64).

Jephthah is the only judge among the major judges not given to the people as judge/deliverer directly by Yahweh. Rather, this rejected one (11:2) now becomes the accepted one by popular acclaim (11:6, 8, 10). It is not difficult to connect Jephthah's words in 11:7 ("Are you not the very ones who rejected me. . . . So why do you come to me now when you are in trouble?") with Yahweh's words to Israel in the previous section ("You have abandoned me. . . . Go and cry to the gods you have chosen" [10:13–14]). Jephthah drives a hard bargain, for which he holds most of the chips. He spurns the offer of (temporary) military commander ("be our commander" [11:6]), only to press for the (permanent) civilian leadership of Gilead ("become head over us" [11:8]; "I will be your head," [11:9]). He obtains both positions ("and the people made him head and commander" [11:11]; note which comes first).

(3) Before he becomes militant, Jephthah attempts to be diplomatic (11:12–28). Via messengers, he reminds the king of the Ammonites of Israel's past history in the Transjordan area in the Mosaic era, in what one author has called "a remarkable but entirely credible command of the minutiae of the ancestral migration from Nile to Jordan" (Sternberg 1985: 116).

Jephthah recalls Israel's previous interactions with Edom (v. 17a), Moab (vv. 17b–18), and King Sihon of the Amorites (vv. 19–21), ending with Israel's occupation of all the territory "from the Arnon [north] to the Jabbok," about fifty miles (v. 22). Moab first occupied this strip of land in the Transjordan, but then it was conquered by Sihon (Num. 21:26, "Sihon . . . fought against the former king of Moab and captured all its land as far as the Arnon"). By the time of Jephthah, the Ammonites have claimed it (cf. Jer. 49:1–2).

This Moabite/Ammonite occupation of the same strip of land may explain why Jephthah says in v. 24, "Should you not possess what your god Chemosh gives you to possess?" This is the one place where Chemosh is the god of the Ammonites. Elsewhere their god is Milcom/ Molech (1 Kings 11:5, 7, 33; Jer. 49:1, 3). Chemosh, on the other hand, is the god of the Moabites (1 Kings 11:7, 33). Or else, Jephthah is guilty of a "diplomatic *faux pas*" (Gunn and Fewell 1993: 115).

And if his knowledge of who's who among the gods of neighboring peoples is false, so is his theology questionable: "You possess what your god Chemosh gives you to possess, and we will possess everything that the Lord our God has conquered for our benefit." Hardly a monotheistic creed! At best, it is henotheism, the worship of one god but recognizing that other people worship other legitimate gods. Again, this may be more a part of the give-and-take for the courtesy of political diplomacy than an expression of Jephthah's theology.

It is predictable that Jephthah's final proposal, "Let the Lord, who is judge, decide today for the Israelites or for the Ammonites" (v. 27), will not be enthusiastically accepted by the Ammonites. Should the Ammonites allow the final arbiter to be the God of Israel (v. 28) (Klein 1988: 89)?

(4) Jephthah is the third judge after Othniel (3:10) and Gideon (6:34) to receive a divine charisma, the gift of the spirit of the Lord (11:29). The parallels between Gideon and Jephthah are particularly telling in that each does something far from commendable and exemplary immediately after receiving Yahweh's spirit:

Gideon	Jephthah
Receives the spirit (6:34).	Receives the spirit (11:29).
↓	↓
Makes a test for God	Makes a vow to God
↓	↓
involving an "if . . . then" construction (6:36–40, esp. v. 37).	involving an "if . . . then" construction (11:30–40).
↓	↓
God responds to the test.	God accepts the payment of the vow.

Jephthah's vow is well known. He promises that if God grants him victory over the Ammonites, "whatever comes out of the doors of my house to meet me . . . shall be the Lord's, to be offered up by me as a burnt offering" (11:30b–31).

This vow is like others in the Old Testament:

1. Gen. 28:20–21: "Then Jacob made a vow saying, 'If God will be with me . . . then the Lord shall be my God.'"
2. Num. 21:2: "Then Israel made a vow to the Lord and said, 'If you will indeed give this people into our hands, then we will utterly destroy their towns.'"

3. 1 Sam. 1:11: "She [Hannah] made this vow: 'O Lord of hosts, if only you will look on the misery of your servant . . . give to your servant a male child, then I will set him before you as a nazirite until the day of his death.'"

4. 2 Sam. 15:8: "For your servant [Absalom] made a vow. . . . If the Lord will bring me back to Jerusalem, then I will worship the Lord in Hebron."

Several characteristics of biblical vows emerge when Jephthah's vow and these four vows are grouped together. First, all vows are directed to God. Second, vows are promissory. The person making the vow promises to do something if the right circumstances eventuate. Third, vows are conditional. They start with a protasis introduced by "if. . ." and conclude with an apodosis introduced by "then. . . ." This is what distinguishes a vow from an oath. An oath is also promissory (see, e.g., the oath made by David that Solomon would succeed him [1 Kings 1:13, 17, 30]), but usually not conditional (Milgrom 1990: 488). Fourth, vows involve dedication of something or somebody to God or the sanctuary (for Jacob, tithing; for the Israelites, the Canaanite spoils of war as *kherem*; for Jephthah, his daughter as a sacrifice; for Hannah, her son as a lifelong Nazirite in the sanctuary; for Absalom, sacrifices offered at Hebron). Fifth, vows are made in situations of anxiety, such as the need of a safe return home after an extended absence, facing a military engagement, or starting a family (Parker 1979: 699).

Scripture speaks of the importance of "paying" one's vows (e.g., Ps. 116:14, 18; Prov. 7:14), and accordingly warns against impulsive vows, which, if unfulfilled, arouse God's wrath (Prov. 20:25; Eccl. 5:4–6). Scripture makes no provision for withdrawing or annulling a vow made to God. That would be done later by postbiblical rabbinic tradition: "Four kinds of vows the sages have declared not to be binding: vows of incitement, vows of exaggeration, vows made in error, and vows of constraint" (*Mishnah Nedarim* 3:1).

It is unlikely that Jephthah anticipated that, upon returning home from battle, he would be met by a servant or some kind of an animal. In fact, the verbs "come out" and "meet" (11:31, and again in v. 34 with the addition of "timbrels" and "dancing") appear in 1 Sam. 18:6–7. In both, female dancers come out to meet returning, successful male warriors/survivors. Exodus 15:20–21 uses the word "come out," but not "meet," to refer to the actions of Miriam and other women just after Yahweh's deliverance of his people from the pursuing Egyptians. Thus, for Jephthah, who better than his daughter to come out and meet him after eliminating the Ammonites?

The clear reading of the text is that Jephthah did indeed sacrifice his daughter: "he did to her according to the vow he had made" (v. 39). Only twice in the Old Testament is a human being a "burnt offering": Jephthah's daughter (Judg. 11:31) and Isaac (Gen. 22:2). There are other parallels between these two stories; for example, Isaac is Abraham's "only" son (Gen. 22:2), and the daughter is Jephthah's "only" child (11:34), and in both somebody goes to the mountains (Gen. 22:2; Judg. 11:37). Unlike the Abraham story, in the Jephthah story God supplies no surrogate sacrifice for the daughter.

To make matters worse, Jephthah places the blame on his daughter! "You have brought me very low [kara', used also to refer to a soldier who has been felled, as earlier in the Song of Deborah: "he [Sisera] sank . . . at her feet" (5:27)]; you have become the cause of great trouble to me" (11:35). Apparently, he is unaware that he has become the cause of great trouble to his daughter and to God.

Her only request is that she be allowed two months to wander on the mountains and bewail her virginity, accompanied by her friends (v. 37). The source of the daughter's tears is manifold. She will die husbandless. She will die childless. She will die without ever being sexual. She will die with an unfulfilled life. She will die an unnatural death. She will die a premature death. She will die a violent death (Trible 1984: 104; Gerstein 1989: 192). It is not without significance that she "opts to spend her remaining days not with Jephthah, but with other young women who will be with her and grieve her fate and remember her" (Gunn and Fewell 1993: 116).

Jephthah is remembered by generations to come (he is cited affirmatively in 1 Sam. 12:11 and Heb. 11:32). But so is his daughter, at least four days of every year (v. 40). The NRSV says that her death is "lamented" on those four days. Elsewhere, this verb (tanah) is translated "sing, tell, recite," as in Judg. 5:11, and maybe means that here too. The daughter's death is "commemorated" four days of every year, lest others forget (Bal 1989: 226–27).

(5) The last unit in the Jephthah story is 12:1–7. The story line does not improve. This time Jephthah is involved with some of his own people, the Ephraimites, who are upset because Jephthah was delinquent in not calling them to battle against the Ammonites (v. 1), suggesting either hurt egos or the loss of war spoils.

Jephthah, who had engaged in such polite diplomacy with the Ammonites (11:12–28), is not nearly so diplomatic with his own flesh and blood. So enraged is he by their diatribe, that he orders the Gileadites into battle against them, and to block the fords of the Jordan and there give the Ephraimite fugitives a word test. If they could say "shibboleth," they were allowed to cross over. But the Ephraimites could only say "sibboleth," thus revealing their tribal connections. Jephthah promptly murdered forty-two thousand of them!

"Shibboleth" is a Hebrew homonym that can mean "ear of corn" (Gen. 41:5, 6, 7, 22, 23, 24—Pharaoh's dream of the seven healthy ears of grain and seven emaciated ears of grain) or "channel of water" (Isa. 27:12; Ps. 69:2, 15). The majority of commentators believe that this shibboleth/sibboleth incident reveals dialectical differences among the tribes of Israel; different tribes pronounced the *s* sign differently. To use a modern example, it is as if the Ephraimites could not say "God save the king," but only "God shave the king."

Possibly it has nothing to do with dialectical differences in early Israel at all. It may indicate merely that the Ephraimites were not only malcontents, but also that they could not even repeat a test word spoken first by the Gileadite guards (Marcus 1992: 100). The text states that the Gileadite troops used the word first: "Say 'shibboleth.'" They did not silently hold up a picture of an ear of corn and ask, "What is this?" To give a modern example, a New Englander, faced with a map of the Caribbean and asked to identify the island immediately to the south of Florida, will probably say "Cubar." But asked to say "Cuba," he or she probably will say "Cuba."

The death count of the Ephraimites is staggering: forty-two thousand. That number is higher than the number of adult male troops of first-generation Ephraimites (40,500 [Num. 1:33]) and of the second-generation Ephraimites (32,500 [Num. 26:37])!

Furthermore, Jephthah kills more of his tribal brothers than all the judges together kill of the enemy:

Jephthah—42,000 Ephraimites	Ehud—10,000 (3:29)
	Deborah—901 (approx.) (4:3, 21)
	Gideon—4 (7:25, 8:21)
	Samson—30 (14:19)
	—1000 (15:15)
	—3000 (16:27)
	TOTAL—14,935

Of course, there are more than some fifteen thousand enemy casualties if one includes phrases like "Othniel went out to war" (3:10), or Gideon's strategy that caused the Midianites in a panic to kill each other (7:22), or Jephthah inflicting "a massive defeat on the Ammonites" (11:33) in which the count of enemy dead is not given. Neverthe-less, Jephthah, it appears, is a far greater threat to Israel than are the Ammonites!

A comparison of the three times that the Ephraimites appear oppo-site a major judge further exposes this downward trend in Judges (Ehud, 3:27–29; Gideon, 8:1–3; Jephthah, 12:1–6). Ehud uses these mighty men of valor to eliminate the Moabites. Gideon assuages them. Jephthah slaughters them.

For the first time in Judges, we do not see "the land had rest for [x] years" (3:11; 3:30; 5:31; 8:28) after/during the career of a major judge. How can there be rest following such a tumultuous period?

And also for the first time, the years of oppression outnumber the years of rest for the land or the tenure of the judge (Stone 1992: 341).

Years of oppression	Years of rest/tenure
Othniel, 8 (3:8)	40 (3:11)
Ehud, 18 (3:14)	80 (3:30)
Deborah, 20 (4:3)	40 (5:31)
Gideon, 7 (6:1)	40 (8:28)
Jephthah, 18 (10:8)	6 (12:7)

I. Samson (13:1–16:31)

The last judge story in Judges is Samson's, spread over four chapters (13–16). In spite of the length of his narrative, and the climactic position of his story, Samson appears very rarely in Scripture outside of these four chapters in Judges. Samuel, in his farewell address (1 Samuel 12), reminds his audience of those individuals Yahweh had sent to rescue the people from their enemies. The list (v. 11) includes Jerrubbaal, Barak, Jephthah, and Samson. This is the reading of the NRSV, which states in a footnote that the Hebrew text has Samuel rather than Samson (cf. NIV). In the New Testament, Heb. 11:32 includes Samson in its hall of fame of the faithful (where, surprisingly, his name precedes that of Jephthah).

While there are various ways to divide up the Samson story accord-ing to scholarly analysis, our study will focus on seven incidents:

1. 13:1–25: Samson's birth announcement and the revelation by the angel of his life work to his parents, his birth, his name, and his first experience with the spirit of Yahweh.

2. 14:1–20: Samson's marriage to a Philistine woman over his parents' protest, the lion episode, the riddle episode, and Samson's second and third experiences with the spirit of Yahweh.
3. 15:1–8: Upon discovering that in his absence his father-in-law gave Samson's wife to another man, Samson traps three hundred foxes, attaches incendiary devices to their tails, and sends them into the grain fields of the Philistines, burning and destroying their crops.
4. 15:9–20: The Philistines respond by raiding Judah, whose warriors in turn bind Samson and turn him over to the enemy. A fourth experience of the spirit enables him to break free of his bonds and kill one thousand Philistines with a donkey's jawbone. Thirsty, he prays.
5. 16:1–3: In Philistine Gaza, Samson sleeps with a harlot, and tears the doors of the city gates off their hinges in response to being "set up" and carries them to Hebron.
6. 16:4–22: Delilah successfully entices Samson to reveal the source of his strength. His hair is shaved. His strength leaves. God leaves. The Philistines capture him and mutilate their prize prisoner.
7. 16:23–31: While the Philistines gloat and praise their god Dagon, Samson prays for a second time. God gives him back his strength one more time, and he takes vengeance on his captors, taking his own life in the process.

1. 13:1–25. The Samson story begins in a traditional fashion ("the Israelites again did what was evil in the sight of the Lord"), but curiously lacks any reference to the people of God "crying out" to Yahweh for relief from the four decades of Philistine oppression. Rather, the text moves immediately into the triad of the angel of the Lord, Manoah and his wife, and the ensuing revelation that is about to unfold.

In many ways the birth announcement of Samson has parallels to other birth announcements in Scripture, especially those of Ishmael (Genesis 16), Isaac (Genesis 17), John the Baptist (Luke 1), and Jesus (Matthew 1; Luke 1).

This type of announcement has five stages (for which see Brown 1977: 156):

1. The appearance of the Lord or his angel to a human (13:3)
2. Fear and/or prostration by the human recipient of the revelation (13:20, 22)
3. The divine message:

> a. the human is addressed by name
> b. some additional information about the human recipient
> c. the recipient is told not to be afraid
> d. a woman is with child or shortly will be (13:3)
> e. the woman will give birth to a son (13:3, 5)
> f. the name by which the child will be called
> g. an etymology explaining the name's significance
> h. the future accomplishments of the child (13:5)

4. The parent-to-be raises an objection or presses for further information or a sign (13:8, 17)
5. A sign is given and the recipient understands or is reassured (13:18–21)

The primary focus in ch. 13 is on Samson's parents—his father, Manoah (the same as "Noah" with a prefixed *ma-*, and meaning something like "place of relief/security"), and his nameless mother—and the appearance of Yahweh's angel to them.

"The angel of the Lord" is the term always used by the narrator to describe the one who speaks to Manoah's wife, except in v. 9 ("the angel of God"). His wife calls the visitor either "a man of God" (v. 6) or simply "the man" (v. 10). Manoah shows the same variation, using both "the man of God" (v. 8) and "the man" (v. 11). Among all the places in Scripture where Yahweh's angel appears to a visionary, Judg. 13:6 is the only one that suggests that the theophanic recipient perceived something significantly different than a normal human form: "his appearance was like that of an angel of God, most awe-inspiring."

Unlike other barren wives, for example, Rachel and her "Give me children, or I shall die" (Gen. 30:1), or Hannah and her "If . . . you will give your servant a male child" (1 Sam. 1:11), who lament their childlessness, nothing indicates that Manoah's wife is languishing over her condition. Nor is anything said about her advanced age, as one finds with Sarah or Elizabeth.

The angel comes uninvited to a barren wife and discloses that she will bear a son (v. 3). She receives three additional pieces of information, two of which apply to her ("Be careful not to drink wine or strong drink" and "Do not eat anything unclean"), and one of which applies to her son ("No razor is to come on his head"). The reason for these avoidances by mother and child is explained in what follows: "For the boy shall be a nazirite to God from birth" (literally, "from the womb"). And what this Nazirite is to do in adult years is "begin to deliver Israel from the hand of the Philistines." Samson will have a beginning ministry, but not a finishing ministry.

Interestingly, when she relays this information to Manoah, she makes some changes (v. 7):

13:3–5	13:7
"You shall conceive and bear a son.	You shall conceive and bear a son.
Be careful not to drink wine or strong drink,	Drink no wine or strong drink,
or eat anything unclean,	eat nothing unclean,
for you shall conceive and bear a son.	X
No razor is to come on his head,	X
for the boy shall be a nazirite to God from birth.	for the boy shall be a nazirite to God from birth to the day of his death."
It is he who shall begin to deliver Israel."	X

Two deletions stand out in the retelling (nothing about no razor on his head and nothing about the lad beginning to deliver Israel from the Philistines), as does one expansion ("a nazirite from birth *to the day of his death*"). It is odd that she would delete information about how God will use their son to throw off the Philistine menace. Does the angel's phrase "begin to deliver" throw her off and maybe confuse her, thus restraining her from sharing this bit of data? And when she adds that their boy will be a nazirite to God "to the day of his death," does "death" carry some kind of independent negative force—their son, before he dies, will sow as much destruction as salvation (Alter 1981: 101; Reinhartz 1992: 31)—or is "until the day of his death" her way of paraphrasing the angel's "he shall begin to deliver Israel from the hand of the Philistines" (Savran 1988: 83)?

A few words are in order about the Nazirite. The verb *nazar* means "separate oneself (by practicing abstinence and self-denial)." Derived from the verb is the noun *nazir* in the form of a passive participle, hence, "one set apart, restricted." The word *nazir* is grammatically analagous to a word like *nasiʾ*, "one elevated, a chief," from the verb *nasaʾ*, "lift up."

Numbers 6:1–21, which details the law of the Nazirite, deals only with the temporary Nazirite. By contrast, Samson and Samuel are lifelong Nazirites. Analogously, we distinguish today between short-term missionaries and career missionaries. One of the differences between the Nazirites is that the vow of the temporary Nazirite (Numbers 6) is taken voluntarily and is self-imposed. By contrast, the vow of the life-long Nazirite is imposed by others, usually a mother-to-be (Judges 13).

As a lifelong position the Nazirite has special parallels with the office of the prophet. Neither inherits the position. Both commence their activities by an experience with God, either through his spirit or his word. Both men and women could fill the office. That Samson is to be a Nazirite to God "from the womb" recalls Yahweh's word to Jeremiah: "Before I formed you in the womb I knew you" (Jer. 1:5); or the words of Isaiah's servant: "The Lord called me before I was born, while I was in my mother's womb he named me" (Isa. 49:1). John the Baptist, an Elijah-like prophet, also reflects this lifelong association. The angel's announcement to Zechariah that his forthcoming son "must never drink wine or strong drink; even before his birth he will be filled with the Holy Spirit" (Luke 1:15) and the parallels between Samson's and John the Baptist's birth announcements are Luke's way of saying that John the Baptist is a Nazirite from infancy.

The same may be true of Jesus. When Matthew states that Jesus made "his home in a town called Nazareth, so that what had been spoken through the prophets might be fulfilled, 'He will be called a Nazorean'" (Matt. 2:23), the question is immediately raised, To what prophets is Matthew referring? There is no Old Testament text that says "he will be called a Nazorean." While it is unquestionable that the primary reason that Jesus is called a Nazorean/Nazarene is because he took up residence at Nazareth, it is possible that in some secondary fashion Matthew is connecting Jesus the Nazorean/Nazarene with the *nazir*, especially of Judges 13 (one dedicated to God's service from birth) and the *netser*, "branch," specifically the messianic branch of the House of David ("A shoot shall come up from the stump of Jesse and a branch [*netser*] shall grow out of his roots" [Isa. 11:1]). Thus, the prophets Matthew is referring to are the author of Judges (in Hebrew tradition, one of the "earlier" prophetic books) and Isaiah. (See Brown 1977: 209–13, 223–25.)

Finally, we may note Luke's reference to Paul having his hair cut at Cenchreae, "for he was under a vow" (Acts 18:18), and Paul's own reference to being set apart by God "before I was born" (Gal. 1:15).

This coupling of Nazirites with prophets is particularly clear in Amos (2:11–12): "And I raised up some of your children to be prophets and some of your youths to be nazirites. . . . But you made the nazirites drink wine." In fact, Amos 2:11 is the only Old Testament text where the Nazirite's selection is described expressly as reflective of God's goodness and favor to his people Israel.

Three vows of absention mark the Nazirite:

1. He must be disciplined in his appetites: no drinking of wine or strong drink, no eating grapes.
2. He must be distinctive in his appearance: no razor shall come upon his head.
3. He must be discreet in his associations: he must not go near a corpse (even of close family members) and thus contact impurity.

It is clear that we know a lot more about what the Nazirite could not do than what he could do or did do. Numbers 6 is not so much a job description as it is a job disqualification description. That Amos couples Nazirites with prophets, both of whom served a divine purpose, indicates, however, that the Nazirites must have enjoyed some status.

The Nazirite office is known in the New Testament period, as evidenced by the reference in Acts 21:23–24 to Paul assuming the costs of four Nazirites for shaving their heads and undergoing the rite of purification. How the Nazirite was viewed in postbiblical Judaism may be observed in the section of the Mishnah known as *Nazir*.

Like the angel who appears to the women at the resurrection, who in turn pass the news along to the absent men, the angel of Yahweh appears to the mother-to-be while she is alone (vv. 3, 9). She then goes quickly to share that news with her husband (vv. 6, 10). And Manoah is much like the male disciples in the Gospels who hear the womens' report—uncertain, unconvinced, wanting more details, wanting to know himself and not able to accept his wife's testimony. When the truth does dawn on Manoah (v. 21), he draws the wrong conclusion (v. 22), only to be set straight by his wife's commonsense, logical response (v. 23).

The child is born and named "Samson" ("Shimshon" in Hebrew) by his mother (v. 24). No etymology is given for his name. While some have connected it with the word *shem* ("name") (Greenstein 1981: 241), more likely we should connect his name with the word *shemesh* ("sun"), and thus render Samson/Shimshon as "Sun Child" (Niditch 1990: 611). Samson is another of the names in Judges ending in *-on*: Eglon, Gideon, Dagon. Given the number of times Samson is involved with fire, with something burning or melting, and his fiery temperament, his name connection with the fiery, hot, blazing sun may be quite appropriate. "Fire has become a metonymic image of Samson himself: a blind, uncontrolled force, leaving a terrible swath of destruction behind it, finally consuming itself together with whatever stands in its way" (Alter 1981: 94–95).

It is not certain how best to translate Samson's first encounter with the spirit of the Lord (v. 25). Both the NRSV and the NIV have "The spirit of the Lord begin to stir him."

Judges uses four different verbs to describe the spirit's engagement of a judge:

hayah ʿal ("be/was upon")	lavash ("clothe, invest")	paʿam ("stir"?)	tsalakh ʿal ("rush upon")
3:10 (Othniel)	6:34 (Gideon)	13:25 (Samson)	14:6 (Samson)
			14:19 (Samson)
			15:14 (Samson)
			1 Sam. 10:10; 11:6 (Saul)

The verb *paʿam* occurs only a few more times in the Old Testament, to describe the troubled spirit of a king after a disturbing dream that the king can neither interpret nor control (Gen. 41:8; Dan. 2:1, 3), and a lament of a distraught psalmist, "I am so troubled that I cannot speak" (Ps. 77:4b). All are used with *ruakh* ("spirit"), except Ps. 77:4. The verb appears to come from a term meaning "foot," and its basic meaning is "to stamp, pound." The noun *paʿam* means "time," for times were counted by stamping the foot. Thus, in Judg. 13:25 the spirit of the Lord begins to "drive" Samson (Alter 1990: 49), "to beat on him" (Gunn 1992: 231), "to pulsate in him" (B. Levine, *Numbers*, New York 1993: 340), "to harass, plague, afflict him" (Stone 1992: 342).

2. 14:1–20. There are either three scenes in this chapter: vv. 1–4, 5–9, 10–20 (Blenkinsopp 1963: 66); or four: vv. 1–4, 5–6, 7–9, 10–20 (Exum 1981:12–13); or maybe even five, each of which is introduced with the verb "went down":

1. v. 1: "Samson went down to Timnah."
2. v. 5: "Samson went down with his father and mother to Timnah."
3. v. 7: "Then he went down and talked with the woman."
4. v. 10: "His father went down to the woman."
5. v. 19: "And he went down to Ashkelon."

Samson "went down" to the Philistine village of Timnah (for reasons unexplained) and there spotted a beautiful Philistine damsel. On another occasion, Jacob's son Judah "went up" to Timnah to sheer his sheep and there spotted a beautiful prostitute who, in fact, was his disguised daughter-in-law (Gen. 38:12–14). Samson does not talk to her. He simply sees and likes what he sees, and following protocol, asks his parents to get her for him. The reason for his request is, "She pleases me" (v. 3; cf. v. 7). The Hebrew actually says, "She is right in my eyes." The expression "right in my eyes" is the exact one we find two times in the concluding sections of Judges, 17:6 and 21:25, "In those days there was no king in Israel; all the people did what was right in their own eyes." "To do what is right in one's eyes" in Judges always carries a sinister nuance—to place my way of doing things over anybody else's way of doing things, including God's.

The narrator knows something that neither Samson nor his parents know (and for a second time in back-to-back chapters, Manoah does not know something—cf. 13:16 with 14:4). None of the actors knows that "this was from the Lord" (v. 4). How is one to explain that "a born deliverer would want to enter into an exogamous marriage with a member of the oppressing nation at that" (Sternberg 1987: 237–38)? The phrase does not imply that Yahweh incited Samson's sexual desire for the Timnite, that he stimulates romance and raging hormones as a prelude to slaughter, or even that Yahweh "itches for a fight" (Crenshaw 1978: 70). Rather, it suggests that Yahweh may use even those who are controlled by carnal self-will to advance his work. Here is one of the great theological themes of the Samson story. "God takes a bully boy and muscle man bent on the gratification of his own drives and instincts, and makes him the instrument of a nation's defense and rescue as well as authenticating the divinity's power of salvation, and therefore his right to be regarded as the true God in contrast to false claimants like Dagon" (Vickery 1981: 61).

The spirit of Yahweh always comes to and upon Samson unbidden. While Samson does pray at times for other things (for water to assuage thirst [15:18]; for a renewal of strength to exact vengeance [16:28]), he never prays for an endowment of the spirit. God comes in the Samson story both sovereignly and in response to petitionary prayer. On this occasion, the spirit renders Samson "Tarzanesque," as he rips to pieces barehandedly the lion that pounced on him as he makes his way to Timnah (v. 6a). That he did not tell his parents (who must have been somewhat geographically removed from the procession) indicates that Samson was aware of his Nazirite status, part of which involved no contact with anything dead (v. 6b).

On a repeat visit to Timnah (v. 8), this time to marry the woman, Samson comes across the carcass of this lion, in which bees are starting to produce honey (by the way, this is the only explicit reference in the Old Testament to bee honey versus wild fruit/date honey; note also that in the expression "swarm of bees," "swarm" is the word [*'edah*] used extensively for the "community" of Israel).

For a second time, Samson conceals his behavior from his parents. He refrains from telling them the source of the honey that he is sharing with them, for this is an intentional contact with something deceased, and thus a flagrant violation of his Nazirite vow (v. 9c). But how will they ever find out? Cannot such "little" sins be kept under wraps? Or will his sins find him out (Num. 32:23; Gal. 6:7)?

Anybody who has ever attended a Little League baseball game knows that what starts out as a bit of innocent fun and games can turn into something deadly serious (for the parents, that is). That is what happens here. Samson, fresh off the honey-from-the-lion episode, proposes a riddle to the wedding guests. The setting is a "feast" (v. 10), and while the word for "feast" (*mishteh*) implies a "drinking bout," we are not sure whether or not Samson partook of the intoxicants. If he did, it is another violation of his Nazirite vow.

Three things stand out about Samson's riddle (v. 14). While the word "know" is not used here, his riddle is based on "I know something you don't know" (Niditch 1990: 620–21), and reflects Samson's hubristic confidence. God could have said that too in ch. 14, but it was left to the narrator. Second, the riddle is in the form of a statement ("Out of the eater came . . . Out of the strong came . . ."), and the answer to the riddle is in the form of a question ("What is sweeter than . . . ? What is stronger than . . . ?"). Normally, the riddle takes the form of a question, and the answer takes the form of a statement (Bal 1987: 46). Third, there is not a chance in a million that the guests could decipher the riddle, for it is based on an isolated incident in Samson's life to which no one is privy except Samson.

This latter point may explain why the wedding guests become as hostile as they do to Samson's bride: "Coax your husband . . . or we will burn you and your father's house with fire" (v. 15). As guests, they have been humiliated and exploited, made to look like fools and nincompoops.

Samson is hardly sympathetic to his bride's entreaty. His "Look, I have not told my father or my mother. Why should I tell you?" (v. 16) is hardly intended to bolster her self-image or buttress their young marriage.

In a rage, Samson goes from Timnah down to Ashkelon (v. 19), one of five main Philistine cities and situated on the southern Mediterranean coast, thirty of whose people he will massacre and then rob to pay off his debts to the party-goers back at Timnah. All this is prefaced by "Then the spirit of the Lord rushed on him." Samson's rage is a spirit-energized rage. Might one compare the plagues that fell on Egypt in Gen. 12:17 because pharaoh plowed with Sarai, Abram's heifer?

3. 15:1–8. When 15:1 states that Samson returned to Timnah to "visit" his wife, this is probably the Old Testament's way of saying that Samson returned to his bride's village to consummate their marriage. This interpretation is reinforced by two items in the text. First, Samson brought a "kid" (*gedi ʿizzim*) for his wife. While this is exactly the same animal that his father, Manoah, brought to God as an offering (13:15, 19), a better parallel is found in Genesis, where Judah offers to give a "kid" for his payment of sex with a prostitute (Gen. 38:17, 20). In both Genesis 38 and Judges 15 a man presents a kid to a woman as a prelude to sexual intimacy. Second, Samson's words "I want to go into my wife's room" are self-explanatory.

High expectations give way to unbridled rage when he discovers that his father-in-law interpreted Samson's return to his father's house as a de facto divorcing of his wife ("I was so sure you had rejected [literally, "hated"] her"), so that the father-in-law gave her to another man. Samson's rejection of the prettier and younger sister shows his real love for his bride. She is not merely a sex object.

Samson prefaces his forthcoming revenge by saying, "This time, when I do mischief to the Philistines, I will be without blame" (v. 3). This suggests an admission of guilt by Samson about his earlier behavior at Ashkelon. What he did there was without justification. Not so on this occasion.

Samson does not need the spirit of the Lord to help him catch three hundred foxes. He simply needs excellent trapping skills. If one wants to do as much damage as possible to the opponents' crops, then the most propitious time to do that is "wheat harvest" (v. 1).

It is now the Philistines' turn to respond in this incessant vendetta marked by retaliation and revenge. Samson's bride and her father are burned by their own countrymen (v. 6). Either way, Samson's bride was doomed. Had she not coaxed the meaning of the riddle, she and father would have been burned to death (14:15). Because she was willing to coax the meaning of the riddle, that provokes Samson to leave abruptly, return, lose his bride, and incinerate their fields, all leading to her and her father's burning by fire (Polzin 1980: 187).

For her death Samson seeks revenge (v. 7). The NRSV's "I swear I will not stop until I have taken revenge on you" and the NIV's "I won't stop until I get my revenge on you" are not good translations of the Hebrew.

The RSV's "I swear I will be avenged upon you, and after that I will quit" is much better. Addictions to anything, however, including retaliation, are not so easily arrested. "Bondage always cries, 'Once more, and I'm through!'" (Stone 1992: 343). Agur was quite correct: "Three things are never satisfied; four never say, 'Enough': Sheol, the barren womb, the earth ever thirsty for water, and *the fire* that never says, 'Enough'" (Prov. 30:15–16).

4. 15:9–20. The crop-deprived Philistines come to seize Samson. Judah will not provide a refuge for Samson; rather, the Judeans will bind Samson and hand him over to the Philistines to do as they wish. There are a number of references, about a dozen, in chs. 15 and 16 to the "binding" of Samson, the word for which is *ʾasar*. Now what makes this interesting is that in the most extended discussion of oaths/vows in the Old Testament, Numbers 30, the verb *ʾasar* is used frequently to refer to a vow/oath by which one binds oneself (e.g., v. 2). Samson is already "bound" by his Nazirite vow. Now the Philistines wish to "bind" him in a different way.

Samson's fourth encounter with Yahweh's spirit (v. 14) enables him to break free of his confinement. In fiery fashion his bonds disintegrate and melt. His hand now free, he uses the jawbone of a donkey (hardly a formidable instrument of war; compare Shamgar's oxgoad in 3:31) to kill one thousand Philistines (v. 16). With mother and father out of the way and out of the story, there is no need for the narrator to inform us that Samson did not tell his parents what he had done with the dead donkey, unlike earlier, when the narrator informed us that Samson kept his parents in the dark about the dead lion (14:6).

Samson briefly becomes a poet (v. 16), composing a four-line celebration victory ode that highlights *his* accomplishments ("*I* have slain a thousand men"). And he memorializes the event by giving the place a name, Ramath-lehi, that is, "Jawbone Hill."

Samson can contest the Philistines with the help of Yahweh's spirit, but he has no resources to deal with his thirst, and so, for one of two times, Samson prays (v. 18), and God graciously provides water (v. 19). Samson's actions in vv. 16–17 and Yahweh's actions in vv. 18–19 "provide a contrast between the self-centeredness of Samson and the power and grace of Yahweh" (Exum 1983: 41). Furthermore, Samson's prayer reveals both Samson's utter dependence on Yahweh and Yahweh's openness to supplication (Exum 1983: 45).

The narrator does what Samson just did with Ramath-lehi. The narrator memorializes the place where God supernaturally supplied (once again) water from the rock by giving it a name: "En-hakkore," that is, "Wailer's Well," or "Crier's Spring," or "Namer's Spring." Actually, the

Hebrew (*ʿen haqqoreʾ*) contains the same verb (*qaraʾ*) found in 14:5 (the lion came to "meet" him) and in 15:14 (the Philistines came to "meet" him).

5. 16:1–3. Four women are involved in the Samson story:

13:3: a mother ("The angel of the Lord appeared to the woman")
14:1: a bride ("Once Samson . . . saw a Philistine woman")
16:1: a prostitute ("Once Samson . . . saw a woman, a prostitute")
16:4: a mistress ("He fell in love with a woman")

In 14:2 Samson says, "I saw a Philistine woman." Here, 16:1 says, "He saw a prostitute at Gaza." Whatever he sees seems always to get him in trouble. It sounds like this is a trap into which Samson has fallen. It is a set-up, and he has foolishly taken the bait. This might explain why Samson acts as violently as he does (v. 3), ripping the doors of the city gates off their hinges, hoisting them on to his shoulders, and carrying them toward Hebron (about forty miles away and uphill all the way!). What a contrast between Samson carrying wooden gates on his back and Jesus carrying a wooden cross on his back! Jesus is walking the *via dolorosa*, while Samson is walking the *via concupiscentia*.

Once to Abraham (Gen. 22:17) and once to Rebekah (Gen. 24:60) the promise was made that they (or their offspring) would "possess the gate(s) of their enemies," a promise that carries the guarantee of a complete victory over one's adversaries (Wharton 1973: 53). Breaking and removing the bars of a city gate marks a decisive stage in the ultimate defeat of the city, for the city is then fully exposed and vulnerable to invasion from without. Thus, Jeremiah refers in his oracle of Babylon's destruction to the breaking of the bars of Babylon's city gate (Jer. 51:30). Jerusalem was vulnerable to invasion because God had "ruined and broken her bars" (Lam. 2:9). God also threatens to "break the gate bars of Damsacus" (Amos 1:5).

6. 16:4–22. The only woman Samson is said to love, and the only woman named, appears here—Delilah. We do not read that Delilah loved Samson. So the love here operates on a one-way street.

As they did with Samson's bride, the Philistines ask Delilah to coax from Samson (14:15 and 16:5 use the imperative verb *patti*) something they cannot themselves discover. But there are two major differences between the two episodes. First, his bride is asked merely to entice him into explaining his riddle. By contrast, Delilah is asked to entice Samson into revealing the source of his strength, so that the Philistines "may overpower him, so that we may bind him in order to subdue him" (v. 5). Their intent is clear. In fact, the last verb (*ʿanah*) elsewhere may carry the meaning of "rape" (as in Amnon's violation of his half-sister Tamar: "No, my brother, do not *force* me. . . . Being stronger than she, he *forced* her. . . . Absalom hated Amnon, because he had *raped* his sister Tamar" [2 Sam. 13:12, 14, 22]).

The second difference between the two episodes is that his bride is threatened with death by burning if she does not cooperate (14:15b). Here, Delilah is herself coaxed into coaxing with the offer of a large sum of money if she accepts and is successful (16:5c). While her willingness to be bribed may be rooted in economic necessity, it is more likely that her willingness is rooted in avarice. One author (Vickery 1981: 69) has argued that both of the women in ch. 16 are prostitutes. "The difference is that the former is an honest one explicitly plying her trade in exchange for money and restricting her involvement to physical functions. Delilah is, as it were, a whore at heart aware of the hero's love for her and how his emotions may be manipulated to serve her greed and lust for power."

The incident with Delilah is an expected and natural sequel to the one with the prostitute in 16:1–3. Gaza is prominent in both (vv. 1, 21), and Samson's destruction of the city gates at Gaza "furnishes the Philistines with the motive for seeking vengeance on Samson through their intrigues with Delilah" (O'Connell 1996: 217). Lack of consensus remains about the meaning of Delilah's name. But here again there may be a connection with 16:1–3, which emphasizes the nightime (when harlots typically work). The Gazites lay in wait "all night" (v. 2) and kept quiet "all night" (v. 2). But Samson lay only until "midnight" (v. 3), then at "midnight" got up (v. 3). Now the consonants of the Hebrew word for "night" are *l-y-l-h* and the consonants of "Delilah" are *d-l-y-l-h*. Delilah is literally a "lady of the night," and Samson, the Sun Child, is seduced by Delilah, the Night Lady (Klein 1988: 119).

Delilah seeks four times to elicit from Samson the source of his incredulous strength and four times he makes a response, "in a game of psychological brinkmanship" (Alter 1990: 53):

1. vv. 6–9 ("if they bind me with seven fresh bowstrings")
2. vv. 10–12 ("if they bind me with new ropes")
3. vv. 13–14 ("if you weave the seven locks of my head")
4. vv. 15–22 ("a razor has never come upon my head")

We meet here a Samson who (1) offers no resistance; (2) lacks any sense of discernment; (3) at least attributes his power to God; (4) is guilty of gross presumption ("I will go out as at other times, and shake myself free" [v. 20c]); and (5) is spiritually ignorant ("He did not know that the Lord had left him" [v. 20d]). The verb used for Yahweh leaving (*sur*) somebody whom he has rejected appears again in Saul's attempts to contact the spirit of Samuel through a medium: "God has turned away from me and answers me no more" (1 Sam. 28:15). What Samson did not know (16:20) is even more tragic than what his parents did not know (14:4): when God departs, he may depart without fanfare. The cutting of Samson's hair marks the third and final violation of his Nazirite vow, and the only part of the vow that earlier had been expressly placed on Samson himself (13:5) rather than on his mother (13:4).

7. 16:23–31. Not only is Samson godless and strengthless, but he is also sightless, thanks to his Philistine captors (16:21; for gouging out the eyes as a punishment on a prisoner, see 2 Kings 25:7; Jer. 39:7; 52:11, all referring to Nebuchadnezzar's treatment of Zedekiah).

Samson represents a prize catch for the Philistines, the end of all their ravagement, or so they think. It is appropriate, therefore, that they celebrate the power and victory of Dagon their god. While the Philistines could easily have killed Samson, he is at the moment of more value to them alive than dead. A hapless entertainer is more fun than a corpse.

At this moment Samson does something for only the second time: he prays (v. 28). His prayer is not quite "Father, forgive them, for they know not what they do." He asks for God to strengthen him one more time "so that with this one act of revenge I may pay back the Philistines for my two eyes" (v. 28b). The verb behind the NRSV's "with this one act of revenge I may pay back" is *naqam*, which appeared earlier in Samson's response upon hearing that the Philistines had burned to death his wife and father-in-law: "I will not stop until I have taken revenge on you" (15:7b).

Samson's prayer is composed of four parts:

1. An *introductory formula* provided by the narrator ("then Samson called to/on the Lord and said"), the exact same introductory formula one finds in Samson's first prayer (15:18). The formula features the verb *qara'* for "call," and here the verb refers to a desperate calling out to God for help by somebody in dire straits. Accordingly, the verb is prominent in the lament prayers in the Psalter (e.g., "I cry aloud to the Lord" [3:4]; "Answer me when I call" [4:1]; "The Lord hears when I call to him" [4:3]; "I call upon you, for you will answer me" [17:6], and many others).
2. An *address/invocation:* "Lord God . . . O God."

3. A *petition:* "Remember me and strengthen me only this once." For other prayers in which the supplicant begins by petitioning God "to remember me," see 2 Kings 20:3 ("Remember now . . . how I [Hezekiah] have walked before you in faithfulness") or Luke 23:42 ("Remember me when you come into your kingdom"). Prayers calling upon God to remember something or somebody are especially prominent in Nehemiah (5:19; 6:14; 13:14, 22, 29, 31).

4. A *motivation:* "so that with this one act of revenge I may pay back the Philistines for my two eyes."

What may surprise some readers of Scripture is that God answers affirmatively even this kind of a prayer. Samson's strength returns one time, not because his hair starts to grow back again (v. 22), or even because of one last rushing of the spirit, but because God chooses to honor Samson's prayer.

Samson desires not revenge (taking the law into one's own hands) but vengeance (appealing to a higher legal power for retributive justice). The word *naqam* has here to do with "punitive vindication in redress of wrong suffered by an individual . . . the concept of Yahweh's granting individual acts of successful exercise of power over enemies in specific situations of jeopardy" (Mendenhall 1973: 92–93). "Here Samson, beyond all hope of ever seeing procedural justice done him for his enemies, entreats God to empower him to exact extraordinary retribution for himself—for him, there can be no other kind; and the God of *nqm* complies" (Greenberg 1983: 13).

Empowered one final time, Samson "leans" his hands on the two middle pillars of the temple (the same verb [*samak*] used in Lev. 1:4; 3:2, 8, 13; 4:4, 15, 24, 29 for the laying of a hand on the sacrifice by the worshiper), causing the building to crash, and sending three thousand Philistines and Samson himself to their death (v. 30). So ends the Samson saga.

There are two different ways of evaluating this last scene and Samson's whole life. One could say that "the best thing Samson ever did for Israel was to die" (Stone 1988: 346, 372; 1992: 343). Or, one might say that "his death is his greatest performance" (Bal 1987: 63). Given that this final episode takes place in a Philistine temple, Dagon's turf, Gunn (1992: 247) states that "to bring low the god of the Philistines is perhaps Samson's real contribution to Yahweh's purposes, and thus his achievement is not a physical one, but a theological one."

3. In Those Days There Was No King in Israel (17:1–21:25)

A. 17:1–18:31. In a nutshell, the incident in these two chapters unfolds as follows. A Levite from Bethlehem, from the "clan" (*mishpakhah*) of Judah, had made his way northward to the hill country of Ephraim (in search of employment and use of his skills?). There he is retained by a well-to-do private citizen, Micah, who already has his own shrine (17:5), complete with a molten image he had made from previously stolen money that he returned to his mother (17:2), plus ephod and teraphim (household gods). Even though he has appointed his own son as priest (17:5c), he installs (literally, "fills the hands of") the Levite as his personal priest (17:12), indicating that in Israel a member of the Levitical tribe was the preferred priest. In return for his services, Micah provides his personal priest support and a modest stipend—ten shekels of silver per year, plus clothing and keep (17:10b).

Subsequently, this Levite relocates to Dan, in northern Galilee, when migrating Danites pass through Micah's town and make him a better offer by appointing him as priest over an entire tribe (18:19). In today's language we would say that he leaves a small, rural pastoral charge to become pastor of an urban megachurch.

This event transpires because the Danites (i.e., Samson's turf), hard pressed by the Philistines, seek a territory of their own elsewhere in Canaan where they can settle unharassed by potent and preying neighbors. Accordingly, they send a group of five spies, who stop off at Micah's house in Ephraim, where they meet and are impressed by this Levite (18:2–6). Continuing on their way, the spies travel north and come to the city of Laish. It is for them an ideal land, for it is an unfortified, undefended territory, and one whose residents are wealthy but unaccustomed to warfare (18:7, 10, 27) and therefore incapable of offering any kind of resistance to militant outsiders. The city is captured and renamed "Dan" (18:29). The Levite at the center of this episode is named only at the end. He is Jonathan (18:30), a grandson of Moses (!), thus allowing the Danite priesthood to claim Mosaic lineage.

Not one of the characters in this story is wholesome. Micah's mother consecrates by oral declaration the eleven hundred pieces of silver to Yahweh, and then transfers them to her son, who uses but two hundred of the silver pieces to make his sculptured image (17:3b–4). Micah (or Micayhu, the longer form of the name in 17:1, 4) never lives up to his name. This one whose name means "Who is like Yahweh?" is a thief along the lines of Prov. 28:24 ("Anyone who robs father or mother . . ."), an idolater, a godmaker ("You take my gods that I made" [18:24]), with his own private clergy. He is an "Israelite betrayer of Israelite values without reason" (Klein 1988: 144).

The Levite is not impressive either. He is "an arch-opportunist" (Polzin 1980: 198), as ready to give God's blessing to the Danite spies (18:6) as were the four hundred prophets to Ahab (1 Kings 22:12), a yes-man without a conscience or the mind of God. Similarly, the migrating Danites appear distasteful. Apostasy now escalates from a family to a tribal level (O'Connell 1996: 239) as they establish their own shrine and worship center at Dan, an alternative to the legitimate house of God at Shiloh (18:31b). In their conquest of Laish one gets the impression "that their confidence lies less in indomitable faith in Yahweh than in the knowledge that they have found easy prey" (Webb 1987: 186).

It cannot be denied that this incident is related in some way to the Danite cult that became important after the northern kingdom of Israel was established in the late 900s B.C. According to 1 Kings 12:29–31, the Israelite king Jeroboam I established a sanctuary at Dan (and Bethel), employed non-Levitical priests to serve, and set up there an idolatrous golden calf.

But what is its function in relationship to the rest of Judges, that is, the sixteen chapters that have preceded it? It is common to refer to the stories of chs. 17–18 and 19–21 as "appendices." By definition, an appendix is a somewhat artificial appendage to a story that can be cut away without serious loss or damage to the whole. That is hardly the case here.

A clue may be found in an expression that occurs four times in these five chapters, twice in a fuller form, twice in a shorter form:

17:6: "In those days there was no king in Israel; all the people did what was right in their own eyes."
18:1a: "In those days there was no king in Israel."
19:1a: "In those days, when there was no king in Israel. . . ."
21:25: "In those days there was no king in Israel; all the people did what was right in their own eyes."

One might suggest that these four passages function as refrains, and are concluding summaries for each respective unit (Stone 1988: 457):

Unit 1: 17:1–5; concluding summary: 17:6
Unit 2: 17:7–13; concluding summary: 18:1a
Unit 3: 18:1b–31; concluding summary: 19:1a
Unit 4: 19:1b–21:24; concluding summary: 21:25

In the case of the longer expression with two parts—really two sentences in apposition to each other—the second may be understood as having a casual relationship to the first: "Because there was no king in Israel in those days, all the people continued to do what was right in their own eyes." Situation A precipitates situation B. Chapters 17–18 are one illustration of autonomy gone amuck at the level of one tribe (Dan), while chs. 19–21 illustrate the same at the level of all Israel.

It is inevitable that if a nation chooses to do "evil in the eyes of Yahweh" (3:7–16:31), then it will also choose to do "what is right in their own eyes" (chs. 17–21). Repudiation of God inexorably leads to exaltation of self and self-determination. Written over 3:7–16:31 is "Not your will be done"; written over chs. 17–21 is "My will be done." Israel's sin is not only apostasy and idolatry (3:7–16:31) but arrogance and presumption (chs. 17–21).

To correct that downward tumble (started in the prologue [1:1–3:6], fleshed out in the judge stories [3:7–16:31], and reaching a climax in chs. 17–21), Israel needs a king, "but not a king who, like the judges, will go to battle against foreign foes. Israel needs a king who will function as a guardian of the covenant, the very thing which the premonarchic order ultimately put at risk. Fundamental to safeguarding Israel's covenant fidelity is confronting the enemy which took more Hebrew lives than any foreign oppressor. A king is needed who will save Israel from its greatest threat: itself" (Stone 1988: 477).

B. 19:1–21:25. If the Levite of chs. 17–18 is Mr. Opportunist, the Levite of ch. 19 is Mr. Insensitivity personified quintessentially. For some unexplained reason, the Bethlehem concubine of this Levite from Ephraim leaves him (in itself, almost unheard of in the rest of the Old Testament) and returns to her father's house (19:2), much as Samson did with his spouse and father (14:19). Although the NRSV's rendering of 19:2, "she became angry with him," is a less faithful reading of the Hebrew than the NIV's "she was unfaithful to him" or the KJV's "played the whore," we need not assume that she literally was sexually promiscuous. After all, she seeks out her father, not a lover. She is more interested in a friendly roof over her head than in cohabitation. Possibly, we should understand "play the harlot" (*zanah*) metaphorically: she, for all practical purposes, played the harlot by walking out on her husband (Webb 1987: 188).

If she is angry or unfaithful, the Levite is conciliatory. He goes in search of his aberrant concubine, to speak tenderly to her, and to return her to his house, much as Jesus told of the shepherd who goes in search of the lost sheep to find it and to restore it to the flock (Matt. 18:12–14). This is the only point in which the Levite appears in commendable light.

Although the woman is consistently called a concubine rather than a wife, her father is the Levite's "father-in-law," who persuades his son-in-law to stay five days before he leaves with his daughter (19:3–9). Throughout this period, the only recorded chit-chat is between son-in-law and father-in-law, a kind of "exercise in male bonding" (Trible 1984: 68). The concubine never speaks and is never spoken to.

The Levite, his male attendant, and his concubine head back to his home, passing near Jerusalem/Jebus, as yet a non-Israelite city and thus potentially hostile, and continue on their way until they reach Gibeah in the territory of Benjamin (19:10–14). Presumably, they are now on friendly turf.

But that hunch is doubly wrong. First, the locals do not roll out the welcome mat to this threesome, and were it not for the kindness of a transplanted Ephraimite sojourning in Gibeah, they would have slept in the open square of the city under the stars (19:15–21). Apparently, Gibeah is not Hospitalityville.

The second surprise for the Levite is his forthcoming shocking discovery that not every Gibeahite trumpets traditional family values. A group of depraved men, which the NRSV calls "a perverse lot" (19:22), and which Boling (1975: 276) calls "the local hell-raisers," descends on the house with the intention of sodomizing the Levite guest: "Bring out the man who came into your house so that we may have intercourse with him [literally, 'so that we may know him']" (19:22).

The host offers an alternative to assuage their lust. He makes available (without consulting them) his own virgin daughter and the Levite's concubine (v. 24). Thus, "To prevent the rape of one man the host offers the rape of two women" (K. Stone 1996: 80). The host also offers "two females to satisfy the gamut of heterosexual preferences. One is virgin property; the other, seasoned and experienced" (Trible 1984: 74). At this point the Levite sends his concubine outside, where she is gang raped and tortured through the night hours (19:25). At dawnbreak they release her (a phrase recalling the "man" who wrestled with Jacob and then said, "Let me go, for for the dawn is breaking" [Gen. 32:26] [both passages use the Piel of *shalakh*]).

The parallels between this passage and the story of the two angels/messengers who visit Lot in Sodom (Genesis 19) are obvious, with scholars arguing either for the dependence of the Genesis story on the Judges story (e.g., Niditch 1982), or the dependence of the Judges story on the Genesis story (e.g., Lasine 1984). The major difference between the two, of course, is that Lot's daughters are not violated, but the concubine is. Maybe the concubine's destiny would have been different if the host's guests were angels, as at Sodom.

As outrageous as is the behavior of the mob vis-à-vis the concubine, it is matched by the Levite's behavior at three points. First, seeing her disheveled, humiliated, and at death's door, he coldly says, "Get up, we are going" (19:28), as if she has been through nothing more than a felicitous night on the town and chose to sleep outdoors. Second, he dismembers his concubine's corpse into twelve sections and "mails" them throughout the tribal area—his way of calling for revenge upon the perpetrators (19:29). (The expression "he took the knife" occurs again in the Old Testament only in Gen. 22:10 with Abraham and Isaac, but what a contrast between a delivered Isaac and a dismembered concubine!) Third, his explanation to the larger assembly of what happened is twisted and perverted (20:4–6). For example, he says that the Gibeahites wanted to "kill" him (20:5), when in fact they wanted to "know" him (19:22). Again, he says nothing about "seizing" his concubine and thrusting her outside (19:25). Nor does he say anything about his host's offer of the two women (19:24), or about his callous words to his concubine as if she had just returned from a refreshing morning aerobic workout (19:28).

The modern reader certainly feels for the unfortunate concubine, a marginal woman without speech or power in a man's world. But can we be sure that the ancient reader felt the same? Thus, Penchansky (1992: 83) asks, "Is there here a deliberately feminist impulse . . . or might one see these texts as anti-feminist, reflecting a general misogynistic polemic . . . or is the entire feminine issue irrelevant to the text?"

As repugnant as is the account of the ravishing of the concubine, as far as Judges 19–21 is concerned, it is "only the pebble that starts the landslide" (L. Stone 1988: 403). What emerges in chs. 20 and 21 is the graphic inability of premonarchic Israel and their judicial apparatus to handle even local disputes without them burgeoning into civil wars.

Chapter 20 focuses on the war of revenge against Benjamin, in which the city of Gibeah is located. Unlike the host and Levite, who are more than ready to hand over women to the mob, the Benjaminites refuse to hand over the culprits (20:13), and so become the villains and the objects of punishment themselves. An enormous civil war ensues in which twenty-five thousand of the Benjaminites are killed (20:46), with only six hundred escaping (20:47), and only after the Benjaminites in self-defense have managed to kill over forty thousand of their Israelite kin (20:21, 25, 31).

The last chapter of Judges describes the nefarious attempts of the prosecuting tribes to repopulate the almost decimated tribe of Benjamin. Given that they have made an oath not to give their own daughters in marriage to the villainous Benjaminites (21:1), what are their options?

There are two. First, because only the city of Jabesh-gilead did not heed the call to arms, it is to be "devoted to destruction" (the only narrative of Israel conducting a *kherem* war against Israel). Only four hundred young virgins are spared, for the sake of becoming wives to the mateless Benjaminites (21:12). Since that number is inadequate, the Benjaminites obtain permission to take for themselves the young dancing women who participate in some kind of a vintage festival at Shiloh (21:14–24).

There can be no doubt that this incident not only looks back to the Lot/Sodom story, but also anticipates the story of King Saul. A few of the parallels and connections (also see Brettler 1989: 412–15; Amit 1994: 31–35) include:

1. The Levite's dismembering of his concubine parallels Saul's dismembering of a yoke of oxen (1 Sam. 11:7), and both times the individual sends out the portions throughout Israel as a call to arms for revenge.
2. The cities of Gibeah and Jabesh-gilead, which appear prominently in Judges 19 and 20, figure in the Saul story as his home and capital (Gibeah: 1 Sam. 10:26; 11:4; 15:34), and as a city he saved from destruction (Jabesh-gilead, 1 Sam. 11:1–13).
3. Saul is a Benjaminite, and it is the Benjaminites who in Judges 20 are almost annihilated.
4. On his return to Ephraim, the Levite makes it as far as Gibeah, but not as far as "Ramah" (Judg. 19:13). Ramah (1 Sam. 7:17) is more than likely the place where Saul first met Samuel when he went looking for his father's donkeys (1 Sam. 9:3).
5. An old man from Ephraim hosts and entertains a Levite, and Samuel, a man from Ephraim, hosts and entertains Saul (1 Sam. 9:22–26).
6. There are six hundred Benjaminite survivors (Judg. 20:47), and Saul has six hundred followers (1 Sam. 13:15; 14:2).
7. In Saul's time, Nahash, the king of the Ammonites, agreed to a treaty with Jabesh-gilead provided he could gouge out everyone's "right eye" (1 Sam. 11:2), and the Benjaminites are "the sons of the right (hand)." Part of the strategy of Jabesh-gilead was to say to Nahash, "Tomorrow we will give ourselves up to you, and you may do to us whatever seems good to you" (1 Sam. 11:10). The latter expression reads literally, "and do for

yourselves what is good in your eyes"—surely a reverberation of Judg. 21:25.

Judges 19–21 also looks forward to First Samuel and Saul in another way. Indeed, the guilt-by-association idea inherent in Judges 19–21 suggests proleptically that Saul is not the final solution to a kingless, confederate Israel in which all the people do what is right in their own eyes. At best, he is an interim solution; at worst, he compounds the problem. Is there one to come after Saul who will be the real savior and deliverer?

This last story in Judges provides another footnote to the grimness of the days of the Judges. Here are the Israelites in Judges who meet a violent death:

The violently killed	The perpetrator	Reference
70 sons of Jerubbaal	Abimelech	9:5
Abimelech	a woman	9:53
a daughter	Jephthah	11:39
42,000 Ephraimites	Jephthah	12:6
Samson	Samson	16:30
40,030 Israelites	Benjaminites	20:21, 25, 31
25,000 Benjaminites	Israelites	20:46
men, women, children from Jabesh-gilead	Israelites	21:10–11

The evidence is clear. Every Israelite in Judges who dies violently at the hand of another dies at the hand of a fellow Israelite! No Israelite is said to be put to death by any Midianite or Moabite or Philistine. It is a book about kindred killing kindred. That is a gruesome part of the savagery of the era.

Bibliography (Judges)

Commentaries and Major Studies

Bal, M. 1988. *Death and Dissymmetry: The Politics of Coherence in the Book of Judges*. Chicago: University of Chicago Press.

Bodine, W. R. 1980. *The Greek Text of Judges: Recensional Developments*. HSM 23. Chico, Calif.: Scholars Press.

Boling, Robert G. 1975. *Judges*. Anchor Bible 6A. New York: Doubleday.

Brenner, A., ed. 1993. *A Feminist Companion to Judges*. The Feminist Companion to the Bible 4. Sheffield: JSOT Press.

Burney, C. F. 1970 [1903]. *The Book of Judges with Introduction and Notes*. New York: Ktav.

Cundall, A. E. 1968. *Judges: An Introduction and Commentary*. Tyndale Old Testament Commentaries. Downers Grove, Ill.: InterVarsity.

Davis, D. R. 1990. *Such a Great Salvation*. Grand Rapids: Baker.

Gray, John. 1986. *Joshua, Judges, Ruth*. New Century Bible. London: Nelson. Pp. 201–396.

Hamlin, E. J. 1990. *At Risk in the Promised Land: A Commentary on the Book of Judges*. International Theological Commentary. Grand Rapids: Eerdmans.

Klein, L. R. 1988. *The Triumph of Irony in the Book of Judges*. JSOT Supplement 68; Bible and Literature Series 14. Sheffield: Almond.

Lindars, B. 1995. *Judges 1–5: A New Translation and Commentary*. Ed. A. D. H. Mayes. Edinburgh: T. & T. Clark.

Martin, J. D. 1975. *The Book of Judges*. Cambridge Bible Commentary. Cambridge University Press.

Mayes, A. D. H. 1974. *Israel in the Period of the Judges*. London: SCM.

Moore, G. F. 1976 [1895]. *A Critical and Exegetical Commentary on Judges*. International Critical Commentary. Edinburgh: T. & T. Clark.

O'Connell, Robert H. 1996. *The Rhetoric of the Book of Judges*. VTSup 63. Leiden: E. J. Brill.

Polzin, Robert. 1980. *Moses and the Deuteronomist: A Literary Study of the Deuteronomistic History*. New York: Seabury. Pp. 146–204.

Simpson, C. A. 1957. *Composition of the Book of Judges*. Oxford: Basil Blackwell.

Soggin, J. Alberto. 1981. *Judges: A Commentary*. Trans. J. Bowden. Old Testament Library. Philadelphia: Westminster.

Stone, Lawson G. 1988. "From Tribal Confederation to Monarchic State: The Editorial Perspective of the Book of Judges." Ph.D. diss. Yale University.

Webb, Barry G. 1987. *The Book of the Judges: Grace Abounding*. The Bible Speaks Today Series. Leicester: Inter-Varsity.

Wood, L. 1975. *Distressing Days of the Judges*. Grand Rapids: Zondervan.

Yee, Gale A., ed. 1995. *Judges & Method: New Approaches in Biblical Studies*. Minneapolis: Fortress.

Shorter Studies

Ahlström, G. W. 1993. *The History of Ancient Palestine*. Minneapolis: Fortress. Pp. 371–90.

Block, D. I. 1988. "The Period of the Judges: Religious Disintegration under Tribal Rule." In *Israel's Apostasy and Restoration: Essays in Honor of Roland K. Harrison*. Ed. A. Gileadi. Grand Rapids: Baker. Pp. 39–57.

Brettler, Marc. 1989. "The Book of Judges: Literature as Politics." *JBL* 108: 395–418.

Bright, John. 1981. *A History of Israel*. 3rd ed. Philadelphia: Westminster. Pp. 173–82.

Brueggemann, Walter. 1981. "Social Criticism and Social Vision in the Deuteronomic Formula of the Judges." In *Die Botschaft und die Boten: Festschrift für Hans Walter Wolff zum 70. Geburtstag*. Ed. J. Jeremias and L. Perlitt. Neukirchen: Neukirchen Verlag. Pp. 101–14.

Buber, Martin. 1967. "The Books of Judges and the Book of Judges." In *The Kingship of God*. 3rd ed. New York: Harper and Row. Pp. 66–84.

Callaway, Joseph A. 1988. "The Settlement in Canaan: The Period of the Judges." In *Ancient Israel: A Short History from Abraham to the Roman Destruction of the Temple.* Ed. H. A. Shanks. Englewood Cliffs, N.J.: Prentice-Hall. Pp. 53–84.

Chalcraft, D. J. 1990. "Deviance and Legitimate Action in the Book of Judges." In *The Bible in Three Dimensions: Essays in Celebration of Forty Years of Biblical Studies in the University of Sheffield.* JSOT Supplement 87. Ed. D. J. A. Clines, S. E. Fowl and S. E. Porter. Sheffield: JSOT Press. Pp.177–96.

Childs, Brevard. 1979. *Introduction to the Old Testament as Scripture.* Philadelphia: Fortress. Pp. 254–62.

Cundall, A. E. 1970. "Judges—An Apology for the Monarchy?" *ExpT* 81:178–81.

Dumbrell, W. J. 1983. "'In Those Days There Was No King in Israel; Every Man Did What Was Right in His Own Eyes': The Purpose of the Book of Judges Reconsidered." *JSOT* 25:23–33.

Exum, J. C. 1990. "The Centre Cannot Hold: Thematic and Textual Instabilities in Judges." *CBQ* 52:410–31.

Fensham, F. C. 1991. "Literary Observations on Historical Narratives in Sections of Judges." In *Storia e tradizoni di Israel: Scritti in onore di J. Alberto Soggin.* Brescia: Queriniana. Pp. 77–87.

Gooding, D. W. 1982. "The Composition of the Book of Judges." *Eretz Israel* 16:70–79.

Gros Louis, Kenneth R. R. 1974. "The Book of Judges." In *Literary Interpretations of Biblical Narrative.* Ed. K. Gros Louis, J. Ackerman, and T. Warshaw. Nashville: Abingdon. Pp. 141–62.

Guest, P. D. 1998. "Can Judges Survive without Sources? Challenging the Consensus." *JSOT* 78:43–61.

Gunn, D. M. 1974. "Narrative Patterns and Oral Traditions in Judges and Samuel." *VT* 24:286–317.

———. 1987. "Joshua and Judges." In *The Literary Guide to the Bible.* Ed. R. Alter and F. Kermode. Cambridge, Mass.: Belknap. Pp. 102–21.

Hauser, A. J. 1979. "Unity and Diversity in Early Israel before Samuel." *JETS* 22:289–303.

Howard, D. M., Jr. 1993. *An Introduction to the Historical Books.* Chicago: Moody. Pp. 99–123.

Ishida, T. 1973. "The Leaders of the Tribal League 'Israel' in the Premonarchic Period." *RB* 80:514–30.

Kort, W. A. 1988. *Story, Text, and Scripture: Literary Interests in Biblical Narrative.* University Park, Pa.: Pennsylvania State University Press. Pp. 29–35.

Lilley, J. P. U. 1967. "A Literary Appreciation of the Book of Judges." *TynB* 18:94–102.

Malamat, A. 1976. "Charismatic Leadership in the Book of Judges." In *Magnalia Dei: The Mighty Acts of God: Essays on the Bible and Archaeology in Memory of G. Ernest Wright*. Ed. F. M. Cross, W. E. Lemke, and P. D. Miller. Garden City, N.Y.: Doubleday. Pp. 152–68.

Mayes, A. D. H. 1977. "The Period of the Judges and the Rise of the Monarchy." In *Israelite and Judaean History*. Ed. J. H. Hayes and J. M. Miller. Philadelphia: Trinity Press International. Pp. 285–331.

McKenzie, D. A. 1975. "The Judge of Israel." *VT* 25 (1975) 118–21.

McKenzie, J. L. 1966. *The World of the Judges*. Englewood Cliffs, N.J.: Prentice-Hall.

Mullen, T. E., Jr. 1993. *Narrative History and Ethnic Boundaries: The Deuteronomistic Historian and the Creation of Israelite National Identity*. SBLSS. Atlanta: Scholars Press. Pp. 121–80.

Patton, C. L. 1996. "From Heroic Individuals to Nameless Victims: Women in the Social World of the Judges." In *Biblical and Humane: A Festschrift for John F. Priest*. Ed. L. B. Elder, D. L. Barr, and E. S. Malbon. Atlanta: Scholars Press. Pp. 33–46.

Roger, M. G. 1970. "Judges, Book of." *IDBSup*, 509–14.

Smend, R. 1970. *Yahweh War and Tribal Confederation*. Nashville: Abingdon.

Stone, Lawson G. 1992. "Judges." In *Asbury Bible Commentary*. Ed. E. E. Carpenter and W. McCown. Grand Rapids: Zondervan. Pp. 329–46.

Vaux, Roland de. 1978. *The Early History of Israel*. Trans. David Smith. Philadelphia: Westminster. Pp. 681–93, 751–63.

Judges 1:1–3:6 (Introduction)

Auld, A. G. 1975. "Judges 1 and History: A Reconsideration." *VT* 25:261–85.

Brettler, Marc. 1989. "Judges 1:1–2:10: From Appendix to Prologue." *ZAW* 101:433–35.

Eslinger, L. M. 1989. "A New Generation in Israel." In *Into the Hands of the Living God*. Bible and Literature Series 24. Sheffield: Almond. Pp. 55–80.

Fretheim, T. E. 1983. *Deuteronomic History*. Interpreting Biblical Texts. Nashville: Abingdon. Pp. 87–98.

Gunn, D. M., and Danna N. Fewell. 1993. *Narrative in the Hebrew Bible*. The Oxford Bible Series. Oxford: Oxford University Press. Pp. 158–63.

Mullen, T. E., Jr. 1984. "Judges 1:1–3:6: The Deuteronomistic Reintroduction of the Book of Judges." *HTR* 77:33–54.

Nelson, R. D. 1981. *The Double Redaction of the Deuteronomistic History*. JSOT Supplement 18. Sheffield: JSOT Press. Pp. 43–53.

O'Doherty, E. 1956. "The Literary Problem of Judges 1, 1–3, 6." *CBQ* 28:1–7.

Weinfeld, M. 1967. "The Period of the Conquest and of the Judges as Seen by the Earlier and the Later Sources." *VT* 17:93–113.

———. 1993. "Judges 1:1–2:5: The Conquest under the Leadership of the House of Judah." In *Understanding Poets and Prophets: Essays in Honor of George Wishart Anderson*. JSOT Supplement 152. Ed. A. G. Auld. Sheffield: JSOT Press. Pp. 388–400.

Williams, J. G. 1991. "The Structure of Judges 2:6–16:31." *JSOT* 49:77–86.

Wright, G. Ernest. 1946. "The Literary and Historical Problem of Joshua 10 and Judges 1." *JNES* 5:105–14.

Younger, K. L., Jr. 1994. "Judges 1 in Its Near Eastern Literary Context." In *Faith, Tradition, History: Old Testament Historiography in Its Near Eastern Context*. Ed. J. K. Hoffmeier, A. R. Millard, and D. W. Baker. Winona Lake, Ind.: Eisenbrauns. Pp. 207–27.

———. 1995. "The Configuring of Judicial Preliminaries: Judges 1:1–2:5 and Its Dependence on the Book of Joshua." *JSOT* 68:75–92.

Judges 3:7–11 (Othniel)

Stone, Lawson G. 1988. "From Tribal Confederation to Monarchic State: The Editorial Perspective of the Book of Judges." Ph.D. diss. Yale University. Pp. 260–89.

Judges 3:12–30 (Ehud)

Alter, Robert. 1981. *The Art of Biblical Narrative*. New York: Basic Books. Pp. 37–41.

Amit, Y. 1988. "The Story of Ehud (Judges 3:12–30): The Form and the Message." In *Signs and Wonders: Biblical Texts in Literary Focus*. Ed. J. Cheryl Exum. Atlanta: Society of Biblical Literature. Pp. 97–123.

Brettler, Marc. 1991. "Never the Twain Shall Meet? The Ehud Story as History and Literature." *HUCA* 62:285–304.

Culley, R. C. 1992. *Themes and Variations: A Study of Action in Biblical Narrative*. Atlanta: Scholars Press. Pp. 99–100.

Halpern, B. 1988. *The First Historians: The Hebrew Bible and History*. San Francisco: Harper & Row. Pp. 39–75.

Handy, L. K. 1992. "Uneasy Laughter: Ehud and Eglon as Ethnic Humor." *SJOT* 6:233–46.

Jobling, D. 1988. "Right-Brained Story of Left-Handed Man: An Antiphon to Yairah Amit." In *Signs and Wonders: Biblical Texts in Literary Focus*. Ed. J. Cheryl Exum. Atlanta: Society of Biblical Literature. Pp. 125–31.

Knauf, E. A. 1991. "Eglon and Ophran: Two Toponymic Notes on the Book of Judges." *JSOT* 51:15–44.

Ogden, G. S. 1991. "The Special Features of a Story: A Study of Judges 3:12–30." *BT* 42:408–14.

Sternberg, M. 1985. *The Poetics of Biblical Narrative*. Bloomington: Indiana University Press. Pp. 331–37.

Yadin, Yigael. 1963. *The Art of Warfare in the Biblical Lands According to Archaeological Finds*. New York: McGraw Hill.

Judges 3:31 (Shamgar)

Craigie, P. C. 1972. "A Reconsideration of Shamgar ben Anath (Judges 3:31 and 5:6)." *JBL* 91:239–40.

Fensham, F. C. 1989. "Shamgar ben Anath." *JNES* 20:197–98.

Shupak, N. 1989. "New Light on Shamgar ben Anath [Judges 3, 31]." *Bib* 70:517–25.

Stone, Lawson G. 1988. "From Tribal Confederation to Monarchic State: The Editorial Perspective of the Book of Judges." Ph.D. diss. Yale University. Pp. 364–66.

Van Selms, A. 1964. "Judge Shamgar." *VT* 14:294–309.

Judges 4:1–5:31 (Deborah and Barak)

Ackerman, J. 1975. "Prophecy and Warfare in Early Israel: A Study of the Deborah-Barak Story." *BASOR* 220:5–12.

Amit, Y. 1987. "Judges 4: Its Content and Form." *JSOT* 39:89–111.

Bal, Mieke. 1988. *Murder and Difference: Gender, Genre, and Scholarship on Sisera's Death*. Trans. M. Grumpert. Bloomington: Indiana University Press.

Block, D. I. 1994. "Deborah among the Judges: The Perspective of the Hebrew Historian." In *Faith, Tradition, and History: Old Testament Historiography in Its Near Eastern Context*. Ed. A. Millard, J. K.

Hoffmeier, and D. W. Baker. Winona Lake, Ind.: Eisenbrauns. Pp. 229–53.

Culley, R. C. 1992. *Themes and Variations: A Study of Action in Biblical Narrative*. Atlanta: Scholars Press. Pp. 100–104.

Exum, J. C. 1985. "'Mother in Israel': A Familiar Figure Reconsidered." In *Feminist Interpretation of the Bible*. Ed. L. M. Russell. Philadelphia: Westminster. Pp. 73–85.

Fewell, D. N., and D. M. Gunn. 1990. "Controlling Perspectives: Women, Men, and the Authority of Violence in Judges 4 and 5." *JAAR* 56:389–411.

Halpern, Baruch. 1983. *The Emergence of Israel in Canaan*. SBLMS 29. Chico, Calif.: Scholars Press. Pp. 116–23, 146–49.

———. 1988. *The First Historians: The Hebrew Bible and History*. San Francisco: Harper & Row. Pp. 76–103.

Hanselman, S. W. 1989. "Narrative Theory, Ideology, and Transformation in Judges 4." In *Anti-Covenant: Counter-Reading Women's Lives in the Hebrew Bible*. JSOT Supplement 81; Bible and Literature Series 22. Ed. M. Bal. Sheffield: Almond. Pp. 95–112.

Margalit, B. 1995. "Observations on the Jael-Sisera Story (Judges 4–5)." In *Pomegranates and Golden Bells: Studies in Biblical, Jewish, and Near Eastern Ritual, Law, and Literature in Honor of Jacob Milgrom*. Ed. D. P. Wright, D. N. Freedman, and A. Hurvitz. Winona Lake, Ind.: Eisenbrauns. Pp. 629–41.

Matthews, V. H. 1991. "Hospitality and Hostility in Judges 4." *BTB* 21:13–21.

de Moor, J. C. 1995. "Deborah." *Daughters of Sarah* 21:34–37.

Murray, D. F. 1979. "Narrative Structure and Techniques in the Deborah-Barak Story (Judges IV 4–22)." In *Studies in the Historical Books of the Old Testament*. VTSup 30. Ed. J. A. Emerton. Leiden: E. J. Brill. Pp. 155–89.

Na'aman, N. 1990. "Literary and Topographical Notes on the Battle of Kishon." *VT* 40:423–26.

Niditch, S. 1989. "Eroticism and Death in the Tale of Jael." In *Gender and Difference in Ancient Israel*. Ed. P. L. Day. Minneapolis: Fortress. Pp. 43–57.

Ogden, G. S. 1994. "Poetry, Prose, and Their Relationship: Some Reflections Based on Judges 4 and 5." In *Discourse Perspectives on Hebrew Poetry in the Scriptures*. Ed. E. R. Wendland. UBS Monograph Series 7. New York: United Bible Societies. Pp. 111–30.

Rasmussen, R. C. 1989. "Deborah the Woman Warrior." In *Anti-Covenant: Counter-Reading Women's Lives in the Hebrew Bible*. JSOT

Supplement 81; Bible and Literature Series 22. Ed. M. Bal. Sheffield: Almond. Pp. 79–93.

Stek, J. H. 1986. "The Bee and the Mountain Goat: A Literary Reading of Judges 4." In *A Tribute to Gleason Archer*. Ed. W. C. Kaiser Jr. and R. F. Youngblood. Chicago: Moody. Pp. 53–86.

Sternberg, M. 1985. *The Poetics of Biblical Narrative*. Bloomington: Indiana University Press. Pp. 270–83.

van Wolde, E. 1995. "Yaᶜel in Judges 4." *ZAW* 107:240–46.

Yee, Gale A. 1993. "By the Hand of a Woman: The Metaphor of the Woman Warrior in Judges 4." *Semeia* 61:99–132.

Judges 5:1–31 (the Song of Deborah)

Alter, Robert. 1985. *The Art of Biblical Poetry*. New York: Basic Books. Pp. 43–50.

Ballentine, S. 1993. *Prayer in the Hebrew Bible*. Overtures to Biblical Theology. Minneapolis: Fortress. Pp. 220–24.

Blenkinsopp, J. 1961. "Ballad Style and Psalm Style in the Song of Deborah: A Discussion." *Bib* 42:61–76.

Coogan, M. D. 1978. "A Structural and Literary Analysis of the Song of Deborah." *CBQ* 40:143–66.

Craigie, P. C. 1969. "The Song of Deborah and the Epic of Tukulti-Ninurta." *JBL* 88:253–65.

———. 1978. "Deborah and Anat: A Study in Poetic Imagery." *ZAW* 90:374–81.

Fokkelman, Jan P. 1995. "The Song of Deborah and Barak: Its Prosodic Levels and Structure." In *Pomegranates and Golden Bells: Studies in Biblical, Jewish, and Near Eastern Ritual, Law, and Literature in Honor of Jacob Milgrom*. Ed. D. P. Wright, D. N. Freedman, and A. Hurvitz. Winona Lake, Ind.: Eisenbrauns. Pp. 595–628.

Freedman, D. N. 1980. *Pottery, Poetry, and Prophecy*. Winona Lake, Ind.: Eisenbrauns. Pp. 147–60.

Gerleman, G. 1966. "The Song of Deborah in the Light of Stylistics." *VT* 36:32–53.

Globe, A. 1974. "The Literary Structure and Unity of the Song of Deborah." *JBL* 93:493–512.

Gray, John. 1988. "Israel in the Song of Deborah." In *Ascribe to the Lord: Biblical and Other Studies in Memory of Peter C. Craigie*. JSOT Supplement 67. Ed. L. Eslinger and G. Taylor. Sheffield: JSOT Press. Pp. 421–55.

Hauser, A. J. 1980. "Parataxis in Hebrew Poetry." *JBL* 99:23–41.

―――. 1987. "Two Songs of Victory: A Comparison of Exodus 15 and Judges 5." In *Directions in Biblical Hebrew Poetry*. JSOT Supplement 40. Ed. E. R. Follis. Sheffield: JSOT Press. Pp. 265–84.

Keller, Stephen. 1979. *Parallelism in Hebrew Poetry*. HSM 20. Missoula, Mont.: Scholars Press. Pp. 156–63.

Miller, P. D., Jr. 1973. *The Divine Warrior in Early Israel*. HSM 5. Cambridge, Mass.: Harvard University Press. Pp. 87–102.

de Moor, J. C. 1993. "The Twelve Tribes in the Song of Deborah." *VT* 43:483–94.

O'Connor, M. 1980. *Hebrew Verse Structure*. Winona Lake, Ind.: Eisenbrauns. Pp. 487–93.

Schloen, J. D. 1993. "Caravans, Kenites and *casus belli*: Enmity and Alliance in the Song of Deborah." *CBQ* 55:18–38.

Shaw, J. 1989. "Constructions of Women in Readings of the Song of Deborah." In *Anti-Covenant: Counter-Reading Women's Lives in the Hebrew Bible*. JSOT Supplement 81; Bible and Literature Series 22. Ed. M. Bal. Sheffield: Almond. Pp. 113–32.

Stager, L. E. 1988. "Archaeology, Ecology, and Sacred History: Background Themes to the Song of Deborah." In *Congress Volume: Jerusalem, 1986*. VTSup 40. Ed. J. A. Emerton. Leiden: E. J. Brill. Pp. 221–34.

―――. 1989. "The Song of Deborah: Why Some Tribes Answered the Call and Others Did Not." *BAR* 15, no. 1:51–64.

Stuart, D. K. 1976. *Studies in Early Hebrew Meter*. HSM 13. Missoula, Mont.: Scholars Press. Pp. 121–36.

Walsh, J. P. M. 1987. *The Mighty from Their Thrones*. Overtures to Biblical Theology. Philadelphia: Fortress. Pp. 70–75.

Judges 6:1–8:35 (Gideon)

Auld, A. G. 1989. "Gideon: Hacking at the Heart of the Old Testament." *VT* 39:393–406.

Buber, Martin. 1967. "The Gideon Passage." In *The Kingship of God*. 3rd ed. New York: Harper and Row. Pp. 59–65.

Clark, G. R. 1993. *The Word Hesed in the Hebrew Bible*. JSOT Supplement 157. Sheffield: JSOT Press. Pp. 221–22.

Culley, R. C. 1992. *Themes and Variations: A Study of Action in Biblical Narrative*. Atlanta: Scholars Press. Pp.104–6.

Emerton, J. A. 1976. "Gideon and Jerubbaal." *JTS* 27:289–312.

Fontaine, Carole R. 1982. *Traditional Sayings in the Old Testament*. Bible and Literature Series 5. Sheffield: Almond. Pp. 76–95.

Garsiel, M. 1993. "Homiletic Name-Derivations as a Literary Device in the Gideon Narrative: Judges VI–VIII." *VT* 43:302–17.

Habel, N. 1965. "The Form and Significance of the Call Narratives." *ZAW* 77:297–323.

Macartney, Clarence. 1948. *The Greatest Questions of the Bible and of Life*. Nashville: Abingdon-Cokesbury. Pp. 68–77.

Malamat, A. 1953. "The War of Gideon and Midian: A Military Approach." *PEQ* 85:61–65.

Sakenfeld, K. 1978. *The Meaning of Hesed in the Hebrew Bible*. HSMS 17. Missoula, Mont.: Scholars Press. Pp. 54–58.

Standaert, B. 1996. "Adonai Shalom (Judges 6–9): The Persuasive Means of a Narrative and the Strategies of Inculturation of Yahwism in Context." In *Rhetoric, Scripture and Theology*. JSNT Supplement 131. Ed. S. E. Porter and T. H. Olbricht. Sheffield: Sheffield Academic Press. Pp. 195–202.

Tanner, J. P. 1992. "The Gideon Narrative as the Focal Point of Judges." *BSac* 149:141–61.

Zakovitch, Y. 1985. "Assimilation in Biblical Narratives." In *Empirical Models for Biblical Criticism*. Ed. J. H. Tigay. Philadelphia: University of Pennsylvania Press. Pp. 192–95.

Judges 9:1–57 (Abimelech)

Boogart, T. A. 1985. "Stone for Stone: Retribution in the Story of Abimelech and Shechem." *JSOT* 32:45–56.

Campbell, E. F., Jr. 1983. "Judges 9 and Biblical Archaeology." In *The Word of the Lord Shall Go Forth: Essays in Honor of David Noel Freedman in Celebration of His Sixtieth Birthday*. Ed. C. L. Myers and M. O'Connor. Winona Lake, Ind.: Eisenbrauns. Pp. 263–71.

Crown, A. D. 1961–1962. "A Reinterpretation of Judges IX in the Light of Its Humour." *Abr Nahrain* 3:90–98.

Fokkelman, J. P. 1992. "Structural Remarks on Judges 9 and 19." In *Sha'arei Talmon: Studies in the Bible, Qumran and the Ancient Near East Presented to Shemaryahu Talmon*. Ed. M. Fishbane and E. Tov. Winona Lake, Ind.: Eisenbrauns. Pp. 33–45.

Halpern, Baruch. 1978. "The Rise of Abimelek ben-Jerubbaal." *HAR* 2:67–100.

Janzen, J. G. 1987. "A Certain Woman in the Rhetoric of Judges 9." *JSOT* 38:33–37.

Lindars, B. 1973. "Jotham's Fable—A New Form-Critical Analysis." *JTS* 24:355–66.

Maly, E. 1960. "The Jotham Fable—Anti-Monarchical?" *CBQ* 22:299–305.

Ogden, G. S. 1995. "Jotham's Fable: Its Structure and Function in Judges 9." *BT* 46:301–8.

Vater Solomon, Ann M. 1985. "Fable." In *Saga, Legend, Tale, Novella, Fable: Narrative Forms in Old Testament Literature*. JSOT Supplement 35. Ed. G. W. Coats. Sheffield: JSOT Press. Pp. 114–25.

Judges 10:1–5; 12:8–15 (the Minor Judges)

Hauser, A. J. 1975. "'The Minor Judges'—A Re-evaluation." *JBL* 94:190–200.

Mullen, T. E., Jr. 1982. "The 'Minor Judges': Some Literary and Historical Considerations." *CBQ* 44:185–201.

Stone, Lawson G. 1988. "From Tribal Confederation to Monarchic State: The Editorial Perspective of the Book of Judges." Ph.D. diss. Yale University. Pp. 383–85.

Judges 10:6–12:7 (Jephthah)

Bal, M. 1989. "Between Altar and Wandering Rock: Toward A Feminist Theology." In *Anti-Covenant: Counter-Reading Women's Lives in the Hebrew Bible*. JSOT Supplement 81; Bible and Literature Series 22. Ed. M. Bal. Sheffield: Almond. Pp. 211–32.

———. 1990. "Dealing with Women: Daughters in the Book of Judges." In *The Book and the Text: The Bible and Literary Theory*. Ed. R. Schwartz. Oxford: Blackwell. Pp. 16–39.

Claasens, L. J. M. 1996. "Notes on Characterisation in the Jephtah Narrative." *JNSL* 22:107–15.

———. 1997. "Theme and Function in the Jephthah Narrative." *JNSL* 23:203–19.

Courtledge, T. W. 1992. *Vows in the Hebrew Bible and in the Ancient Near East*. JSOT Supplement 147. Sheffield: JSOT Press. Pp. 175–85.

Culley, R. C. 1992. *Themes and Variations: A Study of Action in Biblical Narrative*. Atlanta: Scholars Press. Pp. 106–8.

Day, P. L. 1989. "From the Child Is Born the Woman: The Story of Jephthah's Daughter." In *Gender and Difference in Ancient Israel*. Ed. P. L. Day. Minneapolis: Fortress. Pp. 58–74.

Ellington, J. 1992. "More on *Shibboleth* (Judges 12:6)." *BT* 43:244–45.

Exum, J. C. 1988. "The Tragic Vision and Biblical Narrative: The Case of Jephthah." In *Signs and Wonders: Biblical Texts in Literary Focus*. Ed. J. C. Exum. Atlanta: Scholars Press. Pp. 59–83.

Fuchs, E. 1989. "Marginalization, Ambiguity, Silencing: The Story of Jephthah's Daughter." *JFSR* 5:35–45.

Gunn, D. M., and Danna N. Fewell. 1993. *Narrative in the Hebrew Bible*. The Oxford Bible Series. Oxford: Oxford University Press. Pp. 112–19.

Humphreys, W. L. 1989. "The Story of Jephthah and the Tragic Vision: A Response to J. Cheryl Exum." In *Signs and Wonders: Biblical Texts in Literary Focus*. Ed. J. C. Exum. Atlanta: Scholars Press. Pp. 85–96.

Kaiser, Walter, Jr. 1988. *Hard Sayings in the Old Testament*. Downers Grove, Ill.: InterVarsity. Pp. 101–5.

Marcus, David. 1986. *Jephthah and His Vow*. Lubbock: Texas Tech Press.

———. 1989. "The Bargaining between Jephthah and the Elders (Judges 11:4–11)." *JANES* 19:95–100.

———. 1990. "The Legal Dispute between Jephthah and the Elders," *HAR* 12:105–14.

———. 1992. "Ridiculing the Ephraimites: The Shibboleth Incident (Judges 12:6)." *Maarav* 8:95–105.

Mendelsohn, I. 1954. "The Disinheritance of Jephthah in the Light of Paragraph 27 of the Lipit-Ishtar Code." *IEJ* 4:116–19.

Milgrom, Jacob. 1990. *Numbers*. JPS Torah Commentary. Philadelphia: The Jewish Publication Society. Pp. 488–90.

Parker, S. B. 1980. "The Vow in Ugaritic and Israelite Narrative Literature." *UF* 11:693–700.

Reis, P. T. 1997. "Spoiled Child: A Fresh Look at Jephthah's Daughter." *Prooftexts* 17:279–98.

Swiggers, P. 1981. "The Word *šibbolet* in Jud. xii.6." *JSS* 26:205–7.

Trible, P. 1981. "A Meditation in Mourning: The Sacrifice of the Daughter of Jephthah." *USQR* 31:59–73.

———. 1984. "The Daughter of Jephthah: An Inhuman Sacrifice." In *Texts of Terror: Literary and Feminist Readings of Biblical Narrative*. Overtures to Biblical Theology. Philadelphia: Fortress. Pp. 93–116.

———. 1987. "A Daughter's Death: Feminism, Literary Criticism, and the Bible." In *Backgrounds for the Bible*. Ed. M. P. O'Connor and D. N. Freedman. Winona Lake, Ind.: Eisenbrauns. Pp. 1–14.

Judges 13:1–16:31 (Samson)

Alter, R. 1990. "Samson without Folklore." In *Text and Tradition: The Hebrew Bible and Folklore*. SBL Semeia Studies. Ed. S. Niditch. Atlanta: Scholars Press. Pp. 47–56.

Bal, M. 1987. *Lethal Love: Feminist Literary Readings of Biblical Love Stories*. Bloomington: Indiana University Press. Pp. 37–67.

Blenkinsopp, J. 1963. "Structure and Style in Judges 13–16." *JBL* 82:65–76.

Brooks, S. S. 1996. "Saul and the Samson Narrative." *JSOT* 71:19–25.

Brown, Raymond. 1977. *The Birth of the Messiah*. New York: Doubleday & Co.

Camp, C. V., and C. Fontaine. 1990. "The Words of the Wise and their Riddles." In *Text and Tradition: The Hebrew Bible and Folklore*. Ed. S. Niditch. Atlanta: Scholars Press. Pp. 127–51.

Crenshaw, James. 1974. "The Samson Saga: Filial Devotion or Erotic Attachment?" *ZAW* 86:470–504.

———. 1978. *Samson: A Secret Betrayed, A Vow Ignored*. Atlanta: John Knox.

Culley, R. C. 1992. *Themes and Variations: A Study of Action in Biblical Narrative*. Atlanta: Scholars Press. Pp. 108–9.

Exum, J. C. 1980. "Promise and Fulfillment: Narrative Art in Judges 13." *JBL* 99:39–59.

———. 1981. "Aspects of Symmetry and Balance in the Samson Saga." *JSOT* 19:2–29.

———. 1983. "The Theological Dimension of the Samson Saga." *VT* 33:30–45.

———. 1996. "Why, Why, Why, Delilah?" In *Plotted, Shot, and Painted: Cultural Representations of Biblical Women*. JSOT Supplement 215. Sheffield: Sheffield Academic Press. Pp. 175–231.

———, and J. W. Whedbee. 1990. "Isaac, Samson and Saul: Reflections on the Comic and Tragic Visions." In *On Humour and the Comic in the Bible*. JSOT Supplement 92; Bible and Literature Series 23. Ed. Y. T. Radday and A. Brenner. Sheffield: Almond. Pp. 117–59.

Freeman, James A. 1982. "Samson's Dry Bones: A Structural Reading of Judges 13–16." In *Literary Interpretations of Biblical Narratives II*. Ed. K. R. R. Gros Louis and J. S. Ackerman. Nashville: Abingdon. Pp. 145–60.

Fuchs, E. 1985. "The Literary Characterization of Mothers and Sexual Politics in the Hebrew Bible." In *Feminist Perspectives on Biblical Scholarship*. Ed. A. Y. Collins. Chico, Calif.: Scholars Press. Pp. 117–36.

Greenberg, M. 1983. *Biblical Prose Prayer as a Window to the Popular Religion of Ancient Israel*. Berkeley: University of California Press.

Greene, M. 1991. "Enigma Variations: Aspects of the Samson Story (Judges 13–16)." *Vox Evangelica* 21:53–79.

Greenstein, E. L. 1981. "The Riddle of Samson." *Prooftexts* 1:237–60.

Gunn, D. M. 1992. "Samson of Sorrows: An Isaianic Gloss on Judges 13–16." In *Reading between Texts: Intertexuality and the Hebrew Bi-

ble. Ed. D. N. Fewell. Louisville: Westminster/John Knox. Pp. 225–53.

Humphreys, W. L. 1985. *The Tragic Vision and the Hebrew Tradition*. Overtures to Biblical Theology. Philadelphia: Fortress. Pp. 68–73.

Kim, J. 1993. *The Structure of the Samson Cycle*. Kampen: Kok Pharos.

Margalit, O. 1985. "Samson's Foxes." *VT* 35:224–29.

———. 1986a. "Samson's Riddles and Samson's Magic Locks." *VT* 36:225–34.

———. 1986b. "More Samson Legends." *VT* 36:397–405.

———. 1987. "The Legend of Samson/Heracles." *VT* 37:63–70.

Mendenhall, G. 1973. *The Tenth Generation*. Baltimore: Johns Hopkins University Press.

Milgrom, Jacob. 1990. *Numbers*. JPS Torah Commentary. Philadelphia: The Jewish Publication Society. Pp. 43–50, 355–58.

Nel, P. 1985. "The Riddle of Samson (Judg 14, 14.18)." *Bib* 66:534–45.

Niditch, S. 1990. "Samson as Culture Hero, Trickster, and Bandit: The Empowerment of the Weak." *CBQ* 52:608–24.

O'Connor, M. 1986. "The Women of the Book of Judges." *HAR* 10:277–93.

Porter, J. R. 1962. "Samson's Riddle: Judges xiv. 18." *JTS* 13:106–9.

Reinhartz, A. 1992. "Samson's Mother: An Unnamed Protagonist." *JSOT* 55:25–37.

Sasson, J. M. 1988. "Who Cut Samson's Hair? (And Other Trifling Issues Raised by Judges 16)." *Prooftexts* 8:333–39.

Savran, G. W. 1988. *Telling and Retelling: Quotation in Biblical Narrative*. Bloomington: Indiana University Press.

Segert, S. 1984. "Paronomasia in the Samson Narrative in Judges xiii-xvi." *VT* 34:454–61.

van der Toorn, K. 1986. "Judges xvi 21 in the Light of the Akkadian Sources." *VT* 36:248–53.

Vickery, J. B. 1981. "In Strange Ways: The Story of Samson." In *Images of Man and God: Old Testament Short Stories in Literary Focus*. Ed. B. O. Long. Sheffield: Almond. Pp. 58–73.

Webb, Barry. 1995. "A Serious Reading of the Samson Story (Judges 13–16)." *RTR* 54:110–20.

Wharton, J. A. 1973. "Secret of Yahweh: Story and Affirmation in Judges 13–16." *Int* 27:48–66.

Judges 17:1–18:31 (the Levite and the Danites)

Amit, Y. 1990. "Hidden Polemic in the Conquest of Dan: Judges xvii-xviii." *VT* 40:4–20.

Davis, D. R. 1984. "Comic Literature—Tragic Theology: A Study of Judges 17–18." *WTJ* 46:156–63.

Greenspahn, F. E. 1982. "An Egyptian Parallel to Judges 17:6 and 21:25." *JBL* 101:129–30.

Malamat, A. 1970. "The Danite Migration and the Pan-Israelite Exodus-Conquest." *Bib* 51:1–16.

Noth, Martin. 1962. "The Background of Judges 17–18." In *Israel's Prophetic Heritage: Essays in Honor of James Muilenburg*. Ed. B. W. Anderson and W. Harrelson. New York: Harper & Brothers. Pp. 68–85.

Satterthwaite, P. 1993. "'No King in Israel': Narrative Criticism and Judges 17–21." *TynB* 44:75–88.

Spina, F. 1977. "The Dan Story Historically Reconsidered." *JSOT* 1:60–71.

Judges 19:1–21:25 (the Levite and the Concubine)

Amit, Y. 1994. "Literature in the Service of Politics: Studies in Judges 19–21." In *Politics and Theopolitics in the Bible and Postbiblical Literature*. JSOT Supplement 171. Ed. H. G. Reventlow, Y. Hoffman, and B. Uffenheimer. Sheffield: JSOT Press. Pp. 28–40.

Bach, A. 1998. "Rereading the Body Politic: Women and Violence in Judges 21." *BibInt* 6:1–19.

Culley, R. C. 1976. *Studies in the Structure of Hebrew Narrative*. Missoula, Mont.: Scholars Press. Pp. 54–59.

Currie, S. D. 1971. "Biblical Studies for a Seminar on Sexuality and the Human Community, I: Judges 19–21." *Austin Seminary Bulletin* 87:13–20.

Fokkelman, J. P. 1992. "Structural Remarks on Judges 9 and 19." In *Sha'arei Talmon: Studies in the Bible, Qumran and the Ancient Near East Presented to Shemaryahu Talmon*. Ed. M. Fishbane and E. Tov. Winona Lake, Ind.: Eisenbrauns. Pp. 33–45.

Hudson, D. M. 1994. "Living in the Land of Epithets: Anonymity in Judges 19–21." *JSOT* 62:49–66.

Keefe, A. 1993. "Rapes of Women/Wars of Men," *Semeia* 61:79–97.

Lasine, S. 1984. "Guest and Host in Judges 19: Lot's Hospitality in an Inverted World." *JSOT* 29:37–59.

Matthews, V. 1992. "Hospitality and Hostility in Genesis 19 and Judges 19." *BTB* 22, no. 1:3–11.

Niditch, S. 1982. "The 'Sodomite' Theme in Judges 19–20: Family, Community, and Social Disintegration." *CBQ* 44:365–78.

Penchansky, D. 1992. "Staying the Night: Intertexuality in Genesis and Judges." In *Reading between Texts: Intertexuality and the Hebrew Bible*. Ed. D. N. Fewell. Louisville: Westminster/John Knox. Pp. 77–88.

Revell, E. J. 1985. "The Battle with Benjamin (Judges xx 29–48) and Hebrew Narrative Techniques." *VT* 35:417–33.

Satterthwaite, P. E. 1992. "Narrative Artistry in the Composition of Judges xx:29ff." *VT* 42:80–89.

Stone, K. 1993. "Sexual Practice and the Structure of Prestige: The Case of the Disputed Concubines." In *SBLSP 1993*. Ed. E. H. Lovering Jr. Atlanta: Scholars Press. Pp. 554–73.

———. 1995. "Gender and Homosexuality in Judges 19: Subject-Honor, Object-Shame?" *JSOT* 67:87–107.

———. 1996. *Sex, Honor, and Power in the Deuteronomistic History*. JSOT Supplement 234. Sheffield: Sheffield Academic Press. Pp. 69–84.

Trible, P. 1984. "An Unnamed Woman: The Extravagance of Violence." In *Texts of Terror: Literary-Feminist Readings of Biblical Narratives*. Overtures to Biblical Theology. Philadelphia: Fortress. Pp. 65–91.

Wright, R. A. 1989. "Establishing Hospitality in the Old Testament: Testing the Tool of Linguistic Pragmatics." Ph.D. diss. Yale University. Pp. 135–36, 145–47, 182–97.

Ruth

If the New Testament has its parable of the good Samaritan (recorded only in Luke 10:29–37), the Old Testament has its parallel, the story of the good Moabite. Few Judeans in Jesus' day ever thought of any Samaritan as "good"; similarly, the first adjective that popped into the mind of an Israelite who thought "Moabite" more than likely was not "good."

The setting for the book of Ruth is "in the days when the judges ruled." That means anytime between Othniel of Judges 3 and Samson of Judges 13–16. Given that Ruth's husband, Boaz, is but three generations before David (Boaz > Obed > Jesse > David [4:21–22]), the story may be set in the latter portions of this period, a time, as we saw in our study of Judges, that Israel's unfaithfulness and disloyalty to the ways of Yahweh had mushroomed.

The pastoral calmness of Ruth contrasts vividly with the chaos and turbulence of Judges. Judges focuses on times of wars of conquest and liberation. Ruth focuses on times of peace, the kind of family events that take place during years of rest in the land. To a certain degree, the relationship between Judges and Ruth parallels that between Homer's *Iliad* (with its focus on war) and *Odyssey* (written thirty years later by Homer, and detailing Odysseus's postwar, ten-year homeward journey from the siege of Troy to his wife in Ithaca).

The eighteenth-century philosopher Thomas Paine, in his celebrated *Age of Reason*, while going overboard with his choice of some of the adjectives and adverbs, described Ruth this way: "The book of Ruth, an idle, bungling story, foolishly told, nobody knows by whom, about a strolling country girl, creeping slyly to be with her cousin Boaz. Pretty

187

stuff indeed, to be called the Word of God! It is, however, one of the best books of the Bible, for it is free from murder and rapine" (I take this quotation from a modern publication of this 1794 work. See Thomas Paine, *Age of Reason* [Secaucus, N.J.: 1991], 121). The "murder and rapine," so rampant throughout Judges, is, as Paine notes, absent in Ruth.

It is, of course, only in the Septuagint and Christian canon that Ruth comes between Judges and Samuel. In contrast, the Jewish canon places Ruth in its third and final section of canonical books, known as the "Writings." It is the first of five books in a subcategory of the "Writings" known as the "Megilloth" ("festal scrolls"). After Psalms, Job, Proverbs, the five occur in this (probably chronological) order: Ruth (the judges), Song of Songs/Solomon (youthful Solomon), Ecclesiastes (older Solomon), Lamentations (Jeremiah), Esther (postexilic Persian period).

The placement of Ruth between Judges and Samuel (by the way, the Christian canon also divides one book, Samuel, into two, First and Second Samuel) reinforces its role in legitimating the kingship of David. It does so in two ways (Jobling 1993: 131). First, its presence here produces three canonical books in sequence that end with a statement about monarchy:

> *Judges 21:25.* The urgent need for a king: "In those days there was no king in Israel; all the people did what was right in their own eyes."
> *Ruth 4:22.* David is the answer to that dilemma: "Obed of Jesse, and Jesse of David" (and the only biblical book whose last word is a personal name).
> *1 Sam. 31:1–13.* Saul's death and burial ends an interim monarchy and paves the way for the emergence of the everlasting existence of the house of David.

Second, the book of Ruth not only precedes First Samuel in the Septuagint and Christian canon, but historically it parallels it in that both are bookended by the judges' epoch at one end and the emergence of David at the other:

Ruth: The era of the judges <Ruth> David
First Samuel: The era of the judges <Samuel and Saul> David

Ruth gets us to David by means of an idyllic romance story featuring a Moabite heroine. First Samuel gets us to David by means of a protracted struggle between "Bishop" Samuel and King Saul, and the latter's fall from God's grace.

That Ruth's setting is the era of the judges in no way helps us to determine the date of its writing or the author. It is an exercise in futility to try to determine the author, whoever he or she may have been. The book's very anonymity compels the reader to focus exclusively on what is written rather than on who wrote it.

As for the possibilities of date, the spectrum ranges from as early as David's reign to some time after Judah's resettlement in Zion following captivity in Babylon (539 B.C.), possibly even into the next century, when the careers of Ezra and Nehemiah were in full swing. The most widely espoused date is during the reign of Solomon, that is, the latter portion of the tenth century B.C. (see Hubbard 1988: 23–35).

But even if Ruth was penned as early as the tenth century B.C., that is no guarantee that it was shortly thereafter given a wide hearing and the truth of its message started to trickle down into society. It is conceivable that the book was composed at an earlier date, but its use and acceptance came much later (Nash 1995: 353). One thinks, for an analogy, of Lincoln's Gettysburg Address and the gap between its composition and the subsequent recognition of its monumental significance.

There are five different geographical settings in Ruth, with the first two highlighting the theme of emptiness, and the last showing the transformation of emptiness into fullness (Gottwald 1985: 556).

Chapter 1	Chapter 2	Chapter 3	Chapter 4
Elimelech and his family journey to Moab (vv. 1–5).	Ruth meets Boaz as she gleans in his field in the daytime.	Ruth meets Boaz on the threshing floor at night.	Twelve men at the city gate of Bethlehem (vv. 1–12).
Naomi returns with Ruth to Bethlehem (vv. 6–22).			Boaz marries Ruth, who gives birth to Obed (vv. 13–17).
			A ten-generation genealogy ending with David (vv. 18–22).

Famine		Plenty
Barrenness	⟶	Fruitfulness
Isolation		Community

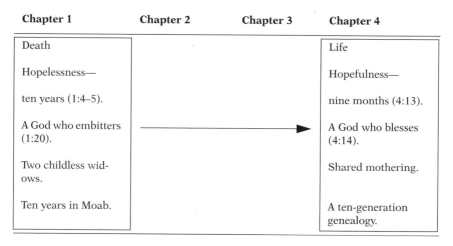

Chapter 1	Chapter 2	Chapter 3	Chapter 4
Death			Life
Hopelessness—			Hopefulness—
ten years (1:4–5).			nine months (4:13).
A God who embitters (1:20).		→	A God who blesses (4:14).
Two childless widows.			Shared mothering.
Ten years in Moab.			A ten-generation genealogy.

1:1–5. The reference at the opening of Ruth to a family from Bethlehem links Ruth with the end of Judges, which recounted two incidents of Bethlehemites: first, the Levite from Bethlehem (Judg. 17:7–13); second, the concubine from Bethlehem (Judg. 19:1–30). Together the stories form a "Bethlehem trilogy" (Merrill 1985: 131), with the third standing in bold contrast to the first two.

It is ironic for two reasons that a family from Bethlehem, because of a famine, should travel to Moab for food and sustenance. First, the very name "Bethlehem" means "House of Bread." But there is no "lehem" in "Beth-lehem." Beth-lehem has become "Bethraʿav" ("House of Famine"). Second, apart from all the other unsavory references to Moab throughout Scripture (e.g., Moab's origin is in an incestuous relationship between a drunken father and his firstborn daughter [Gen. 19:30–37], or the exclusion of Ammonites and Moabites from admission to the Israelite assembly even down to the tenth generation [Deut. 23:3–6]), we have the incident recorded in Numbers 25. Right after Balaam the diviner, much to the consternation of Balak king of Moab, has prophesied a great and noble destiny for Israel (Numbers 23–24), Israel participates with the women of Moab in the awful act of sin and apostasy at Shittim and Baal-peor. (The lofty predictions for the people of God in Numbers 23–24 do not match the behavior of the people of God in Numbers 25!). Part of that indulgence involved the Israelites eating (Num. 25:2) with the Moabites (Fewell and Gunn 1988: 103). So two times Israelites eat with Moabites on Moabite soil. First, Moab is a place of destruction; second, Moab is a place of salvation.

Already experiencing the distress of being a refugee, Naomi ("my pleasant one") additionally bears the pain of the death of a spouse.

Elimelech ("my God is king"), her husband, is dead. Can one still affirm that "my God is king" when "my-God-is-king" is dead and the surviving spouse is a refugee, an alien, and a woman? That pain will be exacerbated with the subsequent death of her two sons, Mahlon and Chilion. A woman who is already a refugee, an alien, and a widow now becomes childless as well. All that she has are her two Moabite daughters-in-law, Orpah and Ruth.

1:6–22. Upon hearing of the end of the famine back home and the restoration of food supplies, Naomi sets out to return from Moab to Bethlehem. In the process she tries to discourage her two daughters-in-law from accompanying her. What future is there for two Moabite childless widows on Judahite soil? Naomi's reference to the fact that she is too old to remarry and have sons who might in the distant future replace her deceased sons in the lives of Ruth and Orpah (vv. 11–13) is surely a veiled allusion to the institution of levirate marriage (a marriage between a childless widow and a brother of her husband), on which we will say more when commenting on chs. 3 and 4.

Naomi's words in 1:8–9 are one of six or seven prayers scattered throughout Ruth (Thompson 1993; Miller 1994). It is a prayer by a woman for Yahweh's blessing for two other women in a time of crisis. There are three interesting items about Naomi's prayer. First, it is one of the relatively few times in the Old Testament when one person invokes Yahweh's *khesed* (devotion, loyalty, kindness, mercy, favor) on behalf of others ("May the Lord deal kindly with you"). See also Gen. 24:12 ("O Lord, . . . show steadfast love to my master Abraham"), and 2 Sam. 2:6 ("And now may the Lord show steadfast love and faithfulness to you [the residents of Jabesh-gilead]"). Second, her prayer is that Yahweh's *khesed* for them will correspond to their *khesed* for her ("as you have dealt with the dead and with me"). Thus, in her prayer the actions of "these two female foreigners become a model for Yahweh" (Trible 1978: 170). Third, the rest of the book of Ruth is the outworking of this prayer of Naomi—the manifestation of Yahweh's *khesed* to a Moabite woman who follows her mother-in-law to Bethlehem. Little did Naomi recognize the ramifications of her brief prayer.

Orpah decides to take Naomi's advice and return to family and her religion ("your sister-in-law has gone back to her people and her gods" [v. 15]). She is not condemned for this choice, and Naomi is hardly evangelistic at this point. But Orpah is never mentioned again after this.

By contrast, Ruth chooses to "cling" to her mother-in-law. There are two interesting verbs in the first and last chapters of Ruth that are used in the Old Testament only in this book to define a relationship between two women. The first of these is "cling" (*davaq*). While this verb frequently appears in the Old Testament to describe an individual clinging to God, it appears only eight times in reference to one human clinging to another human (and four of these are in Ruth—1:14; 2:8 ["keep close to"] 2:21, 23 ["stay close by"]). The other four refer to an act of a male: a man leaves father and mother and clings to his wife (Gen. 2:24); Shechem is "drawn" to Dinah the daughter of Jacob (Gen. 34:3); Joshua forbids intermarriage with the women of those nations Yahweh left among Israel (Josh. 23:12); Solomon marries foreign women (1 Kings 11:1–3).

The balancing unique use of a common verb in Ruth 4, and corresponding to *davaq* in ch. 1, is the verb "love" (*ʾahav*) in 4:15 ("for your daughter-in-law, who loves you"). Ruth 4:15 is the only instance in the Old Testament where one woman is said to love another woman.

We also need to note that Ruth's now famous words to Naomi in vv. 16–17, which appear as poetry in most Bibles, record the commitment of a woman to a woman, a younger woman to an older woman, a daughter-in-law to a mother-in-law, a Moabite to a Bethlehemite. These two verses of Scripture are among the most popularly used in wedding ceremonies, and well they should be. But let us note that such use lifts the passage out of its original context. The passage is about Ruth and her commitment to a future with her mother-in-law rather than to a future with a husband. Trible (1978: 173) has noted that in many respects Ruth's leap of faith is greater than even Abraham's in Genesis. Unlike Abraham, Ruth breaks with her past and her home, and heads west to a new land without being told by God to do so, and without any promise of blessing from God such as Abraham received (cf. Gen. 12:1–3).

The response of Naomi to Ruth at this point is "She said no more to her" (v. 18b). Naomi's silence has been interpreted by some as Naomi's anger at Ruth (Fewell and Gunn 1988: 100), but more likely means that Naomi ceased trying to persuade Ruth not to go with her and consented to having Ruth return with her (Coxon 1989: 26).

There is no record of Naomi introducing Ruth to the people of Bethlehem (vv. 19–21), and so her second silence vis-à-vis Ruth. What we do have here is her lament, a request that the Bethlehemites no longer call her "Naomi" but "Mara" ["bitter one"] because "the Almighty has dealt bitterly [*marar*] with me." This statement represents "the nadir of the Ruth narrative" (Grant 1991: 431), with Naomi making the mistake that many loyal but hurting believers have committed: interpreting and trying to figure out God in light of our circumstances, rather than interpreting and trying to figure out our circumstances in light of God and his character.

Normally, a change of name means a change for the better: "No longer shall your name be Abram, but your name shall be Abraham" (Gen. 17:5); "You shall no longer be called Jacob, but Israel" (Gen. 32:28); "You are Simon son of John. You are to be called Cephas" (John 1:42); "I do not call you servants any longer . . . but I have called you friends" (John 15:15). Naomi's request is the opposite of that trend. Henceforth the pleasant one should be identified as the embittered one.

So for Naomi, Ruth has not done what Naomi wanted her to do (return to her own people/god), and God has done what Naomi did not want him to do. Perhaps paradoxically, she prays for Yahweh's kindness to Ruth and Orpah in their respective futures (vv. 8–9), while reflecting on God's painful treatment of her in her own past (vv. 20–21).

2:1–23. This chapter begins at Naomi's home (vv. 1–2), moves to Boaz's field (vv. 3–17), and finishes back at Naomi's home (vv. 18–22). It starts "at the beginning of the barley harvest" (1:22), in late April to early May, and finishes at "the end of the barley and wheat harvests" (2:23), sometime in June.

The beginning of barley harvest provides Ruth with the opportunity to go and glean in someone's field. Ruth's activities illustrate the law of Leviticus (19:9–10; 23:22) and of Deuteronomy (24:19–22) in operation regarding the legality of allowing the poor and the alien to glean in the fields at harvest time. Specifically, Lev. 19:9–10 specifies four gifts for the poor: two from the grain harvest (the unharvested edges of fields/vineyards, and the gleanings [v. 9]), and two from the vineyards (the fruit not yet mature and hence not to be stripped, and the fruit that has already fallen from the trees [v. 10]).

The second chapter of Ruth focuses on the second of these four, gleaning. At harvest time the harvesters would cut the stalks of grain with one hand while catching what was reaped with the other. Inevitably some would fall to the ground. This is what is meant by the gleanings—that which falls to the ground.

Ruth does this gleaning by herself. Naomi does not join her, and not necessarily because she is too old and feeble, for after all, was she not strong enough to make the return voyage (by foot?) from Moab to Bethlehem?

Verse 3 makes the interesting point that Ruth just "happened" to glean in a part of a field belonging to Boaz, a wealthy relative of Naomi. "Just happened?" we ask. Mere coincidence? As luck would have it? While some commentators (e.g., Sasson) downplay any theological significance here, most (e.g., Hals, Hubbard) find in 2:3 a major contribution to one of the book's key theological emphases, and that is its emphasis on the hidden, yet providential, hand of God that directs the movement of a Moabite widow.

Upon seeing Ruth in the fields and being unsure who she is, he asks this question: "To whom does this young woman belong?" (v. 5; NIV: "Whose young woman is that?"). For Boaz, a young woman is somebody who belongs to a man, is a man's possession (Trible 1978: 176, 183). He moves beyond that perception later in the narrative when, upon waking at the threshing floor, he asks of Ruth, "Who are you?" (3:9). "Whose are you?" versus "Who are you?"; ownership versus personal identity. The one sure place where ownership does take priority over identity is found in Paul's affirmation to the crew and passengers on board ship heading to Rome and caught in a savage storm at sea: "Last night an angel of the God *whose I am* and whom I serve stood beside me and said, 'Do not be afraid.'" (Acts 27:23–24 NIV).

Boaz urges Ruth to continue to glean in his field and to stay close to his young women (v. 8). He also orders the young men working his fields not to bother her (v. 9), using the verb "bother" (*naga*ʿ), which runs the range from "strike" (Gen. 32:26) to "touch" (Gen. 26:11) to "touch sexually, foreplay" (Gen. 20:6). Clearly, Boaz is concerned about Ruth's safety. But his counsel and warning may also betoken an immediate arousal of romantic attachment to Ruth.

Somehow Boaz already knows about Ruth's second-mile assistance and devotion to Naomi (v. 11). His source of information is not disclosed. There is, interestingly, no account of Naomi and Boaz ever meeting each other. Their only communication with each other is by proxy—Ruth. Boaz's words to Ruth about her leaving—"your father and mother and your native land and came to a people that you did not know before"—are very similar to those used of Abraham in Gen. 12:1. Their closeness to each other may even suggest that the narrator conceives of Ruth as a kind of "matriarch by adoption" (Alter 1981: 59).

How appropriate it is that right after Boaz meets Ruth (vv. 8–11) he prays for her (v. 12). And this Moabite damsel he affirms for seeking refuge under the "wings" (*kanaph*) of Yahweh, the God of Israel. At this point Ruth may know as little about the God of Israel as she does about the land of Israel. So far, from Naomi, she has received mixed signals on what kind of a God this Yahweh is. He is a blessing-with-kindness-God, yes (1:8–9); but he is also an embittering, void-creating, harsh, calamity-bringing deity (1:20–21). Now in Boaz's prayer she hears that this Yahweh is a rewarding God, one who honors acts of devotion and loyalty with appropriate acts of divine benefaction. One wonders if

Boaz knows (or hopes!) that he himself will be the reward Yahweh will supply.

After a meal with Boaz (v. 14), Ruth heads back to Naomi, carrying the results of her gleaning. It is only when Ruth tells Naomi that she has gleaned in the field of Boaz (v. 19) that Naomi speaks to Ruth for the first time about Boaz (v. 20). Why has she not mentioned him before, especially since he is rich, he is a relative, he has fields, it is harvest time, and she and Ruth are impoverished and hungry?

We can speculate. Is Naomi for one reason or another not particularly happy that Ruth has decided to come with her, for Ruth is now an albatross around her neck (Fewell and Gunn 1988: 101)? Is Naomi's silence about Boaz the narrator's way of adding tension to the story (Coxon 1989: 27)? Or, having been gone for ten years, does Naomi even know whether or not Boaz is still alive and still farming? Or, if we wish to pursue the parallel with Abraham back in v. 11, does Naomi simply give Ruth as few directives as possible ("Go, my daughter" [v. 2]), just as God gave Abraham minimal directives ("Go to a land I will show you")? Such a modicum of information calls for obedience and trust rather than looking for an address.

Naomi uses two phrases to describe Boaz's connection with her family. Boaz is "a relative of ours" and "one of our nearest kin" (NIV: "one of our kinsman-redeemers"). This second expression is the word *go'el*. The root is a key one in chs. 2–4 of Ruth. It occurs there no fewer than twenty-two times. The verb form (*ga'al*) appears eleven times (3:13 [4x]; 4:4 [4x]; 4:6 [3x]). The participle/noun form (*go'el*) appears nine times (2:20; 3:9, 12 [2x]; 4:1, 3, 6, 8, 14). The cognate noun *ge'ullah* ("redemption") appears in 4:6, 7. Since all but one of these twenty-two uses of this root appear in chs. 3–4, we shall reserve comment on its significance until then. Suffice it to ask here, What might Ruth, a Moabite, understand by this term when she heard Naomi use it the first time? While it is appropriate to show how this verb is used throughout Ruth in conjunction with the Torah's injunctions about land and kin redemption, which also use this root, it is hardly likely that this Moabite woman had been briefed on the technicalities of land redemption addressed in Lev. 25:25–26, or the technicalities of redemption of kin sold to a non-Israelite owner addressed in Lev. 25:47–55.

But because Naomi calls Boaz "one of *our* nearest kin" rather than "one of *my* nearest kin," she raises the hopes of both herself and Ruth. For the first time in a long while a light turns on in Naomi's life. Boaz—he is alive! He will be our savior! He will be our rescuer! God's *khesed* has come in the form of a *go'el*.

3:1–18. Three different scenes at three different times of day fill this chapter: (1) vv. 1–5, Ruth and Naomi at home late in the afternoon or early evening; (2) vv. 6–15, Ruth and Boaz at the threshing floor from evening until midnight and through the hours of the night; (3) vv. 16–18, Ruth returns to Naomi around dawn.

Naomi assumes the role of matchmaker (Berquist 1993: 31). She instructs Ruth to bathe and perfume herself and put on her best attire. This would be a change from Ruth's work clothes and sweaty appearance after the backbreaking work of gleaning in the fields. Nowhere does the text state that Ruth was beautiful, but her subsequent way of acting and speaking serve to emphasize Ruth as a beautiful subject rather than as a beautiful object (Landy 1994: 291).

Her mother-in-law further tells Ruth to station herself on the threshing floor, where Boaz at the end of the day and after mealtime will bed down for the night. Ruth is simply to uncover the feet of the sleeping Boaz and wait (v. 4). Presumably, Boaz is sleeping on the threshing floor rather than in his own bed and in his own home because the harvested grain has been transported to the threshing floor for winnowing. Boaz is there either to guard the produce against theft, or to engage in a ritual of thanksgiving to celebrate the end of the harvest, or possibly both. If it is the former, he is not particularly vigilant, for he is sound asleep!

Threshing floors do not get good "press" in the Old Testament. In 1 Kings 22:10, King Ahab of Israel and King Jehoshaphat meet together at the threshing floor, where four hundred prophets give them disastrous counsel on whether or not to attack Syria/Aram. However, Micaiah, the 401st prophet, delivers prophetic judgment on Ahab. Even closer to Ruth is Hosea's indictment of Israel, who has "played the whore. . . . You have loved a prostitute's pay on all threshing floors" (Hos. 9:1). And it was on a threshing floor that Gideon put his notorious test to God (Judg. 6:36–40). It is also possible that the threshing floor, like the "gate" to the city in Ruth 4:1, functions as a legal site where matters like the rights of widows might be raised (Matthews 1987: 29, 35).

Admittedly, the plan is full of risk. So much so, that later (v. 14) Ruth departs at dawn before her presence with Boaz during the night becomes public knowledge. It is not that Boaz is trying to hide anything. His concern is that the uninformed might jump to the wrong conclusion and misread the situation.

Since Boaz already knows about Ruth and Naomi and their circumstances (2:11), but for one reason or another has done nothing to alleviate those circumstances by approaching them as a go'el, Naomi (and

Ruth) will take the initiative. Ruth agrees fully with the plan (v. 5). In ch. 1 she had said, in effect, to Naomi who urged her to stay in Moab, "All that you tell me I will *not* do." Here she says, "All that you tell me I *will* do."

Ruth's word to the now awakened and startled Boaz is, after she identifies herself, "Spread your cloak over your servant, for you are next-of-kin" [*go˒el*] (v. 9). The expression "spread one's cloak over (a female)" occurs in Scripture only twice, here in Ruth 3:9 in reference to a human pair, and in Ezek. 16:8 in reference to God and Jerusalem personified as a nubile maiden ("I spread the edge of my cloak over you and covered your nakedness. I pledged myself to you and entered into a covenant with you . . . and you became mine"). The phrase clearly refers to marriage. Henceforth the woman is covered to all except her husband. The law in Deut. 22:30 expresses the illicitness of sexual relations of a son with the (former) wife of one's father as "uncovering/removing his father's garment." That is to say, the son is in violation of the law because he has seen nakedness that is reserved for his father.

The second part of Ruth's statement ("for you are next-of-kin") presents a bit of a problem. Boaz is to marry Ruth because he is her *go˒el*, her redeemer. Now in no Old Testament passage that deals with the responsibilities of a *go˒el* (Lev. 25:28–55) is marriage spelled out as one of those responsibilities. What a redeemer must do is redeem property that one of his kin who is in financial straits has sold (Lev. 25:25–28), or else redeem a kinsman who, in financial straits, sells himself to a non-Israelite (Lev. 25:47–55). The law knows also a Levite redeeming property from an Israelite (Lev. 25:32), and an Israelite redeeming property of a Levite (Lev. 25:33). (Intentionally, there is no *go˒el* for the indebted Israelite [Lev. 25:35–38], for "redemption" applies only to what is "sold," be it field or kin, not to mere indebtedness.)

A classic case of such redemption of property of a relative is found in Jer. 32:6–9. Jeremiah purchases/redeems the property of his cousin Hanamel, which is on the verge of being lost to the family. The difference between Jeremiah 32 and Leviticus 25 is that in the former, Jeremiah obtains the title deed to the property, whereas in the latter, the property is restored reasonably soon to the original owner. Or does the redeemer retain possession of the property until the jubilee (Milgrom 1995: 67)?

Even though Ruth calls Boaz *go˒el* and not *yavam* ("husband's brother, *levir*"), Boaz is not stunned by her request. He does not "correct her confusion" vis-à-vis her understanding of redemption and marriage. On the contrary, he prays for Yahweh's blessing on her, and says that her loyalty in seeking him out, rather than a younger man, is even a greater loyalty than Ruth demonstrated in her devotion to Naomi in ch. 1 (v. 10). Again, these words of Boaz may contain an allusion to levirate marriage, and not be purely romantic. That is to say, Boaz is commending Ruth for keeping herself available to him rather than pursuing marriage with a man outside their clan (Levine 1983: 105). So it would seem that while redemption and levirate marriage are two separate issues, they cannot be totally isolated from each other. Not only would levirate marriage provide a son for the childless widow, but it also would protect that same childless widow from social isolation and economic disaster. If Ruth does not illustrate the extension of levirate marriage beyond a biological one, then it may illustrate the extension of redemption to include support for a childless widow by the *go'el*.

Earlier Naomi had said, "I am *too old* to have a husband," and here Boaz commends Ruth for not going after *young* men. We need to be cautious, however, in reading too much into these age-qualifying adjectives, "old" and "young." Campbell (1975: 67) puts it well: "If usual Ancient Eastern procedure was followed, Naomi was probably married in her early to mid-teens, and had her two sons by the time she was 20. They in turn would have married by the time they were 15 or so, to girls a bit younger. Ten years of childless marriage for them would bring us to the mid-forties for Naomi. Given the rigors of life in ancient Palestine, that would be years enough, almost certainly, for her to have reached menopause. The storyteller will establish that Boaz and Naomi are of the same generation, and we can assume that Ruth was between 25 and 30 when the events in the story took place." If that is the case, ch. 3 pictures a meeting between a woman in her twenties and a man in his forties. Ruth is hardly guilty of raiding the geriatric ward!

Some commentators have wondered if anything more than just conversation happened between Ruth and Boaz during that night on the threshing floor. She asks him to marry her (in code): "spread your cloak over your servant." He accepts (in code): "I will do for you all that you ask." She uncovers his feet. She lies at his feet until morning. They are off by themselves. But it is the events of ch. 4 that put the cap on such speculation, for if there was sexual intercourse on the threshing floor and the relationship was consummated there and then, "the scene in the city [viz., ch. 4] would be fake" (van Wolde 1997: 21). And would Ruth have engaged in sexual congress, knowing there is another *go'el* more closely related to the family, as Boaz had told her (v. 12)?

At dawn Ruth returns to Naomi. The one place where the text quotes Ruth quoting Boaz to Naomi is not found earlier in the chapter: "He said, 'Do not go back to your mother-in-law empty-handed'" (v. 17).

And none of what Boaz actually said to Ruth or vice-versa is recapitulated. It is all subsumed under "then she told her all that the man had done for her" (v. 16). These words of the narrator about Ruth in 3:16b sound like another woman who has been alone with a man and then returned to her village to tell what happened: "The woman left her water jar and went back to the city. She said to the people, 'Come and see a man who told me everything I have ever done!'" (John 4:28–29).

4:1–12. For the first time in Ruth there is a scene with no women present. Ruth 4:1–12 is an all-male forum, eleven of them altogether, trying to decide legally the future of Elimelech's property. It is not clear whether the sudden appearance of the twelfth man (and the closer redeemer) is planned or just happens (just as earlier Ruth "happened" into Boaz's field).

Boaz introduces this closer redeemer as "friend" (NRSV; NIV). The Hebrew is *peloni 'almoni*, which cannot mean "friend." Many commentators render something like "Mr. So-and-So." Perhaps it is the Hebrew equivalent of "John Doe" (Pardes 1992: 107). That the closer redeemer is denied a personal name and identity may be the narrative's way of pronouncing a condemnation upon him for withdrawing from his (levirate/*go'el*) responsibilities.

In speaking earlier to Ruth, Boaz had used language reminiscent of the levirate law of Deuteronomy 25:5–10. His words to her in 3:13, "if he is not willing [*khapats*]," are exactly the same as Deut. 25:7, "but if the man is not willing [*khapats*]." But in speaking to the man directly he does not use this expression, possibly out of respect for his relative and his desire to preserve harmony in a moment of tension (Brin 1994: 59).

When informed that on the day when he redeems Elimelech's property from Naomi he also acquires Ruth (v. 5), the closer redeemer backs off and says, "I cannot redeem it" (v. 6). The verb used for avoiding levirate responsibilities in Deut. 25:7 and Ruth 3:11 is "not willing." Here, the closer redeemer uses the verb "cannot" (*yakol*); that is, he uses the argument of inability rather than of unwillingness. He feels that he cannot do so for it would damage his own inheritance, and so he backs off at acquiring Ruth as part of a package deal. (By the way, the use of the verb "purchase" [*qana*] with "wife" as object in 4:5, 10, is not designed to reduce women to mere property. The choice of the verb here is stylistic and not technical, as noted by Levine [1983: 101].) (Note that later [v. 13] the text simply says, "So Boaz took Ruth," using one of the standard verbs for marriage [*laqakh*]. It does not say, "So Boaz purchased Ruth.") In whatever way taking Ruth would damage his own inheritance, this unnamed man marks himself as dramatically different from Ruth in their respective scale of values. For Ruth, loyalty (*khesed*) stands head and shoulders over everything else. For this person, loyalty is expendable, especially when it may mean sacrifice.

A crowd larger than the ten elders ("all the people who were at the gate") witnesses the decision, and to Boaz they wish a fertile future, using a double simile, and with the content of each drawn from Genesis: "May the Lord make the woman who is coming into your house like Rachel and Leah" (v. 11); "May your house be like the house of Perez whom Tamar bore to Judah" (v. 12).

In the first simile, two women, Rachel and Leah, in a sense notorious rivals, are spoken of in what is the one place in the Old Testament where "matriarchs are called up from the past to serve as a model for future building" (Pardes 1992: 98).

The second simile points to the incident in Genesis 38 involving Judah, his three sons, and his daughter-in-law Tamar, by whom Judah fathers two (grand)sons, Perez and Zerah. In fact, there are a number of similarities between the book of Ruth and Genesis 38 (see, among others, the study of van Wolde 1997):

Genesis 38	Ruth
1. Judah separates from his brothers	1. Elimelech separates from his kin
2. Judah marries a Canaanite	2. Boaz marries a Moabite
3. Death of spouse and two sons	3. Death of spouse and two sons
4. In-law child urged to return to her father's house (v. 11)	4. In-law child urged to return to her mother's house (1:8)
5. Onan willing to have sex with Tamar, but not willing to inseminate her (v. 9)	5. Closer redeemer willing to acquire the land, but not willing to acquire Ruth (4:6)
6. Tamar takes bold initiatives	6. Ruth takes bold initiatives
7. Through such intiatives Tamar achieves the purpose of the levirate with one who was not her *levir* (her father-in-law)	7. Through such initiatives Ruth achieves the purpose of the levirate with one who was not her *levir* (a relative [cousin?] of her father-in-law)
8. Judah praises Tamar (v. 26)	8. Boaz praises Ruth (3:11)
9. Tamar produces a messianic child (Perez)	9. Ruth is the great-grandmother of the messianic child David

10. The use of the verb *nakar* ("recognize, take note of") in vv. 25, 26	10. The use of *nakar* ("recognize, take note of") in 2:10, 19
11. Chapter 38 interrupts the flow of the Joseph story, with 39:1 picking up where 37:36 left off	11. The book of Ruth interrupts the flow of the story from the judges to Samuel

One can go back further in the Old Testament than even Genesis 38 for connections with the Ruth story, and that would be the Lot story that is spread over Genesis 13–19. Lot is the ancestor of Ruth (a Moabite), and Judah is the ancestor of Boaz. All three stories feature a widow or daughter(-in-law) who seizes the initiative: Lot's daughters, who get him drunk, then have sex with him in a cave; Tamar, who disguises herself as a prostitute and has sex with her sheep-farming father-in-law, Judah; Ruth, who approaches Boaz in the darkness of the night, sleeps at his feet, and ends up marrying him in a society that operates with laws and customs. As Frisch (1982: 434) has pointed out, there is a moral advance in each of these three stories when they are placed side-by-side, from (1) the morally objectionable to (2) the morally questionable to (3) the morally sanctioned.

4:13–17. Boaz, at least according to the book of Ruth, becomes for the first time a husband and a father, and not just redeemer. (There is a tradition in the Babylonian Talmud, *Baba Batra* 91a, that Boaz was married, but his wife died on the very day Ruth arrived back in Bethlehem with Naomi.) Ruth becomes for the first time a mother. Naomi becomes for the first time a grandmother and foster mother. The child is named "Obed," which means "worker, worshiper," and contains the same root as that in the name of the prophet Obadiah. The baby's name, given not by the parents or by Naomi but by the neighborhood women, is a "celebration of the work, service, devotion to God of Naomi and Ruth" (Feeley-Harnik 1990: 174).

Interestingly, the women talk only to Naomi. The baby's biological parents are not present. Ruth is not identified by name but by relationship ("your daughter-in-law"), by her affection for Naomi ("who loves you"), and by her worth to Naomi ("who is more to you than seven sons"). Of this last phrase, Campbell (1975: 168) astutely says, "What more appropriate way to praise Ruth than to say she is worth seven times what the story has made such an absorbing concern—a son!" The women's words to Naomi about Ruth are very similar to words found in the very next chapter of the Old Testament (Elkanah's words to Hannah about himself): "Am I not more to you than ten sons?" (1 Sam. 1:8).

Not only because of any legal requirement but because of her devotion to Naomi, Ruth will share parenting responsibilities in the raising of Obed. Obed will have a foster mother who is his legal mother (Naomi) and a biological mother (Ruth). In this sense the text can say, "A son has been born to Naomi" (v. 17). (By the way, the phrase "a son/ child is/was born to X" is used elsewhere always of the father: Abraham [Gen. 17:17; 21:5]; David [2 Sam. 3:2, 5; 12:14; 1 Chron. 3:1; 22:9]; Job [Job 1:2]; Hezekiah [Isa. 39:7]; Hilkiah, father of Jeremiah [Jer. 20:15]. See Exum 1996: 169.) Naomi is grandmother, legal mother, foster mother, and nanny to Obed. No wonder she took the child and pressed him against her bosom (v. 16a). One can imagine Naomi, like Simeon who took another child in his arms and blessed God (Luke 2:28), saying, "Master, now you are dismissing your servant in peace . . . for my eyes have seen your salvation."

4:18–22. The book of Ruth ends with a ten-generation genealogy in which Boaz and David occupy the critical seventh and tenth positions respectively:

1. Perez
   ↓
2. Hezron
   ↓
3. Ram
   ↓
4. Amminadab
   ↓
5. Nahshon
   ↓
6. Salmon
   ↓
7. Boaz
   ↓
8. Obed
   ↓
9. Jesse
   ↓
10. David

While scholarly arguments abound about the originality or secondary nature of this genealogy (see Hubbard 1988: 15–21), it fits in well with what has immediately preceded. For example, by ending the book with David (the only biblical book that ends with a personal name), the writer has shown how admirably the prayers of the women were answered. They had prayed not just for a child but for one whose name would "be renowned in Israel" (v. 14c). Who fulfills that better than David?

But there is a problem here. Both 4:17 and 4:18–22 designate David as the great-grandson of Ruth, a Moabite. How is that reality to be squared with the law of Deut. 23:3, which states, "No Ammonite or Moabite shall be admitted to the assembly of the Lord. Even to the tenth generation, none of their descendants shall be admitted to the assembly of the Lord"?

Two crucial kings in the Old Testament traced their respective ancestry to these two excluded peoples: David (descended from Ruth the Moabite), and his grandson Rehoboam, the founder of the Judean monarchy, whose mother was Naamah the Ammonite (1 Kings 14:31). In the Babylonian Talmud there is an attempt by the rabbis to square the two. The Mishnah, which forms part of the Talmud, is arranged in six "orders," which in turn are divided into "tractates." The third of these six orders is called "Nashim" ("Women"), and its first of seven tractates is "Yebamoth" ("Sisters-in-law").

In the Babylonian Talmud (*Yebamoth* 63a) we encounter this concern in the following words: "R. Eleazar further stated: 'What is meant by the text, *And in thee shall the families of the earth be blessed?* The Holy One, blessed be He, said to Abraham, I have two godly shafts to engage on you: Ruth the Moabitess and Naamah the Ammonitess.'"

A little later the Mishnah (*Yebamoth* 76b) makes the legal ruling that the prohibition on Moabites and Ammonites in Deut. 23:3 applies to males and not to females ("their women, however, are permitted at once"). To that legal interpretation the Talmud supplies the following homiletical/haggadic commentary (*Yebamoth* 77a): "Raba made the following exposition: What was meant by *Thou hast loosed my bonds* [Ps. 116:6]! David said to the Holy One, blessed be He, 'O Master of the world! Two bonds were fastened on me; and you loosed them: Ruth the Moabitess and Naamah the Ammonitess.'" (I take my quotations from *The Babylonian Talmud: Seder Nashim*, [London: 1936], 1:420, 516, 519. See also Milgrom 1982: 174.)

There is only one mention of Ruth in the New Testament, and that is in v. 5 of Matthew's genealogy of Jesus (Matt. 1:1–17). She joins Tamar, Rahab, Bathsheba, and Mary in the line of Jesus' ancestors. While the inclusion of women in a genealogy is not unheard of, it is rare.

Why these four from the Old Testament and Mary? Why not Sarah, Rebekah, Rachel, and Leah? Two suggestions are among the most likely. Because all these women were not only sinners, but sinners who engaged in sexual sin or what might be interpreted as sexual sin, their inclusion here accomplishes two things. First, it underscores the ministry of Jesus as savior of all kinds of sinners. Second, these four Old Testament women become prototypes of Mary, who conceived a child apart from her husband. It is as if Matthew is saying to the "critics" of his presentation of Mary's virginal conception (i.e., a cover-up for an act of fornification), "You criticize Mary. But look at your own history. What about the likes of Tamar, Rahab, Ruth, and Bathsheba?" But if that is Matthew's point, it appears that he is almost agreeing with the critics, and thus, unintentionally, calling into question Mary's faithfulness and Jesus' legitimacy.

More likely, Matthew, by including these women, all of whom were Gentiles (Bathsheba by virtue of her marriage to Uriah the Hittite), is saying something about the scope of Jesus' messianic ministry. All people, Jew and non-Jew alike, are welcomed in Messiah's kingdom, a kingdom over which Jesus alone is king.

Accordingly, both the book of Ruth and Matthew's genealogy of Jesus affirm three truths (cf. Gage 1989: 373–75): (1) the particularity of the Gospel story: Ruth, through confession and marriage, becomes more than an alien Moabite on Judahite soil; she joins the family of God, and Jesus is the crown and climax of that family; (2) the universality of the Gospel story: none are excluded on the basis of ethnicity, language, geography, or gender; entrance into God's family is not by face or race, but by grace; (3) the mystery of the Gospel story: God's sovereign plan is often implemented through the most unlikely events and people. To those who say, "How odd of God to choose a Jew!" this tiny book of the Bible responds, "How odd of God to choose a Moabite!"

Bibliography (Ruth)

Commentaries and Major Studies

Atkinson, D. 1983. *The Wings of Refuge: The Message of Ruth*. The Bible Speaks Today. Downers Grove, Ill.: InterVarsity.

Brenner, A., ed. 1993. *A Feminist Companion to Ruth*. The Feminist Companion to the Bible 3. Sheffield: JSOT Press.

Campbell, Edward F. 1975. *Ruth*. Anchor Bible 7. Garden City, N.Y.: Doubleday.

Caspi, M. M., and R. S. Havrelock. 1996. *Women on the Biblical Road: Ruth, Naomi, and the Female Journey*. Lanham, Md.: University Press of America.

Cundall, A. E., and Leon Morris. 1968. *Judges and Ruth: Introduction and Commentary*. Tyndale Old Testament Commentaries. Downers Grove, Ill.: InterVarsity. Pp. 217–318.

Fewell, D. N., and D. M. Gunn. 1990. *Compromising Redemption: Relating Characters in the Book of Ruth*. Literary Currents in Biblical Interpretation. Louisville: Westminster/John Knox.

Gow, M. G. 1992. *The Book of Ruth: Its Structure, Theme and Purpose*. Leicester: Apollos.

Hals, Ronald M. 1969. *The Theology of the Book of Ruth*. Philadelphia: Fortress.

Hubbard, Robert L., Jr. 1988. *The Book of Ruth*. New International Commentary on the Old Testament. Grand Rapids: Eerdmans.

Kates, J. A., and G. T. Reimer, eds. 1994. *Reading Ruth: Contemporary Women Reclaim a Sacred Story*. New York: Ballentine.

Levine, E. 1973. *The Aramaic Version of Ruth*. Analecta Biblica 58. Rome: Pontifical Biblical Institute.

Nielsen, Kirsten. 1997. *Ruth, A Commentary*. Old Testament Library. Louisville: Westminster/John Knox.

Sasson, Jack M. 1979. *Ruth: A New Translation with a Philogical Commentary and a Formalist-Folklorist Interpretation*. Baltimore: Johns Hopkins University Press.

Shorter Studies

Alter, Robert. 1981. *The Art of Biblical Narrative*. New York: Basic Books. Pp. 58–60.

Bauckham, R. 1997. "The Book of Ruth and the Possibility of a Feminist Canonical Hermeneutic." *BibInt* 5:29–45.

Beattie, D. R. G. 1974. "The Book of Ruth as Evidence for Israelite Legal Practice." *VT* 24:251–67.

———. 1978a. "Redemption in Ruth, and Related Matters: A Response to Jack M. Sasson." *JSOT* 5:65–68.

———. 1978b. "Ruth III." *JSOT* 5:39–48.

Berlin, A. 1983. *Poetics and Interpretation of Biblical Narrative*. Sheffield: Almond. Pp. 83–110.

———. 1988. "Ruth." In *Harper's Bible Commentary*. Ed. J. L. Mays. San Francisco: Harper & Row. Pp. 262–67.

Bernstein, M. J. 1991. "Two Multivalent Readings in the Ruth Narrative." *JSOT* 50:15–26.

Berquist, J. L. 1992. *Reclaiming Her Story: The Witness of Women in the Old Testament*. St. Louis: Chalice. Pp. 141–53.

———. 1993. "Role Dedifferentiation in the Book of Ruth." *JSOT* 57:23–37.

Bertman, S. 1965. "Symmetrical Design in the Book of Ruth." *JBL* 84:165–68.

Brenner, A. 1983. "Naomi and Ruth." *VT* 33:385–97.

Brenner, G. 1990. "Readers Responding: An Interview with Biblical Ruth." *Soundings* 73:233–55.

Brin, G. 1994. *Studies in Biblical Law from the Hebrew Bible to the Dead Sea Scrolls*. JSOT Supplement 176. Trans. J. Chipman. Sheffield: JSOT Press.

Bos, J. W. H. 1988. "Out of the Shadows: Genesis 38; Judges 4:17–22; Ruth 3." *Semeia* 42:58–64.

Carmichael, C. M. 1980. "'Treading' in the Book of Ruth." *ZAW* 92:248–66.

Childs, Brevard. 1979. *Introduction to the Old Testament as Scripture.* Philadelphia: Fortress. Pp. 560–68.

Coxon, P. W. 1989. "Was Naomi a Scold? A Response to Fewell and Gunn." *JSOT* 45:25–27.

Davies, E. W. 1981. "Inheritance Rights and the Hebrew Levirate Marriage." *VT* 31:138–44, 257–68.

———. 1983. "Ruth 4:5 and the Duties of the *goʾel.*" *VT* 33:231–34.

Day, L. 1998. "Otherness and Gender in Biblical Short Stories." *HBT* 20:109–27.

Exum, J. C. 1996. "Is This Naomi?" In *Plotted, Shot, and Painted: Cultural Representations of Biblical Women.* JSOT Supplement 215. Sheffield: Sheffield Academic Press. Pp. 129–74.

Feeley-Harnik, G. 1990. "Naomi and Ruth: Building Up the House of David." In *Text and Tradition: The Hebrew Bible and Folklore.* Ed. S. Niditch. Atlanta: Scholars Press. Pp. 163–84.

Fewell, D. N., and D. M. Gunn. 1988. "'A Son is Born to Naomi!' Literary Allusion and Interpretation in the Book of Ruth." *JSOT* 40:99–108.

———. 1989. "Boaz, Pillar of Society: Measures of Worth in the Book of Ruth." *JSOT* 45:45–49.

Fisch, H. 1982. "Ruth and the Structure of Covenant History." *VT* 32:425–37.

Gage, W. A. 1989. "Ruth upon the Threshing Floor and the Sin of Gibeah: A Biblical-Theological Study." *WTJ* 51:369–75.

Gordis, Robert. 1974. "Love, Marriage, and Business in the Book of Ruth: A Chapter in Customary Hebrew Law." In *A Light unto My Path: Old Testament Studies in Honor of Jacob M. Myers.* Ed. H. N. Bream, R. D. Heim, and C. A. Moore. Philadelphia: Temple University Press. Pp. 241–64.

Gottwald, N. K. 1985. *The Hebrew Bible: A Socio-Literary Introduction.* Philadelphia: Fortress. Pp. 554–58.

Goulder, M. D. 1993. "Ruth: A Homily on Deuteronomy 22–25." In *Of Prophets' Visions and the Wisdom of Sages: Essays in Honour of R. Norman Whybray on His Seventieth Birthday.* JSOT Supplement 162. Ed. H. A. McKay and D. J. A. Clines. Sheffield: JSOT Press. Pp. 307–19.

Gow, M. D. 1984. "The Significance of Literary Structure for the Translation of the Book of Ruth." *BT* 35:309–20.

———. 1990. "Ruth Quoque—A Coquette? (Ruth 4:5)." *TynB* 41:302–11.

Grant, R. 1991. "Literary Structure in the Book of Ruth." *BSac* 148:424–41.

Green, B. 1982. "The Plot of the Biblical Story of Ruth." *JSOT* 23:55–68.

Greenstein, E. L. 1990. "On Feeley-Harnik's Reading of Ruth." In *Text and Tradition: The Hebrew Bible and Folklore*. Ed. S. Niditch. Atlanta: Scholars Press. Pp. 185–91.

Howard, D. M., Jr. 1993. *An Introduction to the Historical Books*. Chicago: Moody. Pp. 125–39.

Hubbard, R. L., Jr. 1989. "Theological Reflections on Naomi's Shrewdness." *TynB* 40:283–92.

Hunter, A. 1981. "How Many Gods Had Ruth?" *SJT* 34:427–36.

Hyman, R. T. 1983–1984. "Questions and Changing Identity in the Book of Ruth." *USQR* 38:189–201.

Jackson, G. S. 1994. "Naomi, Ruth, and Orpah." *TBT* 32:58–73.

Jobling, D. 1993. "Ruth Finds a Home: Canon, Politics, Method." In *The New Literary Criticism and the Hebrew Bible*. JSOT Supplement 143. Ed. J. C. Exum and D. J. A. Clines. Sheffield: JSOT Press. Pp. 125–39.

LaCocque, A. 1990. *The Feminine Unconventional: Four Subversive Figures in Israel's Tradition*. Overtures to Biblical Theology. Minneapolis: Fortress. Pp. 84–116.

Landy, F. 1994. "Ruth and the Romance of Realism, or Deconstructing History," *JAAR* 62:285–317.

Larkin, K. J. A. 1996. *Ruth and Esther*. Old Testament Guides. Ed. R. N. Whybray. Sheffield: Sheffield Academic Press. Pp. 17–56.

Levine, Baruch. 1983. "In Praise of the Israelite *Mišpāḥâ:* Legal Themes in the Book of Ruth." In *The Quest for the Kingdom of God: Studies in Honor of George E. Mendenhall*. Ed. H. B. Huffman, F. A. Spina, and A. R. W. Green. Winona Lake, Ind.: Eisenbrauns. Pp. 95–106.

Matthews, V. H. 1987. "Entrance Ways and Threshing Floors: Legally Significant Sites in the Ancient Near East." *Fides et Historia* 19, no. 3:25–40.

Merrill, E. H. 1985. "The Book of Ruth: Narration and Shared Themes." *BSac* 142:130–41.

Milgrom, Jacob. 1982. "Religious Conversion and the Revolt Model for the Formation of Israel." *JBL* 101:169–76.

———. 1995. "The Land Redeemer and the Jubilee." In *Fortunate the Eyes That See: Essays in Honor of David Noel Freedman in Celebration of His Seventieth Birthday*. Ed. A. B. Beck, A. H. Bartelt, P. R. Raabe, and C. A. Franke. Grand Rapids: Eerdmans. Pp. 66–69.

Miller, P. D. 1994. *They Cried to the Lord: The Form and Theology of Biblical Prayer*. Minneapolis: Fortress. Pp. 290–93.

de Moor, J. C. 1984. "The Poetry of the Book of Ruth." *Orientalia* 53:262–83.

———. 1986. "The Poetry of the Book of Ruth." *Orientalia* 55:16–46.

Moore, M, S. 1998. "Ruth the Moabite and the Blessing of Foreigners." *CBQ* 60:203–17.

Murphy, R. E. 1981. *Wisdom Literature: Job, Proverbs, Ruth, Canticles, Ecclesiastes, Esther*. Forms of Old Testament Literature. Grand Rapids: Eerdmans. Pp. 83–96.

Nash, P. T. 1995. "Ruth: An Exercise in Political Correctness or a Call to Proper Conversion?" In *The Pitcher is Broken: Memorial Essays for Gösta W. Ahlström*. Ed. S. W. Holloway and L. K. Handy. JSOT Supplement 190. Sheffield: Sheffield Academic Press. Pp. 347–54.

Ozick, C. 1987. "Ruth." In *Congregation: Contemporary Writers Read the Jewish Bible*. Ed. D. Rosenberg. New York: Harcourt Brace Jovanovich. Pp. 361–82.

Pardes, I. 1992. *Countertraditions in the Old Testament: A Feminist Approach*. Cambridge, Mass.: Harvard University Press. Pp. 98–117.

Prinsloo, W. S. 1980. "The Theology of the Book of Ruth." *VT* 30:330–41.

Rauber, D. F. 1970. "Literary Values in the Bible: The Book of Ruth." *JBL* 89:27–37. (Repr. in *Literary Interpretations of Biblical Narratives*. Ed. K. Gros Louis, J. Ackerman, and T. Warshaw. Nashville: Abingdon, 1974. Pp. 163–76.)

Rebera, B. A. 1992. "Translating a Text to Be Spoken and Heard: A Study of Ruth 1." *BT* 43:230–36.

Sasson, Jack. 1987. "Ruth." In *The Literary Guide to the Bible*. Ed. R. Alter and F. Kermode. Cambridge, Mass.: Belknap. Pp. 320–28.

Strouse, E., and B. Porten. 1979. "A Reading of Ruth." *Commentary* 67, no. 2:63–67.

Thompson, M. E. W. 1993. "New Life amid the Alien Corn: The Book of Ruth." *EvQ* 65:197–210.

Tigay, Jeffrey H. 1996. *Deuteronomy*. The JPS Torah Commentary. Philadelphia: The Jewish Publication Society. Pp. 482–83.

Trible, Phyllis. 1978. *God and the Rhetoric of Sexuality*. Overtures to Biblical Theology. Philadelphia: Fortress. Pp. 166–99.

———. "Ruth, Book of." *ABD* 5:842–47.

———. 1997. "Ruth: A Text in Therapy." *USQR* 51:33–42.

van Wolde, E. 1997. "Texts in Dialogue with Texts: Intertexuality in the Ruth and Tamar Narratives." *BibInt* 5:1–28.

Weinfeld, M. 1971. "Ruth, Book of." *EncJud* 14:518–22.

1 Samuel

We can be fairly certain that originally First and Second Samuel formed one book. The division into two books may have been done early in the Christian era, but was anticipated by the Septuagint, the translation of the Hebrew Bible into Greek, in the pre-Christian centuries. The Septuagint (represented by the symbol LXX, the Roman numeral for 70) considered Samuel and Kings one unified composition called "The Book of Kingdoms." Hence, the four subparts of the Book are Kingdoms Alpha, Kingdoms Beta, Kingdoms Gamma, and Kingdoms Delta.

The Latin Vulgate followed the LXX at this point, except that it changed "Kingdoms" to "Kings" and used Roman numerals instead of letters of the Greek alphabet: I Kings; II Kings; III Kings; IV Kings. This practice is still followed by some Roman Catholic Bibles.

A Hebrew manuscript from the 1400s A.D., undoubtedly relying on a much older precedent, divides Samuel into two books. This division was adopted by the famous Bomberg Bible of 1517 and by all subsequent Protestant Bibles.

The point in the biblical narrative where the story is divided into two different books is, admittedly, strange, but not without rhyme or reason. For example, it is somewhat unexpected that the story of King David does not end in the last chapter of Second Samuel, but rather in the second chapter of First Kings, after Solomon has ascended the throne. Or again, Saul's death is recorded in the last chapter of First Samuel. But then there follows another "account" of his death in 2 Sam. 1:1–16 and David's elegy over Saul and Jonathan (2 Sam. 1:17–27). Most likely, the commencement of Second Samuel with material primarily about Saul is intended to shift the focus, even of Saul's death, to the figure of David (Childs 1979: 272). What does Saul's demise mean for David not only in terms of opportunity, but also in terms of his own feelings for his predecessor?

It is interesting that the next two books after Ruth bear the name "Samuel." He certainly cannot be the author of them, for his death is recorded in 1 Sam. 25:1. Again of interest, Samuel, now old and gray, delivers his last words in 1 Sam. 12:1–25 (like Moses in Deut. 31:1–8 and Joshua in Josh. 24:1–28), but he goes on living until 1 Sam. 25:1, some years later! Certainly, Samuel must be responsible for some of the material in First Samuel. We can adduce that from 1 Chron. 29:29, which says, "Now the acts of King David, from first to last, are written in the records of the seer Samuel," and from 1 Sam. 10:25 which says, "Samuel told the people the rights and duties of the kingship; and he wrote them in a book."

If Samuel's primary connection with the book(s) that bears his name is not authorship, then that primary connection must be the monumental spiritual stature of Samuel and the far-reaching shadow of influence he cast over his own generation and generations to come. Judging from Jer. 15:1 ("Though Moses and Samuel stood before me"), one concludes that these two men are the two great spiritual forces of premonarchic Israel. One finds a possible similar coupling in the words of the eighth-century prophet Hosea: "By a prophet [Moses] the Lord brought Israel up from Egypt, and by a prophet [Samuel?] he was guarded" (Hos. 12:13).

Several factors underscore Samuel's significance. First, he bridges the transition from Israel's confederacy in the days of the judges to monarchy. Second, in conjunction with the first, he bridges the gap between the former charismatic age and the forthcoming prophetic era. Third, he bridges the gap between an exclusively entrenched hierarchy of religious functionaries—the priests—and an upsurge of prophetic spiritual leaders. History is replete with the ongoing struggle in religious communities between hierarchy and charism.

In the opening chapters of First Samuel we find the established clergy (the house of Eli) replaced by a new leader (Samuel) from the ranks of the laity (Albright 1963: 44). For similar movements, one thinks of the Essenes, who turned their back on a corrupt Jerusalem priesthood; or the Pharisees, who began preparing teachers/rabbis to replace priests as leaders of the community; or the Lutherans and Calvinists ordaining pastors instead of priests; or John Wesley, a Tory Anglican, ordaining lay preachers; or parachurch movements, often led by laity and often having a much wider sphere of influence than main-line denominational ministries.

There seems to be a discrepancy about Samuel's tribal background. According to 1 Sam. 1:1, Samuel is from the tribe of Ephraim, one of the laic tribes. Yet, according to 1 Chron. 6:27–28 (see especially the NIV), he is a Levite from a family of singers. Is Samuel from a laic tribe or a clerical tribe? These two traditions may be harmonized by suggesting that though technically a layperson from the tribe of Ephraim, as a Nazirite devoted by his mother to service at the sanctuary in Shiloh and there performing Levitical functions, he may well have been considered by later genealogists as a Levite.

In one sense, what we call "First Samuel" could as well be called "The Book of Samuel and Saul." If Samuel occupies center stage in chs. 1–12, Saul occupies center stage in chs. 13–31. But Eli is present in the first portion of the book and David in the latter. Accordingly, we suggest a threefold division of First Samuel with a human pair in each division, usually in some kind of an adversarial relationship:

I.   1–7: Samuel and Eli (prophet versus priest)
II. 8–15: Samuel and Saul (prophet/archbishop versus king)
III. 16–31: Saul and David (king versus successor)

I. 1–7: Samuel and Eli

1:1–28. We owe to Brevard Childs (1979: 272–73) the observation about the significance of the placement of poems near the beginning (1 Sam. 2:1–10, the Prayer of Hannah) and end (2 Sam. 22:1–51; 23:1–7, the Song of David) of Samuel. It is as if these two poems, one sung by a woman, one sung by a man, act as bookends to Samuel. Both celebrate in thanksgiving form the faithful workings of Yahweh.

However, the Prayer of Hannah does not begin First Samuel, nor does the Song of David end Second Samuel. Preceding the Prayer of Hannah is the narrative about Samuel's birth and consecration, and how a barren wife is blessed with a child (1:1–28). And following the Song of David is the narrative about David taking a census (2 Sam. 24:1–25). At the beginning of this episode David appears as a proud, vain man glorying in his resources. By narrative's end David is reduced to contrition and penitence. Thus, Hannah in 1 Samuel 1 and David in 2 Samuel 24 are traveling in different directions: she from abasement to a position of honor; he from a position of honor to abasement.

Thus, if we should connect the poems that come near the beginning of First Samuel and the conclusion of Second Samuel, then we should also connect the narratives with which First Samuel begins and Second Samuel ends. They also are bookends framing the whole (Brueggemann 1990: 44).

First and Second Samuel

1 Sam. 1:1–28	1 Sam. 2:1–10	2 Sam. 22:1–51; 23:1–7	2 Sam. 24:1–25
narrative	poem	poem	narrative
barren woman	new mother responds	triumphant king gives	self-exalting king
blessed and	in thanksgiving and	thanks for victories	judged and
exalted	exalts God		abased

One can quickly see that Hannah's poem is an appropriate response to the narrative details of ch. 1 of First Samuel. The barren one becomes the doxological one. But the narrative of 2 Samuel 24 is not an appropriate sequel to the poems of 2 Samuel 22 and 23. The victorious, thankful one becomes the egocentric, self-exalting one.

First Samuel 1 falls into two basic parts: (1) vv. 1–8, which provide the necessary background information that follows in (2) the narrative of vv. 9–28. We are first introduced to Samuel's father, Elkanah, whose family tree is traced quickly back through four generations of Ephraimites. "The names in Elkanah's genealogy are important because of their unimportance" (Eslinger 1985: 67). Whatever later claim to fame Samuel may have, it is not because his ancestry is a biblical who's who.

Further, we are told he had two wives (not unlike many other men in the Old Testament), one of whom is fertile (Peninnah), and one of whom is barren (Hannah ["the gracious one"]).

Three people are particularly unhelpful and insensitive to Hannah. The first is her rival co-wife and provocateur, Peninnah, who taunted and insulted Hannah year after year (vv. 6–7). The second is her husband, Elkanah, who "hammers" (Fokkelman 1993: 31) her with four staccato questions (v. 8). His questions are not just probing but actually plaintive, especially his last one: "Am I not more to you than ten sons?"—as if to say, "Am I not all the men in your life you really need?"

The third culprit is Eli the priest, who interprets Hannah's silent praying, with only the moving of her lips, as drunkenness (vv. 13–14)—hardly an indication of pastoral sensitivity. To be sure, it would appear from other texts throughout the Old Testament that prayer recited aloud was the normal practice. (Interestingly, later Jewish practice urged that the faithful recite their central prayer, known as the ʿAmida or *Shemoneh ʿEsreh*, in a whisper, using Hannah's prayer as the model. See in the Babylonian Talmud *Berakot* 31a and in the Jerusalem Talmud *Berakot* 4:1.)

Hannah is capable of admonishing her "pastor" and setting him straight about the nature of her activities (vv. 15–16).

At the heart of all this is Hannah's vow (v. 11). It is in most ways like other biblical vows (see our discussion on pp. 144–45), but with one fundamental difference. All of the other vows we mentioned earlier went something like this: "If you [God] do such-and-such, then I will do such-and-such." Hannah's is a bit different. She says, "If you [God] give me so-and-so, I will give you back so-and-so." To put it a bit differently, the other vows say, "If you will do X, then I will do Y," in a sort of quid pro quo fashion (Polzin 1989: 24). But Hannah says, "if you will give me X, then I will give you X" (Fokkelman 1993: 29). This means, then, that Samuel is not only a gift from God, but also a gift to God (Walters 1988: 399).

A key word throughout this section is "ask," root *shʾl*. It occurs no fewer than nine times:

> v. 17: "Then Eli answered, '. . . the God of Israel grant your *asking* that you have *asked* of him.'"
>
> v. 20: "She named him Samuel, for she said, 'I have *asked* him of the Lord.'"
>
> v. 27: "And the Lord has granted me my *asking* that I *asked* of him."
>
> v. 28: "Therefore I have caused [or, 'lent'] him to be *asked* for by the Lord. All the days of his life he is the *asked-for* one [or, 'he is Saul/ *Shaʾul*']."
>
> 2:20: "Then Eli . . . would say, 'May the Lord repay you with children by this woman for the *asking* that she *asked* of the Lord.'"

Now several things may be noticed about the uses of "ask" in chs. 1 and 2. First, the name "Samuel" is not per se to be connected with the verb "ask." Samuel probably means something like "the name of God" or "his name is God." Second, what we have here is not a case of literal etymology, but alliterative etymology. That is to say, both "Samuel" and "ask" begin with the consonant *sh—shemuʾel, shaʾal—*just as both end with the letter *l*. Third, Hannah is not so much interested in explaining why she named the child "Samuel," as much as she is in proclaiming that this baby is a gift from God in divine response to petitionary prayer.

Fourth, we may notice that one more time in Samuel somebody asks God or his representative for something, and that is the occasion when the people "ask" Samuel to appoint a king over them (8:10; 12:13, 17, 19, all using *sha'al*). Polzin (1989: 24–25) creatively suggests that Hannah's asking God for a child is a parabolic foreshadowing of Israel asking Samuel (and God) for a king. Peninnah has sons; Hannah does not. Israel's neighbors have kings; Israel does not. Hannah appears drunk, but is not. Kingship appears inherently evil, but is not. Elkanah is worth more to Hannah than ten sons—or so he believes, and Yahweh is worth more to Israel than ten kings.

It is this connection between these two episodes that makes most sense out of Hannah's comments on her newborn's name. At first look they seem to explain more the name of "Saul" than of "Samuel." In fact, many scholars assert that ch. 1 actually describes the naming of Saul, which only later unadvisedly was transferred to Samuel.

There are two "asked-for" ones in this era in the Old Testament. There is the *sha'ul*, who is the son of Hannah, and later there is the *sha'ul*, who is the son of Kish. "An important and divinely acceptable Saul . . . will have already been at work for decades before the birth of the Benjaminite we know as king Saul" (Fokkelman 1992: 56).

2:1–10. It is not infrequent in Scripture to encounter a praiseful, poetic response by an individual on the heels of a gracious act by God. One thinks, for example, of the Songs of Moses and Miriam (Exod. 15:1–21) as a celebratory response to God's deliverance of Israel at the sea as the Egyptians pursued them, or of the Song of Deborah that celebrates Yahweh's victory over the Canaanites and their charioteers (Judg. 5:2–31). That is what we have here. God has given barren Hannah a child. Mother Hannah consecrates that child to God. Then she prays.

There are a number of significant items in her prayerful canticle. First, only a few of the phrases in the prayer appear to touch directly on Hannah's own circumstances. To whom might she be referring other than Peninnah when she says, "My mouth derides my enemies [plural!]" (v. 1)? When she proclaims in v. 5, "Those who were hungry are fat with spoil," this is surely a reference back to her own refusal to eat (1:7), and to her subsequent enjoyment of food and drink with her husband (1:18). And similarly, the reference to "the barren bearing seven" and the forlornness of she who has birthed many (v. 5) harks back to Hannah and Peninnah in ch. 1. Was it Peninnah whom Hannah had in mind in v. 3 when she says, "Talk no more so very proudly, and let not arrogance come from your mouth"?

There are, however, numerous other phrases that do not flow out of the narrative of ch. 1—for example, "the bows of the mighty are broken" (v. 4), or "the Lord kills and brings to life" (v. 6), or "for not by might does one prevail" (v. 9). The inclusion of such ideas tells us that 1 Sam. 2:1–10 is not simply Hannah's private prayer that we may read for curiosity and to discover how people "back then" prayed. Hannah's prayer has both specificity and universality, allowing her to pray it and allowing any of God's children to pray it.

Second, Hannah does not offer this prayer right after Samuel is born. If she had, the prayer would appear after 1:20 rather than after 1:28. She offers this prayer after she weans him, brings him to the sanctuary at Shiloh and presents him to Eli, and prepares to return to Ramah. The prayer at this point means that it is not simply a prayer of thanksgiving for the birth of Samuel, but for all she believes the child will be and for the ministry Yahweh will work through that child (Walters 1994: 75).

Third, the use of the first-person singular pronoun "I" and pronominal adjective "my" is confined to the first verse of the prayer. The pronouns or pronominal adjectives used subsequently are either about God ("you," v. 2; "our," v. 2; "he," vv. 6–10) or about other individuals ("your," v. 3; "those," v. 5; "she," v. 5). Hannah's autobiographical references give way to references about her God.

Fourth, the prayer makes not one petition (Clements 1985: 62). Hannah does not ask God for a thing. Her petitionary praying of ch. 1 has as its sequel in ch. 2 her doxological praying.

Fifth, the prayer has parallels and associations with other Old Testament passages. Hannah's prayer and Psalm 113 share some almost identical phrases. Compare her "He raises up the poor from the dust; he lifts the needy from the ash heap, to make them sit with princes and inherit a seat of honor" (v. 8) with Ps. 113:7–8, "He raises the poor from the dust, and lifts the needy from the ash heap, to make them sit with princes, with the princes of his people." Compare also her "There is no Holy One like the Lord, no one besides you" (v. 2) with Ps. 113:5, "Who is like the Lord our God?" Finally, note how her reference to the "barren" bearing seven (v. 5) parallels Ps. 113:9, "He gives the barren woman a home."

Parallels also are evident between Hannah's prayer in 1 Samuel 2 and David's song in 2 Samuel 22 (Polzin 1989: 33–34):

1 Samuel 2:1–10	2 Samuel 22
In the Lord my horn is lifted high (v. 1).	The Lord is . . . the horn of my salvation (v. 3).
My mouth derides	I am saved

1 Samuel 2:1–10	2 Samuel 22
my enemies (v. 1).	from my enemies (v. 4).
There is no rock like our God (v. 2).	My God, my rock, in whom I take refuge (v. 3).
The Most High will thunder in heaven (v. 10).	The Lord thundered from heaven (v. 14).
He will give strength to his king (v. 10).	He is a tower of salvation for his king (v. 51).
He exalts the power of his anointed (v. 10).	He shows steadfast love to his anointed (v. 51).

But while the Prayer of Hannah anticipates the Song of David, at least to a certain degree (there are some fundamental differences between the two), it also looks back to the Song of Deborah in Judges 5 (Jobling 1993: 27). Although the same vocabulary crossovers as in 1 Samuel 2 and 2 Samuel 22 are lacking, the basic theme in both is the same: the sweeping away and abasement of the powerful by mighty acts of Yahweh.

Sixth, the Prayer of Hannah resonates most clearly in the Song of Mary in Luke 1:46–55, known as the "Magnificat." Mary, the "maidservant" of the Lord (Luke 1:38), has "found favor" with God (Luke 1:30). When Hannah discovers, via Eli, that God will grant her petition for a son, she responds, "Let your maidservant find favor in your sight" (1 Sam. 1:18).

In one line, Mary says, "For he has looked with favor on the lowliness of his maidservant" (Luke 1:48). The Greek word used there for "lowliness" (*tapeinōsis*) is the same one that appears in the Septuagint text of 1 Sam. 1:11 when Hannah prays, "If only you will look on the misery [*tapeinōsis*] of your maidservant."

In fact, we may observe numerous parallels between Luke's account of the birth of John the Baptist and Jesus and the account of Samuel's birth (Brown 1979: index references under "Hannah" and "Samuel").

The Greek word for the "inn" (*katalyma*) that was unavailable to Mary and Joseph and their newborn (Luke 2:7) is the same word used in the Septuagint for the place where Elkanah and Hannah, the future parents of Samuel, stayed in Shiloh (1 Sam. 1:18; "quarters," NRSV).

Luke tells us that every year Jesus' parents went to Jerusalem for the festival of the Passover (Luke 2:41). This parallels the information about Samuel's parents, who also would go up year after year to worship and sacrifice to the Lord at Shiloh (1 Sam. 1:3; 2:19).

Mary, the mother, names her child (Luke 1:31), as does Hannah (1 Sam. 1:20). After his birth, Mary brings Jesus to the temple (Luke 2:22–24), where the parents are blessed by the elderly Simeon (Luke 2:25–35). While there, they also encounter an aged prophetess, Anna, who served God (Luke 2:36–38 [incidentally, "Anna" in the Greek text is *Hanna*]). Similarly, after his birth, Hannah brings Samuel to the sanctuary at Shiloh (1 Sam. 1:24–28). There Hannah encounters the aged priest Eli, who blesses Samuel's parents (1 Sam. 2:20). Also, 1 Sam. 2:22 refers to women who, like Anna, "served at the entrance to the tent of meeting."

Luke 2:39 informs us that when all the above was completed, Mary and Joseph "returned to Galilee, to their own town of Nazareth." Elkanah and Hannah do the same: "and then they would return to their home" (1 Sam. 2:20).

Finally, there is a twofold statement about Jesus: (1) "the child grew and became strong, filled with wisdom; and the favor of God was upon him" (Luke 2:40); and (2) "Jesus increased in wisdom and in years, and in divine and human favor" (Luke 2:52). This matches a twofold statement made about young Samuel: (1) "and the boy Samuel grew up in the presence of the Lord" (1 Sam. 2:21); and (2) "now the boy continued to grow both in stature and in favor with the Lord and with the people" (1 Sam. 2:26).

2:11–36. This section narrates in contrastive detail the emergence of young Samuel as one who ministers faithfully before Yahweh and the disappearance of the family of Eli, whose sons minister unfaithfully.

Samuel (v. 11)
sons of Eli (vv. 12–17)
Samuel and his family (vv. 18–21)
sons of Eli (vv. 22–25)
Samuel (v. 26)
sons of Eli (vv. 27–36)

The sons of Eli are condemned by the narrator (vv. 12–17), by their own father (vv. 22–25), and by a "man of God" (vv. 27–36). The narrator's condemnation and that of the anonymous man of God match each other in that both condemn the Elides for taking their portion of the animal sacrifice before God receives his portion on the altar, that is, the fat (vv. 16, 29 [esp. in the Septuagint]). In other words, the priests' working philosophy was "Me first, God second." Furthermore, the text is not talking about a one-time lapse. The majority of the verbs throughout 2:11–36 are in forms that describe habitual action. For the Elides, a slip had become a slide, a mistake had evolved into a pattern. An infraction had evolved into a modus operandi.

Three vocabulary items reinforce this contrast between Samuel and the brothers Hophni and Phinehas. First, twice Samuel is called a "boy," *na'ar* (vv. 11 and 18). The servant of Eli's sons (or maybe even the sons themselves) is also styled as "servant [boy] of the priest" (vv. 13, 15) or "young men, boys, lads" (v. 17). Thus, the text presents a ministering *na'ar* and an impious *na'ar*.

Second, twice the verb *gadal* is used to describe Samuel's growth and maturation, both physically and spiritually (vv. 21, 26). The same verb is used to describe the greatness of the sins of the sons of Eli: "Thus the sin of the young men was very great (*gedolah*) in the sight of the Lord" (v. 17). Samuel is growing in grace and the sons of Eli are growing in sin.

Third, the first word used by the narrator to describe Eli's sons is "scoundrels" (v. 12; "wicked" [NIV]). The Hebrew for this is *beliya'al*. It is the exact term used by Hannah in the preceding chapter in her response to Eli on her supposed state of drunkenness: "Do not regard your servant as a worthless [NIV, wicked] person" (1:16). Thus, the text depicts a godly mother who others think is wicked, but is not, and priests who think they are righteous, but are not.

Father Eli's concern is a bit different. He is informed of his sons "lying with the women who served at the entrance to the tent of meeting" (v. 22); cf. Exod. 38:8 for a reference to the female personnel who worked in the sanctuaries. That he is not himself aware of his sons' misbehavior is not an indictment of his own ineptness and insensitivity (Willis 1971: 292); rather, it reflects Eli's advanced age. He is pushing the century mark (4:15), and is just not connected into the daily goings-on about the sanctuary (Eslinger 1985: 123) (but see God's word in 3:12–14).

That Eli rebukes his sons in the next three verses (vv. 23–25) indicates his problem is not ineptness or callousness. For Eli, his sons' lecherous behavior is nothing less than a sin against God. Hence come his famous words in v. 25, which we may render thus: "If one persons offends against another, God will defend him; but if a person offends against Yahweh, who will undertake his vindication?"

The man of God goes further than either the narrator or the father. To words of rebuke he adds (1) a prophecy of the end and impoverishment of the house of Eli (vv. 27–34), and (2) a prophecy of a divinely raised-up faithful priest to take the place of the house of Eli (vv. 35–36). Historically, these prophecies are fulfilled a century or so later. In 1 Kings 2:27, 35, we read, "So Solomon banished Abiathar from being priest to the Lord, thus fulfilling the word of the Lord that he had spoken concerning the house of Eli in Shiloh. . . . And the king put the priest Zadok in the place of Abiathar."

But could the prophecy be fulfilled in Samuel himself long before Abiathar appears on the scene (Polzin 1989: 41)? Two elements reinforce this possibility. First, the same adjective (*ne'eman*) is used twice in 2:35 to refer to the "faithful" priest whom God will raise up and the "sure" house that God will establish for him. This same adjective appears in the next chapter in reference to Samuel: "And all Israel . . . knew that Samuel was a *trustworthy* prophet of the Lord" (3:20). It is a word that takes on the two related connotations of "trusted, reliable, faithful" and "secure, guaranteed." Second, Samuel works in the sanctuary precincts under the supervision of Eli, and he wears a "linen ephod" (v. 18; cf. King David in 2 Sam. 6:14). We know that the priests wore linen raiment when officiating at the sacrifices (Lev. 6:10). The high priest also wore linen on the Day of Atonement (Lev. 16:4). (For angels wearing linen, see Ezek. 9:2–3, 11; 10:2; Dan. 10:5.) The ephod, an apronlike garment covering the body from waist to thigh, was also worn by the priest (Lev. 8:7). And while we cannot be sure about the nature of the "robe" Samuel wore (v. 19), the word *me'il* for the priest's robe is described at length in Exod. 28:31–35 and 39:22–26. Jonathan wears one (1 Sam. 18:4), as do Saul (1 Sam. 24:5, 12) and even Samuel's spirit (1 Sam. 28:14).

3:1–4:1a. Unlike prophets whose divine call comes to them when they are doing something quite different (e.g., Amos, "the Lord took me from following the flock" [Amos 7:15], or Moses, working with his father-in-law's flock in Midian [Exod. 3:1]), Samuel receives his call when he is already in the sanctuary "ministering to the Lord under Eli" (v. 1). His status seems to be that of a novitiate or acolyte, and the verb for "minister" (*sheret*), used here and back in 2:11 and 2:18, is often associated with the Levites who serve under the supervision of the priests (Num. 8:26; 18:2; Ezek. 44:11–12, 16). Levites "serve/assist" while priests "approach the altar." In the rare time *sheret* is used of priests, it means "officiate" (Exod. 39:26).

The incident recorded in 3:1–4:1a has five parts (Fishbane 1982):

1. vv. 1–3: Samuel ministers in the midst of a paucity of divine words and visions.

2. vv. 4–9: Yahweh calls Samuel three times, but without success.
3. vv. 10–15: Yahweh gets through on the fourth try, and delivers to Samuel an oracle against the house of Eli.
4. vv. 16–18: Samuel transmits the substance of the oracle to Eli only upon Eli's insistence that Samuel conceal nothing.
5. vv. 3:19–4:1a: Yahweh confirms and all Israel affirms that Samuel is God's appointed prophetic spokesman.

The normal day-to-day operations of the religious aspect of worship and religion continue. The sanctuary at Shiloh has not shut down or ceased operations. Priests are there to take appropriate action with the sacrifices brought by the people. Only one thing is absent, or at least rare, and that is a word from God or a vision of/from God (v. 1). A beehive of religious activities, but no word from God and no vision of/from God! It is a time of ritual without experience.

Throughout the chapter there is an emphasis on a God who reveals himself visually (e.g., "the Lord came and stood there" [v. 10]) and verbally (e.g., "Speak, for your servant is listening" [v. 10]). Of further interest is that the emphasis on verbal revelation is greater than on visual revelation (Eslinger [1985: 144] notes six references to visual revelation but sixteen to verbal revelation). Thus, the thrust is not so much on what God looks like, but on what he says when he comes. Fifteen times the noun "word" and the verb "speak" appear. Samuel does not say, "Show yourself, Lord, for your servant is watching." He does say, "Speak, Lord, for your servant is listening." Samuel needs not the gifts of eyes or of tongues, but of ears. As the prophet of Patmos put it, "Let anyone who has an ear listen to what the Spirit is saying to the churches" (Rev. 2:7, 11, 17, 29; 3:6, 13, 22).

Three times Yahweh calls Samuel, and three times Samuel mistakes the voice of God for that of Eli (vv. 4–9). That misunderstanding suggests two ideas. First, the divine voice may be indistinguishable from a human voice. And two, it is not always a simple, easy matter even for God to communicate with and get through to his servants (Fokkelman 1993: 162). But at least let us give Samuel credit. He is still a "lad" (v. 1). God's heard word in those days is "rare" (v. 1). He does "not yet know the Lord" (v. 7), meaning that he had not yet received any revelation from God. His obtuseness aside, he is, nevertheless, responsive and enthusiastic.

Note the double use of "not yet" (*terem*) in this paragraph:

v. 3: "The lamp of God had *not yet* gone out."
v. 7: "Now Samuel did *not yet* know the Lord."

The first of these two refers to the menorah that is to be kept burning continually throughout the night hours in the sanctuary (Exod. 27:20–21). The lamp will be extinguished as the dawn approaches. But there is another dawn approaching (Eslinger 1985: 149) to end the darkness of the era of the Elides, and that dawn is Samuel. Accordingly, v. 7 implies that Samuel, who does "not yet" know Yahweh, shortly will. The expression "did not know the Lord" is for the sons of Eli a condemnation (2:12); for Samuel it is a promise (3:7).

For a fourth time, an overt condemnation comes upon the house of Eli (3:10–15; cf. 2:12–17; 2:22–25; 2:27–36). The condemnation in 3:10–15 is closest to that in 2:27–36, for on both occasions Eli hears a divine oracle about his family's demise from somebody who speaks for God (a man of God; Samuel). Two things separate 3:10–15 from 2:27–36. First, Samuel himself is now informed about the defrocking of Eli's house. And two, this time Eli's response to the bad news is registered: "It is the Lord; let him do what seems good to him" (v. 18b). Such a response may be either "a model of piety and acquiesence" (Brueggemann 1990: 26) or "an expression of despair in which Eli hides his cynicism about Yahweh beneath the guise of submission and piety" (Eslinger 1985: 154).

We are introduced at the start of this chapter to Samuel as a "boy" (v. 1). By chapter's end he is a prophet (v. 20). The double reference to "at Shiloh" in v. 21 is not without significance. God's word of judgment had fallen earlier at Shiloh. Now, God's hopeful, liberating word for the future comes "at Shiloh." For Eli, there is no future; for Shiloh, there is a future. The place-name repetition "emphasizes that the renewal through Samuel reaches to the very heart of the damages done by the Elides" (Eslinger 1985: 159). For a New Testament analogy, note that Jerusalem, the place where the disciples so often failed Jesus, is the very place where the Pentecostal Spirit falls on them, renewing and empowering them for ministry (Acts 2).

While it is customary and legitimate to use this story to encourage simple faith and obedience in the young to the Lord (à la Samuel), that is not its primary focus. The parallels with young Jesus in the temple (Luke 2:41–52) tell us more about God than about youth. In young Samuel, God is commencing a new prophetic era. In young Jesus, God again is launching a new prophetic epoch. "The degree to which God has chosen to be dependent upon good leadership in the spreading abroad of the Word is striking" (Fretheim 1983: 106).

4:1b–7:1. Verse 1a of chapter 4, which we included with the previous section, states, "And the word of Samuel came to all Israel." But surprisingly, Samuel disappears from the narrative, and does not resurface until 7:3: "Then Samuel said to all the house of Israel. . . ." This has led many scholars (e.g., Miller and Roberts 1977) to suggest that this portion of First Samuel is not original, but is rather a secondary insertion into the text. And because there are so many references in these few chapters to the "ark" (thirty-seven in 4:3–7:2 of the NRSV), it is common to refer to the unit as the "Ark Narrative." But one wonders if the glaring absence of Samuel is more of theological significance than compositional significance. The absence and silence of Samuel point to Israel's neglect of prophetic ministry at this critical time in their history, what with both the priesthood corrupting and the Philistines threatening to make themselves permanent rulers of Palestine. It is surely not without significance that when the Israelites are hard-pressed by the Philistines, they send for the ark but not for Samuel.

These opening seven chapters have a natural flow and development of plot. Willis (1971: 298) puts it well: "(a) The writer tells how Yahweh prepares a man to lead Israel through some crisis (1 Sam. 1:1–4:1a); (b) he describes this crisis (1 Sam. 4:1b–7:1); and finally (c) he relates the successful manner in which that man guides Israel through the crisis (1 Sam. 7:2–17)."

Israel's defeat by the Philistines at Aphek (4:1), with the loss of about four thousand troops (4:2), leads to the bright idea of bringing the ark from Shiloh and engaging the Philistines in battle a second time (4:3). But Israel is routed again, this time at Ebenezer (5:1), and to add insult to injury, the Philistines capture the ark (4:11). Israel loses without the ark; Israel loses with the ark; Israel loses the ark.

There are at least three possibilities why the ark was fetched. One, the Israelites were defeated because of an oversight. Somebody forgot to send the ark along. That oversight is now corrected. Two, by bringing the ark into battle the Israelites are admonishing Yahweh and reminding him of his covenantal obligations. Three, the Israelites believed that the mere presence of the ark was a guarantee of survival and victory. If their thinking includes this third point, then the Israelites are guilty of turning what God intended to be a symbol into an idol.

This way of thinking may suggest why centuries later, in his famous "Temple Sermon," Jeremiah drove home his point by referring to what had happened earlier to Shiloh: "Go now to my place that was in Shiloh. . . . I will do to the house that is called by my name . . . just what I did to Shiloh" (Jer. 7:12, 14); "I will make this house like Shiloh" (Jer. 26:6). Compare also the reference to Shiloh's judgment in Ps. 78:60: "He abandoned his dwelling at Shiloh, the tent where he dwelt among mortals."

It cannot be merely the fact of Shiloh's destruction that fuels the analogy between Jeremiah's Jerusalem and Samuel's Shiloh, for many other Israelite cities were destroyed. What provides the punch for the analogy is (1) Shiloh is the only other sanctuary we know of that actually housed the ark; and (2) in both Shiloh and Jerusalem the people prostituted their relationship with God by trusting (falsely) in a symbol to save them. The ark did not save them; neither did the temple. Had he spoken, Samuel would have matched Jeremiah's "Do not trust in these deceptive words: 'This is the temple of the Lord'" (Jer. 7:4) with his own "Do not trust in these deceptive words: 'This is the ark of the Lord.'" What the people really need to do is not bring the ark, but get rid of foreign gods and turn in repentance to Yahweh (1 Sam. 7:3).

Interestingly, what causes the ninety-eight-year-old and overweight Eli to fall off his chair, break his neck, and die is not the death of his wayward sons Hophni and Phinehas but the capture of the ark by the Philistines (4:17–18). Similarly, his daughter-in-law, before she dies, names her newborn "Ichabod" primarily because "The glory has departed from Israel" (4:20–22). The "glory of Israel" is Yahweh himself, the ark, and maybe even the priest's sons now dead.

It is difficult to overestimate the importance of the ark for Israel. Where God goes, the ark goes; where the ark goes, God goes. Can you imagine, then, the reaction to Jeremiah's startling words "They shall no longer say, 'The ark of the covenant of the Lord.' It shall not come to mind, or be remembered, or missed, nor shall another one be made" (Jer. 3:16)? Rank heresy, or liberating truth and prophecy? The next verse answers: "Jerusalem shall be called the throne of the Lord" (Jer. 3:17).

The ark is as much, if not more, a problem for the Philistines as it was for the Israelites (ch. 5). For the Philistines, getting rid of the ark is like "defusing a bomb that might explode at any time" (Brueggemann 1990: 38). Three evidences support that. First, the Philistine god Dagon is discovered face to the ground before the ark, either worshiping or fallen in defeat (5:3), and then on the next day in the same position after being propped up, this time without head or hands (5:4). Second, Yahweh strikes the Philistines with "tumors" (5:6). The word for "tumors," *'apolim*, is related to the word *'opel* ("tower"), and both come from the verb *'apal* ("surge ahead/up, storm" [cf. Num. 14:44]). The latter two words may explain how the first one came to mean "tumor, hemorrhoid." Third, the Philistines shunt the ark from Ashdod to Gath (5:8) to Ekron (5:10). Brueggemann (1990: 38) compares this moving the ark from city to city with the authorities moving Jesus from Annas to Caiaphas to Pilate (John 18:13–28).

Chapter 6 describes the return of the ark to Israel at the suggestion of the Philistine priests and diviners. But it is not sufficient merely to send the ark back to its source. The ark captors are to send a guilt offering of five gold tumors and five gold mice (6:4). Interestingly, the verb used of this guilt offering is "return," *hashev* (6:3, 4, 8, 17). In Old Testament cultic literature the "guilt/ *ʾasham*" offering differs from all other offerings by its unique use of the Hiphil of *shuv*, "return, restore, make restitution" (Num. 5:7, 8; 18:9). See also Lev. 6:4, which in the context of a guilt offering speaks of "restoring" (*heshiv*) what one took by robbery. Leviticus 6:5 uses the verb *shillem*, "repay," instead of *heshiv*. The implication is that with an *ʾasham* offering damage has been done vis-à-vis one of the Lord's "holy things," and restitution is mandated. For this reason, some prefer to translate the *ʾasham* offering not as "guilt offering" but as "reparation offering."

The reason for using mice was the possibility that the plague sent by Yahweh had been brought on by some kind of rodents. Each part of the offering is significant. First, that five tumors and five mice are sent indicates submission, with the number five representing the five cities of the Philistine pentapolis (Gaza, Gath, Ashdod, Ekron, and Ashkelon [6:17]), that is, the entire nation. Second, the gold represents the value of the offering; only the best is given. Third, the aim of the offering is the riddance of the plague from the land. The tumors and the mice are not only a reparation to Yahweh, but also are a means of sending the plague back to its divine source.

The ark's first stop on its way back to Israel is at Beth-shemesh in the field of one called "Joshua" (6:14). (Here is another Joshua who is connected with somebody or something coming into the Promised Land after an extended absence.) But there seventy (or fifty thousand, or 50,070; see the NRSV and NIV footnotes) perish for looking into the ark (6:19). This is the tragic result of even inadvertent contact with the high voltage of the *supersancta* (cf. 2 Sam. 6:6–7).

Accordingly, the Philistines are happy to rid themselves of the ark, and they send it on to Kiriath-jearim (6:21–7:2). It should be obvious why the ark was not returned to Shiloh. After all, that is where it was to start with. Anything so explosive as to cause the death of thousands for viewing it is best kept out of populous urban areas and placed instead in "an out-of-the-way hamlet" (Eslinger 1985: 227). Additionally, as Eslinger points out, the messengers are careful not to tell the real story of why the residents of Kiriath-jearim should come and claim the ark: "The Philistines have returned the ark of the Lord" (6:21). They do not say, "Oh, by the way, we housed the ark for a while here, but fifty thousand of our citizens died for looking into it." Nor do they say, "We want to get rid of Yahweh and the ark" (6:20; the Hebrew allows us to read "him" or "it"). What is offered as privilege is really a subterfuge.

7:2–17. For twenty years the ark remains at Kiriath-jearim. It is a time during which Israel "lamented" (NRSV), "mourned and sought after" [NIV] Yahweh (v. 2). The meaning is either that the people mourned Yahweh as though he were dead (Eslinger 1985: 230), or that the people longed for a rehabilitation of their relationship with God (Fokkelman 1993: 296). The latter seems more likely in light of v. 3, where Samuel says, "If you are returning to the Lord with all your heart. . . ." Samuel reappears in the narrative when any hope for the future seems impossible. What Eli and his sons failed to accomplish, Samuel accomplishes.

Samuel sounds like Joshua in urging the people to put away the gods they have embraced and to serve Yahweh only (v. 3; cf. Josh. 24:14). And the people did (v. 4). As Polzin (1989: 74) has pointed out, the addition of the word "only" in 7:3, 4, is important, for while the expression "serve the Lord" is quite common in Deuteronomy and the corpus of Deuteronomic literature, these are the only two places in that portion of Scripture where "serve the Lord *only*" occurs.

Although repudiation of idolatrous gods is a good start, it is not enough. While the people fast and confess their sin, Samuel intercedes before Yahweh at Mizpah on their behalf (vv. 5–6). Thus Samuel fills the role of revivalist and mediator. Earlier, Eli had asked, "If someone sins against the Lord, who can make intercession [*mi yitpallel*]?" (2:25). Samuel is the answer to that question: "I will make intercession [*we'etpallel*] with the Lord for you" (v. 5). Samuel's reputation as a godly intercessor is well established not only in 7:5–9, but also in 12:19–25; 15:11 ("he cried out to the Lord all night"); Ps. 99:6 ("Samuel was among those who called on his name"); Jer. 15:1 ("Though Moses and Samuel stood before me").

So there is no forgiveness without repudiation of sin (v. 4). There is no forgiveness without confession (v. 6). There is no forgiveness without an intercessor and mediator (v. 5). And finally, there is no forgiveness without a sacrifice (v. 9). That Samuel offers a burnt offering on behalf of the people (literally, "an entire whole-burnt offering" [*'olah kalil*]) to Yahweh, and not a "sin" offering, demonstrates that the burnt offering itself could serve as the sole expiatory sacrifice for the entire nation (cf. 13:12; 2 Sam. 24:25), or for an individual (Job 1:5, 42:7–9). This is in accord with Lev. 1:4, which speaks of the burnt offering being "acceptable in your behalf as atonement for you."

Assuming this gathering at Mizpah (for other gatherings at Mizpah, see Judg. 20:1, 3; 21:1, 5, 8; 1 Sam. 10:17) to be a prelude to battle, the Philistines take the offensive and attack Israel (v. 7). The Philistines are defeated not by Israel, but by Yahweh (v. 10). The victory is something for which no person or group of persons can claim credit. Hannah earlier had said of God, "the Most High will thunder in heaven" (2:10). That "prophecy" is fulfilled here when "the Lord thundered with a mighty voice" (v. 10). Thus, rather than interpreting God's intervention as a reward for prayer and sacrifice, we should interpret that intervention "from the perspective of God's mercy . . . he is responding to an appeal to act on Israel's behalf when she does not deserve it" (Miscall 1986: 39).

To commemorate this spectacle, Samuel raises a stone between Mizpah and Shen, a stone he names "Ebenezer" ("stone of help"), a name made famous in one of the stanzas of the hymn "Come, Thou Fount of Every Blessing": "Here I raise mine Ebenezer" (v. 12). Two things are of interest about this naming. First, for the first time in Samuel a male names something. The previous namings were done by women (1:20; 4:21). Second, this is the second appearance of "Ebenezer" in First Samuel. It first appeared as the place where the Philistines slaughtered Israel and captured the ark (4:1; 5:1). Is there any relationship between the two Ebenezers, one a place of defeat and massacre, the other a place of testimony about a God who intervenes to save and rescue? Theologically, yes. The two Ebenezers commemorate a God who can turn defeat into victory. "The battle that was lost at Ebenezer had to be won at Ebenezer" (Willis 1971: 304).

Samuel adds in his explanation of Ebenezer near the end of v. 12 the words "thus far" or "as far as here the Lord has helped us." By this addition Samuel is making two points, one geographical and one theological. "Yahweh has helped them back to Ebenezer and has there reversed the ill-effects of the previous disaster; he has helped the Israelites back to the place where they were undone and their relationship with Yahweh seemed at an end" (Eslinger 1985: 243).

The chapter concludes (vv. 15–17) by drawing attention to Samuel's circuit-riding judging responsibilities through four northern cities: Bethel, Gilgal, Mizpah, and back home to Ramah. These three verses sound like the conclusion to many of the judges' cycles in Judges. After the enemy is "subdued" (v. 13), the land enjoys rest for X number of years. What does one do in those years of rest? Well, people work and get married (Ruth). Others resume their more regular responsibilities (1 Sam. 7:15–17).

That Samuel built an altar at Ramah (v. 17) indicates that his times of prayer and sacrifice were not limited to times of national emergency and trauma. Who would not pray when the Philistine predators are breathing down one's neck? Samuel does not worship a God who inhabits a fire-alarm box on which is inscribed "In case of emergency, pull." An altar at Ramah is as important as fasting and a prayer meeting at Ebenezer.

II. 8–15: Samuel and Saul

These eight chapters focus on the emergence of the institution of the monarchy in Israel, Samuel's on-again, off-again position on the idea, and the selection of Saul as Israel's first king, with his turbulent, bungling start in that office.

This is not the first time, however, that kingship was a possibility in Israel. In the days of the judges, particularly the era of Gideon, leading citizens approached Gideon and urged him (1) to appoint himself as ruler over them and (2) to establish a hereditary rulership (Judg. 8:22). In fact, Gideon's son by a concubine, Abimelech ("my father is a king"), seized that position in Shechem after an incredible act of fratricide; but it is a position that turns out to be short-lived (Judges 9).

Even earlier, in the canonical ordering of Israel's sacred text and traditions, the issue of kingship appears first as a part of the promises that God made about kings coming forth from Abraham and Sarah (Gen. 17:6, "kings shall come from you"; 16, "kings of peoples shall come from her") and from Jacob (Gen. 35:11, "kings shall spring from you"), and second in the laws and precepts of Deuteronomy 12–26. Within that larger unit of Deuteronomy is a section that deals specifically with civil and religious authorities (Deut. 16:18–18:22). Four are mentioned: (1) the judiciary—local judges and officials (16:18–17:13); (2) the king (17:14–20); (3) the clergy (18:1–8); (4) the prophet (18:9–22).

Several unique items are found in the seven brief verses devoted to the issue of a king (Deut. 17:14–20). First, it is the only one of the four authorities whose appointment is optional: "You may [are free to] set a king over yourself" (Deut. 17:15 NRSV, but rendered as a command in NIV: "be sure to appoint over you"). Second, all four subunits emphasize the duties of the respective office holders, but only the other three mention the rights and authority of the office holders, that they are individuals whose pronouncements must be obeyed; for example, see the insistence on heeding the final verdict given in the high court by a Levitical priest or magistrate (Deut. 17:8–13), or the disastrous consequences for not heeding the words of a prophet (Deut. 18:15, 19). No such warning appears for disregarding the word of a king. Third, specific roles are assigned to the other office holders. By contrast, nothing is said about the role of the king in government or any exercise of royal power.

What Deut. 17:14–20 does do is limit the power of the king by curbing three excesses to which kings were prone: large cavalry, large harem, and great wealth (Deut. 17:16–17). His one and only positive responsibility is writing out a copy of and reciting God's law (Deut. 17:18–20), and this is the same Torah that God gave to all the people. There is one law and one God for both ditch digger and royal sovereign. And his citizens are his "brothers" (Deut. 17:20), not his "subjects" or "footstool."

The insistence that God alone choose the king (Deut. 17:15) is, to be sure, not restricted to the king. Yahweh also "chooses" (*bakhar*) the priest (Deut. 18:5) and "raises up" (*qum*) the prophet (Deut. 18:15, 18). But in point of fact, only four Old Testament kings are divinely chosen (via a prophetic representative): (1) Saul (1 Sam. 9:16–17; 10:20–24); (2) David (1 Sam. 16:1–3); (3) Jeroboam (1 Kings 11:29–39); (4) Jehu (2 Kings 9:1–13). The infrequency with which God selected the king of Israel or the king of Israel/Judah may be the stimulus behind Hosea's indictment, "They set up kings without my consent, they choose princes without my approval" (Hos. 8:4).

Some of this concern or ambivalency vis-à-vis monarchy in Israel spills over into 1 Samuel 8–12. It has been common since the days of Wellhausen to divide these five units into different sections, depending upon whether the particular section speaks in terms either favorable or disfavorable to the monarchy. And given that Israel had a monarchy before their exile to Babylon but no monarchy after their return from exile, Wellhausen dates the "pro-monarchy" passages to the preexilic period (anytime before 587 B.C.), and the "anti-monarchy" passages to the postexilic period (anytime after 587 B.C. or 539 B.C.).

The breakdown is as follows:

Anti-monarchy:	8:1–22		10:17–27		12:1–25
Pro-monarchy:		9:1–10:16		11:1–15	

If this breakdown is valid (and major questions about its validity remain, some of which we shall shortly raise), then some observations emerge (Childs 1979: 277–78). First, the anti-monarchy passages dominate the pro-monarchy ones. This is indicated in two ways. Both times pro-monarchy passages appear, they are ringed by anti-monarchy passages (8:1–22 <9:1–10:16> 10:17–27; 10:17–27 <11:1–15> 12:1–25). And note, the overall unit commences (8:1–22) and concludes (12:1–25) with an anti-monarchical tone. Second, the very fact that the pro-monarchy tradition is intertwined with the anti-monarchy tradition indicates that the monarchy is an institution whose origin is in the Israelites imitating the pagan, non-covenant nations, but nevertheless is a phenomenon in which God is vitally involved and gives his imprimatur. God does not overrule the people and veto their request, their questionable motives notwithstanding. Nor does he withdraw into indifference, exasperated because it hasn't been done his way. Rather, he uses the realities of the moment, and in all things he works for good.

It is not an argument against the validity per se of Israel's monarchy that the nation wanted a king or had a king like other nations. If that were the case, then any Israelite institution having any parallels with similar institutions in other religions (temple personnel, tabernacle, priesthood, holy days, sacrificial system, etc.) would also be suspect. Now to be sure, no Israelite group ever approached Moses and Aaron and said, "Give us a sacrificial system so that we can be like all the nations." Imperialism on the other side of the fence is normally more attractive than ritual on the other side of the fence. Yet, it is to the credit of Israel that they were able to hear, and be defined by, that direct word from God, but also by discriminatingly being open and receptive to borrowings and adaptations from surrounding cultures. As J. J. Roberts (1987: 380) has said, "It is difficult to speak of the essence of Yahwism without speaking of its ability to take up elements of its environment, even hostile elements, and transform them into supporting structures for the Yahwistic faith. . . . The mere presence of foreign elements in the development of the Israelite monarchy is hardly sufficient grounds for rejecting it as pagan aberration."

8:1–22. Most of this chapter is about the elders' request to Samuel to appoint a king over them, Samuel's attempt to dissuade them from what he perceives as foolishness, and God's decision on the matter. But it is Samuel's advanced age (v. 1) and his two delinquent judge-sons (vv. 2–3) that precipitate the whole incident. As Eli was old (2:22; 3:2; 4:15, 18), so is Samuel. As Eli had two very lackluster sons (1:3; 2:12–13, 22–25), so does Samuel. Thus, Samuel indirectly plays a role in the establishment of the monarchy that he vigorously opposes. That Samuel resides in Ramah (7:17) while his sons are stationed at Beersheba (8:2), some fifty miles to the south of Ramah, may indicate something of Samuel's desire to distance himself from his crooked sons by putting them in the "boonies."

It is difficult for a nation to change the fundamental model by which it governs itself. (Witness the painful struggle of Russia to shift from a communist, Marxist model to a democractic, free-market model.) Three reasons motivate the request: (1) the hopelessly and irreversibly corrupt current system of judges (the solution is not replacing the office holders but the system); (2) the desire to conform to surrounding nations and their government by monarchy; (3) a deep sense that a national leader such as a king would unite a deeply fractured nation, which then could present a much stronger front against invading nations. There is, of course, a bit of simplistic thinking in this: the problems are primarily structural. Change the skeleton and the problems will leave via the back door, while success comes walking in the front door. But what if the problems are not structural and external?

One gets the distinct impression that Samuel sees the peoples' request more as a rejection of his judgeship than as a rejection of Yahweh's rule, and hence the reason why Yahweh clarifies in v. 7 that it is Yahweh, not Samuel, on whom the people are turning their backs. This is most evident in Samuel's quotation in v. 6 of the elders' words in v. 5. He deletes two items in his quotation. One is their reference to his advanced age and reprobate sons; the other is their use of the phrase "like other nations." He quotes the middle of their request but omits the first and last parts. What sticks in Samuel's mind is their request for a king "to govern us" (*leshophtenu*), not for a judge, a *shophet*, which Samuel is.

Samuel tries his diplomatic best to talk the group out of such nonsense, but he is no more successful with dissuasion than was Pilate with another group. It is debatable whether the items listed by Samuel in vv. 11–18 describe cruel and oppressive kingship or reasonable and responsible kingship. For example, can one be a legitimate king without conscription (v. 11), war machinery (v. 12), and taxation (v. 15)? These can be implemented without necessarily being abusive. Rather, it is in the way he says it that Samuel tries to arouse second thoughts. "The king is the grammatical subject of fourteen lines" (Fokkelman 1993: 347) in this unit, and the expression "he will take" (meaning "confiscate") comes penetratingly five times in succession (vv. 11, 13, 14, 15, 16).

God's response to this is most interesting. Not once but three times he instructs Samuel to "listen to the voice of the people," adding to this on the third occasion "and set a king over them" (vv. 7, 9, 22). The judge and the prophet (i.e., Samuel) are the individuals par excellence to whom the people are to listen. Here, that is reversed. Samuel, the judge/prophet, is to listen to the people (Miscall 1986: 47). It is as if the writer is drawing a contrast between "a God who reveals his love in spite of being rejected" and "a judge who fails to conceal his selfish reluctance to become the maker of kings" (Polzin 1989: 88).

Samuel's response in v. 22b to God's instruction in v. 22a seems amiss. He sends the elders back to their homes. He does not appoint a king or initiate any procedures. Is he stalling? Is he putting everything on hold? Maybe the elders will think differently after they've slept on it. Maybe even God will reconsider. Or does Samuel need time to do all the necessary legwork on this major reformation?

We indicated previously that it is common to label 8:1–22 as an "anti-monarchy" section. But is this the case? While Samuel himself is undoubtedly an anti-monarchist, it is less clear that this is God's position (but see v. 7). And we must not assume that the narrator's position is Samuel's position. The narrator nowhere evaluates the elders' request negatively or speaks in opposition to the monarchy. In fact, this entire section (chs. 8–12) has only two pejorative editorial evaluations by the narrator, 8:2–3 and 10:27 (Eslinger 1983: 68).

9:1–27. Saul is introduced in the Scripture in ways that parallel Samuel's introduction. First is the reference to the father of each and his genealogical roots over four preceding generations:

1 Sam. 1:1	1 Sam. 9:1
Zuph	Aphiah
↓	↓
Tohu	Becorath
↓	↓
Elihu	Zeror
↓	↓
Jeroham	Abiel
↓	↓
Elkanah	Kish

Second, both fathers are introduced with phrases that are quite similar: "There was a certain man of Ramathaim, a Zuphite, from the hill country of Ephraim, whose name was Elkanah" (1:1); "There was a man of Benjamin whose name was Kish . . . a man of wealth" (9:1). In each case, both fathers, although mentioned first, will shortly be eclipsed by their better-known son, Elkanah by Samuel, and Kish by Saul. Third, Saul's search for his father's lost donkeys takes him as far as the land of Zuph (v. 5), and back in 1:1, Elkanah was identified as a Zuphite. Fourth, if Samuel is the answer to Hannah's request for a son, Saul is the answer to the people's request for a king.

The story of Saul begins when his father dispatches him and a servant ("one of the boys") on a wide-ranging mission to find Kish's straying donkeys (vv. 3–4). The two would have returned empty-handed to Kish had it not been for the boy's astute suggestion that they just happened to be in the very town where a "man of God" with a reputation for truthful prediction resides (v. 6). It is ironic that a "boy" knows of the whereabouts and reputation of this individual, but Saul, the tall, handsome son of a wealthy farmer, does not. Apparently, there were a few exceptions to the claim made earlier for Samuel: "All Israel from Dan to Beersheba knew that Samuel was a trustworthy prophet of the Lord" (3:20). That fact has escaped Saul. This is partly what makes the Saul of 1 Samuel 9 so attractive. While destined by God for pivotal leadership, he is so unpretentious, delightfully uninformed, and healthily naïve.

It is also ironic that Saul is the son of "a man of wealth" (v. 1) but does not have a nickel in his pocket to give as an honorarium or fee to the man of God (vv. 7–8). The boy knows what Saul does not know, and has money that Saul does not have. Later in the narrative Samuel will ask the boy to go on ahead and leave Samuel and Saul alone to discuss some important matters in private (v. 27). And Saul eclipses the boy as he had eclipsed his father. But where would Saul be were it not for the sagacity and boldness and generosity of this anonymous "boy"?

In a scene reminiscent of other biblical scenes in which a man meets a woman or women coming out to draw water (Gen. 24:15–20; 29:9–10; Exod. 2:15–16; John 4:6–7), Saul and his companion on their way to the unnamed town encounter some girls who are on a water mission much as Saul is on a lost donkeys mission (vv. 11–13). Their counsel is that Saul and his companion make haste (*maher* [v. 12]) to the town where Samuel the seer will preside at a sacrificial meal, at least in offering a table grace ("he must bless the sacrifice" [v. 13]). While it is not normal for a prophet/seer to perform sacrificial duties, one must remember that Samuel is the one individual in whom prophetic and priestly jurisdictions are fused.

Two items in this pericope connect with the account of Saul's ritual sin and rejection by God, which begins at 13:8. First, in ch. 9 Saul's haste in running to meet Samuel leads to success; in ch. 13, Saul's haste in not waiting for Samuel leads to failure and rejection (Gunn 1980: 62). Second, the women state that none of the invited guests will eat anything until Samuel arrives (v. 13); in ch. 13, Saul waits seven days and then does the inadmissable before Samuel comes.

Samuel is as uninformed about what is really going on as is Saul until God speaks to him. The Ephraimite prophet is told by the God of Israel to anoint as "ruler" (*nagid*) [not "king," *melek*] over his people a Benjaminite man who will seek him out (v. 16). This Benjaminite (recall their near demise in Judges 19–21) will "rule over" Israel (v. 17). And again, the Hebrew uses a different verb (*'atsar*) for "rule" than, say, a more standard verb like *mashal* or *malak*. Its normal meaning is "hold back, put the brakes on, restrain," and if it means "rule, reign" in 1 Sam. 9:17, then this is the only place in the Old Testament where it carries that meaning.

After easing Saul's mind about his father's lost donkeys (v. 20a), revealing to Saul his unique destiny (v. 20b), and providing a sumptious dinner and overnight stay (vv. 22–27), Samuel knows that the "moment for Saul's enlightenment arrives" (Eslinger 1985: 317) and expresses his intent to make known to Saul "the word of God" (v. 27d).

Several ideas jump from the story. For one thing, Saul went to look for his father's donkeys and he found a royal crown. Columbus went to look for a shorter route to India and he rediscovered a forgotten continent. Alexander Graham Bell was looking for a way to help the deaf, and he found the telephone. If Saul had not been looking for his father's animals, he would not have found the royal crown. If you do not look, nothing happens. "Seek and ye shall find," (Matt. 7:7) said Jesus. But find what? Maybe what you are looking for. But maybe something totally unexpected. Remember another Saul, also a Benjaminite, who went in pursuit and search of people of the Way. What he ended up actually finding was the Christ of the Way (Acts 9). In search of the Messianists, he found (or was found by) Messiah.

Again in this chapter, "the seeker turns out to be the sought" (i.e., the seeking farmer becomes the sought leader), and "whilst seeker$_1$ [Saul] is seeking seeker$_2$ [Samuel], seeker$_2$ is on the lookout for seeker$_1$" (Fokkelman 1993: 363, 368). The seeker, then, is actually the sought. Another place where this is true is in a verse of an old hymn: "I sought the Lord, and afterward I knew He moved my soul to seek Him seeking me; it was not I that found, O Saviour true, No, I was found of Thee."

10:1–16. Now alone with Saul, Samuel proceeds to anoint Saul as ruler/*nagid* by pouring oil on him from a "vial" (NRSV) or "flask" (NIV). The Hebrew word is *pak*, and is to be distinguished from the "horn" (*qeren*) of oil from which Samuel anointed David (1 Sam. 16:13), from the "horn" (*qeren*) from which Zadok anointed Solomon (1 Kings 1:39), and even from Hannah's reference to "God exalting the horn (*qeren*) of his anointed" (1 Sam. 2:10). The use of *pak* in 1 Sam. 10:1 may function to "dissociate Saul from David and from the closing statement of the Song of Hannah" (Miscall 1986: 59).

For a second time in Samuel, a prophet offers a sign that points to the significance of something on the horizon. The first was 1 Sam. 2:30–33, in which Samuel pronounces the forthcoming destruction of the entire house of Eli. The sign is in 2:34: "The fate of your two sons, Hophni and Phinehas, shall be a sign to you—both of them shall die on the same day." The purpose of the sign is to confirm Samuel's threat.

But in ch. 10 the sign has a different function. The sign serves to confirm Saul's anointing, not the certainty of Samuel's word: "Now this shall be the sign to you that the Lord has anointed you ruler over his heritage" (NRSV, which follows the longer reading of the Septuagint in 10:1, versus NIV, which follows the shorter reading of the Masoretic Text).

As Eslinger (1985: 321–22) has pointed out, each of these three signs corresponds to incidents in the preceding chapter:

Sign one: You will meet two men who will tell you that your father's donkeys have been found (10:2; cf. 9:3–4, 20).

Sign two: You will meet three men carrying, among other items, three loaves of bread, of which they will give you two (10:3–4); cf. 9:7, where Saul wonders what they can give to the man of God, since the bread in their sacks is gone.

Sign three: Saul will meet a band of prophets coming down from the shrine (NRSV), or the high place (NIV) (10:5); cf. 9:14, where Saul and the boy, as they entered the town, spotted Samuel on his way up to the shrine (NRSV), or the high place (NIV).

Verses 9–13 develop and report only on this third sign, although all three were fulfilled. Two things happen to Saul. First, God gives him another heart (v. 9), and then, as the spirit of God possesses him, Saul begins to engage in prophetic ecstasy (v. 10). One fundamental difference stands between these two. The heart change (v. 9) is permanent. "Saul puts off the Old Adam and becomes a new person" (Fokkelman 1993: 418). The ecstatic prophesying is temporary: "When his prophetic frenzy had ended, he went home" (v. 13). The form of the Hebrew verb used here (literally, "to experience prophetic ecstasy") describes what happens physically and emotionally to an individual when seized by the irresistable spirit of God.

Saul is the only Old Testament king who is called a prophet (v. 11b), and the only one who is said to prophesy (v. 11a). What arouses the cautious interest of the people is what they *saw:* "When all who knew him before saw how he prophesied . . ." (v. 11a). This may be contrasted with the reaction of another crowd that was puzzled, but by what they *heard* (at Pentecost): "Each one heard. . . . How is it that we hear? . . . We hear them speaking" (Acts 2:6, 8, 11).

The questions raised by the observers ("What has come over the son of Kish? Is Saul also among the prophets?") are their way of raising their own questions about the legitimacy of Saul's identification with the prophets. After all, they want a king, not another prophet. They want someone to fight their battles, not someone who would be "lost in wonder, love and praise" before God. As Brueggemann (1990: 77) states, "[Saul] is transformed in ways that others find embarrassing. They wanted a planner and a budgeter who would manage the economy and the army. They surely did not intend a king who would be moved by the wind of God out beyond their own hoped-for vision of Israel."

The unit closes (vv. 14–16) with a brief conversation between Saul and his uncle (presumbably, the father is absent when Saul returns home). Saul is careful to speak to his uncle only about the missing donkeys. He keeps the wraps on his anointing (how difficult that must have been!), apparently at Samuel's request. Saul is like those individuals in the Gospel narratives whom Jesus touched, restored, and told, "Don't tell anybody what I've done to you" (Mark 1:44). Like Samson (Judg. 14:6), he did not share with a relative a recent experience of his.

10:17–27. For a second time, Samuel summons the people to Mizpah (7:5–12 describes fasting and repentance and renewal at Mizpah), where now Saul will be chosen as king by lot.

If Saul is present, he is hardly excited about Samuel's opening words at the convocation (vv. 18–19). They take the form of a prophetic oracle of judgment: (1) a call to attention (v. 17); (2) a messenger formula (v. 18a); (3) a recital of Yahweh's saving acts (v. 18b); and (4) an accusation (v. 19a), which is reinforced by Samuel quoting the people (v. 19b). While quotations of the type "X quoting Y to Y" are common enough in the Old Testament, a double quotation is rare. The double quotation of 8:19 ("appoint a king over us") here in 10:19 and again in 12:12 underscores Samuel's severe reservations and his inclination to cast blame on the people.

Only two other times in the Old Testament is an individual identified by lot: Achan (implied in Josh. 7:14–26 but "lot" [goral] does not appear) and Jonathan (1 Sam. 14:38–45). In both cases the drawing of lots is designed to identify an individual who is guilty of a serious infraction. One might also include the casting of lots aboard the ship on which Jonah is a passenger (Jon. 1:7), and argue that in this case the casting of lots is designed either to pinpoint an individual who can explain the reason for the storm or to pinpoint the villain.

Leaving aside Saul being chosen by lot, all other Old Testament instances of lot casting are in contexts of illicit action. Does this then raise serious questions about Saul's election by lot (Miscall 1986: 22) and make Saul's lottery a "sham" or a "trap" (Eslinger 1985: 344, 350)? Or, these negative incidents notwithstanding, could lot drawing be a legitimate means of doing such things as selecting national leaders?

Perhaps the best parallel to the Saul selection is the New Testament story of the choice of a successor to Judas Iscariot (Acts 1:15–26). By lot it turns out to be Matthias. Acts does make a point (which 1 Samuel 10 does not) that the assembly first made the topic a matter of fervent prayer (Acts 1:24–25). What makes the two stories so close is that both speak of lots and the spirit of God. Saul is first possessed by the spirit (1 Sam. 10:10) and then taken by lot (1 Sam. 10:21). Matthias is taken by lot (Acts 1:26) and then filled with the Holy Spirit (Acts 2:4). (See Brueggemann 1990: 79.)

In this lottery section the action of a drawing of a lot is expressed three times by the passive of *lakad*, "was taken by lot" (vv. 20, 21 [2x]). This same verb is used with Saul a few chapters later (14:47), but this time the active voice:—"Saul took/seized the kingship over Israel." This is the only place in the Old Testament where *lakad* is used for assuming royal office or any other office. Is this part of Saul's later downfall? Not content to be seized by God's call, he tries to seize royal authority.

For some reason (modesty? discomfort? apprehension? he knows too much?), Saul is absent when his lot is drawn (v. 21). The words "when they sought him, he could not be found" sound much like the woman's search for her lover in the Song of Solomon, "I sought him, but did not find him" (5:6), and even like Saul's futile search for his father's lost donkeys. Only a further revelation by God reveals his whereabouts among the "baggage" (v. 22), a word (*hakkelim*) that "can refer to almost any kind of equipment or paraphernalia, so that exactly where Saul was hiding is something we cannot know with certainty" (McCarter 1980: 193). Whatever it was, it must have been large enough to conceal a person who was "head and shoulders taller than any of them" (9:2; 10:23). A six-foot-ten person cannot hide behind a suitcase!

Samuel, enthusiastically or reluctantly, publicly affirms the chosenness of Saul (v. 24a). The expression he uses of Saul, "there is no one like him," while common enough as a designation for God, is used elsewhere only of Moses (Deut. 34:10) and Josiah (2 Kings 23:25). Samuel has either had some genuine second thoughts about Saul and the monarchy or he is a great actor who knows how to play to the gallery.

Saul discovers three items that accompany kingship. The first item is a monarchic constitution (v. 25a), which is a document spelling out the rights and limitations of the king, and something not nearly as polemical as Samuel's words in 8:11–18. The second item is supporters, "warriors" [NRSV] or "valiant men" [NIV] whose hearts God had touched (v. 26). The Hebrew word for "warriors" or "valiant men" is *hakhayil*, and it reminds the reader of 9:1, where Saul is described as the son of a *gibbor khayil* ("a man of wealth" [NRSV]; "a man of standing" [NIV]).

The third item is opposition: some "worthless fellows" despised him and withheld any acts of courtesy and recognition (v. 27). Apparently, Gibeah, to which Saul has returned, is a beehive of "worthless fellows," as Judg. 19:22 labels some of the men of the city "a perverse lot."

Saul's response is silence (end of v. 27), and such silence is due to "astonishment, or inexperienced ability to respond, or forbearance, or perhaps all of these" (Eslinger 1985: 358).

11:1–15. While God had earlier made it clear that Saul would deliver his people from the Philistines (9:16), Saul's first test turns out to be with the Ammonites in the Transjordan area, precisely the same people whom the judge Jephthah had defeated (Judges 10–11) Their king is Nahash (which is the same as the Hebrew word for "serpent" in Genesis 3), and he and his troops attack the Transjordanian Israelite city of Jabesh-gilead.

Nahash agrees to an arrangement whereby instead of killing the Jabeshites, he will let them live, but it is mutilation and submission in lieu of execution. Little does Nahash know that he, who would gouge out the *right* eye of the Jabeshites, will himself be defeated by Saul from the tribe of Benjamin, literally, "a son of the *right*." That he grants a respite of one week before imposing the brutality while the Jabeshites seek assistance (v. 3) is because he sees it as "the last desperate floundering of his victims which he allows with the charitable sarcasm of a generous nature" (Fokkelman 1993: 463).

The elders of Jabesh make it appear that they will search "throughout Israel" (v. 3); in fact, they head straight to Saul's home in Gibeah (v. 4). They know where to go, and whom to seek after. Samuel and the "worthless fellows" may have their doubts about Saul, but the Jabeshites do not.

That the people of Gibeah hear about the possible atrocity before Saul does (vv. 4–5) does not diminish Saul's importance (as he finds out by accident). Rather, it provides Saul with the opportunity to be the take-charge person and to turn weeping into action.

But he does so not in his own strength or position. For a second time the spirit of God comes mightily on Saul (both 10:10 and 11:6 use *tsalakh 'al* for this charismatic anointing), suggesting that we should see the spirit's coming in 11:6 as a "booster shot" (Eslinger 1985: 366). The spirit's seizure of Saul moves him in this case to "care, rage, and risk" (Brueggemann 1990: 84).

Saul's interesting way of rousing and mobilizing supporters and conscripts works (v. 7): three hundred thousand from Israel and thirty thousand from Judah (v. 8), a 10:1 ratio for what will later be the two halves of a divided people. The larger number of responses to Saul's

SOS "expresses the energy and strength to which the breaking through of the Spirit can lead, raising people above their all-too-human dimensions and day-to-day routine" (Fokkelman 1993: 458).

Little do the Ammonites know that the words of the Jabeshites in v. 10 are 100 percent deception. They anticipate victory and deliverance, not surrender, in light of the news that reached them in v. 9. And deliverance they get (v. 11).

Now is not a propitious time to be anti-Saul (v. 12). The people (the Jabeshites? the 330,000 troops? those whose hearts God had touched [10:26]?) turn on those who earlier railed against Saul and insulted him (10:27). The passage reads literally: "Who is the one saying [*ha'omer* is a participle with the prefixed definite article] 'Saul, he shall reign over us'?" As it stands, the people's words are a statement. Many modern translations (NRSV, NIV) make it a question: "Shall Saul reign over us?" Or else they follow the Septuagint and read it as a negative: "Saul shall not reign over us" (e.g., McCarter 1980: 199).

We are inclined to think that it is a rhetorical question, or even an exclamation. The order subject-verb (*sha'ul yimlok*) rather that the expected sequence of verb-subject brings this out. So we read v. 12 this way: "The people then said to Samuel, 'Who is the one saying "Saul! He shall reign over us!"?'" A lynch mob is about to form.

That Saul answers a question addressed to Samuel (v. 13) is not an "impetuous interruption" (Eslinger 1985: 376). Saul's quick response continues his aggressiveness and leadership so ably illustrated throughout this chapter. It is a comment on Saul's character as well. He is charitable and magnanimous. (It is too bad that he did not perpetuate that perspective vis-à-vis David later on.) And his answer lets Samuel off the hook, and saves Samuel from being forced to make a savory statement about Saul, with whom he has not been lavish in his praise.

It is Samuel's idea (not God's, not the people's, not the narrator's) that they go to Gilgal to "renew" (NRSV) or "reaffirm" (NIV) the kingship (v. 14). There are only eight other places in the Old Testament where the verb used in v. 14 for "renew, reaffirm" (what Hebrew grammarians call the Piel stem of the verb *khadash*) appears. Perhaps the best known of these is David's penitential prayer in Ps. 51:10: "Create in me a pure heart, O God, and *renew* a steadfast spirit within me" (NIV). That Psalm reference makes it clear that the verb means to restore something (or somebody) that has been damaged or has deteriorated to its original condition. Perhaps Samuel's choice of this verb is his way of indicating his abiding reservations about the whole idea of monarchy.

Can God's people have two kings? Must monarchy be "either . . . or," or can it be "both . . . and"?

The people making Saul king in Gilgal (v. 15) fulfills God's word in 8:22: "give them a king." What we have in chs. 10 and 11 are three different ways by which Saul became king: (1) God chose and anointed him (10:1); (2) he is made king by lot (10:21); (3) the people made him king after his successful deliverance of Jabesh-gilead (11:15). To put it a bit differently, Saul is made king (1) by God, (2) by chance, and (3) by his own proven capacity for leadership.

Might we apply the same three phenomena to Jesus? Jesus was chosen by God to be the King of Glory. But by chance (we might say), from our point of view, he was born at the right time, in the right place, and into exactly the right family. But what really made (and makes) him king in the hearts of his followers was that when he had the opportunity either to retreat and avoid his mission or to advance, he chose to advance toward death and life.

12:1–25. It is common to refer to this portion of Scripture as Samuel's farewell address, but unlike other places, where the farewell address and the death notice of the speaker are in proximity (Moses: Deut. 33:1–29 and 34:5–8; Joshua: Josh. 24:1–28 and 24:29–30), Samuel's farewell address (1 Sam. 12:1–25) is separated considerably from the notice of his death (1 Sam. 25:1). But that Samuel even presents a speech that may be styled "a farewell address" is a witness to his stature. He is in good company (Moses and Joshua), and no other judge/prophet is accorded such a platform.

There are two parts to the unit (Polzin 1989: 117):

1. a Samuel-centered dialogue between Samuel and his audience (vv. 1–5)
2. a people-centered dialogue (vv. 6–25)
   a. Samuel's prophetic judgment speech (vv. 6–17)
   b. the narrator's reference to the thunderstorm and the people's fear of Yahweh and Samuel (v. 18)
   c. Samuel's concluding speech (vv. 20–25)

In the first section, Samuel talks in a way that may sound like he is "defensive and self-protective" (Gunn 1980: 64), "is piqued about the fact he is being pushed out" (Fokkelman 1993: 495). He reminds his audience that his own leadership has been exemplary, and challenges anybody to provide evidence to the contrary. His quadruple use of "taken" is surely a subtle throwback reference to the leadership that the king will assume:

1 Samuel 8 (the king)	1 Samuel 12 (Samuel)
Your sons he will *take* (v. 11).	Whose ox have I *taken?* (v. 3).
Your daughters he will *take* (v. 13).	Whose donkey have I *taken?* (v. 3).
The best of your fields he will *take* (v. 14).	From whose hand have I *taken* a bribe? (v. 3).
One-tenth of your grain he will *take* (v. 15).	You have not *taken* anything from the hand of anyone (v. 4).
Your male and female servants he will *take* (v. 16).	

The closest parallel to Samuel's words are Paul's denials that he defrauded communities in matters of money (see 1 Cor. 9:1–14; 2 Cor. 7:2; 11:7–9; 1 Thess. 2:1–12), and the prototypical expression of such disclaimers is 1 Sam. 12:3–5. Samuel's apologia recalls that of Moses in Num. 16:15 in that both passages refer specifically to the denial of the misappropriation of a donkey.

Samuel moves from defending himself (vv. 3–5) to defending Yahweh (vv. 6–17)—as if he needs defending. He covers the time from Jacob (v. 6a) through Moses and Aaron (v. 8) down to the present moment, the encounter with the Ammonite Nahash (v. 12; cf. 11:1–13). His point is that if he has done nothing to incur the wrath of his people by his actions, neither has Yahweh. In fact, whenever God's people rebelled and went into a tailspin, whenever they "cried" (vv. 8, 10), Yahweh "sent" (vv. 8, 11) deliverers. Now, instead of crying out to God in repentance (v. 10), they are crying out to God for a king (v. 12). Samuel is befuddled. Why this sudden shift in strategy when in need from weeping to whining, from repentance to recklessness?

In this prophetic judgment speech Samuel carefully crafts his indictment. To that end, he glosses over any mention of his sons' corruption and waywardness, which were partly the stimulus for the people's request for a king in the first place (8:5). "Obviously the sons are the chink in his armor, so he is careful to hide their failing behind his own merits" (Eslinger 1985: 386). Again, in his brief overview of the judges' period, Samuel discusses "none of the problems and complexities of the actual experience of judgeship. . . . Judgeship is right and adequate and should not be giving way to monarchy" (Jobling 1986: 51). Again, note his silence about Saul's victory over Nahash (v. 12), and his attribution of the people's request for a king to this event when in fact they said this back in ch. 8 (8:19) (Miscall 1986: 75). And finally, note how Samuel uses, judiciously, a double quotation, one from an earlier generation (v. 10, quoting Judg. 10:10), and one from the present generation (v. 12, quoting 8:19), the purpose of which is to glorify and put on a pedestal the earlier generation while condemning his own.

A thunderstorm in dry season (vv. 17–18) is some indication that Samuel's sentiments are not simply the tattered ramblings of a rejected, embittered old man. He is a prophet. He still "has clout with God" (Brueggemann 1990: 94) and can call upon God for "an audiovisual teaching aid" (Eslinger 1985: 417).

In response to the people's request for prayer (v. 19), Samuel preaches (v. 20–25), with only a promise of the former (v. 23). He stops short, however, of asking the people to withdraw their request for a king, and neither do the people explicitly volunteer to do so. Apparently trying to make the best of a bad and irreversible situation, Samuel urges loyalty and service to Yahweh (vv. 20, 24), as had Joshua in Joshua 24. His exhortation is addressed only to the people. He only once uses the word "king" and never "Saul." Here, "king/Saul" is merely part of the people.

On the one hand, Samuel affirms that the survival of the people, their foolish request notwithstanding, is guaranteed: "For the Lord will not cast away his people, for his great name's sake" (v. 22). Lest, however, that promise breed a sense of false security and indifference, he says a few verses later, "But if you still do wickedly, you shall be swept away, both you and your king" (v. 25). Interestingly, the Hebrew verb for "be swept away" (*saphah*) is one that David later will use about Saul's death: "The Lord will strike him down; or his day will come to die; or he will go down into battle and perish [be swept away]" (1 Sam. 26:10). And David uses the same verb of himself to describe the death he might meet at Saul's hands (1 Sam. 27:1).

One can only imagine what the newly crowned Saul, on what ought to have been his magical day, is thinking as he listens silently to Samuel's fulminations against the people for requesting a king, like the nations. If you are Saul, it is a classic case of somebody raining on your parade.

13:1–23. This chapter begins (vv. 1–7) and ends (vv. 15b–23) with Israel, led by King Saul, engaging the Philistines in battle. In between is a section (vv. 8–15a) in which Samuel comes to Saul and, because of Saul's disobedience, announces that God has withdrawn the kingdom from Saul. So the chapter moves from Saul versus the Philistines to

Saul versus Samuel to Saul versus the Philistines. And it is difficult to say which of these two opponents is more intimidating to Saul, thousands of Philistines or one Samuel. If the Philistines have a monopoly on weapons production so that Israel has to go to them for supplies, Samuel has a monopoly on the commandments of God so that Saul has to go to him. What the Philistines possess metalurgically, Samuel has theologically.

The chapter begins with what is more than likely a textual error, for v. 1 states, literally, that "Saul was one year old when he began to reign, and he reigned two years over Israel." Youthful kings are not unheard of (e.g., Josiah began to reign at the age of eight [2 Kings 22:1], and in Greek tradition, Minos, son of Zeus, was nine years old when he ruled Knossos [*Odyssey* 19.179]), but a one-year-old king? The textual problem notwithstanding, the regnal formula used here is a standard one ("So-and-So was X years old when he began to reign and he reigned X years"), so that 13:1 marks the beginning of a new era in Israel's history. Saul the *nagid* (chieftain) is now Saul the *melek* (king).

We are also surprised to find out that Saul is married (see 14:50 for Ahinoam) and has a son Jonathan (vv. 2–3, 16). Enigmatically, Jonathan is not identified as the son of Saul when he first appears in the narrative (vv. 2–3), but only later (v. 16). Nothing in the Saul story had given us even an inkling that he has both spouse and son.

The heart of the chapter is the showdown between Saul and Samuel (vv. 8–15a). Hard-pressed by the Philistines, and with Samuel a no-show after the mandatory seven-day waiting period (v. 8), Saul takes matters into his own hands and offers the sacrifices (v. 9); and then, with perfect timing, Samuel shows up (v. 10). Samuel proceeds to scorch Saul and brand him a fool (v. 13). Not only has Saul aborted his role as the nation's king, but also, God already has his replacement in mind, "a man after his own heart" (v. 14). (Paul quotes this part of 1 Sam. 13:14 and combines it with the Septuagint of Ps. 89:20 in Acts 13:22: "I have found David, son of Jesse, to be a man after my heart.") Samuel gives Saul no chance to respond; instead, Samuel storms off by himself, not to his own town of Ramah but to "Gibeah of Benjamin," Saul's home town (v. 15a)!

Throughout this incident, Saul is presented sympathetically. Consider these facts: (1) On this occasion Saul can muster only three thousand troops (v. 2). On a previous occasion against Nahash and the Ammonites, a lesser foe, Saul had well over 300,000 (11:8). This represents a reduction in troops by some 99 percent. (2) Saul is facing, without adequate weapons, a well-armed foe (vv. 19–22). (3) Many of Saul's own troops are panicking and deserting their leader, either by hiding out

(v. 6) or by crossing the Jordan in the wrong direction (v. 7). (4) Saul waits seven days, as Samuel requested (10:8), but Samuel is a no-show. (5) Saul explains that he offered the sacrifice only as a last resort: "I forced myself" (NRSV); "I felt compelled" (NIV) (v. 12). In his explanation to Samuel he is not pompous or presumptuous, but deferential.

What, then, has Saul done that is such a terrible gaffe? The most obvious explanation is that he has overstepped his bounds as king in doing what only priests are supposed to do—offer sacrifices to God. But the problem with this is that other kings offered sacrifices to God, and did so without censure (David: 2 Sam. 6:13, 17–18; Solomon: 1 Kings 3:3, 15 [as he stood before the ark of the covenant]; 8:64 [in front of the house of the Lord]; Ahaz: 2 Kings 16:12–13 [against the altar]).

The one king who is condemned for offering sacrifices is Uzziah (2 Chron. 26:16–21). His sin is offering incense inside the temple, for which he is stricken with leprosy. But something here is not present in the other narratives. King Uzziah's encroachment upon the temple is prefaced with "But when he had become strong he grew proud, to his destruction" (2 Chron. 26:16). There is a world of difference between an act of arrogant defiance (Uzziah's) and an act of desperation (Saul's).

Interestingly, in his rebuke (v. 13) Samuel does not say, "Why did you not wait?" or "Why did you offer the sacrifice?" Nor does he say, "Why have you not kept the commandment I gave you?" (cf. 10:8). Rather, he says, "You have not kept the commandment of the Lord your God, which he commanded you." But in point of fact, it was Samuel who issued that command, not God, and God never speaks in ch. 13. One wonders if the only stipulation that Saul has broken is "Thou shalt not violate Samuel's authority" (Brueggemann 1990: 100), and thus that it is "a trumped-up charge to keep Saul on the defensive and under prophetic control" (Polzin 1989: 129). For Samuel, it is not only "what God says, I say," but also, "What I say, God says," and although that can be empowering for one's ministry, it can also be lethally dangerous.

For some analysts of this story, "What is at stake here is the danger of autonomous political authority extending its control even into the realm of sacred and religious institutions" (Birch 1991: 211). For others, the issue is not the usurpation of the authority and privileges of another; rather, Saul's real sin is his preoccupation with liturgical matters at the expense of saving God's people from the hand of the Philistines (9:16), and his doing whatever he sees fit to do, for God is with him (10:7) (Miscall 1986: 87). Saul's divine calling is to be a militarist, not a liturgist. If sacrifices really need to be offered to "entreat the favor of the Lord" (v. 12) prior to battle, then why did Saul not feel similarly before he engaged the Ammonites at Jabesh-gilead, where nobody offered any sacrifices (11:1–15)? Of course, on that occasion he had a fighting force of 300,000 troops against a much less formidable foe.

14:1–52. Sandwiched between two chapters that highlight the tension between Saul and Samuel comes ch. 14, highlighting the tension between Saul and Jonathan. In these three chapters Saul finds himself embroiled either in a king and prophet/priest fracas or in a father and son fracas. Interestingly, when Saul and Samuel are "going at it," Jonathan is nowhere to be found; and when Saul and Jonathan are "going at it," Samuel is nowhere to be found. As far as we know, Samuel and Jonathan are never in the same place at the same time.

The first part of the chapter (vv. 1–23) focuses primarily on Jonathan and a colleague ("one who carries Jonathan's armor" [v. 1]; cf. Saul's companion Ahijah, the priest who carries an ephod [v. 3]), and how this twosome managed to strike terror into the camp of the menacing Philistines (vv. 14–15). Jonathan will act against the Philistines independently of Saul the king, as will David later on against one imposing Philistine (1 Samuel 17).

Jonathan is impressive not only in his aggressiveness and boldness, but also in his honesty. He can affirm categorically that "nothing can hinder the Lord from saving by many or by few" (v. 6d), but he also says immediately before this, "It may be that the Lord will act for us" (v. 6c). Maybe Yahweh will deliver; maybe he will not. The phrase "it may be" is one used several times in Scripture by a person about a potential action by God (Exod. 32:30; Num. 23:3; 2 Sam. 16:12; Jer. 21:2; Jon. 1:6; Amos 5:15). God cannot be boxed into a guaranteed course of action. (Possibly of even greater interest are those passages in which God, the omniscient one, uses "it may be" about a person or a group of persons: Isa. 47:12; Jer. 36:3, 7; 51:8; Ezek. 12:3; and especially Jesus' parable in Luke 20:9–18, "I will send my beloved son; it may be that they will respect him" [v. 13].)

Everything seems to be going Israel's way until Saul, for some unexplained reason, imposes an oath on his troops that they will fast until evening, by which time, hopefully, Saul will have vanquished the Philistines (v. 24). Possibly, he thinks self-affliction via deprivation will move God to provide support and victory—as if God can be so seduced and manipulated. An oath in the Old Testament, to be distinguished from a conditionally stated vow, comes in one of two forms. First, there is what we shall call the "oath of purgation," whose purpose is to clear the accused of a charge. Examples of this kind of oath are Gen. 14:22–

23 (Abram's words): "I have sworn to the Lord . . . that I would not take a thread"; Exod. 22:8: "If the thief is not caught, the owner of the house shall be brought before God, to determine whether or not the owner had laid hands on the neighbor's goods"; Lev. 6:3–5 (a charge or suspicion of thievery): "If you swear falsely regarding any of the various things . . . or anything else about which you have sworn falsely"; Num. 5:19 (the wife suspected by her husband of infidelity): "Then the priest shall make her take an oath"; Rom. 1:9: "For God . . . is my witness that without ceasing I remember you always in my prayers."

The second kind of an oath is what we shall call a "promissory oath," which imposes some kind of an obligation on the oath taker. Examples are Abraham's servant who takes an oath not to get a wife for Isaac from the Canaanites (Gen. 24:2–4); Joseph, who takes an oath that he will bury his father in Canaan rather than leave his corpse behind in Egypt (Gen. 47:29–31; 50:5); David, who by oath, which he is now asked to honor, allegedly promised that Solomon would succeed him as King (1 Kings 1:13, 17, 30). Of course, by definition a covenant is a promissory oath ("let there be an oath between you and us, and let us make a covenant with you" [Gen. 26:28]).

Saul's oath is the latter type. It imposes a fast on his soldiers. If there are instances in the Old Testament of oath taking that spring from the sublime and solemn, Saul's oath is an instance of a noble institution used trivially and irrationally. The rigors of battle are debilitating enough, especially when one is up against a superior foe, and now add to that abstinence from food!

Jonathan is absent when his father imposes the oath, and not having heard about it, he sins inadvertently by helping himself to some honey for nourishment and strength (v. 27). Hearing makes one culpable: "when any of you sin in that you have heard a public adjuration" (Lev. 5:1); "all who hear the words of this oath and bless themselves" (Deut. 29:19); "the eleven hundred pieces of silver that were taken from you, about which you uttered a curse, and even spoke it in my hearing" (Judg. 17:2). If Jonathan can be exonerated for violating his father's oath, it is because he has not heard it.

This section of 1 Samuel 14 has many connections with Judges:

1. Saul, who defeated the Ammonites, imposes an unexplained oath; Jephthah, who also defeated the Ammonites, made a silly vow.
2. Saul's oath places his son's life in potential jeopardy; Jephthah's vow placed his daughter's life in actual jeopardy.

3. Jonathan does something without telling his father (14:1); Samson did something without telling his parents (Judg. 14:6).
4. Saul wants vengeance on the Philistines (14:24); so did Samson (Judg. 16:28).
5. Jonathan eats forbidden honey (14:27); so did Samson (Judg. 14:9).

Actually, the parallels go back as far as Joshua and the story of Achan (Joshua 7). Apart from both stories featuring the identification of the wrongdoer through lot drawing, they both use the verb "trouble" (*akar*): Joshua says to Achan, "Why did you trouble us?" (Josh. 7:25); Jonathan says about Saul, "My father has troubled the land" (14:29). In the former case, Achan brought trouble to the land by taking booty; in the latter case, Saul brought trouble to the land by forbidding access to booty/honey (Miscall 1986: 94).

It is difficult to know whether Jonathan's "guilt" is established merely by a lottery or by lot drawing that included the Urim and Thummim. That is because of a significant difference between the Masoretic Text and the Septuagint text of v. 41:

Masoretic Text: "Then Saul said to the Lord, the God of Israel, 'Give me the right answer.'" (or, "Then Saul prayed to the Lord, the God of Israel, 'Show *tamim*.'")

Septuagint: "Then Saul said to the Lord, the God of Israel 'Why have you not responded to your servant today? If this inquity was due to my son Jonathan or to me, O Lord God of Israel, show Urim, but if it was due to your people Israel, show Thummim.'"

In either case, Jonathan is identified as the culprit. Saul's inquiry in response, "Tell me what you have done" (v. 43), is exactly the same as Samuel's to Saul in the preceding chapter, "What have you done?" (13:11). Both statements follow palpable violations of a transparent mandate. Thus, in ch. 14 Saul becomes Samuel and Jonathan becomes Saul. The accusee of ch. 13 is the accuser of ch. 14.

Jonathan should die for this oath violation. Saul says so (v. 44). But Jonathan is not put to death, because of his unawareness of the oath and because of the intervention of the people. In ch. 11 the Jabeshite people owe their salvation to Saul; in ch. 14 Jonathan owes his salvation to the people (v. 45). Another (rare) instance of a popular challenge to the official royal verdict of death is the people's rejection of Jehoiakim's death sentence on Jeremiah after that prophet's Temple Sermon. Jeremiah is rescued by Ahikam and is not handed over to the king's officials to be put to death (Jer. 26:24). In 1 Samuel 14, Saul listens to and respects the voice of the people, and that is salutary. However, in the next chapter he again listens to the voice of the people (15:24), but this time it spells his doom (Brueggemann 1990: 107).

The last few verses of the chapter are surprising. In between references to Saul's battles (vv. 47–48, 52) is a reference to Saul's immediate family and his army commander (vv. 49–51). There are three things of significance about the placement of vv. 47–52 at the end of ch. 14 (Miscall 1986: 98). First, that there is a summary here and not at the end of his reign hints that Saul's reign is, for all practical purposes, already over. Second, no mention of Yahweh is made anywhere in these six verses. Third, while vv. 47–48 and 52 speak of the battles in which Saul engaged and in which he punished his enemies, only v. 48 speaks of an actual victory: "he rescued Israel out of the hands of those who plundered them."

15:1–35. This chapter describes a further incident in Saul's life that seals his permanent rejection by God. The story begins with Samuel quoting the Lord to Saul to the effect that Saul is to attack and utterly destroy (*kherem*) the Amalekites. No person or thing is to be spared (*khamal* [v. 3]; cf. vv. 9, 15). This gruesome assignment is in retaliation for something these people did to Israel that antedates Saul's time by centuries. While there is no indication that the Amalekites were a menace to Israel in Saul's era, in the time of Moses these people gained infamy by preying on the sick and the weak—those who traveled at the rear—as the Israelites made their way to Canaan (Deut. 25:17–19), much like a wolf preys on the straggling sheep.

Surprisingly perhaps, the lengthy corpus of Deuteronomic laws, begun in ch. 12 of Deuteronomy and ending in ch. 25, comes to a conclusion in 25:17–19 with a law different from any that preceded it. God commands Israel, once securely settled in the land, "to blot out the remembrance of Amalek from under heaven" (Deut. 25:19). Perhaps, the placement of this law to exact vengeance on the Amalekites for their acts of hostility is prompted by similar language in another law that appears a few verses earlier. The purpose of levirate marriage ("so that his name might not be blotted out of Israel" [Deut. 25:6]) and the fate of the Amalekites ("you shall blot out the remembrance of Amalek" [Deut. 25:19]) share vocabulary ("blot out") and interchangeable expressions ("name" and "remembrance").

It is not without interest that when Samuel later requotes what he was instructed to tell Saul, he makes a slight change by addition. The Lord was first quoted as saying, "Now go and attack Amalek, and utterly destroy all that they have" (v. 3). When Samuel repeats that quotation, this is how it comes out: "Go, utterly destroy *the sinners*, the Amalekites" (v. 18). Surely, Samuel's addition of "the sinners" is his way of making his case against Saul as tight and condemnatory as possible.

Saul's first move, after assembling a fighting force (v. 4), is to exempt the Kenites who inhabit Judah and the Negeb area. Saul's reason for doing so is because they "showed kindness" to Israel when Israel exited Egypt (v. 6). We are not sure what this refers to, but if the Kenites and Midianites are somehow to be connected (Moses' father-in-law is both Midianite [Exod. 3:1; 18:1] and Kenite [Judg. 4:11]), then Saul is probably thinking of Jethro/Hobab and his assistance to Israel in Exodus 18 and Num. 10:29–32. There is precedent for exempting one group from punishment. Joshua spared Rahab and her house for exactly the same reason Saul spares the Kenites: both "showed kindness" (*'asah khesed*) to Israel (Josh. 2:12; 1 Sam. 15:6).

For reasons either sinister or rational, Saul, says the narrator, chose to spare the Amalekite king Agag and the best of the sheep, cattle, and fatlings (vv. 7–9). Viewed from one perspective, Saul's activities are patent disobedience, for the ban mandated at the beginning of the chapter required the total destruction of Amalekite spoil, human and nonhuman alike. Viewed from another perspective, Saul's selective implementation of the ban could appear to be quite legitimate. For one thing, in the account of Joshua's campaign against Ai we see a precedent for taking the king alive in a *kherem* war and reserving his execution until later (Josh. 8:23–29; see Miscall 1986: 101). Hence, it would not appear that "devote to destruction" is something that had to be done at one place and all at one time. Again, the instruction was to kill "ox and sheep, camel and donkey" (v. 3). Saul spares only "the sheep and cattle" (v. 9), that is, the animals that may be sacrificed to God, but not those (camel and donkeys) that may not be sacrificed to God. And in saving the "valuable" and destroying "the despised and worthless," Saul is being faithful to the Old Testament tradition of offering to God only the best and the unblemished. Furthermore, Lev. 27:28 and Num. 18:14 state that *kherem* animals, if fit for the altar, and even proscribed property, need not be put to the sword, but can be sacrificed and given to the priests. How can we know that Saul did not intend to slaughter Agag as a sacrifice "before the Lord" before Samuel preempted him (v. 33)?

It is clear from Yahweh's word in v. 11 and Samuel's words in the ensuing conversation with Saul that neither is as impressed by Saul's behavior as the reader might be inclined to be. Yahweh states, "I am sorry [NRSV]; I am grieved [NIV] [literally, 'I repent'] that I made Saul king" (v. 11). For emphasis, the narrator repeats this sentiment at the end of the narrative: "And the Lord was sorry/grieved [literally, 'repented'] that he had made Saul king over Israel" (v. 35c). One suspects that Yahweh's sorrow is prompted not by this singular aberration of Saul, but by an accumulation of the same. Evidence to support this comes from the fact that in v. 13 Saul claims to have carried out "the command" (singular) of the Lord, while in v. 11 Yahweh indicts him for not carrying out "my *commands*" (plural) (Brueggemann 1990: 111).

Samuel's response to this startling statement by Yahweh is that he "was angry" (a rendering superior to the NIV's "was troubled"). But angry at whom and for what? At God because of sadness over God's change of mind and his own compassion for Saul (Sternberg 1985: 504–5)? At Saul because of his continual lackluster performance while in royal office (Eslinger 1988: 353)?

Three other places in the Old Testament have the same Hebrew idiom as in v. 11, *wayyikhar le*, with the preposition prefixed to the name of the angry person:

Gen. 4:5: the Lord rejects Cain's offering, "so Cain was very angry."
2 Sam. 6:8: after the Lord kills Uzzah for touching the ark to keep it from falling, "David was angry."
Jon. 4:1: after the Lord has forgiven the contrite Ninevites, "he [Jonah] became angry."

One might also note Jesus' parable of the father and two sons in Luke 15:11–32. Upon hearing that his father was having a welcome-home party for his vagabond brother, the older brother became angry and refused to join the celebration (Luke 15:27–28). What these four instances have in common is anger at God. God has done something that the angered individual, had he been God, would not have done, or would have done differently. Given Samuel's persistently negative feelings toward the idea of monachy and toward Saul, it is likely that he is angry at God for even allowing Israel to have a king. What God permitted, Samuel would have vetoed, had he been God.

The rest of the chapter is a dialogue (if we may call it that) between Samuel and Saul.

Saul moves from a witness of his obedient implementation of the divine command (v. 13), to explaining the role of his people (v. 15), to another statement of fulfillment of the command to which he now adds that the spared animals are for sacrifice to Yahweh (v. 21), to a confession of sin and a request for forgiveness (vv. 24–25), and finally to another confession of sin, but this time with no request for forgiveness but for public honor from Samuel (v. 30).

Samuel starts with a question (much as did God in Gen. 3:9) (v. 14), accuses Saul of the sin of omission (vv. 16–19), shifts from his sarcastic question of v. 14 to a rhetorical question in v. 22, pronounces Yahweh's rejection of Saul (v. 23b), reinforces that rejection (v. 26), speaks in vague terms of a successor (v. 28), and finally, offers a statement about God that is either a profound theological truth or a pious platitude (v. 29).

Yahweh himself has said that he repents of a previous reaction (v. 11). The narrator concurs (v. 35b). Samuel does not: "The Glory of Israel [a title for God used only here in the Old Testament] will not recant or change his mind; for he is not a mortal, that he should change his mind" (v. 29). And Samuel uses the same verb, *nakham*, for "change his mind" as do God (v. 11) and the narrator (v. 35b) for God's "regret" and God saying "he was sorry." In support of Samuel's position one might cite Balaam's statement on the topic in Num. 23:19, although Balaam may not be the best theological ally to have in one's corner. So, then, does God recant, repent, change his mind (vv. 11, 35) or does he not (v. 29)?

There are five ways to look at this quesiton in regard to Samuel's statement in v. 29. First, this is an illustration of the Bible's rejection of the law of contradiction, which says that two contradictory truths cannot simultaneously be true. Second, Samuel is wrong and his statement is misleading (Eslinger 1988: 352). Third, Samuel's statement is a later redactional gloss inserted into the text to affirm a more "orthodox" position on God's immutability (McCarter 1980: 268). Fourth, Samuel's statement refers only to God's irreversible rejection of Saul, and not to a universally true theological principle. God will not change his mind about changing his mind vis-à-vis Saul (Polzin 1989: 255). It is God's "will not" rather than God's "cannot." Fifth (and the view we prefer), the statement made by Samuel is not that God is incapable of changing his mind (vv. 11 and 35 state that he is), but that God's standards and the decisions he makes on the basis of those standards are not arbitrary like those of humankind or of pagan deities. God's decision to shift his position from acceptance to rejection or vice-versa, from punishment and justice to forgiveness and mercy or vice-versa, is rooted in God's constancy rather than in any divine caprice. As Moberly (1998:115) has stated, "How people respond to God *matters* to God, and *affects* how God responds to people." It appears that Samuel's words about God not repenting (v. 29) find a clue for their meaning in the words Samuel uses just before these ones: "The Lord has torn the kingdom of Israel from you this very day, *and has given it to a neighbor of yours, who is better than you*" (v. 28). It is this of which God will not repent, that is, his commitment to give royal leadership of his people to David and his house. And it is this indirect reference by Samuel that prepares us for the entry of David into the very next chapter of 1 Samuel, chapter 16. For Saul, it will be crucial to see how he responds to that. Hopefully, he will not respond to David as Abel did to Cain, but only time will tell.

III. 16–31: Saul and David

16:1–23. This chapter details the emergence of David as the divinely chosen replacement to the disqualified Saul to be Israel's king (vv. 1–13), and David's first meeting with Saul when he is called to the royal court to be Saul's minstrel or harpist during the king's bouts with torment (vv. 14–23).

God gives Samuel two assignments: go to Jesse of Bethlehem (presumably somehow known to Samuel) (v. 1b), and anoint one of his sons as king (v. 12b). Understandably, Samuel is hesitant about implementing these, for should Saul hear about it, it will not be music to his ears (v. 2). "It is hazardous to anoint a king when there already is a king" (Brueggemann 1990: 121). Samuel's fears that Saul might kill him anticipate the capacity for violence that Saul will demonstrate later in his life against David. That Saul already had such a reputation may be gleaned from the fact that the elders of Bethlehem panic when Samuel shows up (v. 4). What will Saul do to Bethlehem if he finds that he is to be replaced, and that by a Bethlehemite?

But God's decisions are determinative, the risks notwithstanding. What the people had earlier done to God, God has now done to Saul:

"They have rejected [ma'as] me from being king" (8:7).
"I have rejected [ma'as] him from being king" (16:1).

In Saul's place God has chosen one of the eight sons of Jesse but withholds from Samuel which one (hence opening the door to Samuel successfully or unsuccessfully exercising some discernment). God's intentionally vague "one of his sons" may remind the reader of another deliberately vague divine disclosure to a father (and son): "Sacrifice him there . . . on one of the mountains" (Gen. 22:2).

God's announcement, "I have chosen one of [Jesse's] sons to be king," reads literally, "I have seen for myself [ra'iti . . . li] a king among his sons." The verb ra'ah ("see, look") occurs, in some form, ten times in this chapter:

v. 1: "I have seen for myself a king among his sons"
v. 6: "When they arrived, Samuel saw Eliab"
v. 7: "The Lord does not look at the things man looks at"
v. 7: "Man looks . . . but the Lord looks"
v. 12: "He was . . . good-looking"
v. 17: "See for me one who plays well"
v. 18: "I have seen a son of Jesse . . . a good-looking man"

The whole chapter is about looking and seeing, especially that of God, Samuel, David, and even Jesse (who does not seem to see). That the story begins with Yahweh saying "I have seen for myself" is deliberate and contrastive with what God had said before about Saul (Gunn 1980: 125). Compare these two verses:

8:22: "Appoint a king for them."
16:1: "I have provided a king for myself."

Saul is the king appointed for the people (*lahem*), but David is the king appointed for God (*li*).

Samuel is not that impressive. God twice rebukes him, once for being too far behind the Lord, "How long will you mourn for Saul, for I have rejected him?" and once for being too far ahead of the Lord, "Do not consider [Eliab] . . . for I have rejected him" (Kessler 1970: 547). Samuel's "surely" (v. 6) in respect to Eliab sounds like that of Agag in the previous chapter (Polzin 1989: 155). The "surely" of each man was inaccurate:

15:32, Agag: "Surely the bitterness of death is past." It was not.
16:6, Samuel: "Surely the Lord's anointed is now before the Lord." He was not.

Samuel assumes that Eliab is the son of Jesse to be anointed for two reasons. He is the oldest of the brothers, and in appearance is—like Saul—handsome and tall (as if Israel needs another Saul!). As Sternberg (1985: 97) asks, "What would be more natural than to disqualify or at least distrust . . . the candidate who shares the rejected king's most salient feature?"

In this second rebuke of Samuel, Yahweh chides him for going only by external appearances (v. 7), and urges Samuel to go to the heart of the matter, which *is* the heart. Yahweh's assumption is that Samuel, while not possessing God's omniscience, to be sure, should be far more perceptive than he is. Earlier, Samuel himself had declared that Yahweh, in his rejection of Saul, was now seeking out a man "after his own heart" (13:14).

We need, however, to go easy on Samuel, even though the "seer" cannot always see as God sees. His mistake is not so much an egregious one as it is an honest one. The only precedent Samuel has for God choosing a king is Saul, and he too was handsome and tall. And there is no inherent vice in being handsome and tall, anymore than there is inherent virtue in being ugly and short. It appears, in one respect, that God did look on the external, or at least that the narrator did (9:2; 10:23). And apparently God did not like the heart that he saw in Saul, for we read in 10:9 that he gave Saul "another heart" (Eslinger 1988: 348–50). God chose, then changed, the candidate. By contrast, God never gives David "another heart." However, later in his life David will be well aware of his own heart irregularities and ask God to create in him a "pure heart" (Ps. 51:10).

That David is presented in the scene as the eighth brother after the first seven may be another illustration of the Old Testament pattern of seven/eight in which eight expresses the idea of culmination or climatic finish. One thinks of the following parallels:

1. Circumcision is to be practiced on the eighth day (possibly referring to the completion of creation in seven days, but here applied to the individual) (Gen. 17:12).
2. The firstborn of cattle and sheep stay with their mother for seven days, but are given to God on the eighth day (Exod. 22:30).
3. The days of ordination for Aaron and his sons total seven days (Lev. 8:33–35), but on the eighth day they begin their ministry (Lev. 9:1).
4. The individual with an infectious skin disease must stay outside the camp for seven days, and on the eighth day re-entry procedures start (Lev. 14:8–10). The same applies for those rendered unclean by bodily discharges (Lev. 15:13–14).
5. The feast of Tabernacles lasts for seven days, and on the eighth day the people are to conduct a sacred assembly and present their offerings to God (Lev. 23:34–36).
6. Amos, prophet to Israel, begins his preaching with oracles to eight different nations, climaxing with his words to Israel: Damascus, Gaza, Tyre, Edom, Ammon, Moab, Judah, Israel (Amos 1–2).

After all of Yahweh's insistence that Samuel not be misled by external appearances, it is somewhat surprising to see the text highlighting David's external features—reddish complexion (or hair), a fine appearance, good-looking (v. 12). Such external features are not a deterrent to being used by God, but they cannot be a substitute for the coming of the spirit of the Lord in power (v. 13). To public charisma must be added divine empowerment.

When the spirit came mightily on Saul, he immediately began to prophesy (10:6, 10), or to deliver the Jabesh-gileadites from Ammonite oppression (11:6). When the same spirit comes on David, he does nothing, at least not immediately. Is David himself aware of this pneumatic rush, and if so, how does he understand it, or experience it? We do not yet know.

To be sure, ch. 16 is about transition, a transition in leadership from Saul to David. Yet, even though the spirit leaves Saul (v. 14), he is not removed from office. And even though David is anointed, he does not immediately become king. Hence, in one case rejection is not immediately followed by death or removal, and in the other case anointing is not immediately followed by coronation (Miscall 1993: 195). Saul retains all the external trappings of his office, but he is an empty shell. David, meanwhile, is anointed, but is on hold.

Readers of Scripture will be surprised that an "evil spirit from the Lord" tormented Saul (v. 14; cf. 18:10; 19:9). The word "devil" never appears in the Old Testament, and of the eighteen or nineteen times "Satan" occurs there, fourteen of those are in Job 1–2, and always with the definite article, indicating a title ("the satan") more than a name. Given that Israel was surrounded by nations who believed in multiple gods and demons, it is remarkable that the Old Testament has only one instance of demon posession, Saul (contrast how many are in just the Gospels), and it comes from Yahweh! The Old Testament worldview is not one in which Yahweh shares power or competes for power with other supernatural forces. He alone is the power.

Saul's torment leads one of his servants to suggest David and his musical skills as a solution to the king's problems. In fact, the servant is superlative in his listing of David's qualifications—plays the harp well, a brave man, a warrior, good speaker, good-looking, Yahweh is with him (v. 18)—in what is certainly a case of "overnomination" (Brueggemann 1990: 125). It is also a fairly typical listing of the traits that "make a man a man" (Clines 1995). The last of these phrases ("and the Lord is with him") is set apart from the preceding ones as if to give it special prominence by a peculiarity in the Hebrew text. It is normal to find what is called an *atnach*, which divides the verse into two approximately even halves. Here, the *atnach* comes under "good-looking," which is the third-to-last word of a twenty-two-word verse. So, the "second half" of the verse is made up (in Hebrew) of just two words: "and-the-Lord [was] with-him." This is David's real claim to significance (Walters: 1988: 571). Interestingly, this servant of Saul is more optimistic about David than is David's own father, Jesse (v. 11). Little does Saul know what this meeting with David as court minstrel and musical therapist will lead to in months and years to come. "While Saul and his court think they are welcoming a musician, we realize that the Saulide monarchy is dragging in a Trojan Horse" (Fokkelmann 1986: 135).

Somehow, Saul knows David's name, which has not yet been mentioned in Saul's presence. The servant had simply said, "I have seen a son of Jesse" (v. 18), and to Jesse Saul sends this message: "Send me your son David" (v. 19). Possibly, the servant said more about David than is recorded in v. 18. That Saul further identifies David as "one who is with the sheep" indicates that Saul also knows David's vocation, and it chimes with what Jesse earlier said about David and sheep (v. 11). It is significant that while Saul is associated only with (his father's) donkeys, David is associated with sheep. Given that the metaphor of the king as shepherd is so common in the ancient Near Eastern world, perhaps these associations are one way the Old Testament suggests that David is the real king while Saul is king pro tem.

The spirit of the Lord that came mightily on David did not teach David how to play the lyre. He already possessed that skill. What the spirit does for David is take that resident, acquired skill and use it to bring trouble and comfort to a hurting, distressed soul. It is not difficult to move from this single instance of David ministering therapeutically to an individual through music to the Psalter, much of which is connected with Israel's "sweet singer," and from which Jewish and Christian believers, like Saul, have drawn comfort, relief, and hope.

17:1–58. Few, if any, stories in the Bible involving David are as familiar as this one, which describes the David versus Goliath episode, the small guy taking on and being victorious over the big guy. Goliath is an impressive sight. His height, following the Hebrew text, is "six cubits and a span" (v. 4), which transfers to approximately nine feet and nine inches. The Greek text reads "four cubits and a span," which equals six feet and nine inches, still quite an imposing stature.

Furthermore, his armor and weapons accentuate his height (vv. 5–7). "Goliath did indeed have the whole armor, but it was not 'the whole armor of God'" (Brueggemann 1990: 127). It is rare in the Bible for a writer to comment on what a character is wearing unless that article of clothing is central to the theme of the story, such as Adam and Eve's loincloths of fig leaves and garments of skins (Gen. 3:7, 21), Joseph's long robe with sleeves (Gen. 37:3), David's linen ephod (2 Sam. 6:14), Jesus' scarlet robe and crown of thorns (Matt. 27:28–29).

Is the sight of Goliath intimidating or comical? Miscall (1986: 120) asks, "Is this a powerful and fearsome warrior or a big oaf weighed down with armor and with little mobility?" Alter (1981: 81) describes Goliath as "a hulking monument to an obtusely mechanical conception of what constitutes power," and again (1992: 99) as "an allegorical satire on displaced faith in the realm of quantified material implements."

Israel (and Saul) is terrified both by Goliath's words ("When Saul and all Israel heard these words . . . they were dismayed and greatly afraid" [v. 11]) and by his appearance ("All the Israelites, when they saw the man . . . were very much afraid" [v. 24]). Israel might easily have taken to heart Yahweh's words to Samuel in the preceding chapter vis-à-vis Eliab: "Do not look on his appearance or on the height of his stature . . . for the Lord does not see as mortals see; they look on the outward appearance, but the Lord looks on the heart" (16:7). Interestingly, in this incident it is Eliab (17:28), whose own appearance and stature had been played down, who scolds David for thinking he can fight against one who dwarfs even Eliab. Fokkelman (1986: 162) correctly observes, "To the extent that Israel has been frightened by a giant, it runs the risk of being corrupted by subscribing to that ideology and the delusion that height or mindless force is required as an answer to that challenge."

Apart from his intimidating appearance, Goliath's strategy is to taunt the enemy (vv. 8–10, 43–44). David also knows how to taunt (vv. 45–47). Taunting is a time-honored part of war texts in which one side tries to obtain psychological advantage over the other via insults. "A taunt is a challenge, a dare that cannot be ignored unless the object of the challenge and implicit insult wishes to admit cowardice, womanishness, and defeat" (Niditch 1993: 93).

Jesse's sending of the youngest brother to check on his older brothers who are elsewhere (v. 17) is reminiscent of Jacob sending his young son Joseph to check on his older brothers who are elsewhere (Gen. 37:13–14). In both cases the older brother(s) look with distaste on the younger brother when he shows up (Gen. 37:18; 1 Sam. 17:28–30). And while Saul is not hostile to David as was Eliab, Saul assumes that David can fight Goliath only if he is dressed as a miniature Goliath (vv. 38–39). To this, David objects (v. 39b). "If you want to be killed by the Philistines, imitate the Philistine, dress like him, think like him, and talk like him" (Brueggemann 1987: 6). If God could say that his ways are not our ways (Isa. 55:9), so here, David could say to Saul, "Your way is not my way" (Gunn 1980: 79).

While this is a relatively long chapter (fifty-five verses), only two verses are given to the description of the showdown between David and Goliath (vv. 48–49). As in ch. 16, God used a skill already possessed by David (playing the lyre, slinging stones to frighten away predatory animals that got too close to his flocks) in a situation that surfaces unexpectedly (Saul's sickness, Goliath's intimidating taunts of Israel). One instrument is musical; the other is lethal. David plays and slings. He ends bouts of depression, and he ends a life. The spirit of the Lord that comes mightily on David (16:13) is the real source of enablement behind David's ministry to Saul, and his elimination of Goliath.

The battle of "champions" (see Hoffner 1968) now over, David presents the head of Goliath to Saul (v. 57), and the chapter ends with David reaffirming his paternity ("I am the son of your servant Jesse the Bethlehemite" [v. 58]). It is as if, in presenting Goliath's head as a war trophy, David says, "Here is Goliath's head, but my head is Jesse."

It is not difficult to see why this story has such fascination for children, or why it has served as biblical background for many a homily on defeating the giants in one's life, or on how the little guy can win, and so forth. Suffice it to say, David was not always successful in fighting giants, especially when they were giants of his own making. For example, while he is eminently successful against the Philistine giant Goliath, a giant external to him, he is a failure in his fight against lusting (an internal giant) for Bathsheba (2 Samuel 11).

We shall briefly touch on three problems in the interpretation of 1 Samuel 17. The first has to do with the fact that the Hebrew text and the Greek text (Septuagint) of this chapter diverge sharply in their length. The Greek text contains about 55 percent of the Hebrew text. Here is the breakdown:

Verses present in the Hebrew and the Greek	Verses present only in the Hebrew
1–11	12–31
32–40	41
42–48a	48b
49	50
51–54	55–58

Scholars who have addressed such textual matters offer several suggestions for the differences: (1) the longer Hebrew version is the more
original one, which later was abbreviated in the Greek text (Jason 1979;
Rofé 1987); (2) the shorter Greek version is the original one, and the
Hebrew text represents an expanded version (Tov 1986); (3) there never
were two versions of the story worked on one way or the other by a re-
dactor, but rather the incident (all the verses that is) is a recomposi-
tioning of the story of Saul in 1 Samuel 9–10 in which David's rise to
power is modeled on that of Saul, indicating David is Saul's legitimate
heir (Auld and Ho 1992); (4) via a form-critical analysis of the passage
one can demonstrate that the chapter is the end product of a long literary history, one that passed through four or five stages of compilation
(DeVries 1973).

The second issue in this chapter is the problem raised in vv. 55–58
(absent from the Septuagint). We know from 16:14–23 that David and
Saul have already met, that David has played his lyre before Saul in the
royal court, that Saul "loved David greatly," and that David became
Saul's armor bearer. The two of them speak to each other in 17:31–39
(all but v. 31 present also in the Septuagint). Yet, after David has killed
Goliath, Saul does not appear to know who David is (vv. 55–58, absent
from the Septuagint)! When does David first meet Saul, in the palace
(ch. 16) or on the battlefield (ch. 17)? Are we dealing here with "variant
accounts of the 'first' meeting of the two men or a sequential development of their relationship" (Sternberg 1987: 231)?

Can the whole of ch. 17 be read as a unified narrative? We believe it
can, and we begin by quoting Polzin's forceful question (1989: 172):
"Why would some guiding intelligence take care in v. 15 ["David went
back and forth from Saul to feed his father's sheep at Bethlehem"] to
make David's situation there consistent with the events of the preceding chapter, but then allow to stand, or worse still incorporate, a conclusion that is inconsistent not only with chapter 16 but also with
Saul's and David's meeting in the middle of chapter 17?"

One could conceivably argue that by the time of the Goliath incident
several years had passed since David's service to Saul as court musician
and armor bearer, but this possibility loses its validity because of the
claim of 17:15 and because of David's and Saul's dialogue in 17:31–39.
Again, it is possible to suggest that Saul is asking about David's lineage
("Whose son are you?") in order to ascertain more about David's stock
and roots. Saul's question thus becomes a command, "Tell me about
your family." But Jesse was first introduced in the narrative (16:1) as
one sufficiently known at least to Samuel so that God does not need to

tell Samuel who Jesse is. And in 16:17–19 Saul's servant has informed Saul already about David's lineage.

One might also argue that Saul asks the question in v. 55 of Abner, "Whose son is this young man?" simply because he cannot see who it is that is going out to fight Goliath. But how, then, is one to explain Saul's later question to David ("Whose son are you, young man? v. 58) when David stands right in front of him? The problem here is obviously not a visual one.

Polzin has noticed the frequent use of the demonstratives "this" and "these" throughout ch. 17, and almost always the demonstrative is used in a derisive sense:

> v. 25: The Israelites to David: "Have you seen this man who has come up?"
>
> v. 26: David to the Israelites: "What shall be done for the man who kills this Philistine?" ("this Philistine" occurs also in vv. 32, 33, 37)
>
> v. 26: David to the Israelites: "Who is this uncircumcised Philistine?" (and see also v. 36)
>
> v. 28: Eliab to David: "Why have you come down?"—literally, "Why this coming down of yours?"
>
> v. 39: David to Saul on Saul's armor: "I cannot walk with these."
>
> v. 47: David to Goliath: "All this assembly may know that the Lord does not save by sword and spear."

Then come the first two of Saul's three inquiries:

> v. 55: "Whose son is this young man?"
>
> v. 56: "Inquire whose son this stripling is."

If Saul's "this" of vv. 55 and 56 carry the same force of earlier uses of "this" in the chapter, then Saul is not asking for information. He knows well who this young Bethlehemite is. It appears that Saul is asking this question "as much out of derision as amazement" (Polzin 1989: 173).

What, then, of Saul's question directly to David in v. 58, "Whose son are you, young man?" Might it be that Saul, now well aware of David's prowess and hence usefulness to Saul in the future, is asking David to renounce Jesse as his father and proclaim himself Saul's son (Polzin 1989: 175)? After all, had not Samuel earlier predicted that Israel's king(s) "will *take* your sons and appoint them to his chariots" (8:11)? That seems literally to be fulfilled in 18:2, where we read that "Saul *took* him [David] that day and would not let him return to his father's house."

The third issue here is: who actually killed Goliath?

1. "David . . . struck down the Philistine and killed him" (17:50). (See also 18:6; 19:5; 21:9; 22:10, 13 and the statement in Sir. 47:4.)
2. "Elhanan son of Jaare-oregim the Bethlehemite killed Goliath" (2 Sam. 21:19).
3. "Elhanan son of Jair killed Lahmi the brother of Goliath" (1 Chron. 20:5).

There are several ways to approach this, the least acceptable of which, in our judgment, is to suggest that David and Elhanan are the same person, with Elhanan being his original name and David his throne name.

A second way is to believe that there are two variant traditions of who killed Goliath—David or Elhanan—and that 2 Sam. 21:19 is the more plausible tradition. It would be more natural for a heroic incident like this to be transferred from a minor person to a national hero, from a GI to a general, rather than vice versa. The Chronicler, when confronted with these variant traditions, harmonized them by making El-hanan the executioner of Goliath's brother.

A third way is to try to harmonize all three references. But this can be done only by extensive changing and "correcting" some of the texts. For example, the conservative scholar R. K. Harrison, in his celebrated *Introduction to the Old Testament* (1969: 704), suggests no fewer than three textual changes to achieve harmonization: (1) changing Elha-nan's father's name, Jaare-oregim, in 2 Sam. 21:19, to Jair, and deleting "oregim" to make it conform to 1 Chron. 20:5; (2) changing the sign of the accusative ʾet before "Goliath" in 2 Sam. 21:19 to ʾakh, "brother," again conforming 2 Sam. 21:19 to 1 Chron. 20:5; (3) changing "Lahmi" into "Bethlehemite" in 1 Chron. 20:5 to obtain the reading there, "and Elhanan, the son of Jair the Bethlehemite, slew the brother of Goliath."

Is it possible that David had some kind of assistance in his contest with Goliath and the Philistines? After all, even the 2 Samuel 21 account that credits the victory over Goliath to Elhanan ends by including Goliath in the group of four warriors who "fell at the hands of David and his men" (2 Sam. 21:22). Most of us need co-combatants when facing giants.

18:1–30. David's victory over Goliath brings him contact with Saul's family: first Jonathan, on his own initiative (vv. 1–5), and then his daughters Merab and Michal, by their father's initiative (vv. 6–30). We are introduced first to Jonathan in the following sequence (Jobling 1978: 12):

1. Jonathan establishes identification with David (v. 1).
2. Saul confirms the identification of Jonathan with David by taking David into his house (v. 2).
3. Jonathan makes David his replacement (vv. 3–4).
4. Saul confirms the replacement of Jonathan by David by sending David out to fight the battle Jonathan had previously fought (v. 5).

David is certainly a recipient of just about everybody's love. Somebody is loving (ʾahav) David at some stage in his life:

1. "Saul loved him greatly" (16:21).
2. "Jonathan loved him" (18:1).
3. "Jonathan made a covenant with David because he loved him" (18:3).
4. "All Israel and Judah loved David" (18:16).
5. "Michal loved David" (18:20).
6. "The king is delighted with you, and all his servants love you" (18:22).
7. "When Saul realized . . . that Saul's daughter Michal loved him" (18:28).
8. "Jonathan made David swear again by his love for him; for he loved him as he loved his own life" (20:17).
9. "Saul and Jonathan beloved and lovely" (2 Sam. 1:23).
10. "Your love [Jonathan's] to me [David] was wonderful, passing the love of a woman" (2 Sam. 1:26).

We should avoid interpreting these references simply to mean that Jonathan and David were good, close friends. Similarly, we should avoid the conclusion that Jonathan and David were homosexual lovers (Horner 1978). Jonathan loves David; he does not "know" David. One study of the word "love" (Thompson: 1974) observes that within the lexicon of (political) treaty terminology, "love" connotes loyalty and faithfulness. Thus, when Amos castigates Tyre for not remembering "the covenant of kinship" with Israel (1:9), this surely refers back to the political/diplomatic covenant made between David and King Hiram of Tyre. This relationship is expressed by "for Hiram had always been a lover [ʾohev] of David" (1 Kings 5:1).

Does, then, the phrase "Jonathan loved David" mean merely that Jonathan was loyal to David? There is another verb in addition to "love" that describes Jonathan's feelings for David, and that is "took great delight in" (NRSV), "was very fond of" (NIV), in 19:1, and the Hebrew for that is *khapats be*. In fact, Saul uses this verb in an insincere fashion to describe his feelings for David, "See, the king is delighted in you" (18:22), and in 18:25, "the king desires no marriage present except. . . ." These two verbs describe a man's feeling for a woman in the Shechem/Dinah story of Genesis 34: "And he [Shechem] loved the girl" (Gen. 34:3); "And he [Shechem] was delighted with Jacob's daughter" (Gen. 34:19). (In *The Book of Genesis: Chapters 18–50* [Grand Rapids: 1995], I render Gen. 34:19 as "was infatuated with.")

Is there a middle ground between friendship and connubiality? Without in any way indicating homoeroticism, might we say that David was Jonathan's "significant other" and vice versa (Clines 1995: 241)? There was an intimacy between these two that David did not experience with any of his wives. It is interesting that David is always the object of love. He is not said to love anyone; rather, people love him. (The possible exception to this is 16:21, where in the expression "Saul loved him greatly," "Saul" is assumed to be the subject. The text simply says, "He loved him greatly," and David is the subject of the three other verbs in the sentence [Wong 1997: 544–46].)

The reader is impressed by Jonathan's spirit. David is a friend, not a competitor or rival. Contentedly he steps aside, happy to stand in the shadow of David. Jonathan does not believe that equality (and hence, eventual succession) with Saul is something to be grasped at, but empties himself and takes the form of a follower.

Upon returning home after the victorious battle, Saul, David, and the rest are met by a group of singing, dancing women (cf. Exod. 15:20–21; Judg. 11:34). Their song is "Saul has killed his thousands, and David his ten thousands" (v. 7).

It is unlikely that this song is intended to elevate David's accomplishments over Saul's. These women would hardly choose this occasion to denigrate their king. Rather, the two lines are reflective of a feature of Hebrew poetry in which a number in the first line is increased by one unit in the next, for example, "three . . . four" or "six . . . seven." In the case of one thousand, the next number would be ten thousand (Gevirtz 1964: 17). Another illustration of this sequence is present in Deut. 32:30: "How could one have routed a thousand, and two put ten thousand [a myriad] to flight?"

But these fine points of the stylistics of Hebrew poetry escape Saul. He knows nothing about the significance of "fixed pairs" in poetry. In fact, each of the three times this refrain occurs (18:7; 21:11; 29:5), something unpleasant follows.

Saul has several ways he believes he can eliminate David: (1) try to kill him outright—Saul with his spear in hand versus David with his lyre in hand (vv. 10–11); (2) make David a commander of a military militia, and hence "kick David upstairs by promoting him to colonel" (Fokkelman 1986: 224) (vv. 12–16); (3) marry him to his daughter Merab, and let the Philistines kill him in battle while David represents his father-in-law (vv. 17–19); (4) marry him to his daughter Michal, and ask only for a hundred Philistine foreskins as a modest marriage present (vv. 20–29). Saul's hope is that before David can get any of the foreskins, the Philistines will skin him.

Throughout this chapter we are allowed to hear not only Saul's words, but also his thoughts (both "said" and "thought" are conveyed by 'amar). By contrast, we hear David's words, but never his musings. With Saul there is an interesting chiastic use of "said/thought" (Alter 1981: 118):

> v. 17: "Then Saul *said* to David"
> "For Saul *thought*"
> v. 21: "Saul *thought*"
> "Therefore Saul *said* to David"

Everything Saul tries to do backfires. He misunderstands poetry. He is a poor shot with a spear. David has unprecedented success in leading the army. And David doubles Saul's request for a hundred foreskins to two hundred (v. 27)! David tops Saul twice: ten thousand to one thousand, and two hundred to one hundred. David tops Saul twice and he eludes him twice.

To collect two hundred foreskins of the Philistines is interesting, for throughout the Old Testament the Philistines are referred to as "the uncircumcised ones" (e.g., 17:26, "this uncircumcised Philistine"). This event may be referred to in Ps. 118:10–12, where the writer says three times, "All nations surrounded me; in the name of the Lord I cut them off." The verb "cut off" is really "circumcise (by removing the foreskin)," so that one could translate, "All nations surrounded me, but in Yahweh's name indeed I cut off their foreskins" (M. Dahood, *Psalms III: 101–150* [Garden City, N.Y.: 1970], 154, 157–58).

19:1–24. Saul tries to eliminate David—much as David will later try to eliminate Uriah—beginning with a more subtle strategy (ch. 18), then becoming much more overt and blatant (ch. 19). So here, Saul speaks with Jonathan about wanting to have David killed (v. 1). Saul makes no attempt to cover his tracks.

Jonathan succeeds in restraining his father by reminding Saul that David has done nothing worthy of death; in fact, David had put his life on the line for Saul and for Israel (vv. 4–5). Saul agrees, and takes an oath that he will not have David killed (v. 6). But one wonders. Is Saul really persuaded by the forcefulness of Jonathan's logic, or is this merely a charade to get David back to the court, where one more time Saul may get his hands on him (Miscall 1986: 127)?

If it is a charade, maybe it has worked. Saul has another chance to use David for target practice. This time David does not merely avoid the weapon. He escapes (vv. 8–10). Being the object of three throws of a spear from one's father-in-law ought to convince anybody that for the father-in-law you are *persona non grata*, and he would like to make you *persona non exista!*

Saul sends messengers to David's house (v. 11), just as later, David would send messengers to Uriah's house (2 Sam. 11:3–4). Both want to get their hands on somebody inside the house. The messengers plan to kill David in the morning (as the Gazites intend to kill Samson in the brothel in the morning [Judg. 16:2]).

It is now Michal's time to come to David's rescue as Jonathan had in the earlier part of the chapter. Like Rahab (Josh. 2:15), she lowers David to the ground through an open window so that he may escape under cover of darkness. David, Michal, and a window appear together twice in the biblical narrative (Fokkelman 1986: 273), the first window representing the love between Michal and David, the second window representing the alienation between Michal and David:

1 Sam. 19:12: "So Michal let David down through the window."
2 Sam. 6:16: "Michal . . . looked out of the window, and saw King David leaping and dancing before the Lord."

In the previous chapter we observed that Michal loved David (18:20), the only instance in the Old Testament where we read that a woman loved a man (apart from the unnamed woman in the Song of Solomon; e.g., "I sought him whom my soul loves" [3:1]). Now, in ch. 19, Michal is putting that love into practice. She fulfills literally the teaching of 1 John 3:18, "Little children, let us love, not in word or speech, but in truth and action."

To that end, Michal made a David look-alike dummy, using, of all things, life-size household idols/teraphim (what are *they* doing in Michal and David's house?) with goats' hair and clothes for the covering. When her ruse is discovered, she exclaims, "He [David] said to me, 'Let me go; why should I kill you?'" (v. 17b).

An overwhelming number of commentators believe that Michal's explanation is a fabrication. This, then, is another illustration of outright lies in unverifiable quotations using the XYZ (X told Y that Z said) format (see pp. 49–50). For a dissenting view, that David probably did so threaten Michal, see Edelman 1991: 147–48. As trickster, Michal joins a host of other women who outwit men. Not having the "clout" in a patriarchal society like a man, women often survived using wit and deception. Compare the following:

Rebekah and Isaac (Gen. 27:5–23)
Rachel and Laban (Gen. 31:34–35)
Tamar and Judah (Gen. 38:12–30)
the midwives and pharaoh (Exod. 1:15–19)
Jochebed/Miriam and pharaoh (Exod. 2:2–10)
Rahab and the officials of Jericho (Josh. 2:3–21)
Jael and Sisera (Judg. 4:17–21; 5:24–27)
Esther and Mordecai/Haman (Esth. 5–7)

Saul now launches a search-and-destroy mission for David (vv. 18–24). On three occasions Saul sends messengers to capture David, but on each occasion they are thrown off track when the spirit of God comes upon them and they engage in frenzied, ecstatic, abnormal behavior. It is somewhat like Balaam in Numbers 22–24. His mission is to curse, but what comes out is blessing. Their mission is to capture, but what comes out is praise and worship.

Half curious, half frustrated, Saul himself goes to capture David at Ramah. Upon Saul too comes the spirit of the Lord (an echo of a later Saul who also went to capture fugitives only to find himself on the ground [Acts 9:1–4]?). This particular incident produces a second instance in the Saul story of the proverbial question "Is Saul also among the prophets?" (cf. 10:12).

However, some major differences stand between these two events. Samuel predicted the first one (10:6) but not the second one. In the first one, Saul's charismatic experience is the third of three "signs" that God will perform authenticating Saul's election. There is no "sign" significance for the second one. At the first experience, God gave Saul "another heart" (10:9). There is no heart transplant in the second experience. And finally, only in the second experience does Saul "strip off his clothes" (19:24) and lay on the ground nude for an extended period of time. In such condition—frenzied and totally naked—he is hardly in any condition to pursue David up and down Ramah's streets and boulevards. This time of trance provides David ample time to escape Saul.

This chapter's ending with Saul's stripping and nakedness is a commentary on Saul's life from this point on. Note the emphasis on "stripping" at these two key points:

19:24: "He [Saul] stripped off his clothes."
31:8–9: "When the Philistines came to strip the dead, they found Saul. . . . They cut off his head, stripped off his armor."

His nudity (or near nudity) is a picture of an individual reduced to a state of impotency. Thus Gunn (1980: 83) remarks that "Saul's helplessness before Samuel is marked symbolically by his nakedness." Alter (1992: 20) says that "the nakedness reduces him to abject equality with all the other victims of the spirit; and even more significantly . . . nakedness signifies divestment of kingship." Brueggemann (1990: 45) observes that the "pitifully embarrassing scene is that of this once great man, still tall but no longer great . . . now rendered powerless in a posture of submissiveness." And finally, Jobling (1978: 10) quotes the German scholar Stoebe: "The clothes which are here torn off are the clothes of a king, who now, not only in disgraceful nakedness, but stripped likewise of power, lies impotently on the ground."

20:1–42. Saul may have lost his clothes, but he has not lost his anger at David. "Is Saul also among the prophets?" ch. 19 ended by asking. Chapter 20 chimes in with its own question, in essence, "Is Saul also among those so consumed by anger and revenge that he will stop at nothing to eliminate any imaginary threat?"

Chapter 20 is really a chapter more about Jonathan than about either his father, Saul, or his brother-in-law, David. There are three main scenes, and in each, Jonathan is a major character:

Scene 1: Jonathan and David talk together (vv. 1–23)
Scene 2: Jonathan and Saul talk together (vv. 24–34)
Scene 3: Jonathan and David talk together (vv. 35–42)

In scene one, David is bewildered as to why Saul wants to kill him. David has done nothing to goad Saul into such behavior (v. 1). Jonathan's words to David about his father will impress some as naïve (v. 2). After all, did not Saul in 19:1 speak to Jonathan about killing David? But at the last meeting, father and son had reassured David that his life was safe (19:4–7, esp. Saul in v. 6). So, Jonathan's comments in 20:2 go back to 19:6 rather than to 19:1.

It is David, not Jonathan, who comes up with a litmus test to determine whether Saul's mood is hostile or conciliatory. Jonathan is to explain to his father at the family feast that David is absent because he has returned to Bethlehem to celebrate some yearly sacrifice with his own family (vv. 5–8). Jonathan is to let David know of his father's reaction to David's absence by shooting arrows in the direction of David's hiding place (vv. 18–23). David will celebrate at Bethlehem, the "house of bread," rather than share Saul's bread.

The occasion is the "new moon" (vv. 5, 18, 27), an important festival celebrated by families and clans if they were in a state of ritual purity. On four occasions in the Old Testament the new moon festival is connected with the Sabbath observance (2 Kings 4:23; Isa. 1:13–14; Hos. 2:11 [Heb. v. 13]; Amos 8:5), but only one of these (Amos 8:5) explicitly refers to the cessation from work on the new moon festival as on the Sabbath.

In scene two, Saul's hunch is that David is absent from festival observance because he is disqualified by some form of ritual impurity (v. 26), possibly a nocturnal emission. David would then be conforming to a teaching like Lev. 7:20, "But those who eat flesh from the Lord's sacrifice of well-being while in a state of uncleanness shall be cut off from their kin" (as if David has not already been cut off from his kin!). This ruse, however, will work for one day but not for two. For example, Lev. 15:16 teaches that an emission of semen merely requires bathing, and one is unclean only "until the evening."

Saul cannot say "David" to Jonathan. He calls him "the son of Jesse" (vv. 27, 30, 31). In response, however, Jonathan does not use "the son of Jesse" but "David" (v. 28). (Compare, later, how Michal will sneeringly refer to David as "the king of Israel" in face-to-face conversation with her husband [2 Sam. 6:20].)

Jonathan attempts to cover for David (vv. 28–29). His repetition in vv. 28–29 is longer than David's own suggested wording (v. 6)—from two lines of fourteen words to five lines of twenty-one words (Fokkelman 1986: 330). Here are a few of the changes: (1) Jonathan substitutes "go" (v. 28) for David's "run" (v. 6); (2) Jonathan changes David's "a yearly sacrifice" (v. 6) into "a sacrifice" (v. 29); (3) David's "all the family" (v. 6) becomes "our family," and Jonathan adds "and my brother has commanded me to be there" (v. 29); (4) Jonathan has David say to Jonathan in v. 29, "Let me go . . . let me *slip away*" (*malat*, a key verb used in ch. 19 to refer to David's escape from and eluding of Saul: [19:10, 11, 12, 17, 18]). Fokkelman (1986: 332) says that the use of this verb "must act like a red flag to a bull. Placed in the mouth of the (feigned) David, and addressed to Saul, it is a first-class Freudian slip."

Saul loses all control. "It takes almost nothing to set Saul off when the subject is David" (Brueggemann 1990: 151). In effect he "curses out" Jonathan (for an attempt to put Saul's name for his son into equivalent profane English, see the rendering of v. 30a in the *Living Bible*, but not reproduced in its successor, the *New Living Translation*). To shameless speech (v. 30) Saul adds shameless action (v. 33), as he attempts to kill Jonathan with his spear, just as he had done with David. For Saul, Jonathan has become David.

The final scene (vv. 35–42) brings Jonathan and David together once more. It is the last time they will see each other alive, except for the brief episode in 23:15–18. The next time they are spoken of together David will compose a eulogy/elegy over Saul and Jonathan (2 Sam. 1:17–27). It is an emotionally wrenching scene. It is a weeping scene and a parting scene. David bows before Jonathan, even though both know that David is the heir-elect (v. 41). And Jonathan wishes David peace (v. 42), an appropriate parting blessing for one whose life has been anything but peaceful in recent days and months.

21:1–15. Many things happen in twos in this chapter: (1) David makes two journeys, first to Nob (v. 1) and later to Gath (v. 10); (2) David commits two acts of duplicity, one involving speech (v. 2), the second involving action (v. 13); (3) two individuals are duped, Ahimelech the priest of Nob, and Achish the Philistine king of Gath; (4) David asks two questions of Achish, "Now then, what do you have at hand?" (v. 3) and "Is there no spear or sword with you?" (v. 8), and in both, David is "more imperious than entreating" (Alter 1981: 72); (5) two shepherds are present in this narrative, David (16:11; 17:15) and Doeg the Edomite who is "the chief of Saul's shepherds" (21:7); (6) Ahimelech is afraid of David (v. 1), and David is afraid of Achish (v. 12).

David flees first to Nob, which is situated to the north of Jerusalem and is in the southern portion of the territory of Benjamin (Neh. 11:32; Isa. 10:27–32). In the wake of the destruction of Shiloh (Jer. 7:14), the sanctuary that had been at Shiloh (1 Sam. 14:3) has now been moved to Nob.

Ahimelech, the priest, meets David, just as earlier the elders of Bethlehem greeted Samuel upon his arrival in their city:

"Ahimelech came trembling to meet David" (21:1).
"The elders of the city came to meet him [Samuel] trembling" (16:4).

David responds to the questions of the priest (which, by the way, presuppose previous contact between the two) by concocting the lie that he is on a secret mission for Saul (v. 2).

Ahimelech offers David the holy bread that is supposed to be set before Yahweh on the shewbread table in the sanctuary in two rows of six loaves each (Exod. 25:30; Lev. 24:5–9). We cannot be certain whether the bread given to David is the old bread that has been on the table undisturbed for a week, then to be eaten by the priests in the sacred precincts, or the twelve freshly baked loaves.

David (and his men!) may have this bread "provided that the young men have kept themselves from women" (v. 4b). Hence, a matter of ritual purity surfaces in ch. 20 (v. 26) and again in ch. 21 (v. 4b). Leviticus (see Lev. 15:16–18) teaches that sexual intercourse causes impurity (cf. Exod. 19:15b "do not go near a woman"). The concern in 1 Samuel 21 is with the holiness of the military camp (Deut. 23:10–15). Even more so than for the residential camp of Israel is the requirement of purity in Israel's military camp. The idea is that God is present in such a camp to fight for Israel, and impurity is incompatible with the presence of God. Accordingly, soldiers on a campaign would abstain from contact with women (possibly, this is behind Uriah's refusal to go down to his wife's house [2 Sam. 11:11]), which is one source of such impurity. One cannot miss the irony in David's affirmation of his own purity while at the same time telling Ahimelech a blatant lie.

"Doeg the Edomite" (v. 7) maybe is like "Uriah the Hittite," a mercenary in the army of an Israelite king. He, as far as David is concerned, is in the wrong place at the wrong time. As an "eavesdropper" (Alter 1981: 66) he sees all, hears all, and can pass that information on to Saul. Hence, David must be on the move again, this time to Gath, the city of Goliath.

The Synoptic Gospels have Jesus comment on this story of David eating the holy bread (Matt. 12:1–8; Mark 2:23–28; Luke 6:1–5) to teach the subordination of even very sacred institutions to the importance of people. Institutions are servants, not masters. The point of the parallel between the two is the satisfying of the hunger of the followers of David and the followers of the Son of David (the former with holy bread, the latter with hand-harvested grain on the Sabbath). Some differences stand between the account in 1 Samuel 21 and that in the Gospels. There is, for example, no mention of a Sabbath in 1 Samuel 21, nor is there an explicit mention of David actually entering the sanctuary (cf. Mk. 2:26). Most interesting is Mark's identification of the priest as Abiathar (Mk. 2:26), who is the son of Ahimelech (and maybe the reason why neither Matthew nor Luke mentions any priest's name?). Either Mark is incorrect, or else something like "the father of" [Abiathar] has been accidentally omitted from the text.

David now heads some distance to Gath in Philistine territory. Note the reverse order of place name and person name in David's two journeys: Nob . . . Ahimelech (v. 1), Achish . . . Gath (v. 10).

This indicates that in v. 1 David's primary target is to get to Nob (for sanctuary shelter?), but in v. 10 his primary aim is to get to King Achish (for a hideout beyond Saul's turf). But he finds out, to his dismay, that his reputation has preceded him (v. 11). The songs of David's prowess are familiar (but not appreciated) on Philistine soil. David's spontaneous move on this occasion is to fake insanity (v. 13; and for a second time in this chapter he illustrates an uncanny ability to think "fast on his feet"). And it works (vv. 14–15). He is a convincing actor. Achish sends David away, never realizing that he "let slip the golden opportunity of liquidating the man who will later prove to be the only man who can break Philistine might" (Fokkelman 1986: 366). Achish can tell, verily, the fisherman's story of "the big one that got away."

For a second time David is the object of a double derisive demonstrative:

17:55–56 (Saul to Abner): "Whose son is *this* young man? . . . Inquire whose son *this* child is."

21:15 (Achish to his officials): "you brought *this* fellow to play the madman. . . . Shall *this* fellow come into my house?"

Psalm 34 refers to this incident in its superscription: "Of David, when he feigned madness before Abimelech, so that he drove him out, and he went away." In this alphabetical acrostic psalm that celebrates and gives thanks to Yahweh for deliverance from tribulations there is no actual reference in the internal parts of the psalm to the incident in 1 Samuel 21. And, of course, we note that the title names the king as "Abimelech" rather than "Achish." It might be that "Abimelech" is not so much a mistake in Psalm 34 as it is that "Abimelech" is the Semitic name of a line of Gath's kings (see Gen. 26:1: "Isaac went to Gerar, to King Abimelech of the Philistines," coming after Gen. 20:2, another Abimelech).

22:1–23. From Gath, David flees to Adullam, a small site southwest of Bethlehem, where he will be joined by "all his father's house" (including his oldest and very resentful brother, Eliab [17:28]) and by a motley group of four hundred have-nots (v. 2)—the distressed, the indebted, the discontents. For Mendenhall (*The Tenth Generation* [Baltimore 1973], 135–36), this group of poor, marginal desperadoes attracted to David is the best Old Testament example of a socially marginal group in the ancient Near East called the Habiru: "He [David] lost status in the Israelite community by flight caused by the enmity of the king. There gathered about him other refugees motivated by economic as well as other concerns. All were similarly without legal protection and had to maintain themselves by forming a band under the leadership of David, which was then able to survive by cleverness combined with a considerable degree of mobility." Such individuals, interestingly, never found Saul to be a magnet. David attracts them; Saul repels them. And here David foreshadows "David's greater son," who will attract to himself those whom the Herods either ignore or bully.

Ever mindful of the Torah's injunction to honor one's mother and father, David, sensing the danger of the situation to himself and to his family, takes his parents to Moab as a hideaway (v. 3). This is one of the very few times in the Old Testament that the Moabites are spoken of appreciatively and admirably, and how appropriate it is for David to select Moab, given that Ruth, his great-grandmother, was Moabite.

The bulk of the chapter (vv. 6–23) describes Saul's horrendous massacre of Ahimelech and all the priests serving at the sanctuary there. This is Saul's way of retaliating against anybody he suspects of being in collusion with David in any way.

Saul rebukes his fellow Benjaminites for conspiracy in that they have not jumped on his anti-David bandwagon (vv. 6–8). Saul still can refer to David only as "the son of Jesse" (vv. 7–8). Note that among his insults Saul says of David, "Will he make you all commanders of thousands and commanders of hundreds?" (v. 7c). Saul's use of a descending pattern ("thousands . . . hundreds") may be deliberate, for an ascending pattern ("hundreds . . . thousands") would be a painful reminder of the song celebrating David's victory over Goliath (thousands . . . ten thousands) in 18:7 (Fokkelman 1986: 385). It is Doeg, however, who offers the information about his observance of Ahimelech's hospitality toward David (vv. 9–10). For Ahimelech, the sharing of that information is the kiss of death.

It is interesting to compare Doeg's words (vv. 9b-10) with Saul's repetition of those charges in v. 13:

1. Note the change of order. Doeg speaks of (a) Ahimelech inquiring of the Lord, (b) provisions, (c) the sword of Goliath. Saul speaks of (a) bread, (b) a sword, (c) Ahimelech inquiring of the Lord. Thus, a-b-c becomes b-c-a. In other words, the charge Doeg starts with is the one with which Saul ends, as if to rearrange the charges in "an ascending order of treason" (Sternberg 1985: 420).
2. Doeg speaks of Ahimelech's inquiring of "the Lord"; Saul speaks of Ahimelech inquiring of "God."
3. Doeg speaks of "the sword of Goliath," which is surprisingly glossed over by Saul's "a sword."

4. Doeg speaks of "provisions" (did he know or not know it was "holy bread"?); Saul speaks of "bread."

Ahimelech tries to defend himself before Saul (vv. 14–15), something about as useless as trying to stop an avalanche by holding one's hand aloft.

In defending David (unlike Saul, Ahimelech does call him "David" [v. 14], not "the son of Jesse"), Ahimelech uses language reminiscent of that used by Yahweh about the great Moses:

Num. 12:7: "Not so my servant [*avdi*] Moses; he is entrusted [*ne'eman*] with all my house [*beti*]."
1 Sam. 22:14: "Who among all your servants [*avadekah*] is so faithful [*ne'eman*]? . . . and he is honored in your house [*betekah*]."

Saul's pronouncement of death on Ahimelech ("you shall die" [v. 16]) is exactly the same as that which he earlier pronounced on Jonathan for an act of sacrilege (14:44). And just as the people then refused to obey the royal edict (14:45), so do they here (22:17b).

But Doeg has no such scruples about Yahweh's anointed priests. His only loyalty is to Saul. He is "an evil genius" (Gunn 1980: 87), "a hired gun" (Brueggemann 1990: 159). Tragically, using an Edomite mercenary, Saul does to Nob (v. 19) what Joshua did to Jericho. "Through the hand of a foreigner Saul perpetrates upon Israelites, priests of the Lord, what he himself did not perpetrate upon foreigners, the Amalekites" (Miscall 1986: 136).

The escape of just one Nobite survivor (Abiathar) from a massacre (v. 20) recalls another massacre from which one person escaped (Jotham [Judg. 9:5]). In one, seventy are killed; in the other, eighty-five are killed. And both times the bloodbath is perpetrated by kin against kin.

Not for the last time will David admit (v. 22c) that he is the cause of the death of innocent persons. Compare his words after his census and the judgment of God for that act: "I alone have sinned . . . but these sheep, what have they done?" (2 Sam. 24:17). David's parents will be safe with the king of Moab (v. 3), and Abiathar will be safe with David (v. 23).

23:1–29. In this cat-and-mouse game, there is one significant difference between Saul the "cat" and David the "mouse." Both Saul and David have access to human informants—Saul: "it was told Saul" (v. 7); "when Saul was told" (v. 13); "when Saul heard" (v. 25); David: "they told David" (v. 1); "when David learned" (v. 9); "when David was told"

(v. 25). But what David has, and Saul does not have, is access to divine information—"David inquired of the Lord" (v. 2); "then David inquired of the Lord again" (v. 4); "David said, 'O Lord, the God of Israel'" (vv. 10–11); "then David said [to Yahweh]" (v. 12). The one who relies only on human informers is frustrated, but the one who combines proper listening to others and seeking the will of God is successful (in evading the "cat"). Or to put it differently, "Saul's preponderant military resources are counterbalanced by David's divine sources" (Polzin 1989: 200).

The very town that David has delivered from the Philistines, Keilah (vv. 1–5), now intends, so David finds out by divine oracle, to hand David over to Saul (vv. 6–14). Not an awful lot of gratitude there, unless their motivation is fear of sharing the Nobites' fate (cf. the language of v. 10 with 22:19).

David's next hideout is the wilderness of Ziph (v. 14) and of Maon (v. 24). And the Ziphites, on their own initiative, are prepared to hand David over to Saul (vv. 19–20). (Cf. in the superscription that introduces Psalm 54: "A Maskil of David, when the Ziphites went and told Saul, 'David is in hiding among us.'") "Ziph and Maon are one or two hours' walk to the southeast of Hebron" (Fokkelman 1986: 436). It is more than likely, then, that they are part of the territory of Judah. (For the contrary view that the two represent an independent buffer zone between Judah and the Philistines, see Edelman 1991: 182–83.) Neither Judahite Keilah nor Judahite Ziph nor Judahite Maon proves to be a real sanctuary for the Judahite David. Gunn (1980: 90) says tellingly, "As chapter 23 makes clear, apart from *his own son*, his own countrymen are all on his [Saul's] side, prepared to give up David and demonstrate their loyalty to the king. It is not treachery that defeats Saul but the will of Yahweh."

Two things do happen in this chapter that work in David's favor. One is the sudden and brief appearance of Jonathan (his last with David) in vv. 16–18. While all previous meetings of the brothers-in-law have been salutary, what distinguishes this one from the previous ones is Jonathan's bold assertion to David, "You shall be king over Israel," followed up by his "I shall be second to you" (v. 17). David will be number one, and Jonathan will be number two, and, of course, few people celebrate the position of runner-up or second fiddle, as does Jonathan. The celebratory cry "We're number two!" is seldom heard on fields or diamonds or courts or in arenas.

Jonathan is right in his first prophecy (concerning David), but wrong in his second prophecy (concerning himself). One wonders about the source of Jonathan's statement vis-à-vis David. Is he stating "knowledge, belief, or hope? Or is this persuasive flattery?" (Miscall 1986: 142).

The second gracious thing that happens to David is the sudden arrival of an unbidden "messenger" (v. 27) who informs Saul of a raid the Philistines are making that requires Saul's intervention, thus forcing him, temporarily at least, to suspend his chase of David. And just when he had David within hand's grasp!

David will say, "Blessed be this messenger." Saul will say, "Cursed be this messenger." Given that "messenger" (*mal'ak*) may also be rendered "angel," could it be that "Providence itself is the Sender" (Fokkelman 1986: 450)?

24:1–22. So preoccupied is the writer with Saul's relentless search-and-destroy pursuit of David (and Saul himself is so preoccupied with it) that he devotes not so much as a syllable to the results of Saul's campaign against the Philistines (23:27–28; 24:1a). How did the battle go? Was it successful? Was Saul victorious? Who cares when personal vendettas outweigh the significance of national concerns? Saul will take one dead David over a thousand dead Philistines.

That Saul and David should meet where and when and how they do in this chapter is an instance of burlesque humor or divine providence or both. Saul enters a cave to "relieve himself," and it is the very same cave in which David and his men are hiding (v. 3). The Hebrew "to relieve himself" reads literally "to cover his feet." Saul defecates in a cave while in a squatting position that causes his cloak to fall over his feet; hence the phrase "to cover one's feet." There are caves all over the area of En-gedi. And yet Saul answers "the call of nature" in the very cave in which David and his party have hidden out.

David's allies, thankfully lacking any interest in scatological humor, suggest a theological interpretation of this bathroom improvisation incident. God has used "nature" to deliver Saul, our enemy, into our hands (v. 4). They make exactly the same mistake that Saul made in the previous chapter when it was David who was in a vulnerable position—"God has given him into my hand" (23:7b). Those who are inclined to justify a certain course of action as "God's will" merely because the circumstances are perfect may do well to ponder these two incidents in 1 Samuel 23 and 24.

David does not cut off Saul's head as he did Goliath's and as his associates urge him to, but he does "cut off [a key verb in this chapter] a corner of Saul's cloak" (v. 4). David does not derobe Saul; he cuts off just a snippet of his robe in the darkness of a cave. And yet this relatively minor act is enough to make David feel guilt immediately after (v. 5). Does he have the right to scissor away a three-inch-square patch from the clothing of the "Lord's anointed" (v. 6)? It is a credit to David that he is capable of being distraught even over the doing of a little thing (Swindoll 1997: 85).

But is it a little thing? The reader should connect this tearing of clothing with Saul earlier tearing the hem of Samuel's robe (15:27), which prompts Samuel to say that Yahweh "has torn the kingdom from you . . . and has given it to a neighbor of yours who is better than you" (15:28). Also, 18:4 tells us that Jonathan stripped himself of his robe and gave it to David. All three passages (15:27; 18:4; 24:4, 5, 11) use the Hebrew word meʿil for "cloak, robe." Does the transference of clothing from Saul (or Jonathan) to David represent the transference of the kingship from Saul to David (Gunn 1980: 95; Fokkelman 1986: 458)?

Outside the cave David attempts to clear the air about his own behavior vis-à-vis Saul (vv. 9–15) in what is David's longest speech recorded in the Bible (Fokkelman 1986: 461). Saul is listening to the wrong people (v. 9), and David refused to end Saul's life when Saul was a sitting duck (vv. 10–11). If Saul is to suffer any consequences, it will be because of Yahweh's hand, not David's (vv. 12, 15).

Saul is not even sure if it is David who is talking: "Is this your voice, my son David?" (v. 16), sounding for all the world like blind Isaac, who inquired about the identity of the speaker in front of him—Esau? Jacob? (Gen. 27:18, 22, 24, 32). Have Saul's eyes been blinded by his tears? If so, it is an "apt emblem of his moral blindness that has prevented him from seeing David as he really is" (Alter 1981: 37).

Verse 16c is the only occasion on which Saul weeps (Fokkelman 1986: 468). There has been, thus far, plenty of gnashing of teeth, but no weeping. Hannah weeps over barrenness (1:7, 8, 10). Saul upbraids people for weeping (11:4–5). Jonathan and David weep on each other's shoulders (20:41). David weeps over a devastated city (30:4). But Saul's weeping is different from all these in that his weeping alone is prompted by his own obtuseness and vileness.

Saul sounds like Judah talking to his daughter-in-law Tamar upon the exposure of his own immorality (Gen. 38:26) when he says to David, "You are more righteous than I" (v. 17). Both use the same Hebrew construction:

Gen. 38:26: *tsadeqah mimmenni ki*
1 Sam. 24:18: *tsaddiq ʾattah mimmenni ki*

For the first time Saul concedes, without making a concession speech, that David "shall surely be king" (v. 20). Saul does not say how or when. He does manage to get a promise from David that David will not "cut off" any of Saul's descendants (v. 21) (as he had cut off the corner of Saul's cloak). This raises the question of whether David's word will be like Saul's promissory word, unreliable or reliable. Will David honor this oath?

A lot of talk and action in this chapter involves Saul and David. From David we have self-exoneration (vv. 9–15) and an oath directed to future Saulides (v. 22). From Saul we have confession, concession, tears, and a concern for posterity (vv. 16–21). The one thing we do not have is any real reconciliation between Saul and David. That David goes one way and Saul goes another way at the end (v. 22) indicates that the meeting of the two "has not led to a rapproachment between the King and King-elect" (Edelman 1991: 203). This suggests to the reader that ahead in the narrative there may be a déjà vu of 1 Samuel 24.

25:1–44. With Saul momentarily absent from the narrative, David finds himself in another tense situation. It concerns a wealthy herder, Nabal, and his wife, Abigail, from Carmel, a village in the Maon district of Judah (see Josh. 15:55) south of Hebron (not to be confused with the prominent mountain of the same name on the coast of Palestine made famous in the Elijah narrative).

Before we are told Nabal's name (v. 3a), we are told details of his wealth (v. 2). This odd sequence functions to indicate the important place Nabal's possessions will have in the ensuing narrative (Bar-Efrat 1989: 115). After their names (Nabal's first, Abigail's second) come two phrases describing each (Abigail first, Nabal second). In what Sternberg (1987: 327) calls "moral and psychological portraiture by epithet," Abigail is "clever and beautiful" while Nabal is "surly and mean" (v. 3b). Such descriptors, coming as early as they do in the chapter, have a proleptic function vis-à-vis the unfolding narrative.

Since David and his supporters are on the run from Saul in wildernesses and more than likely are getting by only on rations, David sends ten of his men to Nabal with the request that Nabal share with them out of his bounty on this feast day (vv. 5–8). Nabal owes this to David in return for the protection that David has given (either solicited or unsolicited) to Nabal's shepherds, or in return for David not having harmed the vulnerable shepherds. It is pay-up time! To Nabal this delegation may appear to be "the Mafiosi" (Gunn 1980: 101), "protection racketeers" (Miscall 1986: 151), or "terrorists" (Brueggemann 1990: 176). Or contrariwise, David is referring to an earlier and gracious act of his, according to the old principle of reciprocity, "entirely analagous to the content of the historical prologue in Late Bronze Age covenants" (Mendenhall 1973: 94).

Nabal's response is far from sensitive and charitable. He insults David in good Saul-like fashion (v. 10a), and also the delegation David has sent (v. 10b). Those whom David called "my young men" (v. 8) Nabal calls "servants" (v. 10c) (Levenson 1978: 16). Not only is Nabal "surly and mean," but he is also a parsimonious ingrate.

David's response to this is to declare war on Nabal and put Nabal and his men to the sword as Saul has done to the priests of Nob (22:19). Compare the threefold use of "sword" in v. 13 with the threefold use of "peace" back in v. 6 (Miscall 1986: 151). Jesus said, "I have not come to bring peace, but a sword" (Matt. 10:34). David said, in essence, "I have come to bring peace, but now I bring a sword."

At this point Abigail, Nabal's wife, enters the narrative when informed of her husband's suicidal rebuttal (vv. 14–17). Armed with welcomed and copious gifts for David and his group (e.g., wine not water), Abigail rides off to meet David, but without telling her husband (v. 19b). Her secretive behavior parallels that of Jonathan to Saul: "but he did not tell his father" (14:1 [and Samson with his parents, Judg. 14:6b]).

Abigail's impassioned speech to David covers vv. 23–31. She prostrates herself before David (v. 23), accepts the responsibility for her asinine husband's behavior (v. 24), and comments on the suitability of her husband's name (v. 25). Now, it is well known that "Nabal" is the Hebrew word for "fool, foolish one"—for example, "the fool [*naval*] has said in his heart, 'There is no god'" (Ps. 14:1).

It is unlikely that parents would ever give the birthname of "Fool" to a child. And who would ever marry somebody whose name is "Fool"? Nabal possibly is a nickname, but nicknames, especially pejorative ones, are rare in the Old Testament. And if it is only a nickname, then Abigail is merely agreeing with what others have said about her spouse.

Is it possible that Nabal is a perfectly normal name, and that we are dealing here with homonyms? There are Semitic roots with the consonants n-b-l that suggest something like "fire, flame" or "send" (Barr 1969: 25–27). If such is the case, Abigail did not know the original meaning of her husband's name (how many spouses know the meaning of their spouse's name anyway?), but years of living with Nabal caused her to connect his lifestyle with the qualities that the Hebrews termed *naval*.

Note too, as Barr (1969: 27–28) has pointed out, that Abigail does not say in v. 25, "Nabal is his name for he is a *naval*" or "for he is *naval*-like." She does not use an adjective but a noun—"Nabal is his name, and folly [*nevalah*] is with him"—and an indicting noun at that! In the Old Testament, *nevalah* often describes gross sexual sin or the violation of major commandments, doing "what is not done in Israel." Examples (with translation of *nevalah* in the NRSV in quotation marks):

1. Gen. 34:7: Shechem's violation of Dinah, "an outrage"
2. Deut. 22:21: loss of virginity, "a disgraceful act"
3. Josh. 7:15: violation of the *kherem*, "an outrageous thing"
4. Judg. 19:23–24 and 20:6, 10: Gibeah's ravaging of the concubine, "a vile thing," "a vile outrage," "a disgrace"
5. 2 Sam. 13:12: Ammon's violation of Tamar, "anything so vile"

Hence, in Abigail's understanding, Nabal's sin is not merely a breach of etiquette, being a skinflint, but a morally outrageous and deplorable act. This alone explains why God took Nabal's life (vv. 37–38).

Throughout her speech Abigail is very deferential towards David. The Hebrew word for "master, lord" (*ʾadon*) occurs thirty-eight times in 1 Samuel, and eighteen of these (about 50 percent) are in ch. 25. And in her speech in vv. 24–31, Abigail refers to David as "master, lord" fourteen times (Miscall 1986: 152). Furthermore, her reference to Yahweh "slinging out as from the hollow of a sling" David's enemies (v. 29) is surely her way of referring to David's victory over Goliath with a "sling," as is the narrator's reference to Nabal's death in v. 37, where he says of Nabal, "he became like a stone." A sling and a stone(s) in ch. 17 and ch. 25.

David is impressed by her mediation. She is the one, he testifies, who has been used by God to restrain David from taking the law into his own hands and requiting Nabal's insult (vv. 33–34). Had he gone ahead with his own recrimination play, David would have become a *Naval*.

The Old Testament frequently, as here, associates "insult" (*kherpah*) with "fool" (*naval*):

1 Sam. 25:39: "Blessed be the Lord who has judged the case of Nabal's insult [*kherpati miyyad naval*]."

2 Sam. 13:12–13: "Do not do anything so vile [*nevalah*]. As for me, where could I carry my shame [*kherpati*]? As for you, you would be one of the scoundrels [*nevalim*] in Israel."

Ps. 39:8: "Do not make me the scorn of the fool [*kherpat naval*]."

Ps. 74:22: "Remember how the impious scoff at you [*kherpatekah minni naval*] all day long."

After Nabal's death (v. 38), Abigail is a widow, a rich widow, an attractive widow. Abigail thereafter becomes David's wife (v. 42). And we wonder if David has not picked up three new things: (1) a new wife; (2)

access to his new wife's wealth (do Nabal and Abigail have children; and could a widow inherit her deceased husband's wealth?); and (3) a needed support base in the Hebron area, which David will later make his first capital city. David also marries Ahinoam of Jezreel (either a local Jezreel or, less likely, the Jezreel to the far north) (v. 43).

But what of Michal through all this? Saul has arbitrarily ended her marriage with David and married her off to someone named Palti (v. 44). Saul is mentioned, for the only time in a long chapter of forty-four verses, in the last verse. His motive for taking Michal from David is purely political. David is no longer connected with the royal family and therefore has no claim on the throne (Alter 1981: 121). Saul, his recent concessions and statements about David's kingship notwithstanding, is still looking for a way to remove David permanently, or at least to disqualify him from succeeding Saul. And now the stage is set for the drama of ch. 26.

26:1–25. As in ch. 24, upon receiving appropriate and vital information about David's whereabouts from the Ziphites, Saul sets out in pursuit of David. Unlike ch. 24, where the meeting between Saul and David was accidental (Saul entered a cave to relieve himself in which David was hiding), here the meeting is initiated intentionally by David, first by spies (v. 4), then by David's own two trips to Saul's camp, the first alone (v. 5), the second with Abishai (v. 7). The darkness of the cave covered David's movements in ch. 24, while the darkness of the night covers David's movements in ch. 26 (Fokkelmann 1986: 540).

When David and Abishai come into Saul's camp they find Saul and his bodyguards in "a deep sleep" (the same Hebrew word used of Adam in Gen. 2:21, of Abram in Gen. 15:12, of Jonah in Jon. 1:5–6). They're not just napping, but comatose! Saul's deep sleep is like Jonah's. It comes at an unexpected time: Saul's while hotly pursuing somebody in a search-and-destroy mission, Jonah's while on a sinking ship in a storm at sea.

Abishai thinks like David's men did in 24:4. Saul is vulnerable; this must be of God; let's kill him (v. 8). David might well have responded to Abishai with "Put your sword back into its place; for all who take the sword will perish by the sword" (Matt. 26:52). Abishai illustrates the principle that those who are most loyal may also be most ruthless, that those who are prepared to die for a cause may also be prepared to kill for that cause. David's restraint and Abishai's lack of restraint probably explain why in v. 11 David instructs Abishai to remove the spear stuck in the ground by the head of the slumbering Saul, only to remove it himself in v. 12. There is a "sudden distrust of his lieutenant's impulsiveness" (Sternberg 1987: 244).

David takes Saul's spear and water jar (v. 12), removes himself some distance from Saul's camp (v. 13), and calls back to the camp in a voice loud enough to stir the campers from their deep sleep (vv. 14–16).

Directing his comments at Abner and his fellows, he says that they deserve to die for dereliction of duty, not protecting Yahweh's anointed. The combination of verbs is interesting: "As the Lord lives, you deserve to die" (v. 16). At no point does David say the same thing to Saul—"you deserve to die."

Then David speaks to Saul (vv. 18–20), again defending himself (cf. 24:9–15). David has been forced by Saul into exile (v. 19d) and into "serving other gods" (v. 19e).

Saul confesses: "I have sinned" (v. 21). It sounds like Pharaoh in Exod. 9:27. Both men confess their sin ("I have sinned") and then go right on sinning. He then proceeds in v. 21b to use "elementary language here. It is a promise only one step removed from the words that children use when they want to show remorse: I won't ever do it again; words that they often have ready rather too quickly to avert a crisis" (Fokkelman 1986: 548).

One difference in this chapter is that while both Saul and David speak to each other (from a distance), Saul never mentions Yahweh, while David does (vv. 16, 23, 24). In his very last words to Saul (vv. 23–24), David starts by talking about Yahweh (v. 23a) and concludes by talking about Yahweh (v. 24b). In the middle he talks about himself (vv. 23b, 24a).

27:1–12. David has, he thinks, two options with regard to Saul's pursuing him: remain in the country and hope for the best or cross the border and live (temporarily) elsewhere. The chapter begins with David talking to himself—"said in his heart" (as God does [Gen. 8:21; 18:17], and as Abraham does [Gen. 17:17], and as Saul does [1 Sam. 18:17b, 21]). By the way, this brief chapter also ends with David again talking to himself (v. 11b) and with Achish talking to himself (v. 12).

His decision is to flee to an adjacent land, the land of the neighboring Philistines, and particularly to Gath, city of King Achish and Goliath. Will David be able to sing "the Lord's song in a foreign land" (Ps. 137:4)? Will Saul honor national boundaries or will he go in pursuit of David, much as Jehoiakim sent a search party down to Egypt to extradite and then execute the prophet Uriah (Jer. 26:20–23)? It is not difficult to reflect on "the painful and ambiguous predicament of the future king of Israel forced to seek refuge among his people's hated enemies" (Alter 1981: 69). Can one imagine an aspiring leader-to-be in modern Israel fleeing for refuge to an Arab country inimical to Israel?

Achish rolls out the welcome mat for David, either offering him political asylum or taking him on board as a mercenary (Edelman 1991: 233), with vv. 8–11 suggesting the latter.

Once ensconced in Ziklag (v. 6) and deliberately removed from Achish's supervision (v. 5), David goes to work in ways partly necessary for his survival but surely not honoring to his Lord. He makes raids on nearby non-Israelite peoples, killing the entire human population ("dead men tell no tales") and taking the rest as spoils for himself, his men, and Achish (vv. 8–9, 11). Furthermore, David deceives Achish (as he did in ch. 21) into believing that it is against David's own people that he has conducted these raids, thus endearing himself to Achish (v. 10).

We may understand David's actions as "a pragmatic act necessary for David to maintain his position and perhaps his life" (Niditch 1993: 129). For Mendenhall (1973: 218), David's sorties illustrate how "an ʿApiru group conducted raids upon villages outside the sovereignty of the immediate overlord." These incidents, however, also illustrate that David can be "clever, rough, capable, ambitious, and courageous. He does what he must to survive" (Birch 1991: 214). Or as Miscall (1986: 165) says, "The man who knows well the strategic value of restraint and flight also knows well the strategic value of battle and wholesale massacre."

And Achish buys it (v. 12)! The phrase "Achish trusted David" uses the same Hebrew construction (ʾaman be) as Gen. 15:6, "and he [Abram] believed the Lord." Abram put his faith in a God of truth. Achish put his faith in a master of duplicity.

28:1–25. Panic-stricken by the gathering-for-war Philistines (v. 1a), and with Samuel dead (v. 3a), to whom shall Saul turn? To Yahweh, naturally (v. 6a). But there is a problem. Yahweh does not respond by dreams (Saul's own? somebody else's?), or by Urim (via the priests), or by prophets (v. 6b). All three normal means of receiving a divine message (dreams, cult objects, and prophecy) are shut down. (For the close connection of two of these, dreams and prophets, see Deut. 13:2, "If prophets or those who divine by dreams appear among you . . ."; Joel 2:28, "your sons and your daughters shall prophesy, your old men shall dream dreams.")

For a second time (cf. 14:37b) Yahweh refuses to answer Saul. An absence of revelation that deprives an individual of a divine word is always a portent of God's forthcoming wrath. That is the truth Amos points to when he says, "The time is surely coming, says the Lord God, when I will send a famine on the land; not a famine of bread or a thirst for water, but of hearing the words of the Lord" (8:11).

Brueggemann (1990: 192) compares Saul's actions to those of a person who, diagnosed with a terminal illness, turns to medical quacks and charlatans when "official" medical practitioners are unable to do anything. Even though Saul had expelled in Josiah-like fashion the mediums and spiritists (v. 3b; perhaps as one last attempt to please the deity? [Humphreys 1985: 36]), he resorts to what he once banned.

Disguising himself (v. 8a), both to camouflage his identity from the medium at Endor and to enable him to pass undetected through the Philistine ranks through which he must go to get from Gilboa to Endor (Edelman 1991: 242), Saul asks this anonymous medium to make contact with the deceased Samuel (vv. 8b, 11b). There is a world of difference between Saul coming to the medium at night (v. 8b), and Nicodemus coming to Jesus at night (John 3:2), but perhaps both feel safer traveling under the cloak of darkness.

What Saul asks the medium to perform is a form of divination known as necromancy, that is, making contact with the dead, even if, as in this case, such contact is against the will of the departed (v. 15a). The Torah condemns to death any who are practitioners of necromancy (Lev. 20:27) and discourages Israelites from consulting necromancers (Lev. 19:31).

Note here that the divining powers of the woman are not employed. Samuel simply "comes up" (Miscall 1986: 168). The text does not state that Samuel came up from Sheol, as we might expect, but that he came up "out of the ground" (v. 13b). Presumably, "ground" (ʾerets) here carries the special meaning of "netherworld," and hence is a synonym for Sheol.

It is of interest that in the dialogue that follows between the two, Saul only once uses "God" (v. 15), while Samuel uses "Lord" seven times (vv. 16–19). The nail in the coffin of any possible Saulide dynasty is Samuel's "tomorrow you and your sons shall be with me" (v. 19). Saul's desperate last straw turns out to be, in fact, the handwriting on the wall. "To speak with the dead is to join the dead" (Miscall 1986: 172).

29:1–11. As in 4:1, the Philistines prepare for battle against Israel at Aphek. Achish's generals are understandably concerned that David and his party are permitted to march with the Philistine ranks. Will not David and his men be fifth columnists? And Achish does little to squash their reservations by referring to David in their presence as "the servant of King Saul of Israel." Why not at least identify David as a *former* servant of Saul (Edelman 1991: 254)? For a parallel, one thinks of the early followers of Jesus in Jerusalem who had grave misgivings about allowing the new Messianist, Saul of Tarsus, to join their ranks (Acts 9:26).

David follows the dictum of Prov. 27:2, "Let another praise you, and not your own mouth." Three times Achish affirms David's integrity (vv. 3, 6, 9). Moreover, Achish compares David to an angel of God (v. 9). David enjoys this comparison three more times (2 Sam. 14:17, 20; 19:27), and is the only individual in the Old Testament to do so. He shares the analogy with Stephen, who had an angel-like face (Acts 6:15).

Achish's defense of David is much like Pilate's of Jesus. Achish and Pilate refute the accusations brought against their respective charges, and both do it three times in succession (1 Sam. 29:3, 6, 9; Luke 23:4, 14–15, 22). (See Brueggemann 1990: 200.)

God receives no mention in this chapter except for Achish's perhaps surprising "As the Lord lives" (v. 6). The Philistine king acquiesces to his commanders' concern and releases David from war responsibilities (v. 10). This means that David, Israel's future king, is spared the embarrassment of fighting against his own people and possibly having a role in deposing the Lord's anointed. Is divine providence at work here?

30:1–29. Returning to Ziklag, David discovers that it has been razed and its occupants abducted, including David's two wives, Ahinoam and Abigail (vv. 1–5). Like Moses, David experiences recrimination from within his own ranks (v. 6a). His crime is one of oversight, leaving behind only women and children in very vulnerable Ziklag.

It is at this point in the narrative that we encounter a fundamental distinction between Saul and David (Brueggemann 1990: 201). Both find themselves in a very tense, disturbing moment that is conveyed by the word *tsarar*.

28:15: "Saul answered, 'I am in great distress' [*tsar li me'od*]."
30:6: "David was in great danger [*wattetser ledawid me'od*]."

What did Saul do? He consulted a medium. What does David do? "He strengthened himself in the Lord his God" (v. 6b). It's the same situation, but radically different responses. For an analogy, compare Kings Josiah and Jehoiakim. Both hear the reading of the word of the Lord. Josiah, when he heard that word, "cut" his clothes in contrition (2 Kings 22:11). Jehoiakim, when he heard that word, "cut" the scroll into shreds in an act of defiance (Jer. 36:23). Again, the same situation elicits radically different responses.

Upon receiving divine approval, David sets out in pursuit of the aggressors (vv. 7–10). But who are they? In which direction is David to go? A "chance" meeting with an Egyptian solves those dilemmas. It is he who divulges to David that the Amalekites are the villains behind the raid on Ziklag (vv. 11–15).

With this information in hand, David turns his attention to slaughtering the Amalekites (something Saul had only partially done in ch. 15), rescuing his wives, and returning to Ziklag with war spoils (vv. 16–20).

The story invites comparison with Abram in Genesis 14 (Niditch 1993: 102). A place is invaded; a family member is abducted; Abram and David are each informed by an individual of what has happened (Gen. 14:13; 1 Sam. 30:11–15), one an escapee, the other left behind. Abram and David each pursue successfully the abductors and reclaim the family member. Both stories end with the distribution of booty taken from the enemy (Gen. 14:20–24; 1 Sam. 30:21–31).

In addition to being intensely spiritual (v. 6b), David is wise, diplomatic, and generous. He shares the spoil not only with those who engaged the enemy in battle on the front lines, but also with those who remained in the rear guard (vv. 23–24) (over the protest of his vanguard fighters), as well as with various communities throughout Judah (vv. 26–31). It is especially this last group that will later appoint David as king of Judah, and headquarter him in Hebron, the last Judahite beneficiary mentioned in 1 Sam. 30:26–31.

31:1–13. While David is in the deep south fighting the Amalekites sucessfully (ch. 30), Saul is in the north (Mount Gilboa) fighting the Philistines unsuccessfuly (ch. 31). Knowing that the handwriting is on the wall, Saul asks his armor bearer to kill him (v. 4). This unnamed armor bearer is like Saul's first armor bearer, David (16:21), in that both refuse to strike down Yahweh's anointed. Their restraint vis-à-vis their master contrasts with the armor bearer of the pretentious and short-lived-king Abimelech, who shared no such scruples (Judg. 9:54). When he refuses, Saul falls on his own sword (v. 4). This is one of the very few instances of suicide in Scripture. But it is a suicide of honor (if one can use that oxymoron) like Samson's, not allowing the enemy to claim the credit for finishing him off.

The Philistines (accidentally?) stumble on the corpse of Saul. Then these Philistines do to an Israelite king what an Israelite David did to a Philistine hulk—decapitate him (v. 9a).

For the Philistines, this is a day of good news and they cannot keep silent (v. 9c; cf. 2 Kings 7:9), and so they send out messengers to tell it. Brueggemann (1990: 208–9) captures well the significance of this: "The death of an enemy king, when discovered, is good news. Strategically, the King's death means that the military threat has lost its main force. Theologically, it means that the enemy god has been defeated, for when the king dies, the king's god has failed."

Saul is not without those who remember his kindness to them and "owe him one." The residents of Jabesh-gilead, recalling their own salvation due to the intervention of Saul (ch. 11), fetch the bodies of Saul and his three sons from the wall at Beth-shan, where the slain are cremated (v. 12c; cf. Achan and his family in Josh. 7:25–26; Achan, like Saul, violated the command to apply *kherem* to a city, and after their deaths both corpses are burned and then buried [v. 13]).

If, as we suggested at the beginning of our comments on ch. 31, the events of chs. 30 and 31 are simultaneous, then it is interesting that the text devotes twenty-nine verses to David's relatively minor battle with the Amalekites, but only thirteen verses to Saul's monumental life-ending battle with the Philistines (Miscall 1986: 181). Even in death Saul is subordinated to David, and does not receive "the press" given to his successor.

Saul in First Chronicles

First Chronicles has only one chapter for the Saul story, and that is ch. 10, almost all of which is a parallel to 1 Samuel 31, the account of Saul's death at the hands of the Philistines.

Before ch. 10 there are two brief genealogical references to Saul. In fact, we have here two duplicates. First, there is a genealogy of the Benjaminites that does not mention Saul (7:6–12), and then a duplicate of that Benjaminite genealogy that does mention Saul (8:1–40; note v. 33). The genealogical repetition allows the introduction of Saul into this history of the people of God that goes back not only to Sinai, not only to the patriarchs, but to Adam and creation (1 Chron. 1:1). But even here (8:29–40), the emphasis is on Saul's family's connections with Gibeon rather than with the Benjaminites per se, suggesting perhaps that the Saulides are more geographical Benjaminites than they are ethnic Benjaminites (Walters 1991: 71). No wonder that Israel (= "Judah" in Chronicles) later says to David at Hebron, "We are your bone and flesh" (11:1)!

Second, one finds a genealogy of the line of Saul in 8:29–40, and a duplicate of that data in 9:35–44. The duplicate (9:35–44) comes on the heels of a section (9:2–34) that describes worship in Jerusalem after the Babylonian exile, and which is the only passage in all of First and Second Chronicles to speak of an actual return from exile. So 9:2–34, which precedes 9:35–44 in the text, actually follows 9:35–44 historically. It is as if the two are set into bold contrast with each other: 9:2–34 a release from death; 9:35–44 (Saul and his kin) a sinking into death.

A few differences stand between the Chronicler's account of Saul's last military campaign and death and that of 1 Samuel 31. Here are some examples: (1) 1 Sam. 31:10 says that the Philistines fastened Saul's body to the wall of Beth-shan and put his armor in the temple of Astarte, while 1 Chron. 10:10 says that the Philistines impaled Saul's head in the temple of Dagon; (2) the account in Chronicles deletes any reference to the Philistine advancement even into Transjordanian cities (cf. 1 Sam. 31:7); (3) the Chronicler does not mention the cremation of the corpses (1 Sam. 31:12; 1 Chron. 10:12).

But perhaps the most significant difference is the assertion in 1 Chronicles 10 (but not in 1 Samuel 31) that Saul died because of his unfaithfulness (v. 13) (Walters 1991: 64), for which the Hebrew word is *ma'al*.

This word occurs several times throughout Chronicles, but at three especially critical points:

> 1 Chron. 9:1: "Judah was taken into exile . . . because of their unfaithfulness."
> 1 Chron. 10:13: "So Saul died for his unfaithfulness; he was unfaithful to the Lord."
> 2 Chron. 36:14: "All the leading priests and the people also were exceedingly unfaithful."

Chronicles begins (1 Chron. 9:1) and ends (2 Chron. 36:14) its historical narrative by delineating unfaithfulness/*ma'al* as the reason for Judah's exile. In using the same word to sum up Saul's life (1 Chron. 10:13), the Chronicler makes Saul a sinister parallel to God's disobedient people as a whole and to Judah's last king, Zedekiah, in particular. Israel's first king and last king are done in by unfaithfulness.

Bibliography (1 Samuel)

Commentaries and Major Studies

Ackroyd, P. 1971. *The First Book of Samuel*. Cambridge Bible 9. Cambridge: Cambridge University Press.

Alter, R. 1981. *The Art of Biblical Narrative*. New York: Basic Books.

Brueggemann, W. 1990. *First and Second Samuel*. Interpretation. Louisville: John Knox.

Eslinger, L. 1985. *Kingship of God in Crisis: A Close Reading of I Samuel 1–2*. Bible and Literature Series. Sheffield: Almond.

Fokkelman, J. P. 1986. *Narrative Art and Poetry in the Books of Samuel*. Vol. 2, *The Crossing Fates* (*I Sam. 13–31 and II Samuel 1*). Studia semitica Neerlandia 23. Assen: Van Gorcum.

———. 1993. *Narrative Art and Poetry in the Books of Samuel*. Vol. 4, *Vow and Desire* (*I Sam. 1–12*). Studia semitica Neerlandia 31. Assen: Van Gorcum.

Gordon, R. P. 1986. *I & II Samuel: A Commentary*. Library of Biblical Interpretation. Grand Rapids: Zondervan.

Jobling, D. 1993. "What, If Anything, Is 1 Samuel?" *SJOT* 7:17–31.

———. 1998. *1 Samuel*. Berit Olam. Collegeville, Minn.: Liturgical Press.

Klein, R. 1983. *1 Samuel*. Word Biblical Commentary 10. Waco, Tex.: Word.

McCarter, P. K., Jr. 1980. *1 Samuel*. Anchor Bible 8. Garden City, N.Y.: Doubleday.

Miscall, P. 1986. *1 Samuel: A Literary Reading*. Bloomington: Indiana University Press.

Polzin, R. 1980. *Samuel and the Deuteronomist*. San Francisco: Harper and Row.

Robinson, G. 1993. *Let Us Be Like the Nations: A Commentary on the Books of 1 and 2 Samuel*. International Theological Commentary. Grand Rapids. Eerdmans.

Sternberg, M. 1985. *The Poetics of Biblical Narrative*. Bloomington: Indiana University Press.

1 Samuel 1–7 (Samuel and Eli)

Albright, W. F. 1963. *The Biblical Period from Abraham to Ezra*. New York: Harper and Row.

Brettler, M. 1997. "The Composition of 1 Samuel 1–2." *JBL* 116:601–12.

Brueggemann, W. 1990. "1 Samuel 1: A Sense of Beginning." *ZAW* 102:33–48.

Campbell, A. F. 1975. *The Ark Narrative (1 Samuel 4–6; 2 Samuel 6): A Form-Critical and Tradition-Historical Study*. Decatur, Ga.: Scholars Press.

———. 1979. "Yahweh and the Ark: A Case Study in Narrative." *JBL* 98:31–43.

Fishbane, M. 1982. "1 Samuel 3: Historical Narrative and Narrative Poetics." In *Literary Interpretations of Biblical Narratives*. Vol. 2. Ed. K. R. R. Gros Louis and J. S. Ackerman. Nashville: Abingdon. Pp. 191–203.

Fretheim, T. E. 1983. "God Provides New Leadership (1 Samuel 3:1–10)." In *Deuteronomic History*. Nashville: Abingdon. Pp. 99–108.

Gitay, Y. 1992. "Reflections on the Poetics of the Samuel Narrative: The Question of the Ark Narrative." *CBQ* 54:59–73.

Janzen, J. G. 1983. "Samuel Opened the Doors of the House of Yahweh (1 Samuel 3:15)." *JSOT* 26:89–96.

Lewis, T. J. 1994. "The Textual History of the Song of Hannah (1 Samuel ii 1–10)." *VT* 44:18–46.

Miller, P. D., and J. J. M. Roberts. 1977. *The Hand of the Lord: A Reassessment of the 'Ark Narrative' of 1 Samuel*. Baltimore: Johns Hopkins University Press.

Moberley, R. L. W. 1995. "To Hear the Master's Voice: Revelation and Spiritual Discernment in the Call of Samuel." *SJT* 48:443–68.

Simon, U. 1981. "Samuel's Call to Prophecy: Form Criticism with Close Reading." *Prooftexts* 1:120–32.

Spina, F. 1991. "A Prophet's 'Pregnant Pause': Samuel's Silence in the Ark Narrative (1 Samuel 4:1–7:12)." *HBT* 13:59–73.

———. 1994. "Eli's Seat: The Transition from Priest to Prophet in I Samuel 1–4." *JSOT* 62:67–75.

Tsevat, M. 1980. "The Death of the Sons of Eli." In *The Meaning of the Book of Job and Other Biblical Studies*. New York: Ktav. Pp. 149–53.

———. 1992. "Was Samuel a Nazirite?" In *Sha'arei Talmon: Studies in the Bible, Qumran and the Ancient Near East Presented to Shemaryahu Talmon*. Ed. M. Fishbane and E. Tov. Winona Lake, Ind.: Eisenbrauns. Pp. 199–204.

Van der Toorn K., and C. Houtman. 1994. "David and the Ark," *JBL* 113:209–31.

Walters, S. D. 1994. "The Voice of God's People in Exile." *Ex Auditu* 10:73–86.

Willis, J. T. 1971. "An Anti-Elide Narrative Tradition from a Prophetic Circle at the Ramah Sanctuary." *JBL* 90:288–308.

———. 1973. "The Song of Hannah and Psalm 113." *CBQ* 34:139–54.

———. 1979. "Samuel Versus Eli," *TZ* 35:201–12.

1 Samuel 8–15 (Samuel and Saul)

Birch, B. 1971. "The Development of the Tradition of the Anointing of Saul in 1 Sam 9:1–10:16." *JBL* 90:55–68.

———. 1976. *The Rise of the Israelite Monarchy: The Growth and Development of 1 Samuel 7–15*. SBLDS 27. Missoula, Mont.: Scholars Press.

Blenkinsopp, J. 1964. "Jonathan's Sacrilege. 1 Sm 14, 1–46: A Study in Literary History." *CBQ* 26:423–29.

Clements, R. E. 1974. "The Deuteronomic Interpretation of the Founding of the Monarchy in 1 Sam viii." *VT* 24:398–410.

Edelman, D. K. 1991. *King Saul in the Historiography of Judah*. JSOT Supplement 121. Sheffield: JSOT Press.

Eslinger, L. 1983. "Viewpoints and Points of View in 1 Sam. 8–12." *JSOT* 26:61–76.

Gordon, R. P. 1994. "Who Made the Kingmaker? Reflections on Samuel and the Institution of the Monarchy." In *Faith, Tradition, and History: Old Testament Historiography in Its Near Eastern Context*. Ed. A. R. Millard, J. K. Hoffmeier, and D. W. Baker. Winona Lake, Ind.: Eisenbrauns. Pp. 255–69.

Gunn, D. 1980. *The Fate of King Saul*. JSOT Supplement 14. Sheffield: JSOT Press.

Halpern, B. 1981. *The Constitution of the Monarchy in Ancient Israel.* HSM 2. Chico, Calif.: Scholars Press.

Howard, D. M. 1988. "The Case for Kingship in Old Testament Narrative Books and the Psalms." *TJ* 9:19–35.

———. 1990. "The Case for Kingship in Deuteronomy and the Former Prophets." *WTJ* 52:101–15.

Jobling, D. 1976. "Saul's Fall and Jonathan's Rise: Tradition and Redaction in 1 Sam. 14:1–46." *JBL* 95:367–76.

———. 1986. "Deuteronomic Political Theory in Judges and 1 Samuel 1–12." In *The Sense of Biblical Narrative: Structural Analyses in the Hebrew Bible II.* JSOT Supplement 39. Sheffield: Almond. Pp. 44–87.

Long, V. P. 1994. "How Did Saul Become King? Literary Reading and Historical Construction." In *Faith, Tradition, and History: Old Testament Historiography in Its Near Eastern Context.* Ed. A. R. Millard, J. K. Hoffmeier, and D. W. Baker. Winona Lake, Ind.: Eisenbrauns. Pp. 271–84.

Mayes, A. D. H. 1978. "The Rise of the Israelite Monarchy." *ZAW* 90:1–19.

McCarthy, D. 1973. "The Inauguration of Monarchy in Israel." *Int* 27:401–12.

Miller, J. M. 1974. "Saul's Rise to Power: Some Observations Concerning 1 Sam 9:1–10:16; 10:26–11:15 and 13:2–14:46." *CBQ* 36:157–74.

Moberly, R. W. L. 1998. "'God is Not a Human That He Should Repent' (Numbers 23:19 and 1 Samuel 15:29)." In *God in the Fray: A Tribute to Walter Brueggemann.* Ed. T. Linafelt and T. K. Beal. Minneapolis: Fortress. Pp. 112–23.

Polzin, R. 1987. "The Monarchy Begins: 1 Samuel 8–10." In *SBLSP 1987.* Ed. K. H. Richards. Atlanta: Scholars Press. Pp. 120–43.

———. 1988. "On Taking Renewal Seriously: 1 Sam 11:1–15." In *Ascribe to the Lord: Biblical and Other Studies in Memory of Peter C. Craigie.* JSOT Supplement 67. Ed. L. Eslinger and G. Taylor. Sheffield: JSOT Press. Pp. 493–507.

Roberts, J. J. M. 1987. "In Defense of the Monarchy: The Contribution of Israelite Kingship to Biblical Theology." In *Ancient Israelite Religion: Essays in Honor of Frank Moore Cross.* Ed. P. D. Miller Jr., P. D. Hanson, and S. D. McBride. Philadelphia: Fortress. Pp. 377–96.

Tsevat, M. 1980. "The Biblical Account of the Foundation of the Monarchy in Israel." In *The Meaning of the Book of Job and Other Essays.* New York: Ktav. Pp. 77–99.

Williams, J. G. 1994. "Sacrifice and the Beginning of Kingship." *Semeia* 67:73–92.

Yamit, Y. 1992. "The Glory of Israel Does Not Deceive/Change His Mind." *Prooftexts* 12:201–12.

1 Samuel 16–31 (Saul and David)

Ackroyd, P. 1975. "The Verb 'Love'—*'aheb* in the David-Jonathan Narratives: A Footnote." *VT* 25:213–14.

Alter, R. 1999. *The David Story: A Translation with Commemtary of 1 and 2 Samuel.* New York: Norton.

Auld, A. G. and C. Y. S. Ho. 1992. "The Making of David and Goliath." *JSOT* 56:19–39.

Bar-Efrat, S. 1989. *Narrative Art in the Bible.* Sheffield: Almond.

Barr, J. 1969. "The Symbolism of Names in the Old Testament." *BJRL* 52:11–29.

Barthélemy, D., et al. 1986. *The Story of Goliath and David: Textual and Literary Criticism.* Göttingen: Vandenhoeck and Ruprecht.

Berlin, A. 1983. *Poetics and Interpretation of Biblical Narrative.* Sheffield: Almond.

Beuken, W. A. M. 1978. "1 Samuel 28: The Prophet as 'Hammer of Witches.'" *JSOT* 6:3–17.

Blenkinsopp, J. 1975. "The Quest of the Historical Saul." In *No Famine in the Land.* Ed. J. W. Flanagan and A. W. Robinson. Missoula, Mont.: Scholars Press. Pp. 75–99.

Boogart, T. A. 1985. "History and Drama in the Story of David and Goliath." *RefR* 38:204–14.

Brooks, S. S. 1996. "Saul and the Samson Narrative." *JSOT* 76:19–25.

Brueggemann, W. 1987. "Before the Giants/Surrounded by Motherhood," *PSB* 8:1–13.

———. 1989. "Narrative Intentionality in 1 Samuel 29." *JSOT* 43:21–35.

———. 1993. "Narrative Coherence and Theological Intentionality in 1 Samuel 18." *CBQ* 55:225–43.

Clines, D. J. A. 1995. "David the Man: The Construction of Masculinity in the Hebrew Bible." In *Interested Parties: The Ideology of Writers and Readers of the Hebrew Bible.* JSOT Supplement 205. Sheffield: Sheffield Academic Press. Pp. 212–43.

Cohen, K. I. 1994. "King Saul—A Bungler from the Beginning." *BRev* 10, no. 5:34–39, 56–57.

DeVries, S. J. 1973. "David's Victory over the Philistine as Saga and as Legend." *JBL* 92:23–36.

Edelman, D. K. 1991. *King Saul in the Historiography of Judah.* JSOT Supplement 121. Sheffield: JSOT Press.

Eslinger, L. 1988. "A Change of Heart: 1 Samuel 16." In *Ascribe to the Lord: Biblical and Other Studies in Memory of Peter C. Craigie*. JSOT Supplement 67. Ed. L. Eslinger and G. Taylor. Sheffield: JSOT Press. Pp. 341–61.

Gevirtz, S. 1964. *Patterns in the Early Poetry of Israel*. Chicago: University of Chicago Press. Pp. 15–24.

Gordon, R. 1980. "David's Rise and Saul's Demise: Narrative Analogy in 1 Samuel 24–26." *TynB* 31:37–64.

Gunn, D. 1980. *The Fate of King Saul*. JSOT Supplement 14. Sheffield: JSOT Press.

Halpern, B. 2001. *David's Secret Demons*. Grand Rapids: Eerdmans.

Hawk, L. D. 1996. "Saul as Sacrifice: The Tragedy of Israel's First Monarch." *BRev* 12, no. 6:20–25, 56.

Hoffmeir, J. K. 1991. "The Aftermath of David's Triumph over Goliath: 1 Samuel 17:54 in Light of Near Eastern Parallels." *Archaeology in the Biblical World* 1:18–19.

Hoffner, H. A., Jr. 1968. "A Hittite Analogue to the David and Goliath Contest of Champions." *CBQ* 30:220–25.

Horner, T. 1978. *Jonathan Loved David: Homosexuality in Biblical Times*. Philadelphia: Fortress.

Howard, D. M., Jr. 1989. "The Transfer of Power from Saul to David in 1 Sam. 16:13–14." *JETS* 32:473–83.

Humphreys, W. L. 1985. *The Tragic Vision and the Hebrew Tradition*. Philadelphia: Fortress. Pp. 23–66.

Jason, H. 1979. "The Story of David and Goliath: A Folk Epic?" *Bib* 60:36–70.

Jobling, D. 1978. "A Structural Study in 1 Samuel." In *The Sense of Biblical Narrative I*. JSOT Supplement 7. Sheffield: JSOT Press. Pp. 4–25.

Kessler, M. 1970. "Narrative Technique in 1 Sm 16, 1–13." *CBQ* 32:543–54.

Lawton, R. B. 1993. "Saul, Jonathan and the 'Son of Jesse.'" *JSOT* 58:35–46.

Lemeche, N. 1978. "David's Rise." *JSOT* 10:2–25.

Levenson, J. 1978. "1 Samuel 25 as Literature and History." *CBQ* 40:11–28. (Repr. in *Literary Interpretations of Biblical Narratives*. Vol. 2. Ed. K. R. R. Gros Louis. Nashville: Abingdon, 1982. Pp. 220–42.

Long, V. P. 1989. *The Reign and Rejection of King Saul: A Case for Literary and Theological Coherence*. SBLDS 118. Atlanta: Scholars Press.

Malul, M. 1996. "Was David Involved in the Death of Saul on the Gilboa Mountain?" *RB* 103:517–45.

Mavrodes, G. 1983. "David, Goliath, and Limited War." *RefR* 33:6–8.

McCarter, P. K. 1973. "The Apology of David." *JBL* 99:489–504.

McKenzie, S. L. 2000. *King David: A Biography.* Oxford/New York: Oxford University Press.

Mendenhall, G. E. 1973. *The Tenth Generation.* Baltimore: Johns Hopkins University Press.

Miscall, P. D. 1983. *The Workings of Old Testament Narrative.* Philadelphia: Fortress. Pp. 47–138.

Niditch, S. 1993. *War in the Hebrew Bible.* New York: Oxford University Press.

Preston, T. R. 1982. "The Heroism of Saul: Patterns of Meaning in the Narrative of the Early Kingship." *JSOT* 24:27–46.

Reis, P. T. 1994. "Collusion at Nob: A New Reading of 1 Samuel 21–22." *JSOT* 61:59–73.

Rofé, A. 1987. "The Battle of David and Goliath: Folklore, Theology, Eschatology." In *Judaic Perspectives on Ancient Israel.* Ed. J. Neusner, B. A. Levine, and E. S. Frerichs. Philadelphia: Fortress. Pp. 117–51.

Rosenberg, J. 1986. *King and Kin: Political Allegory in the Hebrew Bible.* Bloomington: Indiana University Press.

Steussy, M. J. 1999. *David: Biblical Portraits of Power.* Columbia, S.C.: University of South Carolina Press.

Swindoll, C. 1997. *David: A Man of Passion and Destiny.* Dallas: Word.

Thompson, J. A. 1974. "The Significance of the Verb *LOVE* in the David-Jonathan Narratives in 1 Samuel." *VT* 24:334–80.

Tov, E. 1986. "The David and Goliath Saga: How a Biblical Editor Combined Two Versions." *BRev* 11, no. 4:35–41.

Walters, S. 1988. "The Light and the Dark." In *Ascribe to the Lord: Biblical and Other Essays in Memory of Peter C. Craigie.* JSOT Supplement 67. Ed. L. Eslinger and G. Taylor. Sheffield: JSOT Press. Pp. 567–89.

———. 1991. "Saul of Gibeon." *JSOT* 52:61–76.

Willis, J. T. 1973. "The Function of Comprehensive Anticipatory Redactional Joints in 1 Samuel 16–18" *ZAW* 85:294–314.

Wong, G. C. I. 1997. "Who Loved Whom? A Note on 1 Samuel xvi 21." *VT* 47:544–46.

2 Samuel

The consensus among many biblical scholars is that the life of David found in 1 Samuel 16–1 Kings 2 is comprised of several different compositions. These would include (to use common labels):

1. the History of David's Rise (1 Samuel 16–2 Samuel 5)
2. the Ark Narrative (2 Samuel 6, and originally a part of 1 Samuel 4–6)
3. a Dynastic Oracle Establishing the Supremacy of David and His Family (2 Samuel 7)
4. the Succession Narrative/Court History (2 Samuel 9–20; 1 Kings 1–2)
5. a "Samuel Appendix" inserted between the main body and conclusion of the Succession Narrative/Court History (2 Samuel 21–24)
6. the above five compositions were amalgamated into a single composition by the Deuteronomic historian.

There are also numerous suggestions to reconfigure some of the above. For example, is the designation "Succession Narrative" (see the work of L. Rost mentioned in the bibliography for a pioneering study in this area) sufficiently accurate to capture the thrust of 2 Samuel 9–20 and 1 Kings 1–2? Is the main concern of this corpus the issue of which of David's sons will succeed him, or is this emphasis a one-dimensional focus that fails to capture adequately the richness and complexity of these chapters? Inclined toward the latter view, many commentators now prefer the designation "David's Court History" over "Succession

Narrative." Again, there is much debate among interpreters about Rost's view that the Succession Narrative begins with 2 Samuel 9. Even while retaining the label "Succession Narrative," may it start, some suggest, as early as ch. 6, or ch. 4, or even ch. 2 (Gunn 1978: 65–84)?

Furthermore, some would argue that the Succession Narrative presents a view of David so at odds with the Deuteronomist (e.g., sinful versus pious) that the Deuteronomist would hardly have included it in his work, despoiling as it would his exemplary David. Hence, the Succession Narrative must be a post-Deuteronomic tradition to the Deuteronomic History that delegitimates David (Van Seters 1983: 289). But this playing-off of the Deuteronomist's pious David against the Succession Narrative's sinful David is surely exaggerated, and avoids much material (e.g., the Deuteronomist's inclusion of the Samuel Appendix [2 Samuel 21–24]) that suggests that the Deuteronomist's David is not quite as pristine as Van Seters would have us believe (see Gordon 1994: 288–95).

One might note two other tendencies in the modern scholarly studies of David. One tendency is to emphasize the propagandistic and apologetic nature of much of the David material. This is especially true of the data in 1 Samuel 16–2 Samuel 5. That is to say, most of this material, so it is claimed, is not reporting factual history at all. Rather, its concern is rhetorical and not historical. The data has been chosen and told in such a way that it defends David against the accusation of any illegal, unethical activity in the transfer of the crown from Saul to himself, or with parties favorable to the deceased Saul. For some reason, many scholars cannot accept as historical (i.e., "real") a David who is not driven by wild ambition, a David who entertains no fantasies of usurpation, a David who is genuinely grief-stricken at the tragic death of Saul. Such a David would be too good to be true; hence, the writer must be reconstructing an imaginary David.

The second tendency grows out of the first. The "real" David that emerges from such reconstruction is a David who flies directly in the face of the David of Jewish and Christian piety. Rather than David being "a man after God's heart," he is first of all a man after Saul's throne, and then a man after Bathsheba's body. Did David have anything to do with Saul's death (1 Samuel 31; 2 Sam. 1:1–16)? Yes. Was David expressing his true feelings for Saul when he delivered his eulogy (2 Sam. 1:17–27)? No. Was David involved in any way in the deaths of Abner (2 Sam. 3:22–30) and Ishbosheth (2 Sam. 4:1–12), pro-Saul individuals, even though the text clears him of complicity? Yes (Vanderkam 1980; Cryer 1985). Did David wait on God for directions and did he conduct himself honorably and charitably at this time of transition, or was he a co-conspirator, an orchestrator, a manipulator, a megalomaniac? The latter. In such a scenario Saul becomes the saint and David the sinner! Or at least we feel a twinge of sorrow for Saul but only revulsion for David.

The canonical presentation of David's life would suggest one that is analogous to Saul's (and others in Scripture)—a life of noble beginnings and painful endings. One might suggest that both Saul's and David's life follow a "rise-fall" pattern:

Saul (1 Samuel 9–31)

David (1 Samuel 16–1 Kings 2)

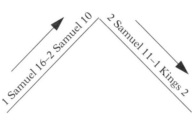

But ascents do not suddenly become descents. There is normally an event or two that dramatically changes the direction of one's life. Hence, maybe in the lives of Saul and David we should speak of three periods: (1) a rise; (2) a turning point; and (3) a decline (and see Exum 1992: 120–49).

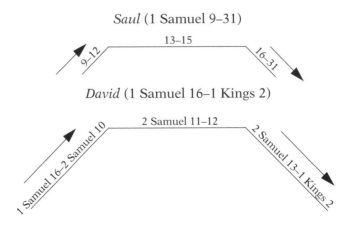

Saul (1 Samuel 9–31)

David (1 Samuel 16–1 Kings 2)

As far as David's life goes, this schema does not suggest that everything in 1 Samuel 16–2 Samuel 10 presents David at his best or that everything in 2 Samuel 13–1 Kings 2 presents him at his worst. For example, in his spat with his reclaimed wife, Michal, over his public behavior in bringing the ark into Jerusalem, his acid remarks to her are not designed to fuel harmony in their marriage (2 Sam. 6:21–22). Regardless of how many Philistines David can kill, if he cannot talk to his wife without insulting and degrading her, he has major problems.

In that portion of Scripture that paints David in decline (2 Samuel 13–1 Kings 2), we find David singing a moving thanksgiving song subsequent to God's deliverance of him from all his enemies (2 Samuel 22). While David makes striking claims here about his life of purity and obedience to God (vv. 21–25)—striking in light of the David we know from 2 Samuel 11–12—the primary focus is on a delivering, saving God.

Below is the outline I will follow in my analysis of the David story in Second Samuel.

Outline of David's Life in 2 Samuel

I.   1:1–27: David as Loyalist and Lamenter
II. 2:1–4:12: David as Regional King
III. 5:1–25: David as National King
IV. 6:1–23: David as Ark Custodian
V.   7:1–29: David as Head of a House
VI. 8:1–10:19: David as Warrior
VII. 11:1–12:31: David as Adulterer, Murderer, and Penitent
VIII. 13:1–14:33: David as Father of a Family in Turmoil
IX. 15:1–18:33: David as Refugee and Distraught Father
X.   19:1–20:26: David as One Who Fights Adversity
XI. 21:1–24:25: David as Executioner, Militarist, Hymnist, and Census-Taker

I. 1:1–27: David as Loyalist and Lamenter

1:1–27. The opening of Second Samuel parallels that of two other Old Testament books:

Josh. 1:1: "After the death of Moses . . ."
Judg. 1:1: "After the death of Joshua . . ."

2 Sam. 2:1: "After the death of Saul . . ."

Through these parallel introductions (and the only three books in the Old Testament to begin so), three periods of Israel's history are tied together: the liberation from Egypt, the conquest of Canaan, and the institution of the Israelite monarchy. Is there a future for Israel after Moses? Yes. Is there a future for Israel after Joshua? Yes. Is there a future for Israel after Saul? Yes.

But there will be little future for the unnamed Amalekite who brings word to David that Saul and Jonathan are dead (v. 4), and in the process takes credit for finishing off a wounded Saul before the Philistines wade in looking for the kill of the enemy's king (v. 10). He believes he has done David a favor. With Saul dead, a void has been created that David is now able to fill, as if David has been chomping at the bit, salivating over the forthcoming demise of Saul. The Amalekite's presentation to David of Saul's crown and armlet, the two most distinguishing royal insignia, indicates two things. First, it demonstrates that this Amalekite (assuming his story is fabricated) got to Saul's corpse before the Philistines did, for surely the latter would have removed these articles from the lifeless body of Israel's king. Second, in giving them to David, the Amalekite is himself symbolically transferring the kingship to David. In return, of course, he expects some kind of reasonable reward for his efforts, some kind of compensation. What we have is not disinterested action or absolute loyalty to David, but a case of "opportunistic self-aggrandizement" (Arnold 1989: 298).

For some reason, the Amalekite mentions the deaths of Saul and Jonathan only. Yet, the narrator tells us that Saul lost two other sons, Abinadab and Malchishua (1 Sam. 31:2). Why does the Amalekite not mention them? Did he not know them, or not know of their deaths? Did David not know them? Or does he mention only Saul and Jonathan because these are the only two Saulides who stand in the way of a straight, uncontested path to the throne for David?

Saul may be comfortable with a henchmen like Doeg, who will raise his hand against the Lord's servant priests when the king's own soldiers refuse to do so (1 Sam. 22:17–19), but David "goes ballistic" at this Amalekite's revelation. For Saul, Doeg is a breath of fresh air, the epitome of what the king's yes-men should be. For David, the Amalekite is a disgrace, one whose actions, however well intentioned, are completely uncalled for and totally unacceptable. Saul will take all the Doegs and Amalekites he can get in his camp; David will shun either, for "those who draw the sword will perish by the sword" (Matt. 26:52).

David grills the Amalekite, first verbally, then literally. David's questions, "Who are you?" (v. 8) and "Where are you from?" (v. 13), recall Saul's earlier questions about David, "Whose son is that young man" (1 Sam. 17:55) and "Whose son are you?" (1 Sam. 17:58).

Throughout the conversation between the two are five quotations:

1. v. 7: the Amalekite quotes his own earlier words to Saul to David.
2. v. 8a: the Amalekite quotes Saul's words to him to David.
3. v. 8b: the Amalekite quotes his response to Saul to David.
4. v. 9: the Amalekite quotes Saul's words to him to David.
5. v. 16: David quotes the Amalekite's words to the (now dead) Amalekite.

So we have four quotations by the Amalekite and one by David. David's quotation is most interesting. First, it is the only one of the five that is verifiable. We know that the Amalekite did say before David that he had killed Saul. Second, in the NRSV (but not in the NIV with its pluperfect "had said to him") David speaks to the Amalekite after he has had him executed. Third, David puts words in the mouth of the (dead) Amalekite that make his dastardly deed more incriminating than it already is. David quotes the Amalekite as having said, "I killed the Lord's anointed." Nowhere in the earlier conversation did the Amalekite ever refer to Saul as "the Lord's anointed" or claim that he had killed the Lord's anointed. He simply said, "I killed him" (v. 10a).

The king before David, Saul, is good at "striking down" (*paga‘ be*) the innocent (1 Sam. 22:17b, 18 [2x]). The king after David, Solomon, is also proficient at "striking down" the innocent (1 Kings 2:25, 29, 31, 32, 34, 46). In both cases the "innocent" are imaginary rivals, conspirators, loyal supporters of the opposition, potential fifth columnists. In contrast, David "strikes down" one guilty of regicide (v. 15).

David's words to the deceased mercy killer, "Your blood be on your head" (v. 16) provide background to illuminate the meaning of the crowd's response to Pilate's declaration of his own innocence in regard to Jesus: "His blood be on us and on our children" (Matt. 27:25). Unfortunately, this phrase has fueled much anti-Semitism from the Christian community over the centuries. That certainly is not its purpose for inclusion in the Passion Narrative. Rather, it seems that David's "Your blood be on your head" and the crowd's "His blood be on us and on our children" reflect a formula of acceptance of responsibility for the shedding of blood. One finds a parallel in Lev. 20:9, 11, which list certain kinds of criminals and criminal acts, and then add "their blood is on them." In Josh. 2:19 the two spies say to Rahab, "If any of you go out of the doors of your house, they shall be responsible for their own death [literally, 'his blood [is] on his head'], and we shall be innocent; but if a hand is laid upon any who are with you in the house, we shall bear the responsibility [literally, 'his blood [shall be] on our heads'] for their death."

One thing of interest in David's lament over Saul and Jonathan (vv. 17–27) is the absence of any negative feelings expressed by David toward Saul. We expect David to speak lovingly and gratefully of Jonathan (v. 23a, 25b–26), but will he extend those feelings to Saul? Either David has a heart that is genuinely free of malice, or he is a great actor (and a liar) who knows how to "play to the gallery" and diplomatically establish a bridge with Saul's supporters who might have qualms about signing on with a southern/Judean successor.

Here are some of David's descriptors for Saul (and Jonathan): "your glory (or the fleet-footed, clean "gazelle," *tsevi*) (v. 19); "the mighty" (vv. 19, 21, 22, 25, 27); "beloved and lovely" (v. 23); "swift and strong" (v. 23); provider of clothing and jewelry for the daughters of Israel (v. 24). So moved is David by the deaths of these two men that he "puts down a security blackout on the news" (Briscoe 1984: 97): "Tell it not in Gath, proclaim it not on the streets of Ashkelon" (v. 20).

Furthermore, David's words in v. 21, "You mountains of Gilboa, let there be no dew or rain upon you," reflect an idea widespread throughout the biblical world that the tragic slaying of a hero brings drought and famine to the area. Thus, in the Canaanite story from ancient Ugarit known as the "Aqhat Epic," Danel, father of the slain Aqhat, after being informed of the violent slaying of his son, utters this curse:

> Seven years may Baal afflict you,
> Even eight, the Rider of Clouds:
> Without dew, without rain,
> Without the surging of the deeps,
> Without the goodness of Baal's voice.

It is interesting to compare David's response on this occasion to the announcement of somebody's death with his response to similar announcements on later occasions. In addition to the case in 2 Samuel 1, David is informed of (1) Abner's death (3:22–39); (2) the death of the unnamed son whom Bathsheba gave birth to (12:16–23); and (3) Absalom's death (18:19–33). Here are some of the correspondences:

1. Somebody close to David dies tragically: Saul and Jonathan; Abner; an unnamed son; Absalom.

2. David is informed of the death through a messenger: an Ama-lekite who "escaped" from Saul's camp (1:1–2); David "heard" of Abner's death (3:28); the servants of David tell him about the death of his newborn (12:19); a Cushite tells David of Absalom's death (18:32).
3. David (and others) weep, fast, or tear their clothes in distress (1:11, 12; 3:31; 12:16, 21–22; 18:33).
4. David speaks out of the brokenness of his heart (1:17–27; 3:33–34; 18:33; 19:4; but *not* in 12:16–23).
5. People around David respond to or evaluate David's actions on each occasion: "And all the men who were with him did the same. They mourned and fasted (1:11b–12a); "All the people took notice of it [David's grieving over Abner], and it pleased them" (3:36); "Then his servants said to him 'What is this thing you have done? You fasted for the child while it was alive, but when the child died, you rose and ate food'" (12:21); Joab re-bukes David for mourning for Absalom (19:5–7).

This last point is most telling. In the first two instances David com-poses a poetic lament, first for Saul, then for Abner. But he composes no lament for his own two sons when news of their deaths reaches him. Again, in the first two instances those near David are moved by his out-pouring of grief for the deceased. But in the third instance the observ-ers are perplexed by his lack of grief and his speedy return to business as usual after so traumatic an incident. And in the fourth instance Joab angrily rebukes David for his stupid sentimentalism. How different are the last two scenes from the first two! Together, these four scenes present "a single, evolving portrait of the king's personal and political decline . . . a way to measure David's psychological disposition and public standing at key moments in his reign, depicting a leader who in-creasingly loses control over his emotions and public image even as the tragedies of life grow less politically expeditious and more personal" (Weitzman 1997: 138).

II. 2:1–4:12: David as Regional King

2:1–32. The opening of this chapter pictures a David who does not act without first a word from God (vv. 1–4a), and a David who will not force himself as king over the late Saul's subjects (vv. 4b–7). He prays for himself (v. 1) and he prays for others (vv. 5–6). One is a prayer for guidance; the other is a prayer for blessing. And yet, even the language at the beginning of the chapter points to David's "rise" by its fourfold use of the verb "go up" (*ᶜalah*), which we will translate "ascend" to bring out the force of David's ascent (Polzin 1993: 32):

v. 1: "Shall I ascend into any of the cities of Judah?"
v. 1: "The Lord said to him, 'Ascend.'"
v. 1: "To which city shall I ascend?"
v. 2: "So David ascended there."

After this brief introduction to David, he drops out of sight for the rest of the chapter. The emphasis now is on Joab, David's nephew and commander-in-chief, and Abner and Ishbaal, the former being Saul's surviving commander-in-chief, and the latter Saul's only surviving son (vv. 8–32).

Two things are of interest about Ishbaal/Ishbosheth. First, where does he come from? 1 Sam. 14:49 informs us that Saul had three sons: Jonathan, Ishvi, and Malchishua. In 1 Chron. 8:33 and 9:39 the number of sons increases to four: Jonathan, Malchishua, Abinadab, and Eshbaal/Ishbosheth. And 1 Sam. 31:2 says that the Philistines killed Jonathan, Abinadab, and Malchishua. Common to all three lists are Jonathan and Malchishua, but what of Ishvi, Abinadab and I/Eshbaal? If all the data we had was 1 Samuel 14 and 31, the obvious sense would be to make Ishvi and Abinadab the same person. It is also possible that Ishvi of 1 Samuel 14 and Ishbosheth of 2 Samuel 2, given the "Ish" at the start of both names, are the same person. Admittedly, this leaves unresolved the issue of why Ishbosheth is not mentioned in 1 Samuel 31 as a participant in and survivor of the war at Mount Gilboa at which his father and three brothers perished. His omission from that event cannot be due to his being a minor, for just two chapters later we are told that he was "forty years old" when he began to reign (2 Sam. 2:10).

The second thing of interest about him is his name. "Ishbosheth" means "man of shame," and as a birth name it sounds as unlikely as Nabal, "fool" (1 Samuel 25). Now we note that in First Chronicles his name is consistently I/Eshbaal, "man of Baal" (1 Chron. 8:33; 9:39). Another example of a Baal name in Chronicles that disappears in Second Samuel is David's son Beeliada/Baaliada (1 Chron. 14:7), but which appears in 2 Sam. 5:16 simply as Eliada. Presumably, "Baal" was once a legitimate epithet for Yahweh (see Hos. 2:16: "On that day . . . no longer will you call me 'My Baal'"), but when the Baal cult of Canaanitism became a threat to Israel's monotheistic creed, the label was shunned, and either deleted or replaced in personal names. This, then, avoided the idea that Saul and David had honored the Canaanite deity. That Second Samuel has no Baal names for this period and First

Chronicles does simply indicates that the Hebrew text of Second Samuel comes from manuscripts that underwent such revisions, whereas the Hebrew text of First Chronicles comes from manuscripts that did not. Or possibly, Baal names in Chronicles were left unmolested because by the time of the Chronicler the Baal cult had lost its appeal and no longer presented an inducement to syncretistic idolatry for Israel.

The theme of violence and death sounded in ch. 1 continues into ch. 2. Two death scenes occupy the remainder of the chapter. First (vv. 12–16), evolving out of the burgeoning civil war between forces favorable to Saul and those favorable to the insurgency of David, Abner suggests a contest between a dozen of his men and a dozen of Joab's men. Their goal is "to have a contest" (v. 14, NRSV) or "fight hand to hand" (NIV). The actual Hebrew word is *sakhaq* and means "to play, entertain." (Cf. Judg. 16:25, 27: "'Call Samson, and let him *entertain* us'. . . . there were about three thousand men and women, who looked on while Samson *performed*.") While the word refers to sexual dalliance (Gen. 26:8, Isaac "playing with, fondling" Rebekah, and there spelled *tsakhaq*), it may also refer to deadly combat, as 2 Sam. 2:14 indicates. The employment of "play" in a hostile context "implies a particular way of looking at war that equates war with games" (Niditch 1993: 95). This turns out to be a "game" in which all the contestants died (v. 16), and the death toll in Second Samuel climbs to twenty-five.

The second death scene emerges from vv. 18–32, involving the same two parties. Asahel, fleet-footed and impetuous brother of Joab, pursues Abner with the intention of overtaking him and killing him. Like Lot, who offered his two daughters to the crazies assaulting his house in lieu of his guests (Gen. 19:8), Abner offers an easier target for Asahel, a younger, less-experienced warrior (v. 21). Both offers of surrogates were rejected. Abner has no choice but to kill Asahel (v. 23). And the death toll in Second Samuel climbs to twenty-six.

Inevitably, this killing sparks a blood duel with Joab, and only Abner's request for a common-sense truce (v. 26) puts an end (momentarily, anyway) to the violence—but not before nineteen of David's servants and 360 followers of Abner perish (vv. 30–31). And the death toll in Second Samuel rises to 405.

Joab is like Absalom (2 Samuel 13). Both have a relative (a brother, a sister) who has been killed or violated. The perpetrator is well known to the kin of the assaulted. Both are crimes involving "brothers" (brothers in the sense of an all-Israelite designation in 2 Samuel 2 and literal half-brothers in 2 Samuel 13). The desire for immediate revenge and retaliation runs high. "Vengeance is mine; I will repay," say Joab and Absalom. But the timing is not right. Be patient. The propitious time will come. It may be after your king fathers six sons (3:2–5) or "two years later" (13:23).

3:1–39. Indeed, David's house does grow stronger over that of Saul through both protracted war (v. 1) and multiplying the number of "Mrs. Davids" with the male progeny they will produce (vv. 2–5). For starters, David has six wives during his tenure at Hebron, each of whom bears him a son. In a chapter that will shortly focus on Abner taking a woman who is Ishbosheth's (vv. 6–11), it is interesting to note that one of David's wives, maybe two, he took from another man, after the first husband's death. One of them is Abigail, formerly married to Nabal (1 Sam. 25:39–42). The other may be his wife Ahinoam (2 Sam. 2:2; 3:2). Only one other person in the Old Testament bears this name, Saul's wife: "The name of Saul's wife was Ahinoam, daughter of Ahimaaz" (1 Sam. 14:50). To what else might Nathan be referring when he, speaking for God, says to David after the Bathsheba/Uriah incident, "I gave you your master's house, and your master's wives into your bosom" (2 Sam. 12:8)? (See Levenson 1980: 507, 513–14.)

There is war not only between the house of David and the house of Saul, but also within the house of Saul. What precipitates it is Abner taking Rizpah, Saul's concubine, and the vehement protest from Ishbosheth (vv. 6–11). The narrator does not actually say that Abner "went into" Rizpah. We merely hear Ishbosheth's denunciation of the fact (v. 7), which identifies "a full-blown and explosive affair of which we have had no inkling" (Sternberg 1985: 241).

It is common for commentators to suggest that by "going into" a king's widow/concubine, Abner has designs on Ishbosheth's throne and would like to replace him. Reference can be made to similar ideas in 2 Sam. 12:8 (David taking Saul's wife); 2 Sam. 16:21 (Ahithophel urges Absalom, who would like to overthrow his father, to "go into your father's concubines"); 1 Kings 2:17 (Adonijah requested as a wife Abishag, the lady who nursed David during his last illness, an act Solomon interpreted as his half-brother's attempt to lay claim to the throne [1 Kgs. 2:22–25]). This does not mean, of course, that usurping Ishbosheth's throne was the actual intention of Abner (and Adonijah). It simply means that this is the interpretation that Ishbosheth (and Solomon) placed on the sex. There has been no indication that it was Abner's intent to take the throne. And was it not Abner who had recently played a major role in making Ishbosheth king?

Note also that Ishbosheth never expresses any concern about Rizpah's well-being and never even uses her name. She is simply "my father's concubine" (Stone 1996: 85). Rizpah is much like Michal later in the chapter (vv. 13–16). Rizpah is caught in the middle between Abner and Ishbosheth. Michal is caught in the middle between her former husband, David, and her present husband, Paltiel. Abner goes into Rizpah—for sex? to assert or strengthen his claim to the throne? As a precondition of becoming Israel's king, David insists that Michal be restored to him—he loved her? she had been illegitimately taken from him by Saul? he had risked his life to raise the bride price for her father? she is useful in cementing David's claim to the support of Saul's subjects? How does Rizpah feel—used? abused? confused? What does Michal feel—gratitude? love? contempt (for Paltiel? for David?)? Eight women appear in 2 Samuel 3, but not one of them ever speaks.

Abner's willingness to transfer his allegiance to David and David's happy acceptance of that loyalty (vv. 17–21) alarms Joab, David's commander-in-chief (vv. 22–25). Interestingly, Joab accuses Abner of deception (v. 25), only to use deception himself and lure Abner to his death (vv. 26–27). Joab, like many of us, accuses another of his own sin.

This part of the story is often cited as an illustration of the ancient practice of blood vengeance. When a person is killed, his or her kinsmen are obliged to avenge the death of the deceased by slaying the killer. So Joab is obliged to kill Abner for murdering his brother Asahel. But this is certainly not a perfect example of blood vengeance, for Joab obviously had political motives. If Abner is allowed to join forces with David, might he not replace Joab as David's commander-in-chief? Jonathan may be willing to step aside for David, but Joab is not willing to step aside for Abner. And the death toll in Second Samuel rises to 406.

For a third time the question of (hidden) motivation arises in this chapter (and we add a later fourth one):

1. Abner went into Rizpah. Why?
2. David insisted that Michal be restored to him. Why?
3. Joab killed Abner. Why?
4. David lamented for Abner (vv. 31–36). Why?

There is little mention of God throughout this chapter (Brueggemann 1990: 232). David never speaks to or about God, nor does his top soldier, Joab, nor does David's counterpart, Ishbosheth. Abner is the only one to speak of God (v. 9, when he was furious at Ishbosheth; and v. 18, when he is seeking to persuade his people to unite under David.)

4:1–12. In another incident with minimal talk about God (see v. 8), Abner's death makes Ishbosheth a sitting duck, an easy target for anybody who desires his removal. Two men from the Gibeonite city Beeroth (one of the cities of the Gibeonite pentapolis [Josh. 9:17]), Rechab and

Baanah, slaughter Ishbosheth and behead him, taking his head (Goliath-like [1 Sam. 17:51, 54, 57]) to David in Hebron. And the death toll in Second Samuel rises to 407. Possibly, their actions were in revenge for what Saul, Ishbosheth's father, had done to the Gibeonites (2 Sam. 21:4).

What makes their act of execution so bold is that it is done around the noon hour or shortly thereafter, "about the heat of the day," the same part of the day in which Saul had fought against the Ammonites (1 Sam. 11:11). They do not even use the cover of darkness. The text calls them "captains of raiding bands," raiding bands such as the Amalekite ones we read about in 1 Sam. 30:8, 15, 23. Mendenhall (1973: 86) calls them "two disreputable turncoats [who] commit political assassination in order to ingratiate themselves with the man who will inevitably win power." Brueggemann (1990: 234) calls them "two paramilitary thugs."

If these two executioners were aware of what David did to the Amalekite when he claimed to have killed Saul, then their actions in bringing Ishbosheth's head to David are incredibly stupid. But maybe they did not know. The two hit-men also manage to drag Yahweh's holy name into the mud by ascribing their brutal criminal activity to God (v. 8). They have acted for God, so they believe, with a posture not all that different from the militant crusaders of the medieval and modern period.

But how can David reward evil with good, the killing of a "righteous man" (v. 11) by reprobates? What David does is (1) order their execution (v. 12a); (2) have their corpses mutilated (v. 12b); (3) have their torsos impaled (4:12—with shades of Josh. 8:29; 10:26; 1 Sam. 31:10b). And the death toll in Second Samuel rises to 409. Any remaining roadblocks (Abner was a real roadblock, Ishbosheth a quasi-roadblock) to the extension of David's reign over Judah in directions northward are now removed.

For some reason, David composes passionate laments over Saul and Jonathan when informed of their deaths (1:17–27), and over Abner (3:33–34), but not over Ishbosheth. There is weeping in ch. 1 (v. 24), weeping in ch. 3 (v. 32), but no weeping in ch. 4. The progression over these four chapters has been death and weeping (ch. 1); death but no weeping (ch. 2); death and weeping (ch. 3); death but no weeping (ch. 4).

III. 5:1–25: David as National King

5:1–25. Deprived of their de facto leader Abner (3:30) and their de jure leader Ishbosheth (4:6), the northern Israelites turn to David to fill the vacuum of leadership (vv. 1–5). David then relocates his capital from Hebron to Jerusalem (vv. 6–9), has a house built for himself (v. 11), and expands his family (vv. 13–16). And twice God answers his inquiries about whether or not to go against the Philistines (vv. 17–25). This is the essence of ch. 5.

It is a chapter about David obtaining new things:

1. a new empire (vv. 1–5)
2. a new capital city (vv. 6–9)
3. a new palace (v. 11)
4. a new family (vv. 13–16)
5. a new confidence in God and himself because of victories over harassing neighbors (vv. 17–25)

There is more upbeat talk about God here than in the previous four chapters. The Israelite elders quote the Lord to David (v. 2). David makes a covenant (a constitution?) with these elders "before the Lord" (v. 3). The narrator, in a rare move, comments twice on the powerful workings of God in David's life (vv. 10, 12). David himself inquires twice of the Lord (via the priestly Urim and Thummim?) on God's will in the matter of confronting the approaching Philistines (vv. 19, 23). Both times the Lord responds, the first time with basically a "yes" answer (v. 19c), the second time with an answer involving a complex military stratagem (vv. 23–24) (indicating, by the way, that consulting the Urim and Thummin, if David used them, could involve more than merely a "yes" or "no" answer). And finally, David gives proper recognition to the Lord for turning back and routing the Philistines (v. 20).

It is obvious that most of this talk about God comes toward the beginning and end of the chapter. While David first consulted the Lord about whether or not to fend off the Philistine threat, he did not first consult the Lord about attacking Jerusalem (and the Jebusites), which he then named after himself and made his new capital city. He did it on his own. In other words, in the two defensive wars in this chapter David first seeks the divine will. In the one offensive war in this chapter David acts independently.

And what about a Phoenician king building a house in Jerusalem for a king of Judah/Israel (v. 11)? And what about David's taking additional wives and concubines (vv. 13–14), presumably from the Jebusite Canaanites whom David overpowered? Is God's will to be sought first in these things too, or not? A Phoenician builds David's house literally, and Jebusite women build David's house metaphorically.

And note that while David is quick to give praise to God for victory over the Philistines (v. 20), he says nothing similar to that after he has conquered Jerusalem. But then again, the Jebusites and the Philistines are not comparable threats. The Jebusites are a cocky group of city dwellers who suffer from feelings of invincibility ("even the blind and the lame will turn you back" [v. 6b]), even though in Joshua's time the Jebusites successfully resisted Judahite (Josh. 15:63) and Benjaminite (Judg. 1:21) takeovers. By contrast, the Philistines constituted a herculean war machine.

Almost everything in this chapter has a parallel in First Chronicles:

(a) Israel anoints David king (2 Sam. 5:1–5; 1 Chron. 11:1–3 and 12:23–40).
(b) David captures Jerusalem (2 Sam. 5:6–10; 1 Chron. 11:4–9).
(c) Hiram builds David a house (2 Sam. 5:11–12; 1 Chron. 14:1–2).
(d) David expands his family (2 Sam. 5:13–16; 1 Chron. 14:3–7) (but Chronicles mentions no concubines, only wives).
(e) David has two victories over the Philistines (2 Sam. 5:17–25; 1 Chron. 14:8–17).

One notes several differences when the two accounts are compared. Four especially stand out. First, Chronicles moves directly from Saul's sorry end (1 Chron 10:13–14) to David's accession as king of Israel (1 Chron. 11:1–3), thus deleting all the gore and mess and violence of 2 Samuel 1–4. This also removes any possibility of viewing David as an opportunistic usurper. He is God's servant, chosen by God to replace a failed king.

Second, Chronicles does not mention the taunt that the Jebusites hurled at David, nor does it mention David's vengeful answer to that taunt ("'Let him attack the lame and the blind, those whom David hates.' Therefore it is said, 'The blind and the lame shall not come into the house'" [2 Sam. 5:8]). In Chronicles, David says nothing. He lets his actions do the talking.

Third, 2 Samuel 5 presents (a) through (e) as if they are sequential, one happening right after the other. Yet Chronicles narrates (a) and (b) in ch. 11 while (c) through (e) are delayed until ch. 14. And in between (a) and (b) and (c) through (e) Chronicles inserts a portion of the account of David bringing the ark to Jerusalem (1 Chronicles 13, resumed in ch. 15 and 16). Let us put it thusly:

2 Samuel	1 Chronicles
(a)—(e), ch. 5	(a)—(b), ch. 11 (and 12)
ark brought to Jerusalem, ch. 6	ark brought to Jerusalem, ch. 13 (resumed in ch. 15 and 16)
	(c)—(e), ch. 14

This difference in sequence indicates that maybe neither Samuel nor Chronicles has presented its data strictly chronologically. In the case of Chronicles, for example, the author/editor may have placed the account of David bringing the ark into Jerusalem before the two battles with the Philistines as a way of emphasizing David's greater concern with cultic/worship matters than with military ones.

The fourth interesting difference between the two accounts is the information about what David and his troops did with the spoil they captured from the Philistines:

> 2 Sam. 5:21: "The Philistines abandoned their idols there, and David and his men carried them away."
>
> 1 Chron. 14:12: "They abandoned their gods there, and at David's command they were burned."

In other words, Chronicles makes explicit what in Second Samuel is implicit. This is in line with Deut. 7:5, which forbids taking the physical objects of Canaanite religion as booty or bringing them to God ("But this is how you must deal with them: . . . burn their idols with fire").

IV. 6:1–23: David as Ark Custodian

6:1–23. With the exception of the cursory reference to it in 1 Sam. 14:18, the sacred ark of the covenant has not been mentioned since 1 Sam. 7:1–2, when the Philistines returned the ark they had captured first to Bethshemesh, then to Kiriath-jearim, where it was placed in the home of Abinadab.

David, acting on his own initiative, leads a delegation of thirty thousand to fetch the ark from its resting place and bring it to Jerusalem. The number thirty thousand recalls an earlier ark incident:

> 2 Sam. 6:1: "David gathered all the chosen men of Israel, thirty thousand."
>
> 1 Sam. 4:10: "There was a very great slaughter, for there fell of Israel thirty thousand foot soldiers."

There are other correspondences between the ark narratives of 1 Samuel 4–7 and that of 2 Samuel 6 (Van der Toorn and Houtman 1994: 222):

1. the reference to a "new cart" (1 Sam. 6:7; 2 Sam. 6:3—the only two Old Testament occurrences) as the means of the ark's transportation
2. the use of rhetorical questions expressing fear before the ark
   a. the Philistines: "Who can deliver us from the power of these mighty gods?" (1 Sam. 4:8)
   b. the Bethshemeshites: "Who is able to stand before the Lord, this holy God?" (1 Sam. 6:20)
   c. David: "How can the ark of the Lord come into my care?" (2 Sam. 6:9)

There is at least one difference between the two units. In 1 Samuel 7 the ark is at Kiriath-jearim and is under the supervision of Abinadab's son Eleazar (1 Sam. 7:1). In 2 Samuel 6 the ark is at Baale-judah (2 Sam. 6:2) and is transported by Abinadab's sons Uzzah and Ahio (2 Sam. 6:3). As to the discrepancy in the personal names, one may suggest either that Eleazer is no longer a part of the picture or that Eleazar and Uzzah are the same person, the first name being the longer form of the two. As to the discrepancy in the place name, Baale-judah probably refers to a town in Judah (cf. "Bethlehem of Judah" in 1 Sam. 17:12). And Josh. 15:9 explicitly identifies Baalah with Kiriath-jearim.

The procession is halted when the ark is in danger of falling off the ox-pulled cart. To prevent the ark from crashing to the ground, Uzzah reaches out, touches, and steadies the ark. But in touching the ark, however well-intentioned his actions and instincts were, he dies (v. 7). Uzzah's death, resulting from an obviously unpremeditated act, demonstrates that there can be no appeal to inadvertency in the realm of the most sacred.

Understandably, David is angry at God (v. 8; see p. 251 for other expressions of anger directed at God). The Lord who "burst forth" against David's enemies, the Philistines (5:20), is the same Lord who "bursts forth" (v. 8) against David's assistant.

After a three-month cooling-off period, David resumes the task of bringing the ark to Jerusalem. If God has blessed the house of Obed-edom for storing the ark (v. 11b), surely God will bless David and his house for building a real "house" for the ark in Jerusalem. David wants what Obed-edom is experiencing.

The occasion is a festive one, with singing, dancing, and sacrifices (vv. 13–15, 17–19). Everybody is euphoric except Michal. What is about to happen between David and Michal is an "exchange of whipsaw sarcasms" (Alter 1981: 124).

The story begins by saying that David (with the people) was dancing (*sakhaq*) before the Lord with all his might (v. 5). Later, the narrator again says that David was "dancing" before the Lord with all his might (v. 14), but this time the verb is *karkar*. And still later, we read that Michal saw David "leaping" (*pazzaz*) and "dancing" (*karkar*) (v. 16). It is as if the narrator first uses the normative word for "dancing" (v. 5), then shifts to a word that expresses more movement and animation (v. 14), and then uses a double expression to describe what Michal saw—not just dancing or whirling, but leaping and whirling—all as the narrator's way of building up the hostility that Michal harbors toward David (Berlin 1983: 73).

We cannot be sure why Michal is in such a rage. Alter (1981: 123) suggests the following possibilities: "the undignified public spectacle which David is now making of himself; Michal's jealousy over the moment of glory David is enjoying while she sits alone, a neglected co-wife, back at the provisional palace; Michal's resentment over David's indifference to her all these years, over the other wives he has taken, over being torn away from the devoted Palti; David's dynastic ambitions—now clearly revealed in his establishing the Ark in the 'City of David'—which will irrevocably displace the house of [her father] Saul." In ventilating her displeasure at David, she is somewhat like God vis-à-vis Uzzah in the first half of the chapter (Polzin 1993: 65). God kills and David is angry. Michal rebukes and David taunts. God and Michal, each in their own way, throw water on David's party.

David does little to help the misunderstanding. In what is the only instance in the Old Testament of an individual using the first-person singular pronoun as the object of the verb "choose" (along with its parallel in 1 Chron. 28:4), David says "the Lord chose me in place of your father" (v. 21). And to add insult to injury, he promises further and even more risqué exhibitionisms (v. 22). Regardless of how many Philistines David can kill on the battlefield, if he cannot speak to his wife without insults, he has a big problem, he is a big problem.

For the rest of her life Michal remains childless (v. 23), and she is about the only wife of David to be so. Michal is unlike David's Hebronite wives (3:2–5) and his Jebusite wives (5:13–16). "Whereas the Jebusite women *of* Jerusalem help David build his house (2 Sam. 5), Michal *in* Jerusalem does not" (Polzin 1993: 71). The narrator avoids attributing Michael's barrenness to a formal, dead marriage from this point on, or to David divorcing her, or to a judgment of God for raising her voice against the Lord's anointed.

First Chronicles treats this episode a bit differently than does 2 Samuel 6, a point we observed briefly when discussing 2 Samuel 5. Like

2 Samuel 6, 1 Chron. 15:25–16:3 records the transfer of the ark to Jerusalem. It notes very briefly Michal's displeasure (15:29), but records no words between her and David. Chronicles also substitutes poles and the shoulders of the Levites for transferring the ark (15:15) and says nothing about a new cart, or the Uzzah incident, or the blessing on Obed-edom and his house. Chronicles then adds data not found in 2 Samuel 6. (1) David appoints individuals of the Levites to play musical instruments before the ark (1 Chron. 16:4–6). (2) David encourages the singing of a psalm of praise by professional Levitical singers (1 Chron. 16:7–36). This song is actually drawn from three sections of the Psalter: 1 Chron. 16:8–22 = Ps. 105:1–15; 1 Chron. 16:23 = 33 = Ps. 96:1–13; 1 Chron. 16:34–36 = Ps. 106:1, 47–48. Here is David composing psalms for the temple even before there is a temple, and unlike some of his other compositions (2 Sam. 1:17–27; 22; 23), this is his only song that is assigned a specific cultic setting by its narrative setting (Weitzman 1997: 101). (3) David establishes a Levitical family to perform cultic rituals before the ark (1 Chron. 16:37–42). Unlike Second Samuel, First Chronicles strongly emphasizes David's take-charge role in this scene. More than legitimating worshiping God in Jerusalem, the Chronicler's version highlights the role of David in supervising, stimulating, and organizing the proper worship of God (Wright 1998: 53–54).

The Samuel story of the ark's transfer suggests several truths (Peterson 1995):

1. Places where God is can be not only beautiful, but also dangerous. And serving God can be both beautiful and dangerous. The story plays off Uzzah who died in God's service against David who danced in God's service.
2. It can be fatal to think that one is responsible for God's safety and well-being. Uzzah has God in a box, and must keep God free of the world's dirt.
3. We are not responsible for keeping God from falling, but he has pledged to keep us from falling ("Now to him who is able to keep you from falling . . ." [Jude 24]).
4. Uzzah is busy taking care of God, while David knows the reality of being taken care of by God (before Goliath, before Saul, etc.).
5. Even in his anger David is alive to God. One can get angry with God, but one does not get angry with a box.
6. Michal may have preferred to be married to Uzzah. He is more predictable than David, more proper.

7. We talk and sing too much about marching ("We're marching to Zion" or "Onward, Christian soldiers, marching as to war") and not enough about dancing.

V. 7:1–29: David as Head of a House

7:1–29. The chapter falls into three parts: (1) David wants to build God a house (vv. 1–7); (2) The Lord responds with a "Thanks, but no thanks" answer, but promises to build a house for David different from the house he currently occupies (vv. 8–17); (3) David's prayerful response to that revelation (vv. 18–29).

While it is common among commentators to attribute different parts of the chapter to different authors, and to designate the chapter as a later intrusion into the David story, thanks to its Deuteronomistic language and messianic emphases, the arguments for both the unity of the chapter and its congruence with its context are compelling (Van Seters 1983: 274). For example, David's desire to give the ark a home other than a tent home (7:2) accords well with 6:17–19, which informs us of a tent that David pitched for the ark once he transferred it to Jerusalem. Also, David's reference to his own royal house (7:1–2) presupposes 5:11 with its reference to King Hiram of Tyre building David a house. Finally, the reference to the Lord having given rest to David from all his enemies (7:1b) points back to his victories over the Philistines recorded in 5:17–25.

It is understandable that David would desire to build a house for his God. Near Eastern royal ideology is replete with instances of kings building temples with consequent divine benevolence toward the king and his seed (Laato 1997a; 1997b). As Fretheim (1983: 114–15) observes, the utility of a sanctuary is threefold. First, it brings order to the worship of God versus an "anything goes" perspective. Second, a sanctuary provides a tangible aspect of the divine presence, and not merely a "spiritual" presence. Third, a sanctuary provides a point of assurance of the divine presence. God has promised to dwell there, and his people can be confident that they will encounter him there when they enter the holy place.

David has two choices if he is interested in equalization. Since David lives in a house and the ark is in a tent, David can put his house on the market and move into a tent. But kings, upwardly mobile persons that they are, never downsize. Hence, the only other option is to bring God up to David's level. Let him have a house, too.

Nathan the prophet, to whom we are introduced for the first time, baptizes the project (v. 3). That Nathan turns out to be wrong in the counsel he gives David demonstrates that even good, anointed prophets may be guilty of assuming that how and what they feel and think is what the Lord God feels and thinks. Like Samuel earlier, Nathan is looking too much at external appearances (1 Sam. 16:7). At the same time, let us not be too hard on Nathan. What preacher would not get excited about a church building program when the richest person in town offers to bankroll the project?

Not only is Nathan wrong, but also he is gracious enough to admit it. Instead of blankly endorsing David's brainstorm, Nathan brings a message from God to David (vv. 5–16). The text does not repeat the repetition of this divine message to David (as in Exodus where God speaks to Moses and then comes the account of Moses relaying that message to the people either exactly or with some modification). Instead, v. 17 summarizes by saying, "Nathan spoke to David."

The gist of this message is that while God declines David's thoughtful offer, God will build a house for David that will be carried on by his sons and will last forever. The two most important words in this chapter are "house" and "forever."

The word "house" is used fifteen times in this chapter: once by the narrator (v. 1); six times by God (vv. 5, 6, 7, 11, 13, 16); eight times by David (vv. 2, 18, 19, 25, 26, 27, 29 [2x]). It carries four different connotations:

1. house = royal palace (vv. 1, 2) (NIV, "palace")
2. house = temple (vv. 5, 6, 7, 13)
3. house = royal dynasty (vv. 11, 16, 19, 25, 26, 27, 29)
4. house = family (v. 18) (NIV, "family")

The second key word is "forever." It occurs eight times in this chapter. It appears more often in this chapter than in any other chapter in the books of Samuel and the books of Kings, and accounts for eight of its thirty-three uses in these books. It is used by God three times (vv. 13, 16 [2x]) and by David in his prayer five times (vv. 24, 25, 26, 29 [2x]), with David's "forevers" thus topping God's "forevers" by an almost 2:1 ratio.

It is this emphasis in the chapter on God's promise to build for and of David "a house that will last forever" that has led commentators to contrast the unconditional covenant God makes with the house of David with the conditional covenant he made with the house of Israel at Sinai ("if you obey my voice and keep my covenant" [Exod. 19:5]). But perhaps the promise to the house of David is not all that unilaterally unconditional, and perhaps the dynastic oracle here is firmly set in the Sinaitic covenant (Eslinger 1994). We can agree with Brueggemann (1990: 259) when he says, "While the covenantal 'if' is silenced in this theology, it has not been nullified."

This is particularly true when the Lord speaks of David's son: "When he commits iniquity, I will punish him with a rod such as mortals use, with blows inflicted by human beings" (v. 14b). Interestingly, here is the major difference between 2 Samuel 7 and its parallel in 1 Chronicles 17. Unlike 2 Samuel 6, which Chronicles significantly reworks, there is little change in Chronicles retelling of 2 Samuel 7 except at this point—it deletes 2 Sam. 7:14b:

> 2 Sam. 7:14–15: "I will be a father to him, and he shall be a son to me. When he commits iniquity, I will punish him with a rod such as mortals use, with blows inflicted by human beings. But I will not take my steadfast love from him, as I took it from Saul."
> 1 Chron. 17:13: "I will be a father to him, and he shall be a son to me. I will not take my steadfast love from him, as I took it from him who was before you." (The Chronicler cannot even bring himself to say "Saul.")

But there is another way in which the unconditional nature and eternality of God's promise to David's house needs qualification. First, we may look at an earlier "forever" that God directed to another house, and then subsequently rescinded when the bearers of that promise disgraced the promise giver by their sinful living. It is God's promise to Eli and his seed in 1 Sam. 2:30: "I promised that your family and the family of your ancestor should go out and in before me forever; but now the Lord declares. . . ." It is this withdrawal of God's "forever" vis-à-vis the house of Eli that is partially behind Jeremiah's comparison of Jerusalem's fate to Shiloh's, where the house of Eli ministered (Jer. 7:12, 14; 26:6). Had not Yahweh, a century earlier, said to Jerusalem through Isaiah that he would protect, deliver, spare, and rescue it (Isa. 31:5)? "No longer," says Jeremiah, as at Shiloh ("No longer, Eli").

The second thing to note is that the very next "forever" God or his prophet speaks to David and his house after all the "forevers" in 2 Samuel 7 is in 2 Sam. 12:10, after David's affair with Bathsheba and Uriah: "Now therefore the sword shall not depart from your house forever." The combination of 2 Samuel 7 with 2 Samuel 12 demonstrates that God's "forevers" can be both salutary and sobering. In fact, as Polzin (1993: 80) states, "God may keep a house in existence forever in order that its punishment may be kept in force forever."

In what may be the longest declaration of praise in the context of address to God in prayer, David responds to God's announcement (vv. 18–29). It is a prayer that follows this pattern (Miller 1994: 345–46):

1. Occasion—David sits before the Lord after Nathan has delivered the dynastic oracle to him.
2. Address—"O Lord God" repeated eight times (vv. 18, 19 [2x], 20, 22, 25, 28, 29); "O Lord" (v. 24).
3. Praise—vv. 18–24 are virtually entirely praise, and focus on the greatness of God in establishing David and his royal line (vv. 18–21), and on the redemption and establishing of the nation Israel (vv. 23–24).
4. Petition—"And now, O Lord God, as for the word you have spoken . . . confirm it forever; do as you have promised" (v. 25).
5. Motivation—"Thus shall your name be magnified forever. . . . and you have promised this good thing to your servant" (vv. 26–28).
6. Petition—"Now therefore may it please you to bless the house of your servant" (v. 29a).
7. Motivation—"so that it may continue forever before you . . . and with your blessing the house of your servant shall be blessed forever" (v. 29b).
8. Divine Response—None immediately; the history of the Judahite monarchy will spell out the response.

The story suggests crucial ideas for any faith community (for some of these thoughts I thank Lawson Stone, formerly my student and now my colleague):

1. We have to accept the possibility that God may say no to some of our loftiest, noblest dreams and aspirations. Paul knew that. Among the clearest times of evidence that the Spirit was directing him was when the Spirit said no: "having been forbidden by the Holy Spirit to speak the word in Asia" (Acts 16:6); "When they had come opposite Mysia, they attempted to go into Bithynia, but the Spirit of Jesus did not allow them" (Acts 16:7). God said no to Bithynia and opened the door to Troas, which opened the door to the spread of the gospel into Europe. Wanting Bithynia, but getting Troas! "When God says 'no' it is not necessarily rejection but redirection" (Swindoll 1997: 162).

2. When God says no, it does not necessarily mean we are sinful. It may only indicate that the best of us are fallible. And fallibility must not be confused with sinfulness.

3. God's plans for us are infinitely greater than any plans we have for God. God's plan to build a house for David is far more strategic than any plans David has to build a house for God.

4. David is interested in a project (building a house); God is interested in people (building a household).

5. David is interested in achieving; God wants to teach him something about receiving. For many it is difficult to receive. It is much easier to wash feet than it is to have one's feet washed. A TV star much beloved by children, Fred Rogers, put it succinctly: "It's so very hard receiving. When you give something you're in much greater control. But when you receive something, you're so vulnerable. I think the greatest gift you can give people is an honest receiving of what they have to offer."

VI. 8:1–10:19: David as Warrior

8:1–18. The chapter falls into two uneven sections: (1) the expansion of David's empire to the southwest (v. 1), eastward (v. 2), to the northeast (vv. 3–8), northward (vv. 9–10), southward (vv. 13–14); (2) the formation of the bureaucracy with which David will surround himself—military personnel (vv. 16a, 18), administrative personnel (vv. 16b, 17b), priestly personnel (v. 17a). Mendenhall (1973: 11) describes those expansionist policies narrated in vv. 1–14 as the "incorporation of the old Canaanite city states under King David."

Several things may be observed about the cataloging of David's wars in vv. 1–14. First, they are the first offensive wars in which David engages, and accordingly are to be distinguished from those defensive wars mentioned in 5:17–25. In those wars David defends himself against the Philistines, who have "come up." In the defensive wars David first sought guidance from God (5:19a, 23a)—none of that in ch. 8. In ch. 5 God speaks directly to David (5:19b, 23b)—none of that in ch. 8. In ch. 5 David gives credit to God for his victories (5:20b)—none of that in ch. 8. In ch. 8 the narrator speaks glowingly of David ("David won a name for himself" [v. 13a])—none of that in 5:17–25.

Second, the chapter goes out of its way to say that David did not hoard the trophies of war for his own coffers. Both captured weapons (v. 8) and captured vessels (vv. 10b–12) he brought to Jerusalem and dedicated to his Lord, and the captured horses he eliminated (v. 4b).

Like the good king of Deut. 17:14–20, David does not accumulate for himself horses (Deut. 17:16) or silver and gold (Deut. 17:17).

Third, David is quite capable of inflicting incredible pain on the captured enemy. This is true particularly of his treatment of the Moabites (v. 2). The meaning of the verse is not entirely clear. It may mean either that David had two-thirds of the population put to death or that he killed only the tallest, ablest Moabites and hence used "genetic selection to weaken Moabite stock" (Niditch 1993: 130). Add to this David's vanquishing twenty-two thousand Arameans (v. 5) and eighteen thousand Edomites (v. 13).

The Chronicles version of this episode (1 Chronicles 18) preserves the enormous numbers of 2 Sam. 8:5 (1 Chron. 18:5) and of 2 Sam. 8:13 (1 Chron. 18:12), but totally eliminates the information in 2 Sam. 8:2 about David having the Moabites lie on the ground and measuring them off with a cord of two lengths or one length. For the first time we are seeing David in a new role. Up to this point in the Bible, David has been the hunted. Now he becomes the hunter. It is difficult to move from being prey to being predator.

Of all of David's bureaucratic appointments (vv. 15–18), most interesting is the appointment of the hitherto unknown Zadok as one of the priests (v. 17a), along with some of David's own sons (v. 18b). Zadok (after whom the Sadducees [Zadokees] are named) appears later in the David story (2 Sam. 15:24; 1 Kings 1:34; 2:35), but is especially prominent in Ezekiel's vision of the reconstructed temple as the leader/founder of the Levitical priests who serve in this temple (Ezek. 40:46; 43:19; 44:15; 48:11).

That David could even, or would even, appoint priests suggests that for this king, priests were regarded as royal appointees who could be dismissed by royal decree, as was the Abiathar family for siding with Adonijah (1 Kings 2:27, 35b). Even more unexpected is David's appointment of his own sons as priests (v. 18b; the NIV strangely reads "royal advisers" instead of "priests" for *kohanim*, relegating the better reading to a footnote, but note that the Septuagint renders *kohanim* not by the usual *hiereis*, "priests," but by *aularchai*, "princes of the court"). David is not Levite. He is Judahite. Either there is some leeway in priestly appointments or David is culpable of some old-fashioned nepotism. Bloodlines become more important than guidelines. We do not know which of his sons he designated as priests, but we do know that all of David's sons named in the following narratives are not sons who brought euphoria to their father's heart. By contrast, the Cherethites (Cretans) and Pelethites (of Caphtorian origin?) (v. 18a), foreign mercenaries in David's army, never betrayed him as did his own sons.

To be sure, the narrator twice gives the glory for victory to the Lord (vv. 6c, 14c). Nevertheless, one comes away from this chapter with some misgivings. As Brueggemann (1990: 264) notes, "Such enormous blessings constitute for David (as for us all) enormous temptations. Well-being seduces us into forgetting the God who blesses." When Paul says that he knows the experience of "having plenty" and "of being in need" (Phil. 4:12), one suspects that maybe he found living with plenty more spiritually challenging then living with little or nothing.

9:1–13. Sandwiched between two chapters dealing with David's foreign wars and the expansion of his empire is this little chapter in which David seeks out any surviving members of Saul's household so that he may extend kindness (*khesed*) to them. The Saulide survivalist turns out to be Jonathan's handicapped son, Mephibosheth (or Merib-baal, as he is called in 1 Chron. 8:34 and 9:40, with this being another instance of a "Baal" name in Chronicles appearing as a "Bosheth" name in Samuel as with Ishbosheth and Eshbaal). The end of the matter is that David invites Mephibosheth to eat for the rest of his life at the royal table. Mephibosheth could have said of David, "Thou preparest a table before me in the presence of Mine enemies."

David does not appear to know some people whom the reader might expect him to know. For all of his close, intimate camaraderie over the years with Jonathan, he seems to be uninformed about the existence of Jonathan's son Mephibosheth. Similarly, even though Bathsheba's house cannot be that far away from David's house—he can see her with his naked eye (no pun intended)—David has no idea who the woman is (11:2–3).

We cannot be sure why David is suddenly so solicitous toward any of Saul's family. On the surface it appears to be an aboveboard, charitable act rooted in David's agapic love for Jonathan. In bygone days Jonathan had said to David: "Never cut off your faithful love [*khesed*] from my house, even if the Lord were to cut off every one of the enemies of David from the face of the earth" (1 Sam. 20:15). Well, the Lord is trimming off these enemies in 2 Samuel 8 and 10. But when one is preoccupied with international affairs and military skirmishes, should they be so consuming that they cause one to forget the request of a loyal, trusted friend to whom one owes one's own survival? David is a survivor. Mephibosheth is a survivor. One survivor seeks out the welfare of another survivor out of loyalty to a friend who is not a survivor.

Commentators, however, are not so sure about David's motives. For many of them, David's request is more sinister than it is solicitous. Here is a sampling of views. Is David interested in taking care of Mephibosheth, or taking custody of him, and trying to unearth any potential contenders to his throne (Gunn and Fewell 1993: 104, 69)? Is David really magnanimous to Mephibosheth or is he being prudent in arranging to have him under his eye (Whybray 1968: 36)? Is David's making Mephibosheth a dining-room fixture the price David is willing to pay for keeping an eye on the last of Saul's line (Sternberg 1987: 255)? In relocating Mephibosheth from his own home to David's home has David in effect made Mephibosheth a political prisoner (Perdue 1984: 75) and put him under house arrest (Ackerman 1990: 43)? And thus, will David succeed in forestalling a rebellion in Saul's name (Flanagan 1972: 180)? Are David's actions analogous to what Brueggemann (1990: 267) calls "a White House media event with a poor family"?

It is unlikely that David would be all that paranoid about an individual being an insurrectionist and inciting a coup who is crippled in his feet (4:4; 9:3, 13) and lives far away in the town of Lo-debar (v. 5), a site generally identified with Tell el-Hammeh, north of the Jabbok River in the Ammonite territory of the northern part of Gilead (and a place name that has no fewer than four different vocalizations/pronunciations in the Old Testament).

We can imagine what Mephibosheth feels when he is summoned to David's house. What fate awaits him? Despite being lame in both feet, he is able to come to David and fall and bow before him, and David merely says his name (in what tone of voice?): "Mephibosheth" (v. 6).

We may compare this with another scene in which a sovereign merely utters the name of the one who is in front of him:

2 Sam. 9:6: "David said, 'Mephibosheth!'"
John 20:16: "Jesus said to her, 'Mary!'"

One doubts that Mephibosheth immediately returned to Lo-debar and said, "I have seen David." Mephibosheth expresses servitude; Mary becomes an evangelist.

This event in David's life points back to earlier events in First Samuel as well as ahead to events in Second Kings (Polzin 1990: 102–6, from whom I draw heavily for my remarks on the rest of this chapter). First of all, there are parallels between the fallen royal house of Saul and the fallen priestly house of Eli:

1. "Is there still anyone left of the house of Saul to whom I may show kindness?" (2 Sam. 9:1), and "Everyone who is left of your [Eli's] family" (1 Sam. 2:36).
2. "Mephibosheth . . . came to David and fell on his face and bowed" (2 Sam. 9:6), and "Everyone who is left in your family

shall come to bow before him [the faithful priest]" (1 Sam. 2:36).
3. "Mephibosheth ate at David's table" (2 Sam. 9:11; similarly, 9:13), and "Everyone who is left in your family shall come to bow before him for . . . a loaf of bread . . . that I may eat a morsel of bread" (1 Sam. 2:36).

But later in biblical history, when the house of David is in shambles, as was Saul's house earlier, one of David's descendants eats at somebody else's table: King Jehoiachin eats at the table of King Evil-merodach of Babylon (2 Kings 25:27–30 = Jer. 52:31–34).

Fallen House	Survivor	Benefactor (who allows survivor to eat at his table)
Eli's	those left in his family	the faithful priest
Saul's	Mephibosheth	David
David's	Jehoiachin	Evil-merodach, king of Babylon

The connection between the last two of these scenes is especially powerful by their repeated emphasis on "ate always." Mephibosheth ate "always" at David's table (2 Sam. 9:7, 10, 13), and Jehoiachin ate "every day of his life" (literally "always," *tamid*, as in 2 Samuel 9) at Evil-merodach's table (2 Kings 25:30).

A parallel also exists between David's preservation of the house of Saul and God's preservation of the house of David. The reason David shows kindness to a survivor of the house of Saul is "for the sake of" Jonathan (9:1, 7). And the reason God shows kindness to the survivors of the house of David, disreputable and violent lot that they often were, and tempers his judgment is "for the sake of" David (1 Kings 11:12, 13, 32, 34; 15:4; 2 Kings 8:19; 19:34; 20:6).

But then, God is benefactor to Israel because of somebody else. Through Moses, God tells his people that they are obtaining the blessing of land not because of their worthiness to possess it, but because of the wickedness of the nations already living there, and, most important for the sake of the promise God made to the patriarchs (Deut. 9:4–5).

10:1–19. Chapter 10 connects with ch. 9 in that both show David wanting "to do kindness" to a deceased person of whom David is fond by rewarding that person with some charitable act to his family or descendants. In addition to 2 Sam. 9:1 and 10:2, see 2 Sam. 19:32–40, in which elderly Barzillai requests that David's favor be granted not to

Barzillai, since he has so little time left to live, but to Chimham, possibly Barzillai's son. So alongside the idea in the Old Testament of cross-generational retribution (e.g., Exod. 20:5; Deut. 5:9) is the idea of cross-generational benefaction.

We are perhaps surprised to read that David wishes to do kindness, or deal loyally, with Hanun, who has succeeded his father, Nahash, as king of the Ammonites, all in response for Nahash's dealing loyally with David (v. 2). Nahash had been a source of terror to the Transjordanian Israelites in Saul's day (1 Samuel 11). Is the Nahash of Saul's era the same Nahash of David's era? And if so, has the breach between Israelite king and Ammonite king been repaired by David's time? Or could David be making all this up as an excuse to get a delegation onto Ammonite soil for less-than-cordial reasons?

This is what Hanun's advisers suspect (v. 3). Accordingly, Hanun had David's delegation subjected to various demeaning miseries. These measures involved mutilation of their beards and forcible indecent exposure by tearing their clothing. Apparently, the Ammonites inflict punishment on their enemies in halves—gouge out the right eye, but not both eyes (1 Sam. 11:2); cut off half the beard, but not the whole beard; cut off half the clothing at the waist or just below (and thus feminize them [Niditch 1993: 118]), but not all the clothing. Hanun is like Rehoboam, Solomon's son, who likewise listened to misguided counsel from his advisers and paid a mighty big price as a result (1 Kings 12:10–11).

David is sensitive to the embarrassment caused his men and sends them to Jericho, "the City of Palms," for a time of physical and emotional healing (v. 5). But rather than lead an army himself to even the score against the Ammonites, he sends Joab (v. 7), as he does again in 11:1.

Joab is the only one in this chapter to speak of the Lord: "Be strong . . . for the cities of our God; and may the Lord do what seems good to him" (v. 12). Exhortations before battle normally are delivered by the priest (stated explicitly in Deut. 20:2 and implied in Num. 31:6; 1 Sam. 4:4; 14:3, 18), but could be given by nonpriests such as the judges (Judg. 4:14; 7:15).

Joab and his brother Abishai are successful in forcing the Arameans and Ammonites to flee (vv. 13–14). David knows a lot about what it means to flee somebody who does not have your best interests in mind (1 Sam. 19:10, 18; 20:1; 21:10). There is no mention of war casualties in Joab's fighting with the Ammonites. But in David's war with the Arameans, who had joined forces with the Ammonites, David kills thousands of the fleeing enemy—forty thousand for starters (v. 18).

David's treatment of the Arameans (v. 19) follows Deuteronomy's teaching on the treatment of defeated peoples. To offer a defeated city "peace" means to offer that city the opportunity to surrender in return for a promise to spare the city if they agree to serve you (Deut. 20:10–12). The victorious party granting terms of submission is expressed by "make a treaty with us" (Josh. 9:6, 7, 11, 16; 1 Sam. 11:1). The defeated party's submitting to the terms of the victor is described either with some verb and the noun *shalom* (e.g., "offer it *shalom*") or with a verb derived from *shalom*, that is, *hishlim* ("respond peaceably," Deut. 20:12; Josh. 10:1, 4; 11:19).

Here the Arameans make peace with victorious Israel (*yashlimu*) and become subject to them (*ya'avdum*) (v. 19). In ch. 9 it was Saul's servants who became servants to David (9:3, 6, 8, 11), who earlier was styled as a servant of Saul (1 Sam. 17:32, 34; 26:18, 19). Saul's former servants become servants of David, a former servant of Saul. And what happens in ch. 9 on the home front takes place in ch. 10 in international affairs. David picks up new servants—the Arameans/Syrians.

VII. 11:1–12:31: David as Adulterer, Murderer, and Penitent

11:1–27. It is not enough for the Ammonites to flee (10:14). They must be punished for their humiliating of David's legates (11:1), and to that end David dispatches Joab on this punitive sortie against Rabbah ("the Great"), the capital city of the Ammonites, which today is Amman, the capital of Jordan. David himself remains behind in Jerusalem (end of v. 1) for reasons that are not clear. It is common for interpreters to root the blame for David's sins in the rest of this chapter in this irresponsible shirking of royal functions. Had he been where he should have been, the Uriah/Bathsheba scenario would never have taken place. But that is not necessarily a correct deduction. To be sure, the people in Samuel's days longed for a king who would "govern us and go out before us and fight our battles" (1 Sam. 8:20). But that this was the people's vision for their earthly king does not necessarily mean that it was also the Lord's vision for Israel's king.

This is not the first time David has not accompanied his troops into battle. In the first stage of the Ammonite war (10:7–14) he sent Joab (10:7), as he does here in 11:1. Other military occasions where David may be represented by proxy include the Chronicler's account of Israel's battle with the Edomites (where Abishai's is the only name mentioned [1 Chron. 18:12–13]), and one in the title to Psalm 60 ("and when Joab on his return killed twelve thousand Edomites in the Valley of Salt"; and see 1 Kings 11:15). Undoubtedly, killing the opposition's king in the heat of battle would be a great morale booster for the other side (as happened to Saul in 1 Samuel 31, and to Ahab of Israel in 1 Kings 22:31–37, reducing his soldiers to being like "sheep that have no shepherd" [1 Kings 22:17]).

A late afternoon stroll on the roof of his palace unintentionally provides David with a chance sighting of a beautiful woman bathing in her house. Even though she lives just a few houses away from the royal house, David does not know who she is. She must be a person of some importance and probably of wealth, for what sort of people have houses just a stone's throw from the palace? And she is more than likely married, for no single woman in that day would own a house in that quarter of town. Or is she a maid in that home?

The use of the verb "inquire" (*darash*) with David (v. 3) is very interesting in light of its use with David earlier:

2:1: "David inquired of the Lord"

5:19: "David inquired of the Lord"

5:23: "When David inquired of the Lord"

11:3: "David sent someone to inquire about the woman"

Apparently, this would have been a great time for David to inquire of the Lord, as he had done in the past, rather than inquire about this bathing beauty. He has not learned that if your inquiry causes you to sin, then you are to tear out your inquiry and throw it away (Matt. 5:29).

David finds out her name (Bathsheba), her father's name (Eliam), and, alas, her husband's name (Uriah). That last piece of information especially should put an end to any fantasy David may be feeding. Uriah, a Hittite mercenary in David's army with a beautiful Yahwistic name, "Ya (Yahweh) [is] my light," is unlikely an ordinary foot soldier, just a "GI." That he has a house, rather than barracks, close to the king's house suggests this.

The same goes for Bathsheba. About her father Eliam we know little. But her grandfather (and Eliam's father) is none other than Ahithophel (see 2 Sam. 23:34), an invaluable advisor sought out by David, then by Absalom (2 Sam. 16:23). At some point Ahithophel threw his support behind Absalom (17:1–4, 14), much to the chagrin of David (15:31). It is surely ironic that it is Ahithophel, into whose granddaughter David "went on his rooftop," who later advises Absalom to "go into" David's concubines on the roof of David's house (16:20–22).

The note at the end of v. 4, placed in parentheses in many translations, is an important one: "Now she [Bathsheba] was purifying herself after her period." First, it shows that the "bathing" of v. 2 is a ritual bath of purification after a woman's normal menstruation, spoken of in Lev. 15:19–24. Second, that Bathsheba has had a menstrual period since last being with her husband, Uriah, demonstrates that the child she will soon conceive (v. 5a) cannot be Uriah's, and so must be David's. In fact, there is a play here on the word "wash, bathe" (*rakhats*).

v. 2: "He saw a woman washing."
v. 8: David to Uriah: "Go down to your house, and wash your feet."

David sees Bathsheba washing, and he invites Uriah to wash his own feet in his own house. As Yee (1988: 246) has pointed out, the first of these two washings insures David's paternity, while the second washing is David's attempt to cover up his paternity. Third, we note that in Psalm 51, whose title connects this psalm with 2 Samuel 11, one of David's prayers is that God will wash him and make him whiter than snow (Ps. 51:7; but using *kavas* for "wash" instead of *rakhats*). God needs to wash the one who observed a washing and tried to encourage another washing.

We cannot be sure if Bathsheba came willingly or protesting vigorously, anymore than we can be sure why David did not go to war. Was the sex forced or consensual? Nor can we be certain whether her words "I am pregnant" are a "cry of triumph or an S.O.S. signal" (Blenkinsopp: 1965: 52). How, for example, is Bathsheba's "I am pregnant" different from Eve's "I have produced a man with the help of the Lord" (Gen. 4:1)?

Upon discovering Bathsheba's pregnancy, David sends a message to his chief soldier requesting that Uriah be sent back home to David in Jerusalem from Rabbah—so that David might confess? might ask for Uriah's forgiveness? might apologize? or something else? What unfolds next in the narrative is David's "something else" rather than any of his first three options.

His first proposal is that Uriah go down to his house, accompanied by a present from the king, and "wash his feet" (v. 8), which, if not an actual euphemism for sex, at least leans in that direction. To be sure, an invitation to somebody to wash their feet may be simply a courtesy extended by a host to their guest (e.g., Gen. 18:4, where three men show up at the entrance of Abraham's tent, and Abraham fetches water for them so they may wash their feet). But this case is different. It is not a guest entering his host's house. It is a husband entering his own and his wife's house, and seeing a spouse he has not seen or been with for some while. Earlier David "slept" (*shakav*) with Uriah's wife (v. 4). Now, rather than sleeping with his wife, Uriah "sleeps" (*shakav*) outside David's house (v. 9), even though his own house (and wife) is but a short walking distance away.

His explanation to David is a compelling one (v. 11). Out of loyalty to his military colleagues still slugging it out on the battlefield, and who are not favored with any R and R, Uriah renounces all the comforts of home—not only sex with Bathsheba, but even eating or drinking with her. This is the second time David offered somebody an opportunity to be in a house of their own. But just as the Lord rejected David's offer of a house of his own (ch. 7), so Uriah refuses David's offer to take up residence in his own home (Schwartz 1991: 43).

Behind Uriah's statement may be the ancient doctrine in Israel of the holiness of the war camp. A military camp, where God is present to fight for his people, is subject to even greater regimentation than is a residential camp. Accordingly, anything that causes impurity, and that includes sexual congress, is to be avoided. Hence, sexual relations for the fighting men would constitute a violation of terms of their enlistment. See Lev. 15:16, 18, and Deut. 23:9–12 for the Torah injunctions, and besides 2 Sam. 11:11, see 1 Sam. 21:5–6 (where David reassures the priest of Nob that his warriors had not had recent sexual relations with women, and so they were permitted to eat of the holy bread recently taken out of the sanctuary). If that explanation is correct (and there are dissenters), then David's coitus with Bathsheba, a soldier's wife, compounds his crime. "Violating a marriage is bad enough; violating a marriage under sacred conjugal suspension is a particularly cruel and nasty offense" (Rosenberg 1989: 111).

David's second plan is to invite Uriah to the palace for a royal banquet, get him intoxicated, and then have him taxied to his house and wife (v. 13), possibly for an alcohol-induced tryst with Bathsheba before he returns to the battle. David would not be the first to provide alcohol to excess as a prelude to sex. Lot's daughters did this with their father (Gen. 19:30–38). Another example may be present in Ruth 3:7, where only after Boaz had eaten and drunk, Ruth came, uncovered his "feet," and lay down (*shakav*) at his feet. That Uriah refuses to join his wife even for eating and drinking, but does not hesitate to join David for eating and drinking, demonstrates that the real activity in which Uriah will not participate with Bathsheba is sex.

Rebuffed for a second time, David's third plan is to send a letter back with Uriah for Joab, ordering Uriah to be placed in the very front line of battle, where most likely he will be killed (vv. 14–15). Little does Uriah know that he is carrying back his own death sentence to Joab.

This horrendous and despicable scheme invites comparison with Ahab's coveting of Naboth's vineyard, and the role of the king's wife, Jezebel, in the narrative of 1 Kings 21 (White 1994: 68):

1. A king covets a commoner's property (a wife, a vineyard) that is in close proximity to his palace (2 Sam. 11:2–3; 1 Kings 21:1–2).
2. A royal letter is sent to subordinate(s) directing Uriah's/ Naboth's murder through devious means (2 Sam. 11:14–15; 1 Kings 21:8–10).
3. The contents of that letter are revealed (2 Sam. 11:15; 1 Kings 21:9–11) and implemented, resulting in the death of the innocent (2 Sam. 11:17; 1 Kings 21:13). There is a report made back to the king of the finished deed (2 Sam. 11:18–24; 1 Kings 21:14).
4. The king takes/seizes the property after the husband's/owner's murder (2 Sam. 11:27; 1 Kings 21:16).
5. There is a surprise encounter by the king with a prophet who announces God's judgment and retribution (2 Sam. 12:1–12; 1 Kings 21:17–24).
6. The king, upon hearing the condemnation of the prophet, confesses and repents (2 Sam. 12:13; 1 Kings 21:27).
7. A son of the sinning king suffers for the sin of his father (2 Sam. 12:15–19; 1 Kings 21:29).

As Fretheim (1983: 127) has reminded us, David's sin is certainly adultery and murder, but is more than these, as reprehensible as they are. It is a sin committed by a person with power over the lives of others against a person(s) with little or no power. And to sin against the weak and most vulnerable is among the most heinous sins. It is a sin committed by a man against a woman. It is a sin committed by a commander-in-chief against one of his soldiers. It is a sin committed by a king against two of his subjects.

As with other matters in this story, there are gaps in the reader's knowledge of who knows what and how much, and why somebody does what he does in the way he does it. Sternberg (1987: 205–12), for example, raises hypotheses/questions like these, then probes for answers: (1) does Uriah know what David has done? (2) Uriah does not know what David has done; (3) David has decided Uriah knows; (4) David thinks Uriah does not know; (5) David, like the reader, cannot tell whether Uriah knows or does not know.

Very interesting is the message Joab sends back to David (vv. 18–21). In it (v. 21), Joab has David refer back to the story of Abimelech, who was killed when a woman threw a millstone on him (Judg. 9:52–53). The connection of the Abimelech story of Judges 9 with 2 Samuel 11 is twofold. First, in Judges 9 a man is killed (or severely injured) by a woman, whereas in 2 Samuel 11 a man kills for a woman. Second, Abimelech asks a subordinate to finish him off with the sword to prevent news spreading that this two-bit thug was killed by a woman. Similarly, David does what he thinks is necessary to prevent news spreading about his dastardly deed involving Uriah and Bathsheba. (See Sternberg 1987: 221.)

As it turns out, the messenger alters the message Joab gave him for David (vv. 22–24), changing Joab's aggressively laying seige against Rabbah (vv. 16, 20) to the Rabbahites coming out of the city aggressively against Joab, an attack Joab managed to repel, but in which Uriah died (vv. 23–24).

David's last remark in this chapter is a return message to Joab via the courier, part of which is, "Do not let this matter trouble you" ("upset you," NIV) (v. 25). Two things are of interest here. First, what is David referring to when he says "this matter"—the adultery with Bathsheba (about which Joab may or may not know), or Uriah being set up (about which Joab knows)? The second item is the use of virtually the same phraseology two verses later by the narrator to describe the Lord's feelings about David's behavior (v. 27). Let us translate literally to bring out the connection in these two verses:

v. 25: "Do not let this matter [thing] be evil in your eyes."
v. 27: "But the matter [thing] which David had done was evil in the eyes of the Lord."

Maybe to Joab it is not outrageous, but to Yahweh it is. At least nine months have passed since that rooftop affair, and David gives no evidence of a guilty conscience, no conviction of sin. Maybe he has covered his tracks successfully, but then again, maybe he has not, for "No one who conceals transgressions will prosper; but one who confesses them and forsakes them will obtain mercy" (Prov. 28:13).

12:1–31. If David thinks he is scot-free, then he is in for a rude awakening. The first time the Lord sent Nathan to David was to announce a grand and glorious destiny for the house of David (ch. 7). The second time the Lord sends Nathan to David is to announce that the sword shall never depart from David's house (v. 10) because of something that started on the roof of David's house. Nathan is both prophet and parablist, as vv. 1–15a indicate. These fourteen and one-half verses cover two movements (Linafelt 1992: 103):

> Nathan comes to David (v. 1a)
>   *Movement One:*
>   Nathan's parable (vv. 1b–4)
>   David's response (vv. 5–6)
>   Nathan's verdict (v. 7a)
>   *Movement Two:*
>   the Lord's speech (vv. 7b–12)
>   David's response (v. 13a)
>   Nathan's verdict (vv. 13b–14)
> Nathan leaves David (v. 15a)

Presumably, Nathan could have strode prophetically into David's house, pointed an incriminating finger toward David, and condemned him in a Jonathan Edwards–like tone: "Israelite Kings in the Hands of an Angry God." But he has a different strategy, and this is telling a parable, storytelling. Although used sparingly in the Old Testament, the parable is a pedagogical device that Jesus used often and effectively.

The didactic effect of a story over other forms of communication is illustrated beautifully in the short story of early-twentieth-century novelist Anton Chekhov called "Home" (Anton Chekhov, *The Cook's Wedding and Other Stories* [New York: 1984 (1920)], 65–78). A father is trying to convince his seven-year-old son not to smoke. But the young son is not at all interested in or persuaded by his father's arguments. In exasperation the father tries to sound like Moses, who had just descended Sinai: "Give me your word of honor that you won't smoke again." The son responds with "Word of honor," but it is obvious that he does not mean a word of it. Feeling himself to be a failure, the father tells his son to go to bed. The son asks the father to tell him a bedtime story first, and so the father makes up a fictional story of an emperor who had a son who smoked:

> The emperor's son fell ill with consumption through smoking, and died when he was twenty. His infirm and sick old father was left without anyone to help him. There was no one to govern the kingdom and defend the palace. Enemies came, killed the old man, and destroyed the palace, and now there are neither cherries, nor birds, nor little bells in the garden. . . . That's what happened.

Chekhov describes the impact of the story on the young lad:

His eyes were clouded by mournfulness and something like fear; for a minute he looked pensively at the dark window, shuddered and said, in a sinking voice: "I am not going to smoke any more. . . ."

After telling his son this story, the father says to himself:

Why must morality and truth never be offered in their crude form, but only with embellishments, sweetened and gilded like pills? It's not normal. . . . It's falsification . . . deception . . . tricks.

The reader (and maybe David too) should not miss some of the subtle connections between Nathan's parable and the events of the preceding chapter. Here are a few:

1. The word Nathan uses for "traveler" (v. 4) is the very rare word *helek*, which we could translate literally as "walker." Now let us put together 11:2 with 12:4: "David was walking (*yithallek*) on the roof of his house"; "Now there came a walker (*helek*) to the rich man."
2. Chapter 11 begins with David "sending" Joab, and ch. 12 begins with the Lord "sending" Nathan.
3. David sent messengers for Bathsheba and he "took" her (*laqakh*) in 11:4, while in the parable the rich man would not "take" one of his own flock, and so he "took" (*laqakh*) the poor man's lamb (12:4).
4. Nathan's emphasis of the ewe lamb who "ate" at table with her master and "drank" from his cup, and who "lay in his bosom" (12:3) surely recalls Uriah's refusal to "go to my house, to eat and to drink, and to lie with my wife" (11:11).
5. Nathan's suggesting in v. 3 that the ewe lamb was like a daughter ("she was to him like a daughter [*bath*]") would be powerful in light of David's behavior with *Bath*sheba. To be sure, Bathsheba is Uriah's wife, not his daughter, but Nathan's use of the daughter analogy makes his point all that more powerful.

It is important that Nathan not merely tell the story, but that he tell the story in the right way and at the right time so that the desired response from the hearer will be forthcoming. What, for example, would have happened if David had responded with "Very interesting story, tell me another one"?

David responds with righteous indignation, first pronouncing a death sentence upon the man ("The man [the rich man? the traveling man?] who has done this deserves to die" [v. 5], or literally, "A son of death is the man who does this"). Earlier, Saul had called David a "son of death" (1 Sam. 20:31), as David had called Abner (1 Sam. 26:16). The expression "son of death" means either "deserve to die" or some disparaging term such as "scoundrel" (McCarter 1980: 299).

David's second expression of wrath is his demand that the culprit "restore the lamb fourfold" (v. 6). This is in line with the Torah's teaching about restitution: "When someone steals . . . a sheep, and slaughters it or sells it, the thief shall pay . . . four sheep for a sheep" (Exod. 22:1). The Septuagint has David saying "He shall restore sevenfold," and while some argue that this is the original reading, the Septuagint's "sevenfold" is likely a change in the text, and could be based on a teaching like Prov. 6:30–31, which states that thieves, if they are caught, must repay sevenfold. If the Septuagint's reading is the original one, then David's words are still telling: he who took Bathsheba, "daughter of seven," demands that the pitiless taker of the lamb restore sevenfold to the poor man.

David's use of "fourfold" anticipates later developments in the David story. Does David himself end up paying fourfold? He does lose, in tragic contexts, four of his sons to death: his and Bathsheba's first child (12:18); Amnon (13:29); Absalom (18:14–15); Adonijah (1 Kings 2:25).

Nathan's "You are the man!" (v. 7a) provides one of three dramatic two-word sentences (in Hebrew) in this whole scenario (Brueggemann 1990: 282):

1. "I-[am] pregnant" (11:5).
2. "You-[are] the-man" (12:7a).
3. "I-have-sinned against-the-Lord" (12:13a).

Bathsheba informs; Nathan rebukes; David repents.

Several things stand out in David's repentance. First, although David has sinned against Uriah and Bathsheba, he confesses that he has sinned against the Lord. To put it a bit differently, David does not say that he has sinned against the Sinai commandments—although he has violated the sixth (murder), seventh (adultery), and tenth (coveting your neighbor's wife)—but that he has sinned against the Lord. This indicates the real nature of David's sin. Despite all the things God had done for him and given him ("I anointed . . . I rescued . . . I gave . . . I would have added" [vv. 7–8]), David still sinned. Because God's gracious acts are the basis for God's accusation, rather than law violation, David's sin is a "rebellion against grace, and not disobedience of the commandments" (Fretheim 1983: 126). We might also note that even though the commandments David has broken (sixth, seventh, and tenth) come in the second half of the Decalogue (those dealing with parents and neighbors), the fact that David says he has sinned against the Lord should warn against a simplistic splitting of the Ten Commandments into God-related ones (nos. 1–4 or 1–5) and neighbor-related ones (nos. 5–10 or 6–10). To sin against another is to sin against God.

The second thing of interest in David's repentance is that he does repent, and does not order the execution of Nathan. He easily enough found a way to silence Uriah. Why not Nathan too? That a prophet could openly condemn as powerful a person as a king and not suffer death or other consequences points to one of the truly unique concepts of the Old Testament, prophetic immunity.

The third thing we note is how infrequently any king of Israel and/or Judah repents in the face of prophetic preaching. Solomon does not. Rehoboam does not. Jeroboam does not. And the list goes on and on. Hence, for all his sordidness, David stands out as an exemplar in allowing the word of and from God to strike home to his own heart. It is as if David says, Truman-like, "The buck stops here."

Two other kings who do repent in the face of prophetic preaching are Ahab before Elijah (1 Kings 21:27–29) and Josiah before Huldah (2 Kings 22:18–20). But precisely here is the fourth point of interest. In the case of David, his repentance mitigates retribution (i.e., he himself will not die), but does not cancel retribution. Similarly, in the case of Ahab and Josiah, retribution is postponed (in Ahab's case to his succeeding family; in Josiah's case until the time of Zedekiah). Again, in Moses' prophetic preaching to the hypothetical exiles of the future (Deut. 4:29–30; 30:1–10), he says that repentance can only terminate judgment ("from there you will seek the Lord your God" [Deut. 4:29]), but not prevent it. All of this is to be distinguished from the prophets who teach not only that repentance can mitigate, postpone, or terminate divine judgment, but also that repentance can actually avert divine judgment. A parade example is Nineveh's repentance at the preaching of Jonah, by which it escaped God's judgment completely (Jon. 3:6–10).

David not only makes a penitential prayer (v. 13), but he also offers an intercessory prayer (v. 16) as he pleads before God for the life of his gravely ill son. Even though the prophet had unequivocally pronounced the forthcoming death of the child (v. 14), David prays for a reversal of that judgment. For David, "supplication is more humbling than resignation" (Simon 1967: 239). A later instance will demonstrate that even a prophet's unqualified prediction of death (Isaiah of Hezekiah) can be reversed through prayer, and is not necessarily as fixed as (in Dan. 6:8) "the laws of the Medes and Persians" (2 Kings

20:1–6). David's "Who knows? The Lord may be gracious to me, and the child may live" (v. 22) sounds like the Ninevites' "Who knows? God may relent and change his mind" (Jon. 3:9). In two totally different ways, both ch. 11 and ch. 12 raise the question "Who knows?"

Unlike Saul, David will not seek out a medium for contact with the deceased. At some point one has to get on with living, even though painful memories of the past persist. And this David does. He consoles ("comforted," NIV) his wife, and the narrator uses a verb, *nakham* (v. 24), that means both to "comfort" and "repent, change one's mind," especially when God or the Lord is the subject of the verb. Although the verb is not used in that latter sense in ch. 12, one can suggest that David hopes that God will "nakham" and not let the child die. When God does not "nakham," the child dies, and David "nakhams" Bathsheba, then marries her. They have another child, Solomon, and this chapter (12:24) records the only time he appears in 2 Samuel (v. 24). But here comes Nathan again (v. 25a). By now David has learned to duck whenever Nathan shows up. Will the prophet deliver another scorching ultimatum? Will child number two be taken also? No, not this time. On the contrary, David and Bathsheba get another son, and their son gets another name, Jedidiah, "beloved of the Lord."

The last unit in ch. 12, vv. 26–31, narrates the conclusion of the war against the Ammonites (see ch. 10). Joab does most of the dirty work (vv. 26–27), but leaves the mopping-up tasks for David (vv. 28–31), speaking to David as bluntly as Nathan ever spoke to David ("take the city . . . or I myself will take the city, and it will be called by my name" [v. 28b]). David took a wife who belonged to another. Joab threatens to take Rabbah, which ought to belong to David. Not as predatory as David, Joab will not make Rabbah his Bathsheba.

VIII. 13:1–14:33: David as Father of a Family in Turmoil

13:1–39. If God's heart was pained and he was grieved when he saw in Noah's day an earth that was evil, corrupt, and full of violence (Gen. 6:5–6, 12), how did his heart feel when he looked on the house of David and again saw evil and corruption and violence? Chapter 11 detailed a sordid instance of adultery (maybe rape?) in David's house, followed by murder. Bathsheba's blood flows because of her gender (11:4); Uriah's blood flows because of his husband role. Now, ch. 13 details the unconscionable sexual abuse of one of David's children (his daughter Tamar) by one of David's other children (Amnon, a half-brother to Tamar). In retaliation for her violation, Absalom has Amnon murdered, and he himself flees from David's court. So the movement in this chapter is from rape (vv. 1–22) to revenge (vv. 23–39).

These two sections are tied together by common motifs and language (Polzin 1993: 134–35):

vv. 1–22	vv. 23–39
1. Amnon invites Tamar to have sex with him (v. 11), but she refuses (v. 12).	Absalom invites David to join him in Baal-hazor for sheepshearing (v. 24), but David refuses (v. 25).
2. Tamar responds with a double refusal: "No, my brother, do not force me" (v. 12).	David responds with a double refusal: "No, my son, let us not all go" (v. 25).
3. Jonadab counsels Amnon (v. 5), and Amnon accepts his counsel (v. 6).	Jonadab counsels David (vv. 32–33), and his knowledge turns out to be accurate (v. 35).
4. The way to set up Tamar focuses on food and eating (vv. 5–10).	The way to set up Amnon is at a feast (vv. 27–28).
5. Absalom says to Tamar after she has been raped, "Do not take this to heart" (v. 20).	Jonadab, after informing David of Amnon's death, says to David, "Do not let my lord the king take it to heart" (v. 33).
6. In grief Tamar tears her clothes (v. 19).	In grief David tears his clothes (v. 31).
7. Tamar remains (v. 20).	Absalom flees (vv. 34, 37, 38).

It is not without interest that the chapter begins (v. 1) by identifying Tamar as the beautiful sister of Absalom (who does not appear again until v. 20), rather than as the beautiful daughter of David. It is the sibling-sibling relationship that is emphasized rather than the child-parent relationship. Hence, as early as v. 1 there is a hint that Absalom, rather than David, will stand up for Tamar.

Both the narrator (v. 1) and Amnon himself (v. 4) use the normal Hebrew word for "love" (ʾahav) to express Amnon's feelings for Tamar (a verb, by the way, not used for any feelings David had for Bathsheba). But how shall we understand "love"? Ask Amnon, and he will tell you it is the real thing. Others might say it is infatuation or lust masquerading as love. Maybe we should substitute a more ambiguous word like "desired" (Trible: 1984: 38, 58).

We do know from later in the narrative that Amnon engages in sex with Tamar against her will (v. 14). If Bathsheba protested as vigorously as Tamar did (v. 12), ch. 11 has not recorded that protest. Such a "private" conversation between David and Bathsheba might have been recorded, given the number of private conversations that the narrator records in ch. 13 (vv. 3–5, Jonadab with Amnon; vv. 10–19, Amnon with Tamar behind the closed doors of his bedroom; v. 20, Absalom with Tamar), as well as a public conversation (vv. 24–26, Absalom with David).

One question that ch. 13 raises is whether Amnon's sin is rape or incest or both. There are those texts that explicitly forbid sexual relationships with a (half-)sister, such as Lev. 18:9 ("You shall not uncover the nakedness of your sister"); Lev. 18:11 ("You shall not uncover the nakedness of your father's wife's daughter"); Deut. 27:22 ("Cursed be anyone who lies with his sister, whether the daughter of his father or the daughter of his mother"); Ezek. 22:11 ("another defiles his sister, his father's daughter").

Absalom's words to Tamar, "Has Amnon your brother been with you?" (v. 20; using the same phrase as the narrator did with Joseph and Potiphar's wife, "He would not consent to lie beside her or to be with her [Gen. 39:10]"), may be read as an accusation of incest or rape. If the charge is incest, then the following situation comes into being: "If the incest with which he [Absalom] accuses Amnon (2 Sam. 13:20) violates the strongest taboo of the kinship system, fratricide creates a paradox vis-à-vis its strongest obligation: blood vengeance. As Amnon rapes a sister whom he is bound to protect and avenge, so Absalom kills a brother whom he is bound to protect and avenge" (Propp 1993: 47).

It would appear from other verses that the crime is more rape than incest. Note, for example, that v. 2 says, "Amnon was so tormented that he made himself ill because of his sister Tamar, for she was a virgin, and it seemed impossible to Amnon to do anything to her" (Fokkelman 1981: 103). What deters Amnon is that Tamar is a virgin, not that she is his sister (and for the law about the rape of an unengaged virgin, see Deut. 22:28–29). One also notes that when Tamar attempts to dissuade Amnon from violating her (v. 12), among her arguments she does not mention family relationships (Bar Efrat 1989: 264). In addition to saying, or instead of saying, "For such a thing is not done in Israel," she might have said, "For I am your sister." Also, when she says to Amnon, "Speak to the king, for he will not withhold me from you" (v. 13), we best understand her to be saying that a father might permit such a marriage at certain periods in biblical history (cf. Abraham and Sarah, according to Gen. 20:12).

For Amnon, it is simply a matter of asking Tamar to lie (*shakav*) with him (v. 11). That is not how Tamar sees it. She does not respond with

"I will not lie with you," but rather with "Do not force me" (v. 12), using her own imperative to veto Amnon's imperative.

The verb for "force" (*ʿanah*) is used again in v. 14 ("being stronger than she, he forced her") and in v. 22 ("Absalom hated Amnon, because he had forced his sister Tamar"). The verb does not always refer to forced sex. For example, the Lord says to Abram, "Your offspring shall be aliens in a land that is not theirs, and shall be slaves there, and they shall be oppressed [*ʿanah*] for four hundred years" (Gen. 15:13). Four centuries of *ʿanah!* A woman can "*ʿanah*" another woman, as Sarah "dealt harshly" with Hagar (Gen. 16:6), and a man could treat his wife so ("if you ill-treat my daughters," Laban says to Jacob [Gen. 31:50]).

The nature of Amnon's love is evident in his treatment of Tamar after the rape. He burns for her (v. 1), then he banishes her (v. 15). He cannot stand to be apart from her, and shortly thereafter he cannot stand to be in the same room with her. It is understandable why Tamar says to Amnon that post-rape expulsion is as evil as rape itself (v. 16). It is not a case of two wrongs making a right. "The hate of one man will become collective hate. A deflowered virgin is a blot on a patriarchal order" (Van Dijk-Hemmes 1989: 143). Only two individuals in the Old Testament wear "a coat of many colors": Joseph (Gen. 37:3, 23, 32) and Tamar (vv. 18–19). Both coats are torn, one by a fictitious wild animal presumably, and one by the wearer herself in an act of painful mourning and grief. Joseph is incarcerated. Rape ends Tamar's future.

What is David's response to this? "David became very angry" (v. 21). The Septuagint shows a longer reading that is supported by a copy of Samuel from the Dead Sea Scrolls: "But he would not punish his son Amnon, because he loved him, for he was his firstborn" (cf. the NRSV and the NIV). This is the third time David has become angry (cf. his anger at God [6:8], and his anger at the sheep stealer in the parable [12:5]). While most commentators argue for the longer reading as the more original one, this is not necessarily the case (Conroy 1978: 152–53).

Either reading makes David appear unappealing. Is he just angry, and that's it (shorter reading)? At whom is David angry—Amnon? Absalom? Tamar? himself? And why does he take no swift, decisive action against Amnon? Is it only because he is soft-hearted and sentimental, allowing love for somebody to outweigh justice (longer reading), just as Amnon allowed "love" to outweigh decency and morality? Is he disqualified from being family disciplinarian by virtue of his own track record? Or is it that David, "hoping that time will heal all wounds, does not want to take any action that will exacerbate family unity and jeopardize dynastic continuity" (Ackerman 1990: 46)?

Absalom, too, takes no immediate action other than to house his sister (v. 20c). He is as passive and quiet as is his father. But the two silences are radically different. "For the king, the failure to speak is a sign of domestic and political impotence. . . . For Absalom, the refusal to say anything—to the perpetrator of the sexual crime, the narrator specifies [v. 22]—is ominous in an opposite way because it clearly betokens a grim resolution to act in due time" (Alter 1981: 79).

For two years (v. 23) Absalom ("father of peace") plans and plots and waits for the perfect circumstances in which to pay back Amnon in a very unpeaceful way. As David foolishly sent Tamar to Amnon (v. 7), so now he foolishly sends Amnon to Absalom miles away to the north at Baal-hazor in Ephraim (v. 27). It is akin to Jacob sending Joseph to his brothers in Shechem and Dothan (Gen. 37:12–17). In both, a father sends a son on what is essentially a suicide mission, given the enormity of fraternal rage in both cases.

Absalom is better than his father at accomplishing his goals by getting his intended victim intoxicated (v. 28). The setup works, and Amnon is executed (v. 29). We should not overlook the fact that Absalom may have had another reason to have Amnon out of the way, apart from avenging his sister's rape. According to 2 Sam. 3:2–3, Amnon is the oldest of David's children. Chileab, the second oldest, is either deceased or not a factor. Absalom is now the oldest surviving son and hence David's logical successor. Is it possible that Absalom's heart "perhaps is as swelled with ambition as it is darkened with hate" (Long 1981: 30)? Could it be that Absalom's "desire to possess the throne is likely mixed with, or may even outweigh, his desire to avenge his sister" (Fewell and Gunn 1993: 151)?

The chapter ends with David mourning "for his son" (v. 37). But for which son—the executed Amnon or the vanished Absalom? Absalom hides out for three years in the house of his mother's father (v. 38). "Three years is a long time for a son to be in exile" (Brueggemann 1990: 291).

Two other equally grisly scenes in the Old Testament invite comparison with this one: Shechem's rape of Dinah, daughter of Jacob (Freedman 1997) in Genesis 34; and the rape of the Levite's concubine (Polzin 1993: 137–38) in Judges 19–21.

Genesis 34	2 Samuel 13
1. v. 2: "Shechem . . . seized her and lay with her by force" (*shakav* and *'anah*)	v. 14: "Amnon forced her and lay with her" (*'anah* and *shakav*)

2. v. 7: "because he had committed an outrage [*nevalah*] in Israel . . . for such a thing ought not to be done"	v. 12: "for such a thing is not done in Israel, do not do anything so vile [*nevalah*]"
3. love and sex lead to a desire for marriage (vv. 8, 11–12)	love and sex lead to hate and dismissal (vv. 15, 17)
4. Jacob has four principal sons (Reuben, Simeon, Levi, Judah), and the last of these four follows his father	David has four principal sons (Amnon, Absalom, Adonijah, Solomon), and the last of these four follows his father
5. Jacob has only one daughter whose name we know—Dinah	David has only one daughter whose name we know—Tamar
6. the first three sons are chastened by their father, and forfeit blessing and tribal territory (Gen. 49:3–7)	the first three sons die violent deaths

Judges 19–21	2 Samuel 13
1. brother vs. brother, or kin vs. kin at the national level (19:23; 20:13, 23, 28; 21:6)	brother vs. siblings at the family level
2. fraternal rape (by residents of Benjaminite Gibeah)	fraternal rape
3. 20:13: "but the Benjaminites would not listen to their kinsfolk"	v. 14: "but he would not listen to her"
4. 19:28: the Levite says to his recently raped concubine, "Get up [*qum*], we are going [*halak*]"	v. 15: Amnon says to the recently raped Tamar, "Get up [*qum*], get out [*halak*]"
5. the rape is a "vile thing" (*nevalah*) (19:23, 24; 20:6, 10)	the rape is a "vile thing" (*nevalah*) (v. 12)
6. 19:30: "Has such a thing ever happened since the day that the Israelites came up from the land of Egypt?"	v. 12: "for such a thing is not done in Israel"
7. 19:24: "Here are my virgin daughter and his concubine"	v. 2: "for she was a virgin"
8. 19:23: "No, my brothers, do not act so wickedly"	v. 12: "No, my brother, do not force me"
9. revenge for a crime ending in a bloodbath (20:29–48)	revenge for a crime ending in a bloodbath (v. 29)

14:1–33. Joab, who most recently sent a messenger to David inform-
ing him of Uriah's death in battle (11:18–21), now sends an unnamed
wise woman from Tekoa to tell David a fictional story. Tekoa, the home
of the prophet Amos (Amos 1:1), is located a few miles south of Bethlehem. People are being sent to David frequently in chs. 11–14. Joab
sends a messenger (ch. 11). God sends a prophet (ch. 12). Joab sends a
wise woman (ch. 14).

The reason why Joab dispatches this woman is not clear, and the
ambiguity is due to how best to render the Hebrew of v. 1. The verse
says, as literally as possible, "Joab . . . knew that the heart of the king
[was] ʿal [to? toward? for? against? over? on?] Absalom."

The NRSV renders the last part of the verse as "that the king's mind
was on Absalom." Close to this is the NIV's "that the king's heart longed
for Absalom." These translations suggest that David is beside himself
with grief over the three years of Absalom's absence and longs for reconciliation. Joab is, therefore, trying to do what he can to bring about
that reconciliation.

But here is another translation for the last part of v. 1: "that the
king's heart was inclined against Absalom" (Polzin 1993: 139), or "that
the king was ill-disposed toward Absalom" (Fokkelman 1981: 126).
Here, Joab believes that David may be on the verge of hunting down
Absalom and giving vent to his hostility. Can Joab head off that vengeance mission by getting the two men together to work out their differences, and hence spare Absalom from becoming Amnon number
two?

We do not read the actual words of the story Joab told the wise
woman to relay to David. All that we read is how he told her to dress
and behave like a grieving widow (v. 2). (For another daring act of a
woman involving wearing a certain type of clothing to catch a guilty
man in self-entrapment, compare Gen. 38:14. In one [2 Samuel 14], a
woman who is not a widow pretends she is a widow. In the other [Gen-
esis 38], a woman who is a widow pretends to be somebody other than
a widow).

There are numerous examples in Old Testament narrative where A
instructs B to tell C something. Those examples fall into one of three
patterns. The first pattern records both the speech of A to B and the
speech of B to C. There are numerous illustrations of this in Exodus.
One example is the Lord's speech to Moses (A to B) about how the people are to observe that first Passover in Egypt (Exod. 12:1–20), followed
by Moses' speech relaying those instructions to the people (B to C) in
Exod. 12:21–27. Another example is the Lord's speech to Moses (A to
B) about how the people are to build the wilderness tabernacle in Exod.

25:1–31:18 followed by Moses' speech to the people (B to C) on this topic in Exod. 35:1–19. When both speeches are preserved, in total or in part, we have the opportunity to compare the relayed speech with the original speech, looking for things like duplication, deletion, addition, rephrasing, and so on.

The second pattern is the one in which only A's speech is recorded. All that the text records of B's part is that B relayed the assigned message spoken by A. A parade example of this is the Lord's oracle to establish David and his house forever, to be transmitted to David through Nathan. The Lord's message to Nathan is given in full (2 Sam. 7:5–16). All that the text records for Nathan's delivery to David is "In accordance with all these words . . . Nathan spoke to David" (2 Sam. 7:17). This pattern highlights the importance and words of the original speaker. Nathan is transmitter, not improviser.

The third pattern is what we have here in 2 Samuel 14. The original speech is not a part of the record. The text merely records that "Joab put the words into her mouth" (v. 3b). What the text does record is the Tekoaite's speech to David and the dialogue with David that follows (vv. 4–20). We have no way of comparing what the woman said to David with what Joab said to the woman. Is what she said to David in vv. 4–7 the essence of what Joab told her to say, or does it include what she said to David in vv. 9, 11, 13–17? Does she simply transmit? Is she only Joab's alter ego? Or does she improvise, expand? Is she artless automaton or creative storyteller? Which would we expect a "wise woman" to be, she of "agile mind and persuasive tongue" (Camp 1981: 20)?

In the dialogue with David she speaks eight times (vv. 4b, 5b, 9, 11a, 12a, 13–17, 18b, 19b–20). David speaks seven times (vv. 5a, 8, 10, 11b, 12b, 18a, 19a). She gets the first word (v. 4b), the last word (vv. 19b–20), and the longest word (vv. 13–17). She is deferential to the king, referring to herself repeatedly as "your servant" (using the Hebrew word *shipkhah* in vv. 6, 7, 12, 15, 17, 19), and "his servant" (using the Hebrew word *ʾamah* in vv. 15, 16), yet she will not hesitate to be confrontational and speak to David bluntly (vv. 13–14). This sage clearly illustrates the truth of Prov. 25:15, "With patience a ruler may be persuaded, and a soft tongue can break bones."

To be sure, similarities exist between the wise woman's story of ch. 14 and Nathan's parable of ch. 12 (Sternberg 1987: 429; Waldman 1986/87). Both times David is under the illusion that he is listening to a telling rather than a retelling. Both times he is tricked into making fiction into history that appears unrelated to his own circumstances. And both times the "judge" declares himself guilty (12:13; 14:21).

But the two accounts have differences as well (Willey 1992: 122–23). While this woman has only the authority of Joab behind her mission, Nathan has the authority of God behind his mission. It is likely that a king will listen to a person who is a man and a prophet of God and a personal acquaintance. Can we be as sure that the king will listen to a woman, a woman without a name, a woman he has never met before, a woman without "official" credentials? The connection between David's actions and the rich man and the ewe lamb is transparent enough so that Nathan's point is readily clear and applicable. By contrast, the woman tells a story of one of her sons who murdered her only other son (v. 6), resulting in the family wanting to seek blood revenge against their criminal relative (v. 7a). If that happens, she will be without sons and without heir (v. 7b). But David has killed nobody (at least not directly). And in what way may the awfulness and decisiveness of blood revenge have any bearing on whether or not David should restore Absalom to family graces? After all, David did not banish Absalom. His exile, rather, was self-imposed.

She is, however, as successful as Nathan, so successful, in fact, that the text has David speaking to Joab as if it were a threesome (v. 21). But for Joab and the wise woman, it turns out to be a qualified success. Absalom may return to Jerusalem, but not to his father's house (v. 24). If Absalom had said, "I will get up and go to my father" (Luke 15:18), he would have discovered that David had hung out the "Not Welcome" sign.

The text pauses to give us some description on Absalom's physical assets, his attractiveness, and an enormous head of hair to boot (vv. 25–26). One cannot help but connect v. 11b, where David says to the "mother," "As the Lord lives, not one hair of your son shall fall to the ground," with the references to Absalom's hair in vv. 25–26. We might also connect the woman's concern about the blood avenger who would cut off both her and her son from God's heritage (v. 16) with the reference in v. 26 to Absalom's annual haircut.

These references to Absalom's physical features accomplish two things. First, they are told in such a way that suggests that Absalom likes Absalom. When he models before a mirror, he likes what he sees. Rosenberg (1986: 156, 158) suggests that Absalom "cultivates a certain narcissism centered in the hair . . . is a kind of Nazirite showpiece, a Samsonlike strutter." Similarly, Fokkelman (1981: 148) states, "We develop a picture of a prince constantly engaged with himself and his beauty."

Second, these references to Absalom's good looks in light of his aging father, whom he might one day succeed, recall another earlier time of transition in monarchy when the present king, himself once very handsome (1 Sam. 9:2) would be succeeded in later years by another handsome and younger man (1 Sam. 16:12).

For two years Absalom lives in Jerusalem, but he and his father never meet (v. 28). Absalom may as well be on the other side of the planet.

Absalom not only looks like Samson, but he also acts like him when he sets the fields of Joab on fire for not answering his request to speak to David on his behalf (v. 30; cf. Judg. 15:4–5). Poor Joab! "The tragedy of Joab . . . is presaged in the scene in which his efforts to serve the State by reconciling Absalom and David receive as their only reward the destruction of his property by the man whose cause he championed" (Whybray 1968: 24).

Eventually, father and son meet (v. 33). There is prostration and kissing, but one still senses a coolness. Not one word of conversation is recorded between father and son. No admission of guilt comes from either side. There is no hugging, no running, as in Luke 15:20. And there is no weeping, as in Gen. 33:4 (when Esau and Jacob reconcile), or as in Gen. 45:2, 14 (when Joseph and his brothers reconcile). One suspects that Absalom is a ticking time bomb.

IX. 15:1–18:33: David as Refugee and Distraught Father

15:1–37. Unlike David, who never plotted (openly at least) a revolt or coup against Saul while the latter was king, Absalom does not exercise the same restraint vis-à-vis David that David did toward Saul. Absalom has no compunction about raising his hand against the Lord's anointed, even if that anointed one is a blood relative.

To that end, Absalom rounds up some horses and a chariot (telltale signs of one with royal aspirations, according to Deut. 17:16 and 1 Sam. 8:11). Saul worked with donkeys (1 Sam. 9:3) and with oxen (1 Sam. 11:5). David worked with sheep (1 Sam. 16:11, 19; 17:15). But now Absalom will work with horses, and throw in an advance squad of fifty cheerleaders (v. 1).

Not one to do anything too hastily, Absalom plots his moves over four years (v. 7, the Septuagint reading; the Hebrew text says "forty"), stirring up discontent by way of a lot of irresponsible talking. James's remarks in his New Testament epistle about the power of the tongue to wreak havoc (James 3:1–12) are right on target.

Being an incumbent can be a liability, and being a new candidate can be an asset. For the challenger can easily recite the wrongs and shortcomings of the incumbent, and promise that if elected, he or she will do better for the voters than the current occupant of the office. That is Absalom's strategy (vv. 2–6).

These opening verses of ch. 15 connect Absalom's behavior with that of the king of ch. 14 whom he would displace (Bar-Efrat 1989: 157):

ch. 14	ch. 15
v. 33: "and he [David] summoned [*qara*ʾ] Absalom"	v. 2: "and Absalom would summon [*qara*ʾ] him and say"
v. 33: "so he [Absalom] came [*boʾ ʾel*] to the king"	v. 4: "all who had a suit or cause might come to me" [*boʾ ʿal*]
v. 33: "so he [Absalom] prostrated [*hawah*] himself"	v. 5: "whenever people came near to do obeisance [*hawah*] before him [Absalom]"
v. 33: "the king kissed [*nashaq*] Absalom"	v. 5: "he [Absalom] would put out his hand and . . . kiss [*nashaq*] them"

After accumulating a sizeable number of supporters and "stealing the hearts" of Israel (v. 6b), Absalom decides it is time to strike. He wants to steal a crown, not just hearts.

His strategy is to ask his father's permission (and here is protocol masking ambition) to return to Hebron to fulfill a vow to God he had made there earlier (v. 7). Unlike the freewill offering that the worshiper promised to God simply as an expression of devotion or gratitude, the votive (or vow) offering was a gift that was promised to God on condition that he grant some kind of benefaction. (For other such votive offerings, compare Gen. 28:20–22 [Jacob]; Judg. 11:30–31 [Jephthah]; 1 Sam. 1:11 [Hannah].)

Of course, we have no way of verifying that Absalom had ever made such a vow. It provides an illustration of a claim made by somebody about something said or heard that we cannot verify. Did Jacob really say what Joseph's brothers claimed he said (Gen. 50:17)? Did Mephibosheth really say what his servant Ziba claimed he said (2 Sam. 16:3)? Did David really say what Bathsheba claimed he had said (1 Kings 1:17)? If Absalom is making this up, then not only is he a candidate who excels in empty promises and smear campaigning, but also he is a liar to boot, and one who will use religion as a vehicle for political prevarication. And he also may know how to exploit buried feelings of resentment toward the incumbent by certain members of the incumbent's constituency who feel wronged or let down. Absalom's choice of Hebron from which to start the fireworks may fuel the hostility of some Judeans toward David for abruptly leaving the ancient Judean capital Hebron in favor of upstart Jerusalem.

Blowing of a trumpet followed by a massive shout (v. 10) is a prelude to a conquest (Josh. 6:16) or a coup. The shout of Joshua's time honors the Lord ("for the Lord has given you the city"). This shout honors Absalom ("Absalom has become king at Hebron").

Possibly, the rebellion could have been nipped in the bud if David had not been so obtuse. He sent Tamar to Amnon's house, being completely taken in by Amnon's ruse (13:6–7). He sent Amnon with Absalom to a sheepshearing festival in Baal-hazor, or so he thought (13:23–27). And now for a third time a son perpetrates a subterfuge on his father, and the father buys it (v. 9). There is precious little wisdom and discernment here.

David's discovery of the plot is something he takes very seriously, leaving him no option but to flee Jerusalem (v. 14). The favored one of God becomes a fugitive; a king becomes an exile.

But he does not empty his house. He leaves behind ten concubines to take care of his house (v. 16), possibly never imagining that they will become fair game for Absalom (at Ahithophel's urging), according to 16:21. That the concubines stay in Jerusalem may be an indication that in David's mind his exodus from Jerusalem is temporary. And in any case, who has time for indulging in some normal royal "pleasures" while running for life and limb?

While none of David's sons appear especially loyal to David, David does have loyal supporters outside his family, and some of them become co-refugees with David. The list of adherents includes:

1. Cherethites, Pelethites (Aegean mercenaries) (v. 18)
2. Six hundred Gittites from the Philistine city Gath (v. 18)
3. Ittai, the Philistine Gittite (vv. 19–23)
4. the Levites Abiathar and Zadok and other Levites (vv. 24–29)
5. Hushai, David's friend and counselor (vv. 32–37)

It is perhaps surprising that so many Philistines (the six hundred Gittites, Ittai, and maybe the Cherethites and Pelethites) are pro-David, and especially Philistines from Gath, the city of Goliath. David had defeated, killed, and decapitated their skyscraper showpiece in an earlier day (1 Samuel 17). The camaraderie between these groups and David goes back to David's mostly cordial relationship with the Philistines in

Saul's day (1 Sam. 21:10–15; 27:1–12; 29:1–11). In fact, Ittai sounds as loyal to David as Ruth was to Naomi:

> Ruth 1:16–17: "Do not press me to leave you or to turn back from following you! Where you go, I will go. . . . where you die, I will die— there I will be buried. May Yahweh do thus and so to me . . . if even death parts me from you."
>
> 2 Sam. 15:21: "As Yahweh lives, and as my lord the king lives, wherever my lord the king may be, whether for death or for life, there also your servant will be."

A woman affirms unconditional loyalty to another woman. A man affirms unconditional loyalty to another man. The woman and the man are both "outsiders" (Moabite, Philistine), but both use the special name of Israel's God—Yahweh—when addressing the Judean whom they pledge to follow, no matter what. The very name "Ittai" is made up of the preposition *ʾet* and a pronominal suffix, and means something like "with me," a name suggesting deep friendship. Notice the wordplay in v. 19, "Then the king said to Ittai [*ʾittay*] the Gittite, 'Why are you coming with us [*ʾittanu*]?'" and in v. 22, "So Ittai [*ʾittay*] the Gittite marched on . . . and all the little ones who were with him [*ʾitto*]." (See Polzin 1993: 151.)

David turns down the Levites' request to carry the ark out of Jerusalem. If it is God's will to restore David to Jerusalem, that will happen, ark or no ark (vv. 25–26). This is a fine expression of casting oneself on the grace of God. At the same time, David wants to "plant" Zadok and Abiathar in a strategic place where they can funnel him vital information about Absalom's movements (v. 28). They are "more valuable to him in Jerusalem spying than in the wilderness praying" (Brueggemann 1990: 303–4). Here is something God must do (vv. 25–26), and something David can do (vv. 27–28). "David's return is entirely the work of God [vv. 25–26] and at the same time entirely the work of David himself [vv. 27–28]" (Fokkelman 1981: 187).

In addition to Zadok and Abiathar, Hushai, who is both David's "servant" (v. 34 and 16:19) and "friend" (v. 37 and 16:16), is more useful to David staying in Jerusalem, where he can be part of a Davidic fifth column too. His name means "the hasty one" (from *hush*, "hurry, make haste"), an interesting name for a friend to the king who is making a hasty retreat from the city ("Hurry [*mahar*], or he [Absalom] will soon overtake us" [v. 14]).

Hushai will counteract any counsel that Ahithophel, formerly a friend and counselor to David but now a defector to Absalom, will share with Absalom (vv. 30–31). Ahithophel plays a role in David's life similar to that of Judas Iscariot in Jesus' life during Passion Week:

1. David crosses the Kidron (2 Sam. 15:23).
   Jesus crosses the Kidron (John 18:1).
2. David goes to the Mount of Olives (2 Sam. 15:30).
   Jesus goes to the Mount of Olives (Mark 14:26).
3. Ahithophel betrays David (2 Sam. 15:12, 31).
   Judas betrays Jesus (Matt. 26:47–50; Mark 14:43–45; Luke 22:47–48; John 18:2–5).
4. When things do not work out as planned, Ahithophel commits suicide by hanging (2 Sam. 17:23).
   Judas commits suicide by hanging (Matt. 27:5).

16:1–23. The chapter divides into two sections:

(A) vv. 1–14: Further indignities are heaped on David as he flees Jerusalem.
(B) vv. 15–23: Absalom sets up shop in Jerusalem.

Several elements tie the two sections together:

1. In (A) there is a triumvirate of David, Ziba [vv. 1–4], and Shimei [vv. 5–14]; and in (B) there is a triumvirate of Absalom, Hushai, and Ahithophel.
2. In both (A) and (B) the characters other than David have something in common. Ziba and Shimei are both Benjaminites; Ahithophel and Hushai are both royal counselors.
3. In both (A) and (B) somebody tricks somebody else. Ziba puts words in Mephibosheth's mouth (v. 3a) that Mephibosheth probably did not say, but Ziba convinces David that he did say it. Hushai fools Absalom into believing that he has shifted his loyalty from David to Absalom (vv. 16–19).
4. In both (A) and (B) somebody takes something that belongs to somebody else, thanks to the intervention of another. Ziba claims the inheritance that belonged to Mephibosheth, thanks to David's confiscatory powers (v. 4a). Absalom takes his father's concubines, thanks to Ahithophel's power of suggestion (vv. 21–22).
5. David expresses surprise through a "why" question when Ziba shows up with much more food than a picnic lunch ("Why have you brought these?" [v. 2a]). Absalom expresses surprise with a

"why" question when Hushai shows up in Jerusalem instead of being with David ("Why did you not go with your friend?" [v. 17b]).

6. Both sections emphasize "chosen." Shimei, son of Gera, curses David at Bahurim (v. 5), which means "the chosen ones" (from *bakhar*, "to choose"). Hushai says he will throw his support behind the one whom the Lord and Israel has "chosen," *bakhar* (v. 18).

7. Shimei accuses David of being a "man of blood," and screams that the Lord is avenging on David the blood of Saul's house (vv. 7–8). Abishai (and where is Joab his brother in all this?) will be a man of blood and bring vengeance on Shimei for his blatant rudeness and disrespect toward David (v. 9).

8. Something in both sections of the chapter recalls an earlier event in David's life. Shimei's throwing stones at David (v. 6) recalls David slinging a stone at Goliath (1 Sam. 17:49). Absalom's going into David's concubines upon the roof of his father's house (v. 22a) recalls David's tragic involvement with Bathsheba that started on the roof of his house (11:2).

9. Cursing the king eventually brings death to Shimei (1 Kings 2:8–9, 36–46). Counseling the king eventually brings death to Ahithophel (17:23) (for this last point see Polzin 1993: 167).

Next to Shimei or Abishai or Absalom, David comes across in this chapter as an appealing individual. His calm and magnanimity (vv. 11–12) contrasts with Shimei's rage and railing. His restraint contrasts with Abishai's thuggish tactics. His piety and trust in a God of justice (v. 12) contrasts with Absalom's opportunism. Unlike his father, Absalom engages in no talk of God.

One note of interest to those reading this story in the Hebrew: in v. 13, in between the words "so David and his men went along the road" and "while Shimei went along on the hillside," there is a space of about an inch with the Hebrew letter *samek* in the middle of the space. This is a marking that goes back to the Masoretes, and the term for such a phenomenon is *pisqaʾ beʾemtsaʿ pasuq*, "a space within a verse." There are more of these in Samuel than in any other book of the Old Testament.

What is of interest about those in Samuel is that many of them occur in historical contexts referred to in some of the individual psalm titles in the Psalter, and where one might expect a prayer. This is what we have in 2 Sam. 16:13, which, for the Masoretes, seemed to be the background for Psalm 3, whose title says, "A Psalm of David, when he fled from his son Absalom." We have the same feature in 2 Sam. 12:13, where there is a space with a *samek* in the middle of the space between "And David said 'I have sinned against the Lord,'" and "Nathan said to David. . . ." At this point, so the Masoretes, David prayed his prayer of confession in Psalm 51, whose title says, "A Psalm of David, when the prophet Nathan came to him, after he had gone in to Bathsheba." The Hebrew reader can also compare 1 Sam. 23:4 with Psalm 54. In 1 Sam. 21:10 (cf. Psalms 34 and 56) and 2 Sam. 7:4 (cf. Psalm 132), the space occurs at the beginning of the verse.

17:1–27. This chapter has two main sections. The first (vv. 1–14) narrates Ahithophel's advice to Absalom on how best to eliminate David (vv. 1–4), Hushai's alternative plan (vv. 5–13), and which of the two Absalom accepted and why (v. 14). In the second section (vv. 15–27) David learns through his surveillance agents of Absalom's intentions and heads across the Jordan. He lays low for a while in, of all cities, Mahanaim (v. 24, 27). How paradoxical! Absalom is successful (for a while) in Hebron and Jerusalem, David's capitals, while David seeks refuge in Mahanaim, the capital city of David's former northern counterpart, Ishbosheth (see Flanagan 1972: 179).

The speechs of Ahithophel and Hushai to Absalom differ considerably:

Ahithophel (vv. 1–4)	Hushai (vv. 5–13)
1. difference in length—shorter, about forty words	—much longer, three and one-half times longer
2. difference in proposed strategy—a quick strike with a smaller force, giving David no chance to fight back	—recruit an enormous army, which will take time to do, and overwhelm David with size
3. difference in rhetoric—straightforward, unpolished language	—flowery, persuasive language using no fewer than four similes (vv. 8, 10, 11, 12)
4. David—Ahithophel uses his name (v. 1)	—Hushai avoids using his name, preferring instead "your father" (vv. 8, 10)
5. who gets the credit?—Ahithophel does ("Let me . . . I will . . . I will . . . I will . . . I will" [vv. 1–3])	—Absalom does ("all Israel be gathered to you . . . and that you go to battle in person" [v. 11])
6. self-mention?—Ahithophel mentions himself	—Hushai never mentions himself

Absalom at first finds Ahithophel's plan appealing (v. 4), but then finds Hushai's counterproposal even more persuasive (v. 14a). As Prov.

18:17 says, "The first to present his case seems right, till another comes forward and questions him" (NIV). But there are deeper issues here than simply persuasive rhetoric. The real reason why Absalom accepts Hushai's plan is because "the Lord had ordained to defeat the good counsel of Ahithophel, so that the Lord might bring ruin on Absalom" (v. 14b). (By the way, the Hebrew text uses the same verb [*tsawah*] in v. 23 for Ahithophel "setting his house in order"—giving final instructions concerning one's household before dying—as it does here for "ordained.") Hushai is well aware that he is an agent of David. What he may not be as aware of is that he is also an agent of the Lord. Through a cunning counselor, God is having his way (see Brueggemann 1990: 313). God could have stopped Absalom's rebellion dead in its tracks with some Sinaitic display of thunderous power. Instead, he works off-stage, unseen and unheard.

It is of interest that only two kings we know of (David [and Absalom, would-be king], Rehoboam) sought counsel. Both Absalom and Rehoboam were given two mutually exclusive bits of counsel (2 Sam. 17:1–4, 5–13; 1 Kings 12:6–7, 9–11). Both listened to the wrong group (2 Sam. 17:14a; 1 Kings 12:13–14). The wrong advice led to disaster for Absalom and Rehoboam. But the sovereign hand of God ruled in both situations (2 Sam. 17:14b; 1 Kings 12:15).

David's well-placed intelligence network keeps him informed of Absalom's movements, first through Hushai, then through the Levites Zadok and Abiathar (v. 15) and their two young sons, Jonathan and Ahimaaz (v. 17), who are couriers between Jerusalem and David's hideout. The latter two were almost caught (v. 18). If they had been, David's future would be in doubt, Hushai's life would be on the block, and Absalom may have succeeded. But thanks to a quick-thinking woman who conceals their presence and makes up a story about their departure, the boys' whereabouts are undetected by the Absalomites (vv. 19–20). A Rahab in the book of Second Samuel! A persuasive Hushai, a fast-on-her-feet unnamed housewife, and an ordaining God all work together for David's salvation.

As the chapter ends, Ahithophel loses his life via suicide (v. 23), Joab loses his job to Amasa (v. 25; the name "Amasa" contains the same root as "Amos," i.e., "carry"), and David gains three new Transjordanian friends—Shobi, Machir, and Barzillai—who provide food and shelter for David and his troops (vv. 27–29). They cannot provide David with counsel, as Hushai does, but they can provide David with comfort. They may not share in Hushai's oratorical skill but they know how to share a cup of cold water.

18:1–33. It is showdown time for Absalom and David. David can either remain a refugee and concede the throne to Absalom or try to regroup and reclaim his throne in Jerusalem. He chooses the latter. But for a second time (see 11:1) David remains at the home base while his troops go off to battle. But we need not worry that this opens the door to Bathsheba scenario number two. This time his military advisers urge David to remain in Mahanaim because his safety and aliveness are more important to his partisans than his physical presence in combat (v. 3). Also there is the possibility, in the minds of his inner circle, that at David's age, his presence might be more of a liability than an asset.

Although Joab seems to be the person in charge from v. 10 on, v. 2 notes that Joab had charge of only a third of David's army. For the first time Joab must share authority with two others, his brother Abishai (which is probably acceptable to Joab), and with the Philistine Ittai (which is probably unacceptable to Joab). Possibly, it is both David's grief over Absalom's death and Joab's own demotion in authority that compounds Joab's overt frustration with David in 19:5–7.

David's only directive is that if Absalom is apprehended, his captors should deal gently with him (v. 5). Repeatedly, David (or somebody else) refers to Absalom as "the young man" in this chapter (vv. 5, 12 [a man who saw Absalom hanging from the tree and quotes David to Joab], 29, 32a), as does the Cushite informer (v. 32b). David is caught between a rock and a hard place, just as Absalom is caught in the branches of a tree by his hair. Absalom is both kin and king, royal and renegade. The most intimate expression David can use for Absalom is "the young man." But all that changes when he is told of Absalom's death. He does not say, "O the young man Absalom." Rather, he says, "O my son Absalom." In fact, he calls Absalom "my son" eight times in two verses (18:33 and 19:4).

Once again we encounter the sorry spectacle of Israel fighting Israel, brother fighting brother, so prevalent in First and Second Samuel. The combat is between "David's servants" and the "men of Israel" (v. 7a), and the outcome is mass fratricide (v. 7b). Even the topography of the area works against Absalom and his troops, as indicated by v. 8b: "and the forest claimed more victims that day than the sword." The "forest" refers to the dense, tough growth of plants, trees, and vines that hid a very uneven and rugged terrain. If the stars fought against Sisera (Judg. 5:20), the forest fought against Absalom.

Of all the other accounts of fratricidal war in First and Second Samuel, the one in ch. 18 has the most parallels with the account in 2 Samuel 2, the war between David's family and Saul's family (Polzin 1993: 183–85). Three are particularly prominent:

1. 2:17: "The battle was very fierce that day; and Abner and the men of Israel were beaten by [*nagap lipne*] the servants of David."
   18:7: "The men of Israel were defeated there by [*nagap lipne*] the servants of David, and the slaughter there was great on that day."
2. 2:28: "Joab sounded the trumpet and all the people stopped; they no longer pursued [*radap*] Israel or engaged in battle any further."
   18:16: "Then Joab sounded the trumpet, and the troops came back from pursuing [*radap*] Israel."
3. 2:16: "Each grasped [*khazaq*] his opponent by the head [*roʾsh*]."
   18:9: "Absalom was riding on his mule. . . . His head [*roʾsh*] caught fast [*khazaq*] in the oak."

In both scenarios David emerges as the winner. He who dares to oppose or eliminate David loses. Absalom, who desired to be head of Israel, is left hanging by his head. For Absalom's troops, their downfall was the forest (v. 8). For Absalom himself, his downfall was one oak tree in that forest (v. 9). Absalom is impaled (v. 9), then executed (v. 15). Other kings are executed by hanging (the king of Ai [Josh. 8:29]), or else executed and then impaled (the five kings of the Amorites [Josh. 10:26]; Saul [1 Sam. 31:10]), as are other individuals who have done something evil to the people of God (the brothers Rechab and Baanah [2 Sam. 4:12]; Holofernes, Nebuchadnezzar's chief army general [Jth. 14:11]; Nicanor, oppressive governor of Judea during the era of Judas Maccabeus [2 Macc. 15:33]). Deuteronomy 21:23 sums up such spectacles: "for anyone hung on a tree is under God's curse."

The individual who first observed the hanging Absalom (v. 10) may be compared with Uriah in ch. 11 (Fokkelman 1981: 245). Neither would do what his superior wanted him to do (go to his house; kill Absalom). Each refused out of a sense of loyalty ("The servants of my Lord are camping in the open field; shall I then go to my house?"; "I would not raise my hand against the king's son, for in our hearing the king commanded"). David has Uriah killed; Joab has Absalom killed.

It is understandable why both Ahimaaz (vv. 28–30) and the Cushite (vv. 31–32) are eager to share with David the news about the victories of his troops over Absalom's (vv. 28b, 31) but reluctant to tell about Absalom's death. They cannot say, "Your majesty, we have good news and bad news. Which do you wish to hear first?" Ahimaaz avoids it altogether (v. 29b), and the Cushite suggests it in a roundabout way ("May the enemies of my lord the king . . . be like that young man" [v. 32]), carefully avoiding saying "Absalom." In the past, David has demonstrated an incredible capacity for rage, when informed of Saul's death (2 Sam. 1:11–16) and of Ishbosheth's death (2 Sam. 4:10–12). How will he respond when informed of the violent death of his own son Absalom, and in defiance of his command at that? That Ahimaaz and the Cushite are merely bearers of information rather than the self-proclaimed assassins as in 2 Samuel 1 and 4 may be a fine point lost on David in this time of anguished trauma.

What David does is unleash a Niagara of tears. David's tears are prompted by and for his sons, the one who dies at birth (12:21), and the one who flees home (13:37) and later dies a violent death (18:33). But David's tears are more than paternal grief. His words "Would that I had died instead of you" imply that Absalom has taken David's place. David was the perpetrator of the evil; Absalom was the sacrificial lamb. It should have been David who died. The story contains parallels with Abraham's near offering of Isaac (Genesis 22). The angel's words to Abraham, "Do not lay your hand on [*shalakh yad ʾel*] the boy" (Gen. 22:12), resemble the servant's to Joab, "I would not raise my hand against [*shalakh yad ʾel*] the king's son." And David's words "Would that I had died instead of [*takhat*] you" (2 Sam. 18:33 [Heb. 19:1]) recall Abraham offering up the ram as a burnt offering "instead of" [*takhat*] his son (Gen. 22:13). Both Isaac and Absalom are bound, one on an altar, one in a tree. The differences between the two fathers, however, is drastic. Abraham's faithful response to testing "resulted in blesssing and continuity for the next generation, [and contrasts with] the judgment on King David, which brings disaster and threatens the dynastic continuity of his line. Abraham becomes a model against which the kings of Israel can be measured and critiqued" (Ackerman 1990: 51).

X. 19:1–20:26: David as One Who Fights Adversity

19:1–41. Absalom's death is not the last of David's crises. In this nineteenth chapter we will observe a David at a low ebb, but then a David who acts magnanimously. David finds himself in five different settings:

1. with Joab (vv. 1–15)
2. with Shimei (vv. 16–23)
3. with Mephibosheth (vv. 24–30)
4. with Barzillai (vv. 31–40)
5. with the people of Israel and Judah (vv. 41–43)

Of these five, David's conduct is exemplary only in the fourth. David kindly accepts elderly Barzillai's suggestion that David lavish his gratitude and gracious offer of residence in the royal court on a member of the younger generation, Chimham, possibly Barzillai's son. In ch. 18 David wishes that he might have died instead of his son Absalom. In ch. 19 father Barzillai wishes that the honor may go to a younger person (his son?) instead of to himself.

But the other incidents are not as smooth. To begin with, Joab rebukes David with incredibly forceful language (vv. 5–7). It is hard to imagine a commander commanding his commander-in-chief so commandingly! Whybray (1968: 42) calls these words of Joab "some of the plainest words spoken by a loyal official to his king in the whole of ancient literature." Brueggemann (1990: 324) says that "Joab talks tougher than even Nathan," while Conroy (1978: 79) draws attention to Joab's "whiplash imperatives" (see v. 7).

David's replacement of Joab with Amasa (v. 13) is partially in response to Joab's impudence of vv. 5–7. As Prov. 15:1 says, "A soft answer turns away wrath, but a harsh word stirs up anger." But Joab's dismissal may also reflect that David, like many a weak leader, resents and is intimidated by the presence of such a proficient and dynamic person as Joab.

David's forgiveness of Benjaminite Shimei (vv. 16–23) for Shimei's earlier cursing of David (16:5–8), and David's restraining of Abishai, who wishes to execute Shimei on the spot (vv. 21–22), seem salutary (see Swindoll 1997: 253–59). But note that Shimei does not approach David alone. He has quite a large support group around him (vv. 16–17). Would David exact revenge publicly, especially when he is trying to restore himself and win the support of otherwise distrustful groups? And if David's forgiveness of Shimei is real, what about David's deathbed charge to Solomon to get rid of Shimei (1 Kings 2:8–9)?

David's meeting with Mephibosheth is interesting (vv. 24–30). Earlier, Ziba, servant of Mephibosheth, claimed that Mephibosheth was openly disloyal to David at the time of Absalom's rebellion, causing David unthinkingly to transfer Saul's estate from Mephibosheth to Ziba (16:1–4). Now, Mephibosheth points out to David that he was not disloyal at all. Rather, the reason he had not gone with David earlier is that he is lame and nobody provided him with a donkey to ride. Clearly, either Ziba is lying in ch. 16 or Mephibosheth is lying in ch. 19. Like Solomon (1 Kings 3:16–28), David is confronted by two people who make opposing claims. Both cannot be right. One is a truthteller and one is a fabricator. And like Solomon, whose solution is to divide the living baby in half, David's solution is to divide the estate in half. He acts arbitrarily and in a way to make both Ziba and Mephibosheth half-winners, and does not pursue the matter to get at the truth.

The fifth section involves David being caught between the people of (northern) Israel and the people of Judah concerning who is more loyal to David, who more rightly may claim David as their king, and who is more entitled to escort him back to Jerusalem (vv. 41–43). Note that in v. 41 the people of Israel ask David a question about the Judahites, but it is the Judahites, not David, who answer the question (v. 42). David sits by silently, caught in the middle of a verbal crossfire between quarreling Israelites and Judahites. And long before Judah and Israel formally split into two distinct entities after Solomon's death, the roots of that cleavage are already forming.

20:1–25. David moves from the frying pan to the fire, from being caught in the middle of tribal antagonism (19:41–43) to having to confront a secessionist movement led by a Benjaminite called Sheba. Sheba uses three lines of poetry to broadcast and fuel his revolt, and these same three lines are used later by northern Israelites when they distance themselves from Solomon (1 Kings 12:16):

> We have no portion in David,
> no share in the son of Jesse!
> Everyone to your tents, O Israel.

There is no doubt how the narrator feels about Sheba. He, not David, calls Sheba a "scoundrel" (v. 1), the same term that another Benjaminite, Shimei, had used of David (2 Sam. 16:7). Christ has no agreement with Beliar (2 Cor. 6:15), that is, Satan and his cohorts, and David has no agreement with Sheba, an *ish beliyaʿal*, a scoundrel, an evildoer. (There is probably some connection in meaning and derivation between *beliyaʿal* and "Beliar.")

David's role in this revolt is minuscule. Sheba wants to break away and establish independence. All that David does is take away any independence and future his ten concubines may ever have by locking them in his house and subjugating them to lifelong celibacy (v. 3). What a contrast between how David treats men and women! Shimei, who openly cursed the king, is forgiven (19:16–23). Mephibosheth, who earlier may have been disloyal to David, receives back half of his estate (19:24–30). But ten anonymous women who have never done anything disloyal to David are placed under lock and key, held incommunicado, and denied a future except for three meals a day and a bed to sleep on at night.

The northern Israelites in the previous chapter had argued that they had ten shares in David (19:43). Here now are ten concubines whom David has shared, but who now have absolutely no share in David.

If David's role is minuscule, Joab's role is major. Thanks to the tardiness of the newly appointed Amasa (v. 5), Joab and his brother Abishai take leadership roles in the pursuit of Sheba. But first, Amasa must be eliminated. Joab acts like Ehud in Judges 3. He approaches his victim secretly armed, feigns friendship, and then delivers one lethal blow (vv. 8–10). That the text says "He [Joab] did not strike a second blow" points to Joab as a "proficient butcher" (Fokkelman 1981: 329). The concubines are gone, and now Amasa is gone.

This portion of ch. 20 parallels the incident in 2:12–32 (Polzin 1993: 199):

1. Joab and Abishai pursue Abner (2:24)
    Joab and Abishai pursue Sheba (20:10b)
2. "How could I show my face to your brother Joab?" (2:22b)
    "Joab said, 'Is it well with you, my brother?'" (20:9a)
3. "So Abner struck him in the stomach" (2:23a)
    "Joab struck him in the stomach" (20:10a)
4. "And all those who came to the place where Asahel had fallen and died, stood still" (2:23b)
    "Since he [Joab] saw all who came by him [Amasa] were stopping" (20:12b)
5. tribal fratricide at Gibeon (2:12, 16)
    familial fratricide (Amasa is Joab's cousin) at Gibeon (20:10)
6. "Joab sounded the trumpet and all the people stopped; they no longer pursued Israel" (2:28)
    "So he [Joab] blew the trumpet, and they dispersed from the city" (20:22c)

Joab would have destroyed the entire city, Abel of Beth-maacah (v. 15), where Sheba sought refuge, had not a wise woman (v. 16) persuaded Joab that there is no sense in obliterating an entire community when the head of the villain would serve the issue (v. 21b). There are eleven women in this chapter. Ten have no voice. One is eloquent, pragmatic, wise, and persuasive. The only thing she shares with the other ten is anonymity. To be wise in this situation is to be able to "think of an alternative way around the present set of circumstances" (Brueggemann 1990: 331). Joab, who had done little listening in the first half of the chapter, is now willing to listen to the voice of sanity (vv. 16–17).

That the wise woman identifies her city as "a mother in Israel" (v. 19b) is crucial. If Joab were to destroy the entire city, a mother city at that, he would then be guilty of killing a cousin (familial fratricide) and killing a mother (matricide)—all that by one whose name means "Yahweh is father" (see Fokkelman 1981: 334).

There are times when David metaphorically lost his head. But if you hang around David long enough for whatever reason, you have a good chance of losing your head literally (Polzin 1993: 199–200). Goliath did (1 Sam. 17:46, 54, 57). Saul did (1 Sam. 31:9). Ishbosheth did (2 Sam. 4:7–8, 12). Shimei almost did (2 Sam. 16:9). Sheba did (2 Sam. 20:21–22). Ahithophel hanged himself by his head (2 Sam. 17:23); and Absalom hung from his head (2 Sam. 18:9). For the sake of one's own head, David may not be the best head with which to be in proximity!

The chapter concludes (vv. 23–26) with a listing of David's cabinet—a military commander (one wonders if Joab is not only in command of all Israel's army, but in command of David too!), one in charge of the mercenary soldiers, one in charge of the forced labor, a recorder, a secretary, two priests, and, interestingly, in addition to these legitimate priestly households who functioned in the service of the national cult, David's own private priest, Ira the Jairite. The list of David's officials is analogous to the list of his officers in 8:15–18. As such, these two bureaucratic listings are bookends to the poignant story of David covering chs. 9–20:

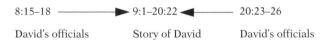

8:15–18	9:1–20:22	20:23–26
David's officials	Story of David	David's officials

Certainly, the external trappings of leadership are all in place, but the national trust in that leadership has severely waned. There is much bureaucracy, but little buoyancy. David is more like a bird flapping about on one wing rather than a soaring eagle.

XI. 21:1–24:25: David as Executioner, Militarist, Hymnist, and Census-Taker

It is all but unanimous among commentators to treat chs. 21–24 as a patchwork of miscellaneous materials about David that have been added on to 2 Samuel 9–20 as an appendix. Comparison may be made with Deut. 23:10–25:19, the last section in the laws of Deuteronomy (chs. 12–25), which is a lengthy series of laws about various and sundry issues with no obvious topical connection. But is 2 Samuel 21–24 all that miscellaneous and disconnected? For example, the emphasis at the start of this unit on three years of famine because of Saul's atrocities (21:1) must be connected with the three years of famine toward the end of the unit (24:13 [Septuagint and 1 Chron. 21:12]; the Hebrew text has "seven years"), the first of three forms of punishment David must accept from God.

Again, many have observed that these last four chapters are arranged in the form of a chiasm (e.g., Sternberg 1987: 40):

a_1 Saul's sin against the Gibeonites and its collective punishment
    (21:1–14)
   b_1 David's heroes and their exploits (21:15–22)
     c_1 David's psalm (22:1–51)
     c_2 David's psalm (23:1–7)
   b_2 David's heroes and their exploits (23:8–39)
a_2 David's sin against the census taboo and its collective punishment
    (24:1–25)

One of the functions of ordering material chiastically is to highlight the central section. Here, that means that the focus is on David as hymnist (22:1–51; 23:1–7), or more particularly, the focus is upon David's God. Hence, Second Samuel concludes not with a "regocentric" emphasis but with a theocentric one.

21:1–14. In v. 1, God does not volunteer an explanation for this three-year famine until David "sought the Lord's face" (something he probably had not done a lot of lately). It turns out that the famine is the expression of God's judgment on Israel for the sin of the deceased Saul against the Gibeonites whom he massacred in violation of Joshua's treaty with the Gibeonites made centuries earlier (Josh. 9:15). For reasons that are not clear, the Old Testament nowhere refers to Saul's slaughter of the Gibeonites. Our only knowledge of it is the reference here in 2 Samuel 21. To compensate for Saul's abuse of the oath, and since he himself is deceased, two of his sons by his concubine Rizpah and five of his grandsons (by Merab?) are put to death (vv. 8–9). This is not because of God's response (v. 1a) but because of the Gibeonites' request (vv. 4–7). And David complies.

As readers we have two options in assessing David's actions. One is that he is using God and using prayer to get rid of, as conveniently and religiously as possible, any and all vestiges of the house of Saul. He uses a hoax to create hell. The second option is to trust David, accept his motives, and believe that this was a painful, traumatic incident for him. Better that seven die than that a nation die. In ch. 24 David cries out,

"But these sheep, what have they done?" (v. 17) when the innocent suffer the effects of the sin of the guilty. But not here.

The incident looks back to two sections of the Torah. First, Deut. 5:9 (= Exod. 20:5) speaks of God "punishing children for the iniquity of the parents" as part of the second commandment, while Deut. 24:16 says that "children shall not be put to death for their parents." It appears that 2 Sam. 21:1–14 supports Deut. 5:9 but disagrees with Deut. 24:16. But note that Deut. 5:9 and 24:16 do not really contradict each other. The first deals with divine punishment, while the second deals with execution by human judicial authorities. What God may do (Deut. 5:9), people may not do (Deut. 24:16). In the very few cases in the Old Testament where children are put to death because of a parent's action, we are dealing not with criminal cases but with offenses against God, such as violation of the *kherem* (Josh. 7:24–25) or a national oath taken in God's name (2 Sam. 21:1–14).

Second, this narrative invites comparison with Numbers 25, the story of Israel's immorality with the Moabite women of Baal-peor. In response God sends pestilence and orders that the ringleaders be impaled.

These are the only two places in the Old Testament where the Hiphil stem of the verb *yaqaᶜ* ("impale" [NIV, "expose"]) occurs (Num. 25:4; 2 Sam. 21:6, 9, 13). There are other similarities:

Numbers 25	2 Sam. 21:1–14
1. God sends a plague (v. 9).	God sends famine (v. 1).
2. The cause is the violation of the Sinaitic covenant not to worship other gods.	The cause is Saul's violation of Joshua's treaty oath made in God's name.
3. Somebody is to be killed and the corpse hung for public display (v. 4).	Somebody is to be killed and the corpse hung for public display (vv. 6, 9, 13).
4. God's wrath is assuaged and the plague stops (v. 8b).	God's wrath is assuaged and the famine ends (v. 14b).

The only woman in this last unit of Second Samuel (which lists a lot of men) is Rizpah, who was compelled to give up two of her sons as part of the ransom (v. 8). Contrary to the law of Deut. 21:22–23, which states that a corpse is not to remain on the stake even overnight, Rizpah's sons, and the others, were exposed to birds of prey and field predators for months, from late April or May through the summer months (vv. 9–10). During that time Rizpah shielded the corpses from abuse (v. 10b), acting like Abram once did (Gen. 15:11). The reality of Deut.

28:26—"Your corpses shall be food for every bird of the air and animal of the earth, and there shall be no one to frighten them away"—does not take place here. Rizpah's "response to a savage massacre was to affirm her own ability to continue being human in the midst of a dehumanizing situation. Surrounded by corpses, she testified to life" (Winters 1997: 153). For the first and only time in his life, David is shamed into action by the behavior of a virtuous, honorable woman, and gives the remains of Saul and Jonathan an appropriate burial (vv. 11–14).

21:15–22. From famine to war, from God to four huge Philistines—so goes this unit. But as the Gibeonites did the killing in vv. 1–14, several of David's men do the killing here: Abishai (vv. 15–17), Sibbecai (v. 18), Elhanan (v. 19), and his nephew Jonathan (vv. 20–21), who engages a Philistine with a particularly curious digital structure (six fingers on each hand and six toes on each foot).

Seven (grand)sons of Saul "fell" (v. 9 [NRSV, "perished"]), and now four Philistines "fall" (v. 22). But David is passive in both incidents. In this second incident the text states that David "grew weary" [NIV, "became exhausted"] (v. 15b). He is no longer the David of old, with boundless energy. As such, he is more dependent on others than he has ever been in his life—dependent upon his troops, to be sure, but even more importantly, dependent upon God, as his hymns in chs. 22 and 23 will make clear. In fact, one may suggest with Childs (1979: 274) that "the description of his [David's] weakness serves to shift the focus of this summary of David's achievements away from his glorification and forms a transition to his praise of God in ch. 22."

22:1–51. David may no longer be able to muster the physical energy and stamina needed to lead his troops into battle, but he can still worship. Days of fighting may be behind him, but days for singing still exist. In fact, so special is David's hymn of praise here in 2 Samuel 22 that it is reproduced in the Psalter as Psalm 18, with only grammatical and orthographic variants between the two versions.

The first thing one notices about this hymn is that David composed it not toward the end of his reign (although it comes near the end of Second Samuel) but at a much earlier time, even before he was anointed king in Hebron. At the time of its composition David is still on the run from Saul. Thus, the occasion for it is, as v. 1 states, "the day when the Lord delivered him from the hand of all his enemies, and from the hand of Saul." (Dahood, in his Anchor Bible commentary on Psalms, notes that v. 6a could just as easily read "the cords of Saul (*shaʾul*) entangled me" instead of the more traditional "as the cords of Sheol (*sheʾol*) entangled me.")

Why, then, is this hymn, by its own testimony composed at a much earlier period, placed in the text at a point where David's career is winding down? For one thing, its placement here informs us that David, all his personal problems notwithstanding, has not lost sight of the indispensable significance of the reality and presence of God in his life. When all hell breaks out in one's life for whatever reasons, God is a fortress, an impregnable city in whom one can take refuge. He is a rock on whom one can stand, safe from the swirling waters of a wadi's flash flood.

For another thing, the placement of this hymn here allows for a parallel with the life of Moses. Both Moses and David near the end of their lives record a song/hymn that gives lavish praise to God (Deut. 31:30–32:43; 2 Sam. 22:1–51) and highlights God as "Rock" (Deut. 32:4, 15, 18, 30, 31; 2 Sam. 22:2, 3, 32, 47). Each hymn is followed by a second and shorter poetic piece (Deut. 33:1–29, Moses' final blessing to the Israelite tribes; 2 Sam. 23:1–7, David's last words). There seems to be a tradition elsewhere in the Old Testament of linking the writing career of David with that of Moses. The division of the Psalter, for example, into five books (chs. 1–41; 42–72; 73–89; 90–106; 107–150) allows for a connection between Moses' five books and David's five books.

Almost all of David's hymn here is talk about God directed to God. So v. 1 begins, "David spoke to the Lord the words of this song." He is not putting on a public performance by singing to the galleries. It is interesting that throughout the first part of the poem (vv. 1–25) David speaks to God primarily in the third person ("He . . ."), but in the second half of the poem (vv. 26–51) he speaks to God primarily in the second person ("You . . ."). The progression of speaking first to God in the third person and then in the second person (as in Ps. 23:1–3 ["he"] and 4–5 ["you"]) suggests a rise in the level of intimacy with which one talks and sings to God.

Note also that the hymn begins in reference to David's past ("encompassed, assailed, entangled, confronted" [vv. 5–6]; "called, heard, came" [v. 7]; to say nothing of God's dramatic intervention in the form of a theophany [vv. 8–20]). But if the psalm begins retrospectively, it ends prospectively, referring to David's future: "[The Lord] shows steadfast love to his anointed, to David and his descendants forever" (v. 51). Whether it is David and his enemies or David and his descendants, God is there as a rock, a fortress, a savior, a lamp, a tower, and as the source of profuse, steadfast love.

The portion of this hymn that has provoked most commentary is David's claims about himself in vv. 21–25. When David says things like "The Lord rewarded me according to my righteousness" (v. 21a), or "I have kept the ways of the Lord" (v. 22a), or "I was blameless before him" (v. 24a), does this sound like the David we've been reading about since ch. 11? Is the David of 11–21 righteous, blameless, clean?

David's statements here have moved two commentators to say, "One effect of this lengthy self-adulation, therefore, is to proclaim not righteousness but self-righteousness, not piety but hypocrisy" (Gunn and Fewell 1993: 124). Another speaks of "the self-promotion of the poetry" (Polzin 1993: 207), while yet another (Weitzman 1997: 118) wonders whether the entire hymn "was added as a kind of damage control to restore the reputation of Israel's greatest king."

Are David's words in vv. 21–25 hyperbolic lies, hypocritical self-promotions, and "Phariseeisms" of the worst sort ("I thank you, God, that I am not as other people")? Or are they authentic statements of an individual in whose life God has decisively worked his forgiving and transforming grace?

Note in the first place that David does not claim to be sinlessly perfect. The purpose of this unit (vv. 21–31) is to acknowledge and affirm God's justice, as the last verse of the section, v. 31, makes clear ("This God—his way is perfect"), rather than to put David's character on a pedestal. God honors those who live in ways that honor him.

Also, if David uttered these words in his pre-Hebron, pre-Jerusalem days, as v. 1 maintains, then he said them long before the Bathsheba/Uriah debacle of ch. 11 and even longer before the census taking incident of ch. 24, the only two sins for which David repents and acknowledges wrongdoing. By the end of First Samuel, David's life is exemplary and unsoiled (although, of course, some would beg to disagree).

We may note that David is not the only person to testify to being "righteous" (vv. 21, 25) and "blameless" (vv. 24, 26). Job, too, says of himself that even though he is a righteous (*tsaddiq*) and blameless (*tamim*) man, he is still a laughingstock (Job 12:4).

God's challenge to Abram to walk obediently before God and be blameless (*tamim* [Gen. 17:1]) on the heels of Abram sleeping with and fathering a child by someone other than his wife (16:1–16), and several years after putting his wife in a physically and sexually vulnerable position by persuading her to be deceptive about her identity (12:10–20), demonstrates that by God's grace, and only by God's grace, may the hitherto foolish and carnal become *tamim*.

It is not without significance that Scripture again and again affirms David's integrity. David himself did it earlier (David to Saul: "The Lord rewards everyone for his righteousness and faithfulness" [1 Sam. 26:23]). So does Solomon ("my father David, because he walked before you in faithfulness, in righteousness, and in uprightness of heart"

[1 Kings 3:6]). So does the narrator of the Solomon story ("his [Solomon's] heart was not true to the Lord his God, as was the heart of his father David" [1 Kings 11:4b]). So does God, speaking to the wife of Jeroboam through the prophet Ahijah ("yet you have not been like my servant David, who kept my commandments and followed me with all his heart, doing only that which was right in my eyes" [1 Kings 14:8]). And so does Paul, alluding to 1 Sam. 13:14 and Ps. 89:20: "I have found David, son of Jesse, to be a man after my heart, who will carry out all my wishes" [Acts 13:22]).

It is not that these sources are sporting blinders. In fact, 1 Kings 15:5 states, "David did what was right in the sight of the Lord, and did not turn aside from anything that he commanded him all the days of his life, *except* in the matter of Uriah the Hittite." The story of David is the story of a God who is a rock and a refuge, a God of grace who can mitigate that "except" that lies buried as a skeleton in one's closet. Grace, grace, God's grace, grace that is greater than anybody's "except"—who would not want to sing to and about a God like that?

23:1–7. David's last words find a parallel in Jacob's last words (Gen. 49:1–28), Moses' last words (Deut. 33:1–29), and Joshua's last words (Josh. 24:1–28). What 2 Sam. 23:1–7 does that none of the other three does is to refer to David's last words as "the oracle [*neʾum*] of David." The word *neʾum* most often refers to an announcement or message from God, usually about forthcoming judgment. Accordingly, it is a popular word in the prophets (e.g., Nah. 1:1; Hab. 1:1; Zech. 9:1; 12:1; Mal. 1:1). Some form of "oracle of Yahweh" occurs twenty-one times in Amos alone.

A parallel to 2 Sam. 23:1 where *neʾum* is followed by a person's name in the genitive is Num. 24:3, "The oracle of Balaam son of Beor," which introduces Balaam's third poem in Num. 24:3–9. And both times the sentence "the oracle of Balaam/David" is followed by a line that begins, "the oracle of the man [*gever*] whose/whom. . . ." But what both Balaam and David do after they use this phrase is make explicit in the next verse or phrase that what they are about to say is inspired by God: Balaam, "The oracle of one who hears the words of God, who sees the vision of the Almighty" (Num. 24:4); David, "The spirit of the Lord speaks through me, his word is upon my tongue" (2 Sam. 23:2). So, then, 22:1–51 is a human utterance directed to God, while 23:1–7 is a divine utterance through a human mouthpiece, but with no specified audience for the oracle. (The only other place where *neʾum* occurs with a human speaker is Prov. 30:1: "The words of Agur . . . an oracle.")

Note that David claims not only that God has spoken *through* him (*dibber be* [v. 2]), but also that God has spoken *to* him (*dibber le* [v. 3]).

And this second claim is critical, for it makes clear that God's blessing will be only on the king "who rules over people justly, ruling in the fear of God." There is no blanket approval of kingship per se, and certainly no endorsement of tyranny, insensitivity, and self-preoccupation.

The poem reads much like Psalm 1, for both contain similes, first for the righteous (king), then for the wicked and godless:

Psalm 1	2 Sam. 23:1–7
They [the righteous] are like trees (v. 3).	One who rules justly is like the light of morning (vv. 3–4).
The wicked are like chaff (v. 4).	The godless are like thorns (v. 6).

23:8–39. David is obviously no "one-man show." He has a tremendous and loyal support base. One might compare this listing of David's associates in the next-to-last chapter of Second Samuel with Paul's listing in the last chapter of Romans (16:3–16) of his fellow workers and those who have helped establish the gospel message at Rome, whom Paul desires to visit.

Some of David's associates receive brief coverage of their exploits (vv. 8–23); others are just names in a list (vv. 24–39). It is not without some pathos that in this lengthy listing of those who fought with and for David, who stood by his side and believed in him through thick and thin, the very last person to be mentioned is Uriah the Hittite (v. 39). And note that while Joab, the ever present supreme commander of David's forces, is not included, his brothers Abishai (v. 18) and Asahel (v. 24) are!

Not only do these warriors fight for David, but also they put their lives at risk by stealthily sneaking through the enemy camp to obtain some water to assuage the thirst of their king (vv. 13–17). The verb used to describe David's thirst ("said longingly" or "longed for" [v. 15]) may connote elsewhere a continuous improper and excessive desire, as in Num. 11:4, "the rabble among them had a strong craving," or in Deut. 5:21, "neither shall you desire [crave] your neighbor's house." It is not clear that David's craving for water was excessive and wrong, but it did put the lives of three of his soldiers at risk. And instead of drinking it, he threw it on the ground. While he spiritualized his actions, one wonders what these three men thought of them, after the ordeal they had gone through to obtain the water.

24:1–25. For reasons unstated, God is again (or still) angry with Israel (for their nasty treatment of David, epitomized in the revolts of Absalom and Sheba, and/or the crudeness of Shimei?). As an expression of that indignation the Lord incites David to take a census of Israel and Judah. The Hebrew for "incite against" (*sut be*) was used earlier by David when he was fleeing Saul ("if it is the Lord who has stirred you up against me" [1 Sam. 26:19]), and by God to Satan about Job ("although you incited me against him, to destroy him for no reason" [Job 2:3]).

It is well known that the Chronicles version of this story (1 Chronicles 21) says nothing about God's anger or God inciting David against Israel. Rather it says, "Satan stood up against Israel, and incited David to count the people of Israel" (v. 1). While some have interpreted "Satan" here to be a general term for "adversary" that has nothing to do with the demonic figure (Sailhammer 1989), the better suggestion is that the earlier of these two accounts (2 Samuel 24) explains David's actions in terms of a primary cause (God's anger), while the later of these two accounts (1 Chronicles 21) explains David's actions in terms of a secondary cause. "Satan," because it is used here without the definite article, is a personal name and not just a title, as in Job 1–2.

In the Old Testament, censuses are common enough. Apart from those taken by Moses (Num. 1:2–47; 4:2–49; 26:2–65), they are common in the period of the monarchy. In addition to David's there are Jehoshaphat's (2 Chron. 17:13–18), Amaziah's (2 Chron. 25:5), and Uzziah's (2 Chron. 26:11–13). Those of the monarchy all have to do with military matters.

It is interesting to note that David's census took over nine months to accomplish (v. 8), while Moses' census took less than a month (according to the date lines, only twenty days have passed between Num. 1:1 and Num. 10:11), even though the totals in both are close to each other. Moses' census was efficiently done; David's census was sluggishly done. Moses had each of the clans take its own census (Num. 1:2, 18). He merely had to collate the totals for each clan. David's census was more laborious and time consuming. Joab visited city after city until all had been canvassed (vv. 5–9). In David's instructions to Joab, he says, "Go through all the tribes of Israel" (v. 2). The verb for "go" is *shut*, meaning "to wander over distant places," as in Satan's "going to and fro" on the earth (Job 1:7; 2:2), or the eyes of the Lord, "which range through the whole earth" (Zech. 4:10).

Joab, never far from the action, senses something is wrong with the census (v. 3). He sounds like Moses. His "May the Lord your God increase the number of the people a hundredfold" is similar to Moses' "May the Lord, the God of your ancestors, increase you a thousand times more" (Deut. 1:11), and this parallel makes it clear that neither Joab nor Moses is complaining about Israel's growth. Does Joab think (correctly, maybe) that David is engaging in some kind of "bureaucratic terrorism" in which the crown invades villages and tribal life" (Brueggemann 1988: 392), or does he see the census's "potential for military aggrandizement at the expense of trust in the power of Yahweh" (Gunn and Fewell 1993: 126)?

For a second time David's heart tells him he has done something he should not have done: "Afterward, David was stricken to the heart" (v. 10). The text uses the exact same phrase as in 1 Sam. 24:5—*wayyak lev dawid ʾoto*—when David cut off a corner of Saul's cloak. What David is not aware of is that God is angry at Israel, not at him.

In a rare move, God allows David a choice in the form of the punishment that will befall Israel and David (vv. 11–14). That David chooses three days of pestilence, when choosing three months of fleeing from the enemy would have saved him from personal setback, shows that "David fears God the most. He also trusts God the most" (Brueggemann 1990: 353).

The chapter concludes with the brief account of David purchasing a piece of property from a Jebusite called Araunah (Ornan in 1 Chron. 21:18) on which he builds an altar to the Lord and offers sacrifices, especially the burnt offering, to stop the plague (vv. 18–25). David's famous "I will not offer burnt offerings to the Lord my God that cost me nothing" (v. 24) explains why, in the Old Testament, fish and game were unacceptable as sacrifices. They cost the donor nothing.

David in First Chronicles

The second story of David in the Bible covers 1 Chron. 11:1–29:30. It is interesting to compare Second Samuel's presentation of David with First Chronicles' presentation of David. Some obvious differences stand out.

1. Much material in the Samuel account is absent from the Chronicles account:
    a. *2 Samuel 1–4* are four chapters that deal with the violent death of the Amalekite who claimed to have killed Saul, David's lament for Saul and Jonathan, and the violent death of others, including Ishbosheth, Saul's surviving son and king in northern Israel for a while.
    b. *2 Sam. 6:20b–23*, the angry exchange of words and insults between David and Michal after David brought the ark to Jerusalem.

    c. *2 Samuel 9*, David's display of kindness to Saul's grand-son Mephibosheth.

    d. *2 Sam. 11:2–12:25*, David's affair with Bathsheba, his setup of Uriah's murder, and his encounter with Nathan.

    e. *2 Sam. 13:1–21:17*, the accounts of Absalom's revolt, Sheba's revolt, and David's hanging of seven members of Saul's family.

    f. *2 Samuel 22*, the psalm of David celebrating God's saving him from Saul.

    g. *2 Sam. 23:1–7*, David's last words, in poetic form.

2. Much material in the Chronicles account is absent from the Samuel account. While there are small bits and pieces added here and there, probably the most interesting new items in Chronicles are:

    a. *1 Chron. 10:13–14*, the Lord puts Saul to death and turns the kingdom over to David.

    b. *1 Chron. 15:1–24*, David selects a long list of Levitical families to carry the ark to Jerusalem, for only the Levites may transport the holy ark.

    c. *1 Chron. 16:4–43*, David appoints priestly personnel to sing and play and carry out cultic rituals before the ark.

    d. *1 Chron. 22:2–29:30*, a very long section in which David organizes religious, military, and civil affairs in his king-dom in preparation for appointing Solomon as his suc-cessor. The transition of leadership from David to Solomon is smooth and knows nothing of the bloodbath "hit list" of 1 Kings 1–2 in which leaders of the opposi-tion to Solomon are "gunned down."

3. The same incident is placed at two different junctures in the two stories:

    The story of David's war with the Philistines and a listing of the names of his warriors comes toward the end of the Samuel account (*2 Sam. 23:8–39*), while in the Chroni-cles account this portion is moved to the beginning of the story (*1 Chron. 11:10–47*). And while 2 Sam. 23:39 lists Uriah as the last name in the list, 1 Chron. 11:41 buries his name in the middle of the list.

4. A single story in Samuel becomes two stories in Chronicles, with an insertion between the two halves:

> *2 Sam. 6:1–23* is the account of David bringing the ark to
> Jerusalem. Here is the layout in Chronicles:
> *1 Chron. 13:1–14* (= 2 Sam. 6:1–11), the ark makes it as
> far as Obed-edom's house.
> *1 Chron. 14:1–17* (= 2 Sam. 5:11–25), David defeats the
> Philistines twice.
> *1 Chron. 15:25–16:3* (= 2 Sam. 6:12–19), the ark makes it
> to Jerusalem.

5. Where the same story appears in both accounts, details may
   vary:

   > In the census-taking (*2 Samuel 24*; *1 Chronicles 21*) God
   > incites David in one (2 Sam. 24:1), but Satan does it in
   > the other (1 Chron. 21:1). The total of the headcount in
   > one is 1.3 million (2 Sam. 24:9); in the other the total is
   > more than 1.5 million (1 Chron. 21:5). In one, God first
   > offers David as a punishment seven years of famine
   > (2 Sam. 24:13, Hebrew text); in the other, God first offers
   > David as a punishment three years of famine (1 Chron.
   > 21:12). Does David buy the threshing floor from Araunah
   > the Jebusite (2 Sam. 24:18) or from Ornan the Jebusite
   > (1 Chron. 21:28)?

6. Very few units of the David story are reproduced exactly in
   First Chronicles as they are in Second Samuel:

   > The closest similarity appears in *2 Sam. 7:1–29* =
   > *1 Chron. 17:1–27*, Nathan's oracle to David that God is
   > going to establish his house forever. But even here the
   > threat of chastisement on any of David's disobedient sons
   > (2 Sam. 7:14b) is absent in 1 Chronicles 17.

We may make several observations about all of the above. First, it
appears that the account in Chronicles has added about the same
amount as it has omitted.

Second, for the most part the portions that Chronicles deletes deal
with incidents in David's life that are disturbing, questionable, im-
moral, or inimical toward David. This is not to say that Chronicles
whitewashes David and makes a sinner into a saint. Chronicles does include David's second great sin, the taking of the census, and 1 Chron.
22:8 uses much stronger language ("you have shed much blood"), as
does 28:3 ("you have shed blood"), than 1 Kings 5:3 does to explain why
David cannot build the temple.

Third, the additions in Chronicles focus on David's role in organizing religious, political, and civic matters that relate to worshiping God and running the empire he is about to bequeath to Solomon.

Fourth, more than likely the author of the account in First Chronicles was aware of and had access to the account in Second Samuel. We cannot be sure who wrote this material or when. But the possibility is high that Second Samuel (and the larger corpus of which it is a part) reached its final form at least by the time of the Babylonian exile (587–539 B.C.), and that Chronicles was written some time between the decree of Cyrus of Persia that allowed war prisoners to return home (539 B.C.) and the completion of Israel's second temple (515 B.C.) after the destruction of Solomon's temple in 587 (Newsome 1975: 215–17).

Fifth, it is wrong and irrelevant to ask which of the two is "truer," or more faithful to the facts. Both accounts make their own inspired point in different ways. It is clear that the Chronicler is speaking to a postexilic restored community that is part of an eternal covenant made by God with David, but a community that has just lived through a seventy-year night. Furthermore, it is a covenant in which God is to be both worshiped and praised, and also obeyed. And in this covenant, God is the model covenant maker and David is the model king, as we follow his rise (11:1–14:2), his reign (14:3–22:1), and his preparation for Solomon's succession (22:2–29:30). (See Wright: 1998 for this outline.) "The fact that the book of Chronicles does not replace Samuel and Kings, but stands alongside the earlier tradition, illustrates the function of the canon as a means of enrichment of the biblical tradition in the process of critical reflection" (Childs 1979: 655).

Bibliography (2 Samuel)

Commentaries and Major Studies

Ackroyd, P. R. 1977. *The Second Book of Samuel*. Cambridge Bible Commentary. Cambridge: Cambridge University.

Anderson, A. A. 1989. *2 Samuel*. Word Biblical Commentary 11. Dallas: Word.

Bailey, R. C. 1990. *David in Love and War: The Pursuit of Power in 2 Samuel 10–12*. JSOT Supplement 75. Sheffield: JSOT Press.

Baldwin, J. 1988. *1 and 2 Samuel*. Tyndale Old Testament Commentaries 8. Downers Grove, Ill.: InterVarsity.

Bergen, R. 1996. *1, 2 Samuel*. New American Commentary 7. Nashville: Broadman and Holman.

Briscoe, S. 1984. *David, A Heart For God*. Wheaton, Ill.: Victor Books.

Brueggemann, W. 1985. *David's Truth in Israel's Imagination and Memory*. Philadelphia: Fortress.

———. 1990. *First and Second Samuel*. Interpretation. Louisville: John Knox.

Carlson, R. A. 1969. *David, the Chosen King: A Traditio-Historical Approach to the Second Book of Samuel*. Uppsala: Almqvist & Wiksell.

Conroy, C. 1978. *Absalom, Absalom! Narrative and Language in 2 Samuel 13–20*. Rome: Biblical Institute Press.

Eslinger, L. 1994. *House of God or House of David: The Rhetoric of 2 Samuel 7*. JSOT Supplement 164. Sheffield: JSOT Press.

Fokkelman, J. P. 1981. *Narrative Art and Poetry in the Books of Samuel*. Vol. 1, *King David (II Sam. 9–20; I Kings 1–2)*. Studia semitica Neerlandia 20. Assen: Van Gorcum.

————. 1990. *Narrative Art and Poetry in the Books of Samuel*. Vol. 3, *Throne and City (II Sam. 2–8 and 21–24)*. Studia semitica Neerlandia 27. Assen: Van Gorcum.

Gordon, R. P. 1988. *1 and 2 Samuel*. Grand Rapids: Zondervan.

Gunn, D. 1978. *The Story of King David: Genre and Interpretation*. JSOT Supplement 6. Sheffield: JSOT Press.

Hertzberg, H. W. 1964. *I and II Samuel*. Old Testament Library. Philadelphia: Westminster.

Jones, G. H. 1990. *The Nathan Narratives*. JSOT Supplement 80. Sheffield: Sheffield Academic Press.

McCarter, P. K., Jr. 1984. *II Samuel*. Anchor Bible 9. Garden City, N.Y.: Doubleday.

Polzin, R. 1993. *David and the Deuteronomist: 2 Samuel*. A Literary Study of the Deuteronomic History, Part 3. Bloomington: Indiana University Press.

Rost, L. 1982 [1926]. *The Succession to the Throne of David*. Trans. M. Rutter and D. Gunn. Historic Texts and Interpreters in Biblical Scholarship 1. Sheffield: Almond.

Swindoll, C. 1997. *David: A Man of Passion and Destiny*. Dallas: Word.

Whybray, R. N. 1968. *The Succession Narrative: A Study of II Samuel 9–20 and I Kings 1–2*. London: SCM.

Youngblood, R. F. 1992. "1, 2 Samuel." In *Deuteronomy, Joshua, Judges, Ruth, 1, 2 Samuel*. Expositor's Bible Commentary 3. Grand Rapids: Zondervan. Pp. 551–1104.

Shorter Studies

Ackerman, J. S. 1990. "Knowing Good and Evil: A Literary Analysis of the Court History in 2 Samuel 9–20 and 1 Kings 1–2." *JBL* 109:41–60.

Ackroyd, P. R. 1981. "The Succession Narrative (so-called)." *Int* 35:383–96.

Alter, R. 1981. *The Art of Biblical Narrative*. New York: Basic Books.

Arnold, B. 1989. "The Amalekite's Report of Saul's Death: Political Intrigue or Incompatible Sources?" *JETS* 32:289–98.

Bar-Efrat, S. 1989. *Narrative Art in the Bible*. JSOT Supplement 70. Sheffield: Almond. Pp. 239–82.

Barrick, W. B. 1997. "Saul's Demise, David's Lament and Custer's Last Stand." *JSOT* 73:25–41.

Bellefontaine, E. 1987. "Customary Law and Chieftainship: Judicial Aspects of 2 Samuel 14:4–21." *JSOT* 38:47–72.

Berlin, A. 1983. *Poetics and Interpretation in Biblical Narrative.* Sheffield: Almond.

Blenkinsopp, J. 1965. "Theme and Motif in the Succession History and the Yahwist Corpus." *VTSup* 15:44–57.

Bright, J. 1981. *A History of Israel.* 3rd ed. Philadelphia: Westminster. Pp. 195–211.

Brueggemann, W. 1988. "2 Samuel 21–24: An Appendix of Deconstruction?" *CBQ* 50:383–97.

Camp, C. V. 1981. "The Wise Women in 2 Samuel: A Role Model for Women in Early Israel?" *CBQ* 43:14–29.

Childs, B. S. 1979. *Introduction to the Old Testament as Scripture.* Philadelphia: Fortress. Pp. 263–80.

Coats, G. W. 1981. "Parable, Fable, and Anecdote: Storytelling in the Succession Narrative." *Int* 35:368–82.

Cryer, F. 1985. "David's Rise to Power and the Death of Abner: An Analysis of I Samuel xxvi 14–16 and the Redactional-Critical Implications." *VT* 35:385–94.

Daube, D. 1998. "Absalom and the Ideal King," *VT* 48:315–25.

Exum, C. 1992. *Tragedy and Biblical Narrative: Arrows of the Almighty.* Cambridge: Cambridge University Press. Pp. 120–49.

———. 1996. *Plotted Shot and Painted.* JSOT Supplement 215. Sheffield: Sheffield Academic Press. Pp. 19–79.

Flanagan, J. W. 1972. "Court History or Succession Document? A Study of 2 Samuel 9–20 and 1 Kings 1–2." *JBL* 91:172–81.

———. 1983. "Succession and Genealogy in the Davidic Dynasty." In *The Quest for the Kingdom of God: Essays in Honor of George E. Mendenhall.* Ed. H. B. Huffman, F. Spina, and A. R. W. Green. Winona Lake, Ind.: Eisenbrauns. Pp. 35–55.

Fontaine, C. 1986. "The Bearing of Wisdom on the Shape of 2 Samuel 11–12 and 1 Kings 3." *JSOT* 34:61–77.

Freedman, D. N. 1997. "Dinah and Shechem, Tamar and Amnon." In *Divine Commitment and Human Obligation: Selected Writings of David Noel Freedman.* Ed. J. R. Huddlestun. Winona Lake, Ind.: Eisenbrauns. Pp. 485–95.

Fretheim, T. E. 1983. *Deuteronomic History.* Interpreting Biblical Texts. Nashville: Abingdon. Pp. 108–33.

Garsiel, M. 1976. "David and Bathsheba, I." *DorleDor* 5:24–28.

———. 1976. "David and Bathsheba, II." *DorleDor* 5:85–90.

———. 1976. "David and Bathsheba, III." *DorleDor* 5:134–37.

———. 1993. "The Story of David and Bathsheba: A Different Approach." *CBQ* 55:244–62.

Gordon, R. P. 1994. "In Search of David: Literary Reading and Historical Reconstruction." In *Faith, Tradition, and History: Old Testament Historiography in Its Near Eastern Context*. Ed. A. R. Millard, J. K. Hoffmeier, and D. W. Baker. Winona Lake, Ind. Eisenbrauns. Pp. 285–98.

Gros Louis, Kenneth R. R. 1982. "King David of Israel." In *Literary Interpretations of Biblical Narratives*. Vol 2. Ed. K. Gros Louis and J. Ackerman. Nashville: Abingdon. Pp. 204–19.

Gunn, D. 1988. "In Security: The David of Biblical Narrative." In *Signs and Wonders: Biblical Texts in Literary Focus*. Ed. J. C. Exum. SBL Semeia Studies. Atlanta: Scholars Press. Pp. 133–51.

———. 1997. "Reflections on David." In *A Feminist Companion to Reading the Bible: Approaches, Methods and Strategies*. Ed. A. Brenner and C. Fontaine. Sheffield: Sheffield Academic Press. Pp. 548–66.

Gunn, D., and D. N. Fewell. 1993. *Narrative in the Hebrew Bible*. Oxford: Oxford University Press.

Hagan, H. 1979. "Deception as Motif and Theme in 2 Samuel 9–20; 1 Kings 1–2." *Bib* 60:301–26.

Hoftijzer, J. 1970. "David and the Tekoite Woman." *VT* 20:419–44.

Kermode, F. 1990. *Poetry, Narrative, History*. Oxford: Blackwell. Pp. 28–48.

Kleven, T. 1992. "Hebrew Style in 2 Samuel 6." *JETS* 35:299–314.

———. 1992. "Desire, Rivalry and Collective Violence in the 'Succession Narrative.'" *JSOT* 55:39–59.

Laato, A. 1997a. *A Star Is Rising: The Historical Development of the Old Testament Royal Ideology and the Rise of the Jewish Messianic Expectation*. Atlanta: Scholars Press.

———. 1997b. "Second Samuel 17 and Ancient Near Eastern Royal Ideology." *CBQ* 59:244–69.

Lasine, S. 1984. "Melodramas as Parable: The Story of the Poor Man's Ewe-Lamb and the Unmasking of David's Topsy-Turvy Emotions." *HAR* 8:101–24.

Levenson, J., and B. Halpern. 1980. "The Political Import of David's Marriages." *JBL* 99:507–18.

Linafelt, T. 1992. "Taking Women in Samuel: Readers/Responses/Responsibility." In *Reading between Texts: Intertextuality and the Hebrew Bible*. Ed. D. N. Fewell. Louisville: Westminster/John Knox. Pp. 99–113.

Long, B. 1981. *Images of Man and God: Old Testament Short Stories in Literary Focus*. Sheffield: Almond. Pp. 26–34.

McCarter, P. K., Jr. 1981. "'Plots, True or False': The Succession Narrative as Court Apologetic." *Int* 35:355–67.

McCarthy, D. J. 1965. "II Samuel 7 and the Structure of the Deuteronomistic History." *JBL* 84:131–38.

Mendenhall, G. E. 1973. *The Tenth Generation*. Baltimore: Johns Hopkins University Press.

Miller, P. D. 1994. *They Cried to the Lord: The Form and Theology of Biblical Prayer*. Minneapolis: Fortress.

Newsome, J. N., Jr. 1975. "Toward a New Understanding of the Chronicler and His Purposes." *JBL* 94:201–17.

Nicol, G. G. 1997. "The Alleged Rape of Bathsheba: Some Observations on Ambiguity in Biblical Narrative." *JSOT* 73:43–54.

Niditch, S. 1993. *War in the Hebrew Bible*. Oxford: Oxford University Press.

Perdue, L. G. 1984. "'Is There Anyone Left of the House of Saul . . . ?' Ambiguity and the Characterization of David in the Succession Narrative." *JSOT* 30:67–84.

Peterson, E. 1995. "Why Did Uzzah Die? Why Did David Dance? 2 Samuel 6–7." *Crux* 26, no. 3:3–8.

Polak, F. 1994. "David's Kingship—A Precarious Equilibrium." In *Politics and Theopolitics in the Bible and Post-biblical Literature*. Ed. H. G. Reventlow, Y. Hoffman, and B. Uffenheimer. JSOT Supplement 171. Sheffield: Sheffield Academic Press. Pp. 119–47.

Polzin, R. 1993. "Curses and Kings: A Reading of 2 Samuel 15–16." In *The New Literary Criticism and the Hebrew Bible*. Ed. J. C. Exum and D. J. A. Clines. JSOT Supplement 143. Sheffield: JSOT Press. Pp. 201–26.

Propp, W. H. 1993. "Kinship in 2 Samuel 13." *CBQ* 55:39–53.

Prouser, O. H. 1996. "Suited to the Throne: The Symbolic Use of Clothing in the David and Succession Narrative." *JSOT* 71:27–37.

Pyper, H. S. 1993. "The Enticement to Re-Read Repetition as Parody in 2 Samuel." *BibInt* 1:153–66.

Rad, Gerhard von. 1966. "The Beginnings of Historical Writing in Ancient Israel." In *The Problem of the Hexateuch and Other Essays*. Trans. E. W. T. Dickens. New York: McGraw-Hill. Pp. 116–204.

Reis, P. T. 1997. "Cupidity and Stupidity: Woman's Agency and the 'Rape' of Tamar." *JANES* 25:43–60.

Rosenberg, J. 1986. *King and Kin: Political Allegory in the Hebrew Bible*. Bloomington: Indiana University Press.

———. 1989. "The Institutional Matrix of Treachery in 2 Samuel 11." *Semeia* 46:103–16.

Roth, W. M. W. 1977. "You Are the Man! Structural Interaction in 2 Samuel 10–12." *Semeia* 8:1–13.

Sailhammer, J. 1989. "1 Chronicles 21:1–A Study in Inter-Biblical Interpretation." *TJ* 10:33–48.

Schwartz, R. 1991. "Adultery in the House of David: The Metanarrative of Biblical Scholarship and the Narratives of the Bible." *Semeia* 54:35–55.

———. 1991. "The Histories of David: Biblical Scholarship and Biblical Stories." In *Not in Heaven: Coherence and Complexity in Biblical Narrative*. Ed. J. P. Rosenblatt and J. C. Sitterson Jr. Bloomington: Indiana University Press. Pp. 192–210.

Simon, U. 1967. "The Poor Man's Ewe-Lamb: An Example of a Juridical Parable." *Bib* 48:207–42.

Sternberg, M. 1985. *The Poetics of Biblical Narrative*. Bloomington: Indiana University Press.

Stone, K. 1996. *Sex, Honor, and Power in the Deuteronomistic History*. JSOT Supplement 234. Sheffield: Sheffield Academic Press. Pp. 85–127.

Trible, P. 1984. *Texts of Terror: Literary-Feminist Readings of Biblical Narrative*. Philadelphia: Fortress. Pp. 37–63.

Valler, S. 1994. "King David and 'His' Woman: Biblical Stories and Talmudic Discussions." In *A Feminist Companion to Samuel and Kings*. Ed. A. Brenner. Sheffield: Sheffield Academic Press. Pp. 127–42.

Vanderkam, J. 1980. "Davidic Complicity in the Deaths of Abner and Eshbaal." *JBL* 94:521–39.

Van der Toorn, K., and C. Houtman. 1994. "David and the Ark." *JBL* 113:209–31.

Van Dijk-Hemmes, F. 1989. "Tamar and the Limits of Patriarchy." In *Anti-Covenant: Counter-Reading Women's Lives in the Hebrew Bible*. JSOT Supplement 81; Bible and Literature Series 22. Ed. M. Bal. Sheffield: Almond. Pp. 135–56.

Van Seters, J. 1983. *In Search of History: Historiography in the Ancient World and the Origins of Biblical History*. New Haven: Yale University Press. Pp. 264–91.

Waldman, N. 1986–1987. "Two Biblical Parallels: Irony and Self-Entrapment." *DorleDor* 15:11–18.

Weitzman, S. 1997. *Song and Story in Biblical Narrative: The History of a Literary Convention in Ancient Israel*. Bloomington: Indiana University Press. Pp. 117–21; 133–40.

Wharton, J. A. 1981. "A Plausible Tale: Story and Theology in II Samuel 9–20, I Kings 1–2." *Int* 35:341–54.

White, M. 1994. "Naboth's Vineyard and Jehu's Coup: The Legitimation of a Dynastic Extermination." *VT* 44:66–76.

Whitelam, K. W. 1984. "The Defence of David." *JSOT* 29:61–87.

Wiggins, S. A. 1997. "Between Heaven and Earth: Absalom's Dilemma." *JNSL* 23:73–81.

Willey, P. W. 1992. "The Importunate Woman of Tekoa and How She Got Her Way." In *Reading between Texts: Intertextuality and the Hebrew Bible*. Ed. D. N. Fewell. Louisville: Westminster/John Knox. Pp. 115–31.

Winters, A. 1997. *Subversive Scriptures: Revolutionary Christian Readings of the Bible in Latin America*. Valley Forge, Pa.: Trinity Press International. Pp. 142–54.

Worster, W. S. 1985. "Reader-Response, Redescription and Reference: 'You Are The Man' (2 Sam. 12:7)." In *Text and Reality: Aspects of Reference in Biblical Texts*. Ed. B. C. Lategan and W. S. Vorster. Philadelphia: Atlanta; Fortress: Scholars Press. Pp. 95–112.

Wright, J. W. 1998. "The Founding Father: The Structure of the Chronicler's David Narrative." *JBL* 117:45–59.

Yee, G. "'Fraught with Background': Literary Ambiguity in 2 Samuel 11." *Int* 42:240–53.

1 Kings 1–11

The books of First and Second Kings cover the period of history from the reign of Solomon (970–930 B.C.) to the fall of Jerusalem and the deportation of the Judean exiles to Babylon (587/86 B.C.), that is, about four centuries of biblical history.

This long period can be broken down into three segments or "acts":

Act 1: The reign of Solomon (1 Kings 1–11)

Act 2: The parallel account or "split screen" account (Nelson 1998: 135) of the now divided kingdom, alternating between the story of the northern kingdom of Israel and its twenty kings and the story of the southern kingdom of Judah and its kings, ending with the demise of the northern kingdom of Israel (1 Kings 12–2 Kings 17)

Act 3: The account of the surviving southern kingdom of Judah from the time of Hezekiah toward the end of the eighth century B.C. until the time of Josiah and his sons in the seventh and sixth centuries B.C., ending with the destruction of Jerusalem and the deportation of the exiles to Babylon in 587/86 B.C. (2 Kings 18–25)

This chapter comments on the life and reign of Solomon (1 Kings 1–11). A quick reading of these eleven chapters reveals a Solomon who is an amazingly paradoxical character. Here is somebody capable of both loving God (3:3) and loving many foreign women who do not love his God (11:1), of exercising incredible wisdom (3:16–28) and incredible stupidity, of accumulating a great number of proverbs and wise sayings (3,000 and 1,005 [4:32]), and an impressive number of wives and concubines (700 and 300 [11:3]). Solomon is somebody who can wholeheartedly live by the teaching of one portion of Deuteronomy (e.g., Solomon's words and prayer in 8:12–61 contain fifty-nine instances of phrases and language parallel to Deuteronomy phraseology), but at another time flagrantly go against another portion of Deuteronomy (11:1–4; cf. Deut. 7:1–4).

Perhaps Solomon is the original Dr. Jekyll and Mr. Hyde, long before Robert Louis Stevenson penned his famous novel with those names in the late 1800s—an individual patently marked by a dual personality, one aspect of which is good and the other bad. The question among commentators is at what point one side of Solomon gives way to the other. The majority of commentators believe that the Dr. Jekyll side of Solomon continues either through 1–8 or 1–10, with the Mr. Hyde side of Solomon starting in 9:1 (Parker 1988), or 9:29 (Brettler 1991), or 11:1. For others, Solomon betrays both "Jekyllian" and "Hydeian" traits throughout most of his tenure (Walsh 1995), while at least one writer considers Solomon a lifelong, sinister Mr. Hyde (Eslinger 1989).

Solomon is in many ways like his father, David. Neither sought the kingship (in ch. 1 of First Kings, Solomon is singularly passive, if not for the most part absent, and does not speak until the last two verses [vv. 52, 53]). In both cases, brothers or a brother thought that the younger brother was less qualified than they were. For both, their reign reaches a zenith (2 Samuel 10; 1 Kings 8), only to have it plunge into a darkness (2 Samuel 11–21, 24; 1 Kings 11) for which both father and son are culpable. And neither David's nor Solomon's strongest virtue is his relationship with women. We might also note that both father and son leave their thumbprints on other portions of Israel's canonical literature. David is forever linked with Psalms as Israel's "sweet psalmist" (2 Sam. 23:1), and Solomon is forever linked with Proverbs (and Song of Solomon and Ecclesiastes) as Israel's singing sage.

But one thing is missing from Solomon's tenure to which his father was privileged. David enters his reign-to-be when he is anointed by the prophet Samuel (1 Sam. 16:13). Solomon is the recipient of no such prophetic charisma. Rather, he enters office thanks to a well-orchestrated power play by his mother, Bathsheba, and Nathan, who manipulate the aged David. Nathan argues for Solomon's candidacy but he does not anoint Solomon's head until after he has set David up (1 Kings 1:34, 39). When David does veer from the path, the prophets (Nathan or Gad) are there to rebuke him (2 Sam. 12:1–25; 24:11–25). No prophet ever confronts Solomon for deleterious behavior. Ahijah the prophet speaks about Solomon (1 Kings 11:31–39) but never to Solomon. Thus, unlike his father, Solomon is privy neither to genuine,

God-directed prophetic anointing nor prophetic censure. His is a life filled with profits but devoid of prophets.

Throughout Solomon's forty year reign (11:42), God speaks to Solomon only four times, and never through an intermediary whom the text identifies. First, God speaks to Solomon through a dream at Gibeon (3:4–15), then speaks soberingly to Solomon (note the divine "if" in 6:12) in conjunction with the king's building of the temple (6:11–13). The third divine communication is in 9:1–9, another sobering divine address (note the divine "if" in 9:4, 6), after Solomon has completed the temple and dedicated it to the Lord in prayer. This divine speech is not explicitly called a dream, but that might be inferred from 9:2, "The Lord appeared to Solomon a second time, as he had appeared to him at Gibeon." God's fourth and final address to Solomon (11:9–13) is one in which he announces that Solomon's kingdom will be dismantled after the king's death, all because of Solomon's turning away from Yahweh. Saul hears about being rejected from Samuel (1 Sam. 15:22–26); David takes the frontal blast from Nathan's fulminating invective (2 Samuel 12); but Yahweh himself anathematizes Solomon.

The story of Solomon in First Kings is presented in two unequal halves, chs. 1–8 and 9–11. The first is favorable to Solomon and the second is critical (especially ch. 11). Repetition of similar data in both sections ties the two units together. For example, the story of Solomon begins with prophetic support (Nathan) and ends with prophetic condemnation (Ahijah). Three enemies of Solomon "disappear" at the beginning (Adonijah, Joab, Shimei) and three enemies appear near the ending (Hadad, Rezon, Jeroboam). Near the story's start God appears to Solomon in a dream in which God gives Solomon wisdom and a number of other unsolicited gifts, such as wealth and long life. But in the second unit God's other Gibeon-like appearance to Solomon is replete with warnings and caution. And in both sections Solomon makes a trade treaty with Hiram, king of the Phoenician city of Tyre.

Here is the arrangement of the narrative of Solomon (closely following Parker 1988: 27):

Frame Story (1–2)

1. First Dream (3:1–15)

2. Women and Wisdom (3:16–28)

Favorable to Solomon

3. Administration and Wisdom (4:1–34)

4. The Contract with Hiram of Tyre (5:1–12)

5. Forced Labor (5:13–18)

6. Solomon Honors God in His Building (6–8)

Critical of Solomon

1. Second Dream (9:1–9)

2. The Contract with Hiram of Tyre (9:10–14)

3. Forced Labor (9:15–28)

4. Woman and Wisdom (10:1–13)

5. Wealth and Wisdom (10:14–29)

6. Solomon Dishonors God in His Home (11:1–13)

Frame Story (11:14–43)

1:1–53. The resilient David is no more. Although he is not senile, advancing age has enfeebled him and reduced him to a "shivering torpor" (Long 1981: 85). His attendants search for a female body to keep him warm (apparently, none of his wives are available or adequate for this task). For reasons that are not clear, this woman must be young, a virgin, and very beautiful. This selected woman is Abishag, and her assignment is to keep David warm without any responsibility for conjugal favors. (Interestingly, the verb used here for "keep warm" [*khamam*] is used elsewhere for animals in heat that leads to mating [Gen. 30:38, 39]; 30:41 uses the related verb *yakham*.)

Adonijah believes himself to be the heir apparent to his father, and he has some justification for thinking so. He is, after all, David's oldest surviving son, something Solomon himself freely acknowledges (2:22). Again, he is the next oldest son after Absalom; he is handsome like Absalom (v. 6b). And the verb behind "his father had never displeased [*ʿatsav*] him" in v. 6a is the same as that after David finds out about Absalom's death: The king is grieving [*ʿatsav*] for his son" (2 Sam. 19:2). All in all, Adonijah is Absalom redivivus.

Adonijah is anything but passive, waiting around for a definitive word from father. He seizes the moment, indicated by the narrator's language that Adonijah "exalted himself" or "put himself forward" (v. 5a). While the verb form here (the Hithpael of *nasaʾ*) may occasionally carry a positive nuance (e.g., Balaam's prophetic words about Israel, "they rouse themselves like a lion" [Num. 23:24]), more often the verb in this stem conveys arrogance or presumption (e.g., Korah's malcontents against Moses and Aaron, "Why then do you exalt [set] yourselves above the Lord's assembly?" [Num. 16:3]; or Prov. 30:32, "If you have been foolish, exalting yourself").

He assembles token royal symbols (chariots and heralds [v. 5b]), confers with supporters (v. 7), but excludes those who are not in his camp (v. 8), and throws a huge party (vv. 9, 19, 41). One wonders if his mother, Haggith (v. 5), was in attendance. After all, her name, *khaggit*, has some connection with *khag*, one of the Hebrew words for "feast," especially a pilgrimage feast (Garsiel 1991: 380).

To offset Adonijah's aspiration and to make a case for the legitimacy of Solomon's candidacy, Nathan goes into action. Three moving scenes follow, with each building on the previous one:

Scene One: Nathan before Bathsheba (vv. 11–14)
Scene Two: Bathsheba before David (vv. 15–21)
Scene Three: Nathan before David (vv. 22–27)

In scene one Nathan requests that Bathsheba approach David and "remind" him of the fact that at some earlier point David had sworn by oath that Solomon would succeed him as king (v. 13). Of course, we have no way of knowing whether Nathan having Bathsheba quote David to David is based on fact or fiction. Certainly, no earlier record in 2 Samuel stands of David making that statement like that we find David making about Solomon in 1 Chron. 28:4–6. If David had said it, obviously, it is news to Bathsheba.

Bathsheba does not question Nathan's veracity (cannot the word of a "man of the cloth" be trusted?) or press for further details. What is interesting is how she retells the suggested words of Nathan in what amounts to "an extraordinary example of deceptive quotation" (Savran 1988: 64) and "the most persuasive inventiveness" (Alter 1981: 98).

1. She changes Nathan's "swear" into "swore by the Lord your God," thus making her husband's alleged earlier promise even more binding.
2. She changes Nathan's rhetorical question, "Did you not swear?" into fact, "My lord, you swore."
3. She changes Nathan's question to David, "Why then is Adonijah king?" into a fact, "Adonijah has become king," and adds the words "although you do not know it."
4. On her own, she draws attention to Adonijah's banquet (v. 19).

5. She mentions on the excluded list from Adonijah's festivities only Solomon (cf. v. 19c with v. 8).
6. She adds, hyperbolically, that all Israel is waiting with bated breath for his announcement of a successor (v. 20), and that should Adonijah succeed, her life and Solomon's are in great danger (v. 21).

In scene three Nathan shows up at the propitious time, just as the two of them had planned. He, too, reminds David of what the king had said earlier (v. 24), adds comments about Adonijah's celebration (but how does he know, for he has not been there?), and changes Bath-sheba's "Abiathar . . . and Joab" (v. 19) into "Joab . . . and Abiathar" (v. 25). Placing Joab's name first must be intentional. Given that relations between David and Joab have been far from cordial for some time, Nathan knows that "the name Joab is useful in hinting at great rancour," (Fokkelman 1981: 358). Unlike Bathsheba, Nathan names those not invited to Adonijah's feast apart from Solomon, not accidentally starting with himself ("But he did not invite me" [v. 26a]). What now is David to do? "The effect of this whole process of repeating and adding is to overwhelm David with a crescendo of arguments" (Alter 1981: 100).

And overwhelm him they do. Convinced by their arguments, David designates Solomon as his successor (v. 30), and directs Zadok the priest and Nathan the prophet to anoint Solomon (vv. 32–35, 39).

Two final things of interest emerge in the chapter. First, Adonijah, the loser in all this, requests an oath from Solomon ("Let King Solomon swear to me" [v. 51]) that he will not kill Adonijah. Solomon does not swear an oath to that effect in his response; instead, he offers a "carefully hedged" (Walsh 1995: 482) conditional promise: "If he proves to be a worthy man . . . but if wickedness is found in him . . ." (v. 52). Adonijah is not as successful with Solomon as was Jacob with Esau when it came to persuading another to swear an oath: "'Swear to me first.' So he [Esau] swore to him" (Gen. 25:33). Solomon may swear at Adonijah, but he will not swear to Adonijah.

The second thing of interest is the references to God, especially those references where God is invoked as a justifying agent in all of these she-nanigans. Witness the words of Benaiah in v. 36 ("Amen! May the Lord, the God of my lord and king, so ordain"), or the words of David's servants in v. 47 ("May God make the name of Solomon more famous than yours"), or the words of David himself in v. 48 ("Blessed be the Lord, the God of Israel, who today has granted one of my offspring to sit on my throne"). This would not be the first time that people have orchestrated events and then attributed it all to God. As Nicol (1993: 140) has stated, "The dissonance between narrative events and such pious speeches must not be lost in interpretation."

2:1–46. David's last recorded words before he dies (v. 10) are those he addresses to Solomon in vv. 2–9. As a valedictory they may be compared with Jacob's last speech to his sons (Gen. 49:1–27), Moses' last speech to his people (Deut. 33:2–29), and Joshua's final address to his people (Josh. 24:2–15). For language and thematic correspondences, one might find a better parallel with God's first address to Joshua (Josh. 1:2–9). Both God in speaking to Joshua and David in speaking to Solomon tie spiritual faithfulness to military success as cause to effect.

Everything David urges on Solomon in vv. 1–4 is salutary—a summons to courage, faithfulness and obedience to God's ways. The reader should be particularly impressed with David's stating the matter of future success for Solomon and his heirs conditionally in v. 4b ("If your heirs take heed to their way"). What makes this interesting is that David quotes an earlier word of God to him to prove the conditional nature of God's dynastic promise, and yet David's citation is based on 2 Sam. 7:12–16, where the dynastic promise is clearly unconditional and forever!

It is the second part (vv. 5–9) of David's address that presents problems. In what Fokkelman (1981: 386) calls "the vulgar settling of two accounts," David directs Solomon to kill two of his old nemeses, Joab (vv. 5–6) and Shimei (vv. 8–9). Both executions, if carried out, suggests David, would only underscore Solomon's wisdom (vv. 6, 9). This will not, however, be a God-given, God-glorifying wisdom, but an expedient, unscrupulous wisdom, a wisdom tainted by blood. Then again, maybe in suggesting that Solomon commence his reign with two executions, David may be recalling that his own reign began with two executions he carried out, the Amalekite slayer of Saul (2 Sam. 1:13–16) and the killers of Ishbosheth (2 Sam. 4:9–12). In both cases the reason for execution was justice, not revenge (Koopmans 1991: 447). Interestingly, Solomon does not question his father's proposal.

Through the rest of the chapter Solomon proceeds to "clean house," eliminating all possible rivals to his reign:

1. Adonijah (vv. 13–25)
2. Abiathar the priest (vv. 26–27)
3. Joab (vv. 28–34)
4. Shimei (vv. 36–46)

In each case involving death the executioner is Benaiah (vv. 25, 34, 46). He is never heard from again except in the brief list of Solomon's high officials in 4:2–6 (v. 4). His one claim to fame? He is Solomon's hatchet man. Although the commander of Solomon's army, he kills and then he disappears.

One wonders if all these killings were necessary in light of the fact that before the first drop of blood was shed, Solomon's kingdom was already "firmly established" (v. 12). In what sense, after the killings, can the text repeat this with "So the kingdom was *established* in [by?] the hand of Solomon" (v. 46c)? Does the first give the credit to God and to David but the second to Solomon?

In the case of Adonijah, he simply asks Solomon, via Bathsheba, to marry Abishag (v. 17). This is no big deal for Bathsheba, for Adonijah's "I have one request to make of you" (v. 16) becomes in her talk with Solomon "I have one *small* request to make of you" (v. 20). Solomon goes ballistic. He interprets Adonijah's request (rightly? wrongly?) as a last-ditch attempt by his half-brother (by taking over a handmaiden of the previous king) to legitimize his claim to David's throne. Thus, Solomon scores at two points. First, he now has a convenient and legitimate reason to dispose of Adonijah permanently. And second, he implies that Adonijah has deceived Bathsheba, and only Solomon's wisdom and discernment have saved the day (Ishida 1987: 179).

Abiathar, a pro-Adonijah supporter and a priest, Solomon banishes to Anathoth, even though Solomon says he ought to die (v. 26). But why should Abiathar deserve death? Just for throwing his support behind Adonijah? Is not Solomon's response overkill? Abiathar escapes a death sentence only because of his earlier loyalty to David. In fact there is a play on the name Anathoth in Solomon's words: "go to Anathoth [*'anatot*]. . . . But I will not at this time put you to death . . . because you shared in all the hardships [*hit'annita*] my father endured [*hit'annah*]." In such a pun Anathoth becomes "Hardshipville" (see Garsiel 1991: 385).

It is interesting that the narrator, not Solomon, states that the banishment of Abiathar actually fulfills an earlier divine word of indictment against the house of Eli (v. 27b; cf. 1 Sam. 2:27–36). In ways that Solomon may think he is acting as an instrument of God, he is not. In ways that he has no idea he is acting as an instrument of God, he is.

Joab is the third on this list of individuals who are persona non grata. He does not flee the country. He flees to Yahweh's tent and grasps the horns of the altar. The sanctity of the altar is evidenced by the asylum it provided to anyone who seized its horns. But such asylum was not extended to murderers, according to Exod. 21:14: "But if someone willfully attacks and kills another by treachery, you shall take the killer from my altar for execution." Hence, the altar provides no safety for Joab, but even here, Solomon instructed Benaiah to ask Joab to come out of the tent. Upon Joab's refusal to exit, a hallowed place becomes a horrendous place. There is blood on the altar, but it is not blood for atonement or purification. Solomon recalls David's words that Joab killed Abner and Amasa (David: v. 5; Solomon: v. 32), but curiously, neither mentions Joab killing Absalom.

Shimei, the Benjaminite who earlier had cursed David (2 Sam. 16:5–14, cf. 2 Sam. 19:16–23), is the fourth individual to feel the brunt of Solomon's purge (vv. 36–46). Placing Shimei under house arrest in Jerusalem (v. 36) effectively severs Shimei from any possible collusion with Benjaminite colleagues. Three years later Shimei goes in search of two of his servants to the Philistine city of Gath. Upon his return to the city he is put to death for disobeying Solomon's orders. But there are two problems with Solomon's treatment of Shimei. First, he asks Shimei two questions (vv. 42, 43), but gives Shimei no chance to respond. Second, he says to Shimei, "Did I not make you swear by the Lord?" But where did Solomon have Shimei take an oath? Is Solomon not inventing this bit of information after a hiatus of three years?

3:1–28. Three things do not bode well for Solomon in the opening verses of this chapter. The first of these is his marriage to the daughter of the neighboring Egyptian pharaoh (possibly the daughter of Psuennes II, the last pharaoh of the Twenty-first Dynasty). This is the first of six references in the biblical text to Solomon's marriage to this Egyptian princess (3:1; 7:8; 9:16; 9:24; 11:1; 2 Chron. 8:11). There is no condemnation of Solomon's actions in any of the First Kings texts until the fifth one, 11:1, a verse (along with 11:2) that draws its phraseology from the prohibitions of intermarriage with the Canaanites in Deut. 7:1–14 and Josh. 23:12, and the list of foreign nations excluded from the assembly in Deut. 23:3–8.

But one wonders if his marriage to pharaoh's daughter, recorded as early as 3:1, does not function "to establish that the cause of Solomon's eventual fall is already there when he is in his glory" (Jobling 1991: 63). Later texts condemn Solomon for his behavior in 3:1 and 11:1–2: "Did not King Solomon of Israel sin on account of such women?" (Neh. 13:26); "But you [Solomon] brought in women to lie at your side" (Sir. 47:19).

The second dark cloud on the horizon in these opening verses is the second half of v. 1, stating that Solomon brought his new bride to Jerusalem until he had finished building: (1) his own house; (2) the house of the Lord; (3) the wall around Jerusalem. Note the order here: first, something for himself; second, something for God; third, something for his people.

The third bad omen in these opening verses is the notation in v. 3 that "Solomon loved the Lord . . . only [*raq*]; he sacrificed and offered incense at the high places." The "only" is suspiciously similar to the "only/except" (*raq*) in 1 Kings 15:5, "David did what was right in the sight of the Lord . . . except [*raq*] in the matter of Uriah the Hittite."

The Hebrew word for "high place" (*bamah*) means literally "back, shoulder" (Deut. 33:29 NRSV: "you shall tread on their backs"; but NIV: "you will trample down their high places"), and is an illustration of an anatomical term transferred to an architectural/topographical context; hence, a "high place" refers to an open-air cultic installation on a high elevation such as a mountain top. The word occurs only twice in the Torah as an object of divine displeasure (Lev. 26:30; Num. 33:52), with the second of these suggesting that the *bamah* was a feature of the worship system of the Canaanites. Samuel "went up" to the *bamah* at Ramah (1 Sam. 9:13–14, 19), apparently a legitimate move, and later "came down" from there (1 Sam. 9:25; as did the band of prophets Saul met [1 Sam. 10:5]). For later kings, however, not to remove the high places was a grievous offense (1 Kings 15:14; 22:43; 2 Kings 12:3; 14:4; 15:4, 35).

One may observe the uneasiness of the scriptural tradition with Solomon's association with the high place at Gibeon by comparing 1 Kings 3:4 with its parallel in 2 Chron. 1:3:

1 Kings 3:4: "The king went [*wayyelek*, sg.] to Gibeon to sacrifice there, for [*ki*] that was the principal high place [*bamah*]."

2 Chron. 1:3: "Then Solomon, and the whole assembly with him, went [*wayyeleku*, pl.] to the high place that was at Gibeon; for [*ki*] God's tent of meeting, which Moses the servant of the Lord had made in the wilderness, was there."

Thus, according to Chronicles, not just Solomon, but the whole congregation participated in the worship at Gibeon's *bamah*, and the "for" (*ki*) clause in Chronicles attempts to sanctify Gibeon by appealing to hallowed memory ("which Moses the servant of the Lord had made in the wilderness"), which 1 Kings 3:3–4 does not.

In his dream at Gibeon, God offers Solomon a blank check, "Ask what I should give you" (v. 5b), he being the only person in the Bible to whom God makes that kind of an offer. As is well known, Solomon requests "an understanding mind to govern your people, able to discern between good and evil" (v. 9, cf. v. 11b). And in response God does give him a "wise and discerning mind" (v. 12). This is the first of several references to Solomon's God-given wisdom (cf. 3:28; 4:29–34; 5:7, 12;

10:4, 7, 8, 23–24). Never after this is wisdom associated with any Israelite king, nor is wisdom even mentioned anywhere in Kings after the Solomon unit (Lasine 1992: 87).

But in an otherwise beautiful section there are some phrases that call for comment. First, Solomon's modest "I am only a little child; I do not know how to go out or come in" (v. 7), coming directly after he has just wiped out four potential foes (2:13–46), leads one writer to refer to Solomon's "oily efforts at humility" (Eslinger 1989: 134). Second, God commends Solomon for not asking "for the life of your enemies" (v. 11), but that may be because they are all dead!

Third, why does God give Solomon things he did not ask for: riches and honor (v. 13) and longevity (v. 14)? Are these unsolicited "bonuses"? At least one of these items—riches—will play a role in Solomon's spiritual collapse. Is not God's giving Solomon riches analagous to Jesus making Judas the treasurer of their band, knowing all the while his covetous, greedy heart? Long before Jesus taught his followers the Paternoster (Matt. 6:9–13), would it not have been appropriate for Solomon to pray that most enigmatic line of the prayer, "And lead us not into temptation" (Matt. 6:13a, NIV)? This petition is interpreted by Richard Foster (*Prayer: Finding the Heart's True Home* [San Francisco: 1992]: 189) as "Lord, may there be nothing in me that will force you to put you to the test in order to reveal what is in my heart." But apparently, sometimes he must.

Unexpectedly, a circumstance arises that provides Solomon an opportunity to put into practice his recently obtained wisdom (vv. 16–28). Two women, both prostitutes, gave birth in their brothel. One baby dies; one baby is still alive. Both mothers come before Solomon (so even harlots can approach the king), each claiming to be the mother of the living child. Solomon's task is to identify the real mother.

This episode is parallel to others in the Old Testament where contending parties each claim what they are doing is right and what the other party is doing is wrong. In several instances the individuals work out a mutually acceptable resolution without recourse to a third party (Abimelech and Isaac [Gen. 26:26–31]; Laban and Jacob [Gen. 31:43–54]). Sometimes a mediating third party makes the decision with respect to the case in hand. In addition to this story in 1 Kings 3, one recalls the role of Abram in settling the dispute over pasture land between two groups of shepherds (Gen. 13:7–12). The parallel today would be a case tried without a jury before a single magistrate.

The first claimant (the plaintiff) has an extraordinary knowledge of how the second mother got her hands on the first mother's baby, given that she was sound asleep when the alleged act of thievery took place

(vv. 19–20)! If her facts are correct, her wisdom rivals that of Solomon, if in fact it does not surpass his (Beuken 1989). The second claimant (the defendant) is as brief in her statement (v. 22a; six words in the Hebrew) as the first claimant is prolix. And her brief words are directed to the first woman, not to Solomon (she says, "The dead son is yours," not, "The dead son is hers"). When Solomon repeats the harlots' contradictory speeches, he significantly reduces the length of the plaintiff's claim to five words (in the Hebrew) (v. 23a).

Actually, both women are opening themselves to serious charges if it can be verified that one or the other is not a truthteller. In the case of the defendant, if she is lying, then she is guilty of kidnapping. The eighth commandment, "You shall not steal," more than likely includes kidnapping as one form of theft. Furthermore, Deut. 24:7 states, "If someone is caught kidnapping another Israelite, enslaving or selling the Israelite, then the kidnapper shall die."

But what of the plaintiff if she is lying? Then she is guilty of bringing false charges and being a false witness. Deuteronomy 19:16–19 states, "If a malicious witness comes forward to accuse someone of wrongdoing . . . If the witness is a false witness . . . then you shall do to the false witness just as the false witness had meant to do to the other." No wonder Solomon calls for a sword (Sternberg [1987: 169] calls this "shock tactics"). Is it meant for the baby, or for the pseudomother guilty of a capital offence? "For either woman now, what is at stake is not just possession of the child but retention of her head!" (Brichto 1992: 54).

That the plaintiff is willing to give up her child ("Please, my lord, give her the living baby" [v. 26]), and thus risk the chance of being labeled a false witness with its attending legal consequences, clues Solomon that she is indeed the real mother. By contrast, because the defendant would rather have the child killed ("Divide it" [end of v. 26]; a plural imperative, spoken not to Solomon but to his enforcers) than admit to kidnapping, Solomon intuits that the defendant's desire is not to have a baby to hold to her breast but to have her rival's baby suffer the same fate as her own dead child.

To be sure, this story illustrates "how a human being with 'godlike' wisdom about human nature might be able to overcome human cognitive limitations, using the true witness of strong emotions to get past false testimony and deceptive appearances" (Lasine 1989: 61). But it is not just Solomon's wisdom; it is the feelings and kenotic behavior of the true mother that makes resolution possible, a mother who is willing to hear her baby say, "My mother, my mother, why hast thou forsaken me?" In the end, however, only Solomon is praised ("All Israel . . .

stood in awe of the king" [v. 28]), not the mother (van Wolde 1995: 641).

4:1–34. The first nineteen verses provide the names of leaders whom Solomon appointed to their posts as he reorganizes the administrative flowchart of his kingdom. There are eleven high officials (vv. 2–6) and twelve provincial officials (vv. 7–19). It is unlikely that these twenty-three individuals held their positions for all four decades of Solomon's rule (Ash 1995: 73).

The listing of the twelve new administrative districts with the name of each district governor is especially interesting:

	District	District Governor
I.	Ephraim	Ben-hur
II.	Makaz	Ben-deker
III.	Arubboth	Ben-hesed
IV.	Naphath-dor	Ben-abinadab
V.	Taanach, Megiddo, Beth-shean, and Abel-meholah	Baana ben-Ahilud
VI.	Ramoth-gilead and Argob	Ben-geber
VII.	Mahanaim	Ahinadab ben-Iddo
VIII.	Naphtali	Ahimaaz
IX.	Asher and Bealoth	Baana ben-Hushai
X.	Issachar	Jehoshaphat ben-Paruah
XI.	Benjamin	Shimei ben-Ela
XII.	Gilead/Gad	Geber ben-Uri

First, the clear purpose of this reorganization is to charge each new district with the responsibility of maintaining the royal household and the cost of government for one month of the year (v. 7). Curiously, Judah is not one of the twelve; there is the brief note at the end of v. 19, "And there was one official in the land of Judah," but his name is not provided. The conclusion we may draw is that the financial burden for running government fell upon the northern tribes.

Second, with just a few exceptions, these new administrative districts do not correspond geographically to the traditional inheritance of the tribes. Only Naphtali (VIII), Issachar (X), and Benjamin (XI) remain as they existed from the days of Joshua. Solomon's actions would be comparable to an American president realigning the borders of the fifty states and then giving these new territories city names rather than state names (as Solomon does for the most part here). Such realignment casts off tradition and ends time-honored loyalties.

Third, we note the patently pro-Judahite character of most of the district appointees, even though they preside over northern, Israelite territories (Halpern 1974: 529–30). To begin with, two of the governors are sons-in-law of Solomon: Ben-abinadab (IV [v. 11]) and Ahimaaz (VIII [v. 15]). The governor of District IX, Baana ben-Hushai, is likely the son of Hushai, David's counselor (2 Sam. 15:32–37). The governor of District VIII, Ahimaaz, might be the son of the priest Zadok who had a role during the rebellion of Absalom (2 Sam. 15:36). Baana ben-Ahilud, governor of District V, appears to be the brother of Jehoshaphat ben-Ahilud, Solomon's court recorder (v. 3). Ahinadab ben-Iddo, governor of District VII, likely is the son of Iddo who ruled over the half-tribe of Manasseh in David's day (1 Chron. 27:21). And finally, could the father of the governor of District IV, Ben-abinadab, be the Abinadab in whose house the ark was placed before David brought it to Jerusalem (2 Sam. 6:3)? It appears that in Solomon's new administrative system power is passing from the tribal elders to the regional governors, all of whom are appointed by the royal regime in Jerusalem.

Finally, we note that many of the names of Solomon's high officials who are stationed in Jerusalem are names with either a "Yah(weh)" or "El(ohim)" element in them (Azar*iah*, *Eli*horeph, Ahi*jah*, *Jeho*shaphat, Bena*iah*, *Jeho*iada, another Azar*iah*). Only one of his provincial governors has such a theophoric name (*Jeho*shapat ben-Paruah).

Whereas Solomon's name occurs but twice in the first half of the chapter (vv. 1, 7), his name occurs ten times in the second half of the chapter (vv. 20–34). While the first nineteen verses might suggest to the reader that Solomon is a parasitic, self-aggrandizing, tradition-bashing megalomaniac, the next fifteen verses suggest nothing of the sort. We must be careful in interpreting and evaluating this data so as not to "confuse historical deduction with historiographic intention" (Glatt-Gilad 1997: 701). Twice the text affirms the spirit of contentedness that prevailed throughout all his empire: (1) "Judah and Israel . . . ate and drank and were happy" (v. 20); (2) "During Solomon's lifetime Judah and Israel lived in safety, from Dan even to Beer-sheba, all of them under their vines and fig trees" (v. 25). Neighboring nations gave him tribute (v. 21b). His provincial officials gave him monthly provisions from their respective sectors (vv. 22–23, 27–28). And God continued to give him wisdom (vv. 29–34). His empire stretched from the Euphrates River to the borders of Egypt (vv. 21–24).

The extent of Solomon's empire thus fulfills God's original promise to Abram: "To your descendants I give this land, from the river of Egypt to the great river, the river Euphrates" (Gen. 15:18). Both Abraham's offspring and Solomon's wisdom are as vast as the sand on the seashore (Gen. 22:17; 1 Kings 4:29).

5:1–17. Solomon is able to establish the necessary groundwork for his vast building programs first by maintaining political alliances with neighboring kings, especially Hiram of Tyre (vv. 1–12), and second by conscripting forced laborers from his own people (vv. 13–18).

First, Solomon obtains a foreign wife (3:1). Now he obtains a foreign trading partner, and an import/export relationship is launched. Solomon will receive cedars and other evergreens from Lebanon that Hiram's men will cut down, tie into rafts, float down to Joppa, break up, and haul overland to Jerusalem (vv. 6, 8–10). In return, Solomon will send Hiram massive amounts of wheat and olive oil (v. 11). Twenty thousand cors of wheat and of oil may equal 125,000 bushels of the former and over a million gallons of the latter. It seems that Hiram is getting the better of the deal, for while Hiram receives staples (wheat and olive oil), Solomon receives luxuries (very expensive wood for ornate buildings). If this is true, one wonders if Hiram's praise of Solomon in v. 7 ("Blessed be the Lord today, who has given to David a wise son") is, in fact, tongue-in-cheek (Jobling 1991: 66).

Note also Solomon's justification for launching his building operations. Solomon says that David could not build a temple because the Lord had not given him rest. Because of constant warfare it had been necessary for David to have the ark moved from battle to battle. But now God has given Solomon rest (vv. 3–4; see 2 Samuel 7). Note his words toward the end of v. 4 (Heb. v. 18): "there is neither adversary [*satan*] nor misfortune [*pega⁽ ra⁾*]," literally, "a bad/evil stroke."

To begin with the second of these (*pega⁽ ra⁾*), we know that the verb from which the noun *pega⁽* is formed, *paga⁽*, appears frequently in ch. 2 to refer to all of his enemies Solomon had "struck down" (vv. 25, 29, 31, 34, 46). So of course there is no *pega⁽* in ch. 5 because Solomon has "paga⁽ed" the opposition in ch. 2. And regarding the first of these two words (*satan*), how shall we reconcile Solomon's claim here that there is no adversary (*satan*) with 11:25, "He [Rezon] was an adversary [*satan*] of Israel all the days of Solomon, making trouble as Hadad did"?

Solomon's forced laborers come, we are told, "out of all Israel" (v. 13), here meaning Israel to the exclusion of Judah. Those conscripted for such work would spend one month working for the king, followed by two months of respite at home (v. 14). Such servants would do things like operate the mines, assist as laborers in the construction projects, and care for Solomon's chariotry and cavalry. If there is a mitigating factor in Solomon's establishing of the corvée, it is that the conscriptees work a system of one month on, two months off. It is hard to imagine the pharaoh of the oppression/exodus extending a two-month vacation as the Hebrews toiled at Pithom and Rameses (Exod. 1:11). Unlike the pharaoh's laborers, Solomon's laborers do not "cry out" to Yahweh for relief from the oppressive weight under which they labor by decree of the sovereign. It appears that for Solomon's laborers, the king's yoke is easy and his burden is light.

6:1–7:51. Most of the data in these two chapters, with the exception of 7:1–12, focuses on Solomon building the temple and furnishing it. The details are as follows:

6:1–10: the exterior of the temple
6:11–13: a challenging word from Yahweh to Solomon
6:14–38: the interior of the temple
7:13–51: the temple's furnishings

First Kings does not provide a reason why Solomon built the temple or why he built it the way he did. David, in his last words to Solomon (2:2–9), does not specifically mention erecting a temple. But according to Chronicles, David provides Solomon with the plans for the temple, plans David received from God (1 Chron. 28:11–19). David uses the same Hebrew word for divinely revealed architectural plans (*tavnit* [1 Chron. 28:19]) vis-à-vis the temple that God used with Moses in revealing the tabernacle's blueprint (Exod. 25:9). So both Moses and Solomon operate with a plan/*tavnit* whose source is God. And both Moses and Solomon "finish" (*kalah*) their respective project (Exod. 40:33; no fewer than three times does the text say Solomon completed the temple: 6:9, 14, 38). Hence, ch. 6 is ringed with Solomon "began to build" (6:1) and "the house was finished" (6:38). Of Solomon nobody will be able to say, "This fellow began to build but was not able to finish" (Luke 14:30).

And to make Solomon's connections with Moses even more obvious, the text states (6:1) that Solomon began building the temple in the fourth year of his reign, which was 480 years after Moses led the Israelites out of Egypt. Through Moses, God is doing a great work; through Solomon, God is doing a great work. Moses' liberating work makes possible Israel's worship of God geographically; Solomon's building work makes possible Israel's worship of God architecturally. Through

Moses, God gives Israel a home; through Solomon God obtains a home. God the home-giver, now becomes God the home-receiver.

There is one more connection with Moses, and that is the linking of 1 Kings 6:7 with Exod. 20:25 and Deut. 27:5–6. The latter two Mosaic portions stress that outdoor altars must be constructed of natural blocks of undressed, unhewn stone upon which no iron has been used. By mentioning in 1 Kings 6:7 that the temple was built with blocks of hewn stone that were cut to size at a quarry some distance away, thus causing no sound of iron in the temple area itself, the author draws an analogy between earlier open-air altars of Moses' day and the temple of Solomon's day. In neither place may any iron tool be used in sacred precincts. In the case of the temple, however, such stones are permissible if they have been hewn elsewhere. So here is an instance where an earlier "Pentateuchal law has been imbedded in a historical source; and its ancient prescriptions have been deliberately reworked and analogically extended to accommodate a new circumstance" (Fishbane 1985: 159).

The plan of Solomon's temple consists of three rooms joined together by doorways, all oriented toward sunrise in the east. These three areas (in an east-to-west direction) are

1. the *'ulam:* "vestibule" (NRSV); "portico" (NIV)
2. the *hekal:* "nave" (NRSV); "main hall" (NIV)
3. the *devir:* "inner sanctuary" (NRSV and NIV)

The Hebrew word *'ulam* can be connected with the Akkadian word *ellamu,* which means "front" (hence, "vestibule, portico"). The Hebrew word *hekal* likewise derives from the Akkadian *ekallu,* and ultimately from the Sumerian *é.gal,* "great house." There is some uncertainty about the origin of *devir.* Possibly it means "oracle," and connects with the verb *davar,* "speak" (Ouellette 1970), or it may mean "back room" (de Vaux 1965: 313).

Two other features distinguish Solomon's temple. One is the two freestanding pillars of bronze in front of the temple's entrance (7:15–22), one called "Jachin" ("it/he shall stand" or "may he establish") and "Boaz" ("in strength"?). The other unique feature is the *yatsi'a* ("structure," 6:10), a series of rooms, chambers, or balconies that surrounded the temple on all sides except the front, with an entrance to this side structure on the south side (6:8). The temple vessels, utensils, and assorted treasures were stored in these adjacent rooms.

There are some obvious differences between the interior structure of the first temple and that of the tabernacle. For example, the temple had no veil, but rather, doors that separated the main hall from the inner sanctuary (6:31–32). Again, in the tabernacle the cherubim rest on the ark, but in the temple they stand apart from the ark (6:27). Unlike the tabernacle, which housed but one laver (Exod. 30:17–21; Lev. 8:11), Solomon's temple court contained ten lavers (7:38–39) that rested on ten wheeled bronze stands (7:27–37), five on the right side of the main hall and five on the left side. Then there is the reference to a large "molten sea" (7:23–26) in the temple court, which is an enormous cast metal bowl or tank supported on twelve oxen that faced in all four directions in groups of three. It may have been shaped either as a hemisphere (1 Kings 7:26 says that the tank held two thousand *baths* [a liquid measure]) or as a cylinder (2 Chron. 4:5 says that the tank held three thousand *baths*). (While we cannot be certain, one *bath* may equal about five U.S. gallons.)

In the midst of all this building, the word of the Lord comes to Solomon (6:11–13). It is not a commending word, but rather a word of warning that obedience and not temple building is what guarantees the presence of God among his people. Disobedience, on the other hand, forces his departure. This is God's second "if" statement to Solomon (and one stronger than the first) and the fourth of five "ifs" Solomon will hear, the first from David (quoting God), and then four from God:

1. "If your heirs will take heed to their way [God's ways and commandments], to walk before me in faithfulness" (2:4)
2. "If you will walk in my ways, keeping my statutes" (3:14)
3. "If you will walk in my statutes, obey my ordinances" (6:12)
4. "If you walk before me" (9:4)
5. "If you turn aside from following me" (9:6)

So a good bit of Solomon's future, and that of his people, lies within the king's own control. Neither blessing nor judgment is divinely determined apart from human behavior. While the divine promise to David a generation earlier to bless and establish "forever" the king's house (2 Sam. 7:13, 16, 24, 25, 26, 29) has not been erased or canceled; it has been muted during Solomon's reign.

8:1–66. The major portion of this chapter (vv. 22–53) is Solomon's extensive prayer of dedication of the temple. But other matters serve as prelude and postlude to the prayer. We have, then, a chapter composed of the following units:

1. the depositing of the ark in its proper place in the temple (vv. 1–13)

2. Solomon's first blessing of his people (vv. 14–21)
3. the prayer of dedication (vv. 22–53)
4. Solomon's second blessing of his people (vv. 54–61)
5. concluding sacrifices and a festival (vv. 62–66)

The first of these five sections describes the completion of what David originally set into motion. The ark has moved from private house to tent, and now to temple ("its final resting place"). It is probable that we should see some parallel between the dedication of Solomon's temple and the dedication of the tabernacle and its priesthood (esp. Leviticus 8). They exhibit the following parallels:

1. Both accounts use the verb *qahal* ("assemble"), first in the Hiphil, then in the Niphal:
   —"assemble the whole congregation" (*qahal* in the Hiphil [Lev. 8:3])
   —"when the congregation was assembled" (*qahal* in the Niphal [Lev. 8:4])
   —"then Solomon assembled the elders" (*qahal* in the Hiphil [1 Kings 8:1])
   —"all the people of Israel assembled" (*qahal* in the Niphal [1 Kings 8:2])
2. Both Moses and Solomon bless the people after the dedication (Lev. 9:23; 1 Kings 8:55).
3. In both cases it is impossible to enter the sanctuary after the divine presence so effusively fills it (Exod. 40:35; 1 Kings 8:11).
4. The dedication is followed by a divine revelation that is either visual (Lev. 9:23b–24) or auditory (1 Kings 9:2–9).

In vv. 14–21 Solomon begins his royal blessing by talking about God (vv. 15–16), and even quoting God (v. 16). He makes a passing reference to David (v. 17), but then quotes God a second time (vv. 18–19) in such a way that clearly draws attention to Solomon and makes him the fulfillment of a biblical prophecy. Solomon ends his benediction with four first person verbs: "I have risen . . . I sit . . . I have built . . . I have provided" (vv. 20–21).

The bulk of this chapter is, as we have said, Solomon's prayer (vv. 22–53). Commentators vary remarkably in their evaluation of the king's prayer of dedication. For example, Clements (1985: 105) calls it "one of the most searchingly reflective prayers in the whole Bible," but Eslinger (1989) labels the prayer "charlatanic" (153), "ingratiating piety" (168), and "the tendentious rhetorical peregrinations of a desperate king seeking to outfox his divine overlord" (179).

Following the outline of Miller (1994: 347–50), we divide the prayer into the following units:

Introduction: v. 22, "Then Solomon stood"
Address: v. 23a, "O Lord, God of Israel"
Praise: vv. 23b–24, "there is no God like you"
Petition: vv. 25–26, "O Lord . . . keep for your servant"
Series of Circumstance and Petition
General Circumstance: v. 27, "But will God indeed dwell?"
General Petition: vv. 28–30, "Regard your servant's prayer"
First Particular Circumstance: v. 31, "If someone sins against a neighbor"
First Particular Petition: v. 32, "then hear in heaven"
Second Particular Circumstance: v. 33, "When your people . . . are defeated before an enemy"
Second Particular Petition: v. 34, "then hear in heaven"
Third Particular Circumstance: v. 35, "When heaven is shut up"
Third Particular Petition: v. 36, "then hear in heaven"
Fourth Particular Circumstance: vv. 37–38, "If there is famine in the land"
Fourth Particular Petition: v. 39, "then hear in heaven"
Motivation for Fourth Petition: v. 40, "so that they may fear you"
Fifth Particular Circumstance: vv. 41–42, "When a foreigner . . . comes from a distant land"
Fifth Particular Petition: v. 43a, "then hear in heaven"
Motivation for Fifth Petition: v. 43b, "so that they may know"
Sixth Particular Circumstance: v. 44, "If your people go out to battle"
Sixth Particular Petition: v. 45, "then hear in heaven"
Seventh Particular Circumstance: vv. 46–48, "If they sin against you"
Seventh Particular Petition: vv. 49–50, "then hear in heaven"
Motivation for Seventh Petition: v. 51, "for they are your people"
Final General Petition and Circumstance: v. 52, "Let your eyes be open"
Motivation for Final Petition: v. 53, "for you have separated them"

Several things stand out in this prayer. First is that Solomon delivers it from a standing position, spreading his hands heavenward (v. 22). For other instances of prayer in which hands were held palms up, possibly raised in a gesture of devotion and presentation, see Exod. 9:29 (Moses); Ezra 9:5 (Ezra); Ps. 63:4; 88:9; 141:2.

Second is Solomon's use of repeated phrases. The most common is "hear in heaven": "hear in heaven and forgive" (vv. 30, 34, 36, 39, 49–50), "hear in heaven and act" (v. 32), "hear in heaven and do" (v. 43). Throughout this prayer, beginning with v. 27, Solomon repudiates the idea that the temple is God's only dwelling place. Never does Solomon ask God to hear from the *devir*, the inner shrine, but always "from heaven." This is especially important, given that the temple, like the tabernacle before it, functions as a divine residence (Exod. 25:8; 1 Kings 6:13). The notion of divine immanence (expressed by the verb *shakan*) cannot overwhelm the notion of divine transcendence, anymore than the reverse can happen. Yahweh's inaccessibility to human eyes guarantees his transcendence, but his everlasting residence ("a place for you to dwell in forever" [8:13b]) on this rock of Zion guarantees his proximity (Terrien 1978: 196), thus creating the oxymoronic concept of an out-of-sight Immanuel.

The third feature of the prayer is that, notwithstanding Solomon's repeated call upon God to "forgive" where forgiveness is needed (vv. 30, 34, 36, 39, 50), he does not ask for an automatic, routine, cheap-grace forgiveness. Without exception, Solomon's appeal for forgiveness is predicated upon the individual or individuals seeking God in prayer (vv. 30, 38), or confessing (vv. 33, 35), or turning from their sin (v. 35), or repenting (vv. 47–48). Not only is the high priest authorized to confess his people's sins (Lev. 16:21), but also penitents could recite their own confessions. There is room in biblical faith for both personal confession and confession by a surrogate, as there is room for a God who is both transcendent and immanent. It becomes clear from this emphasis that in his prayer, Solomon subordinates the role of sacrifice to that of prayer as the temple's primary function (Balentine 1993: 85). To use Savran's felicitous phrase, Solomon's prayer is actually a "prayer about prayer" (1987: 157).

Fourthly, of Solomon's seven specific circumstances and petitions (see outline above), the first four (vv. 31–40) deal with events inside of Israel, while the last three (vv. 41–50) deal with events outside of Israel (Brettler 1993: 32). In regard to the first four, one may do business with God right in the temple area ("and swears before your altar in this house" [v. 31]; "and plead with you in this house" [v. 33]) or just in the direction of the temple area ("and then they pray toward this place" [v. 35]; "so that they stretch out their hands toward this house" [v. 38]).

The last three specific situations focus on (1) a "foreigner" who comes from afar to pray toward the temple (vv. 41–43); (2) Israel engaging enemies in battle far from home (vv. 44–45); and (3) the case of Israelite exiles dispersed to a foreign land (vv. 46–51). It is clear that (2) supplements the request in vv. 33–34. The difference is that vv. 33–34 deal with engaging the enemy in battle on the home front, and being battered in the process, while vv. 44–45 deal with Israel fighting far from home. And (3), which speaks of the exiles turning back to God while even in exile, sounds very much like what Moses said in Deut. 4:29.

It should not be unexpected that Solomon would include the note about the foreigner coming to Jerusalem (vv. 41–43). It is not simply that the temple is "intended as much to impress foreigners as to serve a domestic function" (Younger 1990: 169). Solomon also wants to attract people from far and wide who are in need of help that they have not succeeded in finding near home. As such, Solomon's temple may have functioned as the precursor of the oracle at Delphi or, in more modern times, of Lourdes in France.

A lengthy prayer, now finished, is followed by the offering of copious sacrifices to God (vv. 62–63). Solomon does nothing on a small scale. The verb for "dedicated" in the expression "So the king . . . dedicated the house of the Lord" (v. 63b) is *khanak*, the word behind the name of the Jewish festival of Hanukkah. The superscription of Psalm 30 identifies the psalm as "a song at the dedication of the temple" (*mizmor shir khanukkat habbayit*), although there is little in the psalm that says anything about the nature of this dedication.

9:1–28. This chapter falls into two uneven halves, one in which God talks to Solomon uninterrupted and without response from the king (vv. 1–9), and one (vv. 10–28) that matter-of-factly describes some of Solomon's activities: (1) Solomon's ceding twenty Galilean cities to Hiram (vv. 10–14); (2) his forced laborers recruited from the ranks of the outsiders for the king's other building programs (vv. 15–22), with the overseers of these groups and the soldiers taken from his own people (vv. 22–23); (3) pharaoh's daughter (Solomon's wife) relocating to a domicile outside of Jerusalem (v. 24); (4) Solomon's efforts at cultic orthodoxy (v. 25); and (5) the king's fleet of ships sailing from Ezion-geber (at the head of the gulf of Aqaba), manned by expert sailors supplied by Hiram of Tyre (vv. 26–28). God speaks in the first half (vv. 3–9). The narrator introduces God's speech (vv. 1–2), and then takes over after God has finished (vv. 10–28). In ch. 8 Solomon does most of the talking; in ch. 9 he does none of the talking.

God begins by talking about himself (v. 3) but quickly shifts to talking to/about Solomon (v. 4–9). This is God's sharpest word to Solomon thus far. It highlights the words "if" and "then":

"if you will walk before me . . . then I will establish your royal throne"
"if you turn aside from following me . . . then I will cut Israel off"

The fact that God speaks so conditionally about Solomon's future means that God has not established or decreed which path Solomon must take. "For God to hold out the possibility of a positive human future, when it was not in fact a possibility, would be an act of deception. . . . If *both* futures are possible for God, then God has not established which future shall come to be" (Fretheim 1997: 9).

It is difficult to know whether or not Solomon's various activities in vv. 10–28 illustrate Solomon walking before God, turning aside from God (the two options God gave him in the preceding theophany), or neither. It is difficult to believe that Solomon's northern subjects were ecstatic about his decision to peddle ten of their cities to Hiram (vv. 10–14) in return for 120 talents of gold (were Solomon's treasuries depleted by his lavish expenditures on the temple and palace complex?). Certainly, Solomon must have been aware of the "deleterious effects" (Sweeney 1995: 615) among the residents of the Galilee area of his empire when he bartered off their land. And while he gives away northern property, he establishes a naval garrison to the south (vv. 26–28) that will bring much-needed wealth to his nation (or himself) and provide a potential for an offensive war against Egypt, should the need for that ever arise. If Eslinger does not like Solomon as a prayer, Halpern does not like Solomon as an impartial administrator. Accusing Solomon of stripping the north to clothe the south, Halpern charges Solomon with "an unabashed act of economic cannibalism" (1974: 525). But nothing explicit in the text of ch. 9 itself is negative toward Solomon. There is warning, but no rebuke. There is potential for evil, but no practiced evil.

10:1–29. Two of the more famous displays of Solomon's wisdom occur in conjunction with women, first in 3:16–28 with the two harlots, and here in vv. 1–13 with the visit of the Queen of Sheba (possibly Yemen in southwest Arabia). She comes from her empire "to test him [Solomon] with hard questions." The Hebrew word for "hard questions" (*khidot*) is the same as the "riddle" (*khidah* [sg.]) that Samson told the Philistines (Judg. 14:12). And the introduction to Proverbs states that one of the purposes of wisdom is "to understand the words of the wise and their riddles [*khidot*]" (Prov. 1:6). Thus, near the beginning of the Solomon story the king confronts a riddle (although the word is not used there) placed before him by two "ladies of the night," and near the end of the story the king confronts riddles placed before him by Her Royal Highness the Queen of Sheba.

It seems that in this meeting between heads of state the queen gets
answers to her questions, but Solomon picks up more wealthy items to
expand his coffers (vv. 2, 10). The dispensing of wisdom does not come
cheaply.

In both what the queen herself says and in what the narrator says
about her there are parallels with other individuals in Scripture. For
example, when she says, "I did not believe the reports until I came and
my own eyes had seen it" (v. 7), she sounds like Thomas (John 20:25).
Or again, when the narrator says of her at the end of v. 5 that upon
hearing Solomon's wisdom and seeing his royal accoutrements, "there
was no more spirit in her" (NRSV) or "she was overwhelmed" (NIV), she
looks like Rahab from Jericho days. Rahab's testimony was, "As soon
as we heard it, our hearts melted, and there was no courage [literally,
'no spirit'] left in any of us because of you" (Josh. 2:11). Two women,
both outsiders, observe individuals blessed inordinately by a God
whom they themselves have not hitherto known and worshiped, and
the result is sheer amazement, almost to the point of speechlessness.
(Foreign kings as well as queens could "no longer have any spirit in
them" when they saw this God of the Hebrews in action—see Josh. 5:1.)
But unlike Rahab (and Ruth), the Queen of Sheba praises the God of
Israel, but does not actually confess loyalty to him.

If the first part of the chapter is about women and wisdom (vv. 1–
13), the second part is about wealth and wisdom (vv. 14–29). This includes descriptions of the shields made of gold (vv. 16–17), the king's
throne (vv. 18–20), his ships at sea bringing their valuable cargo to Solomon (v. 22), and his numerous chariots and horses (vv. 26–29), to say
nothing of the gifts neighboring kings brought him (vv. 15, 25). It is to
the credit of Sheba's queen that she mentions Solomon's wisdom before his wealth ("your wisdom and prosperity far surpass the reports I
hear" [v. 7]), while the narrator reverses the order and starts with Solomon's wealth ("Solomon exceeded all the kings of the earth in riches
and in wisdom" [v. 23]). Furthermore, she, a foreigner, uses the holy
name of Israel's God "Yahweh/Lord" not once but twice (v. 9), while the
Hebrew narrator uses only the more generic "God/Elohim" (v. 24).

We should understand the phrase "The whole earth sought the presence of Solomon to hear his wisdom" (v. 24a) as obvious hyperbole, but
as Younger (1987: 164) reminds us, "Hyperbole is only really effective
when there is an element of truth relative to its basic comparison." Solomon's circle of influence is ever expanding. The text has taken us from
"all Israel heard" (3:28) to "the whole earth sought" (10:24). There is, of
course, nothing inherently evil about being successful, but any form of
success has the potential to lead to self-aggrandizement. One could al-

most view Solomon's life as a movie with the caption "How Success Spoiled Solomon."

11:1–43. While commentators disagree precisely where in the biblical narrative the sinister side of Solomon's reign first emerges, they all agree that this shady side sinks to its most reprehensible level in ch. 11. The progression in the chapter is:

1. Solomon's sins (vv. 1–8)
2. Announcement of judgment (vv. 9–13)
3. The implementation of that judgment (vv. 14–40)
    a. through external foes (vv. 14–23)
        i. Hadad the Edomite (vv. 14–22)
        ii. Rezon from Damascus (vv. 23–25)
    b. through an internal foe (vv. 26–40)
        i. Jeroboam, servant of Solomon
4. The end of Solomon's reign and life (vv. 41–43)

Although the account of Solomon's multiple marriages does not appear until ch. 11, we should probably not assume that until after the visit of the queen of Sheba in ch. 10 Solomon was monogamous, and that the only "Mrs. Solomon" was the Egyptian princess (3:1; 7:8; 9:16, 24). More than likely, the procuring of seven hundred wives and three hundred concubines reflects a harem expansion project that the king pursued over many years. He builds churches and colonies. Foreigners (Phoenicians) build the first; foreigners populate the second.

Note the groups from which Solomon selected his spouses: Egyptian, Moabite, Ammonite, Edomite, Sidonian, and Hittite (v. 1), the nations with which Yahweh had instructed the Israelites not to intermarry (v. 2). The two Torah passages that explicitly warn Israel about intermarriage with foreigners (Exod. 34:11–16; Deut. 7:1–4) do so against the indigenous groups within Canaan (Girgashites, Perizzites, Hivites, Jebusites, etc.), but the territories from which Solomon took his wives are outside of Canaan. It seems that 1 Kings 11:1–2 is drawing from Deut. 23:3–8, which lists in succession four of the five nations of 1 Kings 11:1: Ammonite, Moabite, Edomite, and Egyptian. The issue here, however, is not exogamy but which outside groups living in the land of Israel may enter Yahweh's assembly.

In clear defiance of Deut. 17:17 ("he [the king] must not acquire many wives for himself"), Solomon violates the biblical principle for all peoples (not just the king) of one man for one woman, and one woman for one man. Maybe Solomon needs to hear the counsel of another king's (Lemuel) mother, given to her son in Proverbs: "Do not give your strength to women, your ways to those who destroy kings" (Prov. 31:3).

But as so often happens, one sin becomes the occasion for another sin (recall David the adulterer becoming David the murderer). Solomon has a charitable and ecumenical spirit, and orders the construction of chapels in which his foreign wives may worship their gods (vv. 7–8). And alas, he ends up worshiping his wives' gods (vv. 4–5) rather than his father's God. The sin of exogamous polygamy becomes the occasion for the sin of idolatry.

One may compare Solomon with an earlier figure, Caleb, whose life went in a drastically opposite direction. With both, the expression "follow wholeheartedly/completely the Lord" (literally, "be full [*male*ʾ] of the Lord") appears:

> Num. 14:24: "But my servant Caleb, because . . . he has followed me wholeheartedly" (cf. Num. 32:11–12; Deut. 1:36)
> 1 Kings 11:6: "So Solomon . . . did not completely follow the Lord"

Notice the difference in results between a wholehearted walk with God and a partial walk with God. Because of Caleb's wholehearted following of God, "his descendants shall possess the land" (Num. 14:24b). Because of Solomon's failure to follow Yahweh wholeheartedly, his kingdom shall be torn from him and only a portion of it left for his descendants (1 Kings 11:11–13).

We sense that the writer of 1 Kings 11 is trying to be as kind and gracious to Solomon as possible. This is evident in the opening phrase in v. 4: "For when Solomon was old." The writer will attribute at least some of Solomon's sin to dotage. But this provides an unattractive parallel with his father's last years. Neither father nor son is at his best when old. David is manipulated (1 Kings 1:11–30) and recommends vindictively that Solomon eliminate two of David's foes (1 Kings 2:1–9). And Solomon, when he is old, turns his heart away from Yahweh.

The three instruments of judgment that God brings against Solomon illustrate the pattern of "threefold repetition with intensification" (Edelman 1995: 168). Hadad appears as an adversary against Solomon presumably later in the king's reign. By contrast, Rezon "was an adversary of Israel all the days of Solomon" (v. 25a). And finally, and more intensely, Jeroboam "rebelled against the king" (v. 26b). Because of the first two adversarial individuals the consequences for Solomon are immediate. In Jeroboam's case, however, the consequences fall on subsequent generations. Sometimes your sins find you out now; sometimes they find you out later (and sometimes both now and later).

Hadad and Rezon are called "adversary," for which the Hebrew word is *satan* (vv. 14, 23). (Even the angel of the Lord could be a *satan*/adversary, as in the case of Balaam [Num. 22:22]. And some Philistines thought that David might be a *satan*/adversary to them if allowed to stay in their camp [1 Sam. 29:4].) That God "raises up" these adversaries recalls the use of this phrase in Judges, especially with the earlier judges (Judg. 3:9, 15). God will raise up those who are saviors and deliverers of his people, but God will also raise up those who will become a thorn in the flesh of God's people.

It is of interest that the prophet (Ahijah) who announces to Jeroboam the breakup of Solomon's empire is from Shiloh, a northern city (v. 29). Given Solomon's insensitive treatment of his northern citizenry (4:7–19; 9:10–14), there may be some irony in the fact that a northern prophet is God's mouthpiece to declare the fragmenting of Solomon's kingdom. Jeroboam will become king of ten northern tribal areas (v. 31), but only one will be left to Solomon and his heirs (v. 32)—Judah.

If the writer tried to let Solomon off the hook a bit in the first half of the chapter by placing Solomon's apostasy in his old age, he may do the same in the latter half of the chapter. The reason given in v. 33 for Solomon's forfeiting so much of his kingdom is that "they [a plural subject] have forsaken me, have worshiped Astarte . . . and have not walked in my ways." In other words, the writer spreads the guilt around by implicating not only Solomon but unnamed others. Note that among all the ancient versions (e.g., the Septuagint and the Vulgate) the verse uses the singular verb throughout ("he [Solomon] has forsaken"). (See the footnote to 11:33 in both the NRSV and the NIV.)

Hadad and Rezon appear only to disappear once their work is completed. Not Jeroboam. God has as great aspirations for Jeroboam as he had for David or Solomon. To him God says, "If you will listen to all that I command you . . . I will be with you, and will build you an enduring house, as I built for David" (v. 38). God's "if" to Jeroboam recalls God's "ifs" to Solomon (3:14; 6:12; 9:4, 6). Speaking to 11:38, Fretheim (1997: 10) reminds us that "the text gives us no reason to believe that God is being deceptive here or is playing a game, as if God knows for sure that this future will not come to pass, but lays it out anyway. God's 'if' is a real if."

We know that Solomon's son Rehoboam will succeed him (v. 43b). Two things are of interest here. First, even though Solomon had a thousand wives, we know the name of only one son—Rehoboam. Two named daughters are mentioned in 4:11 and 15. David, by contrast, had far fewer wives and many more named sons. Second, if Solomon reigned for forty years (11:42) and his son Rehoboam began to reign at age forty-one (14:21), then that means Rehoboam was born one year before the start of his father's reign. And yet, there is not one word about this son during his father's four-decade rule. We talk about Moses' neglect of Gershom and his circumcision (if that is what Exod. 4:24–26 is about). What about Solomon's neglect of Rehoboam, at least in the data of the text we have?

Solomon in 2 Chronicles 1–9

There is but one brief mention of Solomon in the Second Samuel portion of King David's reign (2 Sam. 12:24–25). Solomon does not surface again until 1 Kings 1. In the Chronicler's account of David and Solomon, by contrast, Solomon occupies a strategic place in three of the latter chapters of First Chronicles (chs. 22, 28, and 29). Nevertheless, it is David's death, recorded in the last chapter of First Chronicles, that makes it possible for his son Solomon to take over. The first nine chapters of Second Chronicles cover Solomon's reign.

The first thing one observes when comparing the life of Solomon in 1 Kings 1–11 with that in 2 Chron. 1–9 is that in the latter, the omissions are more prominent than the additions. A chart of the two sections brings this out:

1 Kings 1–11	2 Chronicles 1–9
1–2	X
3:3–15	1:1–13
[10:26–29]	1:14–17
3:16–4:34	X
5–8	2–7:11
[7:1–12]	X
9:1–9	7:12–22
9:10–28	8:1–18
10:1–13	9:1–12
10:14–28a	9:13–28

11:1–40	X
11:41–43	9:29–31

The four "X" areas in the right-hand column represent those sections of Solomon's life in First Kings that are not reproduced in Second Chronicles: (1) Solomon's rough-and-tumble succession to the throne, and his elimination of Adonijah and those who were pro-Adonijah (1 Kings 1–2); (2) his secular wisdom and administration (1 Kings 3:16–4:34); (3) the construction of the royal palace (1 Kings 7:1–12); (4) his polygamy, apostasy, and the three individuals (Hadad, Rezon, and Jeroboam) who were adversaries/rebels against Solomon (1 Kings 11:1–40).

Unlike with Solomon's father, David, the Chronicler has deleted all the "bad" stuff about Solomon (1 Kings 1–2; 11:1–40). By contrast, of David's two sins (the Bathsheba/Uriah incident and the taking of the census), the Chronicler deletes only the first, but retains the second (2 Samuel 24 = 1 Chronicles 21). This is probably due to the census incident's connections with David buying the piece of property where, one day, a Davidic king will build the temple (a major concern and interest of the Chronicler). This is not to say, however, that Chronicles represents a whitewashed version of Solomon. Not only does Chronicles eliminate the "bad" stuff, it also eliminates some of the "good" stuff (3:16–4:24; 7:1–12). It appears that Chronicles is interested in Solomon and his wisdom exclusively as they relate to the building of the temple. So, while First Kings devotes four of eleven chapters in the Solomon narrative to temple matters (1 Kings 5–8), Chronicles devotes seven of nine (2 Chronicles 2–8). The deletions or the omissions are "the Chronicler's means of concentrating on what he sees as the lasting significance of Solomon's reign, the fulfillment of the Davidic covenant through the building of the Temple and the establishment of the Davidic dynasty. Consequently, other materials, including those which reflect positively on Solomon, are omitted as extraneous to the writer's purpose" (Kelly 1996: 90).

There are other differences as well. For example, while First Kings has five references to Solomon marrying pharaoh's daughter (3:1; 7:8; 9:16, 24; 11:1), Second Chronicles has only one reference to that (8:11 [on which see Cohen 1984–1985]), and this one and only reference has been relocated from the beginning of the Solomon narrative (as in 1 Kings 3:1) to near its end.

Again, on a couple of occasions the Chronicler appears to write a more orthodox version of something Solomon did in the Kings account or dilutes his apparent acts of cultic indiscretion. We have already drawn attention in our comments on 1 Kings 3:4 to the fact that 2 Chron. 1:3 refers to the incident of Solomon going to the high place at Gibeon to worship but replaces a singular verb (an individual ritual impropriety of Solomon) with a plural verb (all the people, not just Solomon, participated in this ritual).

Another illustration of this kind of change is the account of Solomon's observance of the Feast of Tabernacles (1 Kings 8:65–66 = 2 Chron. 7:8–10) after the prayer of dedication for the temple:

> 1 Kings 8:65–66: "So Solomon held the festival . . . seven days and seven days: [a total of] fourteen days. On the eighth day he sent the people away." (This is the reading of the Hebrew text. The Septuagint says, "So Solomon held the festival . . . seven days. On the eighth day he sent the people away.")
>
> 2 Chron. 7:8–10: "At that time Solomon held the festival for seven days. . . . On the eighth day they held a solemn assembly. . . . On the twenty-third day of the seventh month he sent the people away."

The difference between the two is obvious. In Kings, Solomon sends the celebrants home on the eighth day. By contrast, Chronicles says that Solomon observed the eighth day as a festival, in line with the Torah teaching on the Feast of Tabernacles in Lev. 23:36, 39; Num. 29:35 (although Deut. 16:15 does refer to a festival heptad). He releases the people on the following day, thus bringing the Solomon of Chronicles into correct knowledge of the ritual law.

It is clear that the Chronicler interprets Solomon as a second David (Braun 1973: 507–8). Like David, Solomon is chosen by God for this position. The root bakhar, "choose," occurs in Chronicles with David (1 Chron. 28:4), the Levites (1 Chron. 15:2), Israel (1 Chron. 16:13), and, of course, the temple site (2 Chron. 7:12, 16; 12:13; 33:7 [along with Jerusalem itself]). But the only king in the Old Testament with whom this verb is used, apart from David, is Solomon: "It is your son Solomon who shall build my house . . . for I have chosen him to be a son to me, and I will be a father to him" (1 Chron. 28:6; cf. 29:1). This divine selection of Solomon may explain why 1 Chron. 29:24 can say, "All the sons of King David pledged their allegiance to King Solomon" (including or excluding Adonijah?). If this is God's choice, who are we to oppose?

One might also suggest that not only is the Chronicler's Solomon another David, he is also another Joshua (Williamson 1976). Moses is disqualified from leading the people into the land because of his sin (Num. 20:1–12; Deut. 1:37–38; 31:2), and Joshua will complete Moses' unfinished work. David is disqualified from building the temple because he has shed so much blood and waged so many wars (1 Chron. 22:8; 28:2–3), and so Solomon will complete David's unfinished work. Of both Joshua and Solomon the texts twice say that God "exalted" them (using the verb *gadal;* see Josh. 3:7; 4:14; 1 Chron. 29:25; 2 Chron. 1:1). Both lead Israel to "rest" (*nuakh/shaqat*) as a result of their leadership (Josh. 11:23; 21:44; 1 Chron. 22:9, which labels Solomon *'ish menukhah*, "a man of rest"). And finally, some of the language of exhortation and encouragement that Moses passes on to Joshua, and David to Solomon, are amazingly similar—for example, "Be strong, be bold, do not be afraid" (cf. Deut. 31:6 and 1 Chron. 22:13).

Also, there are some parallels between the Chronicler's Solomon and Bezalel, the craftsman in building the wilderness tabernacle, as Dillard (1980–1981: 296–98) has observed. Both are from Judah. Both are given wisdom that leads to a building program (Exod. 31:2–5; 35:30–33; 2 Chron. 1:7–13). And the only reference to Bezalel in the Old Testament outside of Exodus is in Chronicles (1 Chron. 2:20; 2 Chron. 1:5). Furthermore, Bezalel's assistant, Oholiab, is from the tribe of Dan (Exod. 31:6; 35:34; 38:23), and Solomon's assistant, Huram-abi, has a Danite mother (2 Chron. 2:14). (In the Kings account, Huram-abi's name is Hiram [not be confused with the Phoenician king of the same name], and his mother is from Naphtali [1 Kings 7:13–14].) It seems that in the cases of Moses/Joshua, Bezalel/Aholiab, David/Solomon, and Solomon/Huram-abi, somebody has first planted and then somebody has watered. But in all cases, God has given the success and growth (see 1 Cor. 3:6). Or to change the analogy, a skilled master builder lays the foundation, and then someone else builds on it (1 Cor. 3:10).

Bibliography (1 Kings 1–11)

Commentaries and Major Studies

Brueggemann, W. 1982. *1 Kings*. Knox Preaching Guides. Atlanta: John Knox.

———. 2000. *1 and 2 Kings*. Smyth and Helwys Bible Commentary. Macon, GA: Smyth & Helwys.

Burney, C. F. 1903. *Notes on the Hebrew Text of the Book of Kings*. Oxford: Clarendon.

De Vries, S. 1985. *1 Kings*. Word Biblical Commentary 12. Waco, Tex.: Word.

Fretheim, T. E. 1999. *First and Second Kings*. Westminster Bible Companion. Louisville: Westminster John Knox.

Gray, J. 1970. *I and II Kings: A Commentary*. Old Testament Library. Philadelphia: Westminster.

Jensen, I. L. 1968. *1 Kings and 1 Chronicles: A Self-Study Guide*. Chicago: Moody, 1984.

Long, B. O. 1984. *1 Kings: With an Introduction to Historical Literature*. Forms of Old Testament Literature 9. Grand Rapids: Eerdmans.

McKenzie, S. L. 1991. *The Trouble with Kings: The Composition of the Book of Kings in the Deuteronomic History*. VTSup 42. Leiden: E. J. Brill.

Montgomery, J. A. 1951. *A Critical and Exegetical Commentary on the Books of Kings*. Ed. H. S. Geheman. International Critical Commentary. New York: Scribner.

Nelson, R. 1987. *First and Second Kings*. Interpretation. Atlanta: John Knox.

Rice, G. 1991. *Nations under God: A Commentary on the Book of 1 Kings*. International Theological Commentary. Grand Rapids: Eerdmans.

Skinner, J. 1904. *I and II Kings*. Century Bible. Edinburgh: T. C. and E. C. Jack.

Walsh, J. 1996. *1 Kings*. Berit Olam. Collegeville, Minn.: Liturgical Press.

Shorter Studies

Alter, R. 1981. *The Art of Biblical Narrative*. New York: Basic Books.

Ash, P. S. 1995. "Solomon's? District? List [1 Kgs. 4:7–19]." *JSOT* 67:67–86.

Balentine, S. E. 1993. *Prayer in the Hebrew Bible: The Drama of Divine-Human Dialogue*. Minneapolis: Fortress. Pp. 80–88.

Beuken, W. 1989. "No Wise King without a Wise Woman (1 Kings III 16–28)." In *New Avenues in the Study of the Old Testament*. Ed. A. S. van der Woude. OSt 25. Leiden: E. J. Brill. Pp. 1–10.

Braun, R. L. 1973. "Solomonic Apologetic in Chronicles." *JBL* 92:503–16.

———. 1976. "Solomon, the Chosen Temple Builder: The Significance of 1 Chronicles 22, 28, and 29 for the Theology of Chronicles." *JBL* 95:581–90.

Brettler, M. 1991. "The Structure of 1 Kings 1–11." *JSOT* 49:87–97.

———. 1993. "Interpretation and Prayer: Notes on the Composition of 1 Kings 8:15–53." In *Minḥah le-Naḥum: Biblical and Other Studies Presented to Nahum H. Sarna in Honour of His Seventieth Birthday*. JSOT Supplement 154. Ed. M. Fishbane and M. Brettler. Sheffield: JSOT Press. Pp. 17–35.

Brichto, H. C. 1992. *Toward a Grammar of Biblical Poetics: Tales of the Prophets*. New York: Oxford University Press.

Bright, J. 1981. *A History of Israel*. 3rd ed. Philadelphia: Westminster. Pp. 211–28.

Brueggemann, W. 1990. "The Social Significance of Solomon as a Patron of Wisdom." In *The Sage in Israel and the Ancient Near East*. Ed. J. G. Gammie and L. G. Perdue. Winona Lake, Ind.: Eisenbrauns. Pp. 117–32.

Clements, R. E. 1985. *In Spirit and in Truth: Insights from Biblical Prayers*. Atlanta: John Knox. Pp. 103–12.

Cohen, S. J. D. 1984–1985. "Solomon and the Daughter of Pharaoh: Intermarriage, Conversion, and the Impurity of Women." *JANES* 16–17:23–37.

Deurloo, K. A. 1989. "The King's Wisdom in Judgment: Narration as Example." In *New Avenues in the Study of the Old Testament*. Ed. A. S. van der Woude. OSt 25. Leiden: E. J. Brill. Pp. 11–21.

de Vaux, R. 1965. *Ancient Israel: Its Life and Institutions*. Vol. 2, *Religious Institutions*. Trans. J. McHugh. New York: McGraw-Hill. Pp. 312–30.

Dillard, R. B. 1980–1981. "The Chronicler's Solomon." *WTJ* 43:289–300.

————. 1984. "The Literary Structure of the Chronicler's Solomon Narrative." *JSOT* 30:85–93.

Edelman, D. V. 1995. "Solomon's Adversaries Hadad, Rezon and Jeroboam: A Trio of 'Bad Guy' Characters Illustrating the Theology of Immediate Retribution." In *The Pitcher Is Broken: Memorial Essays for Gösta W. Ahlström*. JSOT Supplement 190. Ed. S. W. Holloway and L. K. Handy. Sheffield: Sheffield Academic Press. Pp. 166–91.

Eslinger, L. 1989. *Into the Hands of the Living God*. JSOT Supplement 84; Bible and Literature Series 24. Sheffield: Almond. Pp. 123–81.

Fishbane, M. 1985. *Biblical Interpretation in Ancient Israel*. Oxford: Clarendon.

Fokkelman, J. P. 1981. *Narrative Art and Poetry in the Books of Samuel*. Vol. 1, *King David (2 Sam. 9–20 and 1 Kings 1–2)*. Assen: Van Gorcum. Pp. 345–410.

Fretheim, T. E. 1997. "Divine Dependence upon the Human: An Old Testament Perspective." *Ex Auditu* 13:1–13.

Frisch, A. 1991. "Structure and Its Significance: The Narrative of Solomon's Reign (1 Kings 1:12–24)." *JSOT* 51:3–14.

Garsiel, M. 1991. "Puns upon Names as a Literary Device in 1 Kings 1–2." *Bib* 72:379–86.

Glatt-Gilad, D. A. 1997. "The Deuteronomistic Critique of Solomon: A Response to Marvin A. Sweeney." *JBL* 116:700–703.

Halpern, B. 1988. "Sectionalism and Schism." *JBL* 93:519–32.

————. 1988. *The First Historians: The Hebrew Bible and History*. San Francisco: Harper and Row. Pp. 144–180.

Hanson, P. D. 1986. *The People Called: The Growth of Community in the Bible*. San Francisco: Harper & Row. Pp. 104–27.

Heaton, E. W. 1974. *Solomon's New Men: The Emergence of Israel as a National State*. New York: Pica.

Hurowitz, V. 1992. *I Have Built You an Exalted House: Temple Building in the Bible in Light of Mesopotamian and Northwest Semitic Writing.* JSOT Supplement 115. Sheffield: JSOT Press.

Ishida, T. "Adonijah, the Son of Haggith and His Supporters: An Inquiry into Problems of History and Historiography in 1 Kings 1–2." In *The Future of Biblical Studies: The Hebrew Scriptures.* Ed. R. E. Friedman and H. G. M. Williamson. Semeia Studies. Atlanta: Scholars Press. Pp. 165–87.

Jobling, D. 1991. "'Forced Labor': Solomon's Golden Age and the Question of Literary Representation." *Semeia* 54:57–76.

Kelly, B. E. 1996. *Retribution and Eschatology in Chronicles.* JSOT Supplement 211. Sheffield: Sheffield Academic Press. Pp. 87–95.

Knoppers, G. N. 1993. *Two Nations under God: The Deuteronomistic History of Solomon and the Dual Monarchies.* Vol. 1, *The Reign of Solomon and the Rise of Jeroboam.* HSM 52. Atlanta: Scholars Press.

———. 1994. "Sex, Religion, and Politics: The Deuteronomist on Intermarriage." *HAR* 14:121–41.

———. 1995. "Prayer and Propaganda: Solomon's Dedication of the Temple and the Deuteronomist's Program." *CBQ* 57:229–54.

Koopmans, W. T. 1991. "The Testament of David in 1 Kings ii 1–10." *VT* 41:429–49.

Lasine, S. 1989. "The Riddle of Solomon's Judgment and the Riddle of Human Nature in the Hebrew Bible." *JSOT* 45:61–86.

Levenson, J. D. 1981. "From Temple to Synagogue: 1 Kings 8." In *Traditions in Transformation: Turning Points in Biblical Faith.* Ed. B. Halpern and J. D. Levenson. Winona Lake, Ind.: Eisenbrauns. Pp. 143–66.

Liver, J. 1967. "The Book of the Acts of Solomon." *Bib* 48:75–101.

Long, B. O. 1981. "A Darkness between Brothers: Solomon and Adonijah." *JSOT* 19:79–94.

McConville, J. G. 1992. "Kings viii 46–53 and the Deuteronomic Hope." *VT* 42:67–79.

Millard, A. R. 1991. "Texts and Archaeology: Weighing the Evidence. The Case for King Solomon." *PEQ* 123:19–27.

———. "Solomon: Text and Archaeology." *PEQ* 123:117–18.

Miller, J. M. 1991. "Solomon: International Potentate or Local King?" *PEQ* 123:28–31.

Miller, P. D. 1994. *They Cried to the Lord: The Form and Theology of Biblical Prayer.* Minneapolis: Fortress.

Myers, C. L. 1983. "Jachin and Boaz in Religious and Political Perspective." *CBQ* 45:167–78.

————. 1983. "The Israelite Empire: In Defense of King Solomon." In *The Bible and Its Traditions*. Ed. M. P. O'Connor and D. N. Freedman. Ann Arbor: University of Michigan Press. Pp. 421–28. (= *Michigan Quarterly Review* 22, no. 3).

Nelson, R. D. 1998. *The Historical Books*. Interpreting Biblical Texts. Nashville: Abingdon. Pp. 129–48.

Nicol, G. C. 1993. "The Death of Joab and the Accession of Solomon: Some Observations on the Narrative of 1 Kings 1–2." *SJOT* 7:134–51.

Ouellette, J. 1970. "The Solomonic *DeBîr* According to the Hebrew Text of 1 Kings 6." *JBL* 89:338–43.

Parker, K. I. 1988. "Repetition as a Structuring Device in 1 Kings 1–11." *JSOT* 42:19–27.

————. 1992. "Solomon as Philosopher King? The Nexus of Law and Wisdom in 1 Kings 1–11." *JSOT* 53:75–91.

Porten, B. 1967. "The Structure and Theme of the Solomonic Narrative." *HUCA* 38:93–128.

Riley, W. 1993. *King and Cultus in Chronicles and the Reinterpretation of History*. JSOT Supplement 160. Sheffield: Sheffield Academic Press.

Rogers, J. S. 1988. "Narrative Stock and Deuteronomic Elaboration in 1 Kings 2." *CBQ* 50:398–413.

Savran, G. 1987. "1 and 2 Kings." In *The Literary Guide to the Bible*. Ed. R. Alter and F. Kermode. Cambridge, Mass.: Belknap. Pp. 146–64.

Sternberg, M. 1987. *The Poetics of Biblical Narrative*. Bloomington: Indiana University Press.

Sweeney, M. A. 1995. "The Critique of Solomon in the Josianic Edition of the Deuteronomistic History." *JBL* 114:607–22.

Terrien, S. 1978. *The Elusive Presence: Toward a New Biblical Theology*. San Francisco: Harper and Row. Pp. 186–213.

Tomes, R. 1996. "'Our Holy and Beautiful House': When and Why Was 1 Kings 6–8 Written?" *JSOT* 70:33–50.

van Wolde, E. 1995. "Who Guides Whom? Embeddedness and Perspective in Biblical Hebrew and in 1 Kings 3:16–28." *JBL* 114:623–42.

Walsh, J. T. 1993. "Symmetry and the Sin of Solomon." *Shofar* 12:11–27.

————. 1995. "The Characterization of Solomon in First Kings 1–5." *CBQ* 57:471–93.

Williamson, H. G. M. 1976. "The Accession of Solomon in the Book of Chronicles." *VT* 26:351–61.

Younger, K. L., Jr. 1990. "The Figurative Aspect and the Contextual Method in the Evalution of the Solomonic Empire (1 Kings 1–11)." In *The Bible in Three Dimensions*. Ed. D. J. A. Clines, S. E. Fowl, and S. E. Porter. Sheffield: JSOT Press. Pp. 157–75.

1 Kings 12–2 Kings 25

The rest of First Kings, following the account of Solomon's death, through the end of Second Kings narrates the respective histories of the kingdoms of Israel and Judah. The northern kingdom ("Israel" henceforth) has nineteen kings over its history of some two hundred years (930–722 B.C.). The southern kingdom ("Judah") has twenty kings over its history of some 350 years (930–587/86 B.C.).

There are several differences between the line of Israelite kings and their southern Judahite counterparts. (1) None of the kings of Israel trace their ancestry to David. All of the kings of Judah trace their ancestry to David. So it is a northern non-Davidic line versus a southern Davidic line. (2) In contrast to the kings of Judah, who form together an unbroken Davidic dynasty, the line of Israelite kings is composed of a series of mini-dynasties, lasting anywhere from two generations to several more. (3) All the kings of Israel are reprobates, leading their people away from God instead of back to God. Most kings of Judah similarly fail to inspire their people with godly living, but with four important exceptions: (a) Asa (end of tenth century, beginning of the ninth century B.C.); (b) Jehoshaphat (early to middle ninth century B.C.); (c) Hezekiah (end of eighth century, beginning of seventh century B.C.); (d) Josiah (last half of seventh century B.C.).

A notoriously difficult problem is trying to make sense of the plethora of chronological notices throughout 1 Kings 12–2 Kings 25, a notice like "In the X year of the reign of So-and-So of Israel, So-and-So became king of Judah and he reigned Y years." Such information we call a synchronism, that is, the beginning of the reign of a Judean king is correlated with a specific year in the reign of an Israelite king, or vice versa. These synchronistic chronological notes have the effect of tying together the history and destiny of the kingdoms of Israel and Judah, their formal schism after Solomon's death notwithstanding.

A second chronological note is that for every king the length of his reign is given ("And So-and-So reigned X years/months"). The only exception to this is the one queen among thirty-eight kings, Athaliah, queen of Judah (2 Kings 11:1–17). And it is precisely here that one of the problems emerges. That is, on several occasions the years mentioned in the synchronisms do not always match up with the years given in the length-of-reign notice.

A third chronological note is the correlation of events in the books of Kings with nonbiblical kings. Such notes may refer either to a year in the reign of a biblical king ("In the ninth year of [Zedekiah's] reign . . . King Nebuchadnezzar came with all his army against Jerusalem" [2 Kings 25:1]), or to a year in the reign of a nonbiblical king ("In the fifth month . . . which was the nineteenth year of King Nebuchadnezzar, king of Babylon" [2 Kings 25:8]). Such notices suggest that not only are the history and destiny of Israel and Judah interlocked with each other, but also the history and destiny of both kingdoms are unavoidably influenced by surrounding nations.

Historians disagree some on the dates for many of these kings simply because they interpret the chronological data differently. Were there different systems used for totaling a king's years at different times in Israel and Judah? Yes or no? Were there a number of co-regencies, when two kings ruled simultaneously over one kingdom, with the years of the co-regency assigned to both kings? Yes or no? Are the years of reign rounded off so that the total is approximate and not exact? Yes or no? Accordingly, we will cite the years of reign calculated by four biblical historians at the start of each new subsection (Bright, Galil, Hayes/Hooker, Thiele).

1 Kings 12:1–16:20: Rehoboam, Jeroboam

Most of this section of First Kings focuses on the reigns of Rehoboam, son and successor of Solomon and king of Judah, and on Jeroboam I, the first king of northern Israel:

1. Rehoboam listens to the wrong people, and as a result Israel separates from Judah (12:1–24).
2. Jeroboam's sin in building the golden calves at Dan and Bethel (12:25–33).

Kings of Israel	Length of Reign	Bright	Galil	Hayes/Hooker	Thiele
Jeroboam I	22 years	922–901	931–909	927–906	930–909
Nadab	2 years	901–900	909–908	905–904	909–908
Baasha	24 years	900–877	908–885	903–882	908–886
Elah	2 years	877–876	885–884	881–880	886–885
Zimri	7 days	876	884	880	885
Kings of Judah					
Rehoboam	17 years	922–915	931/30–914	926–910	930–913
Abijah/m	3 years	915–913	914–911	909–907	913–910
Asa	41 years	913–873	911–870	906–878	910–869

3. A "man of God" from Judah is tricked by an "old prophet" from Bethel (13:1–32).
4. Jeroboam continues his sinning (13:33–34).
5. Ahijah's prophecy about the death of Jeroboam's son and its fulfillment (14:1–18).
6. Jeroboam dies and leadership passes to his son Nadab (14:19–20).
7. Overview of the reign of Rehoboam (14:21–31), who is followed by Abijah (15:1–8) and Asa (15:9–24).
8. Jeroboam I's successors (15:25–16:20).

Throughout this unit, emphasizing the splitting of a united monarchy into a divided monarchy, are a number of events that contrast something with something else. To begin with, two explanations are given for the bifurcation of the kingdom. First Kings 11 explains the division as a result of Solomon's uncontrolled sexuality and idolatry. But in ch. 12 the division is a result of Rehoboam's refusal to lift the heavy yoke off his people imposed on them by his father, Solomon. The first explanation seems more at home in the world of Exodus and Deuteronomy ("If you break God's laws, this is what happens to you"), what we might call a theocentric explanation (Weisman 1998: 102). The second explanation seems more at home in the wisdom themes of Proverbs ("If you listen to the wrong kind of people, this is what happens to you"), what we may call an anthropocentric or sapiential explanation. Speaking to the second explanation, Brueggemann (1979: 172) remarks, "It is important that the split did not happen over a theological dispute, nor was it simply a gradual growing apart, but it was triggered by a concrete issue of political oppression and social liberation . . . the royal consciousness was committed to the maintenance of order at the cost of justice."

It is not that these two explanations are incompatible. If ch. 11 focuses on the "why" of the kingdom's dissolution, ch. 12 focuses on its "how." According to ch. 12, Rehoboam's refusal to listen to the wise counsel of his father's advisers is not due to hardhearted insensitivity, to "a petulant display of brutality" (Halpern 1974: 527), but because "it was a turn of affairs brought about by the Lord that he might fulfill his word, which the Lord had spoken by Ahijah the Shilonite to Jeroboam son of Nebat" (v. 15).

The scene is reminiscent of that involving Absalom in 2 Samuel 17. While plotting to overthrow his father, Absalom first takes counsel from Ahithophel, wise counsel that Absalom rejects. As the (foolish) counsel of the young men supplants the (wise) counsel of the elders, so Hushai's (foolish) advice supplants the (wise) counsel of Ahithophel. And on both occasions Absalom's and Rehoboam's "misjudgment" is attributed to the workings of God (cf. 2 Sam. 17:14 with 1 Kings 12:15).

Another contrast (flowing out of the above) is the conflicting advice offered Rehoboam by the elders (*zeqenim*) and the young men (*yeladim*—literally, "children"), the veterans versus the youngsters. The elders counsel a lifting or lightening of Solomon's oppressive load. The young men counsel Rehoboam to ignore these grievances and press for even greater extraction from the northern Israelites. They do so either because they lack any experience in diplomacy or because they are politically ambitious (the best way to advance themselves would be by war with Egypt, a war that could be possible only by an increase in corvée and taxation [Halpern 1974: 527]).

The young men even urge Rehoboam to preface his remarks to the people with "My little finger is thicker than my father's loins" (v. 10c). The Hebrew simply says, "My little [thing] is thicker than. . . ." And while it is common to render "my little thing" as "my little finger" (cf. the Vulgate's *minimus digitus meus*), in light of the comparison with "loins," "my little thing" might easily be "my little member/organ." Such a defiant, obscene comment may explain why Rehoboam does not repeat it when he speaks to the disgruntled northerners. As Alter (1981: 100) states, "Rehoboam revealingly omits the hyperbolic comparison between his little finger and his father's loins, wisely deciding not to compound his budgetary harshness by making extravagant public claims about his own stature vis-à-vis that of the deceased Solomon."

The whole incident recalls the experience of Solomon in 1 Kings 3:16–28 when confronted by two mothers, each one claiming to be the living child's mother. On both occasions two parties designated by status (harlots, elders, young men) rather than by names present contradictory arguments before the king (Solomon, Rehoboam), about which the king must make a judgment.

Rehoboam's refusal to listen to the appeal for reasonable reform opens the door for Jeroboam to become king of Israel. It appears that what God said about/to Jeroboam through Ahijah the prophet (11:29–40) has come to pass. Jeroboam not only has ten pieces of garments but also leadership over ten tribes. But no sooner is Jeroboam in office than he turns out to be "a leader who takes decisive action to control the people because he believes they are capable of turning against and killing him" (Lasine 1992: 145). (Is Jeroboam another Rehoboam, albeit in different dress?)

Jeroboam's strategy to maintain the loyalty of his new subjects and to deter their return to Jerusalem to worship comes out of both his own apprehensions and his self-counsel. Here is one difference between the two kings in ch. 12. Rehoboam at least took counsel with others (*yiwwaʿats ʾet* [vv. 6, 8]); Jeroboam merely took counsel with himself (*yiwwaʿats* [v. 28]).

Specifically, Jeroboam makes two calves of gold, placing one at his southern boundary city of Bethel and the other at his northern boundary city of Dan. About both he says to his people, "Here are your gods, O Israel, who brought you up out of the land of Egypt" (12:28). He also appoints his own non-Levitical clergy (12:31) and establishes his own religious festival (12:32–33).

That is exactly what Aaron said when he built the golden calf at Sinai's base while Moses was at the summit (Exod. 32:4). In fact, the expression "these are your gods" fits the Jeroboam story better, for he built two calves while Aaron built only one. This does not mean that the calf story of Exodus 32 is a fiction created simply as a polemic against breakaway Jeroboam, as many scholars maintain, for what author would invent a story that indicts the entire nation for idolatry, and so soon after their miraculous deliverance at that? Aaron cannot restrain idolatry, and Jeroboam opens the door to rampant idolatry. The connection of Aaron with Jeroboam looks even stronger when it is recalled that they had sons named Abihu and Nadab (Aaron) and Abijah and Nadab (Jeroboam). Aaron's two eldest sons died prematurely (Leviticus 10), as do Jeroboam's two sons (Abijah, 1 Kings 14:1–18; Nadab,

1 Kings 15:27–28). Note also that Aaron's sin is called "a great sin" (Exod. 32:30–31), as is Jeroboam's (2 Kings 17:21).

Few people cast a shadow over history as much as Jeroboam does through his providing alternate worship and sacrifice centers other than Jerusalem. He does not sleep with somebody else's wife and kill the husband, as David did. He does not have one thousand wives like Solomon. He is neither adulterer nor polygamist, but he does tinker with how and where God is to be worshiped and with the fundamental concept of who God is.

Of the eighteen Israelite kings who follow Jeroboam I, fifteen of them are said to have walked in the way/sins of Jeroboam, or refused to depart from the way/sins of Jeroboam (the three exceptions are Elah, Shallum [both have very brief reigns], and Hoshea, the last king of Israel):

1. Nadab (1 Kings 15:26)
2. Baasha (1 Kings 15:34)
3. Zimri (1 Kings 16:19)
4. Omri (1 Kings 16:26)
5. Ahab (1 Kings 16:31)
6. Ahaziah (1 Kings 22:52)
7. Jehoram (2 Kings 3:3)
8. Jehu (2 Kings 10:29, 31)
9. Jehoahaz (2 Kings 13:2, 6)
10. Jehoash (2 Kings 13:11)
11. Jeroboam II (2 Kings 14:24)
12. Zechariah (2 Kings 15:9)
13. Menachem (2 Kings 15:18)
14. Pekahiah (2 Kings 15:24)
15. Pekah (2 Kings 15:28)

Never does the Old Testament say that "humanity walked in the way/sins of Adam," but it does tell of fifteen royals who walked in the way/sins of Jeroboam. But in spite of the duration of the captivating effects of Jeroboam's two calves, individuals whom we might have expected to fulminate against them do not. Jehu, a later king of Israel who extirpates Canaanite Baalism from Israel in a religious purge (2 Kings 10:18–28), says nothing about them. Nor do Elijah, Elisha, and Micaiah, all northern prophets. This silence would suggest that the calves must have been intended to represent Yahweh worship rather than Baal worship.

Conceivably, Jeroboam intended the calves not as actual representations of Yahweh but merely as functionally equivalent to the cherubs that transported Yahweh. That is, the calves represent the vehicle, not the rider. And that may very well be the case. But this distinction would soon be lost on the masses of people. And that may be Jeroboam's mistake. We know that calf worship was practiced elsewhere, but we are aware of no cherub worship. We know that in ancient Israel certain practices performed by pagans were considered compatible with monotheism and adopted (e.g., altars, sacrifices), while other practices were considered indelibly pagan and hence rejected (e.g., sorcery, cult prostitution). Images of calves were forbidden; images of cherubs were acceptable. Possibly, the use of calves was excluded because of their intrinsic pagan associations.

In 1 Kings 12 there was no word from God except that from Shemaiah the prophet (v. 22), who urged Rehoboam to return home and not engage northern Israelites in battle. We should note that Rehoboam obeyed this word (v. 24b). This is another item that sets Rehoboam off from Jeroboam. He obeys the prophetic message while Jeroboam does not (13:4, 33–34).

If "the word of the Lord" is limited to one instance in ch. 12, it occurs throughout ch. 13 (vv. 1, 2, 5b, 9a, 17a, 18a, 20, 21, 26, 32a). To begin with, a "man of God" from Judah goes north to Bethel. This designation for this unnamed prophet appears fifteen times in this chapter (1, 4, 5, 6 [2x], 7, 8, 11, 12, 14 [2x], 21, 26, 29, 31), more frequently here than anywhere else. It is first used of Moses (Deut. 33:1), the greatest of the prophets. And in what is "a striking, if not unique example of prophetic apostrophe" (Walsh 1989: 358), the man of God speaks to the altar, predicting by name the king (Josiah) whom three centuries later God would raise up to smash this altar (vv. 2–3). Some commentators note that the prophet does not mention the golden calf, but we should understand "altar" as a synecdoche in which a part represents the whole.

After the instantaneous healing of his withered hand, Jeroboam asks the man of God to join him at his home. Whatever the king's motives, the prophet cites as his reasons for refusal that he is not to eat food, not to drink water, and not to return by the way that he came (v. 9). The three prohibitions remind one of the three prohibitions God placed on Jeremiah (no wife and children, no entering a house of mourning, no entering a house of feasting [Jer. 16:1–9]), although Jeremiah's prohibitions were lifelong.

The reason for these prohibitions is unclear, especially the third one. Like the magi (Matt. 2:12), he is to return to Judah by a different route. Simon (1976: 90) draws attention to Deut. 28:68, where God's threatened return of his people to Egypt by the way they came is a nullification of the exodus. And in Isa. 37:34 (= 2 Kings 19:33) the Lord's word about the king of Assyria, "By the way that he came, by the same he shall return; he shall not come into this city," indicates voiding the mission and abandoning the goal. Hence, for the prophet to take a different route on his return reinforces the absoluteness, certainty, and success of the man of God's prediction.

One expects opposition from a king bent on having his own way. But should a "man of God" expect opposition from a colleague, an "old prophet" (vv. 11–32)? Here is another contrast between chs. 12 and 13. In ch. 12 "old" men (*zeqenim*) offer Rehoboam salutary counsel. But in ch. 13 an "old" prophet (*navi' zaqen*) deceives the man of God.

The deception comes when the old prophet convinces the man of God that an angel/messenger told him that he was to bring the man of God back to his place for refreshments (vv. 16–19), precisely the invitation the man of God refused from Jeroboam. While God protects the man of God from the violence of Jeroboam ("'Seize him [the man of God]!' But the hand that he [Jeroboam] stretched out against him withered so that he could not draw it back to himself" [v. 4b]), he does not save him from the deception and lies of the old prophet. And for reneging on the prohibitions and believing the old prophet, the man of God is killed by a lion (vv. 20–25). Yahweh's spirit does not come mightily on this man of God when a lion meets him, as it did with Samson when a young lion roared at him (Judg. 14:5–6). Nor did God shut the mouth of this lion as he did with Daniel's lions (Dan. 6:22).

The word for "dead body," *nevelah*, occurs twenty-three times in the Old Testament, and ten of them are here in 1 Kings 13 (vv. 22, 24 [2x], 25 [2x], 28 [3x], 29, 30). Its repetition recalls God's word to Israel in Moses' day about one result of disobedience: "Your corpses [*nevelah*] shall be food for every bird of the air" (Deut. 28:26). And the closeness of the word for "corpse" [*nevelah*] to the word for "foolishness" [*nevalah*] underscores the man of God's tragic mistake (Dozeman 1982: 390).

Interestingly, the old prophet deceives by fabricating a word from God, but goes unpunished (Gross 1979: 122), even though according to Deut. 18:20 he should have died: "any prophet . . . who presumes to speak in my name a word that I have not commanded the prophet to speak—that prophet shall die." On the other hand, the man of God, who appears to act in good faith, dies. Is the man of God, then, simply guilty of too credulous a faith in the truthfulness of others (Crenshaw 1971: 62)? If a man of God allows himself to be deceived, is it no longer important whether he acts in good faith or not (Gross 1979: 123)? Or does the narrative suggest that far from being duped, the man of God is a "guileful, acquisitive schemer" (Reis 1994: 377) who deserves his punishment? He does appear to soften his choice of verb when declining the invitation from the old prophet in comparison with declining the same invitation from Jeroboam:

> To Jeroboam: "For thus I was *commanded* by the word of the Lord" (v. 9).
> To the old prophet: "For it was *said* to me by the word of the Lord" (v. 17).

Also, his "I will not go with you" to Jeroboam in v. 8 is much more emphatic than his "I cannot return or go with you" to the old prophet in v. 16.

If the man of God is best understood as a schemer, then it is strange that at the end of the unit the old prophet has nothing but praise for the deceased man of God (vv. 29–32). First he condemns the man of God while the two are sharing the table (vv. 20–22), but then honors him after his death (vv. 31–32). The old prophet can speak both spurious revelation (v. 18a) and true revelation (v. 20). It is to the credit of the old prophet that he does not gloat over his ruse; he does not say, "I conned him." He wishes to be buried with the man of God when his time comes (v. 31), and he affirms the certainty of the fulfillment of the man of God's prophecy against Jeroboam's altar (v. 32).

The last two verses (vv. 33–34) comment briefly on Jeroboam's response to the altar prophecy and his own healing, and possibly to the old prophet's "seconding" the altar prophecy. That response is a negative one. In no way do any of these events or pronouncements persuade him to reform his policy. We commented above on the frequency of the word "dead body, corpse" in this chapter. An even more frequently used word in this chapter is "(re)turn" (*shuv*). Toward the end of ch. 12 it is used three times by Jeroboam himself (12:26, 27 [2x]). He wants his northerners returning neither to the house of David nor to Rehoboam. In ch. 13 *shuv* appears sixteen times (vv. 4, 6 [2x], 9, 10, 16, 17, 18, 19, 20, 22, 23, 26, 29, 33 [2x]). The majority of these sixteen deal with the man of God returning or not returning. But suddenly in v. 33 ("Jeroboam did not turn from his evil way") the verb loses its geographical nuance and takes on a religious one. Jeroboam, who at any cost wants to thwart (re)turnings, on the heels of an incident highlighting turnings, himself refuses to turn. Little does Jeroboam seem to realize that if he is to have any future, it is not in preventing the (re)turning of his people, but in allowing the turning of his own heart.

   Among the last incidents in the life of Jeroboam is the one involving
the serious sickness and death of his son Abijah (14:1–18). Jeroboam
instructs his wife to disguise herself and go to Shiloh to ask the prophet
Ahijah about the boy's chances for recovery. Jeroboam wants nothing
to do with the man of God from Judah, but understandably, he believes
that Ahijah will be sympathetic, for after all, it was Ahijah who earlier
spoke glowingly of Jeroboam's future (11:31–39). But as Nathan's second prophetic announcement to David was radically different than his
first announcement to David (compare 2 Sam. 12:7–14 with 2 Sam.
7:5–17), so is Ahijah's second prophetic announcement to Jeroboam
radically different than his first to Jeroboam (compare 1 Kings 14:6–16
with 1 Kings 11:31–39).
   The Old Testament has five stories in which a king or queen is in a
situation involving disguise (Coggins 1991). Four of them use the Hithpael of *khapas*, whose basic meaning is "change," and this one in
1 Kings 14 uses the Hithpael of *shanah* (the only time it is used in the
Old Testament):

   1. 1 Sam. 28:8: "So Saul disguised himself and put on other
      clothes and . . . came to the woman [medium] by night."
   2. 1 Kings 20:38: "Then the prophet departed, and waited for the
      king [Ahab of Israel] along the road, disguising himself with a
      bandage over his eyes."
   3. 1 Kings 22:30 (= 2 Chron. 18:29): "The king of Israel [Ahab]
      said to Jehoshaphat, 'I will disguise myself and go into battle.'"
   4. 2 Chron. 35:22: "But Josiah would not turn away from him
      [Pharaoh Neco of Egypt], but disguised himself in order to
      fight with him."
   5. 1 Kings 14:2: "Go, disguise yourself, so that it will not be
      known that you are the wife of Jeroboam."

In none of these instances does the disguise work where the king or his
wife is the disguiser. And what makes the ineffectiveness of Jeroboam's
wife's disguise more prominent is that Ahijah cannot even see, "for his
eyes were dim because of his age" (v. 4b)! So the aged Ahijah of ch. 14
is more like the old prophet of ch. 13 than the dynasty-promising Ahijah of ch. 11.
   What distinguishes this disguise scene is that in the other four, the
disguiser himself (Saul, Ahab, Josiah) suffers. Here, it is the son of the
royal couple who dies. And here we encounter another contrast in these
few chapters of 1 Kings. God heals Jeroboam's withered hand through
the man of God's intercession (13:6), but he does not heal Jeroboam's

sickly son via the ministry of Ahijah, a fellow northerner (14:6–14, esp. v. 12). The child becomes a symbol of what is ahead for Jeroboam's family. Part of the prophet's announcement is that God "will cut off from Jeroboam every male" (v. 10b). This, of course, cannot be literally true, for Jeroboam is succeeded by his son Nadab (v. 20b). The phrase speaks rather to the short-lived dynasty of Jeroboam.

In v. 5 we read that Yahweh informs his servant Ahijah that Jeroboam's wife is on her way "to inquire [*derosh davar*—literally, "to seek a word"] of you concerning her son."

There seem to be two different avenues in the Old Testament for an individual to make an inquiry of Yahweh (Long 1973). One avenue is through the priests, as in Num. 27:21: "But he [Joshua] shall stand before Eleazar the priest, who shall inquire [*sha'al*] for him by the decision of the Urim before the Lord." The other avenue goes through the prophets, as here, but uses the verb *darash* ("seek") rather than the verb *sha'al* ("ask"). One might inquire of Yahweh through a prophet about personal or public affairs such as the whereabouts of lost family, animals (1 Samuel 9, esp. v. 9), a sickness (1 Kings 14:5; 2 Kings 8:8), or a military situation (1 Sam. 28:6; 1 Kings 22:5; 2 Kings 3:11; Jer. 37:7).

The above verses suggest that the priests used the Urim and Thummim in making inquiry of Yahweh, but what did the prophets use, if anything, apart from intercessory prayer? We know that in pagan religions diviners and sorcerers used all sorts of techniques to ascertain the future and the will of the deities. It is not so in Israel. It is surely no accident that right after Deut. 18:9–14 prohibits Israel from seeking out the likes of diviners or sorcerers, Deut. 18:15 speaks of Yahweh raising up a prophet for Israel. In other words, God's people are to turn to prophets for the services that pagans seek from diviners and sorcerers. The prophet simply either quotes God's response directly or shares data that God has revealed in response to pleas for assistance. The lack of the use of divinatory practices by Old Testament prophets reinforces the fact that their knowledge of future events (in this case, the death of Abijah) owes nothing to their own wisdom but everything to divine revelation.

1 Kings 16:21–2 Kings 10: Omri, Ahab, Jehu, Elijah, Elisha, and Jezebel

In this section of First and Second Kings most of the attention focuses on Elijah the prophet and his successor, Elisha. Elijah's career covers twenty-four years (the twenty-two-year reign of King Ahab of Israel and the two-year reign of his son and successor, Ahaziah). Elisha's

Kings of Israel	Length of Reign	Bright	Galil	Hayes/Hooker	Thiele
Omri	12 years	876–873	884–873	879–869	885–874
Ahab	22 years	869–850	873–852	868–854	874–853
Ahaziah	2 years	850–849	852–851	853–852	853–852
J(eh)oram	12 years	849–842	851–842/1	851–840	852–841
Jehu	28 years	842–815	842/1–815/4	839–822	841–814
Kings of Judah					
Jehoshaphat	25 years	873–849	870–845	877–853	872–848
Jehoram	8 years	849–842	851–843/2	852–841	848–841
Ahaziah	1 year	842	843/2–842/1	840	841
Athaliah (queen)	?	842–837	842/1–835	839–833	841–835
J(eh)oash	40 years	837–800	(842/1)-802/1	832–803	835–796

career covers the twelve-year reign of King J(eh)oram of Israel and a portion of King Jehu's twenty-eight-year reign.

Elijah's story is spread over eight chapters (1 Kings 17–2 Kings 2), and he appears in six of those chapters (1 Kings 17; 18; 19; 21; 2 Kings 1; 2). Elisha's story is spread over eight chapters (2 Kings 2–9), and he is present in all of them. Together, these two prophets appear in thirteen chapters of the books of Kings. Compare this proliferation of data with Chronicles, where neither prophet is even mentioned. Why this extended coverage of two northern ("Israelite") prophets by the editor/compiler of Kings, ostensibly a southern Judean deeply committed to pure worship of Yahweh at the Jerusalem sanctuary? Or why the lengthy treatment of Jehu, king of Israel (2 Kings 9–10)? It can only be because both of these Israelite prophets and this particular Israelite king championed the cause of Yahwism against the Baal cult transplanted by Jezebel and sanctioned by her husband, Ahab.

On the other hand, this section of the Old Testament omits any reference to some fairly significant historical events that took place during the reigns of Omri and Ahab. To judge from Scripture, Omri was a relatively insignificant king whose reign is given short shrift (1 Kings 16:23–28). All that we know of him from that source is when he began to reign, how long he reigned, his purchase of Samaria as the new northern capital to replace Tirzah, his being wicked, his being a "Jeroboamite," and his death. But we know from the famous Moabite Stone that Omri's greatest (military) accomplishment was the conquest of neighboring Moab, an event that the author of Kings was certainly aware of but whose relevance for his purpose he did not see. Furthermore, long after Omri died, the mighty Assyrians from Mesopotamia to the east frequently referred to Israel in their writings as the "House of Omri," much as we still refer to the New York Yankees baseball stadium as the "House That Ruth Built."

Similarly, during the reign of Omri's son Ahab, Shalmaneser III, king of Assyria, desired to extend his empire into Canaan. To that end, in 853 B.C. he launched a battle at Karkar (Qarqar) on the Orontes River in Syria against a union of Canaanite nations that included Israel (but not Judah). Ahab, Shalmaneser tells us, fielded one of the largest forces (ten thousand infantry and two thousand chariots) in this coalition. Once again, not a word about this incident appears in the Ahab portion of First Kings. So, Moab's conquest and the war with the heavyweight Shalmaneser III are out, but Elijah and Elisha are in. One suspects that Ahab's real thorn in the flesh was not Shalmaneser III but Elijah. And what God says through one of his servants the prophets is infinitely more important than the headline-grabbing events of the day.

Four of the six events in which Elijah is prominent relate directly to King Ahab: (1) 1 Kings 17:1–24; (2) 1 Kings 18:1–46; (3) 1 Kings 19:1–21; (4) 1 Kings 21:1–29. The fifth involves Elijah and Ahab's son and successor, Ahaziah (2 Kings 1:1–18), and the sixth Elijah and Elisha, as Elijah is taken up by God and succeeded by Elisha (2 Kings 2:1–25).

The first three of these incidents (1 Kings 17; 18; 19) are tied together by a parallel story-line development in each of the episodes (see Cohn 1982: 343–49; Herr 1985: 292–94):

1. Announcement

Elijah: "There will be neither dew nor rain these years" (17:1).	God: "Go, present yourself to Ahab; I will send rain on the earth" (18:1).	Jezebel: "So may the gods do to me . . . if I do not make your life like the life of one of them" (19:2).

2. Journey

Elijah leaves Israel for Phoenicia at God's command (17:9–10).	Elijah returns to Israel from Phoenicia to confront Ahab (18:2).	Elijah flees Israel and Jezebel (19:3) and returns to Israel (19:19).

3. Two Encounters for Elijah in Ascending Order

(a) ravens (17:6–7)	(a) Obadiah (18:7–16)	(a) an angel (19:5–7)
(b) a Phoenician widow (17:8–16)	(b) Ahab (18:17–18)	(b) Yahweh (19:9–18)

4. Three Prayers by Elijah

address (17:20a)	address (18:36b)	address (19:4c)
complaint (17:20b)	petition (18:36c)	petition (19:4d)
address (17:21b)	motivation (18:37)	motivation (19:4f)
petition (17:21c)	divine response (18:38)	divine response (19:5b–7)
divine response (17:22)		

5. Miracle in a High Place

God cures and resuscitates a widow's son in an upper chamber (17:17–23).	God sends fire on the altar on Mount Carmel (18:21–38).	God reveals himself to Elijah in a "sound of sheer silence" at Horeb, the mount of God (19:9b–12).

6. Transformation

The widow: "Now I know" (17:24).	The Israelites on Carmel: "The Lord indeed is God" (18:39).	Elisha: "Let me kiss my father and mother, and then I will follow you" (19:20).

Chapter 17 has three scenes: (1) Elijah goes into hiding by the Wadi Cherith, where the brook and ravens supply him water and food (vv. 2–7); (2) Elijah proceeds north and west to the Phoenician coastland and the city of Zarephath near Sidon (vv. 8–16); (3) God heals the widow's son through his servant Elijah (vv. 17–24).

The Wadi Cherith is hardly a population center. It is, rather, a no man's land east of the Jordan somewhere between where the Yarmuk and Jabbok Rivers flow into the Jordan. It might be called "Wadi Boondocks" (Brichto 1992: 123), but its literal meaning would be "Cut-off Wadi" ("Cherith" is from the verb *karat*, "cut off"). The use of *k-r-t* in ch. 17 needs to be connected with its use in 18:4 ("when Jezebel was killing off [literally, 'cutting off'] the prophets of the Lord"). It also is in the next verse of ch. 18, v. 5, when Ahab says to Obadiah, "so we will not have to kill [*karat*] some of the animals." So, while Ahab is fearful that he may have to cut off some of his animals due to the prolonged drought, and while Jezebel is cutting off Yahweh's prophets, Elijah is holing up at Cut-off Wadi.

Both Elijah (v. 1) and the widow of Zarephath (v. 12) know that the Lord lives, but will Elijah live (Hauser and Gregory 1990: 13)? If he manages to survive the drought, there is still Ahab and Jezebel. To that end, Yahweh sends Elijah to a widow in, of all places, the Phoenician city of Zarephath (Jezebel's turf). If God can use his creation (a brook, birds) to save Elijah, then he can use a desperate widow of a pagan nation who gave little in promise of being able to help him to save Elijah.

An univited, probably unknown, oddly dressed prophet of Israel shows up at the city gate of Zarephath, where a Phoenician widow, whose cupboards are nearly bare (thanks, in part, to this prophet), is gathering sticks for a fire for cooking or baking over. He asks her for a drink of water and, while she is at it, some bread or a cake. Cannot we hear her exclaim, "Wait a minute, mister"?

Elijah's claim on what little she has—what a powerful witness to faith! What if this woman had refused? What if she had said, "You can't ask me to do that"? Then she and her son would have died. As a result of her faith and charity a miracle takes place, and her cupboards are full. Possibly, Elijah's claim on what little she has reflects God's claim on what little we think we have. But when we give God that little, his power is unleashed to take over and provide.

The corollary of Elijah's claim on this widow is her claim on Elijah. When her only son is at the point of death, she directs a blunt question to the prophet. Is he the cause of the lad's illness? "What have you against me, O man of God?" (v. 18). It is as if she says, "I fed you; I saved you; now heal him." And exercise of faith leads to audacity in petition.

Elijah's taking the son to an "upper chamber" (v. 19) and "stretching himself" upon the child three times (v. 21) has faint verbal echoes with New Testament healings. Peter raised Dorcas in a "room upstairs" (Acts 9:37; Acts 9:37 and the Septuagint of 1 Kings 17:19 both use the Greek word *hyperōon*). And Elijah's stretching himself over the lad is like Paul "bending over" or "throwing himself on" the fallen Eutychus (Acts 20:10). And the healing of a widow's only son recalls a similar incident in Jesus' ministry (Luke 7:11–17). Throughout the Old Testament, while the priest may diagnose (e.g., skin diseases in Leviticus 13), healing comes directly from God alone or through his representative, the prophet.

It is interesting to note that in the following chapter (18), set in the land of Israel, Elijah sarcastically and powerfully demonstrates the ineffectiveness of Baal to do anything. But in this chapter, set in the land of Phoenicia, he calls upon Yahweh the God of Israel to intervene, and intervene he does. Elijah "would deny her [Jezebel's] god power in his land while readily exercising the power of his god in her land" (Trible 1995: 6).

It is a bit of a puzzle why this widow responds so enthusiastically after her son's cure ("Now I know that you are a man of God, and that the word of the Lord in your mouth is truth" [v. 24])—what Cohn (1982: 348) calls a "conversion," and what Jobling (1978: 71) calls an "epistemological turning-point"—when she makes no response after the truly great miracle of the perpetual supply of meal and oil. Does it take two miracles to convince her? Or does no response versus exuberant testimony illustrate that "we acknowledge God's beneficence as it operates in our narrow personal interests . . . and fail to acknowledge the unending miracles of daily existence and the unfailing grace that assures their continuance" (Brichto 1992: 129)?

Jesus made a particularly interesting use of the widow of Zarephath event, as found in Luke 4:16–30. Jesus, in his own synagogue in Nazareth, begins by quoting the good words of Isa. 61:1–2. He is the servant God has sent to let the oppressed go free and bring release to the captives. Understandably, the congregation directed accolades to this young preacher (v. 22), for they assumed they were the captives and the oppressed of whom Jesus spoke. He would liberate them from Roman tyranny. But then Jesus goes on to refer to God sending Elijah only to this Phoenician widow even though there were many widows in Israel (vv. 25–26), and only to Naaman the Syrian leper even though there were many lepers in Israel. At this point, the congregation did a 180-degree turn, and Jesus, whom they moments ago lauded, they now want to tar and feather (vv. 28–29). A sermon that, to begin with, soothed them made them seethe in the end. In speaking the way he did, Jesus was suggesting that no one group had a monopoly on the ministry of God's Messiah. God's heart beats for all peoples, the pagan as well as the elect.

Zarephath is a hiding place (a long one at that—two plus years!), not a dwelling place. In **chapter 18** God instructs Elijah to return to Israel and seek out Ahab. While Ahab and his officer Obadiah are foraging through the land looking for food for the animals, Obadiah stumbles into Elijah (vv. 7–16). Obadiah is a good man. He demonstrated his "fear of the Lord" by hiding one hundred prophets from Jezebel's murderous hands, and feeding them as well (vv. 3–4). He did for these prophets exactly what God had done for Elijah in ch. 17.

But when asked by Elijah to tell Ahab that the prophet has returned to Israel, he refuses, at least at first. Ahab will certainly kill him for returning empty-handed without Elijah. So, Obadiah fears Yahweh greatly, but he tries to get out of delivering Elijah's message to Ahab, for he fears for his life even more. But eventually he does go. In trying to take evasive action but ending up doing what he was asked to do, Obadiah is like Moses in Exodus 3–5 or Esther in Esther 4.

Elijah's meeting with Ahab (vv. 16b–19) is tense, but the king does not have the prophet arrested. For Obadiah, Elijah is "my lord" (v. 7); for Ahab, Elijah is "you troubler of Israel" (v. 17). To get to the root of the problem, the reason for the drought, Elijah proposes a contest on Mount Carmel (situated on the Mediterranean coast and within earshot of Jezebel's Phoenicia) between himself, the prophet of Yahweh, and the 450 prophets of Baal (and four hundred prophets of Asherah, who mysteriously disappear from the story at this point). Each group is to prepare an ox on the altar and then call upon Yahweh or Baal, with the deity who answers by fire being the true God. (Note the striking contrast here between Ahab out foraging for food for his animals while Jezebel feeds 850 prophets at her table [v. 19b].)

The Mount Carmel situation is analogous to Moses and Aaron's showdown with the Egyptian magicians, or the one between Yahweh and Dagon in the days of Samuel. Perhaps an even closer analogy is the contest between Korah and Moses (Numbers 16), which calls for a divine decision in the form of a moving theophany (Num. 16:5–11) and concludes with the death of the reprobates (Num. 16:31–35). There is also a parallel with the golden calf incident in Exodus 32 (both taking place on or near a mountain). In both cases, Moses and Elijah, when they speak, avoid threat or coercion: "Whoever is for the Lord, come to me" (Exod. 32:26); "If Yahweh is God, follow him; but if Baal, then follow him" (1 Kings 18:21b). And both times, divine judgment comes through human hands to those who resist the ways of God (Exod. 32:25–29; 1 Kings 18:40). A radical sin, one threatening the well-being of Israel, calls for radical measures. H. H. Rowley (1960–1961: 219) rightly said a number of years ago, "Without Moses the religion of Yahwism . . . would never have been born. Without Elijah it would have died."

It appears that Baal was not an important deity in Canaan until the second half of the second millennium. Even though the Amorites (i.e., Canaanites) occupied Palestine in the days of the patriarchs (Gen. 15:16), Baal does not appear anywhere in Genesis. Israel first confronts Baal and Baal worship (with disastrous results) when they wind down their wilderness wanderings at Baal-peor (Numbers 25). Baal, whose

name means "owner," was viewed as both a universal god, the Baal of
the earth, and a local god. Hence, in the name Baal-peor (Num. 25:3),
Baal is the name of the god, and Peor is the name of the locale. (Compare Baal-meon, "Baal of Meon" [Num. 32:38]; Baal-zephon, "Baal of
Zephon" [Num. 33:7].) Because Baal is the god of rain and fertility (i.e.,
a thunder-hurling weather god), he controls fire and lightning. So, in
making the test a divine answer by fire, Elijah is taking the battle
smack into Baal's turf, in which contest Baal is, on paper, the favorite.

With which Baal are Jezebel's prophets to be connected? Probably,
it is Baal Melqart, god of Tyre. But 1 Kings 18 does not get that specific.
And maybe the lack of precision is deliberate. Childs (1980: 131, 132)
states, "Could it be that in the very imprecision of the Old Testament
regarding the nature of the Baal involved the biblical writer was making his own theological evaluation as to what these gods were really
worth? . . . The contest for Elijah is not between two gods, but between
one God and a delusion." But if Baal is a delusion, he is a delusion that
is almost ineradicable in Israel. Long after Elijah and Jehu's day, there
are still those in Jeremiah's time who are prophesying by Baal (Jer.
2:8). Worship of Baal is the "kudzu weed" of biblical Israelites.

Throughout this chapter Elijah (and the narrator) always prefaces
"Baal" with the definite article, "the" (not normally reproduced in English translation): "the four hundred fifty prophets of the Baal" (v. 19);
"but if the Baal, then follow him" (v. 21); "but the Baal's prophets number four hundred fifty" (v. 22); "then Elijah said to the prophets of the
Baal" (v. 25); "they called on the name of the Baal . . . saying, 'the Baal,
answer us'" (v. 26); "seize the prophets of the Baal" (v. 40). What is the
thrust of this repeated use of the definite article before "Baal"? It is like
the repeated use of the article before "Satan" in Job 1–2 (fourteen times
in all)—for example, "the Satan also came among them" (Job 1:6). In
both places the article changes the following word from a personal
name to a title. Satan and Baal are not who they are (they are not entitled to the honor of a name) but what they are. So not only through his
taunts and sarcasm (even to the point of suggesting in v. 27 that Baal
is not answering because he is "visiting the privy," using bathroom/
scatological language [Rendsburg 1988]), but also through his designation of Baal as "the Baal," Elijah exudes his confidence in his God. That
he drenches the altar sacrifice with four jars of water three times (vv.
33–35) in the middle of a devastating drought, in effect wasting this
precious commodity, also shows his trust in a God who is about to
open up the heavens.

Elijah's having the prophets of Baal put to death (v. 40) may strike
the reader as going a bit too far. Possibly, Elijah's killing of the Baal

prophets is a quid pro quo (Jobling 1978: 80) for Jezebel's killing of the Yahweh prophets. If that is the case, Elijah not only emulates Jezebel but exceeds her in ordering the execution of almost five hundred clergy. The verb used in v. 40 for "kill, slaughter" is *shakhat*, and it is overwhelmingly a term for animal slaughter. There are ten instances where the verb is used for mass slaughter of persons (Num. 14:16; Judg. 12:6; 1 Kings 18:40; 2 Kings 10:7, 14; Jer. 39:6 [2x]; 41:7; 52:10 [2x]).

In **chapter 19** a direct threat on Elijah's life by Jezebel (v. 2; the first time she speaks in the narrative) sends him into hiding, first at Beersheba (v. 3), and then in a cave at Horeb/Sinai, the mount of God (v. 8). Elijah's experience parallels that of Moses (Coote 1981: 117):

1. Moses kills an Egyptian (Exod. 2:12).
   Elijah kills 450 prophets of Baal (1 Kings 18:40).
2. Pharaoh seeks to kill Moses (Exod. 2:15a).
   Jezebel seeks to kill Elijah (1 Kings 19:2).
3. Moses flees for his life to Midian (Exod. 2:15b).
   Elijah flees for his life to Beer-sheba and Horeb (1 Kings 19:3, 8).
4. Moses comes to a bush (Exod. 3:2).
   Elijah comes to a broom tree (1 Kings 19:4).
5. An angel appears out of nowhere (Exod. 3:2; 1 Kings 19:5).
6. Moses and God dialogue by debate (Exod. 3:7–4:17).
   Elijah and God dialogue by debate (1 Kings 19:9–18).
7. God provides Moses with Aaron as an assistant (Exod. 4:14–16).
   God provides Elijah with Elisha as a successor and assistant (1 Kings 19:16, 19–21).
8. God says to Moses, "Go, return" (*lek shuv*) to Egypt (Exod. 4:19).
   God says to Elijah, "Go, return" (*lek shuv*) to Damascus (1 Kings 19:15).
   Elijah says to Elisha, "Go, return" (*lek shuv*) to your parents (1 Kings 19:20).

A cave is a terrific place to hide; it is a terrible place to be caught, and a dangerous place to be during a windstorm strong enough to split mountains and cause avalanches, and an earthquake (v. 11). Elijah's "cave" equals Moses' "cleft of the rock" (Exod. 33:22). God's glory will "pass by" (*ʿavar*) Moses (Exod. 33:22b; 34:6) in his cleft, and God will "pass by" (*ʿavar*) Elijah's cave (1 Kings 19:11).

At the beginning of the chapter Elijah flees for his life (v. 3), but in the wilderness he wishes God to end his life (v. 4), a request God happily ignores. God's question, which he asks Elijah twice (vv. 9b, 13b), is "What are you doing here?" What would be different if God had asked, "What are you doing *there?*" instead of "What are you doing *here?*" "There" means God is outside the cave. "Here" indicates God is in the cave with Elijah. He is a God who enters our own caves of despondency.

This chapter is a powerful object lesson on how victory and celebration can give way to discouragement and withdrawal in the life of any of God's servants:

1. Where such despondency is found:
    a. in such a man, one of the spiritual giants of Scripture
    b. at such a moment, on the heels of God's miraculous provision during the drought, God's answer of fire at Carmel
    c. over such a matter, the death threat of one woman when 850 men had not fazed him at all
2. How such despondency is fostered:
    a. a sense of failure, "the Israelites have forsaken your covenant, thrown down your altars" (vv. 10, 14)
    b. a sense of loneliness, "I alone am left" (vv. 10, 14)
    c. a sense of weariness, "I have been very zealous for the Lord" (vv. 10, 14)
3. How such despondency is faced:
    a. "Get up and eat" (vv. 5, 7), a very practical ministry
    b. "Go, return" (v. 15), running and hiding are dead-end streets
    c. "I will follow you" (v. 20), God's provision of a ministering servant, Elisha (vv. 19–21); sometimes one must let others wash one's feet

Elijah's experience at Horeb/Sinai in 1 Kings 19 might shed some light on Gal. 1:17, where Paul says that after his conversion he "went away at once into Arabia" rather than go up to Jerusalem. Why go to Arabia, and where is Arabia? Arabia is a wide-stretching area to the south and southeast of Palestine, without specific boundaries. Paul is the only person in the New Testament to mention it, and he does so only in Galatians, here in 1:17 and later in 4:25 ("Hagar is Mount Sinai in Arabia"). This latter reference informs us that Sinai (the mount to which Elijah fled) is in Arabia.

Why go to Arabia? For a period of contemplative reflection on all that has recently happened in his life? For an attempt at evangelism of Gentiles? Or may Paul have gone there for the same reason Elijah did? Note that Elijah left Horeb/Arabia and went to Damascus (1 Kings 19:15), and Paul left Arabia for Damascus (Gal. 1:17b).

When Paul states in Gal. 1:14, "I was far more zealous for the traditions of my ancestors," that zeal is reflected not only in the intense study and scrupulous observance of the Torah but also in his elimination of those persons who were violating the law, moving away from that law; hence, his persecution of those who were followers of the Way (Acts 9:2).

As one who had a zeal for God and for religious purity, Saul of Tarsus had two Old Testament antecedents. One is Phinehas, priest and grandson of Aaron, who observed an Israelite male and his Midianite partner engaging in (ritual) intercourse right in front of the sanctuary and in the sight of Moses and all the people. Phinehas killed both of them and stopped God's plague as a result (Num. 25:8). For this action, Yahweh says, "Phinehas . . . has turned back my wrath from the Israelites by manifesting such a zeal among them on my behalf" (Num. 25:11). The other antecedent is Elijah. Twice (1 Kings 19:10, 14) he says, "I have been very zealous for the Lord," and that zeal included slaughtering the prophets of Baal. So we have the zeal of Phinehas, Elijah, and Saul of Tarsus. (One could also add Jehu, king of Israel, a slaughterer of pagans, who likewise speaks of his zeal for Yahweh [2 Kings 10:16].) In some Semitic languages the root *qn'* means "become intensely red," and refers to the effects of anger on the facial complexion.

In the case of Elijah, he encounters Jezebel and he goes to Arabia. In the case of Saul of Tarsus, he encounters Jesus and goes to Arabia. It is as if Saul of Tarsus, "having taken the Elijah of 1 Kings 18 as his role model in his persecuting zeal, took the Elijah of 1 Kings 19 as his role model when confronted, after his zealous triumph, with a totally new reality that made him question his whole life and mission to date" (Wright 1996: 687–88). And what Saul/Paul will learn is that "it was the death of Jesus at the hands of pagans, not the defeat of the pagans at the hand of the heaven-sent zealous hero, that defeated evil once and for all. . . . The cross offered the solution to the problem that 'zeal' had sought to address" (Wright 1996: 691–92).

Chapter 20 is an interlude in the Ahab and Elijah story, for while Ahab is present, Elijah is absent (although his place is taken by other anonymous prophets [vv. 13, 22, 28, 35]).

While the book of Kings ignores the famous battle of Karkar, in which Ahab was involved, it does devote a whole chapter (ch. 20) to Ahab's defensive border skirmish with Ben-hadad, king of Aram/Syria, Israel's northern neighbor.

In the two chapters of the Ahab story in which Elijah is not present (20; 22), the prevailing designation for Ahab changes radically from those chapters in which Elijah is present (17–19; 21) (see Brichto 1992: 169). In those chapters where Elijah is present, the king is called simply "Ahab" thirty-two times (17:1; 18:1, 2, 3, 5, 6, 9, 12, 16 [2x], 17 [2x], 20, 41, 42, 44, 45, 46; 19:1; 21:2, 3, 4, 8, 15, 16 [2x], 20, 21, 24, 25, 27, 29), but "King Ahab" only twice (21:1, 18). By contrast, in the two chapters where Elijah is absent (20; 22), royal terminology is prominent. Thus, in ch. 20 Ahab is just "Ahab" only once (v. 14), but "the king of Israel" twelve times (vv. 4, 7, 11, 15, 21, 22, 28, 31, 32, 40, 41, 43), "the king" two times (vv. 38, 39), and "King Ahab of Israel" two times (vv. 2, 13). The proliferation of regal terminology for Ahab in ch. 20 has the effect of placing Israel's king in a somewhat better light than he appears when Elijah is around.

It is also possible that the threefold use of "Ahab" in ch. 20 (vv. 2, 13, 14) is redactional (DeVries 1978: 122), and that the Israelite king J(eh)oram, brother and successor of Ahaziah and son of Ahab, is the actual "king of Israel" in ch. 20. This would provide an explanation of why Elijah does not appear in ch. 20, for there is no evidence that J(eh)oram and Elijah knew of each other or met, unlike, obviously, the situation of Elijah with Ahab and Ahaziah.

Except for the last section in this chapter (vv. 35–43), Ahab is like Elijah, and Ben-hadad, Aram's king, assumes the role of Ahab. It is Ben-hadad who attacks Samaria and is intent on plundering Ahab's family and treasures (vv. 1–6); drinks himself drunk (vv. 12, 16); believes that his troops can prevail against Ahab on the plain, for Ahab's god is a god of the hills, not of the flatter plains (v. 23); is the cause of the death of many of his troops (vv. 29–30), and finally is reduced to a pathetic suppliant who seeks clemency from Ahab (vv. 32–34).

On the other hand, not once but three times Ahab listens to a prophet (vv. 13–15, 22, 28) who, for a change, brings good news to Ahab. Elijah's promise of drought is replaced by a prophet's promise of victory. The purpose of these prophetic promises is not so that Ahab can boast, but so that he "shall know that I am the Lord" (vv. 13b, 28b). One would suspect that Ahab should already know this after what he saw happen to the prophets of Baal, as well as the termination of the drought in ch. 18. Maybe he needs a bit more convincing. Maybe he needs to know that Yahweh is indeed Yahweh, and that if Yahweh can triumph over Aramean gods, then faith can triumph over horses and chariots. As Israel was preparing to leave Egypt, the plagues would help them to know that Yahweh is God in a profounder sense than they had heretofore conceptualized (Exod. 6:7), to say nothing of what impact these demonstrations of divine power would have on pharaoh's and Egypt's cognition (Exod. 7:5, 17; 8:10, 22; 9:14, 29; 10:2; 11:7; 14:4, 18).

The last unit of ch. 20 (vv. 35–43) involves an anonymous member of a company of prophets disguising himself à la Jeroboam's wife in ch. 14. He waits for the king to pass by, just as Tamar, also in disguise, waited for her father-in-law to pass by (Gen. 38:14). Using a subterfuge, the bandaged prophet tricks the king into condemning himself for granting Ben-hadad clemency when, in fact, he ought to have executed him.

The ruse of the prophet recalls that of Nathan with David in 2 Samuel 12, and that of the wise woman of Tekoa with David in 2 Samuel 14. In each case, as Sternberg (1987: 429) remarks, "The king labors under the illusion that he is listening to a teller, not a reteller; that he is dealing with a genuine legal case, utterly divorced from his own affairs. Having engineered this ironic discrepancy, the parablist is free from the endemic handicaps of the genre and can exploit its strengths to trick the king into self-judgment."

The Israelite king's specific sin is that he "let the man go whom I [Yahweh] had devoted to destruction [*kherem*]" (v. 42a). We know that the desecration of *kherem* is one of the worst sacrileges of all in the Old Testament. Witness the story of Achan and Jericho (Joshua 7), or of Saul and the Amalekites and their king Agag (1 Samuel 15). But in both of those cases Yahweh had given an explicit command to obliterate the opposition. Not so here. The Israelite king's "crime" is not covetousness (Achan) or rationalization (Saul), but charity, forgiveness, and peaceableness. And are these crimes, or does this last prophet in ch. 20 misspeak?

One thing that connects ch. 20 with **chapter 21** is that at the end of ch. 20 and the beginning of ch. 21, Ahab is "sullen and resentful" (*sar weza'ep*) (20:43; 21:4). A stern prophet in the first and a stubborn neighbor in the second are the causes of his dejection. Chapter 21 is set in Jezreel. Apparently, Ahab had two residences, a winter palace in the warmer Jezreel Valley (v. 1) and his main one in Samaria (v. 18). His neighbor is Naboth, and in return for another vineyard or a fair asking price, Ahab wishes to extend his own real estate in Jezreel by having Naboth transfer ownership to him.

The reason Naboth rejects the king's offer (v. 3) seems to be based on the type of teaching found in Lev. 25:23–24, that the Israelites (either clans or individuals), God's tenants in the land of Canaan, do not have the right to alienate land through its permanent and irretrievable sale to a purchaser. For that reason, family relatives are under obligation to redeem the arable land of their relatives, so vital in an agricultural economy, in the event of possible sale or foreclosure. Hence, not even as powerful a person as the king could legally compel one of his subjects to sell any part of his family estate. The prophets condemn the tendency among the rich and powerful to foreclose on the land of the poor. So Isaiah says, "Ah, you who join house to house, who add field to field until there is room for no one but you" (5:8), and Micah speaks of the wicked who "covet fields, and seize them; houses, and take them away" (2:2).

Behind Naboth's refusal may also be the teaching about the inviolability of boundary markers, as seen in Deut. 19:14 ("You must not move your neighbor's boundary marker, set up by former generations"), Deut. 27:17 ("Cursed be anyone who moves a neighbor's boundary marker"), and Prov. 22:28 ("Do not remove the ancient landmark that your ancestors set up"). The disadvantaged were especially vulnerable to boundary tampering, a crime frequently committed nocturnally and in secret, because they lacked the means to defend their rights. The deep, emotional issue here is the attachment to the land they inherited from their ancestors. Deuteronomy 19:14 makes this clear with the phrase "set up by former generations," as does Naboth with his "what I have inherited from my fathers" (v. 3).

But Jezebel sees matters a bit differently than does her husband, Ahab. Here is a classic case of spouses who bring fundamentally different, and mutually exclusive, core values to their marriage and home. Ahab accepts that he cannot have what is not his, however much he desires it. Jezebel's philosophy is that if you have enough power, you can have whatever you want, and use whatever means necessary to get it. It is not expected that Phoenician Jezebel will order her life by the Israelite tenth commandment, when one of the major Canaanite epics from ancient Ugarit highlights favorably the covetous godess Anat, who, when rebuffed in her attempt to get her hands on young Aqhat's divinely fashioned bow in a fair and square way, resorts to violence.

Jezebel has two "scoundrels" (as if she is not one herself) charge Naboth with cursing God and the king. The Hebrew word in vv. 10 and 13 for "curse" is actually "blessed," the same scribal substitution of "curse" with "bless" when God is the object that is found in Job's wife's words "Curse [Bless] God and die" (Job 2:9). For such blasphemy Naboth is stoned to death, and so are his children, according to 2 Kings 9:25–26, thus removing them as heirs to their father's vineyard.

Neither Ahab nor Jezebel shares the whole truth with the other about what happened. Ahab does not tell Jezebel why Naboth would not sell him the vineyard (cf. v. 3 with v. 6), and Jezebel does not tell Ahab how Naboth died (cf. vv. 9–14 with v. 15). As Sternberg (1987: 408) notes, "Having already done the dirty work on her husband's behalf, Jezebel continues to spare his tender conscience by watering down the brutal 'Naboth has been stoned and he died' into the generalized 'Naboth is not alive, but dead.'" Surprisingly, Ahab makes no inquiry about how Naboth died. He simply "rushed off to embrace his new toy" (Brichto 1992: 149).

But then there's Elijah snooping around again (v. 17–29). He has a word for Ahab's future (vv. 20–22) and for Jezebel's future (v. 23; which reduces her to dog food). Ahab never quite gets around to addressing Elijah as "pastor," but he does call him "you troubler of Israel" (18:17), and here, "my enemy" (v. 20).

To his credit, Ahab (but not Jezebel [either because she was too proud or was given no opportunity]) humbles himself before this prophetic word (vv. 27–29). The consequences of sin, however, are not canceled, only postponed to a later generation ("in his son's days I will bring the disaster on his house"). This is another illustration of the doctrine of vertical retribution, that is, delayed punishment. It happens to David's son (2 Sam. 12:13–14); to Jeroboam's son (1 Kings 14:17–18); to the Phoenician widow's son, so she thinks (1 Kings 17:18); and now to Ahab's son; and it is part of the formulation of the second commandment (Exod. 20:5; Deut. 5:9). See also Exod. 34:7b and Lev. 26:39b (where the exiles' realization that they are suffering for the cumulative sins of previous generations as well as for their own merely adds to their distress). The same idea is stated in Lam. 5:7: "Our ancestors sinned; they are no more, and we bear their iniquities." The issue here is how to reconcile divine holiness and divine grace. As Walsh (1992: 207) remarks, "The law of talion and divine mercy are opposed. . . . But both of these realities are simply aspects of Yahweh's will. . . . We are uneasy because, no matter what happens, Yahweh's will must in some measure be thwarted by Yahweh himself."

The chapter is clearly divided into two parts: vv. 1–16 and vv. 17–29 (Walsh 1992). Part one begins in Naboth's vineyard (v. 1) and ends there as well (v. 16). Part two begins with the word of the Lord coming to Elijah (v. 17) and concludes with another divine revelation to Elijah

(vv. 28–29). In part one, Ahab covets a vineyard he cannot have, but he ends up getting it anyway through lies and violence. In part two, Ahab is condemned by Elijah, but ends up escaping immediate death through repentance. There is phony fasting in part one (vv. 9, 12), but real fasting in part two (v. 27). Jezebel writes a letter in part one, and Elijah delivers an oral message in part two, and both messages lead to somebody's death. In part one, Naboth loses the vineyard he inherited from his fathers; in part two, Ahab's condemnation is bequeathed to his sons.

Throughout this unfortunate incident Ahab and Jezebel managed to break at least five of the commandments: They dishonored Naboth's parents by expropriating what they had passed on to their son (no. 5); they murdered (no. 6); they stole (no. 8); they bore false witness literally against a neighbor (no. 9); and they, especially Ahab, coveted (no. 10). Ahab had not learned to be content with whatever he had (see Phil. 4:11). Such coveting led Ahab to

1. an obsession that was never controlled
   ("Give me"—Ahab [1 Kings 21:2]; the prodigal [Luke 15:12]; Simon Magus [Acts 8:19])
2. a transgression that was never intended
   (like Adam and Eve, another sin involving a garden, they begin so reasonably but end so tragically)
3. a possession that was never enjoyed
   (prophets are the voice of God in one's conscience and soul)

Chapter 22 takes the reader back to ch. 20. Both chapters involve border wars between the king of Israel and the king of Aram. In neither chapter is Elijah present, but other prophets are (ch. 20: unnamed prophets; ch. 22: Micaiah). And as in ch. 20, the name "Ahab" is relatively rare: only in v. 20 of the Ahab and Micaiah scenario (vv. 1–38), twice in his obituary notice (vv. 39–40), and three times as the contemporary of Jehoshaphat or father of Ahaziah (vv. 41, 49, 51). By contrast, in vv. 1–38 the more general "king of Israel" appears seventeen times (vv. 2, 3, 4, 5, 6, 8, 9, 10, 18, 26, 29, 30 [2x], 31, 32, 33, 34), and "the king" ten times (vv. 12, 13, 15 [3x], 16, 27, 35, 37 [2x]).

Jehoshaphat, king of Judah, sounding like Ruth ("Where you go, I will go"), agrees to join forces with Ahab to regain Israelite territory in Transjordan by fighting for the important city of Ramoth-gilead (vv. 1–4). In light of the information in 20:34 that upon his defeat by Ahab, Ben-hadad had promised to restore the towns that his father took from

Ahab's father, either Ramoth-gilead was not a part of that package deal or Ben-hadad reneged on his promise.

Jehoshaphat is a sensible and religiously oriented man. First, he wants to know God's mind on this matter (v. 5). And Ahab is able to so-licit positive reinforcement from four hundred prophets (v. 6). One ought to be suspicious when four hundred preachers agree on any-thing! Inspired individuals seldom appear in droves. Jehoshaphat is not impressed by such consensual optimism. Accordingly, he requests just one more prophetic take on the situation. And it is Micaiah. Let us call Micaiah "the 401st prophet."

Micaiah is not Ahab's favorite preacher. The king says, "He never prophesies anything favorable about me" (v. 8). Note that Ahab says "me," not "us." Here may be one of the major emphases of the chapter: "In promising the well-being of his people, Yahweh does not necessar-ily commit himself to the success of an individual leader seeking to im-pose his political will on the people. The leader is expendable, though the people never are" (De Vries 1978: 38).

In chapter 18 it was one prophet (Elijah) versus 450 (or 850) proph-ets. Here, it is one prophet (Micaiah) versus four hundred prophets. It is not unexpected that a Yahweh prophet will face intense opposition from Baal prophets (ch. 18), but equally severe opposition to a Yahweh prophet may come from other Yahweh prophets (ch. 22). That's the oddity. Where one expects collegiality there is confrontation.

After appearing to agree with the majority view in v. 15b (sarcasti-cally? hopefully? actually?), Micaiah shares a vision, much like that ex-perienced by Isaiah (Isaiah 6), in vv. 19–22. In this vision God is search-ing for somebody to "entice" Ahab into attacking Ramoth-gilead. A "spirit" or "the Spirit" volunteers to entice. Yahweh accepts this super-natural volunteer and his strategy, and even promises him success ("You are to entice him, and you shall succeed" [v. 22b]).

Does God entice or approve of such a strategy (Roberts 1986)? Jer-emiah thinks so. In Jer. 4:10 he says, "Ah, Lord God, how utterly you have deceived this people and Jerusalem" (using a verb for "deceive" different from the one in 1 Kings 22). In Jer. 15:18 he says that God is like "a deceitful brook" to him (using yet another word for "de-ceit"). The most interesting reference is Jer. 20:7, where Jeremiah uses the same verb (patah Piel) as 1 Kings 22, as well as the verb "suc-ceed, prevail":

> 1 Kings 22:22: "You are to entice [patah Piel] him, and you shall suc-ceed [yakol]."

Jer. 20:7: "O Lord, you have enticed me [*patah* Piel], and I was enticed [*patah* Niphal]. . . . and you have prevailed [*yakol*]."

Of course, these are Jeremiah's sentiments, expressed in moments of deep anguish to be sure, and not necessarily statements of mainstream, creedal orthodoxy. And yet, as high an orthodox spokesperson as St. Paul, when speaking of the coming day of the Lord, says, "For this reason God sends them a powerful delusion, leading them to believe what is false" (2 Thess. 2:11).

For so speaking, Ahab has Micaiah locked up (vv. 26–27), and Micaiah's last words recorded in Scripture are addressed to Ahab: "If you return in peace, the Lord has not spoken by me" (v. 28a). Micaiah's words are either feigned suspense (he knows that Ahab will not return), or genuine suspense, what Hamilton (1994: 657) calls "the principle of future uncertainty." That is, even for a prophet, the future may not be known for sure until the future becomes the present or past.

Ahab does not return in peace. In spite of his attempt to decrease his high visibility as king by dressing as an ordinary soldier (v. 30), a Syrian fighter, thinking he has wounded an Israelite "GI," lands an arrow in an exposed spot between portions of Ahab's armor as accurately as David's stone hitting Goliath's exposed forehead (v. 34). Ahab bleeds to death, and the dogs of Samaria lick up his blood and harlots bathe in it (v. 38). A soldier of the Syrian king ends Ahab's life even though Ahab had spared the Syrian king's own life when he had him at his mercy (20:34). It is Ahab's own foolishness, his several good traits nothwithstanding, that leads to his demise, not the "inscrutable" will of God. His life and death are "a tragedy of flaw rather that a tragedy of fate" (Hamilton 1994: 602).

There are two remaining events involving Elijah (2 Kings 1:1–18; 2:1–18). Like John the Baptist (Matt. 3:4; Mark 1:6), Elijah does not go for Armani suits; instead, he prefers the clothes of an asetic (1:8). He confronts messengers of King Ahaziah (son and successor of Ahab) as they go to "Baal-zebub, the god of Ekron" to see if the king will recover from serious injuries he sustained in a fall. That they have to go to Ekron, a neighboring Philistine city, may be testimony to the decisiveness with which Elijah has discouraged soliciting any god on Israelite territory except Yahweh. The situation is the reverse of that in ch. 5, where Naaman, the Syrian general from Damascus, seeks out a Hebrew prophet of Yahweh at Samaria for healing. Fortunately for Naaman, there is no Aramean Elijah who rebukes him with "Is it because there is no God in Damascus that you are going to Samaria to inquire of Yahweh, the god of Israel and of Elijah?"

The identity of the god of Ekron as "Baal-zebub" (usually it is Dagon) is unique to this passage. The name means "lord of flies" or "fly master," and may be an intentional distortion (and therefore an invention) of Baal-zebul, "Baal the Prince" or "princely lord." In the New Testament, Baal-zebub is a name for the archetypal enemy of God (Matt. 10:25; 12:24; Mark 3:22; Luke 11:15–19).

Ahaziah's mistake is his belief that in a time of dire need his appeal for healing and restoration is best brought before a god other than Yahweh. Such deviance costs him the lives of 102 of his men (1:9–12) and his own life (1:16–17). He is followed by his brother J(eh)oram.

It is interesting that for all his involvement, via Jezebel, with Baal worship and the prophets of Baal, Ahab has two sons to whom he gives names that include some abbreviated form of Yahweh. "Ahaziah" means "Yah[weh] has taken [by the hand?]," and "Jehoram" means "Yahweh [has raised?] on high." He does not name them "Ahazbaal" or "Baalram." The name honors God, but unfortunately, the behavior does not. In the case of 2 Kings 1:1–17, King "Yahweh-has-taken" has taken to Baal-zebub.

One last scene with Elijah involves his movement from place to place accompanied by Elisha (Gilgal to Bethel to Jericho), and finally across the Jordan, where he ascends to heaven, but not before giving Elisha a "double portion" of his spirit (2:1–18).

The scene has a parallel before it and after it in Scripture. The earlier parallel is that Moses must "depart" before the spirit comes on his successor, Joshua (Num. 27:18–23; and especially Deut. 34:9: "Joshua son of Nun was full of the spirit of wisdom, because Moses had laid his hands on him"). One cannot find Moses after his departure, and the same is true with Elijah (2:16–18). The later parallel is in the New Testament. Jesus must depart before the Spirit comes on his followers (Acts 1:1–11). Elisha "sees" Elijah depart (2 Kings 2:10, 12). The disciples "see" Jesus depart (Acts 1:9). The Greek word for Jesus' ascension ("taken up" in Acts 1:2, 11) is *analambanō*, the same word used in 2 Kings 2:9–11 (Septuagint) for Elijah's ascension. With the double share of the spirit, Elisha is able to do things that he did not, could not, do earlier. With the effusive, Pentecostal outpouring of the Spirit, the 120 believers in the upper room are able to do what they did not, could not, do earlier.

The "double share of your spirit" (2:9) for which Elisha asks Elijah does not mean that he desires twice as much of the spirit as his mentor had. No disciple would aspire to having twice the predecessor and master's power. What "a double share/portion" means is "two-thirds." The Hebrew expression occurs again only in Deut. 21:17 (the portion that the chief heir gets in contradistinction to his brother(s), who get a single share) and in Zech. 13:8 ("In the whole land . . . two-thirds shall be cut off"). No heir can possibly get twice the estate. So if there are two sons, the chief heir obtains two-thirds, and the other, one-third. If there are three sons, the chief heir obtains one-half, and the other two, one-fourth each. If there are four sons, the chief heir obtains two-fifths, and the other three, one-fifth each. If there are nine sons, the chief heir obtains two-tenths, and the other eight, one-tenth each. So then, in making such a request, Elisha is asking Elijah to make him *the* successor to Elijah, not merely *a* successor.

In contradistinction to the judges, where the spirit rushes, seizes, comes upon the individual, implying an episodic and ephemeral coming of the spirit, the spirit "rests" on Elisha (2:15), implying a permanent and enduring dynamic. The verb for the "resting" of the spirit upon somebody (*nuakh*) is used in Num. 11:25–26 of the elders who would share responsibility with Moses in governing the people ("and the spirit rested on them"). Isaiah also uses it in his prophecy of the messianic king: "The spirit of the Lord shall rest on him" (Isa. 11:2).

A tradition in earlier Judaism says that Elisha actually outdid his famous predecessor in working signs and wonders ("Elisha performed sixteen miracles and eight was all his master performed"), and may mean that to some, "double portion" did mean "twice as much." The origin of "sixteen" is obscure; we can discern maybe thirteen miracles:

1. striking the Jordan with Elijah's mantle, causing the water to part (2:13–14)
2. the transformation of bad water into good water by throwing salt into it (2:19–22)
3. the perfect timing of the filling of a wadi in Edom with a torrent of water for the three kings who march against Moab and Mesha (3:16–18) (sudden heavy storms filling dry river beds rather quickly is not at all unusual)
4. the abundant supply of oil for the widow so she can pay the creditor who is about to take away her children as slaves (4:1–7)
5. a prophecy (which is fulfilled) that a barren woman, who had been Elisha's hostess, will have a son (4:15–17)
6. the subsequent restoration of this son to life after he dies (4:18–37)
7. turning the pot of spoiled stew into edible stew by throwing flour into it (4:38–41)

8. feeding a large group of people with a relatively small amount of food (4:42–44)
9. the cleansing of Naaman the leper (5:1–27)
10. the floating ax head (6:1–7)
11. a mountain full of horses and fiery chariots and the blinding of the invading Aramean army (6:8–23), a miracle of opening somebody's eyes (6:17) and closing of somebody else's eyes (6:18)
12. a prophecy of the end of famine, which happens (7:1, 16), notwithstanding the cynical protest of a doubting Thomas (7:2, 17–20)
13. a dead man whose corpse is thrown into Elisha's grave coming back to life as soon as the corpse touches Elisha's bones (13:20–21)

The preceding list suggests several things. First, Elisha's miracles (and Elijah's too) are more like the miracles of Jesus than those of the Moses and Joshua era. For while the latter (e.g., parting of the sea, the manna, the stopped-up Jordan) are for the benefit of the nation, those of Elisha (and Elijah) are primarily for the benefit of individuals.

Second, some of Elisha's miracles are quite similar to some of Elijah's. Both men part the waters of the Jordan with an article of clothing (2 Kings 2:8; 2:14). Both feed a large number of people or a family that has little food (1 Kings 17:14–16; 2 Kings 4:1–7). Both cure/raise a sick/dead son (1 Kings 17:17–23; 2 Kings 4:18–36). Both make use of fire (1 Kings 18:24, 38; 2 Kings 1:10, 12; 6:17). Both are involved in a miraculous event that focuses on somebody doing something seven times (1 Kings 18:43–44; 2 Kings 5:10, 14). Both end a famine (1 Kings 18:41–45; 2 Kings 7:1, 16).

That Elisha can, by God's spirit, replicate some of Elijah's miracles implies that Elijah is not an absolutely unique, omnipotent prophet. Gros Louis (1974: 183) explains the similarities: "Either Elijah and Elisha are equal in power and magic, or their skill comes from another source. And, of course, everything in Kings points to that other source, the Lord God of Israel."

Third, Elisha is mentioned only once in the New Testament ("There were also many lepers in Israel at the time of the prophet Elisha," Luke 4:27). By contrast, Elijah is mentioned numerous times: (1) in conjunction with the identity of John the Baptist and Jesus (Matt. 11:14; 17:10–13; Mark 6:14–15; 8:28; 9:9–13; Luke 1:17; John 1:19–21); (2) in the preaching of Jesus (Luke 4:25–26); (3) on the Mount of Transfiguration (Matt. 17:1–8; Mark 9:2–8; Luke 9:28–36); (4) as an example of intercessory praying (James 5:17); (5) as one who prayed for God to grant him his own demise, only to be corrected by God (Rom. 11:2–4).

And yet, for all these extra notations in the New Testament about Elijah, it may be that the miracle ministry of Jesus is more like that of Elisha than it is of Elijah (Brown 1971). To begin with, even though the public distinguished John the Baptist from Elijah by suggesting that Jesus was either John the Baptist *or* Elijah (Mark 6:14–15; 8:28), and though John the Baptist expressly denied he was Elijah (John 1:21), Jesus clearly identified John the Baptist in the role of Elijah (Matt. 11:14; 17:10–13; Mark 9:9–13), as did the angel to Zechariah, the Baptist's father (Luke 1:17). Elijah and John the Baptist both "dress down" (2 Kings 1:8; Matt. 3:4; Mark 1:6), and both are ascetic, solitary figures who are not mixers or partiers.

If the connection of Elijah with John the Baptist can be sustained, then it is logical to continue and connect Elisha with Jesus. After all, both their names contain the verb "save" or the noun "salvation," and behind both names is the Hebrew root *yshᶜ*. Elisha receives Elijah's spirit by the Jordan (2 Kings 2:6–15), and Jesus receives the Spirit in his baptism by the Jordan. Unlike either Elijah or John the Baptist, Elisha and Jesus dress like everybody else and are quite at home in the midst of crowds. Elisha can hear and see what is going on elsewhere (2 Kings 5:26, he knows about Gehazi lying to Naaman and tricking him into paying a fee for Elisha's services; 6:12, he knows what the king of Aram says even in his bedroom; 6:32, he knows somebody has been sent to kill him). Jesus, too, can see and hear what is going on elsewhere (John 1:48–49, he already knows Nathaniel; Mark 11:2–3, he already knows the colt and its owner and what he might say; Mark 14:13–14, he already knows the house, and its owner, where he and his disciples will eat the Passover meal). And might we connect the story of the corpse of the man that comes back to life when it touches Elisha's bones (2 Kings 13:20–21) with the note in Matt. 27:52 that after Jesus' death "the tombs also were opened, and many bodies of the saints who had fallen asleep were raised"?

At least three of Elisha's miracles parallel Jesus' miracles: (1) Elisha's cleansing of Naaman's leprosy (2 Kings 5) and Jesus' cleansing of lepers, especially the ten lepers (Luke 17:11–19); (2) Elisha's feeding a large multitude with just twenty barley loaves and fresh ears of grain (2 Kings 4:42–44) and Jesus' multiplication of the loaves in the Gospels (cf. the servant's doubting question, "How can I set this before a hundred people?" [2 Kings 4:43], with Andrew's "But what are they among so many people?" [John 6:9b]); and (3) Elisha's resuscitation of the son of a woman from Sunem (2 Kings 4:8–37) with Jesus' resuscitation of the son of the widow of Nain, which is not far from Sunem (Luke 7:11–17).

Let us compare, for example, the Naaman story and the ten lepers story:

Naaman (2 Kings 5)	Ten Lepers (Luke 17:11–19)
1. Naaman visits Elisha in Samaria (v. 9).	Miracle takes place between Samaria and Galilee (v. 11).
2. There is no cure in the presence of the healer; Naaman must go to the Jordan (vv. 10, 14).	There is no cure in the presence of of the healer; they must go and show themselves to the priests (v. 14).
3. Naaman, a Syrian, returns to thank Elisha (v. 15).	One leper, a Samaritan, returns to thank Jesus (vv. 15–16).
4. Naaman praises God ("Now I know that there is no God . . . except in Israel") (v. 15).	"He turned back, praising God with a loud voice" (v. 15; cf. v. 18).
5. Elisha says to Naaman, "Go in peace" (v. 19).	Jesus says to the Samaritan, "Get up and go on your way" (v. 19).

To be sure, there are also differences between Elisha and Jesus and their miracles. Jesus floats no ax head, for example. Also, the one time that Elijah is subjected to insults (2 Kings 2:23–24 [on which, see the very interesting comments in Brichto 1992: 196–98]), two she-bears come out of the woods and maul the insulters. But when Jesus is insulted painfully and degradingly and criminally, there are no she-bears, only the prayer "Father, forgive them; for they do not know what they are doing" (Luke 23:34).

Elisha's last assignment is to play a role in the anointing of Jehu as king of Israel in place of J(eh)oram (9:1–3), to whom the prophet gives the responsibility for destroying the "house of Ahab" (interestingly, not "the house of Omri") (2 Kings 9:6–10).

And that he does, rather systematically and brutally, as described in 2 Kings 9–10. White (1994: 76) correctly notes that the "sole focus of the Jehu narrative is on the exterminations to the exclusion of anything having to do with his actual rule." Here are his victims: (1) J(eh)oram, king of Israel (9:14–26); (2) Ahaziah, king of Judah (9:27–28); (3) Jezebel (9:30–37); (4) Ahab's seventy sons (10:1–11); (5) relatives of King Ahaziah of Judah (10:12–14); (6) any others left to Ahab in Samaria (10:17); (7) Jehu lures all of the prophets of Baal (some remain after Elijah's fiery episode on Carmel) into a Baal temple for a religious celebration. By stationing well-armed guards at the exits, he has the entire congregation of Baalists killed in cold blood (10:18–27). But even though Jehu wiped out Baal from Israel (10:28), he did not wipe out Jeroboam from his own heart (10:29–31). And apparently, Baal has a way of bouncing back after his excision (see Jer. 2:8).

Hopefully, Jehu's method of purging the nation of sinful deviation, even if authorized by Elisha, is part of our unusable past. But maybe it hasn't been. Cyrus Gordon (*The Ancient Near East* [New York: 1965]: 207) remarks,

> Jehu's purge was fatal not only for the history of Israel but for all Western civilization thereafter, for it was a precedent of exclusivism, of fanaticism, where no toleration for any other cult was permissible. This frightful precedent had its reflexes not only on the rare occasions where Jews were in a position to implement such a policy, but more particularly in the history of Christianity and of Islam. Thus the bloody religious wars of Christian Europe in the sixteenth and seventeenth centuries A.D., echo, though indirectly, Jehu's precedent in ancient Israel.

2 Kings 11–17: Jehoahaz to the End of Northern Israel

Kings of Israel	Length of Reign	Bright	Galil	Hayes/Hooker	Thiele
Jehoahaz	17 years	815–801	819–804/3	821–805	814–798
J(eh)oash	16 years	801–786	805–790	804–789	798–782
Jeroboam II	41 years	786–746	790–750/49	788–748	793–753
Zechariah	6 months	746–745	750/49	747	753
Shallum	1 month	745	749	747	752
Menahem	10 years	745–738	749–738	746–737	752–742
Pekahiah	2 years	738–737	738–736	736–735	742–740
Pekah	20 years	737–732	(750?)–732/1	734–731	753–732
Hoshea	9 years	732–724	732/1–722	730–722	732–722

[end of northern Israel, fall of Samaria: 722/1]

Kings of Judah	Length of Reign	Bright	Galil	Hayes/ Hooker	Thiele
Athaliah (queen)	?	842–837	842/1–835	839–833	841–835
J(eh)oash	40 years	837–800	(842/1)–802/1	832–803	835–796
Amaziah	29 years	800–783	805/4–776/5	802–786	796–767
Uzziah (Aza-riah)	52 years	783–742	788/7–736/5	785–760	792–740
Jotham	16 years	742–735	758/7–742/1	759–744	750–732
Ahaz	16 years	735–715	742/1–726	743–728	735–715

This unit in Scripture does not begin on a hopeful or godly note, but then, few do in this part of the Bible. Most of **chapter 11** focuses on Athaliah, mother of the slain king of Judah, Ahaziah. Athaliah is indicted for two major mistakes. First, following her own son's execution at Jehu's hands, she attempts to wipe out the house of David (11:1b), and would have succeeded had not Jehosheba, sister of the slain son, whisked young J(eh)oram (Athaliah's grandson) away and had the priests hide him in the temple for several years (11:2–3). The reference to J(eh)oram being concealed for "six" years (v. 3) and the beginning of his reign in the "seventh" year (v. 4) recalls the six-seven pattern in the creation story of Gen. 1:1–2:3 (six days of divine activity followed by a seventh day of divine rest), or the "Six things Yahweh hates, seven are an abomination to him" in Prov. 6:16.

Jehosheba's actions in hiding her nephew from the wrath of the monarch parallel those of Jochebed and Miriam in saving their son/brother from an infanticidal pharaoh (Exod. 2:1–4). In one case (Exodus 2), deliverance for the very young child is in one kind of an "ark" (*tevah*). In the other case (2 Kings 11), deliverance for the very young child is in the house of the Lord close to another kind of "ark" (*ʾaron*).

Athaliah's second serious error is her worship of Baal (11:18). Baal worship in the north, such as Elijah had confronted, is bad enough, but what is one to do when not only a Jezebel, an outsider, introduces it far from Jerusalem, but also when an Athaliah, an insider, introduces it so close to the holy temple in Jerusalem? Of course, Baal worship promoted by Athaliah is not all that unexpected, given the fact that she is the (grand)daughter of Omri (2 Kings 8:26; 2 Chron. 22:2) and/or the

daughter of Ahab (2 Kings 8:18; 2 Chron. 21:6 [both of which intentionally avoid using her name]), hence, a daughter of Jezebel.

How far Athaliah lives beneath her name! "Athaliah" means
"Yah[weh] is exalted," or "Yah[weh] is upright," or "Yah[weh] has declared his eminence." Here is a case where the name most definitely
does not reflect the character or the moral value of the one who bears
the name.

It is interesting to note who challenges and confronts Baalism in Israel and Judah at this time. In Israel, prophets (especially Elijah) lead
the anti-paganism revolt. But in Judah, priests (especially Jehoiada
[see vv. 4, 9, 15, 17, 18–19]), in conjunction with "the people of the
land" (vv. 18–19), lead the anti-paganism revolt. During David's reign
priests did play a significant role in political affairs (see the references
in 2 Sam. 15:35–36; 17:15–17; 19:11–15; 1 Kings 1:7–8, 38–39). But
after Solomon takes the throne, the role of the clergy in the affairs of
the empire is negligible.

It is only appropriate that J(eh)oash, he who has been shielded by
and indoctrinated under the teaching and supervision of the priests for
six years, should devote much of his reign to overseeing the repair of
the temple in **chapter 12** (vv. 4–16), much as Josiah, a later and more
famous king of Judah, will do (2 Kings 22).

But after twenty-three years of his reign (v. 6), while the money has
been coming in, no repairs have been made to the temple. Somebody
has been pocketing a lot of cash. What does this suggest about the dis-
honesty and negligence of at least some of the priests? Are the clergy,
the sacred, officiating temple servants of God, any better than a Baal-
worshiping Athaliah? The priests apparently are as capable of hiding
money as they are of hiding children.

J(eh)oash therefore orders that all monies donated by the people are
to go toward temple repairs (vv. 9–15). The only exception is that "the
money from the guilt offerings and the money from the sin offerings
was not brought into the house of the Lord; it belonged to the priests"
(v. 16). This last verse is in keeping with Lev. 6:26 and 7:7, which direct
that the meat from these two offerings be eaten by the priests. But
2 Kings 12:16 speaks of the money, not the animal flesh from these offerings. For the guilt offering this is not an issue, for it is "convertible
into silver" (Lev. 5:15), that is, the offerer had the option of donating
the sacrifice's monetary equivalent. But nowhere is this stated for the
sin offering. What this verse in 2 Kings 12 seems to suggest is that the
money/silver brought to the temple for these two specific offerings was
held by the priests in order to purchase the necessary sacrificial ani-

mals (hence available for resale to the laity) rather than diverted to the temple repair fund.

For all of his positive contributions, J(eh)oash still has his share of blemishes. Not only did he not eliminate the high places (v. 3), but he also bought off king Hazael of Syria with sacred vessels from the temple and valuables from the palace and temple when Hazael invaded Jerusalem (vv. 17–18). Chronicles adds that after the death of the priest Jehoiada, J(eh)oash turned away from God totally and ignored the warnings of God-sent prophets (2 Chron. 24:17–19), thus opening his nation this time to devastation at the hands of the Syrians (2 Chron. 24:23–24).

In northern Israel, as observed in **chapter 13**, Jehu is followed by his son Jehoahaz (vv. 1–9) and Jehoahaz's son J(eh)oash (not to be confused with the Judean king with the same name) (vv. 10–25). Jehoahaz is but a puppet of Syria, his military arsenal reduced to fifty horsemen, ten chariots, and ten thousand foot soldiers (13:7). There may be no Baal facilities left in Israel, thanks to Jehu's purge, but a generation later neither are there any chariots left in Israel. Elisha, who is still around, never surfaces during Jehoahaz's seventeen-year reign. Jehoahaz does pray, however, as intercessor, and God honors that (13:4–5).

Unlike his father, Israel's next king, J(eh)oash, does meet with Elisha (13:14–19), and the prophet, now terminally ill, asks him to shoot arrows as a sign of Yahweh's arrow of victory over Syria, and then to strike the ground with arrows as a sign of how many times J(eh)oash will defeat Syria. Jehoahaz had little arsenal (13:7), and his son has little faith (13:18–19). God promises many victories, but J(eh)oash is content with just three (13:18b, 19, 25b).

Even in death the presence of Elisha makes a difference (13:20–21). A deceased man, interred in the same grave as the prophet, comes back to life when his corpse touches Elisha's bones. Elisha dead is more effective than most people alive! Normally, what is dead defiles (see Numbers 19) and is not to be touched, but here the lifeless bones of Elisha bring life to another. The language of restriction against "touching" (*naga*ᶜ) a corpse in Numbers (Num. 19:11, 13) uses the same word here for the deceased "touching" (*naga*ᶜ) Elisha's bones (13:21b). One touching leads to impurity; the other touching leads to life.

Amaziah follows J(eh)oash as the next king of Judah in **chapter 14** (vv. 1–22). Perpetuating a cycle of violence, he avenges his father's death (14:5), but he does not kill the children of the actual murderers (14:6). This latter deed is said to be done in obedience to the teaching of Deut. 24:16 that children are not to be put to death for the sins of their parents. It is not clear whether this is the king's own reason for his restraint or that supplied by the narrator.

Amaziah is also successful in war against the nearby Edomites (14:7), but such success emboldens him to challenge the stronger King J(eh)oash of Israel (14:8–14). Brother fighting brother! Child of God fighting child of God! And in such challenges David does not always win. Sometimes Goliath does. Israel defeats Judah (14:12), and J(eh)oash plunders the temple and the royal treasury (14:14). The tragic consequences of arrogance and folly!

The end of ch. 14, in seven short verses (vv. 23–29), discusses, almost in a blink-and-you-miss-it style, the lengthy forty-one-year reign of Jeroboam II of Israel. This cursory treatment of the monarch who established the farthest-flung empire ever won by the northern kingdom of Israel is interesting. His political achievements are underscored in 14:25: "He restored the border of Israel from Lebo [or, 'the entrance to'] Hamath [the pass between Mount Lebanon and Mount Hermon and the northernmost boundary of Solomon's kingdom] as far as the Sea of Arabah [the Dead Sea]." Although Jeroboam II is "evil" (14:24), God uses him to "save" Israel (14:27b).

Jeroboam II's expansionist policies are partially stimulated by "Jonah son of Amittai the prophet" (14:25b). Apparently, Jonah is fonder of Jeroboam II than he is of the Ninevites. With his own king, Jonah is optimistic and buoyant even though there is evil present (14:24) yet no repentance, but with the king of Nineveh, he is downright nasty even though the Ninevites repent of their evil. God needs no fish to get Jonah behind the mission of Jeroboam II. Two other prophets of this period, Hosea (himself a northerner), who is preaching during the last part of Jeroboam II's reign, and Amos (a southerner in the northern kingdom, who is preaching during the height of Jeroboam II's reign) are not nearly so supportive.

The note in 14:28b ("he [Jeroboam II] recovered for Israel Damascus and Hamath, which had belonged to Judah") is certainly puzzling. Damascus of Syria never belonged to southern Judah. Possibly by "Judah" is meant not the southern kingdom of Judah but the small kingdom with the same name in far-northern Syria, known in other documents as "Samal."

The first seven verses of **chapter 15** briefly discuss the fifty-two-year reign of Azariah (= Uzziah), Jerobom II's contemporary in Judah, and in the year of whose death Isaiah received his call to be a prophet (Isa. 6:1). He receives much more coverage and more favorable treatment in Chronicles (see 2 Chronicles 26, esp. vv. 5–15).

Second Kings 15:5 merely states that "the Lord struck the king, so that he was leprous to the day of his death." Second Chronicles 26:16–21 explains why. He who "set himself to seek God" (2 Chron. 26:5) detoured from that objective, did a 180-degree turn, so that "when he became strong he grew proud, to his destruction" (2 Chron. 26:16). A God-seeker became a self-promoter. A would-be Lucifer becomes leprous.

The specific nature of Uzziah's sin is his offering of incense inside the temple. His offering is out of line because both place and rite—entering the sanctuary and officiating there—are forbidden to the non-priest (Num. 16:40). Twice, his sin is described with the verb *ma'al* ("transgress, trespass, desecrate, commit sacrilege"): "For he was false to the Lord his God. . . . Go out of the sanctuary, for you have done wrong" (2 Chron. 26:16, 18). As a result, he is stricken immediately with a skin disease on his forehead (2 Chron. 26:20), for which he is banished from the royal compound to live in "a separate house" (2 Kings 15:5 = 2 Chron. 26:21), but apparently not from the city of Jerusalem. His son Jotham takes over as regent in his father's absence (2 Kings 15:5b = 2 Chron. 26:21b). Uzziah tried to go where he was not authorized to go. He ends his life going to a place to which he did not have to go. Unhappy that he is excluded from temple rites, he ends his life excluded from the very places where he could make a difference.

In the last fifteen years of his fifty-two-year reign Uzziah witnesses no fewer than five changes of royal leadership to his north: Zechariah, Shallum, Menahem, Pekahiah, and Pekah (15:8–31). Kings, supposedly foundational persons in their society, become revolving doors. God "strikes" (*naga'*) Uzziah (15:5), but assassins "strike" (*nakah*) these Israelite kings (15:10, 14, 25).

Uzziah has the good fortune of being followed by a son, Jotham, who follows his father's good points (15:34) but happily avoids his father's flaws and brazenness (15:32–38). The one blotch on his record is that like his father (15:4), he did not eliminate the pagan high places (15:35).

Chapter 16 describes the sixteen-year reign of Jotham's son Ahaz. The level of condemnation for Ahaz is more intense than for other Judean kings and even some Israelite kings. He actually worships at the forbidden high places (16:4), the first king since Solomon to do so (1 Kings 3:3). He also "made his son pass through fire" (16:3; 2 Chron. 28:3 says "sons"), possibly a reference to something like the cult of Molech/Moloch, a deity worshiped by some of Israel's neighbors through the sacrificing (by fire) of children. The practice of devoting children to Molech is prohibited to the people of God, according to Lev. 18:21 and 20:2–5. See also the condemnation of fire rituals in Deut.

12:31 and 18:10. The idea behind such a grotesque practice is that to get the "best" from a god, that which is most earnestly desired, the devotee has to offer to that god his or her best, most precious gift. Ahaz should consider himself fortunate that his father, Jotham, was not a practicing Molechite!

The failing of Ahaz that 2 Kings 16 highlights the most is his appeal to Assyria for assistance against Syria and Israel, who have teamed up against him (16:5–9; cf. Isaiah 7). Poor Ahaz! He views Syria and Israel as enemies, and Assyria as a savior. Here is a classic case of an individual who can see the short-range issues but not the long-range issues, and for this short-sightedness Ahaz will pay dearly. According to 2 Chron. 28:19 Ahaz's serious error in judgment (appealing to Assyria) leads to the subjugation of Judah. Wanting to save Judah, he leads Judah into bondage. An alliance means a noose around the neck.

While in Damascus meeting with the Assyrian king Tiglath-pileser, Ahaz sees an altar with which he is so enamored that he redesigns the altar in the Jerusalem temple after it (16:10–16), architectural innovations in the temple about which the Chronicler says nothing directly (see 2 Chronicles 28).

As with Uzziah (see 2 Chron. 26:16–18), Chronicles charges Ahaz with *ma'al* ("faithless" [2 Chron. 28:19, 22]), and again this involves tampering with the temple sancta. Ahaz (2 Chron. 28:27) joins J(eh)oram (2 Chron. 21:20), Joash (2 Chron. 24:25), and Uzziah (2 Chron. 26:23), who, while buried inside Jerusalem, are denied burial in "the tomb of the kings."

Chapter 17 describes the end of the northern kingdom of Israel. It does so in four units:

1. vv. 1–6: the reign of Hoshea, the last king of Israel, and the fall of Israel at the hands of the Assyrian kings Shalmaneser V (727–722 B.C.) (v. 3) and Sargon II (722–705 B.C.) (vv. 5–6)
2. vv. 7–23: a theological explanation of the demise of the northern kingdom (with brief asides to Judah too)
3. vv. 24–33: non-Israelites, forcibly resettled in Israel by Assyria, worshipping Israel's God and their own gods
4. vv. 34–41: northern Israelites addicted to idolatry

Hoshea's sin, apart from the generic condemnation "did evil," is that he plays political football. At first he is a willing vassal of Assyria (v. 3). But then he switches teams, shifting his allegiance to "King So of Egypt" (v. 4). Bad move! No pharaoh named "So" is attested in all the extant Egyptian records we have from the Nile Valley. More than likely,

"So" is Tefnakht I (740–718 B.C.), who founded the Twenty-fourth Dynasty and was the king of Sais in the western Delta (Christensen 1989). "So" would be taken as the Hebrew rendering of "Sais."

Several things are of interest in the section justifying Israel's exile (vv. 7–23). For one thing, condemnation is heaped not on the kings, who have thus far been the preoccupation of First and Second Kings, but on the people at large. They are identified as either "the people of Israel" (vv. 7, 8, 9, 22) or just "Israel" (vv. 13, 18, 23 [2x]). Thus, exile comes about not because of the sins of the few, but because of the sins of the many (even though the kings were influential in seducing their people away from God [v. 8b]). There is both royal sin and rampant sin in Israel.

The only king mentioned is Jeroboam I (explicitly in vv. 21–22 and implicitly in v. 16). Ahab may also be footnoted, for the expression in v. 17 of people "selling themselves to do evil" appears again in Kings only in connection with Ahab (1 Kings 21:20, 25).

In fact, some of the sins listed in this chapter are used elsewhere in Kings only in connection with southern kings and their people (Viviano 198: 552):

v. 11: "There they made offerings [literally, 'burned incense'] on all the high places." See Jehoshaphat (1 Kings 22:43); J(eh)oash (2 Kings 12:3); Amaziah (2 Kings 14:4); Azariah (2 Kings 15:4); Jotham (2 Kings 15:35); Ahaz (2 Kings 16:4). For northern kings "burning incense," see 1 Kings 12:33 and 13:1 (Jeroboam I).

v. 16: "They worshiped all the host of heaven." See Manasseh (2 Kings 21:3, 5)—such practice abolished by Josiah (2 Kings 23:4–5, 12).

v. 17: "They made their sons and their daughters pass through fire." See Ahaz (2 Kings 16:3); Manasseh (2 Kings 21:6).

v. 17: "They used divination and augury." See Manasseh (2 Kings 21:6).

A second thing of interest in vv. 7–23 is that Israel's sin is, first of all, "against the Lord their God, who had brought them up out of the land of Egypt" (v. 7). Before they sin against God's laws and commandments, they sin against the God who has saved them. In other words, "Israel's is a rebellion against grace before it is a disobedience of the law" (Fretheim 1999: 192).

A third thing of interest here is the multitude of sins with which the writer indicts Israel (and Judah), especially vv. 7–17. Brettler (1989: 282) calls it "a chorus of answers to a single question asked in ancient

Israel, 'Why was the north exiled?'" Viviano (1989: 551) says that the author "is piling one sin atop another, overwhelming his audience not simply with the fact of Israel's idolatrous practices but also with their variety and quantity."

In some sense, the pagan peoples compelled to relocate to Israel look better than the Israelites themselves. Their sin is syncretism ("So they worshiped the Lord but also served their own gods" [v. 33; cf. v. 41]). Israel's sin is apostasy. At least the uprooted non-Israelites continue to serve their own gods too.

2 Kings 18–21: Hezekiah, Manasseh, Amon

Kings of Judah	Length of Reign	Bright	Galil	Hayes/Hooker	Thiele
Hezekiah	29 years	715–687/6	726–697/6	727–699	729–686
Manasseh	55 years	687/6–642	697/6–642/1	698–644	696–642
Amon	2 years	642–640	642/1–640/39	643–642	642–640

We are fortunate in having in the Old Testament three accounts of the reign and times of Hezekiah, king of Judah. They are (1) 2 Kings 18–20; (2) 2 Chronicles 29–32; (3) Isaiah 36–39.

	2 Kings 18–20	2 Chronicles 29–32	Isaiah 36–39
Introduction to and evaluation of his reign	18:1–8	29:1–2	X
His passover festival	X	30:1–27	X
The reform	18:4	29:3–36; 31:1–21	X
Shalmaneser attacks Samaria	18:9–12	X	X
Sennacherib invades Judah	18:13–16	32:1–8	36:1
Sennacherib's deputies urge Jerusalem to surrender	18:17–35	32:9–16	36:2–20
Response to that ultimatum	18:36–19:7		36:21–37:7

Sennacherib's letter	19:8–13	32:17–19	37:8–13
Response to the letter and Hezekiah's prayer	19:14–19	32:20	37:14–20
Isaiah's pronouncement	19:20–34	32:20	37:21–35
Assyria defeated	19:35–37	32:21–23	37:36–38
Hezekiah's illness and healing	20:1–11	32:24–26	38:1–8, 21–22
Hezekiah's psalm	X	X	38:9–20
Visit of Merodach-baladan of Babylon	20:12–19	(32:27–31)	39:1–8
Conclusion of Hezekiah's reign	20:20–21	32:32–33	X

It is clear enough that none of the three accounts is identical to either of the other two. But the Kings and Isaiah accounts are closer to each other than either is to that in Second Chronicles. Two of the three accounts includes a significant incident that the other two do not: (1) Hezekiah's great Passover festival, mentioned in 2 Chronicles (30:1–27) but not in Kings or Isaiah; (2) Hezekiah's psalm, mentioned in Isaiah (38:9–20) but not in Kings or Chronicles.

The absence of the psalm in the Kings account of Hezekiah is especially interesting, given the many other close parallels between those two versions. The psalm in content is partly lament, partly thanksgiving. While lament dominates in the middle of the psalm (most of vv. 10–18), thanksgiving is in the title (v. 9) and in the conclusion (vv. 19–20). Its absence from the Kings account of Hezekiah but presence in the Isaiah account means that it was either removed from the former, if in fact it was ever there, or added to the latter. Interestingly, Chronicles (2 Chron. 32:25) laments that Hezekiah, after his prayer for healing, "did not respond according to the benefit done to him, for his heart was proud." If one argues that the psalm of Hezekiah is an interpolation in Isaiah 38, then its inclusion restores Hezekiah's reputation as a pious believer who is thankful to God for his benefactions, and so addresses his sin of omission observed by the Chronicler (Weitzman 1997: 105–8).

Hezekiah begins with some sweeping, religious reforms in his nation (18:4–6). One of these reforms involves Hezekiah having the "high places" removed, that is, torn down. But his son and successor, Manasseh, rebuilds them (21:3). It is left to Josiah to solve the problem permanently not only by razing them, but also by polluting them via burning human bones on the altars at these high places, thus invalidating them irremediably (23:16, 20).

But in the midst of such reforms Hezekiah seems to have joined forces in a massive anti-Assyrian coalition with Egypt, Babylon, and several smaller nations in the area. This move is reflected in the wording of 18:7: "He rebelled against the king of Assyria and would not serve him." The reason for Hezekiah's attack on the Philistines (18:8) more than likely is to persuade them to join this coalition.

Hezekiah's policy vis-à-vis the behemoth Assyrians is the opposite of his father's. Ahaz seeks assistance from the Assyrians (2 Kings 16:7–8); Hezekiah desires to rebel against them via military might. And interestingly, Isaiah rejects both Ahaz's policy of Assyrian dependence (Isa. 9:9b) and Hezekiah's policy of mutiny (Isa. 30:1–7; although the prophet does not name Hezekiah as the instigator). Kaufmann (1960: 389) well remarks,

> Hezekiah's coalition is in essence an Assyrian means to fight Assyria; several little 'Assyrias' have banded against the giant. But their purpose too is nothing but plunder, wealth, and domination; in joining them Israel falls into the idolatrous pattern. But Israel cannot win at Assyria's game. To be sure Zion will be delivered, but not by Assyrian means. Only those who redeem themselves from 'Assyrianism,' from idolatry, will be saved in Zion.

The aborted revolt brings Assyria and King Sennacherib to Jerusalem's walls in 701 B.C. Actually, he sends three of his "big guns": the Tartan, the Rabsaris, and the Rabshakeh, (18:17; in the NIV, his "supreme commander," his "chief officer," and his "field commander").

This unit is all about trust. Whom will Hezekiah trust when Assyria has Jerusalem surrounded? Egypt? Assyria? Himself? Yahweh? There are ten appearances of *batakh*, "trust, rely" in chs. 18–19:

1. 18:5: "He [Hezekiah] trusted in the Lord the God of Israel."
2. and 3. 18:19: "What is this trust in which you are trusting?"
4. 18:20: "On whom do you now rely?"
5. and 6. 18:21: "You are now relying on Egypt. . . . Such is Pharaoh king of Egypt to all who rely on him."
7. 18:22: "But if you say to me, 'We rely on the Lord our God.'"
8. 18:24: "How then can you repulse . . . when you rely on Egypt for chariots and for horsemen?"
9. 18:30: "Do not let Hezekiah make you rely on the Lord."
10. 19:10: "Do not let your God on whom you rely deceive you."

The ten uses of *batakh* in these two chapters (and all except the first spoken by Sennacherib's messenger[s]) contrast with the minimal use of this root as a verb or noun in all the rest of Genesis through Kings—only three times (Deut. 28:52; Judg. 9:26; 20:36; the adverbial sense "securely" occurs thirteen times in this large unit). (See Olley 1999: 62.)

So, in what Brueggemann (1985: 4) calls "the conversation at the wall of the city" (versus "the conversation behind the wall"), Sennacherib's officials, through taunt and insult and arrogance, attempt to persuade Jerusalem to capitulate. Actually, this embassy addresses its message first to Hezekiah (18:19–25), then to the people (18:29–35). The picture of an attacker trying to convince the attacked to give up is familiar from passages like Deut. 20:10–11 ("When you draw near to a town to fight it . . .") and 1 Kings 20:2 ("[Benhadad] sent messengers into the city of King Ahab of Israel . . ."). They even offer the Jerusalemites "sticks and carrots" (Ben Zvi 1990: 80) if they will submit: "Then everyone of you will eat from your own vine and your own fig tree, and drink water from your own cistern" (18:31).

In response, Hezekiah goes to church (19:1) and, by proxy, to Isaiah (19:2–4). This means repentance before God (sackcloth for mourning and repentance) and a word from God. Isaiah speaks for God, as the Rabshakeh speaks for Sennacherib. The Rashakeh said, "Be afraid"; Isaiah says, "Do not be afraid" (v. 6). The Rabshakeh said, "Surrender"; Isaiah says, "Trust." Hezekiah can trust because Yahweh will orchestrate not only Sennacherib's disappearance from Jerusalem but also his demise at home (19:7).

Sennacherib follows his first challenge, delivered orally (18:19–35), with a second challenge, delivered in writing (19:8–13; see v. 14 for the reference to the "letter"). Rather than understanding 19:8–13 as referring to a second invasion by Sennacherib of Jerusalem or a parallel literary tradition, we understand an oral message followed up by a written one to reflect actual military usage.

Hezekiah does what he did earlier: he prays (19:14b–19), then hears a word from God through Isaiah (19:20–34). Miller (1994: 351–52) analyzes the prayer as follows:

1. Address and praise: "O Lord the God of Israel . . . enthroned above the cherubim" (v. 15)
2. Petition for a hearing: "Incline your ear, O Lord" (v. 16ab)
3. Motivation:
   (a) appeal to divine reputation: "he has sent to mock the living God" (v. 16c)

(b) appeal to human need: "the kings . . . have laid waste"
(v. 17)
(c) appeal to divine reputation: "and have hurled their gods"
(v. 18)
4. Petition for deliverance: "O Lord our God, save us" (v. 19a)
5. Motivation: appeal to divine reputation: "so that all the kingdoms of the earth may know that you . . . are God" (v. 19b).

Balentine's division (1993: 92) is similar:

1. invocation (v. 15a)
2. description of Yahweh's exclusive sovereignty (v. 15b)
3. petition (v. 16)
4. description of nations' gods as "not gods" (vv. 17–18)
5. petition (v. 19)

The prayer begins and ends similarly:

"You are God, you alone, of all the kingdoms of the earth [v. 15]. . . . Save
us . . . so that all the kingdoms of the earth may know that you, O Lord,
are God alone [v. 19]."

Such bold affirmations at the peripheries of the prayer tend to nul-
lify and overrule the data in the middle part of the prayer—the pivotal
section (Klaus 1999: 188) about the boasting of Sennacherib and the
Assyrian gods (vv. 16–18).

Note also that Yahweh's subsequent word to Hezekiah through Isaiah about Sennacherib's and Assyria's future (19:21–28) and Judah's future (19:29–34) is tied to Hezekiah's prayer: "I have heard your prayer
to me about King Sennacherib of Assyria" (19:20b). Those who trust
also pray. And those who pray earnestly, hear from a God who speaks
revealingly.

For Sennacherib the future is bleak. For Judah the future is blessed,
even if recovery is several years away (19:29) and will include only a
remnant of Judeans (19:30–31). It would seem from the reference in
19:29 (= Isa. 37:30) that Sennacherib attacked Judah, deliberately or
accidentally, at Judah's most vulnerable point in the Jubilee cycle. During the forty-ninth year the land must lie fallow ("*This year* you shall eat
what grows of itself," that is, what grows naturally in the seventh year
from seeds that had fallen to the ground during reaping in the sixth
year). And the land must remain fallow during the fiftieth year too, that
is, the Jubilee (Lev. 25:11) ("and in the *second* year what springs from
that," that is, what grows a third time after reaping). To say that a two-

year cessation of agricultural cultivation created severe economic problems is to put it mildly. Add to the (probable) shortage of food supplies the reality of the most powerful and vulturous king who has shut you up in your own city "like a bird in a cage" (Sennacherib's own line in his inscription), then you must trust and you must pray.

But Yahweh has the last word. A unit that begins with Sennacherib's attack of Judah (18:13–18) ends with an account of his death at the hands of his own sons (while he is in his own church! [19:37]). Fewell (1986: 87) has caught nicely the chiastic structure of 18:13–19:37:

A Sennacherib's destructive action (18:13–18)
   B Sennacherib's verbal offense (18:19–35 and 19:8–13)
      X Hezekiah's activity (18:36–19:7 and 19:14–19)
   B¹ Yahweh's verbal response (19:20–34)
A¹ Yahweh's destructive action (19:35–37)

Two events remain in the Kings account of Hezekiah: (1) his near-death illness and God's giving him healing and fifteen additional years of life (20:1–11); (2) his reception of Merodach-baladan from Babylon and giving him a tour of his splendidly decorated treasure house, only to be rebuked by Isaiah (20:12–19).

Chapter 20 begins with the expression "in those days." More than likely, the events of ch. 20 come *before* those of 18:13–37, for at least two reasons. First, how could Hezekiah show Merodach-baladan so many royal treasures (20:13) if earlier Sennacherib had taken so many of these treasures from Hezekiah as tribute (18:14–16)? Second, if Hezekiah had stood up to and rebuffed the mighty Assyrian Sennacherib, would not Merodach-baladan, a Babylonian and archenemy of Assyria, have commended the Judean king for that, and not be content simply with a tour of the royal treasury?

What, then, is accomplished by reversing the chronological sequence and reserving Hezekiah's one major flaw for last? For one thing, "Hezekiah's nearness to death and his healing are a parallel to what happens to the city of Jerusalem. . . . But it also implies that, just as Hezekiah has only fifteen years to live, Judah too has a limited time left" (Fretheim 1999: 205).

The sequencing of these chapters reminds us also that the best of human leaders are flawed and fallible, and Hezekiah, although reformist and godly, is not Messiah. There is really only one leader in whom we may put our trust, and that is in one greater not only than Solomon, but in one greater also than Hezekiah. The theological point is even clearer in the Isaiah parallel, where chs. 40–66 prepare for one greater than even Hezekiah. Perhaps, then, the order of materials was set first in Isaiah and then appropriated by the editor of Kings (Oswalt 1986: 693).

Hezekiah is followed by his son Manasseh (2 Kings 21:1–18) and his grandson Amon (2 Kings 21:19–26). In their lack of display of any godliness or moral virtue, both are the direct opposite of their (grand)father. Proverbs 22:6 ("Train children in the right way, and when old, they will not stray") seems not to have worked out for Hezekiah.

If Hezekiah is a reformer, his son Manasseh is a counterreformer who overturns the innovations of his father. Twice, Manasseh's reign is compared to that of the northern Israelite king Ahab (see 1 Kings 16:29–34), husband of Jezebel (21:3, 13), to indicate how sweeping can be the influence of an apostate king on his nation.

Manasseh is both very religious (21:3–7)—but for orthodox faith in the wrong direction—and very violent ("Manasseh shed much innocent blood" v. 16). He is both pro-Baal and pro-bloodbath. That Manasseh is able to "mislead" (v. 9; NIV, "lead astray") his people shows that he is a kind of "false 'teaching' prophet" (Ben Zvi 1991: 370).

So different is he from his father that Fretheim (1999: 207) can state, "If a Hezekiah can be followed by a Manasseh, then no amount of trust can secure the future." Sternberg (1987: 340) likewise speaks of "Manasseh of odious memory, whose catalogue of atrocities gives the impression that he spent his life trying to make himself into his father's opposite." Paradoxically, Judah's most sinful king is Judah's longest-reigning king (fifty-five years [21:1]). Being discreet enough to stage no revolts, to pay tribute promptly, and to keep out of mischief with one's Assyrian suzerain is one way to guarantee longevity.

Verses 10–16 suggest that Manasseh's litany of apostate acts is so great that God will send Judah and Jerusalem into exile as a result (see also 23:26; 24:3–4; Jer. 15:4). God does visit the sins of the fathers to the third and fourth generations, and apparently he also visits the sins of kings unto the citizens of the third and fourth generations. This does not gainsay that the people themselves play a role in determining their own destiny. Most of the exhortations in Deuteronomy to the people warning them to shun other gods or face the consequences would be superfluous if Manasseh's actions had already determined their destiny. It is not a case of "either . . . or" but "both . . . and." Note that the end of v. 15 ("they . . . have provoked me to anger, since the day their ancestors came out of Egypt, even to this day") shows a multigenerational escalation of sin. God's position is not "One corrupt, quintessentially evil king means exile for a later generation." Manasseh is simply an archparticipant in an unceasing move away from covenant obedience to God that at some stage must reach the boiling point.

Interestingly, 2 Chronicles 33, but not 2 Kings 21, reports Manasseh's deportation to Babylon (v. 11), his contrite prayer to Yahweh while incarcerated (vv. 12–13a), his release from captivity (v. 13), his building programs around Jerusalem (v. 14), and his return to sound Yahwism (vv. 15–16). Only two kings in First and Second Kings ever "humbled" (*kanaʿ*) themselves: Ahab (1 Kings 21:29) and Josiah (2 Kings 22:19). In Chronicles, four do: Rehoboam (2 Chron. 12:6, 7, 12); Hezekiah (2 Chron. 32:26); Manasseh (2 Chron. 33:12, 19); Josiah (2 Chron. 34:27).

Thus, we have a contrast between Kings' unrepentant Manasseh and Chronicles' repentant Manasseh. Lasine (1993: 179) remarks, "If the monstrous Manasseh of 2 Kings causes the exile of his people without going into exile himself, the exile and repentance of the Chroniclers' Manasseh ensures that the people will *not* be exiled on his account."

2 Kings 22–25: Josiah to the Babylonian Exile

Kings of Judah	Reign	Bright	Galil	Hayes/Hooker	Thiele
Josiah	31 years	640–609	640/39–609	641–610	640–609
Jehoahaz	3 months	609	609	609	———
Jehoiakim	11 years	609–598	609–598	608–598	609–598
Jehoiachin	3 months	598/97	598/97	———	598–597
Zedekiah	11 years	597–587	597–586	596–586	597–587

Josiah is one of the truly unique and most pious kings of all of Judah. It is his attempts to bring religious reform to his nation by ridding it of pagan religious practices that so qualifies him for that honor.

The two accounts of Josiah's reign (640–609 B.C.) are in 2 Kings 22–23 and 2 Chronicles 34–35. As is usually the case, the two accounts show certain differences. Here are some of the most obvious:

1. Kings limits Josiah's reforms to his eighteenth year (2 Kings 22:3) and says nothing about anything prior to that. Chronicles tells us that in the eighth year of his reign (2 Chron. 34:3a), "while he was still a boy, he began to seek the God of his ancestor David," and in his twelfth year (2 Chron. 34:3b), "he began to purge Judah and Jerusalem of the high places." Then, in his

eighteenth year (2 Chron. 34:8), "he sent Shaphan . . . to repair the house of the Lord his God."

2. Kings devotes seventeen verses to detailing the reforming measures instituted by Josiah (2 Kings 23:4–20), but just three verses to the Passover observance, the climax of the reform (2 Kings 23:21–23). Chronicles reverses the emphasis, devoting just six verses to his reforms (2 Chron. 34:3b–7, 33), but nineteen verses to the Passover observance (2 Chron. 35:1–19).

3. Kings reports Josiah's death by Neco, pharaoh of Egypt without comment (2 Kings 23:29–30). Chronicles expands this incident, adding that Josiah died the way he did because "he did not listen to the words of Neco from the mouth of God" (2 Chron. 35:22b), demonstrating that even "godliness does not eliminate foolishness" (Washburn 1991: 59). It may appear that Kings places Josiah's death at Megiddo ("When Pharaoh Neco met him at Megiddo, he killed him. His servants carried him dead in a chariot from Megiddo" [2 Kings 23:29b–30a]), while Chronicles places his death in Jerusalem ("and his servants . . . brought him to Jerusalem. There he died" [2 Chron. 35:24]). Perhaps the two accounts can be harmonized if one reads "fatally injured" for "killed" in 2 Kings 23:29, and "dying" (the Hebrew participle *met*) instead of "dead" in 2 Kings 23:30 (Washburn 1991: 60).

More than likely, Josiah's reforms began prior to 622 B.C., the eighteenth year of his reign, as suggested by Chronicles. In that case, Kings has telescoped Josiah's reforms into one year, all coming on the heels of (1) the temple repairs (2 Kings 22:3–7), (2) the discovery of the lost book (2 Kings 22:8–13), and (3) the prophetess Huldah's interpretation of that book's message (2 Kings 22:14–20).

Weinfeld (1991: 73–74) offers three compelling reasons why this may be so. First, other kings of Judah instituted reforms without the sanction of a written book (Asa [1 Kings 15:11–14]; Jehoshaphat [1 Kings 22:46]; J(eh)oash [2 Kings 11:17–18]; Hezekiah [2 Kings 18:4, 22]). Second, would Josiah make a covenant before Yahweh in the temple (2 Kings 23:1–3) while pagan icons were still there (2 Kings 23:7)? Third, the prophecy of Huldah is uttered not against the background of Josiah's reforms, but against the history of burdensome sin. Recall also that Josiah has already mandated temple renovations, and this must mean something more than a new paint job, or new vinyl siding, or a new roof.

But for the author of Kings it is the discovery of this lost book that really lights the match of reform. (Luther's fresh "rediscovery" of the truth in Scripture of justification by faith alone, lost to much of the Roman Catholicism of his day, or Wesley's fresh "rediscovery" of the truth in Scripture of the earnest call to holiness of life, lost to much of the antinomian Protestantism of his day, may be parallels.)

One may contrast Josiah's response to the reading of a word from God (2 Kings 22:11b) with his son Jehoiakim's response to a reading of a word from God (Jer. 36:23–24). (See Isbell: 1978.)

Josiah (2 Kings 22:11–23:20)	Jehoiakim (Jer. 36:1–32)
1. the words of the book of the law (22:11)	the words of the Lord (vv. 4, 6, 8, 11)
the words of this book (22:13, 16)	the words of the scroll (v. 32)
2. God will indeed bring disaster (*ra'ah*) (22:16).	Judah will hear of all the disasters (*ra'ah*) (v. 3; cf. v. 31).
3. Great is the wrath of the Lord (*gedolah khamat*) (22:13).	Great is the wrath (*gadol ha'ap*) that the Lord has pronounced (v. 7).
4. Josiah tore (*qara'*) his clothes (22:11, 19).	Jehoiakim tore (*qara'*) the document (v. 23) but not his clothes (v. 24).
5. Josiah burned (*sarap*) vessels for false gods (23:4); the Asherah pole (23:6); the chariots of the sun (23:11); the sacred pole at Bethel (23:15); the bones on the altar (23:16); human bones (23:20) (six times in all).	Five times there is a reference to Jehoiakim burning (*sarap*) the scroll (vv. 25, 27, 28, 29, 32).
6. Hearing leads to repentance (vv. 11, 18–19).	Hearing leads to indifference (v. 24).

There is a consensus among both ancient authorities (e.g., rabbinic sources, Jerome) and modern commentators that "the book of the law" discovered in the temple repairs was some form of our book of Deuteronomy. Several items suggest this. First, the expression "the book of the law" (*seper hattorah;* 2 Kings 22:8, 11) is not found anywhere in Genesis through Numbers, but does appear throughout Deuteronomy (e.g., 28:61, and related expressions in 17:18; 28:58; 29:20). Second, the community celebration of Passover in Jerusalem (as opposed to the household Passover sacrifice of Exodus 12) reflects Deuteronomy's teaching on Passover, a festival to be observed "at the place that the Lord will choose as a dwelling for his name" (Deut. 16:2b). Furthermore, Josiah's "Make [ʿasah] a Passover for the Lord your God" (2 Kings 23:21) parallels Deut. 16:1, "You will make [ʿasah] the Passover for the Lord your God." This particular move of Josiah reflects the reform measure of 2 Kings 23:8 in which he closed down all sanctuaries outside of Jerusalem and consolidated worship in Zion's temple. Undoubtedly, the law restricting sacrificial worship to a single, God-chosen place (Deuteronomy 12) is the most unique and far-reaching law in Deuteronomy. Third, many of the paganistic items that Josiah had removed or destroyed are particularly condemned in Deuteronomy (e.g., vessels for and the image of "Asherah" [2 Kings 23:4, 6–7 and Deut. 7:5; 16:21]; "pillars" [2 Kings 23:14 and Deut. 7:5; 12:3]; "high places" [2 Kings 23:13 and Deut. 12:2–3]). Fourth, if the discovered book was the entire Pentateuch, that would have been a very long scroll, unimaginably long, and it would have been a strenuous exercise (more than fifteen hours!) for Huldah to read it before making her evaluation. Fifth, Josiah is the only king of Judah to fulfill the threefold injunction of Deut. 6:5:

> Deut. 6:5: "You shall love the Lord your God with all your heart, and with all your soul, and with all your might."
> 2 Kings 23:25: "Before him [Josiah] there was no king like him, who turned to the Lord with all his heart, with all his soul, and with all his might."

Josiah institutes twelve reform measures, ten for Judah and two for the northern kingdom (and see Lohfink 1987: 464–65; 1993: 52):

Judah (2 Kings 23:4–14)

1. vessels for Baal and Asherah (v. 4) 2. idolatrous priests (v. 5) 3. Asherah (v. 6) 4. houses of the cult prostitutes (v. 7)	*Foreign Cults*
5. high places in the country (v. 8a) 6. high places at Jerusalem's gates (v. 8b)	*Worshiping Yahweh at High Places*
7. child sacrifice to Molech at Topheth (v. 10) 8. horses and chariots of the sun (v. 11) 9. altars on the roof and in the temple courts (v. 12) 10. high places for Astarte, Chemosh, Milcom (vv. 13–14)	*Foreign Cults*

The Northern Kingdom (2 Kings 23:15–20)

1. high places in Bethel (v. 15)
2. other high places and idolatrous priests throughout Samaria (vv. 19–20)

Lohfink (1993: 52) has astutely observed that Josiah's reforms in Judah parallel the movement in Deuteronomy 12:

	2 Kings 23:4–14	Deuteronomy 12
Foreign cults	vv. 4–7	vv. 2–3
Proper worship of Yahweh	v. 8	vv. 4–28
Foreign cults	vv. 10–14	vv. 29–31

Such reforms by Josiah distinguish him from his predecessors and successors. The language used about him in 2 Kings 23:25 suggests that Josiah is a king nonpareil. He is one of several in Scripture about whom an incomparability formula is used (Knoppers: 1992):

Moses, an incomparable prophet: "Never since has there arisen a prophet in Israel like Moses" (Deut. 34:10).

Solomon, an incomparable wise man: "No one like you has been before you and no like you shall arise after you" (1 Kings 3:12).

Hezekiah, an incomparable man of trust: "There was no one like him among all the kings of Judah after him, or among those who were before him" (2 Kings 18:5).

Josiah, an incomparable reformer: "Before him there was no king like him, who turned to the Lord with all his heart, with all his soul, and with all his might . . . nor did any like him arise after him" (2 Kings 23:25; cf. 23:22).

Yahweh, an incomparable God: "To whom then will you liken God, or what likeness compare with him? . . . To whom then will you compare me, or who is my equal? says the Holy One" (Isa. 40:18, 25).

Jesus, an incomparable Savior: "Lord, to whom can we go? You have the words of eternal life" (John 6:68).

Yet, for all of Josiah's radical, thorough, kingdom-shaking reforms, a little more than two decades later (598/597 B.C.) Jerusalem falls to the Babylonians and the first deportation of exiles to Babylon occurs (2 Kings 24:10–16). Three and a half decades later (587/86 B.C.) Jerusalem falls to Babylon a second time, and a second group of Judeans finds themselves "weeping by the rivers of Babylon" (2 Kings 25:1–12). Revival times followed by ravaging times!

None of Josiah's successors—Jehoahaz (2 Kings 23:31–33); Jehoiakim (2 Kings 23:34–24:7); Jehoiachin (2 Kings 24:8–16); Zedekiah (2 Kings 24:17–25:21)—perpetuates Josiah's agenda. Josiah himself dies rather ignominiously, especially according to 2 Chron. 35:20–24. Josiah confronts the Egyptian Neco at Megiddo (well outside of Judean territory, unless Israelite territory has fallen within the sphere of Judean influence), who is on his way to assist the Assyrian king against the Babylonian menace. The language of Chronicles is stronger than that of Kings. Kings (2 Kings 23:29) says, "Josiah went out to meet him [Neco]." But Chronicles (2 Chron. 35:20) says, "Josiah went out against him." For "went out," Kings uses the verb *halak* (which could suggest nonconfrontation), but Chronicles uses *yatsaʾ* (which suggests hostile confrontation). (See Talshir 1996: 216–17.)

It is ironic that this most Martin Luther–like king of Judah is rebuked theologically by the pagan king of Egypt ("Cease opposing God, who is with me, so that he will not destroy you" [2 Chron. 35:21b]). Josiah listens when God speaks through Huldah, and so he lives; Josiah does not listen when God speaks through an Egyptian pharaoh, and so he dies. So perplexed were later writers by the narrator's statement in 2 Chron. 35:22 that the apocryphal 1 Esd. 1:28 changed "He did not listen to the words of Neco from the mouth of God" into "He did not listen to the words of the prophet Jeremiah from the mouth of the Lord."

Two other points take a bit of the shine off Josiah as reformer. First, 2 Kings 23:26–27 (no parallel in Chronicles) informs us that Josiah's reforms, however orthodox and therapeutic, could not erase the evil unleashed by his grandfather Manasseh. Second, Jeremiah, who commends Josiah for his justice and righteousness (Jer. 22:15–16), says absolutely nothing (in specifics, anyway) about Josiah's reform. This is all the more interesting if Jeremiah had been preaching five years before the reform, in the thirteenth year rather than the eighteenth year of Josiah's reign (if that is what Jer. 1:2 says—there are other interpretations of Jer. 1:2, e.g., the thirteenth year of Josiah is Jeremiah's birthdate). Why is it Huldah who is consulted for a prophetic interpretation, and not Jeremiah? Could it be that Jeremiah saw the reform as external change with no internal change, a "circumcision" of high places but no circumcision of the heart?

Bibliography (1 Kings 12–2 Kings 25)

1 Kings 12:1–16:20 (Rehoboam, Jeroboam)

Barrick, W. B. 1996. "On the Meaning 'House of High Places' and the Composition of the Kings History." *JBL* 115:621–42.

Ben Zvi, E. 1993. "Prophets and Prophecy in the Compositional and Redactional Notes in I–II Kings." *ZAW* 105:331–51.

Coggins, R. 1991. "On Kings and Disguises." *JSOT* 50:55–62.

Cohn, R. 1985. "Literary Techniques in the Jeroboam Narrative." *ZAW* 97:23–35.

Coote, R. B. 1991. *In Defense of Revolution: The Elohist History*. Minneapolis: Fortress. Pp. 61–69.

Crenshaw, J. L. 1971. *Prophetic Conflict: Its Effect upon Israelite Religion*. BZAW 124. New York: de Gruyter. Pp. 39–49.

Deboys, D. G. 1991. "1 Kings xiii—A 'New Criterion' Reconsidered." *VT* 41:210–12.

Dozeman, T. B. 1982. "The Way of the Man of God from Judah: True and False Prophecy in the Pre-Deuteronomic Legend of 1 Kings 13." *CBQ* 44:379–93.

Fox, N. 1996. "Royal Officials and Court Families: A New Look at *yĕladim* in 1 Kings 12." *BA* 59:225–32.

Gottwald, N. 1993. "Social Class as an Analytic and Hermeneutical Category." *JBL* 112:3–22.

Gross, W. 1979. "Lying Prophet and Disobedient Man of God in I Kings 13: Role Analysis as an Instrument of Theological Interpretation of an Old Testament Narrative Text." *Semeia* 15:97–135.

Holder, J. 1988. "The Presuppositions, Accusations, and Threats of 1 Kings 14:1–18." *JBL* 107:27–38.

Lasine, S. 1992. "Reading Jeroboam's Intentions: Intertexuality, Rhetoric, and History in 1 Kings 12." In *Reading between Texts: Intertexuality and the Hebrew Bible*. Ed. D. N. Fewell. Louisville: Westminster/John Knox. Pp. 133–52.

Malamat, O. 1965. "Kingship and Council in Israel and Sumer: A Parallel." *BA* 28:34–65.

Mead, J. K. 1999. "Kings and Prophets, Donkeys and Lions: Dramatic Shape and Deuteronomic Rhetoric in 1 Kings xiii." *VT* 49:199–205.

Reis, P. T. 1994. "Vindicating God: Another Look at 1 Kings xiii." *VT* 44:376–86.

Simon, U. 1976. "1 Kings 13: A Prophetic Sign—Denial and Persistence." *HUCA* 47:81–117.

Van Winkle, D. W. 1989. "1 Kings xiii: True and False Prophecy." *VT* 39:31–42.

———. 1989. "1 Kings xii 25–xiii 34: Jeroboam's Cultic Innovations and the Man of God from Judah." *VT* 46:101–14.

Walsh, J. T. 1989. "The Contexts of 1 Kings 13." *VT* 39:355–70.

Weisman, Z. 1998. *Political Satire in the Bible*. SBLSS 32. Atlanta: Scholars Press. Pp. 101–11.

1 Kings 16:21–2 Kings 10 (Omri, Ahab, Jehu, Elijah, Elisha, Jezebel)

Ackroyd, P. R. 1983. "Goddesses, Women and Jezebel." In *Images of Women in Antiquity*. Ed. A. Cameron and A. Kuhrt. Detroit: Wayne State Univesity Press. Pp. 245–59.

Barré, L. M. 1988. *The Rhetoric of Political Persuasion: The Narrative Artistry and Political Intentions of 2 Kings 9–11*. CBQMS 20. Washington, D.C.: Catholic Biblical Association of America.

Becking, B. 1996. "'Touch for Health . . .': Magic in ii Reg 4, 31–37 with a Remark on the History of Yahwism." *ZAW* 108:34–54.

Blenkinsopp, J. 1983. *A History of Prophecy in Israel*. Philadelphia: Westminster. Pp. 68–79.

Brichto, H. C. 1992. *Toward a Grammar of Biblical Poetics*. New York: Oxford University Press. Pp. 122–230.

Brown, R. E. 1971. "Jesus and Elijah." *Perspective* 12:85–104.

Brueggemann, W. 1987–1988. "The Embarrassing Footnote [II Kings 6:8–23]." *ThTo* 44:5–14.

Childs, B. S. 1982. "On Reading the Elijah Narratives." *Int* 34:128–37.

Cohn, R. 1982. "The Literary Logic of 1 Kings 17–19." *JBL* 101:333–50.
———. "Form and Perspective in 2 Kings v." *VT* 33:171–84.
Coote, R. B. 1981. "Yahweh Recalls Elijah." In *Traditions in Transformation: Turning Points in Biblical Faith.* Ed. B. Halpern and J. Levenson. Winona Lake, Ind.: Eisenbrauns. Pp. 115–20.
———, ed. 1992. *Elijah and Elisha in Socioliterary Perspective.* SBLSS. Atlanta: Scholars Press.
Gros Louis, K. R. R. 1974. "Elijah and Elisha." In *Literary Interpretations of Biblical Narrative.* Ed. K. R. R. Gros Louis, J. S. Ackerman, and T. Warshaw. Nashville: Abingdon. Pp. 177–90.
Hamilton, J. M. 1994. "Caught in the Nets of Prophecy? The Death of King Ahab and the Character of God." *CBQ* 56:649–63.
Hauser, A. J., and R. Gregory. 1990. *From Carmel to Horeb: Elijah in Crisis.* JSOT Supplement 85; Bible and Literature Series 19. Sheffield: Almond.
Herr, D. D. 1985. "Variations in a Pattern." *JBL* 104:292–94.
Hobbs, T. R. 1993. "Man, Woman and Hospitality—2 Kings 4:8–36." *BTB* 23:91–100.
Holt, E. K. 1995. "'Urged on by His Wife Jezebel': A Literary Reading of 1 Kings 18 in Context." *SJOT* 9:83–96.
Jobling, D. 1986. *The Sense of Biblical Narrative: Structural Analysis in the Hebrew Bible.* JSOT Supplement 7. Sheffield: Sheffield Academic Press. Pp. 63–88.
Lasine, S. 1991. "Jehoram and the Cannibal Mothers (2 Kings 6:24–33): Solomon's Judgment in an Inverted World." *JSOT* 50:27–53.
LeBarbera, R. 1984. "The Man of War and the Man of God: Social Satire in II Kings 6:8–7:20." *CBQ* 46:636–51.
Lindars, B. 1965. "Elijah, Elisha, and the Gospel Miracles." In *Miracles: Cambridge Studies in Their Philosophy and History.* Ed. C. F. D. Moule. London: Mowbray. Pp. 63–79.
Long, B. O. 1973. "2 Kings iii and Genres of Prophetic Narrative." *VT* 23:338–44.
Margalit, B. 1986. "Why King Mesha of Moab Sacrificed His Oldest Son." *BAR* 12, no. 6:62–68.
Moore, R. D. 1990. *God Saves: Lessons from the Elisha Stories.* JSOT Supplement 95. Sheffield: JSOT Press.
Nicol, G. G. 1987. "What Are You Doing Here, Elijah?" *HeyJ* 28:192–94.
Olley, J. W. 1998. "Yhwh and His Zealous Prophet: The Presentation of Elijah in 1 and 2 Kings." *JSOT* 80:25–51.
Pippin, T. 1988. "Jezebel Re-vamped." *Semeia* 69–70:221–33.
Rendsburg, G. A. 1988. "The Mock of Baal in 1 Kings 18:27." *CBQ* 50:414–17.

Roberts, J. J. M. 1988. "Does God Lie? Divine Deceit as a Theological Problem in Israelite Prophetic Literature." In *Congress Volume: Jerusalem, 1986.* Ed. J. A. Emerton. VTSup 40. Leiden: Brill. Pp. 211–20.

Robertson, D. 1982. "Micaiah ben Imlah: A Literary View." In *The Biblical Mosaic: Changing Perspectives.* Ed. R. Polzin and E. Rothman. Philadelphia: Fortress; Chico, Calif.: Scholars Press. Pp. 138–46.

Robinson, B. P. 1991. "Elijah at Horeb, 1 Kings 19:1–18: A Coherent Narrative?" *RB* 98:513–26.

Rofé, A. 1988. "The Vineyard of Naboth: The Origin and Message of the Story." *VT* 38:89–104.

Satterthwaite, P. E. 1998. "The Elisha Narratives and the Coherence of 2 Kings 2–8." *TynB* 49:1–28.

Schneider, T. J. 1996. "Rethinking Jehu." *Bib* 77:100–107.

Shields, M. E. 1993. "Subverting a Man of God, Elevating a Woman: Role and Power Reversals in 2 Kings 4." *JSOT* 58:59–69.

Siebert-Hommes, J. 1996. "The Widow of Zarephath and the Great Woman of Shunem: A Comparative Analysis of Two Stories." In *On Reading Prophetic Texts: Gender-Specific and Related Studies in Memory of Fokkelien van Dijk-Hemmes.* Ed. B. Becking and M. Dijstra. Leiden: Brill. Pp. 231–50.

Stern, P. D. 1994. "Of Kings and Moabites: History and Theology in 2 Kings 3 and the Mesha Inscription." *HUCA* 64:1–14.

Trible, P. 1994. "The Odd Couple: Elijah and Jezebel." In *Out of the Garden: Women Writers on the Bible.* Ed. C. Buchmann and C. Spiegel. New York: Fawcett Columbine. Pp. 166–79.

———. 1995. "Exegesis for Storytellers and Other Strangers." *JBL* 114:3–19.

Tromp, N. M. 1975. "Water and Fire on Mount Carmel: A Conciliatory Suggestion." *Bib* 56:480–502.

Walsh, J. T. 1992. "Methods and Meanings: Multiple Studies of 1 Kings 21." *JBL* 111:193–211.

White, M. 1994. "Naboth's Vineyard and Jehu's Coup: The Legitimation of a Dynastic Extermination." *VT* 44:66–76.

Wright, N. T. 1996. "Paul, Arabia, and Elijah (Galatians 1:17)." *JBL* 115:683–92.

2 Kings 11–17 (Jehoahaz to the End of Northern Israel)

Brettler, M. 1989. "Ideology, History and Theology in 2 Kings xvii, 7–23." *VT* 39:268–82.

Christensen, D. L. 1989. "The Identity of 'King So' in Egypt (2 Kings xvii, 4)." *VT* 39:140–53.

Dutcher-Walls, P. 1996. *Narrative Art, Political Rhetoric: The Case of Athaliah and Joash.* JSOT Supplement 209. Sheffield: Sheffield Academic Press.

Long, B. O. 1995. "Sacred Geography as Narrative Structure in 2 Kings 11." In *Pomegranates and Golden Bells: Studies in Biblical, Jewish and Near Eastern Ritual, Law and Literature in Honor of Jacob Milgrom.* Ed. D. P. Wright, D. N. Freedman, and A. Hurvitz. Winona Lake, Ind.: Eisenbrauns. Pp. 231–38.

Vivano, P. A. 1987. "2 Kings 17: A Rhetorical and Form-Critical Analysis." *CBQ* 49:548–59.

2 Kings 18–21 (Hezekiah, Manasseh, Amon)

Ackroyd, P. R. 1974. "An Interpretation of the Babylonian Exile: A Study of 2 Kings 20, Isaiah 38–39." *SJT* 27:329–52.

Balentine, S. 1993. *Prayer in the Hebrew Bible.* Minneapolis: Fortress.

Ben Zvi, E. 1990. "Who Wrote the Speech of Rabshakeh and When?" *JBL* 109:79–92.

———. 1991. "The Account of the Reign of Manasseh in II Reg 21, 1–18 and the Redactional History of the Book of Kings." *ZAW* 103:355–74.

Brueggemann, W. 1985. "II Kings 18–19: The Legitimacy of a Sectarian Hermeneutics." *HBT* 7:1–42.

Childs, B. S. 1967. *Isaiah and the Assyrian Crisis.* London: SCM.

Eynkiel, E. 1997. "The Portrait of Manasseh and the Deuteronomistic History." In *Deuteronomy and Deuteronomistic Literature: Festschrift C. H. W. Brekelmans.* Ed. M. Vervenne and J. Lust. BETL 133. Leuven: Leuven University Press; Leuven: Peters. Pp. 233–61.

Fewell, D. N. 1986. "Sennacherib's Defeat: Words at War in 2 Kings 18:13–19:37." *JSOT* 34:79–90.

Halpern, B. 1998. "Why Manasseh is Blamed for the Babylonian Exile: The Evolution of a Biblical Tradition." *VT* 48:473–514.

Handy, L. K. 1988. "Hezekiah's Unlikely Reform." *ZAW* 100:111–15.

Kaufmann, Y. 1960. *The Religion of Israel.* Trans. M. Greenberg. Chicago: University of Chicago Press.

Klaus, N. 1999. *Pivot Patterns in the Former Prophets.* JSOT Supplement 247. Sheffield: Sheffield Academic Press. Pp. 188–94.

Konkel, A. 1993. "The Sources of the Story of Hezekiah in the Book of Isaiah." *VT* 43:462–82.

Laato, A. 1987. "Hezekiah and the Asyrian Crisis in 701 B.C." *SJOT* 2:49–68.

Lasine, S. 1993. "Manasseh as Villain and Scapegoat." In *The New Literary Criticism and the Hebrew Bible*. JSOT Supplement 143. Ed. J. C. Exum and D. J. A. Clines. Sheffield: JSOT Press. Pp. 163–83.

Miller, P. 1994. *They Cried to the Lord: The Form and Theology of Biblical Prayer*. Minneapolis: Fortress.

Moriarty, F. L. 1965. "The Chronicler's Account of Hezekiah's Reform." *CBQ* 27:399–406.

Na'aman, N. 1995. "The Debated Historicity of Hezekiah's Reform in the Light of Historical and Archaeological Research." *ZAW* 107:179–95.

Olley, J. W. 1999. "'Trust in the Lord': Hezekiah, Kings and Isaiah." *TynB* 50:59–77.

Oswalt, J. 1986. *The Book of Isaiah, Chapters 1–39*. NICOT. Grand Rapids: Eerdmans. Pp. 627–703.

Seitz, C. R. 1993. "Account A and the Annals of Sennacherib: A Reassessment." *JSOT* 58:47–57.

Vaughn, A. 1999. *Theology, History, and Archaeology in the Chronicler's Account of Hezekiah*. Archaeology and Biblical Studies 4. Atlanta: Scholars Press.

Weitzman, S. 1997. *Song and Story in Biblical Narrative*. Bloomington: Indiana University Press.

2 Kings 22–25 (Josiah to the Babylonian Exile)

Begg, C. T. 1986. "The Significance of Jehoiachin's Release: A New Proposal." *JSOT* 36:49–56.

Brettler, M. 1991. "2 Kings 24:13–14 as History." *CBQ* 53:541–52.

Conroy, C. 1990. "Reflections on the Exegetical Task: Apropos of Recent Studies on 2 Kings 22–23." In *Pentateuchal and Deuteronomistic Studies*. Ed. C. Brekelmans and J. Lust. BETL 94. Leuven: University Press. Pp. 255–68.

Eslinger, L. 1986. "Josiah and the Torah Book: Comparison of 2 Kings 22:1–23:28 with 2 Chr. 34:1–35:19." *HAR* 10:37–62.

Handy, L. K. 1994. "The Role of Huldah in Josiah's Cult Reform." *ZAW* 106:40–53.

———. 1995. "Historical Probability and the Narrative of Josiah's Reform in 2 Kings." In *The Pitcher Is Broken: Memorial Essays for Gösta Ahlström*. JSOT Supplement 190. Ed. S. W. Holloway and L. K. Handy. Sheffield: Sheffield Academic Press. Pp. 252–75.

Isbell, C. D. 1978. "2 Kings 22:3–23:24 and Jeremiah 36: A Stylistic Comparison." *JSOT* 8:33–45.

Kalami, I., and J. D. Purvis. 1994. "King Jehoiachin and the Vessels of the Lord's House in Biblical Literature." *CBQ* 56:449–57.

Knoppers, G. N. 1992. "'There Was None Like Him': Incomparability in the Books of Kings." *CBQ* 54:411–31.

Lohfink, N. 1987. "The Cult Reform of Josiah of Judah: 2 Kings 22–23 as a Source for the History of Israelite Religion." In *Ancient Israelite Religion: Essays in Honor of Frank Moore Cross*. Ed. P. Miller, P. D. Hansen, and S. D. McBride. Philadelphia: Fortress. Pp. 459–75.

————. 1993. "Recent Discussion on 2 Kings 22–23: The State of the Question." In *A Song of Power and the Power of Song: Essays on the Books of Deuteronomy*. Ed. D. L. Christensen. Winona Lake, Ind.: Eisenbrauns. Pp. 36–61.

Nakanose, S. 1993. *Josiah's Passover: Sociology and the Liberating Bible*. Maryknoll, N.Y.: Orbis.

Paul, M. J. 1990. "King Josiah's Renewal of the Covenant (2 Kings 22–23)." In *Pentateuchal and Deuteronomistic Studies*. Ed. C. Brekelmans and J. Lust. BETL 94. Leuven: University Press. Pp. 269–76.

Person, R. F., Jr. 1993. "II Kings 24, 18–25, 30 and Jeremiah 52: A Text-Critical Case Study in the Redaction History of the Deuteronomistic History." *ZAW* 105:174–205.

Talshir, Z. 1996. "The Three Deaths of Josiah and the State of Biblical Historiography (2 Kings xxiii 29–30; 2 Chronicles xxxv 20–5; 1 Esdras i 23–31)." *VT* 46:213–36.

Washburn, D. L. 1991. "Perspective and Purpose: Understanding the Josiah Story." *TJ* 12:59–78.

Williamson, H. G. M. 1982. "The Death of Josiah and the Continuing Development of the Deuteronomistic History." *VT* 32:242–48.

1 and 2 Chronicles

Like C. S. Lewis's *The Chronicles of Narnia*, First and Second Chronicles present a story that reflects the writer's creativity, imagination, and theological acumen. That story is the history of God's people Israel/Judah that stretches all the way from Adam (1 Chron. 1:1) to the decree of Cyrus of Persia (538 B.C.) authorizing exiled Judeans to return to their homeland, should they so choose (2 Chron. 36:22–23). That story is told first genealogically (1 Chronicles 1–9) and then narratively (1 Chronicles 10–2 Chronicles 36).

It is the early church father St. Jerome (ca. A.D. 340–420) who has given us the name "Chronicles." This is but one of three designations. The title in the Hebrew Bible is *divre hayamim*, literally, "(the) words of the days," but perhaps to be rendered more idiomatically as "events of the times," or "annals." The Septuagint labels these books *paraleipomenōn tōn basileōn iouda*, literally "things omitted of the kings of Judah," or "miscellanies concerning the kings of Judah." This title might suggest that Chronicles is but a supplement to Samuel–Kings and not an equal, a gap filler, and that it contains miscellaneous data rather than foundational data. But that is hardly the case.

The Old Latin versions of the Bible took over the Septuagint rendering with the title *libri paralipomenorum*. St. Jerome, however, used the expression *chronicon totius divinae historiae* ("the chronicle of the whole sacred history") to refer to these biblical books, and hence the origin of the title "Chronicles."

We do not know who wrote Chronicles or when it was written, as is true of many of the entries in the Old Testament canon. Jewish tradition (see in the Talmud, *Baba Bathra* 15a) suggests Ezra. This is possi-

477

ble but not provable. In fact, there is an ongoing debate among scholars as to whether the same author(s) who wrote Chronicles also produced Ezra–Nehemiah. Much of earlier Old Testament scholarship affirmed the equation, but in more recent times the pendulum has swung toward seeing separate authorship for Chronicles versus Ezra–Nehemiah. Among adherents of the latter perspective are, on the one hand, those who argue for dual authorship because they see such sharp and distinctive emphases between Chronicles and Ezra–Nehemiah, and on the other hand, those who would argue for separate authorship but also affirm that both authors were part of a single tradition or school.

Whoever wrote Chronicles lived after King Cyrus of Persia promulgated his decree in 538 B.C., allowing exiled Jews to return to Judah (2 Chron. 36:22–23). One other bit of data that might help with determining at least the earliest date for Chronicles is the family tree of Zerubbabel (one of the early leaders [around 537–520 B.C.] in the postexilic restored community). First Chronicles 3:19–21 traces Zerubbabel's family through two generations (not six, as some construe):

"The sons of Pedaiah: *Zerubbabel* . . .
the sons of Zerubbabel: . . . and *Hananiah* . . .
the sons of Hananiah: *Pelatiah* . . ."

This data would suggest a date of about 500 B.C. as the earliest possible, and more than likely before 400 B.C. To be sure, some writers date the composition of Chronicles to a pre-500 B.C. date (e.g., Newsome 1975: 216), but to do so they must delete the references to Zerubbabel's descendants as secondary, thus making the text fit their theory. And there are those who date Chronicles' composition after 400 B.C., and some place it as late as the final decades of the third century B.C.

So it appears that whoever wrote Chronicles was writing to an audience of Judean Jews, most of whom not long before had returned from a lengthy exile in Babylon. Possibly, most of the returnees had been born in exile. So this will be the "exilic babies" first experience of the "holy land." What expectations did those who accepted Cyrus's offer bring with them as they trekked homeward? A dream to rebuild the kingdom? A return to the glory and golden years of yesterday? A rebuilt temple? A new Davidic king to be their leader? Or a different agenda altogether? And what was life like in postexilic Judah as depicted in the sources that we know come from that era (Haggai, Zechariah, Malachi, Ezra, Nehemiah)? Robust or difficult? Encouraging or discouraging? Faithful or compromising? The postexilic books we have seem to give more emphases to the second of each of these options: difficult, discouraging, compromising. It is to such a group of people that the Chronicler (as the author of Chronicles is commonly called) writes.

It appears that the Chronicler was aware of and had access to the material now contained in Samuel–Kings. (This does not mean that his audience had access to this material, or if they did, that he expected them to compare his version with that of Samuel–Kings, any more than if Matthew had access to Mark, he expected his readers to have access too, and to hear the two synoptically. Both Chronicles and Matthew are sui generis, and not merely addenda.)

But the Chronicler had access to other sources. Some were of a historiographic nature. Thus, he refers to "the Books of the Kings of Israel" (1 Chron. 9:1; 2 Chron. 20:34; 33:18, and to "the Commentary on the Book of the Kings" [*midrash seper hammelakim*] in 2 Chron. 24:27—keep in mind that in Chronicles "Judah" tends to be called "Israel," e.g., 1 Chron. 1:34; 2:1, but see 1 Chron. 4:1). He also mentions "the Book of the Kings of Israel and Judah" (2 Chron. 27:7; 35:27; 36:8). These books may, in fact, be one and the same book.

He also makes frequent mention of prophetic writings as additional sources for data about the king about whom he has just written: 1 Chron. 29:29 (Samuel, Nathan, Gad); 2 Chron. 9:29 (Nathan, Ahijah, Iddo); 2 Chron. 12:15 (Shemaiah, Iddo); 2 Chron. 13:22 (Iddo); 2 Chron. 20:34 (Jehu); 2 Chron 26:22 (Isaiah); 2 Chron. 32:32 (Isaiah); 2 Chron. 33:19 (the seers); 2 Chron. 36:22 (Jeremiah). All except the last are cited simply as supplementary sources for the interested reader who wishes more data on the particular Judean king. The Chronicler, among his nine citations of prophets, mentions Jeremiah as his only illustration of a prophet who spoke a prophetic word that the Chronicler and his audience have seen fulfilled (2 Chron. 36:22).

In some ways, Chronicles is like Genesis. Both begin with the origin of the human race and end with the promise/hope of return to the land of Israel from exile (cf. Gen. 1:26–31 with 1 Chron. 1:1, and Gen. 50:24–26 with 2 Chron. 36:22–23). Note the use of the verbs *paqad* and *ʿalah* in the last chapter of each:

Gen. 50:24–25: "Then Joseph said to his brothers, 'I am about to die; but God will surely come to you [*paqod yipqod*], and bring you up [*heʿelah*] out of this land to the land that he swore to Abraham, to Isaac, to Jacob.' So Joseph made the Israelites swear, saying, 'When God comes to you [*paqod yipqod*], you shall carry up [*haʿalitem*] my bones from here.'"

2 Chron. 36:23: "Thus says King Cyrus of Persia: The Lord, the God of heaven . . . has charged [*paqad*] me to build him a house at Jerusalem. . . . Whoever is among you of all his people, may the Lord his God be with him! Let him go up [*weyaʿal*]."

There is also some parallel between Chronicles and Samuel–Kings and between Deuteronomy and Exodus–Numbers. Both Chronicles and Deuteronomy retell an earlier story already recorded, but in a different context and to a different audience. In the retelling one finds omissions, additions, and alterations in account B when it is compared with account A. Chronicles begins (1 Chron. 1–9) with a backward look and ends with a forward look (2 Chron. 36:22–23). Similarly, Deuteronomy begins with a backward look (chs. 1–3) and ends with a forward look (chs. 31–34). The scope of the Chronicler's survey is, however, grander than that of Deuteronomy. The Chronicler begins with the creation and Adam, and concludes with Cyrus's edict in 538 B.C. Talmon (1987: 371) appropriately refers to Chronicles as "a kind of Deutero-Biblia," a second Bible.

But the clearest parallels with Chronicles are to be found in Samuel–Kings. The nearly universal consensus is that Chronicles has four main units:

1. 1 Chronicles 1–9: Adam through King Saul
2. 1 Chronicles 10–29: David and his preparation for building and staffing the temple
3. 2 Chronicles 1–9: Solomon's building of the temple
4. 2 Chronicles 10–36: kings of Judah from Rehoboam to Zedekiah

Here is how this data parallels Samuel–Kings in terms of who is the major actor:

Chronicles	Major Figure/Event	Samuel–Kings
1 Chronicles 1–9		X
1 Chronicles 10	Saul	1 Samuel 31–2 Samuel 1
1 Chronicles 11–29	David	2 Samuel 2–1 Kings 2
2 Chronicles 1–9	Solomon	1 Kings 1–11
2 Chronicles 10–12	Rehoboam	1 Kings 11:43–14:31
2 Chronicles 13	Abijah	1 Kings 15:1–8
2 Chronicles 14–16	Asa	1 Kings 15:9–24
2 Chronicles 17–20	Jehoshaphat	1 Kings 22:41–50

2 Chronicles 21	Jehoram	2 Kings 8:16–24
2 Chron. 22:1–9	Ahaziah	2 Kings 8:25–29
2 Chron. 22:10–23:21	Athaliah	2 Kings 11
2 Chronicles 24	Joash	2 Kings 12
2 Chronicles 25	Amaziah	2 Kings 14:1–22
2 Chronicles 26	Uzziah/Azariah	2 Kings 15:1–7
2 Chronicles 27	Jotham	2 Kings 15:32–38
2 Chronicles 28	Ahaz	2 Kings 16
2 Chronicles 29–32	Hezekiah	2 Kings 18–20
2 Chron. 33:1–20	Manasseh	2 Kings 21:1–18
2 Chron. 33:21–25	Amon	2 Kings 21:19–26
2 Chronicles 34–35	Josiah	2 Kings 22:1–23:30
2 Chron. 36:1–4	Jehoahaz	2 Kings 23:31–33
2 Chron. 36:5–8	Jehoiakim	2 Kings 23:34–24:7
2 Chron. 36:9–10	Jehoiachin	2 Kings 24:8–17
2 Chron. 36:11–21	Zedekiah	2 Kings 24:18–25:26
2 Chron. 36:22–23	Cyrus's edict	X
X	release of Jehoiachin	2 Kings 25:27–30

Restricting ourselves to the characterizations given in Chronicles, we note that the kings (and Athaliah) fall into one of three categories:

A. Kings who are uniformly good:
  1. David: 1 Chronicles 11–29 (except for the census incident in ch. 21)
  2. Solomon: 2 Chronicles 1–9
  3. Abijah: 2 Chronicles 13
  4. Jotham: 2 Chronicles 27
  5. Hezekiah: 2 Chronicles 29–32
B. Kings/Queens who are uniformly evil and/or ineffective:

1. Jehoram: 2 Chronicles 21
2. Ahaziah: 2 Chron. 22:1–9
3. Athaliah: 2 Chron. 22:10–23:21
4. Ahaz: 2 Chronicles 28
5. Amon: 2 Chron. 33:21–25
6. Jehoahaz: 2 Chron. 36:1–4
7. Jehoiakim: 2 Chron. 36:5–8
8. Jehoiachin: 2 Chron. 36:9–10
9. Zedekiah: 2 Chron. 36:11–21

C. Kings who are a mixture of good and evil:
    from evil to good:
    1. Manasseh (evil, 2 Chron. 33:1–11; good, 2 Chron. 33:12–20)
    from evil to good to evil to good:
    1. Rehoboam (evil, 2 Chronicles 10; good, 2 Chronicles 11; evil, 2 Chron. 12:1–5; some good, 2 Chron. 12:6–16)
    from good to evil to good to evil:
    1. Jehoshaphat (good, 2 Chronicles 17; evil, 2 Chronicles 18; good, 2 Chron. 19:1–20:34; evil, 2 Chron. 20:35–37)
    from good to evil:
    1. Asa (good, 2 Chronicles 14–15; evil, 2 Chronicles 16)
    2. Joash (good, 2 Chron. 24:1–16; evil, 2 Chron. 24:17–27)
    3. Amaziah (good, 2 Chron. 25:1–2; evil, 2 Chron. 25:3–28)
    4. Uzziah (good, 2 Chron. 26:1–15; evil, 2 Chron. 26:16–23)
    5. Josiah (good, 2 Chron. 34:1–35:19; evil, 2 Chron. 35:20–27)

Throughout their history, the people of Judah have had the privilege or the misfortune of having exemplary heads of state who at one moment were quite godly and at other moments just the opposite. The three models of leadership resemble the seven churches in the first three chapters of Revelation: those uniformly good (Smyrna [Rev. 2:8–11]; Philadelphia [Rev. 3:7–13]); those uniformly evil (Sardis [Rev. 3:1–6]; Laodicea [Rev. 3:14–22]); those embodying positive and negative traits (Ephesus [Rev. 2:1–7]; Pergamum [Rev. 2:12–17]; Thyatira [Rev. 2:18–29]). The Apostle Paul's words for these groups are: (1) the "spiritual" (1 Cor. 3:1); (2) the "unspiritual," or "the natural man" (KJV) (1 Cor. 2:14); (3) "people of the flesh," or "worldly" (NIV), or "carnal" (KJV) (1 Cor. 3:1).

In Chronicles there are, to be sure, some kings who, recognizing the errors of their ways, repent (the verb of choice here for the Chronicler is normally the Niphal stem of *kana*ᶜ ("humble oneself"). They are:

David: "I have sinned greatly in that I have done this thing. But now, I pray you, take away the guilt of your servant for I have acted foolishly" (1 Chron. 21:8).

Rehoboam and his officers: "Then the officers of Israel and the king humbled themselves. . . . the Lord saw that they humbled themselves" (2 Chron. 12:6–7). "Because he [Rehoboam] humbled himself the wrath of the Lord turned from him" (2 Chron. 12:12).

Manasseh: "While he was in distress he entreated the favor of the Lord his God and humbled himself" (2 Chron. 33:12).

Josiah: "Because your [Josiah's] heart was penitent and you humbled yourself before God" (2 Chron. 34:27).

So, at least three Judean kings following Solomon—Rehoboam, Manasseh, and Josiah—literally implemented Yahweh's word to Solomon at the consecration of the temple about the way to forgiveness and healing ("If my people who are called by my name humble themselves" [2 Chron. 7:14]).

But, on the other hand, there are those who refuse to humble themselves: "He [Amon, son of the self-humbling Manasseh] did not humble himself" (2 Chron. 33:23); "He [Zedekiah] did not humble himself before the prophet Jeremiah" (2 Chron. 36:12). And sometimes God must humble those who refuse to humble themselves ("For the Lord brought Judah low because of King Ahaz of Israel" [2 Chron. 28:19]).

Thus, we see that the Chronicler has held out before his kingless and postexilic audience a survey of a preexilic defunct dynasty of Davidic kings with highs and lows. Some of these kings illustrate that it is possible, even for persons in positions of power, to live a good and godly life. Other kings illustrate that the effects of unwise decisions leading to disastrous results can be reversed through self-humbling and contrition. Divine judgment may not be averted, but it may be reduced or terminated. Yet other kings illustrate that there are those who found ways other than Yahweh's ways more attractive and remained adamant in their choice. It is not without significance that in Chronicles, apostate kings are as numerous as penitent kings.

There are numerous ways of proceeding in the attempt to flesh out the meaning, purpose, and theology of Chronicles. One way is to examine the individual discussions by the Chronicler of the various kings of Judah and compare that data with parallel data in Samuel–Kings in

order to discern the Chronicler's *Tendenz*. Numerous profitable studies
do exactly that: (1) David (Wright 1991: 229–42; 1993: 87–105; Bailey
1994: 83–90; Knoppers 1995: 449–70; Wright 1998: 45–59; Klein 1999:
104–16); (2) Solomon (Braun 1973: 503–16; 1976: 581–90; Dillard
1980–1981: 289–300); (3) Rehoboam (Knoppers 1990: 423–40); (4) Abijah (Deboys 1990: 48–62); (5) Asa (Dillard 1980: 207–18); (6) Jehoshaphat (Dillard 1986: 17–22; Knoppers 1991: 500–24); (7) Hezekiah
(Thronveit 1988: 302–11); (8) Josiah (Glatt-Gilad 1996: 16–31). (See
also Fishbane 1985: 380–403.) We have done some of this comparative
analysis ourselves after our earlier discussions of Saul, David, and Solomon in Samuel–Kings, as well as in our earlier comments on Hezekiah and Josiah in Second Kings.

But there are other ways of attempting to discern the Chronicler's
message. To begin with, we must ask what the significance is of the
Chronicler beginning the book(s) with essentially nine chapters of ge-
nealogies (1 Chronicles 1–9). Only two books in the Bible commence
with genealogy, First Chronicles and Matthew, and both trace the family line in a descending order. It is important to note not only that the
Chronicler begins with an extended genealogy, but also the structure of
that line of descendants.

Several items stand out here. First, it was important for the Chronicler to begin the genealogy as far back as possible—Adam. David, who
will turn out to be the major role player in Chronicles, is thus not only
a Jew who traces his ancestry to Abraham, but also is a son of Adam.
(Luke makes precisely the same point about Jesus in his genealogy
[Luke 3:23–38], except that Luke, unlike Chronicles and Matthew, gives
the line of descendants in an ascending order.) That the Chronicler begins with Adam suggests the viewpoint that God's people do not begin
at Sinai, or even at Ur, but in Eden. Human creation is the womb in
which Israel is birthed.

The next thing of interest here is that in the seven chapters devoted
to the genealogy of the sons of Jacob/Israel (1 Chronicles 2–8), Judah's
genealogy is covered first (1 Chron. 2:3–4:23), even though he is Israel's
fourth son. By contrast, the genealogy of the firstborn, Reuben, is delayed until 5:1–10. The decision to ignore strict chronology here is the
Chronicler's way of highlighting the history of the tribe of Judah in the
history that the author is about to unfold.

Furthermore, within the Chronicler's presentation of the line of
Judah, the reporting of David's sons fills the central frame: 2:3–55 >
3:1–24 > 4:1–23. And within this list of nineteen named sons of David
(3:1–24), Solomon is number ten, right in the middle, nine named before him and nine named after him (Johnstone 1986: 138). Thus, al-

ready the Chronicler has highlighted the tribe of Judah, and within that larger group David and his sons, and within that group Solomon.

The Chronicler has also given prominence to the tribe of Levi by placing that tribe in the middle of two clusters to each side of the other tribes (Johnstone 1986: 128):

Judah (2:3–4:23)	Reuben (5:1–10)	Levi (6:1–81)	Isaachar (7:1–5)	Benjamin (8:1–40)
Simeon (4:24–43)	Gad (5:11–17)		Benjamin (7:6–12)	
	Manasseh (5:23–26)		Naphtali (7:13)	
			Manasseh (7:14–19)	
			Ephraim (7:20–29)	
			Asher (7:30–40)	

The prominent placement of the Levites in this genealogy suggests a later prominent role for them in Chronicles, and that is indeed the case (see Knoppers 1999: 49–72). Thus far, then, the Chronicler has through genealogical structuring highlighted Judah, David, Solomon, and Levites.

The last feature of the genealogy in chs. 2–8 on which we shall comment is the strange duplication of the tribe of Benjamin, first in 7:6–12 and then again in 8:1–40. By beginning with Judah (2:3–4:23) and ending (via duplication) with Benjamin (8:1–40), the Chronicler brackets the two tribes, surely amalgamated by the author's time, that survived the Assyrian invasion in 722 B.C. and the fate of the northern tribes, and continued to exist beyond Babylonian exile days. Additionally, the second Benjaminite genealogy provides something that the first one lacks: the identifying of Saul and his roots and family (8:29–40).

But there is one unexpected element here. Not once, but twice, Saul is associated with the city of Gibeon (8:29; 9:35) rather than the city of Gibeah as in First Samuel (1 Sam. 10:10, 26). Thus, in First Samuel it is "Saul of Gibeah," but in First Chronicles "Saul of Gibeon." We recall from stories like Joshua 10 (and esp. 2 Sam. 21:2, "Now the Gibeonites were not of the people of Israel, but of the remnant of the Amorites") that the Gibeonites are at best quasi-Israelites. Is Saul, too, by virtue of his Gibeonite linkage, not even a real Israelite for the Chronicler? Thus, in the genealogy the Chronicler not only has highlighted Judah, David, Solomon, and Levites, but also has rendered Saul a specious and intrusive individual.

The last of the genealogic chapters, ch. 9, is a different animal. Most of it (vv. 2–34) is a list of Israelites (vv. 3–9), priests (vv. 10–13), Levites (vv. 14–16), and gatekeepers (vv. 17–34) who resettled in Judah after the exile (see v. 2). And in fact, this is the only chapter in First and Second Chronicles that mentions the return to Zion (Walters 1991: 62). Chronologically, 1 Chron. 9:2–34 should follow the end of 2 Chronicles (2 Chron. 36:22–23): Cyrus issued his edict freeing captive Jews (2 Chron. 36:22–23); those who accepted the offer returned to the holy land and instituted proper worship in Jerusalem (1 Chron. 9:2–34). Thus, the Chronicler ends his genealogy reporting the return from exile, but ends his book reporting only the hope and possibility of that return.

What is accomplished by such a dischronological perspective? It enables the Chronicler to end the writing not merely as a reporter or annalist, but as one who holds before the audience a hopeful future. Cyrus's words, "Whoever is among you of all his people, may the Lord his God be with him! Let him go up," bespeak such hope. Apart from the ending of Judges ("All the people what was right in their own eyes did" [following the Hebrew word order]), Chronicles is the only book in the Old Testament to end with a verb. But it is not just any verb. Rather, it is the one verb in the Old Testament that speaks most directly to the longing of the people of God for release and redemption and restoration: ʿalah.

The dischronological relationship between 1 Chron. 9:2–34 and 2 Chron. 36:22–23 is parallel to that between Ezra–Nehemiah and Chronicles. Ezra and Nehemiah come before Chronicles (in the Hebrew Bible) and report an actual return full of hope, but in the end one that is flawed, as the reforms of Ezra and Nehemiah bear out. Chronicles follows that with the hope for a return beyond the return of 539 B.C. Such is the eschatology of the Chronicler.

Moving beyond genealogical material, we note that another way to get a handle on the Chronicler's message is to focus on his handling of David and Solomon (1 Chronicles 11–2 Chronicles 9), a portion that accounts for over 40 percent of the whole, or in chapter divisions, twenty-nine of sixty-five chapters.

It is well known (and see our earlier discussion of David in Second Samuel and Solomon in First Kings) that the Chronicler's account of these two kings includes hardly any of the unsavory incidents involving this father and son. For example, Chronicles has no reference to the Uriah-Bathsheba incident or to any problems David had with his children. Similarly, Chronicles lacks any description of Solomon's extirpation of his political foes or his multiple marriages and apostasy.

In Solomon's case, his record is absolutely clean. For David, it is almost absolutely clean. The one exception is the inclusion of his census-taking (1 Chronicles 21). And while it is common among commentators to suggest that this sinful act is reproduced because in the long run it establishes the threshing floor of Araunah/Ornan as the piece of real estate on which the temple will be built, there may be more than that (Knoppers 1995). Another possible negative mark on David is the Chronicler's explanation for why David himself cannot build the temple. The author's language seems stronger and more approaching moral censure than in Kings. First Chronicles 22:8 has Yahweh say to David, "You shall not build a house to my name, because you have shed so much blood in my sight on the earth." This contrasts with what Solomon says in 1 Kings 5:3: "You know that my father David could not build a house for the name of the Lord his God because of the warfare with which his enemies surrounded him." Kings—in Solomon's opinion, anyway—attributes David's inability to his preoccupation with war. In Chronicles, Yahweh disqualifies David because of violence. (See further, Dirksen 1996: 51–56.)

The story in First Chronicles 21 highlights a David who, although guilty of falling prey to an inciting Satan (v. 1) and making a decision that brings divine wrath on his innocent subjects (v. 7), is able to confront his guilt. He acknowledges his wrongdoing and repents (v. 8), intercedes for God's judgment to cease against his people (v. 17), and does what Yahweh's angel tells him to do (v. 18–30). Possibly, the Chronicler is lifting up David to his audience as a model of what part of the hymn "Rescue the Perishing" speaks of when it sings "down in the human heart, crushed by the tempter, feelings lie buried that grace can restore."

But what of David's tryst with Bathsheba and his devious elimination of Uriah? Did he not repent then too (2 Sam. 12:13a)? Why not use that incident? For one thing, David's sin there was a private act, and here it is a public act. There, his repentance is short and subdued (two words in Hebrew: "I-have-sinned against-Yahweh"). Here, it is more, and includes intercession on behalf of innocent persons. There, the consequences of his sin threatened only himself, his lover (victim?), and their newborn. Here, the consequences of his sin threaten the entire nation. There, nothing redemptive follows David's sin. He subse-

quently loses four sons to tragedy and violence. Here, something redemptive follows David's sin: a site for the building of the temple
evolves.

An examination of the material in 1 Chronicles 11–29 covering the
reign of David reveals that essentially two items are discussed at any
length, with each followed by an appropriate liturgical act (Allen 1988:
22):

1. David has the ark brought to Jerusalem (1 Chron. 13:1–16:6)
   and concludes that with a song of praise (1 Chron. 16:7–36,
   portions of which appear again in Ps. 96; 105:1–5; 106:1, 47–
   48).
2. David prepares for the building of the temple (1 Chron. 22:1–
   29:8) and follows that with a prayer (1 Chron. 29:10–19).

It is perhaps a bit more accurate to suggest that the author moves
back and forth between emphasizing David building his kingdom and
David building up the cult (Duke 1999: 121). Here is the alternating
pattern:

1 Chronicles 11–12: kingdom (capturing Jerusalem; support from all
   Israel)
1 Chronicles 13: cult (attempt to transport the ark)
1 Chronicles 14: kingdom (military victories)
1 Chronicles 15–17: cult (bringing the ark to Jerusalem and David's
   desire to build a house for it)
1 Chronicles 18–20: kingdom (military victories)
1 Chronicles 21–29: cult (preparations for the temple)

Thus, for the Chronicler these are the hallmarks of David's reign: a
kingdom builder and one who establishes the foundations for the community's corporate worship of God. It is not that the Chronicler has
whitewashed David's (or Solomon's) life. It is not necessary, when an
author pens a biography of a national leader, to include all that leader's
foibles, especially if they do not contribute to the purpose of the author.
Chronicles raises this question for us about David: In the long run,
what were David's most significant contributions, his enduring legacy,
to the people of God?

Solomon's portrayal in Chronicles (2 Chronicles 1–9) parallels that
of his father. Although Chronicles begins the account of Solomon's
reign in 2 Chronicles 1, Solomon has been prominently present in the
David story since 1 Chronicles 22. Within those chapters, on no fewer

than three occasions, we read that Yahweh has "chosen" (*bakhar*) Solomon to succeed David.

—"It is your son Solomon who shall build my house . . . for I have chosen him to be a son to me" (1 Chron. 28:6).
—"Take heed now, for the Lord has chosen you to build a house as the sanctuary" (1 Chron. 28:10).
—"My son Solomon, whom alone God has chosen, is young and inexperienced, and the work is great" (1 Chron. 29:1).

The import of this triple notation may be gauged by the fact that these three passages are the only times in which *bakhar*/choose is applied to any king after David. The ubiquity of the presence of Solomon in the Chronicles David narrative contrasts vividly with the virtual nonexistence of Solomon in the Samuel David narrative (there, he is mentioned only twice, 2 Sam. 5:14 [a birth announcement]; 12:24–25).

A reading of these passages makes it clear that Yahweh has chosen Solomon for one purpose, and that is to build the temple. Accordingly, just about everything in Chronicles relates in one way or another to this project. He builds it (2 Chron. 3:1–4:22); he has the ark of the covenant installed in it (2 Chronicles 5); he blesses his people after its completion (2 Chron. 6:3–11); he prays over it (2 Chron. 6:12–42); he consecrates it (2 Chronicles 7).

On both sides of the main temple section is the account of Solomon's interactions with two non-Israelite heads of state: Huram (Hiram in Kings), king of Tyre (2 Chron. 2:1–16), and the Queen of Sheba (2 Chron. 9:1–12).

Interestingly, these foreign heads of state are the only individuals anywhere in Chronicles who affirm explicitly Yahweh's love for Israel:

Huram: "Because the Lord loves his people he has made you king over them" (2 Chron. 2:11).
Queen of Sheba: "Because your God loved Israel and would establish them forever, he has made you king over them" (2 Chron. 9:8).

Chronicles highlights, more than anything else, Solomon's role as temple builder by dividing his forty-year role into two unevenly treated twenty-year periods:

1. *2 Chronicles 1–7:* the first twenty years, the temple building era (152 verses). It is a period that commences (1:7–13) and concludes (7:12–22) with God appearing to Solomon at night

("That night God appeared to Solomon" [2 Chron. 1:7; and not specifically identified as a "dream" as in 1 Kings 3:5]; "Then the Lord appeared to Solomon in the night" [2 Chron. 7:12]). A dramatic change occurs in the tone of these two divine revelations. In the first, God says that Solomon may have anything he asks for. In the second, God makes three "if they/you . . . then I will . . ." statements. The first (7:14) is a hopeful one addressed to future penitent Israel. The second (7:17–18) is a promissory one addressed to Solomon. The third (7:19–20) is a threatening one addressed to Solomon and to Israel [the "you" of v. 19 is plural], describing both Israel's and the temple's terrible future if there is a flaunting of God's laws.

2. *2 Chronicles 8–9:* activities that cover the second twenty-year period of Solomon's reign, his post-temple projects ("At the end of twenty years" [8:1]) (49 verses). The relationship of chs. 8–9 to 1–7 is one of cause to effects. What does Solomon enjoy as a result of his faithful building of the temple? The benefits include consolidation throughout his empire (8:2–10), faithful worship (8:11–16), prosperity (8:17–18), recognition of Solomon's greatness by the Queen of Sheba (9:1–12) and by other kings (9:13–28).

The entire life of Solomon in Chronicles is bracketed by references to his wisdom:

2 Chron. 1:10: "Give me now wisdom and knowledge to go out and come in before this people."

2 Chron. 9:23: "All the kings of the earth sought the presence of Solomon to hear his wisdom, which God had put into his mind."

The Chronicler is not interested in retelling all the details of the splitting of the united kingdom into a divided kingdom, and is not interested in any of the kings of the northern and schismatic Israel. Rather, the Chronicler's preoccupation is with the kings of Judah who follow David and Solomon. Do they live up to the standard of David and Solomon, and if so, how and with what results? Or do they not live up to the standard of David and Solomon, and if not, how and with what results? A few do (Abijah [ch. 13]; Asa, to a degree [chs. 15–16]; Jehoshaphat, to a degree [chs. 18–20]; Jotham [ch. 27]; Hezekiah [chs. 29–32]; Josiah, mostly [chs. 34–35]). But most do not. For those kings who model the example of David and Solomon, there is blessing. For those kings who do not, there is disaster. Such a lesson, extended to everybody, must not be lost on this postexilic audience to whom the Chronicler is writing.

In describing incidents of deviation from the divine law, the Chronicler frequently employs the word *maʿal*, in both verb and noun form, to refer to such acts of malfeasance. It appears four times in First Chronicles, all before the David-Solomon sections (2:7; 5:25; 9:1; 10:13), and twelve times in Second Chronicles (12:2; 26:16, 18; 28:19 [2x], 22; 29:6, 19; 30:7; 33:19; 36:14 [2x]). These occurrences in Chronicles of *maʿal* account for sixteen of its sixty-three uses in the Old Testament (about 25 percent). And one thing of interest here is that Samuel–Kings, when discussing this same period and the same acts of malfeasance, never once uses the word *maʿal* in either verb or noun form.

The usual translation for this root in the NRSV and NIV is, in the verb form, "transgress, be unfaithful/faithless," although NRSV opts once for "be false" (2 Chron. 26:16) and "do wrong" (2 Chron. 26:18). The standard rendering of the root in noun form is "unfaithfulness."

Individuals may be guilty of *maʿal* (Uzziah [2 Chron. 26:16, 18]; Ahaz [2 Chron. 28:19, 22; 29:19]; Manasseh [2 Chron. 33:19]). But it can be a community problem as well, either present communities (2 Chron. 12:2) or past communities (2 Chron. 29:6; 30:7: "Do not be like your ancestors"). The word is used with Israel's very first king, Saul (1 Chron. 10:13: "Saul died for his unfaithfulness, he was unfaithful to the Lord"), and for the priests and leaders of Israel's last king, Zedekiah (2 Chron. 36:14: "All the leading priests and the people also were exceedingly unfaithful"). So for Chronicles, monarchy in Israel enters in an act of *maʿal* and exits in an act of *maʿal*.

That we read in adjacent chapters that "Judah was taken into exile in Babylon because of their unfaithfulness" (1 Chron. 9:1) and that "Saul died for his unfaithfulness" (1 Chron. 10:13) suggests that the Chronicler "sees Saul as a figure of God's people in their disobedience" (Walters 1991: 64).

But *maʿal* is not confined to the time of the monarchy for the Chronicler. Achan (see Joshua 7), who secretly stole from Jericho's spoils that were to be devoted completely to God, is thereby guilty of the sin of *maʿal* (1 Chron. 2:7; where Achan is called Achar). This is a case of deliberate *maʿal*, in fact, the worst *maʿal* of all, the desecration of what has been devoted to God.

Given the prominence of the temple in Chronicles, it is significant that three instances of *maʿal*/unfaithfulness involve misuse of the temple and its furnishings;

1. Uzziah commits *ma'al* when he offers incense inside the temple
   (2 Chron. 26:16–18). He is stricken with leprosy on the spot.
2. Ahaz decimates the temple's utensils, locks the temple doors,
   and erects altars and high places elsewhere (2 Chron. 28:24–
   25), thus causing spiritual disaster for the whole nation
   (2 Chron. 28:19).
3. The cause of the exile is stated boldly in 2 Chron. 36:14: "All the
   leading priests . . . were exceedingly unfaithful . . . they pol-
   luted the house of the Lord."

The other form of *ma'al* in Chronicles is idolatry, which like temple
tampering, is a sin against God. Saul commits *ma'al* when he consults
a medium for guidance (1 Chron. 10:13). Rehoboam and his people
abandon Yahweh's Torah and so commit *ma'al* (2 Chron. 12:2). Both
Ahaz (2 Chron. 28:22–23) and Manasseh (2 Chron. 33:19) succumb to
idolatry, an act of *ma'al* against Yahweh, breaking the oath to serve
him only. Manasseh's repentance, by the way, demonstrates that even
sins of *ma'al*—sins of unfaithfulness and betrayal—can be forgiven.

If the not so good kings of Judah are doing things like *ma'al*, then
what are the good and godly kings of Judah doing? They are upholding
and incarnating the model of David and Solomon.

Godly and sensible kings, for example, have learned how to trust
God for security and avoid the perils of political collaboration as a
source of salvation. Every alliance either with a foreign power (Asa
with Ben-hadad of Aram [2 Chronicles 16]; Ahaz with Tiglath-pilneser
of Assyria [2 Chron. 28:16–21]) or even with northern Israel (Jehoshaphat with Ahab [2 Chronicles 18]; Jehoshaphat with Amaziah
[2 Chron. 20:35–37]; Amaziah and the hired troops from northern Israel [2 Chron. 25:5–13]) ends in disaster, both personal and national.
To minuscule Judah in those early postexilic days, the temptation
might be to look to alliances as the best road to survival. If so, they
must learn that trust in anything other than God is a sure recipe for disaster, and that "there is strength neither in numbers nor in material
resources" (Knoppers 1995: 626).

Asa, one of Judah's flip-flop kings, learned that lesson the hard way.
First, when attacked by Zerah the Ethiopian and his troops, Asa
prayed, "Help us, O Lord our God, for we rely [*sha'an*] on you"
(2 Chron. 14:11). And Yahweh did help them. But when attacked by
King Baasha of Israel, Asa goes the alliance route, and as a result is
chided by a prophet: "Because you relied [*sha'an*] on the king of Aram,
and did not rely [*sha'an*] on the Lord your God, the army of the king of
Aram has escaped. . . . Were not the Ethiopians and the Libyans a huge

army . . . ? Yet because you relied [*sha'an*] on the Lord, he gave them into your hand" (2 Chron. 16:7–8). Asa's sad story is one of a shift from trust in God to trust in human power, and the tragic consequences that befall.

The opposite of Asa's latter strategy is that of Jehoshaphat when he is attacked by a military coalition (2 Chronicles 20). The text records absolutely no military response by Jehoshaphat and his soldiers. Instead, they engage in liturgical acts like singing and praying, and Yahweh defeats the enemy ("As they began to sing and praise, the Lord set an ambush against the Ammonites . . . so that they were routed" [2 Chron. 20:22]). Davies (1992: 45) captures well the scene here: "If your cause is just and you are faithful to your deity (and if that deity is YHWH), you will not need an army to protect you. Spend your defense budget on hymnbooks and musical training for your brass band! The only army you need is the Salvation Army."

Good kings/leaders not only avoid the wrong kinds of behavior (*ma'al*, realpolitik, etc.), but also lead their people in the joyous, awesome worship of God, especially as that worship centers on the major festivals of the calendar (De Vries 1997). There are five of these:

1. Solomon's dedication of the temple (2 Chronicles 7), which the parallel account dates to the "seventh month" (1 Kings 8:2). The only Israelite festival observed in the seventh month is Tabernacles. It involves seven days of dedication and seven days of feasting (2 Chron. 7:9).
2. Asa's festival (2 Chron. 15:8–15 [or 19]), held in the "third month" (2 Chron. 15:10). Although not named, this festival would be Weeks/Pentecost. On this occasion Asa oversees a covenant renewal ceremony at the heart of which is an oath to seek Yahweh with one's whole heart (2 Chron. 15:11–14). Neither celebration nor commitment cancels out the other.
3. Hezekiah's cleansing and rededication of the temple (2 Chronicles 29) in the very first month of his reign (2 Chron. 29:3)—he wastes no time getting started undoing what his sinful father, Ahaz, had allowed. The sixteen days (see v. 17) of cleansing activities are described in vv. 3b–19, and the celebration activities in vv. 20–35.
4. Hezekiah's Passover/Unleavened Bread festival in the second month of his reign (2 Chron. 30:15–18, 21–22). Once again, celebration is combined with commitment ("But Hezekiah prayed for them, saying, 'The good Lord pardon all who set their hearts to seek God'" [v. 18b]).

5. Josiah's Passover/Unleavened Bread festival (2 Chronicles 35) in the first month (v. 1). Here, reformation (ch. 34) precedes celebration (ch. 35).

In the first four of these five the narration climaxes by emphasizing the joy/rejoicing present in the community of faith: Solomon: "He sent the people away to their homes, joyful and in good spirits" (2 Chron. 7:10); Asa: "All Judah rejoiced over the oath" (2 Chron. 15:15); Hezekiah: "And Hezekiah and all the people rejoiced" (2 Chron. 29:36); Hezekiah: "The whole assembly of Judah . . . rejoiced. There was great joy in Jerusalem" (2 Chron. 30:25–26). We can assume the same atmosphere for Josiah's celebrations, simply because 2 Chron. 35:18 states, "No passover like it had been kept in Israel since the days of the prophet Samuel; none of the kings of Israel had kept such a passover as was kept by Josiah."

It is surely no accident that it is these four kings who are associated in Chronicles with building and/or repairing the temple, especially the altar. Solomon constructs the altar (2 Chron. 4:1). Asa repairs the altar (like Elijah in 1 Kings 18:30b, who "repaired the altar of the Lord that had been thrown down): "He repaired the altar of the Lord that was in front of the vestibule" (2 Chron. 15:8b). Of Hezekiah the text says, "In the first year of his reign . . . he opened the doors of the house of the Lord and repaired them" (2 Chron. 29:3). Finally, twice the text associates Josiah with repairing the temple: "Josiah sent Shaphan . . . to repair the house of the Lord his God" (2 Chron. 34:8b); "And the workers who were working in the house of the Lord gave it [the offerings] for repairing and restoring the house" (2 Chron. 34:10b).

To sum up, we have isolated a number of distinguishing features in Chronicles: (1) The author is interested in tracing the origins of Israel/Judah back to Adam. (2) Judah is highlighted among Jacob's sons. (3) David is Judah's most strategic descendant. (4) Solomon is David's most important son. (5) The Levites are especially prominent. (6) The description of the return to Zion (1 Chron. 9:2–44) precedes significantly the expression of the hope and possibility of that return (2 Chron. 36:22–23). (7) About 40 percent of Chronicles is filled with the story of David and Solomon. Both are stellar individuals primarily because of their involvement with planning and then building the temple. (8) The kings of Judah are presented as test cases vis-à-vis the integrity of David and Solomon. Those kings who model the paradigm of David and Solomon in terms of Torah and temple observance are favored by God; those who do not, experience God's disfavor. There is both immediate retribution for unfaithful individual kings (Dillard

1984) and ultimate retribution for the entire nation (2 Chron. 36:17–21), but only after several centuries of apostasy and God's repeated attempts, by way of his prophets, to turn it away from certain doom (2 Chron. 36:15–16). (9) The book ends with the Chronicler quoting the decree of King Cyrus of Persia allowing the exiles to return and go up to Zion. In other words, the last word of the author to an audience that has already gone up to Zion is that they may yet go up to Zion!

Everything in Chronicles precedes the time of the audience to whom the Chronicler is writing (from Adam to Cyrus of Persia). The Chronicler says nothing about contemporary times, with the possible exception of 1 Chron. 9:2–44. It is as if the Chronicler is asking, "What can we learn for today—and tomorrow—from yesterday?" One can understand the present the more one understands the past (Goldingay 1975: 108).

Well, then, what is it that one can learn for the present and the future from the past? In the Chronicler's presentation of the past, one learns that the community of faith has deep roots in the past, and is not a "Johnny-come-lately" phenomenon. One also learns that God has provided this community with divinely chosen political and religious leaders who give to the community the means and apparatuses necessary for a dynamic, significant engagement with their God in worship. The chief end of the body of believers is, indeed, to glorify God and enjoy him forever. And because so many of these leaders forgot that God's call is a call not only to communal worship at his house but also to communal holiness, the Chronicler reminds the audience, through vivid royal examples of unfaithfulness, that they should "not laugh this off though as if there is no wages of sin" (North 1963: 374). (Recall that Paul's word in Rom. 6:23 on "the wages of sin is death" is addressed primarily to believers, not nonbelievers, coming as it does in the "Shall we continue in sin?" discussion of Romans 6.)

Perhaps this is the reason why Chronicles ends by talking about a return to those who have returned, saying, "Let him go up." We know from Ezra and Nehemiah that the spiritual commitment among many of the returnees in the sixth and fifth centuries B.C. was less than ideal. But in spite of all the hoopla of 538 B.C. and afterwards, Israel still stands on the brink of an even greater return (Johnstone 1986: 114; 1990: 11). This is more than a geographical return. It is a return to Yahweh, a return to being his set-apart-by-grace people. Without that, they have no future.

God will establish a scion of David as the community's leader "forever" (see the "forevers" of 1 Chron. 17:14; 22:10; 28:7). Will the people of God, in response, serve and worship their God forever? If so, let them go up and claim their inheritance.

Bibliography (1 and 2 Chronicles)

Commentaries and Major Studies

Ackroyd, P. R. 1973. *I and II Chronicles, Ezra, Nehemiah*. Torch Bible Commentaries. London: SCM.

———. 1991. *The Chronicler in His Age*. JSOT Supplement 101. Sheffield: JSOT Press.

Allen, L. C. 1987. *1 and 2 Chronicles*. The Communicator's Commentary 10. Waco, Tex.: Word.

Braun, R. 1986. *1 Chronicles*. Word Biblical Commentary 14. Waco, Tex.: Word.

Curtis, E. L., and A. A. Madsen. 1910. *A Critical and Exegetical Commentary on the Books of Chronicles*. International Critical Commentary. New York: Charles Scribner's Sons.

De Vries, S. J. 1989. *1 and 2 Chronicles*. Forms of Old Testament Literature 11. Grand Rapids: Eerdmans.

Dillard, R. B. 1987. *2 Chronicles*. Word Biblical Commentary 15. Waco, Tex.: Word.

Duke, R. K. 1990. *The Persuasive Appeal of the Chronicler: A Rhetorical Analysis*. JSOT Supplement 88; Bible and Literature Series 25. Sheffield: Almond.

Dyck, J. E. 1998. *The Theocentric Ideology of the Chronicler*. Biblical Interpretation Series 33. Leiden: Brill.

Endres, J. C., and W. R Millar, J. B. Burns, eds. 1998. *Chronicles and Its Synoptic Parallels in Samuel, Kings and Related Biblical Texts*. Collegeville, Minn.: Liturgical Press.

Graham, M. P., and K. G. Hoglund, S. L. McKenzie, eds. 1997. *The Chronicler as Historian*. JSOT Supplement 238. Sheffield: Sheffield Academic Press.

Graham, M. P., and S. L. McKenzie, eds. 1999. *The Chronicler as Author: Studies in Text and Texture*. JSOT Supplement 263. Sheffield: Sheffield Academic Press.

Howard, D. M., Jr. 1993. *An Introduction to the Old Testament Historical Books*. Chicago: Moody. Pp. 231–72.

Japhet, S. 1989. *The Ideology of the Book of Chronicles and Its Place in Biblical Thought*. BEATAJ 9. Frankfurt: Peter Lang.

———. 1993. *I and II Chronicles: A Commentary*. Old Testament Library. Louisville: Westminster/John Knox.

Johnstone, W. 1986. *Guilt and Atonement: The Theme of 1 and 2 Chronicles*. JSOT Supplement 42: Sheffield: Sheffield Academic Press.

———. 1997. *1 and 2 Chronicles*. Vol. 1, *1 Chronicles 1–2 Chronicles 9: Israel's Place among the Nations*. Vol. 2, *2 Chronicles 10–36: Guilt and Atonement*. JSOT Supplement 253–254. Sheffield: Sheffield Academic Press.

———. 1998. *Chronicles and Exodus: An Analogy and Its Application*. JSOT Supplement 275. Sheffield: Sheffield Academic Press.

Jones, G. H. 1993. *1 and 2 Chronicles*. Old Testament Guides. Sheffield: JSOT Press.

Kelly, B. E. 1996. *Retribution and Eschatology in Chronicles*. JSOT Supplement 211. Sheffield: Sheffield Academic Press.

McConville, J. G. 1984. *I and II Chronicles*. Daily Study Bible. Philadelphia: Westminster.

McKenzie, S. L. 1985. *The Chronicler's Use of the Deuteronomistic History*. HSM 33. Atlanta: Scholars Press.

Myers, J. 1965. *I Chronicles*. Anchor Bible 12. Garden City, N.Y.: Doubleday.

———. 1965. *II Chronicles*. Anchor Bible 13. Garden City, N.Y.: Doubleday.

Newsome, J. D. 1987. *A Synoptic Harmony of Samuel, Kings, and Chronicles*. Grand Rapids: Baker.

Noth, M. 1987. *The Chronicler's History*. Trans. H. G. M. Williamson. JSOT Supplement 50. Sheffield: JSOT Press.

Riley, W. 1993. *King and Cultus in Chronicles: Worship and the Reinterpretation of History*. JSOT Supplement 160. Sheffield: JSOT Press.

Sailhamer, J. 1983. *First and Second Chronicles*. Everyman's Bible Commentary. Chicago: Moody.

Schniedewind, W. M. 1995. *The Word of God in Transition: From Prophet to Exegete in the Second Temple Period*. JSOT Supplement 197. Sheffield: Sheffield Academic Press.

Selman, M. J. 1994. *1 Chronicles: An Introduction and Commentary*. Tyndale Old Testament Commentaries. Downers Grove, Ill.: InterVarsity.

———. 1994. *2 Chronicles: An Introduction and Commentary*. Tyndale Old Testament Commentaries. Downers Grove, Ill.: InterVarsity.

Thompson, J. A. 1994. *1, 2 Chronicles*. New American Commentary 9. Nashville: Broadman & Holman.

Thronveit, M. A. 1987. *When Kings Speak: Royal Speech and Royal Prayer in Chronicles*. SBL Dissertation Series 93. Atlanta: Scholars Press.

Wilcock, M. 1987. *The Message of Chronicles*. Downers Grove, Ill.: InterVarsity.

Williamson, H. G. M. 1977. *Israel in the Books of Chronicles*. Cambridge: Cambridge University Press.

———. 1982. *1 and 2 Chronicles*. New Century Bible Commentary. Grand Rapids: Eerdmans.

Shorter Studies

Ackroyd, P. R. 1967. "History and Theology in the Writings of the Chronicler." *CTM* 38:501–15.

———. 1973. "The Theology of the Chronicler." *LTQ* 8:101–16.

Allen, L. C. 1988. "Kerygmatic Units in 1 and 2 Chronicles." *JSOT* 41:21–36.

Bailey, N. 1994. "David's Innocence: A Response to J. W. Wright." *JSOT* 64:83–90.

Ben Zvi, E. 1995. "A Sense of Proportion: An Aspect of the Theology of the Chronicler." *SJOT* 9:37–51.

Braun, R. L. 1971. "The Message of Chronicles: Rally 'Round the Temple." *CTM* 42:502–14.

———. 1973. "Solomonic Apologetic in Chronicles." *JBL* 92:503–16.

———. 1976. "Solomon, the Chosen Temple Builder: The Significance of 1 Chronicles 27, 28, and 29 for the Theology of Chronicles." *JBL* 95:581–90.

———. 1977. "A Reconsideration of the Chronicler's Attitude toward the North." *JBL* 96:59–62.

———. 1979. "Chronicles, Ezra and Nehemiah: Theology and Literary History." *VT* 30:52–64.

Childs, B. S. 1979. *Introduction to the Old Testament as Scripture*. Philadelphia: Fortress. Pp. 639–55.

Davies, P. R. 1992. "Defending the Boundaries of Israel in the Second Temple Period: 2 Chronicles 20 and the 'Salvation Army.'" In *Priests, Prophets and Scribes: Essays on the Formation and Heritage of Second Temple Judaism in Honour of Joseph Blenkinsopp*. JSOT Supplement 149. Ed. E. C. Ulrich et al. Sheffield: JSOT Press. Pp. 43–54.

Deboys, D. G. 1990. "History and Theology in the Chronicles' Portrayal of Abijah." *Bib* 1971:48–62.

DeVries, S. J. 1986. "The Forms of Prophetic Address in Chronicles." *HAR* 10:15–36.

———. 1988. "Moses and David as Cult Founders in Chronicles." *JBL* 107:619–39.

———. 1997. "Festival Ideology in Chronicles." In *Problems in Biblical Theology: Essays in Honor of Rolf Knierim*. Ed. H. T. Sun et al. Grand Rapids: Eerdmans. Pp. 104–24.

Dillard, R. B. 1980. "The Reign of Asa (2 Chronicles 14–16): An Example of the Chronicler's Theological Method." *JETS* 23:207–18.

———. 1980–1981. "The Chronicler's Solomon." *WTJ* 43:289–300.

———. 1984. "Reward and Punishment in Chronicles: The Theology of Immediate Retribution." *WTJ* 46:164–72.

———. 1986. "The Chronicler's Jehoshaphat," *TJ* 7:17–22.

Dirksen, P. B. 1996. "Why Was David Disqualified as Temple Builder? The Meaning of 1 Chronicles 22:8." *JSOT* 69:51–56.

Duke, R. K. 1993. "A Model for a Theology of Biblical Historical Narratives: Proposed and Demonstrated with the Books of Chronicles." In *History and Interpretation: Essays in Honour of John H. Hayes*. Ed. M. P. Graham et al. JSOT Supplement 173. Sheffield: JSOT Press. Pp. 65–77.

———. 1999. "A Rhetorical Approach to Appreciating the Books of Chronicles." In *The Chronicler as Author*. Ed. M. P. Graham and S. L. McKenzie. JSOT Supplement 263. Pp. 100–35.

Dumbrell, W. J. 1984. "The Purpose of the Books of Chronicles." *JETS* 27:257–66.

Eshkenazi, T. C. 1995. "A Literary Approach to Chronicles' Ark Narrative in 1 Chronicles 13–16." In *Fortunate the Eyes That See: Essays in Honor of David Noel Freedman in Celebration of His Seventieth Birthday*. Ed. A. B. Beck et al. Grand Rapids: Eerdmans. Pp. 258–74.

Fishbane, M. 1985. *Biblical Interpretation in Ancient Israel*. Oxford: Clarendon.

Gelston, A. 1996. "The End of Chronicles." *SJOT* 19:53–60.

Glatt-Gilad, D. A. 1996. "The Role of Huldah's Prophecy in the Chronicler's Portrayal of Josiah's Reform." *Bib* 77:16–31.

Goldingay, J. 1975. "The Theology of the Chronicler." *BTB* 5:99–126.

Hanks, T. D. 1981. "The Chronicler: Theologian of Grace," *EvQ* 53:16–28.

Harris, R. L. 1990. "Chronicles and the Canon in New Testament Times." *JETS* 33:75–84.

House, P. R. 1998. *Old Testament Theology*. Downers Grove, Ill.: InterVarsity. Pp. 523–38.

Japhet, S. 1971. "Chronicles, Book of." *EncJud*, 5:517–34.

———. 1985. "The Historical Reliability of Chronicles: The History of the Problem and Its Place in Biblical Research." *JSOT* 33:83–107.

Johnstone, W. 1986. "Guilt and Atonement: The Theme of 1 and 2 Chronicles." In *A Word in Season: Essays in Honour of William McKane*. JSOT Supplement 42. Ed. J. D. Martin and P. R. Davies. Sheffield: JSOT Press. Pp. 113–38.

———. 1990. "Which Is the Best Commentary? 11. The Chronicler's Work." *ExpT* 102:6–11.

Kalami, I. 1993. "Literary-Chronological Proximity in the Chronicler's Historiography." *VT* 43:318–38.

Klein, R. W. 1992. "Chronicles, Books of 1–2." *ABD*, 1:992–1002.

———. 1998. "Prophets and Prophecy in the Books of Chronicles." *TBT* 36:227–32.

Knoppers, G. N. 1990. "Rehoboam in Chronicles: Villain or Victim?" *JBL* 109:423–40.

———. 1991. "Reform and Regression: The Chronicler's Presentation of Jehoshaphat." *Bib* 72: 500–524.

———. 1995. "Images of David in Early Judaism: David as Repentant Sinner in Chronicles." *Bib* 76:449–70.

———. 1996. "'Yhwh Is Not in Israel': Alliances as a *Topos* in Chronicles." *CBQ* 58:601–26.

———. 1998. "Of Kings, Prophets and Priests in the Books of Chronicles." *TBT* 36:214–20.

———. 1999. "Hierodules, Priests or Janitors? The Levites in Chronicles and the History of the Israelite Priesthood." *JBL* 118:49–72.

Murray, D. F. 1993. "Dynasty, People, and the Future: The Message of Chronicles." *JSOT* 58:71–92.

Myers, J. M. 1966. "The Kerygma of the Chronicler: History and Theology in the Service of Religion." *Int* 20:259–73.

Newsome, J. D., Jr. 1975. "Toward a New Understanding of the Chronicler and His Purposes." *JBL* 94:201–17.

North, R. 1963. "Theology of the Chronicler." *JBL* 82:369–81.

Payne, J. B. 1979. "The Validity of the Numbers in Chronicles." *BSac* 136:109–28; 206–20; 285–88.

Pratt, R. L., Jr. 1993. "First and Second Chronicles." In *A Complete Literary Guide to the Bible*. Ed. L. Ryken and T. Longman III. Grand Rapids: Zondervan. Pp. 193–205.

Rad, Gerhard von. 1966. "The Levitical Sermons in I and II Chronicles." In *The Problem of the Hexateuch and Other Essays*. Edinburgh and London: Oliver and Boyd. Pp. 267–80.

Shipp, R. M. 1993. "'Remember His Covenant Forever': A Study of the Chronicler's Use of the Psalms." *ResQ* 35:29–39.

Solomon, A. 1989. "The Structure of the Chronicler's History: A Key to the Organization of the Pentateuch." *Semeia* 46:51–64.

Talmon, S. 1987. "1 and 2 Chronicles." In *The Literary Guide to the Bible*. Ed. R. Alter and F. Kermode. Cambridge, Mass.: Belknap. Pp. 365–72.

Thronveit, M. A. 1988. "Hezekiah in the Books of Chronicles." In *SBL Seminar Papers 1988*. Ed. D. L. Lull. Atlanta: Scholars Press. Pp. 302–11.

Townsend, J. L. 1987. "The Purpose of 1 and 2 Chronicles." *BSac* 144:277–92.

Walters, S. D. 1991. "Saul of Gibeon." *JSOT* 52:61–76.

Williamson, H. G. M. 1976. "The Accession of Solomon in the Book of Chronicles." *VT* 26:351–61.

———. 1977. "Eschatology in Chronicles." *TynB* 28:115–54.

———. 1979. "Sources and Redaction in the Chronicler's Genealogy of Judah." *JBL* 98:351–59.

———. 1991. "The Temple in the Book of Chronicles." In *Templum Amicitae: Essays on the Second Temple Presented to Ernst Bammel*. JSNT Supplement 48. Ed. W. Horbury. Sheffield: JSOT Press. Pp. 15–31.

Wright, J. W. 1991. "The Legacy of David in Chronicles: The Narrative Function of 1 Chronicles 23–27." *JBL* 110:229–42.

———. 1993. "The Innocence of David in 1 Chronicles 21." *JSOT* 60:87–105.

———. 1998. "The Founding Father: The Structure of the Chronicler's David Narrative." *JBL* 117:45–59.

Zalewski, S. 1989. "The Purpose of the Story of the Death of Saul in 1 Chronicles IX." *VT* 39:449–67.

Ezra–Nehemiah

In our modern versions of the Old Testament the books of Ezra and Nehemiah appear after the book of Second Chronicles, the fifteenth and
sixteenth books of the Old Testament, and are followed by Esther. But
in the Hebrew Bible, Ezra and Nehemiah follow Daniel and precede
Chronicles (the last book in the canon of the Hebrew Bible).

The sequence Second Chronicles, Ezra, Nehemiah is a historical
one. Ezra–Nehemiah picks up where Second Chronicles leaves off. The
bridge between these two is emphasized by the beginning of Ezra (1:1–
3) repeating the end of Second Chronicles (2 Chron. 36:22–23). While
not a perfect parallel, the way that Exod. 1:1–6 resumes Gen. 46:8–27
comes to mind.

Why, then, the sequence Ezra, Nehemiah, Chronicles? Historically
speaking, it would be comparable to having Acts precede the Gospels
in the New Testament. So obviously, factors other than historical sequence are at work here. The Hebrew Bible has two great histories of
humanity and the nation Israel: (1) Genesis through Kings and (2)
Chronicles, both of which start with Adam and end by tracing Israel's
history into the post-Babylonian exile days (with Chronicles going a bit
further into that era than does Kings). Note that both of these histories
end on a positive note. The last subject in Kings is the release of King
Jehoiachin after thirty-seven years of incarceration in Babylon, only to
become a permanent dinner guest of the king of Babylon (2 Kings
25:27–30). The last subject in Chronicles is the decree of King Cyrus of
Persia authorizing captured Jews to return to Jerusalem to rebuild
their temple (2 Chron. 36:22–23). Possibly, it was this desire to end the
collection of canonical books on such a joyous and hopeful note that

dictated the sequence Ezra, Nehemiah, Chronicles rather than Chronicles, Ezra, Nehemiah. Nehemiah 13, which would have been the final chapter in such a sequence, would be an "uninspiring 'finis'" (Gordon 1965: 299), given its cataloging of persisting acts of sinfulness among the people even after all the good reforming and rebuilding work that Ezra and Nehemiah inspired.

Ezra and Nehemiah come in the latter part of the period that follows the return of some of the Jewish exiles from Babylon to Judah and Jerusalem. This period begins in the latter half of the sixth century B.C. (before Ezra and Nehemiah) and continues down into the second half of the fifth century B.C. (the time of Ezra and Nehemiah).

The earliest date in Ezra–Nehemiah is in Ezra 1:1: "In the first year of King Cyrus of Persia." This is not a reference to the first year of Cyrus' reign per se (that would be about 559 B.C.), but to the year of Cyrus conquering Babylon and effectively ending the existence of the Babylonian Empire. And that year is 538 B.C. The latest date is that alluded to in Neh. 13:6, where Nehemiah states that now having returned to Babylon in the "thirty-second year of the reign of King Artaxerexes" (433 B.C.), he asked at some point for permission to return to Jerusalem to correct some abuses there. Since Artaxerxes died in 423 B.C., Nehemiah's second visit to Jerusalem must take place sometime during 433–423 B.C. Nehemiah simply says, "After some time I asked leave of the king."

So, chronologically these two books stretch over a century, from 538 B.C. to 433–423 B.C. The lives and ministries of Ezra and Nehemiah fill a smaller window in that period, at most thirty-five years (from 458 B.C. to 423 B.C. [at the latest]).

The controlling imperial power of this era is the Persian Empire, whose kings with dates of reign are

Cyrus (559–529 B.C.)
Cambyses (529–521 B.C.)
Darius I (521–485 B.C.)
Xerxes I/Ahasuerus (485–464 B.C.)
Artaxerxes I (464–424 B.C.)
Xerxes II (423 B.C.)
Darius II (423–404 B.C.)
Artaxerxes II (404–358 B.C.)

Dates given in Ezra–Nehemiah help date the time of the activity of these two reformers:

Ezra: "After this, in the reign of King Artaxerxes [I? II?] of Persia, Ezra . . . went up from Babylonia. . . . in the seventh year of King Artaxerxes . . . in the seventh year of the king" (Ezra 7:1, 6, 7b, 8b). If this king is Artaxerxes I, then the seventh year of his reign and the date of Ezra's arrival in Jerusalem would be 458/57 B.C.

Nehemiah: "In the twentieth year, while I was in Susa the capital . . . in the twentieth year of King Artaxerxes . . . I was appointed to be their governor in the land of Judah from the twentieth year to the thirty-second year of King Artaxerxes" (Neh. 1:1; 2:1; 5:14). The twentieth year of Artaxerxes and the beginning of Nehemiah's work is, then, 445/44 B.C., some thirteen years after Ezra's arrival.

In spite of these apparently clear dating notations of the beginnings of the work of Ezra and Nehemiah, many scholars are skeptical about the correctness of this sequence, and in fact argue that Nehemiah actually came to Jerusalem *before* Ezra. They do so primarily in one of two ways. First, some interpret the references in Ezra 7:1–8 to the Artaxerxes in the phrase "seventh year of King Artaxerxes" as Artaxerxes II, not Artaxerxes I (and of course, the Old Testament does not distinguish between "First" and "Second"). This would make the beginning of Ezra's work 398/97 B.C., thus placing him a good bit later than Nehemiah. The second way to reverse their order is to read the references to the "seventh year" of Artaxerxes in Ezra 7 as a scribal mistake for the "thirty-seventh year" of Artaxerxes, thus placing Ezra's mission in 428/27 B.C., still after the start of Nehemiah's ministry, but not by as much as that suggested by the first alternative dating.

Those who advocate Ezra's following Nehemiah (rather than preceding him) appeal to various data in the text to support their reading. For example, Nehemiah is the contemporary of the high priest Eliashib (Neh. 3:1; 12:22; 13:4), while Eliashib's grandson Jehohanan/Johanan is priest in the time of Ezra (compare Ezra 10:6 with Neh. 12:22). But can we be sure that the priest contemporary with Ezra (and with such a common name at that) is the same as his later namesake who was Eliashib's grandson?

Again, if Ezra actually came to Jerusalem thirteen years before Nehemiah specifically for the purpose of teaching the Lord's "statutes and ordinances in Israel" (7:10), a mission specifically designated by King Artaxerxes for Ezra (7:25–26), then he did not carry that out until thirteen years later, when he does so in Neh. 8:1–12. If he came to Jerusalem before Nehemiah with this express mission, why delay thirteen years to commence it? But might not Ezra have been teaching the law of the Lord on a less grandiose scale than that detailed in Nehemiah 8 all along, and only the rebuilding of the altar and temple (prior to Ezra's time), coupled with the rebuilding of Jerusalem and its wall (in Nehemiah's time), created the necessary circumstances for a reading of the law of Moses before "all the people"?

Third, Nehemiah (like Ezra) cites those repatriated to Judah in the late sixth century under the leadership of Zerubbabel and Jeshua (see Ezra 2 and Nehemiah 7), but Nehemiah makes no mention of those who returned to Judah with Ezra (Ezra 8:1–29) nor does he include Ezra, or any who accompanied Ezra, among the builders of the wall (Neh. 3:1–32). ("Hattush" of Ezra 8:2 is not the person with the same name in Neh. 3:10.) Is the silence about them in Nehemiah because Nehemiah came to Jerusalem before Ezra did? Or do the names of the wall builders in Nehemiah 3 represent only the foremen, the supervisory personnel, who are not recent returnees? And was Ezra too advanced in age for such manual responsibilities, or as priest, were his priorities elsewhere? Note also that Meremoth son of Uriah (Ezra 8:33; Neh. 3:4, 21) and Malchijah son of Harim (Ezra 10:31; Neh. 3:11) are mentioned as contemporaries of both Ezra and Nehemiah.

The issue is a complex one, and probably will not be resolved to everybody's satisfaction. Current biblical scholarship tends more to support the traditional order, a turnaround from what was formerly a consensus on Nehemiah's priority. Either order is plausible on logical grounds alone (Gottwald 1985: 436). Putting Ezra after Nehemiah places the former's religious reforms as an accomplishment within the context of political consolidation expedited by Nehemiah. On the other hand, placing Ezra before Nehemiah suggests that Ezra's religious reforms, perhaps advancing and taking hold slowly at first (as most reforms do), really begin to take hold once Nehemiah had implemented his political and real estate reforms. Of course, it is not imperative that the issue be resolved absolutely in order to hear the biblical message (Childs 1979: 637).

The individuals Ezra and Nehemiah are about as different as day and night. Ezra is called both priest and scribe, the only time in the Old Testament where these two offices are fused in one person. "Priest" is Ezra's Jewish title, and "scribe" might refer to his position in the Persian governmental service. Scholarship in one kind of text translates into scholarship in another kind of text (the law of Moses). Ezra is at home in books and in the Book. Where Ezra is referred to in the same verse as priest and scribe, priest always comes first (Ezra 7:11, 12, 21; Neh. 8:9; 12:26).

Nehemiah, on the other hand, is a layman. Vocationally, he is "cupbearer to the king" (Neh. 1:11). He himself states, "When wine was served him, I carried the wine and gave it to the king" (2:1). The Hebrew word for "cupbearer" is *mashqeh*, which means literally, "one who gives (someone) something to drink." The word is used frequently in Genesis 40 to describe one of Joseph's two cellmates. Older translations rendered *mashqeh* in Genesis 40 as "butler" (KJV, RSV), and this is acceptable as long as one remembers that "butler" comes from the Middle English "boteler," someone who attends to (wine) bottles. (See Yamauchi 1980d: 132.)

This vocational distinction between the two explains why for Ezra the text traces his genealogy through sixteen generations all the way back to Aaron (Ezra 7:1–5). To be a priest one has to have the correct roots and proper bloodlines. For Nehemiah, on the other hand, all we know is the name of his father (Hacaliah [Neh. 1:1]).

Ezra's name is nearly the same as that of his grandfather Azariah, minus the "iah" suffix (see Ezra 7:1). This could reflect the practice known as "papponymy," whereby a name appears in alternating generations so that the names of grandfathers are carried by their grandsons. Both Ezra (*ʿezraʾ*) and Azariah (*ʿazaryah*) come from a Semitic verb (*ʿ-z-r*) meaning "to help." The "Nehem-" part of Nehemiah's name comes from a verb (*n-kh-m*), which means "to comfort." Thus, Ezra and Nehemiah speak, via their names, to their people as "help" and "comfort" from the Lord.

Ezra does what one would expect a priest to do. He reads and explains the Torah of Moses to his people, and urges its implementation in their life. Where they have ignored the divine law, thus defiling themselves and the land, Ezra will initiate whatever measures are necessary to get rid of the pollution (Ezra 10). The reforms of Ezra the priest build upon the rebuilding of the altar (Ezra 3:1–6a) and the rebuilding of the temple (Ezra 3:6b–6:22), both of which take place before he arrives on the scene.

On the other hand, one could not predict Nehemiah's future course of action based on his cupbearer responsibilities. How can a cupbearer become a construction worker? For indeed, his main work, once he returns to Jerusalem, is to oversee the building of the wall around Jerusalem (Nehemiah 1–6) and preside with Ezra at its dedication (Neh. 12:27–43). Nehemiah's career is one that shifts from serving drinks to a king (along with other responsibilities) to moving stones into place around Zion's perimeter. He changes places, careers, and uniforms.

Actually, the text never states precisely what Ezra's motives were for returning to Judah. The closest it comes is in Artaxerxes granting Ezra "all that he asked" (Ezra 7:6b), and in the statement that "Ezra had set his heart . . . to teach the statutes and ordinances in Israel" (Ezra 7:10). But why does he wish to do this?

By contrast, Nehemiah's brother Hanani comes to Babylon with a report about the deplorable state of the city and those who escaped exile (Neh. 1:2–3). Such a report moves Nehemiah to prayer (Neh. 1:4–11; 2:4), and to ask the Persian king to send him to Jerusalem in order to rebuild it (Neh. 2:1–5). The "sad" look in Nehemiah's face when he appears before the king (Neh. 2:1–2) may be compared with the reference in Matt. 6:16 to refer to the long faces of fasting Pharisees and in Luke 24:17 to refer to the two sad-looking disciples on the road to Emmaus who thought Jesus was still dead. Certainly, Nehemiah's weeping over a city (Neh. 1:4) parallels Jesus, who wept over the same city (Luke 19:41), as did Jeremiah (Jer. 9:1; 13:17).

One other item betrays Ezra's priestly background versus Nehemiah's background as a civil servant in the Persian Empire. Ezra refers to the months by using ordinal numerals: "fifth month" (Ezra 7:8); "first month" (Ezra 7:9); "fifth month" (Ezra 7:9); "first month" (Ezra 8:31); "ninth month" (Ezra 10:9); "first month" (Ezra 10:17); "seventh month" (Neh. 7:73b; 8:2). These numerical names for the months are what we find in the Torah and the Prophets, literature in which Ezra would have been deeply immersed. Nehemiah, by contrast, uses Babylonian names for the months: "Chislev" (ninth month) (Neh. 1:1); "Nisan" (first month) (Neh. 2:1); "Elul" (sixth month) (Neh. 6:15)—something that is not unexpected from one whose roots are in governmental work in Babylon. Interestingly, in the introductory section (Ezra 1–6) the author uses Ezra's designations in the Hebrew section ("seventh month" [3:1, 6]; "second month" [3:8]), but in the Aramaic section uses the Babylonian name "Adar" [twelfth month] in 6:15 (Demsky 1994: 11). (Ezra is a bilingual book: (1) 1:1–4:7, Hebrew; (2) 4:8–6:18, Aramaic; (3) 6:19–10:44, Hebrew; see Arnold: 1996.)

The book of Ezra falls into two main sections, chs. 1–6 and 7–10:

1. The release by King Cyrus of the exiles (1:1–4) allows their return to Jerusalem (1:5–2:70), where the returnees first rebuild the altar (3:1–7) and then the temple (3:8–6:22). The period covered is a little more than twenty years (538–516/15 B.C.).
2. Almost sixty years later (516/15–458/57 B.C.) Ezra arrives in Jerusalem with his own delegation (7:1–8:36). Informed about some deviations by the people from their religious heritage, exemplified in mixed marriages (9:1–4), Ezra confesses this sin before God (9:5–15), and supervises the dissolution of such marriages (10:1–44).

The book of Nehemiah falls into three main sections: (1) 1:1–7:73a; (2) 7:73b–10:39; (3) 11:1–13:31. The first focuses on Nehemiah, the second on Ezra, and the third on Nehemiah.

1. In the first section (1:1–7:73a) Nehemiah oversees the rebuilding of the wall of Jerusalem that was in disrepair, thanks to the Babylonians (1:1–6:19), and then adds a list of the original returnees from decades earlier (7:6–73, which is virtually the same as the list in Ezra 2:1–70).
2. In 8:1–12 Ezra reads to the people from the book of the law of Moses (the entire Pentateuch, or a portion of the Pentateuch, possibly the Deuteronomic Code [Deuteronomy 12–25], or some other laws contained in the Torah?). This reading from the law book prompts the Levites (not Ezra, as in NRSV) to utter liturgical prayer (9:6–37). And the spirit of that prayer leads to a commitment to covenant renewal (9:38–10:39).
3. In the last section (11:1–13:31) Nehemiah repopulates Jerusalem (11:1–12:26), presides with Ezra at the dedication of the city wall (12:27–47), and in his second administration as governor (13:1–31) tries to eliminate lingering unacceptable behavior among God's people such as Sabbath violation and mixed marriages.

No fewer than thirteen common emphases in Ezra and Nehemiah link them in theme.

(1) Both men return to Jerusalem from Babylon, Ezra with the full blessing of King Artaxerxes (Ezra 7:11–26), Nehemiah with the restrained permission of the same king ("How long will you be gone, and when will you return?" [Neh. 2:6]).

(2) Both books highlight the rebuilding of a Jerusalem-related object. In Ezra 1–6 it is first the altar (3:1–7) and then the Temple (3:8–6:22). Note the order. All restoration to God's way must begin with restoring the altar (recall the words used of Elijah with the prophets of Baal at Carmel: "First he repaired the altar of the Lord that had been thrown down" [1 Kings 18:30]). The altar has autonomous existence, independent of the temple. In Nehemiah (chs. 1–6) the focus is on the rebuilding of the wall around Jerusalem. This apparently was not an issue or pressing need to Ezra, for he never mentions the wall in ruins. What benefits does a wall offer? "In a real sense the building of the wall signifies not only physical protection, but also the separation of the people of God from foreign intercourse" (Childs 1979: 634).

(3) Both books provide a lengthy list of the names of those who returned under the leadership of Zerubbabel and Jeshua in the reign of Darius I and completed the rebuilding of the temple (Ezra 2:1–70; Neh. 7:6–73). Such long lists are not likely to engage the interest of most modern readers. But they are there. Why? Possibly, to remind us that the activities of this people were not limited to the famous like Ezra or Nehemiah, but included the much less famous individuals. God's work cannot be carried on by a few. Eshkenazi (1988b: 654) suggestively compares in America's capital the presence of the Washington Monument (to honor the high and mighty and famous) and the Vietnam War Memorial (to honor the not so high and mighty and famous). Eshkenazi's interesting suggestion (1988b: 647) that the duplication in Nehemiah 7 of Ezra 2 forms an *inclusio* (end parallels the beginning) that unifies the material and signals the end of a unit would be more convincing if, in fact, one could prove indisputably that Ezra–Nehemiah is one book, not two, as she attempts to do. If Ezra and Nehemiah are two distinct books rather than one, then the repetition of Ezra 2 in Nehemiah 7 no more forms an *inclusio* than the repetition of the Decalogue of Exodus 20 in Deuteronomy 5 or the repetition of the Lord's Prayer of Matthew 6 in Luke 11 forms an *inclusio* (Vanderkam 1992: 68).

(4) Ezra (Ezra 7:28; 8:18, 22, 31) and Nehemiah (Neh. 2:8, 18) bear witness to the fact that "the hand of our God" was upon them, and that assertion also is made about Ezra in the third person (Ezra 7:6, 9). Both Ezra and Nehemiah are able to make their way back to Jerusalem because of the providential hand of their God, the kindness and sensitivity of kings like Cyrus and Darius and Artaxerxes I notwithstanding. One wonders if Cyrus would ever have made his decree releasing the captive Jews (Ezra 1:1–4; 6:3–5) had not Yahweh first "stirred up his spirit" (Ezra 1:1). Yahweh, who can "stir up" the spirit of an outsider for the salvation of his people, can also "stir up" the spirit of an outsider for the judgment of his people (1 Chron. 5:26: "So the God of Israel stirred up the spirit of King Pul of Assyria"; 2 Chron. 21:16: "The Lord stirred up against Jehoram the anger of the Philistines").

(5) In both books the author(s) makes extensive use of lists:

Ezra	Nehemiah
1:9–11: the returned vessels	3:1–32: workers on the wall
2:1–70: the returning exiles	7:6–72: the returning exiles
8:1–14: Ezra's traveling companions	10:1–27: signatories to the covenant

10:18–44: men who separated from foreign wives	11:3–36: settlers and settlements 12:1–26: cultic personnel 12:32–42: procession on the wall of members of the community

In addition, Ezra, but not Nehemiah (except for 6:6–7), frequently quotes verbatim from correspondence and letters: (a) Cyrus's decree (1:2–4); (b) Rehum and Shimshai's letter to Artaxerxes libeling the Jews as insurrectionists (4:11–16); (c) Artaxerxes' response to that letter with his own letter mandating a halt to the rebuilding of the city until he grants authorization (4:17–22); (d) a letter from Tattenai, a neighboring provincial governer, to Darius challenging the claim of the resettled Jews that they have Cyrus's permission and blessing to rebuild the temple (5:7–17); (e) after investigating the charges, Darius discovers that Cyrus had issued such an edict and quotes it (6:2b–5), but without some of the patently theological language in the first quotation of the decree in 1:2–4 (e.g., "The Lord, the God of heaven, has given me all the kingdoms of the earth and he has charged me to build him a house at Jerusalem" [1:2]); (f) Darius's response to Tattenai, telling him to cease his resistance and allow the rebuilding of the temple to proceed, with Tattenai's people furnishing some of the costs (6:6–12); (g) Artaxerxes' letter that he sends with Ezra when he departs for Jerusalem, providing royal support and sponsorship for Ezra's expedition (7:12–26).

Whoever put Ezra and Nehemiah together in the form we have in our Bible surely did not compose these lists or letters, but they certainly were two of the sources that the author(s) had available and used in the writing of the text and story.

(6) Both books mention prophets, one favorably, one unfavorably. In the introductory section to Ezra (1–6), Haggai and Zechariah are credited with the stimulus they provided for the building of the temple (5:1–2; 6:14—"And with them were the prophets of God, helping them" [5:2]; "So the elders of the Jews built and prospered, through the prophesying of the prophet Haggai and Zechariah" [6:14]).

Nehemiah chastises the prophetess Noadiah (not to be confused with the male Noadiah in Ezra 8:33) in Neh. 6:14 for complicity with others in attempting to intimidate Nehemiah and his wall-building project: "Remember Tobiah and Sanballat, O my God, according to these things that they did, and also the prophetess Noadiah and the rest of the prophets who wanted to make me afraid." Only five women are called "prophetess" in the Old Testament: Miriam (Exod. 15:20); Deborah (Judg. 4:4); Huldah (2 Kings 22:14); Isaiah's wife (Isa. 8:3); Noadiah (Neh. 6:14). Two of these five women are rebuked for speaking out in some way against male leadership, Miriam against Moses in Num. 12:1–15 and Noadiah against Nehemiah in Neh. 6:14 (Carroll 1992: 94). Did Noadiah disagree with Nehemiah's endorsement of the expulsion of foreign wives, or with Nehemiah's building project with its promotion by the imperial Persians, who thus were "using" Nehemiah to secure their border against the Greeks and other invaders and antagonists to the west?

(7) Both books highlight the joy experienced by those who were in on the ground floor of new beginnings. When the foundation of the temple was laid, "many shouted aloud for joy," and the sound of "the joyful shout" could be heard everywhere (Ezra 3:12–13). Similarly, at the temple's dedication there was "joy," and a "joyful" celebration of the Festival of Unleavened Bread (Ezra 6:16, 22). Ezra's reading of the law book evokes "great rejoicing" (Neh. 8:12), as there was after the observance of the Festival of Tabernacles (Neh. 8:17). And at the dedication of the wall there was great joy. "Rejoiced" or "joy" occur no fewer than five times in Neh. 12:43. And at both the founding of the temple and the reading of the law, joy overshadows weeping (Ezra 3:10–13; Neh. 8:9–12).

Probably the best-known phrase in Nehemiah, because it is sung as a "Scripture chorus" so often, is in Neh. 8:10: "the joy of the Lord is your strength." And while we normally read this phrase as an objective genitive (the joy we discover and experience in and because of the Lord), the phrase might also be taken as a subjective genitive (the joy the Lord experiences in his people) (see Wong 1995: 383–84). Since the word for "strength" (ma'oz) means "refuge, protection," possibly, the latter interpretation is the better one.

(8) In Ezra, after the altar has been rebuilt, one of the first acts of the community is to observe the Festival of Tabernacles, or Sukkot, as it is known in Hebrew (Ezra 3:4–6). After the temple's dedication comes Passover (Ezra 6:19–21) and the Festival of Unleavened Bread (Ezra 6:22). Of these three, only Sukkot appears again, in Neh. 8:13–18. Ezra 6:22 notes the joy present at the celebration of Unleavened Bread, while Neh. 8:17 connects joy with the observance of Sukkot.

Tabernacles is the most joyous of all the festivals, and here is a connection between item (7) above on "joy" and the Sukkot celebration of item (8). In Leviticus 23, one of the Torah's calendars of sacred days, it is the only festival on which rejoicing is explicitly commanded (Lev. 23:40). In Deut. 16:1–17, another calendar of public sacrifices in the Torah, rejoicing during this festival is again noted (Deut. 16:14; as it is for the Feast of Weeks [Deut. 16:11]). According to Num. 29:12–34, part of yet a third holy days calendar in the Pentateuch, its sacrifices are far and away the most numerous of all the festivals. Later, Sukkot was called *zeman simkhatenu*, "the time of our rejoicing."

It is a festival that celebrates the gathering of grain and wine into the storehouse for the year to come. It is a way of thanking God for the year's harvest, and surely it is no accident that the American colonial Pilgrim Fathers (Clines 1989: 213 refers to the list of repatriates in Ezra 2 as a "list of Pilgrim Fathers") modeled their thanksgiving celebrations for their first harvest on the biblical paradigm. How appropriate, too, that Ezra and Nehemiah, books filled with joy, should both highlight a Tabernacles observance, so joy oriented this occasion is.

Tabernacles is celebrated from the fifteenth to the twenty-first day of the seventh month (Tishri [September–October]). Just a few days before it, on the tenth day of the seventh month, Yom Kippur (the Day of Atonement) is celebrated, but neither Ezra nor Nehemiah records its observance. Would this postexilic community participate in Sukkot but not Yom Kippur? Its absence from Ezra 3 is clear enough. Ezra 3:6 says, "The foundation of the temple of the Lord was not yet laid." The primary focus of the Day of Atonement in Leviticus 16 is the cleansing of the temple. So, if there is no temple (yet), there can be no Day of Atonement. Its absence from Nehemiah 8, however, is harder to explain, for by then the temple has been rebuilt. We suggest this tentative answer: because observance of the Day of Atonement in Leviticus 16 focuses almost exclusively on the prescribed ritual that the high priest must adhere to scrupulously, and because there is little for the people to do, unlike Sukkot, it is not even mentioned by Nehemiah.

(9) Both books emphasize the stiff outside opposition that the (re)builders of the temple and then the wall around Jerusalem encountered. In Ezra it occurs as early as 3:3, where those who set up the altar on its foundations did so "because they were in dread of the neighboring peoples." That dread becomes manifest when "adversaries of Judah and Benjamin" offer their assistance in the rebuilding of the temple. When they are rebuffed, they vent their displeasure through various channels, thus slowing down the project for sixteen to seventeen years (4:1–5). Such harrassment continued from the reign of Cyrus into the reign of Darius (4:5b). One could argue that the rejection by Zerubbabel and Jeshua of assistance was valid, for the volunteers were Samaritans, descendants of mixed marriages between northern Israelites and other peoples. For Judean Jews in the postexilic era, there was no such thing as a "good Samaritan." To be a child of the covenant community meant that one was either Judean or Benjaminite. On the other hand, one could argue against the rejection of assistance. Clines (1989: 214–

15), for example, believes that Zerubbabel made his decision on a textual technicality (would Cyrus have cared one way or the other who helped?). Calling Zerubbabel and his colleagues "petty bureaucrats," Clines says, "A document in the hands of a legalist can destroy both creativity and civility."

The emphasis on opposition to the builders continues with Rehum and other Samaritans and their letter to Artaxerxes (4:11–16) and Artaxerxes' rescript (4:17–22), which effectively stops the reconstruction of the city (4:23). Actually, this section belongs, chronologically, to a later period, when Nehemiah was overseeing the city project. Its inclusion here reinforces the hostility and dashed hopes that this nascent postexilic community often faced.

Another letter, this time by Tattenai to Darius (5:7–17), a much earlier letter than that recorded in the previous chapter (4:11–16), is another attempt to cut the legs out from underneath the temple project.

The opposition does not dissipate in Nehemiah 1–6. The ringleaders are Sanballat, governor of Samaria, and Tobiah, an official of some kind from Ammon who had married the daughter of Meshullam, one of Nehemiah's staff on the wall-building project (cf. 6:17–18 with 3:30). For the provocations of this nasty pair, see Neh. 2:10, 19; 4:7; 6:1, 12, 14. In fact, Neh. 4:7 informs us that Nehemiah faced opposition on all four fronts.

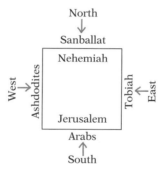

It is no wonder, then, that half of Nehemiah's personnel worked on construction while the other half posted themselves as armed guards around the builders (4:16–17). Apparently, Nehemiah is not ready with a "Father, forgive them" prayer, as the language of Nehemiah's prayer in 4:4–5 and 6:14 bears out. They are "Give them a bit of their own medicine" prayers, as imprecatory in nature as one finds in the Psalter (e.g., Psalm 106) or in the laments of Jeremiah (see Jer. 11:18–20). In neither case does God respond. In fact, God nowhere speaks directly in either Ezra or Nehemiah, although God is spoken to (in prayer) and about (in testimony).

(10) Both Ezra and Nehemiah are concerned about holy things. For Ezra, it is a holy people and holy vessels (8:28), a holy seed (9:2), and a holy place (9:8). For Nehemiah it is a holy day (8:9, 11; 13:22) and a holy city (11:1). Nowhere is there a call to holiness; rather, holiness is stated as a fact, whether the adjective is applied to people, objects, places, or times. This is more like Deuteronomy, which alone in the Pentateuch calls Israel a "holy people" (Deut. 7:6; 14:2, 21; 26:19; 28:9), unlike Leviticus, which invites Israel to be(come) holy (Lev. 11:44–45; 19:2; 20:7, 26; and see also Exod. 19:6; 22:31, verses all addressed to the people and not just to the elite—priests [Lev. 21:6–8]; Nazirites [Num. 6:5]).

(11) In conjunction with this shared emphasis on the community as a holy people in a holy city are the books' mutual reminders that God's people are called to separate themselves from the ways of other nations. Such separation is expressed through the Hithpael (reflexive stem) or the Niphal (reflexive/passive stem) of the verb *badal* ("remove oneself, secede"). See Ezra 6:21 ("all who had separated themselves from the pollutions of the nations of the land"); Ezra 9:1 ("the people of Israel . . . have not separated themselves from the peoples of the lands"); Ezra 10:11 ("separate yourselves from the peoples of the land and from the foreign wives"); Neh. 9:2 ("then those of Israelite descent separated themselves from all foreigners"); Neh. 10:28 ("all who have separated themselves from the peoples of the lands"); Neh. 13:3 ("they separated from Israel all those of foreign descent" [Hiphil stem]).

When Ezra and others issue a proclamation for all the exiles to gather in Jerusalem to address the matter of religious compromise, the penalty for nonattendance is that "all their property should be forfeited [*kh-r-m*], and they themselves banned from [*yibbadel*] the congregation of the exiles" (Ezra 10:8). The message is clear enough: "Separate yourself from them, or else separate yourself from us."

The closest parallel to the reflexive use of *badal* with the meaning of "set oneself apart from" appears in Num. 16:21. Yahweh says, after the revolt of Korah and other malcontents, to Moses and Aaron, "Separate yourselves from this congregation, so that I may consume them in a moment"; otherwise, Moses and Aaron will perish along with the others if they do not desert the arena of punishment. Also, Num. 8:14 and 16:9 use the Hiphil of *badal* for God's act of "separating" the Levites from other Israelites. Ezra uses this verb also with this meaning in the causative stem: "I set apart twelve of the leading priests" (Ezra 8:24); "Ezra the priest selected men . . . to examine the matter" (Ezra 10:16).

(12) This call to separation finds its most graphic portrayal in Ezra and Nehemiah when both books raise and meet head-on the issue of

exogamous intermarriage among the returned exiles (Ezra 9:1–10:44; Neh. 13:1–3, 23–30). The two sections have several items in common. First—and this is crucial—on both occasions the reforms come initially not from Ezra or Nehemiah, but from representatives of a repentant community. Thus, with Ezra, "The officials approached me and said, 'The people of Israel, the priests, and the Levites . . . have taken some of their [the peoples of the land's] daughters as wives for themselves and for their sons'" (Ezra 9:1–2). And in Nehemiah, "When the people heard the law, they [not Nehemiah] separated from Israel all those of foreign descent" (Neh. 13:3). Nehemiah's own follow-up to that appears in Neh. 13:23–30. The significance of this is that the reforms of illicit marriage are imposed not by any pontifical leaders, but emerge from concerns voiced by the community. They work from the bottom up; they are not imposed from above.

Second, both Ezra and Nehemiah condemn only Jewish men for marrying non-Jewish women. Neither condemns Jewish women for marrying non-Jewish men. In other words, the culprits are exclusively male (Eshkenazi 1992: 34).

Third, somebody loses some hair. Ezra says, "When I heard this, I . . . pulled hair from my head" (Ezra 9:3); Nehemiah says, "And I contended with them and cursed them and beat some of them and pulled out their hair" (Neh. 13:25). It is one thing to do this to oneself; it is another thing to do it to somebody else.

Fourth, in Ezra and Nehemiah it is not only the laity who are indicted for this religious infraction, but the clergy as well. Note Ezra 9:1 ("the priests and the Levites"), and in Ezra 10:18–23 names of condemned priests and Levites. In Nehemiah, note 13:28–30, where Nehemiah chides the grandson of the high priest for marrying the daughter of the despised Sanballat. One would hope that at least the clergy would rise above the temptation to dilute their heritage, but apparently that is not the case.

There are, to be sure, some differences in how each book addresses the issue. For example, only Ezra uses the term 'ashma ("guilt") to refer to intermarriage as a sin against God (Ezra 9:6, 7, 13, 15; 10:10), and only he says that one way to obtain forgiveness is to present a "guilt/reparation offering" ['asham] (Ezra 10:19).

Also, Ezra describes such misbehavior using the Hebrew word ma'al ("faithlessness, unfaithfulness") (see Ezra 9:2, 4; 10:6). Nehemiah (13:27) uses the verb once. The noun could be translated more strongly as "sacrilege, act of betrayal." This connection of ma'al with an 'asham offering is in line with earlier priestly teaching (Ezra is a priest) in which ma'al ("trespass") is the legal term for the wrong that is redressed by the *ʾasham* ("guilt/reparation") offering (Lev. 5:15; 6:2; Num. 5:6). In Leviticus and Numbers *maʿal* refers to the misappropriation of property (God's or somebody else's), intentionally or inadvertently, but in Ezra and Nehemiah it is idiomatic for other sorts of betrayal and disloyalty, especially marital infidelity.

The clearest difference between the two is that Ezra takes a far more rigorous approach to the sin of intermarriage than does Nehemiah. Both are outraged, but Nehemiah simply demands of the returned exiles that they desist from such practice in the future (Neh. 13:25b), citing Solomon as an example of what this can lead to (Neh. 13:26). Ezra, on the other hand, mandates not only the bringing of an *ʾasham* offering, but the dissolution of all mixed marriages by ordering the men to divorce their foreign wives (Ezra 10:11). Those who did so are listed in Ezra 10:18–44. One wonders what is the difference, if any, between the community sending away the foreign wives with their children (Ezra 10:44; last verse of the book), and Abraham, at Sarah's insistence, sending Hagar and her child away (Gen. 21:14). In both cases, what futures do the expelled women and their progeny have? Who will protect them and provide for them? In the case of Ezra, those who were formerly exiles now make their spouses exiles? The trauma they have endured they now foist on their partners.

Some scholars have used the difference between Ezra and Nehemiah on intermarriage as an argument in favor of placing Nehemiah before Ezra. The line of reasoning goes as follows: If Ezra returned to Jerusalem before Nehemiah did, he must have "failed" in solving this matter of intermarriage, for Nehemiah later had to correct the same problem, so incompetent was Ezra; and yet, the book of Ezra represents Ezra as a faithful and successful servant of God. Therefore, Nehemiah must have preceded Ezra. This is a specious line of reasoning. By the same logic, one could say that Nehemiah, if he came first, "failed" too, and Ezra had to complete what Nehemiah fumblingly started. Yamauchi (1980c: 11) quotes Cross, who also criticizes this reversal: "I am not impressed by such an argument. One may say that all the prophets and reformers failed in biblical history. A fairly close analogy is found in the reforms of Hezekiah and Josiah, both of which failed." Then again, these reformers "failed" only in the sense that their reforms were not universally embraced, did not have long-lasting consequences, and did not enjoy unmitigated success. Jesus comes to mind here!

If Ezra forces the issue of illicit intermarriage more forcibly than does Nehemiah, then both of these postexilic heroes force the issue more rigorously than do earlier sections of Hebrew history and Scripture. We suggest two major innovations in Ezra and Nehemiah on this matter (see Hayes 1999: 6).

First, Ezra and Nehemiah expand the veto on intermarriage to all peoples. This can be seen in several ways: (1) Deut. 7:1–4 outlaws marriage only with seven groups of Canaanites, not with all the nations (i.e., the people of the "land" [Ezra 10:2, 11], not the people of the "lands" [Ezra 9:1–2]). Deuteronomy 23:3 adds the "Ammonite and Moabite," and here the phrase "shall not be admitted to the assembly of the Lord," does not say "may not marry an Israelite" but surely implies it. And the very fact that only these two groups are singled out suggests that other groups are permitted. (2) Some godly men had wives of foreign background (Joseph and his Egyptian wife [Gen. 41:45]; Moses and his Midianite wife [Exod 2:21]; Boaz and his Moabite wife [Ruth 4:10]; and recall Tamar, the virtuous Canaanite daughter-in-law of Judah [Gen. 38]). (3) Deut. 20:14 allows the taking of foreign women in wartime as slaves, concubines, wives. The exception is wives living in cities in the Promised Land (Deut. 20:15–18). (4) A law in Deuteronomy expanding on Deut. 20:14 is Deut. 21:10–14, where the issue is the legitimate marriage to a (non-Canaanite) woman captured in war. Hence, it appears that Deuteronomy permits, under certain circumstances, marriage between Israelites and non-Israelites. Ezra and Nehemiah say that such a marriage is never permissable.

The second innovation of Ezra and Nehemiah (and especially Ezra) is the rationale for such a universal prohibition. Restored Israel is a "holy seed" (Ezra 9:2). For a holy Judean to marry a Gentile would be mixing the holy with the unholy, and thus an act of profanation. Ezra treats his people (really a priesthood of all believers) the way Lev. 21:1–24 treats the priest. He is holy, and therefore is restricted with regard to whom he may marry (Lev. 21:7). For Ezra, all his people are holy (as in Deuteronomy), and are therefore restricted with regard to whom they may marry.

This is a different rationale from Deuteronomy, where the reason for prohibiting intermarriage is either moral-religious ("for that would turn away your children from following me, to serve other gods" [Deut. 7:4a]) or socio-political ("because they did not meet you with food and water on your journey out of Egypt, and because they hired against you Balaam" [Deut. 23:4]). Now, not all foreign wives turned their husband's heart after their own gods. Asenath does not persuade Joseph to become an Egyptian polytheist. Zipporah does not lure Moses into Midianitism. Tamar does not influence Er toward the gods of Canaan. Where some are not impacted, Solomon succumbs (1 Kings 11:1–8).

Some modern readers may be quick to dismiss Ezra (and Nehemiah) as too harsh, too unrealistic, too legalistic, too racist, too xenophobic, and maybe too misogynistic. But recall that Ezra is part of a chastened community that has lost all sense of cohesion and stability, a community that is just starting to get back on its feet and learn from its earlier mistakes. Things like unrestrained intermarriage would not simply dilute the community's religious boundaries, but be a Trojan horse that would unleash a torrent of problems to compound the ones already present. If the religious heritage of the Hebrew people cannot be maintained and observed at this level—the family as the foundation of society—can it be maintained at all? As readers, we will need to decide whether Ezra is concerned with a matter of spiritual survival, or is he merely magnifying the trivial (see Clements 1985: 156).

(13) Both Ezra and Nehemiah pray. We have one long prayer of Ezra (Ezra 9:6–15) near the end of his book, one long prayer of Nehemiah (Neh. 1:5–11) near the start of his book, and another long prayer in Neh. 9:6–37 that the Septuagint assigns to Ezra ("And Ezra said" [Neh. 9:6]) but is probably a prayer of the Levites (Neh. 9:5). The NRSV goes with the Septuagint, but the NIV follows the Hebrew text.

The three prayers share several things in common. First, they are all prayers of confession. In Ezra 10:1, Ezra "prayed and made confession." In his prayer in Nehemiah 1, Nehemiah refers to his "confessing the sins of Israel" (Neh. 1:6). The prayer in Nehemiah 9 is prefaced with a reference to the Israelites who "stood and confessed their sins. . . . they made confession" (Neh. 9:2–3).

All four of these references to "confession" use the Hithpael stem of *yadah*, "reveal oneself," which connotes the opposite of concealment. For other uses of this verb in the Hithpael, see Lev. 5:5 ("you shall confess the sin that you have committed"); Lev. 16:21 ("then Aaron . . . shall confess over it [the live goat] all the iniquities of the people of Israel"); Lev. 26:40 ("but if they confess their iniquity"); Num. 5:7 ("and that person shall confess the sin that has been committed"); Dan. 9:4 ("I prayed to the Lord my God and made confession"); Dan. 9:20 ("while I was speaking, and was praying and confessing my sin").

In all of these references in Leviticus and Numbers the Hithpael of *yadah* is followed by a direct object. In the references in Ezra, Nehemiah, and Daniel this is true only for Dan. 9:20. In the others the verb either stands alone (Ezra 10:1; Neh. 9:3; Dan. 9:4) or is followed by the preposition *'al* (Neh. 1:6; 9:2). The significance of this is that in these later exilic and postexilic books confession is an independently important act, and does not need to be sequeled by sacrifice.

In the Hiphil stem of this verb the meaning is usually "praise." But even the Hiphil of *yadah* may mean "confess," as in Ps. 32:5 ("I said, 'I will confess my transgressions to the Lord'"), and in Prov. 28:13 ("but one who confesses and forsakes [transgressions] will obtain mercy"). And similarly, the Hithpael of *yadah* may mean "praise," as in 2 Chron. 30:22 ("so the people ate the food of the festival . . . praising to the Lord"). So, the basic meaning of this verb is "declare, speak forth." What comes out of one's mouth is either confession or doxology.

Another parallel between the three prayers is that each features a distinct physical posture for the prayer. Ezra says, "I fell on my knees" (Ezra 9:5), and the narrator says that Ezra "threw himself down" (Ezra 10:1). Nehemiah says, "I sat down" (Neh. 1:4). The Israelites "stood and confessed their sins" (Neh. 9:2), as did the Levites to read from the law (Neh. 9:3). So, no particular posture is *the* posture for prayers of contrition. Kneeling, sitting, and standing are all acceptable.

Yet a third parallel is that fasting accompanies all three prayers of confession: "I got up from my fasting" (Ezra 9:5); "when I heard these words I sat down . . . and mourned for days, fasting and praying" (Neh. 1:4); "the people of Israel were assembled with fasting and in sackcloth" (Neh. 9:1). And both Ezra (Ezra 10:1) and Nehemiah (Neh. 1:4) weep as they fast and pray. Fasting would be out of place in times of celebration, but in times of contrition it can be an essential ingredient. One does not fast at festivals, but neither does one treat a confessional as a buffet line.

A fourth parallel is that the prayers of Ezra and Nehemiah both begin with the first-person singular pronoun "I," but shortly shift to the first-personal plural "we":

Ezra 9:6: "O my God, I am too ashamed and embarrassed to lift up my face to you, for our iniquities have risen higher than our heads, and our guilt has mounted up to the heavens."

Neh. 1:6: "Let your ear be attentive . . . to hear the prayer of your servant that I now pray . . . confessing the sins of the people of Israel, which we have sinned against you. Both I and my family have sinned."

Of course this shift is not present in the prayer of Nehemiah 9, because it is already the prayer of a group, the Levites. A change from "I" to "we" indicates that both Ezra and Nehemiah identify with their people and their faults. They are not only praying for their people as intercessor, but also are praying with their people as mutual supplicant. Absent from both Ezra and Nehemiah is any sense of superiority or elitism, any sense of "I thank you God that I am not as other Judeans." Identifying themselves with their people frees Ezra and Nehemiah from disguising preaching as praying.

A final parallel we shall mention is that in none of these prayers is there any protestation of innocence, any challenge of God's justice. Ezra says in his prayer, "You, our God, have punished us less than our iniquities deserve" (Ezra 9:13). All three prayers seem to veer back and forth between affirming God's virtues and Israel's flaws. For example, one cannot miss the "God has not forsaken/we have forsaken" contrast in Ezra's prayer when in back-to-back verses he says, "Yet, our God has not forsaken us in our slavery" (Ezra 9:9) and then, "We have forsaken your commandments" (Ezra 9:10). Ezra will speak both of Israel's guilt (Ezra 9:6, 7, 13, 15) and iniquities (Ezra 9:7, 13) and of Yahweh's steadfast love (Ezra 9:9) and justice (Ezra 9:15). Compare also what Nehemiah in his prayer says about God (Neh. 1:5, 10) and what he says about himself and his people (Neh. 1:6b–7).

The clearest illustration of this contrast is in the third prayer, that of the Levites (or Ezra) in Neh. 9:6–37. The prayer is essentially a review of history:

creation (v. 6)
Abraham (v. 7–8)
the Red Sea (vv. 9–11)
guidance in the wilderness (v. 12)
Sinai and the law (vv. 13–14)
manna and water (v. 15)
faithlessness and wanting to return to Egypt (vv. 16–17)
the golden calf (v. 18)
guidance in the wilderness (v. 19)
manna and water (vv. 20–21)
conquering land (vv. 22–25)   *ancestral sins*
rebellion and unbelief and the judges (vv. 26–29)
the prophets (v. 30a)
exile (v. 30b)
a God who never terminates or forsakes (v. 31)

acting wickedly and plea for help (vv. 32–37)   *contemporary sins*

As Balentine (1993: 113–14) has noted, the contrast between a good God ("you") and a not so good people ("they/we") is clearest in vv. 16–18 and vv. 19–31:

vv. 16–18: sin/"they" (vv. 16–17a)	—— mercy/"you" (v. 17b)	—— sin/"they" (v. 18)
vv. 19–31: mercy/"you" (vv. 19–25)	—— sin/"they" (vv. 26–30)	—— mercy/"you" (v. 31)

For a people who are in "great distress" (v. 37), their only hope is in a God of "great mercies" (vv. 19, 31). Where distress abounds, mercy abounds all the more.

In addition to these longer prayers, but only in Nehemiah, there are a number of brief prayers inserted here and there in the narrative. Six times Nehemiah calls upon God to remember either him for good (4x) or somebody else for things not so good (2x).

> 5:19: "Remember for my good, O my God, all that I have done for this people."
>
> 6:14: "Remember Tobiah and Sanballat, O my God, . . . and also Noadiah and the rest of the prophets who wanted to make me afraid."
>
> 13:14: "Remember me, O my God, concerning this, and do not wipe out my good deeds."
>
> 13:22: "Remember this also in my favor, O my God, and spare me."
>
> 13:29: "Remember them, O my God, because they have defiled the priesthood."
>
> 13:31: "Remember me, O my God, for good."

Such prayers parallel those of Moses ("Remember Abraham, Isaac, and Israel" [Exod. 32:13; cf. Deut. 9:27]); of Samson ("Lord God, remember me and strengthen me only this once" [Judg. 16:28]); of Hezekiah ("Remember now, O Lord, I implore you, how I have walked before you in faithfulness with a whole heart" [2 Kings 20:3]); of Jeremiah ("O Lord, . . . remember me and visit me, and bring down retribution on my persecutors" [Jer. 15:15]; "Remember how I stood before you to speak good for them" [Jer. 18:20]); of the repentant thief on the cross ("Jesus, remember me when you come into your kingdom" [Luke 23:42]).

To conclude our studies of Ezra and Nehemiah, we note that there are many emphases in these two books that have parallels elsewhere in the Old Testament. For example, the authors of Ezra and Nehemiah present the return to Judah from Babylon as a repetition of the Israelites' return to their land from Egypt. Thus, Ezra 1:11 can speak of the time "when the exiles were brought up from Babylonia to Jerusalem." The use of the passive verb recalls Yahweh's words to Moses at the first exodus: "Go, leave this place, you and the people whom you have brought up out of the land of Egypt" (Exod. 33:1). In both cases the returnees do not come to the land of Israel; they are brought up to the land of Israel.

There is also an intentional desire in Ezra to link the rebuilding of the temple with Solomon's first building of the temple. On both occasions altar/temple building takes place in conjunction with the Festival of Tabernacles. See Ezra 3:4 and 1 Kings 8:2, 65, where the expression "the festival" refers to Tabernacles. (So outstanding was this holy event in comparison to the others that it could be called simply "*the* festival.") In both cases cedar trees from Lebanon are floated down the Mediterranean to Joppa and then hauled over land (Ezra 3:7; 2 Chron. 2:16). In both cases the donors of the cedar trees are "Sidonians and Tyrians" (Ezra 3:7; 1 Chron. 22:4). In both cases temple construction begins in "the second month" (Ezra 3:8; 2 Chron. 3:2 and 1 Kings 6:1).

And certainly a third shared emphasis is Ezra's and Nehemiah's concern over illicit marriages, which may lead to spiritual disarray in the community, even though, as we have seen, they both share and significantly expand Deuteronomy's concern.

But there are other books in the Old Testament whose message seems to go in a fundamentally different direction. Place side by side, for instance, Ezra and Ruth, the latter highlighting a marriage between an Israelite and a non-Israelite, the former outlawing all marriages between Israelite and non-Israelite. There is room for both in the biblical canon, and one does not drown out or overwhelm the other. The canon is not made up of all Ruths, but neither is it made up of all Ezras. The message of God's openness to all nations (Ruth) and his unique concern for the perpetuation of his "treasured possession" (Ezra) form a part of the whole message of Scripture.

There is also a difference in emphasis between Ezra–Nehemiah and Esther. The sentiment expressed in Ps. 137:4–5 ("How could we sing the Lord's song in a foreign land? If I forget you, O Jerusalem, let my right hand wither!") is perfectly at home in the world of Ezra and Nehemiah, but completely out of place in the world of Esther. For Ezra and Nehemiah, all that matters is returning to Zion. For Esther, it is possible for God's people to be "in" the world but not "of" the world, to be in Persia without being Persian. To readapt Jesus' prayer in John 17, "My prayer is not that you take them out of Persia, but that you protect them from the evil one. As you have sent me into the Persias of this world, I have sent them into Persia." Let not an Ezra or a Nehemiah condemn an Esther or a Mordecai as compromisers for choosing to put down roots on alien soil, and let not an Esther or a Mordecai dismiss an Ezra or a Nehemiah as hopelessly overzealous traditionalists and patriots.

From such diversity is woven the tapestry of Scripture. As in the Triune Godhead there is both diversity and unity, so is there in the Scriptures. Goldingay (1994: 336) argues creatively "for seeing the unity of scripture as like the polyphonic unity of a symphony, to which diversity and even dissonance make contributions."

Bibliography (Ezra–Nehemiah)

Commentaries and Major Studies

Batten, L. W. 1913. *A Critical and Exegetical Commentary on the Books of Ezra and Nehemiah*. International Critical Commentary 12. New York: Charles Scribner's Sons.

Blenkinsopp, J. 1988. *Ezra–Nehemiah*. Old Testament Library. Philadelphia: Westminster.

Breneman, M. 1993. *Ezra, Nehemiah, Esther*. New American Commentary 10. Nashville: Broadman.

Brown, R. 1998. *The Message of Nehemiah: God's Servant in a Time of Change*. Bible Studies Today. Leicester: InterVarsity.

Clines, D. J. A. 1984. *Ezra, Nehemiah, Esther*. New Century Bible Commentary. Grand Rapids: Eerdmans.

Davies, G. F. 1999. *Ezra and Nehemiah*. Berit Olam. Collegeville, Minn.: Liturgical Press.

Evers, S. K. 1996. *Doing a Great Work: Ezra and Nehemiah Simply Explained*. Welwyn Commentary. Darlington, England: Evangelical Press.

Fensham, F. C. 1982. *The Books of Ezra and Nehemiah*. NICOT. Grand Rapids: Eerdmans.

Grabbe, L. L. 1998. *Ezra–Nehemiah*. Old Testament Readings. New York: Routledge.

Kidner, D. 1979. *Ezra and Nehemiah*. Tyndale Old Testament Commentaries. Downer's Grove, Ill.: InterVarsity.

Klein, R. W. 1999. "The Books of Ezra and Nehemiah: Introduction, Commentary, and Reflection." In *The New Interpreter's Bible*. Vol. 3. Nashville: Abingdon. Pp. 662–851.

Mason, R. 1987. *Ezra and Nehemiah*. Old Testament Guides. Sheffield: JSOT Press.

Myers, J. M. 1965. *Ezra, Nehemiah*. Anchor Bible 14. Garden City, N.Y.: Doubleday.

Throntveit, M. A. 1992. *Ezra–Nehemiah*. Interpretation. Atlanta: John Knox.

Van Wijk-Bos, J. W. H. 1998. *Ezra, Nehemiah, and Esther*. Westminster Bible Companion. Louisville: Westminster/John Knox.

Williamson, H. G. M. 1985. *Ezra, Nehemiah*. Word Biblical Commentary 16. Waco, Tex.: Word.

Yamauchi, E. 1988. "Ezra–Nehemiah." In *The Expositor's Bible Commentary*. Vol. 4. Ed. F. Gaebelein. Grand Rapids: Zondervan. Pp. 563–771.

Shorter Studies

Allen, L. C. 1999. "'For He is God . . .' Worship in Ezra–Nehemiah." In *Worship and the Hebrew Bible: Essays in Honour of John T. Willis*. Ed. M. P. Graham, R. R. Marrs, and S. L. McKenzie. JSOT Supplement 24. Sheffield: Sheffield Academic Press. Pp. 15–34.

Arnold, B. T. 1996. "The Use of Aramaic in the Hebrew Bible: Another Look at Bilingualism in Ezra and Nehemiah." *JNSL* 22, no. 2:1–16.

Balentine, S. E. 1993. *Prayer in the Hebrew Bible: The Drama of Divine-Human Dialogue*. Overtures to Biblical Theology. Minneapolis: Fortress. Pp. 109–17.

Blenkinsopp, J. 1994. "The Nehemiah Autobiographical Memoir." In *Language, Theology, and the Bible: Essays in Honour of James Barr*. Ed. S. E. Balentine and J. Barton. Oxford: Clarendon. Pp. 199–212.

Bliese, L. E. 1988. "Chiastic Structures, Peaks and Cohesion in Neh. 9:6–37." *BT* 39:208–15.

Boda, M. J. 1996. "Chiasmus in Ubiquity: Symmetrical Mirages in Nehemiah 9." *JSOT* 71:55–70.

———. 1997. "Praying the Tradition: The Origins and Use of Tradition in Nehemiah 9." *TynB* 48:179–82.

Bright, J. 1981. *A History of Israel*. 3rd ed. Philadelphia: Westminster. Pp. 373–402.

Carroll, R. P. 1992. "Coopting the Prophets." In *Essays on the Formation and Heritage of Second Temple Judaism in Honor of Joseph Blen-*

kinsopp. Ed. E. Ulrich et al. JSOT Supplement 149. Sheffield: JSOT Press. Pp. 87–99.

Childs, B. S. 1979. *Introduction to the Old Testament as Scripture*. Philadelphia: Westminster. Pp. 624–38.

Clements, R. E. 1985. *In Spirit and in Truth: Insights from Biblical Prayers*. Atlanta: John Knox. Pp. 147–79.

Clines, D. J. A. 1990. "The Nehemiah Memoir: The Perils of Autobiography." In *What Does Eve Do to Help? And Other Readerly Questions to the Old Testament*. JSOT Supplement 94. Sheffield. JSOT Press. Pp. 124–64.

Cross, F. M. 1975. "A Reconstruction of the Judean Restoration." *JBL* 94:4–18.

Davies, P. R., ed. 1991. *Second Temple Studies*. Vol. 1, *Persian Period*. JSOT Supplement 117. Sheffield: JSOT Press.

Demsky, A. 1995. "Who Came First, Ezra or Nehemiah? The Synchronistic Approach." *HUCA* 65:1–19.

———. "Who Returned First—Ezra or Nehemiah?" *BRev* 12, no. 2:28–33, 46, 48.

Eshkenazi, T. C. 1988a. *In An Age of Prose: A Literary Approach to Ezra–Nehemiah*. SBLMS 36. Atlanta: Scholars Press.

———. 1988b. "The Structure of Ezra–Nehemiah and the Integrity of the Book." *JBL* 107:641–56.

———. 1989. "Ezra–Nehemiah: From Text to Actuality." In *Signs and Wonders: Biblical Texts in Literary Focus*. Ed. J. C. Exum. SBLSS. Atlanta: Scholars Press. Pp. 165–97. (See also the response by D. J. A. Clines, "The Force of the Text," pp. 199–215.)

———. 1992. "Out of the Shadows: Biblical Women in the Post-exilic Era." *JSOT* 54:25–43.

———. 1993. "Current Perspectives on Ezra–Nehemiah and the Persian Period. *Currents in Research: Biblical Studies* 1:59–86.

Eshkenazi, T. C., and K. H. Richards, eds. 1994. *Second Temple Studies*. Vol. 2, *Temple Community in the Persian Period*. JSOT Supplement 175. Sheffield: JSOT Press.

Fleishman, J. 1995. "The Investigating Commission by Tattenai: The Purpose of the Investigation and Its Results." *HUCA* 66:81–102.

Goldingay, J. 1994. *Models for Scripture*. Grand Rapids: Eerdmans.

Gordon, C. H. 1965. *The Ancient Near East*. 3rd ed. New York: W. W. Norton.

Gottwald, N. 1985. *The Hebrew Bible: A Socio-Literary Introduction*. Philadelphia: Fortress. Pp. 432–38, 516, 520–22.

Goulder, M. D. 1992. "The Song of Ascents and Nehemiah." *JSOT* 75:43–58.

Gross, C. D. 1997. "Is There Any Interest in Nehemiah 5?" *SJOT* 11:270–78.

Halpern, B. 1990. "A Historiographic Commentary on Ezra 1–6: Achronological Narrative and Dual Chronology in Israelite Historiography." In *The Hebew Bible and Its Interpreters*. Ed. W. H. Propp et al. Winona Lake, Ind.: Eisenbrauns. Pp. 81–142.

Hayes, C. 1999. "Intermarriage and Impurity in Ancient Jewish Sources." *HTR* 92:3–36.

Holmgren, F. C. 1992. "Faithful Abraham and the *ᵃmana* Covenant: Neh. 9,6–10,1," *ZAW* 104:249–54.

Howard, D. M., Jr. 1993. *An Introduction to the Old Testament Historical Books*. Chicago: Moody. Pp. 273–313.

Japhet, S. 1968. "The Supposed Common Authorship of Chronicles and Ezra–Nehemiah Investigated Anew." *VT* 18:330–71.

———. 1982. "Sheshbazzar and Zerubbabel—Against the Background of the Historical and Religious Tendencies of Ezra–Nehemiah." *ZAW* 94:66–98.

Klein, R. W. 1976. "Ezra and Nehemiah in Recent Studies." In *Magnalia Dei, The Mighty Acts of God: Essays on the Bible and Archaeology in Memory of G. Ernest Wright*. Ed. F. M. Cross et al. Garden City, N.Y.: Doubleday. Pp. 361–76.

Kraemer, D. 1992. "Ezra–Nehemiah, Books of." *ABD*, 2:731–42.

———. 1993. "On the Relationship of the Books of Ezra and Nehemiah." *JSOT* 59:73–92.

Margalith, O. 1986. "The Political Role of Ezra as Persian Governor." *ZAW* 98:110–12.

Mason, R. 1990. *Preaching the Tradition: Homily and Hermeneutics after the Exile*. Cambridge: Cambridge University Press. Pp. 147–83.

McCarthy, D. J. 1982. "Covenant and Law in Chronicles–Nehemiah." *CBQ* 44:25–44.

McConville, J. G. 1986. "Ezra–Nehemiah and the Fulfillment of Prophecy." *VT* 36:205–24.

McFall, L. 1991. "Was Nehemiah Contemporary with Ezra in 458 B.C.?" *WTJ* 53:263–93.

Morgan, D. F. 1990. *Between Text and Community*. Minneapolis: Fortress.

Rendsburg, G. A. 1991. "The Northern Origin of Nehemiah 9." *Bib* 72:348–66.

Rendtorff, R. 1997. "Nehemiah 9: An Important Witness of Theological Reflection." In *Tehillah le-Moshe: Biblical and Judaic Studies in Honor of Moshe Greenberg*. Ed. M. Cogan et al. Winona Lake, Ind.: Eisenbrauns. Pp. 111–17.

Richards, K. H. 1995. "Reshaping Chronicles and Ezra–Nehemiah Interpretation." In *Old Testament Interpretation: Past, Present, and Future*. Ed. J. L. Mays et al. Nashville: Abingdon. Pp. 211–24.

Shaver, J. R. 1992. "Ezra and Nehemiah: On The Theological Significance of Making Them Contemporaries." In *Essays on the Formation and Heritage of Second Temple Judaism in Honor of Joseph Blenkinsopp*. Ed. E. Ulrich et al. JSOT Supplement 149. Sheffield: JSOT Press. Pp. 76–86.

Talmon, S. 1976. "Ezra and Nehemiah, Books and Men," *IDBSup*, 317–29.

———. 1987. "Ezra and Nehemiah." In *The Literary Guide to the Bible*. Ed. R. Alter and F. Kermode. Cambridge, Mass.: Belknap. Pp. 357–64.

Talshir, D. 1988. "A Reinvestigation of the Linguistic Relationship between Chronicles and Ezra–Nehemiah." *VT* 38:165–93.

Throntveit, M. A. 1982. "Linguistic Analysis and the Question of Authorship in Chronicles, Ezra and Nehemiah." *VT* 32:201–16.

Vanderkam, J. C. 1992. "Ezra–Nehemiah or Ezra and Nehemiah?" In *Essays on the Formation and Heritage of Second Temple Judaism in Honor of Joseph Blenkinsopp*. Ed. E. Ulrich et al. JSOT Supplement 149. JSOT Press. Pp. 55–75.

Williamson, H. G. M. 1983. "The Composition of Ezra i-vi." *JTS* 34:1–30.

———. 1987. "Post-exilic Historiography." In *The Future of Biblical Studies: The Hebrew Scriptures*. SBLSS. Ed. R. Friedman and H. G. M. Williamson. Atlanta: Scholars Press. Pp. 189–207.

———. 1999. "Exile and After: Historical Study." In *The Face of Old Testament Studies: A Survey of Contemporary Approaches*. Ed. B. T. Arnold and D. W. Baker. Grand Rapids: Baker. Pp. 236–65.

Wong, G. C. I. 1995. "A Note on 'Joy' in Nehemiah viii 10." *VT* 45:383–86.

Yamauchi, E. M. 1980a. "The Archaeological Background of Ezra." *BSac* 137:195–211.

———. 1980b. "The Archaeological Background of Nehemiah." *BSac* 137:291–309.

———. 1980c. "The Reverse Order of Ezra/Nehemiah Reconsidered." *Themelios* 5, no. 3:7–13.

———. 1980d. "Was Nehemiah the Cupbearer a Eunuch?" *ZAW* 92:132–42.

Esther

Of the thirty-nine (or twenty-four in the Hebrew canon) books in the Old Testament, two are named after women, Ruth and Esther. By contrast, twenty-three are named after men. Ruth and Esther move in opposite directions. In Ruth, a Moabite woman marries a Judean man and remains in Judah. In Esther, a Judean woman marries a Persian man and remains in Persia. Together, the two books form the beginning (Ruth) and end (Esther) of a subsection of the third section of the Hebrew Bible (the "Writings") known as the *megilloth*, "scrolls." These are books that are read at the five festivals of the Jewish year (Ruth at the harvest Feast of Weeks in the third month, Sivan [May–June]; Esther at the Feast of Purim in the twelfth month, Adar [Feb–March]). Ruth is mentioned in the New Testament (Matt. 1:5); Esther is not.

In fact, not only is the person Esther never alluded to in the New Testament, but also the book of Esther is never quoted by any New Testament writer (one of only four or five Old Testament books of which this is true). And the early Christians were slow to see much value in Esther apart from that evidenced in scattered quotations in the church fathers (e.g., Clement of Rome around A.D. 100 viewed Esther as a prototype of the Virgin Mary). The earliest extant commentary on Esther by a Christian was that done by Rambanus Marus, Abbot of Fulda and Archbishop of Mainz in southwest central Germany. He died in A.D. 856, having finished his commentary about twenty-five years earlier, around A.D. 831 (Thornton 1986: 419).

Centuries later, Luther expressed his serious misgivings about Esther: "I am so hostile to the book [2 Maccabees] and to Esther that I wish they simply did not exist, for they Judaize too much and reveal much bad pagan behavior." The second part of this quotation focuses on the grotesque scenes of indulgence and immorality portrayed throughout Esther in the party scenes in the Persian court. The first part of the quotation ("they Judaize too much") more than likely reflects Luther's understanding that Esther contributes nothing substantive to Christian faith. Given Luther's hermeneutical framework that the New Testament is hidden in the Old Testament, and the Old is revealed in the New (and Esther isn't), and the fact that his canon criterion was whether or not the material preached Christ (and Esther doesn't), one Jewish writer (Bickerman 1967: 212) suggests that Luther's reading is "both logical and legitimate."

Some evaluations of Esther by more contemporary Christian writers seem to be quite Luther-like. Thus, in an article entitled "The Place of the Book of Esther in the Christian Bible," celebrated Old Testament scholar Bernhard Anderson (1950: 37–38) writes, "The story unveils the dark passions of the human heart: envy, hatred, fear, anger, vindictiveness, pride, all of which are fused into intense nationalism. . . . The church should recognize the book for what is: a witness to the fact that Israel, in pride, either made nationalism a religion in complete indifference to God or presumptuously identified God's historical purpose with the preservation and glorification of the Hebrew people."

Modern Jewish biblical scholars are capable of expressing sentiments about Esther that share Anderson's perspective. Thus Sandmel (1974: 35–36, 44) writes, "On the negative side it [Esther] has a vindictive, even ferociously vengeful spirit in which retaliation becomes possible and then lamentably indiscriminate. I have no fondness for the close of the book, which describes the slaughter of foes. . . . I should not be grieved if the book of Esther were somehow dropped out of Scripture."

In some early Jewish communities Esther appears to have been ignored. This is true especially in the nonmainstream, separatistic community of Qumran. It is well known that Esther is the only book in the Hebrew Bible of which not even a portion of a verse has been discovered among the Dead Sea Scrolls. This could, of course, simply be an accident (all manuscripts having Esther material have perished), or maybe a text still waiting a serendipitous discovery will reverse matters. This is most unlikely. The community of Qumran must have viewed Esther as an unacceptable oddity—no mention of God anywhere, a Jewess married to a pagan, the incessant debauchery described throughout the book. Susa is not Qumran, any more than Las Vegas resembles a monastery.

The Mishnah, compiled around A.D. 200, is a written compilation of orally transmitted legal practices of Jewish law arranged in six "orders." The orders in turn are divided into "tractates." The tenth tractate in the order *Mo'ed* is called *Megillah*, which means "scroll." Its primary focus is on the reading of Esther on the Festival of Purim. Esther's prominence in the Mishnah, then, suggests that the book's somewhat bumpy journey toward canonicity in both Jewish and early Christian communities reached closure in the Jewish communities that produced the Mishnah, and eventually the Jerusalem and Babylonian Talmuds.

Like many books in the Old Testament (probably the majority), Esther is an anonymous work. There is at least one mention of King Ahasuerus of Persia in every chapter of the book. Since his reign covers the years 486/85–465/64 B.C., the book could not have been written before that. The first reference to Esther (outside of the book) appears in 2 Macc. 15:36 (written near the end of the second century B.C.), where, interestingly, Purim is referred to as "the day of Mordecai," not the "day of Esther." So, it is unlikely that Esther was first written subsequent to that. Accordingly, Esther could have been written anytime between 486/85 B.C. and 100 B.C.

Some matters favor the earlier part of this period, that is, the Persian end. First, the presence of Persian words in Esther and the absence of Greek words suggests an earlier rather than later dating (unless the Persian words are a later author's attempt to give the book a feigned antiquity). Second, if the book had been written toward the end of this period—the Maccabean period, one characterized by fierce loyalty to God—what are the chances that the prized publication of the era would be one that totally omits any reference to God (unless the author is a subterranean anti-Maccabean secularist who writes his tome to tone down the excesses of the religious zealots of his day)? Third, would a book whose Jewish heroine marries a Persian king be heralded in the Hasmonean period (unless, again, the author is bucking the trend of religion by coercion and exclusivism—the expression "an ecumenical Maccabean" would be an oxymoron).

Probably the major argument in favor of a later date is that the Jewish slaughter of Persians in ch. 9 and the "conversion" of some Persians to Judaism out of "fear of the Jews" (8:17) reflect the realities of the Maccabean period, when forced conversions to Judaism were the order of the day. But as we shall see later, ch. 9 is hardly a crusade or inquisition, nor is it nationalism disguised as religion.

A significant number of commentators tend to understand Esther more as a novel than a historical account. Where the expression "historical novel" is used, the emphasis still seems to be more on the word "novel" than on the word "historical."

Why the inclination to view Esther as belletristic and not historical? For one thing, the authorities cite "the improbable elements" (Childs 1979: 601) of the story: (1) in 2:5–6 we read that "there was a Jew . . . whose name was Mordecai son of Jair son of Shimei son of Kish, a Benjaminite who had been carried away from Jerusalem among the captives." Well, if Mordecai was exiled to Babylon in 597 B.C., and since the dateline for Esther 2 is the late 480s B.C. ("the third year of his reign"), Mordecai is now well over one hundred years old! Not too old for a prediluvian like Adam or Methuselah, but quite unique for Mordecai's time—and furthermore, his cousin is the *young* Esther (see 2:2, 8). (2) The prospective replacements for Vashti have to undergo a whole year (two six-month periods) of cosmetic preparations before seeing the king (2:12–14). That's a long time for facial makeovers and hair styling. (3) The Jews are said to kill seventy-five thousand Persians (9:16).

In addition, critics point out that some details in Esther clash with those in the writings of the Greek historian Herodotus (485?–425? B.C.), a near contemporary of the Esther story. Three are normally highlighted: (1) Esther 1:1 speaks of Ahasuerus' "127 provinces," while Herodotus (*History of the Persian Wars* 3.89) speaks only of the king's "twenty satrapies"; (2) Herodotus (*Persian Wars* 7.14 and 9.112) says that Ahasuerus's wife was Amestris, not Vashti or Esther; (3) Herodotus (*Persian Wars* 3.84) says that Persian queens could be selected from only one of seven noble Persian families, a fact at obvious variance with Ahasuerus's selection of Esther.

None of the preceding items are, in our judgment, fatal arguments against historicity. To begin with, it is not at all clear in 2:5–6 that it was Mordecai who was exiled to Babylon in 597 B.C. Quite possibly it is Kish, the last proper name in v. 5 and the great-grandfather of Mordecai, who is the subject of the verb "had been carried away" in v. 6. (Note that the NRSV inserts "Kish" as the subject of the verb in v. 6.)

And given the Persian court's delight in extended partying, along with all the food and drink and games, why not give the young women twelve months to beautify themselves as much as possible?

When Esther differs on a detail with Herodotus, we should not necessarily jump to the conclusion that Herodotus is correct and Esther is incorrect, as if to confer canonical status on Herodotus. Historians have noted that Herodotus was not always the thorough, check-out-the-details-first researcher. Instead, he often relied for his information on the rumor mill, tidbits he picked up here and there.

Of the three "inconsistencies" noted above between Herodotus and Esther, items (1) and (3) can be addressed easily enough. In regard to item (1), it is true that outside of Esther 1:1 there is no reference to Ahasuerus's empire being divided into 127 "provinces." But three other verses in Esther (3:12; 8:9; 9:3) distinguish between "satrapies" and "provinces." The former represents the larger piece of land, possibly comparable to our "regions," while "provinces" refer to smaller sections of lands, comparable to our "states."

As for item (3), yes, according to law the king of Persia is supposed to take his bride from one of seven designated families, and Esther is not from one of those families. But do kings always conduct themselves according to the law? If the king thinks himself ruling either as god or for god, cannot he rationalize certain "adjustments" that work to his benefit? Cannot the king circumvent tradition with impunity?

Item (2), the name of Ahasuerus's wife (Amestris versus Vashti or Esther), is more difficult. First of all, we have no Persian text that identifies the king's wife as Amestris. We have only the Greek historian Herodotus. Clearly "Esther" is closer to "Amestris" than is "Vashti." Both names share the sequence e-s-t-r. What is lacking in the biblical name is the "Am-" at the beginning. Could Esther be a shortened version of Amestris? A parallel might be "Moses," which many scholars think originally included the name of some Egyptian deity that was subsequently deleted, thus producing an abbreviated name.

There are also some interesting "consistencies" in Herodotus and Esther. For example, both agree that Ahasuerus's empire stretched from India to Ethiopia. The reference in 1:3 to Ahasuerus assembling his leaders for an extended banquet in Susa in the third year of his reign seems to correspond to Herodotus' reference (*Persian Wars* 7.8) to Ahasuerus convening an important council in Susa to lay plans for the invasion of Greece. Again, the gap between the third year of his reign (1:3) and the seventh year of his reign (2:16; the time he first meets Esther) points to the three-year campaign that the Persian king waged against the Greeks, and of which Herodotus speaks at length.

Finally, we cannot ignore the fact that the name "Mordecai" is a well-attested name from texts of this period. A fifth-century Aramaic inscription contains the name *M-r-d-k*. The so-called Treasure Tablets (because they were found in the treasury) from the Persian city of Persepolis date from the thirtieth year of Darius I to the seventh year of Artaxerxes I (i.e., 492–458 B.C.). They contain names like *Mar-du-kana-sir*, *Mar-du-uka*, *Mar-duk-ka*. And fifty of these tablets come from the time of Ahasuerus. Now, to be sure, these names are probably not the Mordecai of Esther. If "Mordecai" is to be connected with the divinity

"Marduk," then such a name would more than likely be quite common. There is one Persian text, dating either from the last years of Darius I or the early years of Ahasuerus, that speaks of a government official in Susa named "Marduka" who served the king as an inspector throughout the city. Could this be the Mordecai of Esther? Maybe. Maybe not.

While certainly not a proof of the historicity of Esther, the nearly successful Nazi pogroms, conceived as a "final solution" to the liquidation of European Jewry in the twentieth century, place the book of Esther more in the world of historical reality than in the world of belletristic fiction.

The Text of Esther

What appears in translation in most of our Bibles is a reflection of the Esther that is present in the Hebrew Bible. However, the Septuagint translation, some versions of which were done two centuries before Christ, while fairly close to the Hebrew Esther, also includes six lengthy passages not found in Hebrew manuscripts.

We may line them up as follows:

Hebrew text	Septuagint additions A–F
	A. Mordecai's dream of impending conflict between two dragons, which leads to a discovery of a plot against King "Artaxerxes," and for which Mordecai is rewarded (seventeen verses).
1:1–3:13	
	B. Artaxerxes' first letter, ordering the massacre of the Jews (seven verses).
3:14–4:17	
	C. The prayers of Mordecai (eleven verses) and of Esther (nineteen verses) for God's intervention.
	D. Esther risks her life to appeal to Artaxerxes and faints before the king (sixteen verses and essentially an expansion of 5:1–2).
5:1–2 (absent from the Septuagint but expanded in Addition D)	
5:3–8:12	

	E. Artaxerxes' second letter, condemning Haman and praising the Jews and their God (twenty-four verses).
8:13–10:3	
	F. Mordecai's dream (in A) is clarified or decoded. The plural "Purim" is explained as referring to two lots, one for God's people and one for the nations, and both lots have been fulfilled by God's grace. This addition ends with a colophon stating that Dositheus, a priest and Levite, brought to Egypt a Greek copy of Esther that had been translated by Lysimachus during the fourth year of the reign of Ptolemy and Cleopatra (114–113 B.C.?) (fourteen verses).

It is clear that these additions do two things. Obviously, they expand the book of Esther from 163 verses to 271 verses. But more importantly, these extra 108 verses make Esther more Jewish and more overtly religious. They do so by frequently mentioning the name of God (over fifty times). They record specific prayers (see Addition C). In her prayer, Esther, as penitent, expresses her abhorrence of her position as Persian queen ("I abhor the sign of my proud position. . . . I abhor it like a menstruous rag"), of her marriage to a non-Jew ("I abhor the bed of the uncircumcised and of any foreigner"), and her commitment to a Daniel-like observance of Jewish dietary laws ("Your servant has not eaten at Haman's table, and I have not honored the king's feast or drunk the wine of libations").

In Bibles such as the KJV, NIV, and NASB these extra passages do not appear. In some Bibles, such as the NJB and NAB, they appear in the places indicated in the preceding chart. In a Bible like the NRSV, which contains the apocryphal/deuterocanonical books, the additions are included separately after the book of Judith.

Summarization of the Story

The refusal by a Persian queen (Vashti) to put in a public appearance at her husband's banquet, for whatever reason, and her consequent dismissal open the door to the emergence of the Jew Esther. She will be chosen as Vashti's successor, while all the time concealing her Jewish identity. Esther's four distinguishing features are that she is Jewish, young, very attractive, and unattached. Esther is able to hide her ethnicity, but not her beauty.

An orphan, Esther is cared for and adopted by her cousin Mordecai. When she is taken into the king's palace as his wife (much as Sarai was "taken" to be a foreign king's wife [Gen. 12:15]), Mordecai (unlike Abram) is not far away, sitting just outside at the king's gate. There, he chances to overhear a planned conspiracy on the king's life. He passes this information along to Esther, who in turn transmits it to her husband. The culprits are arrested and hanged for their crime.

King Ahasuerus/Xerxes' second-in-command is Haman. Because Mordecai refuses to bow before and honor Haman, Haman is so enraged that he determines to kill both Mordecai and his people, whom he now knows are Jews. To that end, he persuades Ahasuerus, after he casts a lot to determine the date of genocide, to authorize an edict that will call for the elimination of the Jews (whom he refers to only as "a certain people") on the forthcoming twelfth of Adar.

Upon hearing of that edict, Mordecai implores Esther to use her position to speak as intercessor before her royal husband. At first hesitant, she subsequently agrees to get involved, even if it costs her life. Her strategy is first of all to host a banquet to which her husband and Haman are invited. Without revealing any of her agenda, Esther asks her husband to join her for a second banquet the following day.

In between these two banquets Mordecai manages to enrage Haman a second time. Haman's wife, Zeresh, counsels him to have Mordecai hanged on a seventy-five-foot-high gallows before he attends the second banquet later that evening.

To his surprise, Ahasuerus discovers, during a bout with insomnia, that Mordecai was never honored for saving his life earlier when he found out about the conspiracy on the king's life. How can Ahasuerus appropriately honor Mordecai for his good deed? The king even directs the question to Haman without mentioning Mordecai's name. We can imagine Haman's shock when he discovers that it is not he but the hated, contemptible Mordecai whom the king will honor! And Haman will assist in honoring Mordecai by leading Mordecai on horseback throughout the streets of Susa.

At this second banquet Esther reveals herself as a Jew and Haman as the villain who would mastermind the killing of the Jews, including her. Interestingly, Ahasuerus has Haman hung on the gallows that Haman built for Mordecai, not because Haman is anti-Semitic, but because Haman was observed trying "to make a move" on his beloved Esther. At least, that is the way it looked to the king.

Esther now pleads with her husband to overrule and abrogate the earlier edict. While he cannot cancel this edict, he can publish another edict allowing the Jews to fight and defend themselves.

The Jews fight and defend themselves exceedingly well, and on the very day of the very month that the earlier lot had designated for their annihilation, the grim statistics are five hundred dead Persians in Susa, the ten sons of Haman dead, three hundred more dead Persians in Susa, and seventy-five thousand dead Persians throughout the rest of the empire. But in every instance the Jews do not plunder their slain victims.

The day after the battle, the fourteenth of Adar, Jews throughout Persia celebrate the relief from their enemies. Because fighting continued a day longer in Susa, the Jews living there hold their festive celebrations on the fifteenth of Adar.

Mordecai dispatches letters to all the Jewish families calling on them to celebrate these two days, depending on where they live. These two days respectively are to be identified as "Purim." Esther also sends a letter to her fellow Jews establishing these days of Purim.

At the beginning of the book Esther replaces Vashti as the king's wife. By the end of the book Mordecai has replaced Haman as the king's second-in-command. And the narrative comes to an end.

Structure

One way to ascertain the structure of a biblical book is to search for things or events or words or phrases that are repeated (such as the distribution of the phrase "these are the generations of X" throughout Genesis, or the phrase "when Jesus had finished saying these things" distributed throughout Matthew).

One event that occurs throughout Esther is a banquet/party. (The word *mishteh*, "banquet, feast(ing)," occurs fifty-five times in the Old Testament, twenty of which are in Esther, most often in ch. 5 [6x] and ch. 9 [4x].) In fact, there are nine of them (or ten if one splits the ninth into two feasts):

1. the king's banquet for his officials lasting 180 days (1:3–4)
2. the king's banquet for the locals who live in Susa lasting seven days (1:5–8)
3. Vashti's banquet for women (1:9)
4. the king's banquet when Esther replaces Vashti as queen (2:18)
5. the king and Haman celebrating the edict calling for the annihilation of the Jews over cocktails—"they sat down to drink" (3:15)
6. Esther's first banquet, to which Ahasuerus and Haman are invited (5:5–8)
7. Esther's second banquet, which she hosts with the same guest list (7:1–10)

8. The Jews' festival at which they celebrate authorization by the king to defend themselves against attack (8:16–17)
9. Days of feasting that follow defeat of different Persian groups, the fourteenth and fifteenth of Adar (9:17–19)

So, seven of Esther's ten chapters refer to somebody throwing a party. In several different ways there is a correspondence between these banquet/party scenes. For example, the first two feasts are for officials throughout all of Persia's province (1) (1:3–4) or for those individuals living only in Susa (2) (1:5–8). Both feasts are vulgar and ostentatious. Similarly, the final feasts are for those Jews living all over Persia (9) (9:17, 19) and one only for the Jews who live in Susa (9) (9:18). And here, both feasts are celebratory. And certainly (3), Vashti's last banquet, corresponds to (4), Esther's first banquet, with Vashti as host in (3) and Esther as honoree in (4).

But perhaps the most important item about these banquet/feasting scenes is that the first five are Persian-sponsored banquets, while the last four are Jewish-sponsored banquets (Clines 1990: 37). This shift in emphasis from Persian banquets to Jewish ones points to and underscores a major theme in Esther: the shift or transition of power from Persians to Jews.

This transition of dominion is clearly the focus of the opening verse of ch. 9 (see also 9:22). It speaks of "the very day when the enemies of the Jews hoped to gain power over them, but which has been changed [*wenahaphok hu*ʾ] to a day when the Jews would gain power over their foes" (NRSV). The Hebrew could also be rendered "but now the tables were turned" (NIV), or "the reverse occurred" (Levenson 1997: 118), or "and the opposite happened" (Radday 1990: 311). For the Jews in general and Mordecai in particular, it is a shift from trouble to triumph. For the Persians in general and Haman in particular, it is a shift from success to failure. For the first group (Mordecai and the Jews), life replaces death. For the second group (Haman and [some of] the Persians), death replaces life.

Such reversal in circumstances is brought out through contrasts in the book. Haman's promotion (3:1–6) contrasts with Mordecai's promotion (10:1–3). Both are "advanced" (3:1; 10:2) to their position by the king, but Haman turns out to be a vain (3:5) and vicious (3:6) second-in-command, while Mordecai turns out to be a beneficent second-in-command (10:3).

The gloom that hangs over the Jews in 3:7–4:17 contrasts with the euphoria that engulfs the Jews that begins with the exaltation of Mordecai in 6:1–11 and continues through Purim observances (9:20–32).

So, in 3:7–4:17 the Jews fast (4:3, 16), but in ch. 9 they feast (vv. 17, 18, 19, 22). In 4:1, 2, 3, 4, Mordecai wears sackcloth, but in 6:8, 10, 11, and 8:15 he wears royal robes. In fact, 8:15 points out that the colors of Mordecai's royal robes ("blue and white") are the same as those in the expensive fabrics that hang in the rooms of the royal palace at Susa ("white and blue") (1:6). There is also an interesting shift in these two parts in the use of the verb *naphal*, "fall." First of all, in 3:7 (and referred to in 9:24) the Hamanic Persians "cast" (literally "caused to fall") the Pur/lot in order to determine a date on which to launch the genocide of the Jews. But later, it is Haman's own wife who in 6:13 speaks to Haman of the beginning of his "fall" before Mordecai (who earlier would not fall/bow before him [3:2]). Later, in an act of desperation and plea for mercy, Haman "falls" before Esther (7:8), and still later, fear of the Jews "falls" on the Persians (8:17, 9:2). Thus, in between the two references to falling (in the form of lot casting) in 3:7 and 9:24, which jeopardizes the Jews, are the other fallings, which jeopardize Haman and the Persians.

Theology

One of the unique features of Esther is the total absence of any reference to God. In that one respect the book is Godless. It is the one and only book in the Old Testament never to use any theistic language. Furthermore, as Loader (1978: 418) has observed, "Motifs that suggest a religious quality are introduced, but they are made to function in such a way that any theological significance is immediately veiled again."

For example, Mordecai fasts (4:16), but does he pray and call out to God when he fasts? If he does, the text has not recorded it. Again, when Mordecai says to Esther, "If you keep silence at such a time as this, relief and deliverance will rise for the Jews from another quarter" (4:14), does he mean by "another quarter" that God has a backup plan to Esther should she evade the task? If that is his intention (and one version of the ancient Greek text puts such words in his mouth ["If you neglect your people . . . God will be their aid and deliverance"]), Mordecai could have stated that straightforwardly enough.

The absence of Yahweh's name from such a dynamic narrative raises the following questions: Is God's presence real even if his name is absent? Can the power and sovereignty of God be affirmed even if his name is not sounded? If God is unnamed, is he therefore uninvolved? Are people still entitled to be called "religious and devout" even if the Holy Name is not on their lips? Can one talk about God without using specific God-talk?

All commentators on Esther agree that one of its meanings is the preservation of Israel in Persia when the odds against survival are so overwhelming. But how does one explain such survival? A stroke of good luck? Coincidence? Jewish self-help and ingenuity? A quirk? An enigma? An inept Persian king? An overzealous, bigoted Haman who can keep neither his mouth shut nor his racist feelings under control? All of the above?

Or is the best answer to be found in an affirmation of divine providence that is the saving, sustaining force behind the survival of God's elect? There are so many "what if" situations in Esther that if these are not traceable to a divine hand, then a better title for the book is "Coincidences" (defined by somebody as "miracles in which God prefers to remain anonymous").

What if Vashti had not balked at putting in a public appearance at her husband's banquet, as so requested (1:10–12)? Even the narrator of the story says that she was "fair to behold" (1:11c). We cannot assume that she was expected to show up nude or semi-nude ("wearing the royal crown" in v. 11a does not necessarily mean "wearing *only* the royal crown"), although some ancient interpreters read that into the text.

Nor does the text tell us why she rejected the invitation. It appears that for the king, Vashti is like the king's curtains or couches or goblets, another of his gorgeous possessions to be put on display before an audience, an object for exhibition. She will not be party to this runway, Barbie-doll syndrome. (Her name, "Vashti," bears some semblance to the verb *shata*, "drink," and so her name may point to the excessive drinking of the Persians and her husband [Goldman 1990: 16].) But the fact that the text does not have her supplying a reason for nonconformity may be precisely the point. She does not need to justify her decision with a clarifying response. A decision to act or not act is adequate enough, and does not need justification.

In not jumping at the king's behest she joins others in Scripture who made similar decisions when confronted with options:

Esther 1:12: "But Queen Vashti refused to come at the king's command."

Gen. 39:8, 10: "But he [Joseph] refused. . . . And although she spoke to Joseph day after day, he refused to lie beside her."

Num. 22:13–14: "The Lord has refused to let me go with you. . . . Balaam refuses [at least initially] to come with us."

Heb. 11:24: "By faith Moses, when he was grown up, refused to be called a son of Pharaoh's daughter."

Such refusals are as desirable as refusals such as "How long will you [pharaoh] refuse to humble yourself before me?" (Exod. 10:3), or "How long will they [Israel] refuse to believe in me?" (Num. 14:11), or "He [the elder brother] became angry and refused to go in" (Luke 15:28) are damnable and pathetic.

Here is another "what if." What if some "beautiful young virgin" (2:2–3) other than Esther had first caught the eye of Hegai, the king's eunuch in charge of the royal harem (2:9), and then the eye of Ahasuerus (2:17)? There must have been a good number of candidates, for the search for such a lady was carried out "in all the provinces of his kingdom" (2:3). And because 1:1 says that the king ruled over 127 provinces, one would think that there would be at least that number of contestants or conscriptees.

What if Mordecai had not overheard the conspiracy against Ahasuerus's life, and thus had no such information to relay to the king via Esther (2:19–23)? It is not his guards, his secret service agents, those supposedly most loyal to him, to whom Ahasuerus owes his survival, but to Mordecai. The incident is recorded in official royal documents (2:23b), but Ahasuerus is not informed of the planned assassination, and Mordecai is not rewarded (yet).

Haman, now Ahasuerus's second-in-command, is furious that Mordecai will not bow before him (3:2, 5). If there is one thing proud people resent, it is being upstaged. If there is one thing powerful people resent it is nonconformity. If there is one thing spineless people resent is convictions. Offended by one Jew, Haman wishes to annihilate all Jews (3:6). When that will happen is to be decided by lot (3:7a). The day decided on by casting the lot is almost a year later, "the thirteenth day of the twelfth month, which is the month of Adar" (3:7b). What if the lot for the Jews' execution had been one that was dated twenty-four or forty-eight hours from the present moment? Esther had twelve months to prepare cosmetically to meet Ahasuerus (2:12), and the Jews in Persia have about twelve months before they face their executioners.

What if Esther had not agreed to put her life on the line ("If I perish, I perish") in 4:16? To do that, she will have to divulge her Jewishness, which she will do in 7:3–4. So far, she has effectively kept her ethnicity under wraps (2:10, 20). We are not sure whether "Esther" is to be connected with the Persian *stara* ("star"), or with the goddess "Ishtar" (all three have the *s-t-r* sequence). But there is also a similarity in sound between her name and the Hebrew verb *s-t-r*, "conceal, hide." But what may happen when she lets the cat out of the bag?

What if Haman's suspicions had been aroused when Esther requests a second banquet to which Ahasuerus and Haman are both again invited (5:8)? We need not worry that Ahasuerus is suspicious. He does not know the meaning of the word. For him, a party a day keeps the business away. Esther is taking a risk with this strategy. Humphreys (1998: 341–42) states, "What might have happened had Ahasuerus slept through the night [see 6:1]? Haman could have swayed the king this time and had Mordecai impaled. Esther's second banquet then would have the quality of a wake."

What if during his insomnia Ahasuerus had had his servants read to him a passage from the royal annals that made no mention of Mordecai at all (6:1–2)? Presumably, Mordecai's execution would have proceeded as planned. It is not Esther's intercession that saves Mordecai's life (she is mentioned only once, v. 14, in the chapter), but rather the king's readers "chancing" upon a brief paragraph in the king's autobiography to the effect that Mordecai had foiled an assassination attempt on his life. Why was Mordecai's charitable act ignored and not honored? queries the king.

What if Haman had not thrown himself on the couch where Esther was reclining (7:8a)? For when Ahasuerus reenters the room and observes Haman groveling before Esther, he believes that Haman is throwing himself upon Esther rather than throwing himself upon Esther's mercy. As the king sees it, Haman is trying to "molest" (NIV) or "assault" (NRSV) his wife (7:8b), in the king's palace no less, and right on the heels of having been villified by Esther. Or at least that is what the king said (even if he knew it was not accurate). By ordering Haman's execution for being a rapist rather than a racist (7:9), the king may be distancing himself from any involvement in the extermination plot. And earlier, Esther was very careful to "finger" only Haman in the genocide plot (7:3–6), wisely choosing to omit any reference to the fact that the plot would never have gotten airborne in the first place without Ahasuerus' authorization (3:11).

But if the book of Esther highlights a beneficent providence at work to preserve the Jews in Persia from obliteration, it also highlights the courage, the ingenuity, the wisdom of those Jews. It is not the case that God is active (even if behind the scenes) while his people are passive.

And such courage and ingenuity are evidenced more in the life of Esther than in that of Mordecai. Each character appears in the book about the same number of times (by our count, she fifty-six times, he fifty-nine times). There is no chapter in which only Esther appears; there are, however, two chapters in which Mordecai appears (3:2, 3, 4, 5, 6 [3x]; 10:2, 3) but Esther does not. And the fact that the last chapter of the book speaks only of him and not of her suggests maybe that this book should be called "The Book of Mordecai." We said earlier that the first reference to this Old Testament book is in 2 Macc. 15:36, where Purim is called the "Day of Mordecai."

But note that in the biblical book, Mordecai's words are recorded in direct speech only once, and that is in 4:13–14. Thirty-one words in the Hebrew for him. By contrast, Esther's direct speech has quotation marks eight times (4:11, 16; 5:4, 7–8; 7:3–4, 6a; 8:5–6; 9:13). Two hundred and thirty-two words in the Hebrew for her. All except the first two of these (where she sends a message to Mordecai) are in conversation with her royal husband. It is Mordecai who urges Esther to get involved on behalf of her people (4:14), but it is Esther who sagaciously develops the strategy of that involvement. Haman goes ballistic before Mordecai (3:5; 5:9), but he trembles before Esther (7:6). He is infuriated that Mordecai will not fall and genuflect before him (3:5), but he himself falls in front of Esther (7:8).

The banquets are Esther's idea, nobody else's. The decision to go before Ahasuerus is hers, nobody else's. And the calling for a national and perpetual celebration of Purim is hers and Mordecai's, and nobody else's. Purim is their invention. This is unlike the calendars in the Torah that highlight the various calendrical festivals (Exod. 23:12–19; Leviticus 23; Numbers 28–29; Deut. 16:1–17). In each of those it is God who initiates the festival.

And even here it is Esther, not Mordecai, who gets in the last word. Levenson (1997: 131) has noted that in 9:20–32, the official institution of Purim, Mordecai's role gives way to Esther's:

9:20, 23: Mordecai alone
9:29: Esther and Mordecai
9:31: Mordecai and Esther
9:32: Esther alone

In addition to emphases on providence and human initiative, we should also note the interesting absence of any desire in the book of Esther for any of the Jews to return to Jerusalem. Apparently, Ezra and Nehemiah have not learned to "sing the song of the Lord while in a foreign land" (Ps. 137:4), but Esther and Mordecai seem to have learned how.

The book of Esther suggests that it is possible to be "in" the world, but not "of" the world, to be in Persia without being Persian. To adapt Jesus' priestly prayer in John 17, perhaps we hear a petition like this: "My prayer is not that you take them out of Persia but that you protect them from the evil one. They are not of Persia, even as I am not of it. As you sent me into the Persias of the world, I have sent them into Persia." To put it a bit differently, Esther is about the shift from exile as one way of life (temporary relocation outside Israel) to diaspora as another way of life (permanent relocation outside of Israel).

Some might argue that the Jews do become Persian-like when they, now with the upper hand, engage in mass slaughter of the Persians (five hundred people in Susa [9:6]; Haman's ten sons [9:7–10]; three hundred more Persians in Susa [9:15]; seventy-five thousand Persians throughout the empire [9:16]). And on the next day they turn around and feast (9:17)!

Many commentators are particularly offended by 8:11, which might appear to suggest that the Jews are within their rights to destroy not only the adult males who might attack them, but to destroy their wives and children as well. So reads the NEB: "The king granted permission to the Jews . . . to unite and defend themselves and to destroy, slay, exterminate the whole strength of any people . . . which might attack them, women and children too, and to plunder their possessions." The NAB is similar: "The king authorized the Jews . . . to kill, destroy, wipe out, along with the wives and children, every armed group . . . which should attack them, and to seize their goods as spoil."

But it is not at all clear that this is what 8:11 says. Gordis (1976: 49–53; 1981: 378) argues, convincingly in our judgment, that the "wives and children" are the wives and children of Hebrew men who might be attacked by the Persians. Gordis translates 8:11 as "The king permitted the Jews in every city to gather and defend themselves, to destroy, kill, and wipe out every armed force of a people or a province attacking them, their children and their wives, with their goods as booty." Thus, the issue here is a defensive war, the right to defend oneself, one's family and property from invaders and plunderers. And the Jews may do so only because and after they have been given written, legal permission by the Persian king (see 8:9–14). That the text states twice (9:10b, 15b) that the Jews took no plunder from those they defeated indicates that this is not a war of self-aggrandizement but simply a war of survival.

Finally, the climax in the book of Esther is the institution of Purim. It is a day for "feasting and gladness" (9:18), "gladness and feasting" (9:19), a day for exchanging gifts of food (9:19b), a day of celebration on which the Jews "gained relief from their enemies" (9:22a), a time for giving special presents to the poor among them (9:22b).

Israel's history in the Old Testament falls between Passover and Purim. They are separated by one month in the Jewish calendar (Passover in the first month, Nisan/Abib; Purim in the twelfth month, Adar). These two festivals both dramatically reenact Israel's deliverance (from death and annihilation at Egypt's hands; from death and annihilation at Persia's hands). The parallels between the Passover account in Exodus and the Purim account are obvious: (1) action in a foreign land and court; (2) threat to the existence of God's chosen; (3) deliverance for God's people; (4) Egypt and Persia suffer; (5) establishment of a festival to commemorate the event. (The parallels between Esther and Exodus have been probed most creatively by G. Gerleman in his German commentary *Esther* [Neukirchen-Vluyn: 1982]; see also Wechsler 1997.)

The appropriate response when God intervenes on behalf of his people includes the holiness that goes with Passover and the hilarity that goes with Purim. It encompasses the sobering, reflective mood on Passover, and the less-than-sober Purim, on which, according to the Babylonian Talmud (*Megillah* 7b), "a man is obligated to drink until he is unable to distinguish between 'Blessed is Mordecai' and 'cursed is Haman.'" It embraces a religious celebration (Passover [conjoined with the Feast of Unleavened Bread] is one of the three festivals on which the participants are required to cease work and go to the chosen sanctuary) and a celebration at home (Purim). The two festivals unite piety and partying, raising one's voice to God and raising the roof.

Bibliography (Esther)

Commentaries and Major Studies

Baldwin, J. G. 1984. *Esther: An Introduction and Commentary*. Tyndale Old Testament Commentaries. Downers Grove, Ill.: InterVarsity.

Beal, T. 1998. *The Book of Hiding: Gender, Ethnicity, Annihilation and Esther*. New York: Routledge.

Berg, S. B. 1979. *The Book of Esther: Motifs, Themes, and Structures*. Chico, Calif.: Scholars Press.

Brenner, A., ed. 1995. *A Feminist Companion to Esther, Judith and Susanna*. The Feminist Companion to the Bible 7. Sheffield: Sheffield Academic Press.

Clines, D. J. A. 1984. *The Esther Scroll: The Story of the Story*. JSOT Supplement 30. Sheffield: JSOT Press.

Craig, K. M. 1995. *Reading Esther: A Case for the Literary Carnivalesque*. Louisville: Westminster/John Knox.

Day, L. M. 1995. *Three Faces of a Queen: Characterization in the Book Esther*. JSOT Supplement 186. Sheffield: Sheffield Academic Press.

Fox, M. V. 1991a. *Character and Ideology in the Book of Esther*. Columbia: University of South Carolina Press.

———. 1991b. *The Redaction of the Books of Esther: On Reading Composite Texts*. SBLMS 40. Atlanta: Scholars Press.

Gordis, R. 1974. *Megillat Esther: The Masoretic Text with Introduction, New Translation and Commentary*. New York: Ktav.

Grossfeld, B. 1991. *The Two Targums of Esther*. Collegeville, Minn.: Liturgical Press.

Leniak, T. S. 1998. *Shame and Honor in the Book of Esther.* SBLDS 165. Atlanta: Scholars Press.

Levenson, J. D. 1997. *Esther: A Commentary.* Old Testament Library. Louisville: Westminster/John Knox.

Linafelt, T., and T. K. Beal. 1999. *Ruth and Esther.* Berit Olam. Collegeville, Minn.: Liturgical Press.

Moore, C. A. 1971. *Esther.* Anchor Bible 7B. Garden City, N.Y.: Doubleday.

Paton, L. B. 1908. *A Critical and Exegetical Commentary on the Book of Esther.* International Critical Commentary. Edinburgh: T. & T. Clark.

Rodriguez, A. M. 1995. *Esther: A Theological Approach.* Berrien Springs, Mich.: Andrews University Press.

Stedman, R. C. 1977. *The Queen and I: Studies in Esther.* Waco, Tex.: Word.

Swindoll, C. 1997. *Esther: A Woman of Strength and Beauty.* Nashville: Word.

Whitcomb, J. 1979. *Esther: Triumph of God's Sovereignty.* Chicago: Moody.

Shorter Studies

Anderson, B. W. 1950. "The Place of the Book of Esther in the Christian Bible." *JR* 30:32–43.

Bickerman, E. 1967. *Four Strange Books in the Bible.* New York: Schocken. Pp. 169–240.

Clines, D. J. A. 1990. "Reading Esther from Left to Right." In *The Bible in Three Dimensions: Essays in Celebration of Forty Years of Biblical Studies at the University of Sheffield.* Ed. D. J. A. Clines et al. JSOT Supplement 87. Sheffield: JSOT Press. Pp. 31–52.

———. 1991. "In Quest of the Historical Mordecai." *VT* 41:129–36.

Costas, O. E. 1988. "The Subversiveness of Faith: Esther as a Paradigm for a Liberating Theology." *Ecumenical Review* 40:66–78.

Crawford, S. A. W. 1992. "Esther." In *The Women's Bible Commentary.* Ed. C. A. Newsom and S. H. Ringe. Louisville: Westminster/John Knox.

Darr, K. P. 1989. "Esther and Additions to Esther." In *The Books of the Bible.* Vol. 1, *The Old Testament/The Hebrew Bible.* Ed. B. W. Anderson. New York: Scribner's. Pp. 173–79.

Day, L. M. 1998. "Power, Otherness and Gender in Biblical Short Stories." *HBT* 20:109–27.

Goldman, S. 1990. "Narrative and Ethical Ironies in Esther." *JSOT* 47:15–31.

Gordis, R. 1976. "Studies in the Esther Narrative." *JBL* 95:43–58.

———. 1981. "Religion, Wisdom and History in the Book of Esther—A New Solution to an Ancient Crux." *JBL* 100:359–88.

Greenstein, E. L. 1987. "A Jewish Reading of Esther." In *Judaic Perspectives on Ancient Israel*. Ed. J. Neusner et al. Philadelphia: Fortress. Pp. 225–43.

Hallo, W. W. 1983. "The First Purim." *BA* 46:19–26.

House, P. R. 1998. *Old Testament Theology*. Downers Grove, Ill.: Inter-Varsity. Pp. 490–96.

Humphreys, W. L. 1973. "A Life-Style for Diaspora: A Study of the Tales of Esther and Daniel." *JBL* 92:211–23.

———. 1985. "The Story of Esther and Mordecai: An Early Jewish Novella." In *Saga, Legend, Tale, Novella, Fable: Narrative Forms in Old Testament Literature*. Ed. G. W. Coats. JSOT Supplement 35. Sheffield: JSOT Press. Pp. 97–113.

———. 1998. "The Story of Esther in Its Several Forms: Recent Studies." *RelSRev* 24:335–42.

Jackowski, K. 1988–1989. "Holy Disobedience in Esther." *ThTo* 45:403–14.

Jobes, K. H. 1998. "How an Assassination Changed the Greek Text of Esther." *ZAW* 110:75–78.

Klaasen, M. J. 1996. "Persian/Jew/Jew/Persian: Levels of Irony in the Scroll of Esther." *Direction* 25:21–28.

Lacocque, A. 1990. *The Feminine Unconventional: Four Subversive Figures in Israel's Tradition*. Minneapolis: Fortress. Pp. 49–83.

Larkin, K. J. A. 1995. *Ruth and Esther*. Old Testament Guides. Sheffield: Sheffield Academic Press.

Loader, J. A. 1978. "Esther as a Novel with Different Levels of Meaning." *ZAW* 90:417–21.

Millard, A. R. 1977. "The Persian Names in Esther and the Reliability of the Hebrew Text." *JBL* 96:481–88.

Miller, C. H. 1980. "Esther's Levels of Meaning." *ZAW* 92:145–48.

Niditch, S. 1987. *Underdogs and Tricksters: A Prelude to Biblical Folklore*. San Francisco: Harper & Row. Pp. 126–45.

———. 1993. *War in the Hebrew Bible: A Study in the Ethics of Violence*. New York: Oxford University Press. Pp. 119–22.

———. 1995. "Short Stories: The Book of Esther and the Theme of Woman as a Civilizing Force." In *Old Testament Interpretation: Past, Present, and Future: Essays in Honour of Gene M. Tucker*. Ed. J. L. Mays et al. Edinburgh: T. & T. Clark. Pp. 195–209.

Noss, P. A. 1993. "A Footnote on Time: The Book of Esther." *BT* 44:309–20.

Radday, Y. T. 1990. "Esther with Humour." In *On Humour and the Comic in the Hebrew Bible*. Ed. Y. T. Radday and A. Brenner. JSOT Supplement 92; Bible and Literature Series 23. Sheffield: Almond. Pp. 295–313.

Rosenblatt, N. H. 1999. "Portraits in Heroism: Esther and Samson." *BRev* 15:20–25, 47.

Sandmel, S. 1974. *The Enjoyment of Scripture*. New York: Oxford University Press. Pp. 35–45.

Sasson, J. M. 1987. "Esther." In *The Literary Guide to the Bible*. Ed. R. Alter and F. Kermode. Cambridge, Mass.: Belknap. Pp. 335–42.

Shea, W. H. 1976. "Esther and History." *Andrews University Seminary Studies* 14:227–46.

Stafonovic, Z. 1994. "'Go at Once!' Thematic Reversals in the Book of Esther." *Asia Journal of Theology* 8:163–71.

Sterk, J. P. 1985. "How Many Books of Esther Are There?" *BT* 36:440–42.

Talmon, S. 1963. "Wisdom in the Book of Esther." *VT* 13:419–55.

Thornton, T. C. G. 1986. "The Crucifixion of Haman and the Scandal of the Cross." *JTS* 37:419–26.

Wechsler, M. G. 1997. "Shadow and Fulfillment in the Book of Esther." *BSac* 154:275–84.

———. 1998. "The Purim-Passover Connection: A Reflection of Jewish Exegetical Tradition in the Peshitta Book of Esther." *JBL* 117:321–27.

Weisman, Z. 1998. *Political Satire in the Bible*. SBLSS 32. Atlanta: Scholars Press. Pp. 139–63.

Whedbee, J. W. 1998. *The Bible and the Comic Vision*. Cambridge: Cambridge University Press. Pp. 129–90.

Wiebe, J. M. 1991. "Esther 4:14: 'Will Relief and Deliverance Arise for the Jews from Another Place?'" *CBQ* 53:409–15.

Wills, L. W. 1990. *The Jew in the Court of the Foreign King: Ancient Jewish Court Legends*. Minneapolis: Fortress. Pp. 153–91.

———. 1995. *The Jewish Novel in the Ancient World*. Myth and Poetics. Ithaca: Cornell University Press. Pp. 93–131.

Wright, J. S. 1970. "The Historicity of the Book of Esther." In *New Perspectives on the Old Testament*. Ed. J. B. Payne. Waco, Tex.: Word. Pp. 37–47.

Yamauchi, E. 1980. "The Archaeological Background of Esther." *BSac* 137:99–117.

———. 1992. "Mordecai, the Persepolis Tablets, and the Susa Excavations." *VT* 42:272–75.

Subject Index